The Thought and Writings of
W. E. B. Du Bois

The Seventh Son

Volume II

*Edited and
with an Introduction
by Julius Lester*

Random House   New York

Copyright © 1971 by Julius Lester
All rights reserved under International and Pan-American Copyright Conventions.
Published in the United States by Random House, Inc., New York, and
simutaneously in Canada by Random House of Canada Limited, Toronto.
Library of Congress Catalog Card Number: 77-140716
ISBN: 0-394-47033-8

Unless otherwise specified, the material in this volume is reprinted by permission of Shirley Graham Du Bois, and may not be reprinted or otherwise used without her consent or the consent of the copyright owner.

Acknowledgment is gratefully extended to the following for permission to reprint from their works:

International Publishers Co., Inc.: From *The World and Africa*, by W.E.B. Du Bois. Copyright © 1965 by International Publishers Co., Inc. From *The Autobiography of W.E.B. Du Bois*. Copyright © 1969 by International Publishers Co., Inc.

Harcourt Brace Jovanovich, Inc.: From *Color And Democracy*, by W.E.B. Du Bois. Copyright 1945 by Harcourt Brace Jovanovich, Inc.

Holt, Rinehart and Winston, Inc.: From *Black Folk: Then and Now*, by W.E.B. Du Bois. Copyright 1939 by Holt, Rinehart and Winston, Inc. Copyright © 1967 by W.E. Burghardt Du Bois.

The Atlantic Monthly: "The African Roots of War," May, 1915.

Russell & Russell, Publishers: From *Black Reconstruction in America, 1860–1880*. Copyright 1935, © 1963 by W.E. Burghardt Du Bois.

The Guardian, for articles by W.E.B. Du Bois written from 1953 to 1961.

The Crisis, for articles by W.E.B. Du Bois written from 1910 to 1922.

American Journal of Sociology, for "Prospects of a World Without Race Conflict," March, 1944, published by the University of Chicago Press.

Manufactured in the United States of America
First Edition

CONTENTS

THE THIRD PERIOD: 1934–1948

THE FOURTH PERIOD: 1948–1963

THE SECOND PERIOD
Selections From
The Crisis

In the history of black publications, there has perhaps never been a magazine quite like The Crisis *during the years Du Bois was editor. While the magazine was the official organ of the NAACP, it was more a reflection of Du Bois' personality, thinking and concerns than it was of the organization. Du Bois was always proud of the fact that the circulation of the magazine was more than double the membership of the NAACP at times, and that its readers were overwhelmingly black.*

Published monthly, the magazine was one of the best sources for information about the black world. It featured a compendium of news, a section of excerpts from articles in leading magazines and newspapers, black and white, articles on black history, Africa, and whatever else Du Bois might have been interested in at the particular moment. Each year there were two special issues: one was an "education" issue which featured photographs of the leading black graduates and/or higher degree recipients from black and white colleges, as well as figures on how many blacks had completed college that year. The other special issue was devoted to children, featuring pictures of black babies, as well as stories, especially for children.

The most prominent element of the magazine was its editorial pages, in which Du Bois gave his personal opinions on events of the time. The selection from these editorials which follows can only give a small example of the catholicity of his mind. These editorials have been arranged by theme and subject matter, and chronologically within each section. They have also been selected for their contemporary relevance.

PROTEST

AGITATION

Some good friends of the cause we represent fear agitation. They say: "Do not agitate—do not make a noise; *work.*" They add, "Agitation is destructive or at best negative—what is wanted is positive constructive work."

Such honest critics mistake the function of agitation. A toothache is agitation. Is a toothache a good thing? No. Is it therefore useless? No. It is supremely useful, for it tells the body of decay, dyspepsia and death. Without it the body would suffer unknowingly. It would think: All is well, when lo! danger lurks.

The same is true of the Social Body. Agitation is a necessary evil to tell of the ills of the suffering. Without it many a nation has been lulled to false security and preened itself with virtues it did not possess.

The function of this Association is to tell this nation the crying evil of race prejudice. It is a hard duty but a necessary one—a divine one. It is Pain; Pain is not good but Pain is necessary. Pain does not aggravate disease—Disease causes Pain. Agitation does not mean Aggravation—Aggravation calls for Agitation in order that Remedy may be found.

———

Two Italians were lynched in Florida. The Italian Government protested, but it was found that they were naturalized Americans. The inalienable right of every free American citizen to be lynched without tiresome investigation and penalties is one which the families of the lately deceased doubtless deeply appreciate.

November, 1910. Vol. I, No. 1. p. 21.

TRIUMPH[1]

Let the eagle scream! Again the burden of upholding the best traditions of Anglo-Saxon civilization has fallen on the sturdy shoulders of the American republic. Once more a howling mob

[1]This editorial was written in response to the brutal lynching of a black man in Coatesville, Penna., in August of 1911.

of the best citizens in a foremost State of the Union has vindicated that self-evident superiority of the white race. The case was perfectly clear; it was not that murder had been done, for we Americans are not squeamish at mere murder. Off and on we do more of that kind of thing than most folk. Moreover, there was not much of a murder—only the crazed act of a drunken man quite unpremeditated. The point is he was black.

Blackness must be punished. Blackness is the crime of crimes, as the opera-boufee senator-elect from Mississippi[2] has amply proven. Why is it a crime? Because it threatens white supremacy. A black might—why, civilization might be black! It is therefore necessary, as every white scoundrel in the nation knows, to let slip no opportunity of punishing this crime of crimes. Of course, if possible, the pretext should be great and overwhelming—some awful stunning crime made even more horrible by reporters' imaginations. Failing this, mere murder, arson, barn burning or impudence may do; indeed, must do.

Once the pretext given, then let loose the majesty of American culture. It must warm the hearts of every true son of the republic to read how the brawn and sinew of Coatesville rallied to the great and glorious deed. It deserves a poem; think of the hoary farmers, toilworn with the light of a holy purpose in their eyes and pitchforks in their hands. "The churches were nearly deserted," say the papers. Splendid! Was it not fitting that Coatesville religion should lend its deacons and Sunday-school superintendents to the holy crusade? Did they not choose a noble day? Sunday, the festival of the risen Prince of Peace.

Ah, the splendor of that Sunday night dance. The flames beat and curled against the moonlit sky. The church bells chimed. The scorched and crooked thing, self-wounded and chained to his cot, crawled to the edge of the ash with a stifled groan, but the brave and sturdy farmers pricked him back with the bloody pitchforks until the deed was done.

Let the eagle scream!

Civilization is again safe.

"Oh, say, can you see by the dawn's early light" that soap box of blackened bones and dust, standing in the dew and sunlight on the King's highway to the City of Brotherly Love, while, as the press reports "all day long, not only from Coatesville, but from all Chester County, and even from Philadelphia, people

[2]Vardaman

walked and drove out to the scene of the burning. Men and women poked the ashes and a shout of glee would signalize the finding of a blackened tooth or mere portions of unrecognizable bones. By noon the black heap had been leveled and only the scorched ground was left to tell what had happened there."

Some foolish people talk of punishing the heroic mob, and the Governor of Pennsylvania seems to be real provoked. We hasten to assure our readers that nothing will be done. There may be a few formal arrests, but the men will be promptly released by the mob sitting as jury—perhaps even as judge.

America knows her true heroes.

Again, let the eagle scream!

But let every black American gird up his loins. The great day is coming. We have crawled and pleaded for justice and we have been cheerfully spit upon and murdered and burned. We will not endure it forever. If we are to die, in God's name let us perish like men and not like bales of hay.

September, 1911. Vol. II, No. 5. p. 195.

DIVINE RIGHT

We would like to know what rights the white people of this land are going to be able to retain? Step by step their dearest and most cherished prerogatives are being invaded, and THE CRISIS wants to say right here and now that it does not countenance oppression of the downtrodden whites by arrogant black folk. A few years ago the right to kick a darky off the sidewalk was unquestioned in the most devout circles, and yet to-day they actually complain at being called by their front names.

Everybody knows that for three hundred years the most jealously guarded right of white men in this land and others has been the right to seduce black women without legal, social or moral penalty. Many white mothers and daughters of the best families have helped to maintain this ancient and honored custom by loading the victims of their fathers' and husbands' lust with every epithet of insult and degradation. Thus has the sweet cleanness of their own race virtue shone holier and higher.

Yet what do we see to-day? The black husbands and brothers

are beginning to revolt. In three separate cases, in three consecutive months and in three localities of the southern South have these blind and ignorant fellows actually killed white men who were demanding these ancient rights, and have compelled the chivalry of the land to rise and lynch the black defenders of defenceless virtue; also two strangely illogical black women have been simultaneously killed and a dark and whimpering little girl burned to a quivering crisp.

What does all this mean? Does it portend an unthinkable time when the white man can only get his rights by lynching impudent black husbands and squeamish sweethearts? If so, then, by the Great Jehovah, we can depend on the best friends of the Negro to vindicate the ancient liberties of this land! Anglo-Saxon freedom seems safe at least in the hands of most leaders of Southern society, not to mention the blue blood of Pennsylvania.

Meantime, dear colored brethren, we confess to the error of our ways. We have steadfastly opposed lynching on all occasions, but the South is converting us. We acknowledge our fault. Hereafter we humbly pray that every man, black or white, who is anxious to defend women, will be willing to be lynched for his faith. Let black men especially kill lecherous white invaders of their homes and then take their lynching gladly like men.

It's worth it!

March, 1912. Vol. III, No. 5. p. 197.

OUR OWN CONSENT

We should remember that in these days great groups of men are not long oppressed but by their own consent. Oppression costs the oppressor too much if the oppressed stand up and protest. The protest need not be merely physical—the throwing of stones and bullets—if it is mental and spiritual, if it expresses itself in silent, persistent dissatisfaction, the cost to the oppressor is terrific.

This fact we continually forget. We say: the South is in saddle; what can we do against twenty millions? The white oppressor rules; of what avail is agitation against ninety millions?

If you doubt the efficacy of agitation and protest, ask yourself: Why is the reactionary oligarchic South so afraid of even one protesting voice? Why are the Northern doughfaces, their millionaire backers and their allied teachers in Southern schools so panicstricken at one small voice? Why is the American Negro hater always so anxious to affirm that the Negro assents to his chains and insults, or that the "responsible" Negroes assent, or that "the only real Negro leader" assents? Is it because they know that when one protesting voice finds its fellows it may find soon ten millions? And when ten million voices are raised to say:

Disfranchisement is undemocratic; "Jim Crow" legislation adds insult to theft; "color discrimination is barbarism—"

When ten million voices say this they will, they must, be heard. And when their cause is once heard, its justice will be evident and its triumph sure. Agitate then, brother; protest, reveal the truth and refuse to be silenced. The most damnable canker at the heart of America is her treatment of colored folk.

January, 1913. Vol. V, No. 3. p. 129.

HAIL COLUMBIA

Hail Columbia, Happy Land! Again the glorious tradition of Anglo-Saxon manhood have been upheld! Again the chivalry of American white men has been magnificently vindicated. Down on your knees, black men, and hear the tale with awestruck faces. Learn from the Superior Race. We do not trust our own faltering pen and purblind sight to describe the reception of the suffragists at the capital of the land. We quote from the Southern reporters of the Northern press:

> Five thousand women, marching in the woman-suffrage pageant yesterday, practically fought their way foot by foot up Pennsylvania Avenue, through a surging mass of humanity that completely defied the Washington police, swamped the marchers, and broke their procession into little companies. The women, trudging stoutly along under great difficulties, were able to com-

plete their march only when troops of cavalry from Fort Myer were rushed into Washington to take charge of Pennsylvania Avenue. No inauguration has ever produced such scenes, which in many instances amounted to little less than riots.

More than 100 persons, young and old, of both sexes, were crushed and trampled in the uncontrollable crowd in Pennsylvania Avenue yesterday, while two ambulances of the Emergency Hospital came and went constantly for six hours, always impeded and at times actually opposed, so that the doctor and driver literally had to fight their way to give succor to the injured.

Hoodlums, many of them in uniform, leaned forward till their cigarettes almost touched the women's faces while blowing smoke in their eyes, and the police said not a word, not even when every kind of insult was hurled.

To the white-haired women the men shouted continuously: "Granny! granny! We came to see chickens, not hens! Go home and sit in the corner!" To the younger women they yelled: "Say, what you going to do tonight? Can't we make a date?" and the police only smiled. The rowdies jumped on the running boards of the automobiles and snatched the flags from the elderly women, and they attempted to pull the girls from the floats.

Wasn't it glorious? Does it not make you burn with shame to be a mere black man when such mighty deeds are done by the Leaders of Civilization? Does it not make you "ashamed of your race?" Does it not make you "want to be white?"

And do you know (we are almost ashamed to say it) the Negro again lost a brilliant opportunity to rise in his "imitative" way. Ida Husted Harper says:

"We made the closest observation along the entire line and not in one instance did we hear a colored man make a remark, although there were thousands of them."

Another white woman writes:

"I wish to speak a word in favor of the colored people during the suffrage parade. Not one of them was boisterous or rude as with great difficulty we passed along the unprotected avenue. The difference between them and those insolent, bold white men was remarkable. They were quiet and respectable and earnest, and seemed sorry for the indignities which were incessantly heaped upon us. There were few policemen to protect us as we made our first parade in Washington, and the dignified silence of the colored people and the sympathy in their faces was a great contrast to those who should have known better. I thank them in the name of all the women for their kindness."

Now look at that! Good Lord! has the Negro *no* sense? Can he grasp no opportunity?

But let him not think to gain by any such tactics. The South sees his game and is busy promoting bills to prevent his marrying any wild-eyed suffragette who may be attracted by his pusillanimous decency. Already the Ohio legislature has been flooded by forged petitions from a "Negro advancement society of New York" to push the intermarriage bill!

No, sir! White men are on the firing line, and if they don't want white women for wives they will at least keep them for prostitutes. Beat them back, keep them down; flatter them, call them "visions of loveliness" and tell them that the place for woman is in the home, even if she hasn't got a home. If she is homely or poor or made the mistake of being born with brains, and begins to protest at the doll's house or the bawdy house, kick her and beat her and insult her until in terror she slinks back to her kennel or walks the midnight streets. Don't give in; don't give her power; don't give her a vote whatever you do. Keep the price of women down, make them weak and cheap.

Shall the time ever dawn in the Land of the Brave when a free white American citizen may not buy as many women as his purse permits? Perish the thought and Hail Columbia, Happy Land!

April, 1913. Vol. V, No. 6. pp. 289-90.

THE FRUIT OF THE TREE

Let no one for a moment mistake that the present increased attack on the Negro along all lines is but the legitimate fruit of that long campaign for subserviency and surrender which a large party of Negroes have fathered now some twenty years. It is not necessary to question the motives of these men nor to deny that their insistence on thrift and saving has had its large and beneficent effect. But, on the other hand, only the blind and foolish can fail to see that a continued campaign in every nook and corner of this land, preaching to people white and colored, that the Negro is chiefly to blame for his condition, that he must not insist on his rights, that he should not take part in politics, that "Jim Crowism" is defensible and even advantageous, that he should humbly bow to the storm until the lordly white man grants him clemency—the fruit of this disgraceful doctrine is disfranchisement, segregation, lynching, and that last straw, the cowardly and unspeakable Patterson. Fellow Negroes, is it not time to be men? Is it not time to strike back when struck? Is it not high time to hold up our heads and clench our teeth and swear by the Eternal God we will NOT be slaves, and that no aider, abetter and teacher of slavery in any shape or guise can longer lead us?

September, 1913. Vol. VI, No. 5. p. 232.

DON'T BE BITTER!

Is it not singular that so many white folk in advising black folk —and the ancient industry of advising blacks is booming just now—are careful to say, first and last: "Don't be bitter!" Why is there this insistence on the necessity of a sweet and even temper as an asset in life? Manifestly it is because most Americans who know or who begin faintly to realize the difficulties, complications and insults of a dark man's life today cannot imagine themselves suffering such wrongs without resorting to dynamite or suicide.

With the best will, therefore, they hasten to say: "Don't be bitter—don't mind—look on the bright side—and—and—"— then they trail off helplessly and look you rather miserably and apologetically in the face.

Recently in Atlanta five hundred colored college students met to consider the student volunteer movement. They had been invited, after several years' hesitation, by Mr. John R. Mott, who has been making a desperate attempt for twenty-five years to avoide the "Negro Problem" in his missionary enterprises. He found five hundred earnest, thoughtful young people and he selected among others a southern white man to tell them not to be "bitter!" The white man sailed into his task jauntily. He told of the mission of the races—"strength" from one race, "enterprise" from another, "aggressions" from a third and from Negroes "submission"—then he looked into one thousand eyes and he paused. The sweat began to ooze out of his forehead and his sentences got mixed. Did he see "bitterness" in those eyes? No! but he did not see submission. "At least," he stammered, "your fathers and mothers—I don't know about you all" and he tried a pleasant little interlude which faded to a sickly grin. When at last he sat down even his white friends in the audience knew that he had missed his opportunity. They knew still more when a black man, William Pickens, stood up and with unanswerable logic told Mr. Mott and his friends that Christianity for black men started with the right to vote and nothing less.

If our friends mean by bitterness, the futile, impatient gestures of disgust, the widely boastful word and dumb despair, let them save their advice. Colored Americans are not gesticulating nor yelling, nor committing suicide in numbers large enough to be alarming. But they are looking this nation more and more squarely in the eyes. They are asking in calm, level voice: "How long do you expect to keep up this foolishness and how long do you expect us to submit to it?" That is all. We are just asking. Do you suggest duties for us to attend to? Very good, we shall try to attend to them; we have tried in the past, as you may remember, and we are trying now, as the Census reports prove, but at the same time we keep asking the question: "How long? How much more? What next?" This is what we are doing; if this be bitterness, we are bitter.

August, 1914. Vol. VIII, No. 4. pp. 180-1.

THAT CAPITAL "N"

From time to time persons write us for a brief statement of the reasons for capitalizing the word *Negro.*

The ordinary rules of capitalization enjoin the use of a capital letter for all proper nouns, all names of tribes, races, sects or organized bodies of men.

For this reason the word Negro when referring to a race of men has always been capitalized until late in the Nineteenth Century. With the defense of Negro slavery in those days there grew up the custom of using the small letter for the word since Negroes were looked upon as "real estate" or as moveable property like horses, cows, etc.

At the time the great increase in printing and use of printing machines led to a disuse of capital letters in many cases where they had formerly been used and a great distaste to resorting to them among printers of English. Consequently the rule books used in most printing offices today say that capitals shall be used for the names of all nations and races "except Negro." This has been defended by saying that Negro is not the name of a race but the description of the color of a people, being correlative with white, yellow, etc.

This argument is manifestly false. Black is the correlative of white and Negro does not describe color since all the persons designated as Negroes are by no means black, even in Africa. If, therefore, we follow analogy we cannot refuse to capitalize Negro when we capitalize Caucasian, Malay, Indian, Chinese, etc. Not to capitalize Negro under such circumstances is a direct, and in these days a more and more conscious, insult to at least 150,000,000 human beings and no person or institution will persist in this insult if they realize that these people regard the usage as such.

February, 1916. Vol. XI, No. 4, p. 184.

COWARDICE

No colored man can read an account of the recent lynching at Gainesville, Fla., without being ashamed of his people. The action was characteristic. White officers, knowing themselves in the wrong and afraid of the resistance of colored men, sneaked in at midnight to serve a warrant on a person whom they hoped would be helpless and ignorant of their intentions. Two of them seized the man in his house and after the melee one of the white men was dead and the other seriously wounded. Of the right and wrong of this no one will ever be really sure. There is no proof that he knowingly resisted arrest. There is proof, on the other hand, that after this extraordinary attack his colored fellows acted like a set of cowardly sheep. Without resistance they let a white mob whom they outnumbered two to one, torture, harry and murder their women, shoot down innocent men entirely unconnected with the alleged crime, and finally to cap the climax, they caught and surrendered the wretched man whose attempted arrest caused the difficulty.

No people who behave with the absolute cowardice shown by these colored people can hope to have the sympathy or help of the civilized folk. The men and women who had nothing to do with the alleged crime should have fought in self-defense to the last ditch if they had killed every white man in the county and themselves been killed. The man who surrendered to a lynching mob the victim of the sheriff ought himself to have been locked up.

In the last analysis lynching of Negroes is going to stop in the South when the cowardly mob is faced by effective guns in the hands of the people determined to sell their souls dearly.

October, 1916. Vol. XII, No. 6. pp. 270-1.

LET US REASON TOGETHER

Brothers, we are on the Great Deep. We have cast off on the vast voyage which will lead to Freedom or Death.

For three centuries we have suffered and cowered. No race ever gave Passive Resistance and Submission to Evil longer, more piteous trial. Today we raise the terrible weapon of Self-Defense. When the murderer comes, he shall no longer strike us in the back. When the armed lynchers gather, we too must gather armed. When the mob moves, we propose to meet it with bricks and clubs and guns.

But we must tread here with solemn caution. We must never

let justifiable self-defense against individuals become blind and lawless offense against all white folk. We must not seek reform by violence. We must not seek Vengeance. "Vengeance is Mine," saith the Lord; or to put it otherwise, only Infinite Justice and Knowledge can assign blame in this poor world, and we ourselves are sinful men, struggling desperately with our own crime and ignorance. We must defend ourselves, our homes, our wifes and children against the lawless without stint or hesitation; but we must carefully and scrupulously avoid on our own part bitter and unjustifiable aggression against anybody.

This line is difficult to draw. In the South the Police and Public Opinion back the mob and the least resistance on the part of the innocent black victim is nearly always construed as a lawless attack on society and government. In the North the Police and the Public will dodge and falter, but in the end they wil back the Right when the Truth is made clear to them.

But whether the line between just resistance and angry retaliation is hard or easy, we must draw it carefully, not in wild resentment, but in grim and sober consideration; and then back of the impregnable fortress of the Divine Right of Self-Defense, which is sanctioned by every law of God and man, in every land, civilized and uncivilized, we must take our unfaltering stand.

Honor, endless and undying Honor, to every man, black or white, who in Houston, East St. Louis, Washington and Chicago gave his life for Civilization and Order.

If the United States is to be a Land of Law, we would live humbly and peaceably in it—working, singing, learning and dreaming to make it and ourselves nobler and better; if it is to be a Land of Mobs and Lynchers, we might as well die today as tomorrow.

And how can man die better
Than facing fearful odds
For the ashes of his father
And the temples of his gods?

September, 1919. Vol. XVIII, No. 5. p. 231.

A UNIVERSITY COURSE IN LYNCHING

We are glad to note that the University of Missouri has opened a course in Applied Lynching. Many of our American universities have long defended the institution, but they have not been frank or brave enough actually to arrange a mob murder so that the students could see it in detail. The University of Georgia did, to be sure, stage a lynching a few years ago but this was done at night and the girls did not have a fair chance to see it. At the University of Missouri the matter was arranged in broad daylight with ample notice, by five hundred men and boys who were "comparatively orderly", and it was viewed by some fifty women most of whom we understand were students of the University. We are very much in favor of this method of teaching 100 per cent Americanism; as long as mob murder is an approved institution in the United States, students at the universities should have a first-hand chance to judge exactly what a lynching is.

In the case of James T. Scott everything was as it should be. He was a janitor at the University who protested his innocence to his last breath. He was charged with having "lured" a fourteen year old girl in broad daylight far from her home and "down the railroad tracks". He was "positively identified" by the girl, and while the father deprecates violence he has "no doubt" of the murdered man's guilt.

Here was every element of the modern American lynching. We are glad that the future fathers and mothers of the West saw it, and we are expecting great results from this course of study at one of the most eminent of our State Universities.

June, 1923. Vol. XXVI, No. 2. p. 55.

MOB TACTICS

There has been developed in the United States a regular technique in matters of mob violence. Matters move somewhat as follows:

A crime is committed. The police hasten to accuse a Negro. This, of course, is popular because the white public readily believes in Negro crime. A Negro is arrested. If he is promptly lynched the police are vindicated and the guilty white persons saved from fear of detection. If lynching is delayed but threatened a mob usually attacks the Negro district. This gives a chance for looting and stealing. If any Negroes defend themselves, immediately the police, often assisted by the militia, promptly disarm all Negroes and charge a man with rioting. If any white people are arrested for rioting nearly all of them are discharged; but the Negroes are held and prosecuted. This serves to intimidate the Negro population and keeps it from attempting any self-defense, however innocent the defenders may be, and in no matter how grave danger to life, limb and property.

The result of all this is to mystify and mislead the public. By the time that rioting is over, they are under the impression that the Negroes were partially responsible for starting the trouble and that they were armed and conspiring to kill innocent white people. Thus aggression against Negro Americans becomes an exciting form of sport for the lower order of white folk, in which they have practically nothing to lose and little to fear.

The technique of this procedure is, of course, taken from the acts of England and other countries in dealing with the colonies. Whenever the natives are subdued or punished and compelled to bow to the will of white folk, the explanation is that the natives were the aggressors; that the Colonial Power was acting in self-defense and that civilization was in danger.

The only solution to this kind of problem is not simply to permit but to encourage Negroes to keep and use arms in defense against lynchers and mobs.

August, 1927. Vol. XXXIV, No. 6. p. 204.

PARABLES

EASTER

The land lay smiling in spring splendor, heavy with verdure gleaming with glad sunshine. Athwart it fell the dark shadow of a toiling man; he was great of limb and black, thick of countenance and hard-haired. His face was half-hopeless, half-vacant, with only a faint gleam of something dead and awakening deep in his deep-set eyes. His feet were chained, his neck yoked and his body scarred. They that had driven him and ridden and thrust him threateningly through the thick forest were now afraid of him. They feared the reproach of his dumb, low-burning eyes. They feared the half-articulate sounds of his moving lips, and saw with terror the slow, steady growth of his body, that great, black, undying body. So they took council together to kill him—lying to his ears, crucifying his soul, until he, bent and bowed and heavy with his own weakness, fell and lay his mighty length in stupor along the earth. And the earth trembled.

Sweating and deep of breath the pale-faced murderers worked and delved, digging a cavernous grave and walling it with Oppression. Then shame-faced, yet grim, they turned northward. At daybreak they stood upon the hills of God with faces white and good, crying: "Come, O brothers, Northern brothers, the Thing that hindered our love is dead, dead, long dead." The brothers of the North came trooping, oily tongued, unctuous and rich. Yet they of the North and South looked not each other in the eye, but slunk along false-smiling.

One timid one said:

"O Brother South—I hear chains."

But the South answered:

"Nay, that is the chiming of Negro school bells."

Yet another, quibbling, found his mouth:

"Did the Thing—die—happy?"

The South choked and muttered:

"Happy—so happy—and praising his—Master, and his Best Friends."

"But, Brother, your hands are bloody," quavered a third.

"Blood of the offering burned at the stake for the culture and supremacy of the White Race."

Then hastily the South said in chorus as if to forestall reply:

"See where we have laid Him," and they pointed to that grave, walled with Oppression.

But suddenly the World was wings and the voice of the Angel of the Resurrection beat like a mighty wind athwart their ears, crying:

"He is not here—He is risen."

Risen above half his ignorance; risen to more than six hundred millions of property; risen to a new literature and the faint glimmering of a new Art; risen to a dawning determination to be free; risen to a newer and greater ideal of Humanity than the world has known. RISEN!

April, 1911. Vol. I, No. 6. p. 20.

THE WOMAN

In the land of the Heavy Laden came once a dreary day. And the King who sat upon the Great White Throne raised up his eyes and saw afar off how the hills around were hot with hostile feet, and the sound of the mocking of his enemies struck anxiously on the King's ears, for the King loved his enemies. So the King lifted up his hand and in the glittering silence spake softly, saying, "Call the servants of the King." Then the herald stepped before the armpost of the throne and cried: "Thus saith the High and Mighty One, whose name is Holy: the servants of the King." Now, of the servants of the King there were a hundred and forty-four thousand—tried men and brave, brawny of arm and quick in wit; aye, too, and women of wisdom and marvelous in beauty and grace. And yet on this drear day when the King called their ears were thick with the dust of the enemy, their eyes were blinded with the flashing of his spears, and they hid their faces in dread silence and moved not, even at the King's behest. So the herald called again. And the servants cowered in very shame, but none came forth. But the third blast of the herald struck upon a woman's heart, afar. And the woman straightway left her baking and sweeping and the rattle of tins. And the woman straightway left her chatting and gossiping and the sewing of garments. And the woman stood before the King, saying, "The servant of thy servants, O Lord."

Then the King smiled—smiled wondrously, so that the setting sun burst through the clouds and the hearts of the King's men dried hard within them. And the low-voiced King said, so low that even they that listened heard not well: "Go smite me mine enemies that they cease to do evil in my sight." And the woman quailed and trembled. Three times she lifted up her eyes unto the hills and saw the heathen whirling onward in their rage. And seeing she shrank—three times she shrank and crept to the King's feet. "O King," she cried, "I am but a woman," and the King answered: "Go then, mother of men." And the woman said, "Nay, King, but I am still a maid." Whereat the King cried: "O Maid made Man, thou shall be Bride of God." And yet the third time the woman shrank at the thunder in her ears, and whispered: "Dear God, I am black." And the King spake not, but swept the veiling of his face aside and lifted up the light of his countenance upon her and lo! it was black.

So the woman went forth on the hills of God to do battle for the King on that drear day in the land of the Heavy Laden, when the heathen raged and imagined a vain thing.

May, 1911. Vol. II, No. 1. p. 19.

JESUS CHRIST IN GEORGIA

The convict guard laughed.

"I don't know," he said, "I hadn't thought of that——"

He hesitated and looked at the stranger curiously. In the solemn twilight he got an impression of unusual height and soft dark eyes.

"Curious sort of acquaintance for the Colonel," he thought;

then he continued aloud: "But that nigger there is bad; a born thief and ought to be sent up for life; is practically; got ten years last time——"

Here the voice of the promoter talking within interrupted; he was bending over his figures, sitting by the Colonel. He was slight, with a sharp nose.

"The convicts," he said, "would cost us $96 a year and board. Well, we can squeeze that so that it won't be over $125 apiece. Now, if these fellows are driven, they can build this line within twelve months. It will be running next April. Freights will fall fifty per cent. Why, man, you will be a millionaire in less than ten years."

The Colonel started. He was a thick, short man, with clean-shaven face, and a certain air of breeding about the lines of his countenance; the word millionaire sounded well in his ears. He thought—he thought a great deal; he almost heard the puff of the fearfully costly automobile that was coming up the road, and he said:

"I suppose we might as well hire them."

"Of course," answered the promoter.

The voice of the tall stranger in the corner broke in here:

"It will be a good thing for them?" he said, half in question.

The Colonel moved. "The guard makes strange friends," he thought to himself. "What's this man doing here, anyway?" He looked at him, or rather, looked at his eyes, and then somehow felt a warming toward him. He said:

"Well, at least it can't harm them—they're beyond that."

"It will do them good, then," said the stranger again. The promoter shrugged his shoulders.

"It will do us good," he said.

But the Colonel shook his head impatiently. He felt a desire to justify himself before those eyes, and he answered:

"Yes, it will do them good; or, at any rate, it won't make them any worse than they are."

Then he started to say something else, but here sure enough the sound of the automobile breathing at the gate stopped him and they all arose.

"It is settled, then," said the promoter.

"Yes," said the Colonel, signing his name and turning toward the stranger again.

"Are you going into town?" he asked with the Southern

courtesy of white man to white man in a country town. The stranger said he was. "Then come along in my machine. I want to talk to you about this."

They went out to the car. The stranger as he went turned again to look back at the convict. He was a tall, powerfully built black fellow. His face was sullen, with a low forehead, thick, hanging lips, and bitter eyes. There was revolt written about the mouth, and a hangdog expression. He stood bending over his pile of stones pounding listlessly.

Beside him stood a boy of twelve, yellow, with a hunted, crafty look. The convict raised his eyes, and they met the eyes of the stranger. The hammer fell from his hands.

The stranger turned slowly toward the automobile, and the Colonel introduced him. He could not exactly catch the foreign-sounding name, but he mumbled something as he presented him to his wife and little girl, who were waiting. As they whirled away he started to talk, but the stranger had taken the little girl into his lap, and together they conversed in low tones all the way home.

In some way, they did not exactly know how, they got the impression that the man was a teacher, and of course he must be a foreigner. The long cloak-like coat told this. They rode in the twilight through the half-lighted town, and at last drew up before the Colonel's mansion, with its ghostlike pillars.

The lady in the back seat was thinking of the guests she had invited to dinner, and wondered if she ought not to ask this man to stay. He seemed cultured, and she supposed he was some acquaintance of the Colonel's. It would be rather a distinction to have him there, with the Judge's wife and daughter and the Rector. She spoke almost before she thought:

"You will enter and rest awhile?"

The Colonel and the little girl insisted. For a moment the stranger seemed about to refuse. He said he was on his way North, where he had some business for his father in Pennsylvania. Then, for the child's sake, he consented. Up the steps they went, and into the dark parlor, and there they sat and talked a long time. It was a curious conversation. Afterward they did not remember exactly what was said, and yet they all remembered a certain strange satisfaction in that long talk.

Presently the nurse came for the reluctant child, and the hostess bethought herself:

"We will have a cup of tea—you will be dry and tired."

She rang and switched on a blaze of light. With one accord they all looked at the stranger, for they had hardly seen him well in the glooming twilight. The woman started in amazement and the Colonel half rose in anger. Why, the man was a mulatto, surely—even if he did not own the Negro blood, their practised eyes knew it. He was tall and straight, and the coat looked like a Jewish gabardine. His hair hung in close curls far down the sides of his face, and his face was olive, even yellow.

A peremptory order rose to the Colonel's lips, and froze there as he caught the stranger's eyes. Those eyes, where had he seen those eyes before? He remembered them long years ago—the soft tear-filled eyes of a brown girl. He remembered many things, and his face grew drawn and white. Those eyes kept burning into him, even when they were turned half away toward the staircase, where the white figure of the child hovered with her nurse, and waved goodnight. The lady sank into her chair and thought: "What will the Judge's wife say? How did the Colonel come to invite this man here? How shall we be rid of him?" She looked at the Colonel in reproachful consternation.

Just then the door opened and the old butler came in. He was an ancient black man with tufted white hair, and he held before him a large silver tray filled with a china tea service. The stranger rose slowly and stretched forth his hands as if to bless the viands. The old man paused in bewilderment, tottered and then, with sudden gladness in his eyes, dropped to his knees as the tray crashed to the floor.

"My Lord!" he whispered, "and My God!" But the woman screamed:

"Mother's china!"

The doorbell rang.

"Heavens! Here is the dinner party!" exclaimed the lady.

She turned toward the door, but there in the hall, clad in her night clothes, was the little girl. She had stolen down the stairs to see the stranger again, and the nurse above was calling in vain. The woman felt hysterical and scolded at the nurse, but the stranger had stretched out his arms, and with a glad cry the child nestled in them. "Of such," he whispered, "is the Kingdom of Heaven," as he slowly mounted the stairs with his little burden.

The mother was glad; anything to be rid of the interloper even for a moment. The bell rang again, and she hastened toward the door, which the loitering black maid was just opening. She did not notice the shadow of the stranger as he came slowly down the stairs and paused by the newel post, dark and silent.

The Judge's wife entered. She was an old woman, frilled and powdered into a caricature of youth, and gorgeously gowned. She came forward, smiling with extended hands, but just as she was opposite the stranger, a chill from somewhere seemed to strike her, and she shuddered and cried: "What a draft!" as she drew a silken shawl about her and shook hands cordially; she forgot to ask who the stranger was. The Judge strode in unseeing, thinking of a puzzling case of theft.

"Eh? What? Oh—er—yes—good-evening," he said, "good-evening."

Behind them came a young woman in the glory of youth, daintily silked, with diamonds around her fair neck, beautiful in face and form. She came in lightly, but stopped with a little gasp; then she laughed gaily and said:

"Why, I beg your pardon. Was it not curious? I thought I saw there behind your man"—she hesitated ("but he must be a servant," she argued)—"the shadow of wide white wings. It was but the light on the drapery. What a turn it gave me—so glad to be here!" And she smiled again. With her came a tall and haughty naval officer. Hearing this lady refer to the servant, he hardly looked at him, but held his gilded cap and cloak carelessly toward him; the stranger took them and placed them carefully on the rack.

Last came the Rector, a man of forty, and well clothed. He started to pass the stranger, stopped and looked at him inquiringly.

"I beg your pardon," he said, "I beg your pardon, I think I have met you?"

The stranger made no answer, and the hostess nervously hurried the guests on. But the Rector lingered and looked perplexed.

"Surely I know you; I have met you somewhere," he said, putting his hand vaguely to his head. "You—you remember me, do you not?"

The stranger quietly swept his cloak aside, and to the hostess's unspeakable relief moved toward the door.

"I never knew you," he said in low tones, as he went.

The lady murmured some faint excuse about intruders, but the Rector stood with annoyance written on his face.

"I beg a thousand pardons," he said to the hostess absently. "It is a great pleasure to be here—somehow I thought I knew that man. I am sure I knew him, once."

The stranger had passed down the steps, and as he went the nurse-maid, lingering at the top of the staircase, flew down after him, caught his cloak, trembled, hesitated, and then kneeled in the dust. He touched her lightly with his hand and said, "Go, and sin no more."

With a glad cry the maid left the house with its open door and turned north, running, while the stranger turned eastward to the night. As they parted a long low howl rose tremulously and reverberated through the town. The Colonel's wife within shuddered.

"The bloodhounds," she said. The Rector answered carelessly.

"Another one of those convicts escaped, I suppose; really, they need severer measures." Then he stopped. He was trying to remember that stranger's name. The Judge's wife looked about for the draft and arranged her shawl. The girl glanced at the white drapery in the hall, but the young officer was bending over her, and the fires of life burned in her veins.

Howl after howl rose in the night, swelled and died away. The stranger strode rapidly along the highway and out into the deep forest. There he paused and stood waiting, tall and still. A mile up the road behind him a man was running, tall and powerful and black, with crime-stained face, with convict's stripes upon him and shackles on his legs. He ran and jumped in little short steps, and the chains rang. He fell and rose again, while the howl of the hounds rung harder behind him.

Into the forest he leaped and crept and jumped and ran, streaming with sweat; seeing the tall form rise before him, he stopped suddenly, dropped his hands in sullen impotence and sank panting to the earth. A bloodhound shot into the woods behind him, howled, whined and fawned before the stranger's feet. Hound after hound bayed, leapt and lay there; then silent, one by one, with bowed head, they crept backward toward the town.

The stranger made a cup of his hands and gave the man water to drink, bathed his hot head, and gently took the chains and irons from his feet. By and by the convict stood up. Day was dawning above the treetops. He looked into the stranger's face, and for a moment a gladness swept over the stains of his face.

"Why, you'se a nigger, too," he said.

Then the convict seemed anxious to justify himself.

"I never had no chance," he said furtively.

"Thou shalt not steal," said the stranger.

The man bridled.

"But how about them? Can they steal? Didn't they steal a whole year's work and then, when I stole to keep from starving —" he glanced at the stranger. "No, I didn't steal just to keep from starving. I stole to be stealing. I can't help stealing. Seems like when I sees things I just must—but, yes, I'll try!"

The convict looked down at his striped clothes, but the stranger had taken off his long coat—and put it around him, and the stripes disappeared. In the opening morning the black man started toward the low log farmhouse in the distance, and the stranger stood watching him. There was a new glory in the day. The black man's face cleared up and the farmer was glad to get him.

All day he worked as he had never worked before, and the farmer gave him some cold food toward night.

"You can sleep in the barn," he said, and turned away.

"How much do I git a day?" asked the man.

The farmer scowled:

"If you'll sign a contract for the season," he said, "I'll give you ten dollars a month."

"I won't sign no contract to be a slave," said the man doggedly.

"Yes, you will," said the farmer, threateningly, "or I'll call the convict guard." And he grinned.

The convict shrunk and slouched to the barn. As night fell he looked out and saw the farmer leave the place. Slowly he crept out and sneaked toward the house. He looked into the kitchen door. No one was there, but the supper was spread as if the mistress had laid it and gone out. He ate ravenously. Then he looked into the front room and listened. He could hear low voices on the porch. On the table lay a silver watch. He gazed at it, and in a moment was beside it, with his hands on it. Quickly he slipped out of the house and slouched toward the field. He saw his employer coming along the highway. He fled back stealthily and around to the front of the house, when suddenly he stopped. He felt the great dark eyes of the stranger and saw the same dark, cloaklike coat, where he was seated on the doorstep talking with the mistress of the house. Slowly, guiltily, he turned back, entered the kitchen and laid the watch where he had found it; and then he rushed wildly with arms outstretched back toward the stranger.

The woman had laid supper for her husband, and going down from the house had walked out toward a neighbor's. She was gone but a little while, and when she came back she started to see a dark figure on the doorsteps under the tall red oak. She thought it was the new Negro hand until he said in a soft voice:

"Will you give me bread?"

Reassured at the voice of a white man, she answered quickly in her soft Southern tones:

"Why, certainly."

She was a little woman. Once she had been handsome, but now her face was drawn with work and care. She was nervous, and was always thinking, wishing, wanting for something. She went in and got him some cornbread and a glass of cool, rich buttermilk, and then came out and sat down beside him. She began, quite unconsciously, to tell him about herself—the things she had done, and had not done, and the things she had wished. She told him of her husband, and this new farm they were trying to buy. She said it was so hard to get niggers to work. She said they ought all to be in the chain gang and made to work. Even then some ran away. Only yesterday one had escaped.

At last she gossiped of her neighbors; how good they were and how bad.

"And do you like them all?" asked the stranger.

She hesitated.

"Most of them," she said; and then, looking up into his face and putting her hand in his as though he were her father, she said:

"There are none I hate; no, none at all."

He looked away and said dreamily:

"You love your neighbor as yourself?"

She hesitated—

"I try——" she began, and then looked the way he was looking; down under the hill, where lay a little, half-ruined cabin.

"They are niggers," she said briefly.

He looked at her. Suddenly a confusion came over her, and she insisted, she knew not why—"

"But they are niggers."

With a sudden impulse she rose, and hurriedly lighted the lamp that stood just within the door and held it above her head. She saw his dark face and curly hair. She shrieked in angry terror, and rushed down the path; and just as she rushed down, the black convict came running up with hands outstretched. They met in midpath, and before he could stop he had run against her, and she fell heavily to earth and lay white and still. Her husband came rushing up with cry and oath:

"I knew it," he said; "it is that runaway nigger." He held the black man struggling to the earth, and raised his voice to a yell. Down the highway came the convict guard with hound and mob and gun. They poured across the fields. The farmer motioned to them.

"He—attacked—my wife," he gasped.

The mob snarled and worked silently. Right to the limb of the red oak they hoisted the struggling, writhing black man, while others lifted the dazed woman. Right and left as she tottered to the house she searched for the stranger, with a sick yearning, but the stranger was gone. And she told none of her guest.

"No—no—I want nothing," she insisted, until they left her, as they thought, asleep. For a time she lay still listening to the departure of the mob. Then she rose. She shuddered as she heard the creaking of the limb where the body hung. But resolutely she crawled to the window and peered out into the moonlight; she saw the dead man writhe. He stretched his arms out like a cross, looking upward. She gasped and clung to the window sill. Behind the swaying body, and down where the little, half-ruined cabin lay, a single flame flashed up amid the far-off shout and cry of the mob. A fierce joy sobbed up through the terror in her soul and then sank abashed as she watched the flame rise. Suddenly whirling into one great crimson column it shot to the top of the sky and threw great arms athwart the gloom until above the world and behind the roped and swaying form below hung quivering and burning a great crimson cross.

She hid her dizzy, aching head in an agony of tears, and dared not look, for she knew. Her dry lips moved:

"Despised and rejected of men."

She knew, and the very horror of it lifted her dull and shrinking eyelids. There, heaven-tall, earth-wide, hung the stranger on the crimson cross, riven and bloodstained with thorn-crowned head and pierced hands. She stretched her arms and shrieked.

He did not hear. He did not see. His calm dark eyes all sorrowful were fastened on the writhing, twisting body of the thief, and a voice came out of the winds of the night, saying:

"This day thou shalt be with me in Paradise!"

December, 1911. Vol. III, No. 2. pp. 70-4.

A MILD SUGGESTION

They were sitting on the leeward deck of the vessel and the colored man was there with his usual look of unconcern. Before the seasickness his presence aboard had caused some upheaval. The Woman, for instance, glancing at the Southerner, had refused point blank to sit beside him at meals, so she had changed places with the Little Old Lady. The Westerner, who sat opposite, said he did not care a——, then he looked at the Little Old Lady, and added in a lower voice to the New Yorker that there was no accounting for tastes. The Southerner from the other table broadened his back and tried to express with his shoulders both ancestors and hauteur. All this, however, was half forgotten during the seasickness, and the Woman sat beside the colored man for a full half hour before she noticed it, and then was glad to realize that the Southerner was too sick to see. Now again with sunshine and smiling weather, they all quite naturally reverted (did the Southerner suggest it?) to the Negro problem. The usual solutions had been suggested: education, work, emigration, etc.

They had not noticed the back of the colored man, until the thoughtless Westerner turned toward him and said breezily: "Well, now, what do you say? I guess you are rather interested." The colored man was leaning over the rail and about to light his cigarette—he had several such bad habits, as the Little Old Lady noticed. The Southerner simply stared. Over the face of the colored man went the shadow of several expressions; some the New Yorker could interpret, others he could not.

"I have," said the colored man, with deliberation, "a perfect solution." The Southerner selected a look of disdain from his repertoire, and assumed it. The Woman moved nearer, but partly turned her back. The Westerner and the Little Old Lady sat down. "Yes," repeated the colored man, "I have a perfect solution. The trouble with most of the solutions which are generally suggested is that they aggravate the disease." The Southerner could not help looking interested. "For instance," proceeded the colored man, airily waving his hand, "take education; education means ambition, dissatisfaction and revolt. You cannot both educate people and hold them down."

"Then stop educating them," growled the Southerner aside.

"Or," continued the colored man, "if the black man works, he must come into competition with whites——"

"He sure will, and it ought to be stopped," returned the Westerner. "It brings down wages."

"Precisely," said the speaker, "and if by underselling the labor market he develops a few millionaires, how now would you protect your residential districts or your select social circles or—your daughters?"

The Southerner started angrily, but the colored man was continuing placidly with a far-off look in his eyes. "Now, migration is both costly and inhuman; the transportation would be the smallest matter. You must buy up perhaps a thousand millions' worth of Negro property; you must furnish some capital for the masses of poor; you must get some place for them to go; you must protect them there, and here you must pay not only higher wages to white men, but still higher on account of the labor scarcity. Meantime, the Negroes suddenly removed from one climate and social system to another climate and utterly new conditions would die in droves—it would be simply prolonged murder at enormous cost.

"Very well," continued the colored man, seating himself and throwing away his cigarette, "listen to my plan," looking almost quizzically at the Little Old Lady; "you must not be alarmed at its severity—it may seem radical, but really it is—it is—well, it is quite the only practical thing and it has surely one advantage: it settles the problem once, suddenly, and forever. My plan is this: You now outnumber us nearly ten to one. I propose that on a certain date, shall we say next Christmas, or possibly Easter, 1912? No, come to think of it, the first of January, 1913, would, for historical reasons, probably be best. Well, then, on the first of January, 1913, let each person who has a colored friend invite him to dinner. This would take care of a few; among such friends might be included the black mammies and faithful old servants of the South; in this way we could get together quite a number. Then those who have not the pleasure of black friends might arrange for meetings, especially in "white" churches and Young Men's and Young Women's Christian Associations, where Negroes are not expected. At such meetings, contrary to custom, the black people should not be seated by themselves, but distributed very carefully among the whites. The remaining Negroes who could not be flattered or attracted by these invitations should be induced to assemble among themselves at their own churches or at little parties and house warmings.

"The few stragglers, vagrants and wanderers could be put under careful watch and ward. Now, then, we have the thing in shape. First, the hosts of those invited to dine should provide themselves with a sufficient quantity of cyanide of potassium, placing it carefully in the proper cups, and being careful not to mix the cups. Those at church and prayer meeting could choose between long sharp stilettoes and pistols—I should recommend the former as less noisy. Those who guard the colored assemblies and the stragglers without should carefully surround the groups and use Winchesters. Then, at a given signal, let the colored folk of the United States be quietly dispatched; the signal might be a church bell or the singing of the national hymn; probably the bell would be best, for the diners would be eating."

By this time the auditors of the colored man were staring; the Southerner had forgotten to pose; the Woman had forgotten to watch the Southerner; the Westerner was staring with admiration; there were tears in the eyes of the Little Old Lady, while the New Yorker was smiling; but the colored man held up a deprecating hand: "Now don't prejudge my plan," he urged. "The next morning there would be ten million funerals, and therefore no Negro problem. Think how quietly the thing would be settled; no more bother, no more argument; the whole country united and happy. Even the Negroes would be a great deal happier than they are at present. Instead of being made heirs to hope by education, or ambitious by wealth, or exiled invalids on the fever coast, they would all be happily ensconced in Heaven.

Of course, I admit that at first the plan may seem a little abrupt and cruel, and yet is it more cruel than present conditions, and would it not be well to be a little more abrupt in our social solutions? At any rate think it over," and the colored man dropped lazily into his steamer chair and felt for another cigarette.

The crowd slowly dispersed; the Southerner chose the Woman, but was heard to say something about fools. The Westerner turned to the New Yorker and said: "Now, what in hell do you suppose that darky meant?" But the Little Old Lady went silently to her cabin.

THE STORY OF AFRICA

Once upon a time there lay a land in the southern seas; a dark, grim land, walled well against the world. And in that land rose three rivers and a fourth, all flowing out to seek the sea. One river was born amid the Lakes and Mountains of the Moon, sun-kissed, snow-capped, and fled to the northward silent, swiftly; it clambered over the hills and swam the marshes. It threaded the sands—the narrow, choking sands that grew hotter and narrower as it went; yet the river swept on to wider, greener fields, to a laughing plain until through many mouths it burst like a rocket to the Middle Sea with all its myriads of men.

— In the wake of the river came dark men creeping, dancing, marching, building, until their pyramids and temples dotted the land and dared the Heavens, and the Thought of their souls and cities was the Beginning of the World.

Far, far away to westward another river leapt and sang and lightly turned its back upon the Sea, rushing to northward. But the grim desert shrieked in its fastnesses crying "Not here!" So the river whirled southward till the black forests cried in their gloom, "Not here!" The river bowed and circled westward. Sullenly, silently, yet proudly, she swept into the western sea. As she swept she sang low minor melody; as she sang she scattered gold carelessly to the black children. But ere she died in the depth of the sea she gave to her strongest and blackest sons, Iron—the precious gift of Iron. They fashioned it cunningly and welded it in faery forms and sent it to the ends of earth to make all men awake. And men awoke. They awoke on the cunning breast of the river's self and kingdom on kingdom arose until the empire of the Songhay rivaled the empires of the world. The sound of the might of Negro land echoed in Carthage and grew in Numidia and gave faery tales to the Middle Sea.

Away to the south and eastward and below the Mountains of the Moon the third broad river heard her sisters hurrying seaward. North and westward they had gone but she turned to the eternal east. Golden she lifted up her golden hands and stretched to Ophir, Punt and Tarshish her long, lithe finger. Her voice rose mighty in song until with a million stars in her throat she dropped wild singing in the southern sea and shuddered to the vastness of its silence.

Her black children sat in mine, fortress, temple and flowering field and traded with dark traders beyond the India Sea, till lo: out of the north came a cry, a cry like the anguish of a soul. For back in the bowels of the land men heard the running of three rivers and rushed away madly; for they were those that would not hear and could not see. On they ran, on, on and eastward ringing their spears and crying their great, awful cry of war. As locusts swarming they passed the north of the glooming forest with its dim red faerie; eastward they looked upon the inland oceans and southward they sent their war cry reeling to the Mountains of the Moon.

There came a shouting in the wilderness and again as swarming bees onward they came, and again the war cry echoed to the stars. Over the ruin of things that were passed that black and human flood until its angry surf dashed into the vast, red Heart of the Land, and knew the haunted spell-cursed realm of the Last River. Mighty was this last of rivers—a river of rivers, an endless lacing and swirling and curling and swelling and streaming of wild, weird waters beneath the giant jungle, where the lion, the leopard and the elephant slept with the long, slim snake.

Hand in hand and voice to voice these waters whirled in one vast circle within the bosom of the land saying their incantations. They shouldered past the mountains and sang past all the seas, then shunning the glaring desert and ingathering themselves to one swarming flood they thrilled and thundered on the sea. Snake-like and lion-strong they gathered the children, the little dark and weeping children, and lo, beyond on swelling waters rose a hoarse, harsh cry and slim and sail-like fingers beckoned to the westward deeps. The river paused and rose red and reeking in the sunlight—thundered to the sea—thundered through the sea in one long line of blood, with tossing limbs and the echoing cries of death and pain.

Oh, on! the bloody waters, with those pale ghost fingers of ship and sail, with gold and iron, hurt and hell, rolled, swelled and tumbled, until the laughing islands of the western sea grew dark and dumb with pain and in the world, the great new world a Sorrow was planted and the Sorrow grew.

September, 1914. Vol. VIII, No. 5. pp. 234-5.

OF THE CHILDREN OF PEACE

Come, all my father's children, and sit beside my knee, here with this child of mine, and listen:

Have you ever seen a soldier? It is a brave sight, is it not? Once upon a time, many, many years before your dear little curly heads were born, I remember seeing an army that marched because a King was visiting an Emperor. Berlin was joy mad. Houses streamed with color and music reeled and rioted. Then came the army. Tall, handsome men, all gold and silver and broadcloth, sworded, spurred and plumed, led on horses that curvetted and tossed their shining bits. (Do you not love a horse with his great, sweet eyes and quivery shining softness?) Next came the soldiers, erect, rigid, "Eyes left!" Pit-pat, pit-pat! Clasping their little innocent guns. Next came the artillery: files of wildly prancing horses dragging long leaden things. How the crowd roared. The King bowed to the Emperor and the Emperor bowed to the King, and there rose a great cry of pride and joy and battle from the people. With that cry I seemed suddenly to awake. I somehow saw *through* (you know sometimes how you seem to see, but are blind until something happens and you really see?).

I saw then what I see now. I saw and see the WAR that men said could not be.

Gone was all the brave tinsel, the glitter, sheen and music. The men trudged and limped, naked and dirty, with sodden, angry, distorted faces; their eyes were sunken and bloodshot, with murder in them; they staggered over corpses and severed arms and feet and dead horses and they carried—not little innocent guns, but little innocent children; they dragged, not pale and leaden guns, but pale and bounden women, and before them staggered and crept old women and grandfathers, the sick and the maimed, the weak and the half-grown boys and girls.

I heard the cry that hovered over this fearsome army: it was a wail of hunger and crime, of thirst and pain and death, and the cry rose and met an answering cry that came from beyond the forest to the west.

Two toddling children slipped from their fathers' arms and met in the gloom of that forest, where the beasts cowered and livid, disbodied hands seemed to creep in the darkness.

"Mother," they whispered.

"Mama," they cried.

"Mütterchen," they sobbed.

Wild with horror two bound mothers beat their naked hands against the gun-carriages, groping and struggling through the gloom, as death flamed through their hearts.

Then the armies met. Two fathers leapt from the two armies ahead and each seized the other's child. They strangled and crushed and maimed and murdered it, till each baby lay pale, limp and dead.

(Nay, shrink not, my children, horrible as the tale may be, the truth is worse and you must know it.)

Then War was loose. Then six million human beings left their fields of golden grain and the busy hum of their factories and taking their own children for weapons dashed them against the trees and the lampposts and the churches and wallowed and gasped in their blood!

Come, all my father's children and hear how beyond the blue mists of the Everlasting Sea, the mothers mad with hunger, grief and pain, are fronting the blood-stained heavens with bared and haunted breasts and are shrieking:

"Why?"

"Why?"

Their shriek is the booming of guns, and the booming of cannon is the shriek of mothers.

And you must answer, Children of Peace, you must answer! You must cry: "There is no why!"

"The cause of War is Preparation for War!"

"The cause of Preparation for War is the Hatred and Despising of Men, your and my brothers."

"War is murder in a red coat."

"War is raped mothers and bleeding fathers and strangled children."

"War is Death, Hate, Hunger and Pain!"

"Hell is War!"

And when you believe this with all your little hearts;

And when you cry it across the seas and across the years with all your little voices—

Then shall the mothers of all dead children hear;

Then shall the Sisters of all dead Brothers hear; then shall the Daughters of all dead Fathers hear; then shall the women rise and say:

"War is done."

"Henceforward and forever there shall be no organized murder of men, for the children we bear shall be the Children of Peace, else there shall be no children."

Amen!

But cry, little children, cry and cry loud and soon, for until you and the Mothers speak, the men of the world bend stupid and crazed beneath the burden of hate and death. Behold, this old and awful world is but one slaughter-pen, one tale of innocent blood and senseless hate and strife.

Look yonder! In the gloomy forest all is still, save here a red and flickering flame and there a last trembling sob. Only one living thing passes across the night: a horse—a gaunt, sweating horse, with bloody nostrils, great pain-struck eyes, and bowels trailing on the earth. He hears his Emperor bugling "Victory!" to the King. Turning he staggers toward him and whimpers as he goes.

October, 1914. Vol. VIII, No. 6. pp. 289-90.

AGAIN, SOCIAL EQUALITY

Mr. Paleface entered his parlor mincingly,—"My dear man," he said, expressively.

"I am Brownson," said the dark man quietly.

"Of course—of course—I know you well, and your people. My father was an abolitionist, and I had a black mammy——"

Mr. Brownson looked out of the window, and said rapidly: "I have come to ask for certain rights and privileges. My people——"

"—suffer; I know it; I know it. I have often remarked what a shame it was. Sir, it is an outrage!"

"—yes; we want to ask——"

Mr. Paleface raised a deprecating finger, "Not social equality," he murmured, "—I trust you are not asking for that."

"Certainly not," said Brownson. "I think the right of a man to select his friends and guests and decide with whom he will commit matrimony, is sacredly his and his alone."

"Good—good! Now, my man, we can talk openly, face to face. We can pour out our souls to each other. What can I do? I have already sent my annual check to Hampton."

"Sir, we want to vote."

"Ah! That is difficult—difficult. You see, voting has come to have a new significance. We used to confine our votes to politics, but now—bless me!—we are voting religion, work, social-reform, landscape-gardening, and art. Then, too, women are in politics—you see—well, I'm sure you sense the difficulties. Moreover, what is voting? A mere form—the making and execution of the laws is the thing, and there I promise you that I ——"

"Well, then we would help in carrying out the laws."

"Commendable ambition. Very, very commendable. But this involves even greater difficulties. Administrators and executives are thrown closely together—often in the same room—at the same desk. They have to mingle and consult. Much as I deplore the fact, it is true, that a man will not sit at a desk or work at a bench with a man whose company at a theatre he would resent."

"I see," said Brownson, thoughtfully. "I presume, then, it is our business to demand this right to sit in theatres and places of popular entertainment."

"Good Lord, man, that's impossible! Civil rights like this cannot be forced. Objectionable persons must grow, develop— or wash, before——"

"Then I am sure you will help me clean and train my people. I want to join in the great movements for social uplift."

"Splendid! I will have some movements organized for your folks."

"No, I want to be part of the general movement, so as to get the training and inspiration, the wide outlook—the best plans."

"Are you crazy? Don't you know that social uplift work consists of a series of luncheons, dinners, and teas, with ladies present?"

"Um." said Brownson. "I see. I, also, see that in answering your first question, I made a mistake. In the light of your subsequent definition, I see that social equality, far from being what I don't want, is precisely what I do want."

"I knew it!" screamed Mr. Paleface. "I knew it all the time; I saw it sneaking into your eyes. You want—you dare to want to marry my sister."

"Not if she looks like you," said Mr. Brownson, "and not if she's as big a liar."

"Get out—get out—leave my house, you ungrateful——"

March, 1920. Vol. XIX, No. 5. pp. 236-7.

OF GIVING WORK

"We give you people work and if we didn't, how would you live?"

The speaker was a Southern white man. He was of the genus called "good." He had come down from the Big House to advise these Negroes, in the forlorn little church which crouched on the creek. He didn't come to learn, but to teach. The result was that he did not learn, and he saw only that blank, impervious gaze which colored people know how to assume; and that dark wall of absolute silence which they have a habit of putting up instead of applause. He felt awkward, but he repeated what he had said, because he could not think of anything else to say.

"We give you people work, and if we didn't, how would you live?"

And then the old and rather ragged black man arose in the back of the church and came slowly forward and as he came, he said:

"And we gives you homes; and we gives you cotton; and we makes your land worth money; and we waits on you and gets your meals and cleans up your dirt. And if we didn't do all those things for you, how would you live?"

The white man choked and got red, but the old black man went on talking:

"And what's more: we gives you a heap more than you gives us and we's getting mighty tired of the bargain——"

"I think we ought to give you fair wages," stammered the white man.

"And that ain't all," continued the old black man, "we ought to have something to say about your wages. Because if what *you* gives us gives *you* a right to say what we ought to get, then what *we* gives you gives *us* a right to say what *you* ought to get; and we're going to take that right *some day.*"

The white man blustered:

"That's Bolshevism!" he shouted.

And then church broke up.

April, 1920. Vol. XIX, No. 6. p. 301.

THE RACE

STARVATION AND PREJUDICE

Two utterances by Mr. Booker T. Washington this week illustrate the reasons why so many thinking men, black and white, are coming to doubt Mr. Washington's statesmanship. One statement is in the current *Outlook* and is to the effect that Mr. John E. Milholland and "certain members of my own race in the North have objected because they said I did not paint condi-

tions in the South black enough. . . . I have never denied that
the Negroes in the South frequently meets with wrong and
injustice, but he does not starve." And he quotes facts to show
that there is actual starvation in London.

This argument reduces itself to several propositions:

I. It is not well to tell the whole story of wrong and injustice
in the South, but rather one should emphasize the better aspects.

II. Starvation is worse than other kinds of wrong and injustice.

III. Because there are persons starving in England, neither
England nor black men in America ought to harp on America's
injustices.

The last two propositions are matters of opinion and taste; but
the first proposition has been the keynote of Mr. Washington's
propaganda for the last fifteen years. It has, however, been
ineffective in practice and logically dangerous. It is ineffective
in practice because under its aegis—under the silence, the absence of criticism, the kindly sentiments and wide-spread complacency, we have seen grow up in the South a caste system
which threatens the foundations of democracy, and a lawlessness which threatens all government.

We have seen wholesale disfranchisement of colored votes,
color caste carried to the point of positive cruelty, the rule of
the mob and the lynching of 2,000 men without legal trial,
growing discrimination in schools, travel, and public conven-
iences, and an openly declared determination to stop the development of millions of men at the dead line of color.

To offset this Mr. Washington has a right to point to increased
accumulation of property among Negroes and increased numbers of intelligent and forceful black folk. But what has been the
result of this? It has been an intensified prejudice as shown in
the new Ghetto laws, the strikes against black workers, spread
of civil discrimination, and the crystallization of the disfranchising sentiment. How any intelligent American can calmly and
without hysteria or prejudice look on the development of the
Negro problem in the United States in the last ten years and say
that race and color prejudice has decreased, South or North, or
shows reasonable signs of abating in the near future, passes our
comprehension. And yet Mr. Washington is reported to have

said at the recent Unitarian dinner that "Prejudice still exists, but it is not so bitter as it was," and that the South is an example of the overcoming of race prejudice.

Why now does Mr. Washington persist in making from time to time statements of this kind? It is, we believe, because of a dangerous logical fallacy into which Mr. Washington and his supporters fall. They assume that the truth—the real facts concerning a social situation at any particular time—is of less importance than the people's feeling concerning those facts. There could be no more dangerous social pragmatism. Its basic assumption is that the facts are in reality known, while its whole action prevents the facts from being known. It is a self-contradictory and deceptive position and it has historically led to social damnation in thousands of awful cases. Even where its complacent ignorance has accidentally evolved into good, the good came not because of it but in spite of it. Just here it is that Mr. Washington utterly fails in his English comparisons: It is not starvation that civilization need fear, if civilization faces the awful fact and calls it starvation, knows its gaunt and threatening shape and says with Lloyd George, We will stop it if we shake the economic foundations of the empire. But the starvation which the world and Mr. Washington would do well to fear is that which blinds its eyes to stalking misery in the East End and cries, "Lo, the Power of England!" So, too, in the United States: Awful as race prejudice, lawlessness and ignorance are, we can fight them if we frankly face them and dare name them and tell the truth; but if we continually dodge and cloud the issue, and say the half truth because the whole stings and shames; if we do this, we invite catastrophe. Let us then in all charity but unflinching firmness set our faces against all statesmanship that looks in such directions.

June, 1911. Vol. II, No. 2. pp. 62-4.

LEADERSHIP

At the closing exercises of the privately endowed schools for Negroes you are impressed with the large number of graduates who tell you that they are prepared to return to the homes of their childhood, there to become leaders of their race. And judging from the past, this prophecy will not be without fulfilment. Instead of going to a new land to seek their fortunes, like white boys and girls who have had similar advantages, many of these colored youths will return to the narrow, ugly surroundings of their former homes. They will sacrifice their personal pleasure for what they believe to be the good of the race.

One cannot fail to applaud this missionary spirit, but zeal is discounted when it is coupled with an egregious sense of self-importance, and this unfortunate combination is not infrequent. "I leave these beloved walls," the valedictorian says, with a fine sweep of the hand, "to return to my native home and become a leader of my people. I shall lift them out of the bondage of ignorance into the blessings of today." With this glorious resolve he returns to his people, and before the year is out is counted a nuisance by his fellow townsmen. He went as a missionary where he had not been invited, and he had not the insight to see that he must be taught by his neighbors before he attempted to teach them.

Mr. T. Thomas Fortune has written admirably on the danger of the overemphasis of leadership. "Lift up yourself first," is the gist of his argument. And while appreciating to its fullest the fine desire for helpfulness on the part of the young, educated Negro, we believe that, as far as possible, he should discount his own influence and his own place in the community as he goes about his life of service. What he needs is to gather about him those men and women in the community of best ability and highest power, to encourage all that is strong and virile in his comrades, to forget himself as he brings out the latent ability in others. If, on the other hand, he asserts his leadership, the people who could best help him will stand aside, and he will find himself surrounded only by the second rate and commonplace.

That service is best that is not overwrapped with self-importance, and that leader is greatest who, like Lincoln, is not self-appointed, but is chosen by the people of a democracy.

July, 1911. Vol. II, No. 3. p. 113.

THE BLACK MOTHER

The people of America, and especially the people of the Southern States, have felt so keen an appreciation of the qualities of motherhood in the Negro that they have proposed erecting a statue in the National Capital to the black mammy. The black nurse of slavery days may receive the tribute of enduring bronze from the master class.

But this appreciation of the black mammy is always of the foster mammy, not of the mother in her home, attending to her own babies. And as the colored mother has retreated to her own home, the master class has cried out against her. "She is thriftless and stupid," the white mother says, "when she refuses to nurse my baby and stays with her own. She is bringing her daughter up beyond her station when she trains her to be a teacher instead of sending her into my home to act as nursemaid to my little boy and girl. I will never enter her street, heaven forbid. A colored street is taboo, and she no longer deserves my approval when she refuses to leave her home and enter mine."

Let us hope that the black mammy, for whom so many sentimental tears have been shed, has disappeared from American life. She existed under a false social system that deprived her of husband and child. Thomas Nelson Page, after—with wet eyelids—recounting the virtues of his mammy, declares petulantly that she did not care for her own children. Doubtless this was true. How could it have been otherwise? But just so far as it was true it was a perversion of motherhood.

Let the present-day mammies suckle their own children. Let them walk in the sunshine with their own toddling boys and girls and put their own sleepy little brothers and sisters to bed. As their girls grow to womanhood, let them see to it that, if possible, they do not enter domestic service in those homes where they are unprotected, and where their womanhood is not treated with respect. In the midst of immense difficulties, surrounded by caste, and hemmed in by restricted economic opportunity, let the colored mother of today build her own statue, and let it be the four walls of her own unsullied home.

December, 1912. Vol. V, No. 2. p. 78.

THE HURT HOUND

The editor has received this news note from a colored friend:

"January 22—Revs. G. H. Burks and P.A. Nichols, returning from Louisville to Paducah, Ky., over the I.C. Railroad, on being detained from 5 p.m. to 2 a.m., by reason of a freight wreck, were ushered into the dining car and given supper without one single word of comment or protest from the whites, who were eating at the same time."

The editor read this and read it yet again. At first he thought it was a banquet given to black men by white; then he thought it charity to the hungry poor; then—then it dawned on his darkened soul: Two decently dressed, educated colored men had been allowed to pay for their unobtrusive meal in a Pullman dining car "WITHOUT ONE SINGLE WORD OF COMMENT OR PROTEST!" No one had cursed them; none had thrown plates at them; they were not lynched! And in humble ecstacy at being treated for once like ordinary human beings they rushed from the car and sent a letter a thousand miles to say to the world "My God! Look! See!"

What more eloquent comment could be made on the white South? What more stinging indictment could be voiced? What must be the daily and hourly treatment of black men in Paducah, Ky., to bring this burst of applause at the sheerest and most negative decency?

Yet every black man in America has known that same elation —North and South and West. We have all of us felt the sudden relief—the half-mad delight when contrary to fixed expectation we were treated as men and not dogs; and then, in the next breath, we hated ourselves for elation over that which was but due any human being.

This is the real tragedy of the Negro in America: the inner degradation, the hurt hound feeling; the sort of upturning of all values which leads some black men to "rejoice" because "only" sixty-four Negroes were lynched in the year of our Lord 1912.

Conceive, O poet, a ghastlier tragedy than such a state of mind!

April, 1913. Vol V, No. 6. pp. 290-1.

THE IMMEDIATE PROGRAM
OF THE AMERICAN NEGRO

The immediate program of the American Negro means nothing unless it is mediate to his great ideal and the ultimate ends of his development. We need not waste time by seeking to deceive our enemies into thinking that we are going to be content with a half loaf, or by being willing to lull our friends into a false sense of our indifference and present satisfaction. The American Negro demands equality—political equality, industrial equality and social equality; and he is never going to rest satisfied with anything less. He demands this in no spirit of braggadocio and with no obsequious envy of others, but as an absolute measure of self-defense and the only one that will assure to the darker races their ultimate survival on earth.

Only in a demand and a persistent demand for essential equality in the modern realm of human culture can any people show a real pride of race and a decent self-respect. For any group, nation or race to admit for a moment the present monstrous demand of the white race to be the inheritors of the earth, the arbiters of mankind and the sole owners of a heritage of culture which they did not create, nor even improve to any greater extent than the other great division of men—to admit such pretense for a moment is for the race to write itself down immediately as indisputably inferior in judgment, knowledge and common sense.

The equality in political, industrial and social life which modern men must have in order to live, is not to be confounded with sameness. On the contrary, in our case, it is rather insistence upon the right of diversity;—upon the right of a human being to be a man even if he does not wear the same cut of vest, the same curl of hair or the same color of skin. Human equality does not even entail, as is sometimes said, absolute equality of opportunity; for certainly the natural inequalities of inherent genius and varying gift make this a dubious phrase. But there is a more and more clearly recognized minimum of opportunity and maximum of freedom to be, to move and to think, which the modern world denies to no being which it recognizes as a real man.

These involve both negative and positive sides. They call for freedom on the one hand and power on the other. The Negro must have political freedom; taxation without representation is tyranny. American Negroes of to-day are ruled by tyrants who take what they please in taxes and give what they please in law and administration, in justice and in injustice; and the great mass of black people must stand helpless and voiceless before a condition which has time and time again caused other peoples to fight and die.

The Negro must have industrial freedom. Between the peonage of the rural South, the oppression of shrewd capitalists and the jealousy of certain trade unions, the Negro laborer is the most exploited class in the country, giving more hard toil for less money than any other American, and have less voice in the conditions of his labor.

In social intercourse every effort is being made to-day from the President of the United States and the so-called Church of Christ down to saloons and boot-blacks to segregate, strangle and spiritually starve Negroes so as to give them the least possible chance to know and share civilization.

These shackles must go. But that is but the beginning. The Negro must have power; the power of men, the right to do, to know, to feel and to express that knowledge, action and spiritual gift. He must not simply be free from the political tyranny of white folk, he must have the right to vote and to rule over the citizens, white and black, to the extent of his proven foresight and ability. He must have a voice in the new industrial democracy which is building and the power to see to it that his children are not in the next generation trained to be the mudsills of society. He must have the right to social intercourse with his fellows. There was a time in the atomic individualistic group when "social intercourse" meant merely calls and tea-parties; to-day social intercourse means theatres, lectures, organizations, churches, clubs, excursions, travel, hotels,—it means in short Life; to bar a group from such methods of thinking, living and doing is to bar them from the world and bid them create a new world;—a task to which no single group is to-day equal; it is to crucify them and taunt them with not being able to live.

What now are the practical steps which must be taken to accomplish these ends?

First of all before taking steps the wise man knows the object and end of his journey. There are those who would advise the black man to pay little or no attention to where he is going so long as he keeps moving. They assume that God or his vice-gerent the White Man will attend to the steering. This is arrant nonsense. The feet of those that aimlessly wander land as often in hell as in heaven. Conscious self-realization and self-direction is the watchword of modern man, and the first article in the program of any group that will survive must be the great aim, equality and power among men.

The practical steps to this are clear. First we must fight obstructions; by continual and increasing effort we must first make American courts either build up a body of decisions which will protect the plain legal rights of American citizens or else make them tear down the civil and political rights of all citizens in order to oppress a few. Either result will bring justice in the end. It is lots of fun and most ingenious just now for courts to twist law so as to say I shall not live here or vote there, or marry the woman who wishes to marry me. But when to-morrow these decisions throttle all freedom and overthrow the foundation of democracy and decency, there is going to be some judicial house cleaning.

We must *secondly* seek in legislature and congress remedial legislation; national aid to public school education, the removal of all legal discriminations based simply on race and color, and those marriage laws passed to make the seduction of black girls easy and without legal penalty.

Third the human contact of human beings must be increased; the policy which brings into sympathetic touch and understanding, men and women, rich and poor, capitalist and laborer, Asiatic and European, must bring into closer contact and mutual knowledge the white and black people of this land. It is the most frightful indictment of a country which dares to call itself civilized that it has allowed itself to drift into a state of ignorance where ten million people are coming to believe that all white people are liars and thieves, and the whites in turn to believe that the chief industry of Negroes is raping white women.

Fourth only the publication of the truth repeatedly and incisively and uncompromisingly can secure that change in public opinion which will correct these awful lies. THE CRISIS, our record of the darker races, must have a circulation not of 35,000 chiefly among colored folk but of at least 250,000 among all men who believe in men. It must not be a namby-pamby box of salve, but a voice that thunders fact and is more anxious to be true than pleasing. There should be a campaign of tract distribution—short well written facts and arguments—rained over this land by millions of copies, particularly in the South, where the white people know less about the Negro than in any other part of the civilized world. The press should be utilized—the 400 Negro weeklies, the great dailies and eventually the magazines, when we get magazine editors who will lead public opinion instead of following afar with resonant brays. Lectures, lantern-slides and moving pictures, co-operating with a bureau of information and eventually becoming a Negro encyclopedia, all these are efforts along the line of making human beings realize that Negroes are human.

Such is the program of work against obstructions. Let us now turn to constructive effort. This may be summed up under (1) economic co-operation (2) a revival of art and literature (3) political action (4) education and (5) organization.

Under economic co-operation we must strive to spread the idea among colored people that the accumulation of wealth is for social rather than individual ends. We must avoid, in the advancement of the Negro race, the mistakes of ruthless exploitation which have marked modern economic history. To this end we must seek not simply home ownership, small landholding and saving accounts, but also all forms of co-operation, both in production and distribution, profit sharing, building and loan associations, systematic charity for definite, practical ends, systematic migration from mob rule and robbery, to freedom and enfranchisement, the emancipation of women and the abolition of child labor.

In art and literature we should try to loose the tremendous emotional wealth of the Negro and the dramatic strength of his problems through writing, the stage, pageantry and other forms of art. We should resurrect forgotten ancient Negro art and history, and we should set the black man before the world as both a creative artist and a strong subject for artistic treatment.

In political action we should organize the votes of Negroes in such congressional districts as have any number of Negro voters. We should systematically interrogate candidates on matters vital to Negro freedom and uplift. We should train colored voters to reject the bribe of office and to accept only decent legal enactments both for their own uplift and for the uplift of laboring classes of all races and both sexes.

In education we must seek to give colored children free public school training. We must watch with grave suspicion the attempt of those who, under the guise of vocational training, would fasten ignorance and menial service on the Negro for another generation. Our children must not in large numbers, be forced into the servant class; for menial service is still, in the main, little more than an antiquated survival of impossible conditions. It has always been as statistics show, a main cause of bastardy and prostitution and despite its many marvelous exceptions it will never come to the light of decency and honor until the house servant becomes the Servant in the House. It is our duty then, not drastically but persistently, to seek out colored children of ability and genius, to open up to them broader, industrial opportunity and above all, to find that Talented Tenth and encourage it by the best and most exhaustive training in order to supply the Negro race and the world with leaders, thinkers and artists.

For the accomplishment of all these ends we must organize. Organization among us already has gone far but it must go much further and higher. Organization is sacrifice. It is sacrifice of opinions, of time, of work and of money, but it is, after all, the cheapest way of buying the most priceless of gifts—freedom and efficiency. I thank God that most of the money that supports the National Association for the Advancement of Colored People comes from black hands; a still larger proportion must so come, and we must not only support but control this and similar organizations and hold them unwaveringly to our objects, our aims and our ideals.

April, 1915. Vol. IX, No. 6. pp. 310-12.

BOOKER T. WASHINGTON

The death of Mr. Washington marks an epoch in the history of America. He was the greatest Negro leader since Frederick

Douglass, and the most distinguished man, white or black, who has come out of the South since the Civil War. His fame was international and his influence far-reaching. Of the good that he accomplished there can be no doubt: he directed the attention of the Negro race in America to the pressing necessity of economic development; he emphasized technical education and he did much to pave the way for an understanding between the white and darker races.

On the other hand there can be no doubt of Mr. Washington's mistakes and short comings; he never adequately grasped the growing bond of politics and industry; he did not understand the deeper foundations of human training and his basis of better understanding between white and black was founded on caste.

We may then generously and with deep earnestness lay on the grave of Booker T. Washington testimony of our thankfulness for his undoubted help in the accumulation of Negro land and property, his establishment of Tuskegee and spreading of industrial education and his compelling of the white South to at least think of the Negro as a possible man.

On the other hand, in stern justice, we must lay on the soul of this man, a heavy responsibility for the consummation of Negro disfranchisement, the decline of the Negro college and public school and the firmer establishment of color caste in this land.

What is done is done. This is not fit time for recrimination or complaint. Gravely and with bowed head let us receive what this great figure gave of good, silently rejecting all else. Firmly and unfalteringly let the Negro race in America, in bleeding Hayti[1] and throughout the world close ranks and march steadily on, determined as never before to work and save and endure, but never to swerve from their great goal: the right to vote, the right to know, and the right to stand as men among men throughout the world.

December, 1915. Vol. X, No. 6. p. 82.

[1] A reference to the occupation of Haiti by U. S. troops which had taken place earlier that year.

TO THE RESCUE

The colored troops are leading in the Mexican foray. It is a foolish venture. Just the kind of mistake that we are beginning to think is characteristic of the Wilson administration. Nevertheless "Their's not to reason why," and consequently the Tenth Cavalry with Major Young in command of the Second Squadron is now in Mexico. As one report says: "Especial credit should be given the Tenth." Then, too, the Twenty-fourth, another colored regiment, has been called to support the movement. So in America, in Europe and in Africa black men are fighting for the liberties of white men and pulling their chestnuts out of the fire. One of these bright mornings black men are going to learn how to fight for themselves.

May, 1916. Vol. XII, No. 1. p. 31.

SALUTATIONS

We confess to strong and perfectly legitimate sympathy with the colored lad, Hubert Eaves, of Des Moines, Ia., who refused to salute the American flag. We believe in courtesy and to a certain extent in the thing which is called "patriotism," but we believe that a flag which cannot induce in children natural and spontaneous affection, and which calls for courts and sentences to induce respect, we believe that such a flag represents a seriously defective country. Hubert Eaves if he has any sense at all, and he evidently has, knows perfectly well that the country which this flag represents has treated him with studied insult, dishonesty and cruelty. If in the face of that he could induce himself to salute the country's flag for the hope of the future or in gratitude for little things in the past, very well; but if he cannot do this the most decent thing for the country and for the city of Des Moines would be to fail to see Hubert when he forgets to bob his head.

May, 1916. Vol. XII, No. 1. pp. 31-2.

THE COLORED AUDIENCE

Let us be frank. The colored audience as I have seen it recently in the colored theatres of large cities is not above reproach. We are an appreciative people certainly, but our appreciation need not take the form of loud ejaculations and guffaws of laughter, particularly when that laughter breaks out in the wrong place. Any actor is pleased when the responsiveness of his audience shows him he has got his lines "across", but the most frenzied Othello can hardly conceal his bewilderment when his attempt to strangle Desdemona provokes shouts of merriment.

Is this state of affairs due to ignorance or thoughtlessness? To a combination of both, I fancy. We cannot afford either. It is true one goes to the theater to be amused, in any event to be diverted, but the establishment and maintenance of the colored theater and the colored actor have at this point of our development a peculiar, though obvious significance. Our actors must be encouraged and not put on a level with mountebanks whose slightest gesture is the signal for laughter. There is no truer encouragement than an intelligent appreciation. We shall have to take lessons in its development. Laughter is desirable, tears also, but each in its place.

September, 1916. Vol. XII, No. 6. p. 217.

REFINEMENT AND LOVE

A colored girl writes us from Oswego, N.Y., saying:

"Do you want to know what I like best about THE CRISIS? What I enjoy most? What fires my ambition to struggle on? Well, it is just this: The successes of other members of my race and what they are doing in this United States.

"And do you want to know what I like least? Just such expressions as these: 'The recent Irish revolt may have been foolish, but would to God some of us had sense enough to be fools!' The Great Napolean realized after all that the use of force was not the best way to achieve one's ends. That sort of a foundation is too weak; it cannot last. So is it not better to keep before our people ideas and thoughts of culture, refinement, service and love and in that way build our progress on a sure foundation?"

No one wishes more than THE CRISIS that "culture, refinement, service and love" should triumph in the world; but we continually fear lest easy-going young folk should loll in their parlors toasting their toes and expect the horror of the world's blood sacrifice to be accomplished by someone else while they are practising "refinement and love." Terrible as it may be, the awful fact faces the colored races in this world: That no human group has ever achieved freedom without being compelled to murder thousands of members of other groups who were determined that they should be slaves. Let us hope and deeply pray that this may not happen in the case of colored folk; but at the same time let us set our faces grimly toward the fact, with unwinking eyes, that *it may be necessary*. War is Hell, but there are things worse than Hell, as every Negro knows.

December, 1916. Vol. XIII, No. 2. p. 63.

THREE HUNDRED YEARS

Three hundred years ago this month a "Dutch man of Warre sold us twenty Negars." They were not slaves. They were stolen freemen. They were free in Africa; they were free by the laws of Virginia. By force and fraud they and their children were gradually reduced to a slavery, the legality of which was not fully recognized for nearly a century after 1619. From their loins and the bodies of their fellows of after-years have sprung —counting both "white" and "black"—full twenty million souls. Those still visibly tinged with their blood are still enslaved —by compulsory ignorance, disfranchisement and public insult. In sack-cloth and ashes, then, we commemorate this day, lest we forget; lest a single drop of blood, a single moan of pain, a single bead of sweat, in all these three, long, endless centuries should drop into oblivion.

Why must we remember? Is this but a counsel of Vengeance and Hate? God forbid! We must remember because if once the world forgets evil, evil is reborn; because if the suffering of the American Negro is once forgotten, then there is no guerdon, down to the last pulse of time, that Devils will not again enslave and maim and murder and oppress the weak and unfortunate.

Behold, then, this month of mighty memories; celebrate it, Children of the Sun, in solemn song and silent march and grim thanksgiving. The Fourth Century dawns and through it, God guide our thrilling hands.

August, 1919. Vol. XVIII, No. 4. p. 183.

THE DEMAGOG

From now on in our new awakening, our self-criticism, or impatience and passion, we must expect the Demagog among Negroes more and more. He will come to lead, inflame, lie and steal. He will gather large followings and then burst and disappear. Loss and despair will follow his fall until new false prophets arise. This is almost inevitable in every growing, surging group of low intelligence and poverty. But it is permanently dangerous only as the Demagog finds the cleft between our incipient social classes wide and growing. This, under old economic and social conditions, is the day when we would naturally breed aristocracies of birth, wealth, training and talent, and uncared-for masses of brute and criminal poor. Our common social oppression and serfdom to the white world has saved us from these extremes and left us with smaller inequalities of wealth and education than most groups of 12 millions. Nevertheless the ties between our privileged and exploited, our educated and ignorant, our rich and poor, our light and dark, are not what they should be and what we can and must make them. It is here that the New Negro Demagog thrives and yells and steals. "They are ashamed of their race"; "They are exploiting us"; "They are copying the white man's color line"—he shrieks, as he dexterously fills his own pockets and wastes the pennies of the poor.

Now the difficulty is that back of his exaggerations and dishonesty lies that kernel of truth that gains him his following; there are plenty of black folk who are bitterly ashamed of their color, who shrink with blind repulsion from the uglier aspects of their race's degradation, and who willingly batten on the black poor. They are few in the aggregate, but they exist; and beside them stand the vast number of us who believe in our race and seek its weal, and yet make no effort to reach down and draw up. These latter see no personal duty of theirs toward black thieves and prostitutes, no responsibility for black poverty.

For this attitude we must substitute a feeling of group responsibility, realizing that if we do not know and befriend our unfortunate, scoundrels will use them to their own ends and to our undoing. And such demagogs will be doubly strong because they can count on the applause and backing of the sinister whites; of those who advertise and pat on the back every skunk among us who combines with his filth sufficient ridicule and criticism for our better efforts.

April, 1922. Vol. XXIII No. 6. p. 252.

THE NAME "NEGRO"

South Bend, Ind.

Dear Sir:

I am only a high school student in my Sophomore year, and have not the understanding of you college educated men. It seems to me that since THE CRISIS is the Official Organ of the National Association for the Advancement of Colored People which stand for equality for all Americans, why would it designate, and segregate us as "Negroes", and not as "Americans".

The most piercing thing that hurts me in this February CRISIS, which forced me to write, was the notice that called the natives of Africa, "Negroes", instead of calling them: "Africans", or "natives".

The word, "Negro", or "nigger", is a white man's word to make us feel inferior. I hope to be a worker for my race, that is why I wrote this letter. I hope that by the time I become a man, that this word, "Negro", will be abolished.

Roland A. Barton

My dear Roland:

Do not at the outset of your career make the all too common error of mistaking names for things. Names are only conventional signs for identifying things. Things are the reality that counts. If a thing is despised, either because of ignorance or because it is despicable, you will not alter matters by changing its name. If men despise Negroes, they will not despise them less if Negroes are called "colored" or "Afro-Americans."

Moreover, you cannot change the name of a thing at will. Names are not merely matters of thought and reason; they are growths and habits. As long as the majority of men mean black or brown folk when they say "Negro," so will Negro be the name of folks brown and black. And neither anger nor wailing nor tears can or will change the name until the name-habit changes.

But why seek to change the name? "Negro" is a fine word. Etymologically and phonetically it is much better and more logical than "African" or "colored" or any of the various hyphenated circumlocutions. Of course, it is not "historically" accurate. No name ever was historically accurate: neither "English," "French," "German," "White," "Jew," "Nordic," nor "Anglo-Saxon." They were all at first nicknames, misnomers, accidents, grown eventually to conventional habits and achieving accuracy because, and simply because, wide and continued usage rendered them accurate. In this sense "Negro" is quite as definite as any name of any great group of people.

Suppose now we could change the name. Suppose we arose tomorrow morning and lo! instead of being "Negroes," all the world called us "Cheiropolidi,"—do you really think this would make a vast and momentous difference to you and to me? Would the Negro problem be suddenly and eternally settled? Would you be any less ashamed of being descended from a black man, or would your schoolmates feel any less superior to you? The feeling of inferiority is in you, not in any name. The name merely evokes what is already there. Exorcise the hateful complex and no name can ever make you hang your head.

Or, on the other hand, supposed that we slip out of the whole thing by calling ourselves "Americans." But in that case, what word shall we use when we want to talk about those descendants of dark slaves who are largely excluded still full American citizenship and from complete social privilege with white folk?

Here is something that we want to talk about; that we do talk about; that we Negroes could not live without talking about. In that case, we need a name for it, do we not? In order to talk logically and easily and be understood. If you do not believe in the necessity of such a name, watch the antics of a colored newspaper which has determined in a fit of New Year's Resolutions not to use the word "Negro!"

And then, too, without the word that means Us, where are all those spiritual ideals, those inner bonds, those group ideals and forward strivings of this mighty army of 12 millions? Shall we abolish these with the abolition of a name? Do we want to abolish them? Of course we do not. They are our most precious heritage.

Historically, of course, your dislike of the word Negro is easily explained: "Negroes" among your grandfathers meant black folk; "Colored" people were mulattoes. The mulattoes hated and despised the blacks and were insulted if 'called "Negroes." But we are not insulted—not you and I. We are quite as proud of our black ancestors as of our white. And perhaps a little prouder. What hurts us is the mere memory that any man of Negro descent was ever so cowardly as to despise any part of his own blood.

Your real work, my dear young man, does not lie with names. It is not a matter of changing them, losing them, or forgetting them. Names are nothing but little guideposts along the Way. The Way would be there and just as hard and just as long if there were no guideposts,—but not quite as easily followed! Your real work as a Negro lies in two directions: *First,* to let the world know what there is fine and genuine about the Negro race. And *secondly,* to see that there is nothing about that race which is worth contempt; your contempt, my contempt; or the contempt of the wide, wide world.

Get this then, Roland, and get it straight even if it pierces your soul: a Negro by any other name would be just as black and just as white; just as ashamed of himself and just as shamed by others, as today. It is not the name—it's the Thing that counts. Come on, Kid, let's go get the Thing!

W.E.B. Du Bois

March, 1928. Vol. XXXV, No. 3. pp. 96-7.

PROTEST

There are many legitimate reactions of the Negro to American race prejudice. Some may laugh it off by seeing the absurdity of it; some may ignore and live absorbed in their own groove alone with sea and sun and friends. Some may be silently indignant and some may shout their just resentment to the stars.

Many persons accept every attitude except the last. They are perfectly willing that the Negro should laugh or keep to himself and be silent, no matter what he thinks. But that a black man should stand up openly and protest, is to them monstrous. They stress the undoubted efficacy of cynical humor; they give great weight to the unquestioned dignity and moral splendor of silent self-denial. But they are transported with wrath if a Negro openly complains and sees crimson when a white man pushes his face in the mud.

And yet in the history of the white world, what did modern peoples do to gain freedom for body and soul? They developed a few saints who went to silent death for a Cause. But also they brought forth great prophets who cried aloud and spared not; who spoke with flaming tongue and made men understand the filth and evil they were doing. And without the trumpet tones of prophets many a meek martyr had died in vain. Die, Victim, die! but let's not all die. Laugh, clown, laugh! but for God's sake don't let us all be clowns.

Oct. 1928. Vol. XXVI, No. 4.

OUR CLASS STRUGGLE

In the Marxist patois, the "class struggle" means the natural antagonism and war between the exploiter and the exploited; that is, between those persons who own capital in the form of machines, raw material and money, and who can command credit, and that other large mass of people who have practically nothing to sell but their labor. Between these two classes, there can be no peace because the profit of the capitalist depends on the amount of surplus value he can extract from the work of the laborer.

One no sooner states this than the expert would say immediately that there is no trace of such class struggle among American Negroes. On second thought, however, he might modify this and say that the occupational differences of American Negroes show at least the beginnings of differentiation into capitalists and laborers.

Of Negroes, 10 years of age and over in gainful occupations, there are:

Skilled laborers	331,839
Semi-Skilled laborers	734,951
Farmers	873,653
Common laborers	3,374,545
Trade and Business	52,957
Professional	119,827
Civil Service	15,763
Total	5,503,535

Of the farmers, 181,016 were owners. The others were tenants. We may, therefore, say that the capitalistic class among Negroes would be among the following:

Trade and Business	52,957
Professional	119,827
Farm Owners	181,016
Civil Servant	15,763
Total	369,563

Most of these however depend for their income on labor rather than capital. Those in trade and business, include clerks, as well as about 30,000 investors of capital. And the professional men are not capitalists, except as some of them have saved money. The same thing can be said of the civil servants. The farm owners are by vast majority peasant proprietors, most of whom hire a little or no labor outside the family.

The most that can be said is that many of the people in this group have the American ambition to become rich and "independent;" to live on income rather than labor, and thus their ideology ranks them on the side of the white capitalists. On the other hand, the laborers, skilled and semi-skilled, and the tenants, are all a proletariat, exploited by white capital. One has, therefore, a rather curious arrangement, with the real class struggle not between colored classes, but rather between colored and white folk.

There is, however, an inner division that calls for attention because it emphasizes and foreshadows class distinctions within the race. And that is the existence of delinquency and dependency, of criminals and paupers. What is the extent of this class among American Negroes and what is the relation of the class to the workers and the more prosperous elements who have begun to accumulate property?

During the earlier history of the colored race, there was a natural social and class difference that came through the existence of mulattoes. In the West Indies by French law, these mulattoes were free and often inherited wealth from their fathers. In many cases, they were carefully educated and formed a distinct social class, whose rank depended upon wealth, education and personal freedom. In the later history of the French colonies, and even more in Spanish and American colonies, persistent effort reduced this class to a semi-servile position, and it was the resentment against this that led the mulattoes to unite with the blacks in the Haitian Revolution and overthrow the whites.

In the United States, this color caste was dealt a death blow by the law that made children follow the condition of the mother, so that white fathers sold their colored children into slavery, and the mulatto ceased to be, in most cases, a free man. He inherited no property from his father and lost his right to education; although so far as he was free, he promoted schools, in centers like Washington, Charleston and New Orleans.

The color caste idea persisted after Emancipation, but was gradually driven out by the new economic organization. In this new economy there arose the criminals and paupers;—the direct result of the poverty of a suddenly emancipated class who had little or no capital.

The apparent criminality, however, of the Negro race is greatly exaggerated for two reasons: First, accusation of crime as used systematically in the South to keep Negroes in serfdom after the Civil War; and secondly, Negroes receive but scant justice in the courts. Most writers, today, have assumed on the basis of statistics, that because the Negro population in jails and penitentiary is proportionately much larger than the white population, that, therefore, the Negro is unusually criminal. But as Thorsten Sellin has pointed out in his note on the Negro criminal, "The American Negro lacks education and earthly goods. He has had very little political experience and industrial training. His contact with city life has been unfortunate, for it has forced him into the most dilapidated and vicious areas of our great cities. Like a shadow over his whole existence lies the oppressive race prejudice of his white neighbor, restricting his activities and thwarting his ambitions. It would be extraordinary, indeed, if this group were to prove more law-abiding than the white, which enjoys more fully the advantages of a civilization the Negro has helped to create."*

On the other hand, the peculiar result of the assumed fact that Negroes are criminal is that within the race, a Negro accused or convicted of a crime immediately suffers a penalty, not only of ostracism, but lack of sympathy. Negroes make comparatively little effort to defend the accused; they do not systematically look after them; the churches take little interest in delinquents, and the general attitude of the race is one of irritation toward these members of their groups who have brought the whole race into disrepute. This makes a peculiarly bitter feeling among the unfortunate of the race and the more successful.

So far as dependents are concerned, again the material which we have to measure the amount of dependents is inconclusive and unsatisfactory. There are such differences in policy in various states, such difference in treatment that it is hard to say what the condition is. It would seem, by a study of states where there is a substantial uniform policy toward the feeble-minded and paupers, regardless of race, that there is a higher rate of institutionization among Negroes than among whites. And this would be natural unless corrected by taking into account the unequal economic and social condition.

Here again within the race, there is a certain resentment against a colored person who fails to progress as rapidly as the Negro thinks a black man must. When, therefore, such a person becomes a subject of charity and must be put into an institution, he is regarded not so much as unfortunate as in some vague way blame worthy. He hinders the general advance and even if he

---

*The American Negro. P. 64. American Academy of Political and Social Science.

is not at fault, his existence is a misfortune. The real question, then, in the Negro race, is how far the group can and should assume responsibility for its delinquents and dependents, and cultivate sympathy and help for these unfortunates, and how far in this way differentiation into class can keep economic exploitation from becoming a settled method of social advance.

July, 1933

WILLIAM MONROE TROTTER

Monroe Trotter was a man of heroic proportions, and probably one of the most selfless of Negro leaders during all our American history. His father was Recorder of Deeds for the District of Columbia, at the time when Recorders were paid by fees; and as a result, he retired from office with a small fortune, which he husbanded carefully. Thus, his son was born in comfortable circumstances, and with his talent for business, and his wide acquaintanceship with the best class of young Massachusetts men in his day, might easily have accumulated wealth.

But he turned aside. He had in his soul all that went to make a fanatic, a knight errant. Ready to sacrifice himself, fearing nobody and nothing, strong in body, sturdy in conviction, full of unbending belief.

I remember when I first saw him as a student at Harvard. He was several classes below me. I should like to have known him and spoken to him, but he was curiously aloof. He was even then forming his philosophy of life. Colored students must not herd together, just because they were colored. He had his white friends and companions, and they liked him. He was no hanger-on, but a leader among them. But he did not seek other colored students as companions. I was a bit lonesome in those days, but I saw his point, and I did not seek him.

Out of this rose his life-long philosohy: Intense hatred of all racial discrimination and segregation. He was particularly incensed at the compromising philosophy of Booker T. Washington; at his industrialism, and his condoning of the deeds of the South.

In the first years of the 20th Century, with George Forbes,

Monroe Trotter began the publication of *The Guardian.* Several times young men have started radical sheets among us, like *The Messenger,* and others. But nothing, I think, that for sheer biting invective and unswerving courage, ever quite equaled the *Boston Guardian* in its earlier days. Mr. Washington and his followers literally shrivelled before it, and it was, of course, often as unfair as it was inspired.

I had come to know Trotter, then, especially because I knew Deenie Pindell as a girl before they were married. We were to stop with them one summer. Mrs. Du Bois was already there when I arrived in Boston, and on the elevated platform, I learned of the Zion Church riot. It was called a riot in the newspapers, and they were full of it. As a matter of fact, Trotter and Forbes had tried to ask Booker T. Washington certain pointed questions, after a speech which he made in the colored church; and immediately he was arrested, according to the careful plans which William L. Lewis, Washington's attorney, had laid. I was incensed at Trotter. I thought that he had been needlessly violent, and had compromised me as his guest; but when I learned the exact facts, and how little cause for riot there was, and when they clapped Trotter in the Charles Street Jail, all of us more conservative, younger men rose in revolt.

Out of this incident, within a year or two, arose the Niagara movement, and Trotter was present.

But Trotter was not an organization man. He was a free lance; too intense and sturdy to loan himself to that compromise which is the basis of all real organization. Trouble arose in the Niagara movement, and afterward when the Niagara movement joined the new N.A.A.C.P., Trotter stood out in revolt, and curiously enough, did not join the new organization because of his suspicion of the white elements who were co-operating with us.

He devoted himself to *The Guardian,* and it became one of the first of the nation-wide colored weeklies. His wife worked with him in utter devotion; giving up all thought of children; giving up her pretty home in Roxbury; living and lunching with him in the *Guardian Office,* and knowing hunger and cold. It was a magnificent partnership, and she died to pay for it.

The Trotter philosophy was carried out remorselessly in his paper, and his philosophy. He stood unflinchingly for fighting separation and discrimination in church and school, and in

professional and business life. He would not allow a colored
Y. M. C. A. in Boston, and he hated to recognize colored
churches, or colored colleges. On this battle line he fought a
long, exhausting fight for over a quarter of a century. What has
been the result? There are fewer Negroes in Boston churches
today than when Trotter began a crusade, and colored people
sat in the pews under Phillips Brooks' preaching. There may be
more colored teachers in the schools, but certainly they are
playing no such part as Maria Baldwin did, as principal of the
best Cambridge Grammar School.

When Trotter began, not a single hotel in Boston dared
to refuse colored guests. Today, there are few Boston hotels
where colored people are received. There is still no colored
Y. M. C. A., but on the other hand, there are practically no
colored members of the white "Y," and young colored men are
deprived of club house and recreational facilities which they
sorely need. In the professions, in general employment, and in
business, there is certainly not less, and probably more discrimination than there used to be.

Does this mean that Monroe Trotter's life was a failure?
Never. He lived up to his belief to the best of his ability. He
fought like a man. The ultimate object of his fighting was absolutely right, but he miscalculated the opposition. He thought
that Boston and America would yield to clear reason and determined agitation. They did not. On the contrary, to some extent,
the very agitation carried on in these years has solidified opposition. This does not mean that agitation does not pay; but it
means that you cannot necessarily cash in quickly upon it. It
means that sacrifice, even to blood and tears, must be given to
this great fight; and not one but a thousand lives, like that of
Monroe Trotter, is necessary to victory.

More than that, inner organization is demanded. The free
lance like Trotter is not strong enough. The mailed fist has got
to be clenched. The united effort of twelve millions has got to
be made to mean more than the individual effort of those who
think aright. Yet this very inner organization involves segregation. It involves voluntary racial organization, and this racial
grouping invites further effort at enforced segregation by law
and custom from without. Nevertheless, there is no alternative.
We have got to unite to save ourselves, and while the unending
devotion to principle, such as Monroe Trotter shows, has and

must ever have, its value, with sorrow, and yet with conviction, we know that this is not enough.

I can understand his death. I can see a man of sixty, tired and disappointed, facing poverty and defeat. Standing amid indifferent friends and triumphant enemies. So he went to the window of his Dark Tower, and beckoned to Death; up from where She lay among the lilies. And Death, like a whirlwind, swept up to him. I shall think of him as lying silent, cold and still; at last at peace, dreamless and serene. Let no trump of doom disturb him from his perfect and eternal rest.

May, 1934

WORLD WAR I

WORLD WAR AND THE COLOR LINE

Many colored persons, and persons interested in them, may easily make the mistake of supposing that the present war is far removed from the color problem of America and that in the face of this great catastrophe we may forget for a moment such local problems and give all attention and contributions to the seemingly more pressing cause.

This attitude is a mistake. The present war in Europe is one of the great disasters due to race and color prejudice and it but foreshadows greater disasters in the future.

It is not merely national jealousy, or the so-called "race" rivalry of Slav, Teuton and Latin, that is the larger cause of this war. It is rather the wild quest for Imperial expansion among colored races between Germany, England and France primarily, and Belgium, Italy, Russia and Austria-Hungary in lesser degree. Germany long since found herself shut out from acquiring colonies. She looked toward South America, but the "Monroe Doctrine" stood in her way. She started for Africa and by bulldozing methods secured one good colony, one desert and two swamps. Her last efforts looked toward North Africa and Asia-Minor. Finally, she evidently decided at the first opportunity to seize English or French colonies and to this end feverishly expanded her navy, kept her army at the highest point of efficiency and has been for twenty years the bully of Europe with a chip on her shoulder and defiance in her mouth.

The colonies which England and France own and Germany covets are largely in tropical and semi-tropical lands and inhabited by black, brown and yellow peoples. In such colonies there is a chance to confiscate land, work the natives at low wages, make large profits and open wide markets for cheap European manufactures. Asia, Africa, the South Sea Islands, the West Indies, Mexico and Central America and much of South America have long been designated by the white world as fit field for this kind of commercial exploitation, for the benefit of Europe and with little regard for the welfare of the natives. One has only to remember the forced labor in South Africa, the outrages in Congo, the cocoa-slavery in Portuguese Africa, the land monopoly and peonage of Mexico, the exploitation of Chinese coolies and the rubber horror of the Amazon to realize what white imperialism is doing to-day in well-known cases, not to mention thousands of less-known instances.

In this way a theory of the inferiority of the darker peoples and a contempt for their rights and aspirations has become all but universal in the greatest centers of modern culture. Here it was that American color prejudice and race hatred received in recent years unexpected aid and sympathy. To-day civilized nations are fighting like mad dogs over the right to own and exploit these darker peoples.

In such case where should our sympathy lie? Undoubtedly, with the Allies—with England and France in particular. Not that these nations are innocent. England was in the past blood-guilty above all lands in her wicked and conscienceless rape of darker races. England was primarily responsible for American slavery, for the starvation of India, and the Chinese opium traffic. But the salvation of England is that she has the ability to learn from her mistakes. To-day no white nation is fairer in its treatment of darker peoples than England. Not that England is yet fair. She is not yet just, and she still nourishes much disdain for colored races, erects contemptible and humiliating political and social barriers and steals their land and labor; but as compared with Germany England is an angel of light. The record of Germany as a colonizer toward weaker and darker people is the most barbarous of any civilized people and grows worse instead of better. France is less efficient than England as an administrator of colonies and has consequently been guilty of much neglect and injustice; but she is nevertheless the most kindly of all European nations in her personal relations with colored folk. She draws no dead line of color and colored Frenchmen always love France.

Belgium has been as pitiless and grasping as Germany and in strict justice deserves every pang she is suffering after her unspeakable atrocities in Congo. Russia has never drawn a color line but has rather courted the yellow races, although with ulterior motives. Japan, however, instilled wholesome respect in this line.

Undoubtedly, then the triumph of the allies would at least leave the light of the colored races no worse than now. Indeed, considering the fact than black Africans and brown Indians and yellow Japanese are fighting for France and England it may be that they will come out of this frightful welter of blood with new ideas of the essential equality of all men.

On the other hand, the triumph of Germany means the triumph of every force calculated to subordinate darker peoples. It would mean triumphant militarism, autocratic and centralized government and a studied theory of contempt for everything except Germany—"Germany above everything in the world." The dispair and humiliation of Germany in the eighteenth century has brought this extraordinary rebound of self-exaltation and disdain for mankind. The triumph of this idea would mean a crucifixion of darker peoples unparalleled in history.

The writer speaks without anti-German bias; personally he has deep cause to love the German people. They made him believe in the essential humanity of white folk twenty years ago when he was near to denying it. But even then the spell of militarism was in the air, and the Prussian strut had caught the nation's imagination. They were starting on the same road with the southern American whites toward a contempt toward human beings and a faith in their own utter superiority to all other breeds. This feeling had not then applied itself particularly to colored folk and has only begun to to-day; but it is going by leaps and bounds. Germany needs but the rôle of world conquest to make her one of the most contemptible of "Nigger" hating nations. Just as we go to press, the *Berliner Tageblatt* publishes a proclamation by "German representatives of Science and Art to the World of Culture" in which men like Harnack, Bode, Hauptmann, Suderman, Roentgen, Humperdink, Wundt and others, insult hundreds of millions of human beings by openly sneering at "Mongrels and Niggers."

As colored Americans then, and as Americans who fear race prejudice as the greatest of War-makers, our sympathies in the awful conflict should be with France and England; not that they have conquered race prejudice, but they have at least begun to realize its cost and evil, while Germany exalts it.

If so great a catastrophe has followed jealousies and greed built on a desire to steal from and oppress people whom the dominant culture dispises, how much wilder and wider will be the conflict when black and brown and yellow people stand up together shoulder to shoulder and demand recognition as men!

Let us give then our sympathies to those nations whose triumph will most tend to postpone if not to make unnecessary a world war of races.

November, 1914. Vol. IX, No. 1. pp. 28-30.

LUSITANIA

The last horror of a horrible war is come! It puts a period to what we have already said: European civilization has failed. Its failure did not come with this war but with this war it has been made manifest. Whatever of brutality and inhumanity, of murder, lust and theft has happened since last summer is but counterpart of the same sort of happenings hidden in the wilderness and done against dark and helpless people by white harbingers of human culture. But when Negroes were enslaved, or the natives of Congo raped and mutilated, or the Indians of the Amazon robbed, or the natives of the South Seas murdered, or 2,732 American citizens lynched—when all this happened in the past and men knew it was happening and women fatted and plumed themselves on the ill-gotten gains, and London and Berlin and Paris and New York flamed with orgies of extravagance which the theft of worlds made possible, when all this happened, we civilized folk turned deaf ears. We explained that these "lesser breeds without the law" were given to exaggeration and had to be treated this way. They could not understand "civilization;" but as for the White World, there humanity and Christianity and loving kindness reigned. This was a lie and we know it was a lie. The Great War is the lie unveiled. This world is a miserable pretender toward things which it might accomplish if it would be humble and gentle and poor and honest. It is a great privilege in the midst of this frightful catastrophe to belong to a race that can stand before Heaven with clean hands and say: we have not oppressed, we have been oppressed; we are not thieves, we are victims; we are not murderers, we are lynched!

June, 1915. Vol. X, No. 2. p. 80.

THE PERPETUAL DILEMMA

We Negroes ever face it.

We cannot escape it.

We must continually choose between insult and injury: no schools or separate schools; no travel or "Jim Crow" travel; homes with disdainful neighbors or homes in slums.

We continually submit to segregated schools, "Jim Crow" cars, and isolation, because it would be suicide to go uneducated, stay at home, and live in the "tenderloin."

Yet, when a new alternative of such choice faces us it comes with a shock and almost without thinking we rail at the one who advises the lesser of two evils.

Thus it was with many hasty editors in the case of the training camp for Negro officers which Dr. J.E. Spingarn is seeking to establish.

Does Dr. Spingarn believe in a "Jim Crow" training camp? Certainly not, and he has done all he could to induce the government to admit Negroes to all training camps.

The government has so far courteously refused.

But war is imminent.

If war comes tomorrow Negroes will be compelled to enlist under *white* officers because (save in a very few cases) no Negroes have had the requisite training.

We must choose then between the insult of a separate camp and the irreparable injury of strengthening the present custom of putting no black men in positions of authority.

Our choice is as clear as noonday.

Give us the camp.

Let not 200, but 2,000 volunteer.

We did not make the damnable dilemma.

Our enemies made that.

We must make the choice else we play into their very claws.

It is a case of camp or no officers.

Give us the officers.

Give us the camp.

A word to those who object:

1. The army does not wish this camp. It wishes the project to fail. General Wood refuses to name date or place until 200 apply. The reason is obvious. Up to March 8, sixty-nine men have applied.

2. The camp is a temporary measure lasting four weeks and designed to FIGHT, not encourage discrimination in the army. The New York Negro regiment could not find enough qualified Negroes for its commissions. We want trained colored officers. This camp will furnish them.

3. The South does not want the Negro to receive military training of any sort. For that reason the general staff reduced its estimate from 900,000 to 500,000 soldiers—they expect to EX-CLUDE Negroes!

4. If war comes, conscription will follow. All pretty talk about not volunteering will become entirely academic. This is the mistake made by the Baltimore AFRO-AMERICAN, the Chicago DEFENDER, the New York NEWS, and the Cleveland GAZETTE. They assume a choice between volunteering and not volunteering. The choice will be between conscription and rebellion.

Can the reader conceive of the possibility of choice? The leaders of the colored race who advise them to add treason and rebellion to the other grounds on which the South urges discrimination against them would hardly be doing a service to those whom they profess to love. No, there is only one thing to do now, and that is to organize the colored people for leadership and service, if war should come. A thousand officers of colored blood is something to work for.

Give us the camp!

April, 1917. Vol. XIII, No. 6. pp. 270-1.

WE SHOULD WORRY

The American Negro more unanimously than any other American group has offered his services in this war as officer and soldier. He has done this earnestly and unselfishly, overlooking his just resentment and grievous wrongs.

Up to the present his offer has been received with sullen and ungracious silence, or at best in awkward complaisance.

Nevertheless, the offer stands as it stood in 1776, 1812, 1861, and 1898.

But——

Certain Americans,—Southern Bourbons, and Northern Copperheads—fear Negro soldiers. They do not fear that they will not fight—they fear that they WILL fight and fight bravely and well. Just as in Reconstruction days, it was not bad Negro voters they feared but good, intelligent ones.

Selah!

These Bourbons and Copperheads know that if Negroes fight well in this war they will get credit for it. They cannot "Carrizal" the news and boost the white putty-head who blundered, forgetting the very name of the brave black subalterns. No! those fool French will tell the truth and the Associated Press will not be able to edit "Niggers"; so the Copperheads and Bourbons do not want Negro soldiers. They think they can trust Southern state officers to juggle that little "agricultural laborer joker" and keep us out of the ranks.

Very good.

"We should worry."

If they do not want us to fight, we will work. We will walk

into the industrial shoes of a few million whites who go to the front. We will get higher wages and we cannot be stopped from migrating by all the deviltry of the slave South; particularly with the white lynchers and mob leaders away at war.

Will we be ousted when the white soldiers come back?

THEY WON'T COME BACK!

So there you are, gentlemen, and take your choice,——

We'll fight or work.

We'll fight and work.

If we fight we'll learn the fighting game and cease to be so "aisily lynched."

If we don't fight we'll learn the more lucrative trades and cease to be so easily robbed and exploited.

Take your choice, gentlemen.

"We should worry."

June, 1917

THE BLACK SOLDIER

This number of THE CRISIS is dedicated, first, to the nearly 100,000 men of Negro descent who are today called to arms for the United States. It is dedicated, also, to the million dark men of Africa and India, who have served in the armies of Great Britain, and to the equal, if not larger, number who are fighting for France and the other allies.

To these men we want to say above all: Have courage and determination. You are not fighting simply for Europe; you are fighting for the world, and you and your people are a part of the world.

This war is an End and, also, a Beginning. Never again will darker people of the world occupy just the place they have before. Out of this war will rise, soon or late, an independent China; a self-governing India, and Egypt with representative institutions; an Africa for the Africans, and not merely for business exploitation. Out of this war will rise, too, an American Negro, with the right to vote and the right to work and the right to live without insult. These things may not and will not come at once; but they are written in the stars, and the first step toward them is victory for the armies of the Allies.

June, 1918. Vol. XVI, No. 2. p. 60.

CLOSE RANKS

This is the crisis of the world. For all the long years to come men will point to the year 1918 as the great Day of Decision, the day when the world decided whether it would submit to military despotism and an endless armed peace—if peace it could be called—or whether they would put down the menace of German militarism and inaugurate the United States of the World.

We of the colored race have no ordinary interest in the outcome. That which the German power represents today spells death to the aspirations of Negroes and all darker races for equality, freedom and democracy. Let us not hesitate. Let us, while this war lasts, forget our special grievances and close our ranks shoulder to shoulder with our own white fellow citizens and the allied nations that are fighting for democracy. We make no ordinary sacrifice, but we make it gladly and willingly with our eyes lifted to the hills.

July, 1918. Vol. XVI, No. 3. p. 111.

A PHILOSOPHY IN TIME OF WAR

First, This is Our Country:

We have worked for it, we have suffered for it, we have fought for it; we have made its music, we have tinged its ideals, its poetry, its religion, its dreams; we have reached in this land our highest modern development and nothing, humanly speaking, can prevent us from eventually reaching here the full stature of our manhood. Our country is at war. The war is critical, dangerous and worldwide. If this is OUR country, then this is OUR war. We must fight it with every ounce of blood and treasure.

SECOND, Our country is not perfect. Few countries are. We have our memories and our present grievances. This nation has sinned against the light, but it has not sinned as Germany has sinned. Its continued existence and development is the hope of mankind and of black mankind, and not its menace. We must fight, then, for the survival of the Best against the threats of the Worst.

THIRD, But what of our wrongs, cry a million voices with strained faces and bitter eyes. Our wrongs are still wrong. War does not excuse Disfranchisement, "Jim-Crow" cars and social injustices, but it does make our *first* duty clear. It does say deep to the heart of every Negro American: We shall not bargain with our loyalty. We shall not profiteer with our country's blood. We shall not hesitate the fraction of a second when the God of Battles summons his dusky warriors to stand before the armposts of His Throne. Let them who call for sacrifice in this awful hour of Pain fight for the rights that should be ours; let them who make the laws writhe beneath each enactment that oppresses us,—but we? Our duty lies inexorable and splendid before us, and we shall not shirk.

FOURTH, Calm and with soul serene, unflurried and unafraid we send a hundred thousand black sons and husbands and fathers to the Western Front and behind them rank on rank stand hundreds of thousands more.

We are the Ancient of Days, the First of Races and the Oldest of Men. Before Time was, we are. We have seen Egypt and Ethiopia, Babylon and Persia, Rome and America, and for that flaming Thing, Crucified Right, which survived all this staggering and struggling of men—for that we fight today in and for America—not for a price, not ourselves alone, but for the World.

FIFTH, Protest, my brother, and crumble. I have seen the Vision and it shall not fade. We want victory for ourselves— dear God, how terribly we want it—but it must not be cheap bargaining, it must be clean and glorious, won by our manliness, and not by the threat of the footpad. In the day of our lowest travail we did not murder children and rape women to bring our freedom nearer. We played the game and freedom came. So, too, today our souls are ours, but our bodies belong to our country.

Patience, then, without compromise; silence without surrender; grim determination never to cease striving until we can vote, travel, learn, work and enjoy in peace—all this, and yet with it and above it all the tramp of our armies over the bloodstained lillies of France to show the world again what the loyalty and bravery of black men means.

August, 1918. Vol. XVI, No. 4. pp. 164-5.

FOOD

War necessities may teach the Negro some salutary lessons. For a long time it has been known that as a race we eat too much meat, especially pork, and are ruining our digestions with hot bread made daily. Frugal peoples have long since learned that risen bread thoroughly baked and kept until stale is not only the most economical, but the most nuitritious of dietaries. Modern physicians have long urged us to decrease our meat rations and increase our consumption of vegetables. The war comes now to enforce our common sense. The Hot Biscuit is a lovely institution, but it is too costly in work and money and too dangerous for the digestion to come oftener than once a week. The deceitful Pork Chop must be dethroned in the South and yield a part of its sway to vegetables, fruits and fish. Food—reasonable food —will not only win the war, but it will win health and efficiency if we learn the lesson of the present emergency aright.

August, 1918. Vol. XVI, No. 4. p. 165.

A MOMENTOUS PROPOSAL

A plan of far-reaching constructive effort to satisfy the pressing greivances of colored Americans has been under serious consideration by the military authorities at Washington for two months. On June 15, Dr. Du Bois was called in and asked if he would accept a captaincy in a bureau of the General Staff, if one was established, for the above purposes. Dr. Du Bois replied that he would, provided he could retain general oversight of THE CRISIS, and provided that his captain's salary (which was $1,000 less than his present salary) could be supplemented from THE CRISIS income, so that he would suffer no financial loss. The military authorities saw no objection to these conditions. Dr. Du Bois then consulted the President of the Board of Directors of the N.A.A.C.P., the chairman and the acting chairman of the Board and several members, including Dr. H.C. Bishop, Bishop Hurst, Dr. Bentley, Mr. A.H. Grimke, Colonel Charles Young, Rev. G.R. Waller, Hon. Charles Nagel and Dr. V. Morton-Jones. All of them, except Mr. Grimke, agreed with the conditions and urged acceptance. Mr. Grimke expressed deep sympathy, but asked more time for consideration.

No decision, however, as to establishing the Bureau was arrived at and when the regular July meeting of the Board took place, the priority of the Government's claim on Dr. Du Bois was recognized, but doubt was expressed as to the advisability of his continuing in charge of THE CRISIS.

A puzzling dilemma between devotion to his life work and duty to his country in time of war was thus forced upon Dr. Du Bois. His final conclusion, painful as it had to be, was to accept the commission. When thousands are giving their lives to their country, how could he long hesitate in risking far less? This delicate situation was further complicated by vague rumors which led friends of the Association with more zeal than thought to charge the Government with attempted "bribery" and Dr. Du Bois with being a "traitor." Some who disagreed with the July editorials of THE CRISIS saw in them further evidences of a "corrupt bargain," not knowing that those editorials were written two weeks before Dr. Du Bois had the slightest intimation that his services were to be asked, and were in print before he reached Washington.

Finally, the General Staff, after carefully considering the matter from all angles, has decided not to establish the proposed bureau "at present" as its broad scope might lead "beyond the proper limits of military activity."

Here the matter rests. It is deplorable that this splendid and statesmanlike plan has been abandoned and equally unfortunate that any question as to its desirability should have ever arisen among black folk. The personal side of it is of less consequence and has left Dr. Du Bois in unruffled serenity. No one who essays to teach the multitude can long escape crucifixion.

September, 1918. Vol. XVI, No. 5. pp. 215-16.

OUR SPECIAL GRIEVANCES

The leading editorial in the July CRISIS, called "Close Ranks," has been the subject of much comment. To a few it has seemed to indicate some change of position on the part of the National Association for the Advancement of Colored People and THE CRISIS. It is needless to say that it indicates nothing of the sort. This Association and this magazine stand today exactly where they have stood during the eight years of their work; *viz.*, for the full manhood rights of the American Negro.

The July editorial is not in the slightest degree inconsistent with these principles. It was submitted to prominent members and officers of the board before printing and found no objection.

The editorial seeks to say that the *first* duty of an American is to win the war and that to this all else is subsidiary. It declares that whatever personal and group grievances interfere with this mighty duty must wait.

It does not say that these grievances are *not* grievances, or that the temporary setting aside of wrongs makes them right. But it *does* say, and THE CRISIS repeats the word, that any man or race that seeks to turn his country's tragic predicament to his own personal gain is fatally cheating himself.

What THE CRISIS said is precisely what in practice the Negroes of America have already done during the war and have been advised to do by every responsible editor and leader.

The editorial was in exact accord and almost in the very words of a resolution written by the same hand and passed unanimously by the thirty-one editors of all the leading Negro publications in America.

Did Negroes refuse to serve in the draft until they got the right to vote? No, they stormed the gates of the army for the right to fight. Did they refuse commissions because their army was segregated? No, they were eager to enter and diligent to learn. Have we black men for one moment hesitated to do our

full duty in this war because we thought the country was not
doing its full duty to us? Is there a single Negro leader who
advised by word, written or spoken, rebellion and disloyalty?
Certainly not. Then somebody "forgot his special grievance"
and fought for his country, and to him and for him THE CRISIS
speaks. THE CRISIS says, *first* your Country, *then* your
Rights!

Certain honest thinkers among us hesitate at that last sen-
tence. They say it is all well to be idealistic, but is it not true
that while we have fought our country's battles for one hundred
fifty years, we have *not* gained our rights? There is just enough
fact in this half truth to make it a whole and a very mischievous
lie. No, we have not gained all our rights, but we have gained
rights and gained them rapidly and effectively by our loyalty in
time of trial.

Five thousand Negroes fought in the Revolution; the result
was the emancipation of slaves in the North and the abolition
of the African slave trade. At least three thousand Negro soldiers and sailors fought in the war of 1812; the result was the
enfranchisement of the Negro in many Northern States and the
beginning of a strong movement for general emancipation. Two
hundred thousand Negroes enlisted in the Civil War, and the
result was the emancipation of four million slaves, and the
enfranchisement of the black man. Some ten thousand Negroes
fought in the Spanish-American War, and in the twenty years
ensuing since the war, despite many set backs, we have doubled
our landholding acreage and quadrupled our accumulated
wealth. We have established a strong leadership of education
and character, we have expanded our business interests and we
have established the N.A.A.C.P., with forty thousand members.

God knows we have enough left to fight for, but any people
who by loyalty and patriotism have gained what we have in four
wars ought surely to have sense enough to give that loyalty and
patriotism a chance to win in the fifth.

And we *are* winning right now. Since this war began we have
won:

Recognition of our citizenship in the draft;

One thousand Negro officers;

Special representation in the War and Labor departments;

Higher wages and better employment;

Abolition of the color line in railway wage;

Recognition as Red Cross nurses;

Overthrow of segregation ordinances;

A strong word from the President against lynching.

Blessed saints! Is this *nothing?* Should it not discourage slackers and fools? Come, fellow black men, fight for your rights, but for God's sake have sense enough to know when you are getting what you fight for.

September, 1918. Vol. XVI, No. 5. pp. 216-17.

PATRIOTISM

Curious, indeed, has been the transformation in the souls of most Americans during this war. Before the war nobody *loved* America. The very phrase seemed maudlin and unintelligent. We loved Justice and Freedom; we sought reform and uplift in politics, health protection; a noble art, less class dislike, no race hatred; and we hoped for universal education; but our country? We scarcely had a country—we willed a whole world.

And yet, beneath all this, logically we did love our country because we deemed it capable of realizing our dreams and inspiring the greater world. Else one would no longer have dreamed or worked here. We would have sought a Land of Promise. But did American Socialists emigrate to Germany? No, German Socialists came to America, and worked and believed that here the injustices of private wealth could best and most quickly be remedied. Russian Revolutionists found here no Utopia, but at least a sanctuary and hope which they could not find in Russia. Did Negroes leave America for Mexico, or the West Indies, or Africa? No, they became insulted at the mere suggestion. Despite horrible wrongs, they believed it eventually possible to realize here in America all their highest hopes and aspirations. So with every man who has toiled in this land for higher and better things—even those who longed for the Peace of God, which in these heavy days passeth understanding —all loved and loved passionately not America, but what America might be—the Real America, as we sometimes said.

Men work and fight and sweat for a dream only because they believe it possible. Are the dreams of America less possible now that we fight for common decency in international affairs than before when we strove for the highest things within the nation? If leaving the arena of the heart and intellect, we are forced to contend like very beasts, is the fighting any less necessary? Rather is the call of duty infinitely higher when with gun and knife and clenched hand, we are compelled to strive not simply for the higher life, but for life itself. On some such foundation is building the new Patriotism in America and in the World.

November, 1918. Vol. XVII, No. 1. pp. 8-10.

SPECIAL REPORTS

THE MASSACRE OF EAST ST. LOUIS

The National Association for the Advancement of Colored People, 70 Fifth Avenue, New York, sent Martha Gruening and W. E. Burghardt Du Bois to East St. Louis, as special investigators of the recent outrages. These two collected in person the facts and pictures from which this article is compiled.

On the 2nd of July, 1917, the city of East St. Louis in Illinois added a foul and revolting page to the history of all the massacres of the world. On that day a mob of white men, women and children burned and destroyed at least $400,000 worth of property belonging to both whites and Negroes; drove 6,000 Negroes out of their homes; and deliberately murdered, by shooting, burning and hanging, between one and two hundred human beings who were black.

Such an outbreak could not have been instantaneous. There must have been something further reaching even than an immediate cause to provoke such a disaster. The immediate cause usually given is as follows: On the evening of July 1, white "joy riders" rode down a block in Market Street, which was inhabited by Negroes, and began to fire into the houses. The Negroes aroused by this armed themselves against further trouble. Presently a police automobile drove up containing detectives and stopped. The Negroes thinking that these were the "joy riders" returning opened up fire before this misunderstanding was removed, and two of the detectives were killed. Some of the policemen were in plain clothes.

One naturally wonders why should the white "joy riders" fire in the first place. What was their quarrel with the Negroes? In answering that question we get down to the real story. It is here we meet with the facts that lay directly back of the massacre, a combination of the jealousy of white labor unions and prejudice.

East St. Louis is a great industrial center, possessing huge packing and manufacturing houses, and is, therefore, one of the biggest markets in the country for common unskilled labor. The war, by the deportation of white foreign workers, caused a scarcity of labor and this brought about the beginning of a noticeable influx of Negroes from the South. Last summer 4,500 white men went on strike in the packing plants of Armour & Co., and Negroes from the South were called into the plants as strikebreakers. When the strike ended the Negroes were still employed and that many white men failed to regain their positions. The leaders of various labor unions realized that the supply of Negroes was practically inexhaustible and that they were receiving the same wages as their white predecessors and so evidently doing the same grade of work. Since it was increasingly possible then to call in as many black strike-breakers as necessary, the effectiveness of any strike was accordingly decreased. It was this realization that caused the small but indicative May riots. Evidently, the leaders of the labor unions thought something must be done, some measure sufficiently drastic must be taken to drive these interlopers away and to restore to these white Americans their privileges. The fact that the Negroes were also Americans meant nothing at such a time as this.

The leader of a labor union must be an opportunist. The psychology of any unskilled laborer is comparatively simple. To the knowledge then that his job is being held by an outsider add his natural and fostered prejudice against an outsider who is black and you have something of the mental attitude of the rioters of East St. Louis. Doubtless it was with some such prophetic vision as this that Edward F. Mason, secretary of the Central Trades and Labor Union, issued a letter, the facsimile of which appears on the opposite page.

One point in particular is emphasized, that of color: "The Southern Negro," writes Mr. Mason, "has come into our community. No less than ten thousand of undesirable Negroes," he continues, "have poured in and are being used to the detriment of our white citizens." There is the appeal direct to prejudice. It is not that foreigners—Czechs, Slovaks, Lithuanians—or whatever ethnic division is least indigenous to East St. Louis— it is not that *they* are ousting Americans of any color or hue, but the "Southern Negro," the most American product there is, is being used "to the detriment of our white citizens."

Mr. Mason has no hesitancy in suggesting "that some action should be taken to retard this growing menace" and "to get rid of a certain portion of those who are already here." Was not Mr. Gompers' excuse in Carnegie Hall a faint echo of all this?

Mr. Mason wants to be fair. "This is not a protest against the Negro who has been a long resident"—so runs his superb English—"of East St. Louis, and is a law-abiding citizen of the state." In East St. Louis labor leaders are the arbiters of legal conduct and therefore 10,000 Negroes become undesirable citizens because they are strike-breakers and black.

That the July riot grew out of the meeting called by Mr. Mason (see facsimile), we are not prepared to say; but that it grew out of this attitude is only too apparent. By all accounts of eye-witnesses, both white and black, the East St. Louis outrage was deliberately planned and executed.

Says Richard L. Stokes, writing in the *St. Louis Globe-Democrat* for Sunday, July 8:

> On the night of May 28th a delegation of about 600 union men marched to the City Hall to appeal to the authorities to prevent the importation of any more Negroes. Among them were many of the Aluminum Ore Company strikers. They took possession of an auditorium, and some of the leaders made speeches advising that in case the authorities took no action, they should resort to mob law.

When genuine mob law did finally reign on July 2, the scenes were indescribable. Germany has nothing on East St. Louis when it comes to "frightfulness." Indeed in one respect Germany does not even approximate her ill-famed sister. In all the accounts given of German atrocities, no one, we believe, has accused the Germans of taking pleasure in the sufferings of their victims. But these rioters combined business and pleasure. These Negroes were "butchered to make" an East St. Louis "holiday."

Carlos F. Hurd, an eye-witness, realizes this fact and speaks of it in the article which he publishes July 3 in the *St. Louis Post-Dispatch*, of which he is a staff-reporter. Mr. Hurd writes:

> A mob is passionate, a mob follows one man or a few men blindly; a mob sometimes takes chances. The East St. Louis affair, as I saw it, was a man hunt, conducted on a sporting basis, though with anything but the fair play which is the principle of sport. The East St. Louis men took no chances, except the chance from stray shots, which every spectator of their acts took. They went in small groups, there was little leadership, and there was a horribly cool deliberateness and a spirit of fun about it.
>
> 'Get a nigger,' was the slogan, and it was varied by the recurrent cry, 'Get another!' It was like nothing so much as the holiday crowd, with thumbs turned down, in the Roman Coliseum, except that here the shouters were their own gladiators, and their own wild beasts.

He goes on with another horrible account of which he was also an eye-witness:

> A Negro, his head laid open by a great stone-cut, had been dragged to the mouth of the alley on Fourth Street and a small rope was being put about his neck. There was joking comment on the weakness of the rope, and everyone was prepared for what happened when it was pulled over a projecting cable box, a short distance up the pole. It broke, letting the Negro tumble back to his knees, and causing one of the men who was pulling on it to sprawl on the pavement.
>
> An old man, with a cap like those worn by street car conductors, but showing no badge of car service, came out of his house to protest. "Don't you hang that man on this street," he shouted. "I dare you to." He was pushed angrily away, and a rope, obviously strong enough for its purpose, was brought.
>
> Right here I saw the most sickening incident of the

evening. To put the rope around the Negro's neck, one of the lynchers stuck his fingers inside the gaping scalp and lifted the Negro's head by it, literally bathing his hand in the man's blood.

'Get hold, and pull for East St. Louis!' called a man with a black coat and a new straw hat, as he seized the other end of the rope. The rope was long, but not too long for the number of hands that grasped it, and this time the Negro was lifted to a height of about seven feet from the ground. The body was left hanging there.

These accounts make gruesome reading, but they are all true. Hugh L. Wood paints in the *St. Louis Republic* another horrible picture. He says:

A Negro weighing 300 pounds came out of the burning line of dwellings just north and east of the Southern freight house. His hands were elevated and his yellow face was speckled with the awful fear of death.

"Get him!" they cried. Here was a chance to see suffering, something that bullets didn't always make.

So a man in the crowd clubbed his revolver and struck the Negro in the face with it. Another dashed an iron bolt between the Negro's eyes. Still another stood near and battered him with a rock.

Then the giant Negro toppled to the ground. "This is the way," cried one. He ran back a few paces, then ran at the prostrate black at full speed and made a flying leap.

His heels struck right in the middle of the battered face. A girl stepped up and struck the bleeding man with her foot. The blood spurted onto her stockings and men laughed and grunted.

No amount of suffering awakened pity in the hearts of the rioters. Mr Wood tells us that:

A few Negroes, caught on the street, were kicked and shot to death. As flies settled on their terrible wounds, the gaping mouthed mobsmen forbade the dying blacks to brush them off. Girls with blood on their stockings helped to kick in what had been black faces of the corpses on the street.

The *St. Louis Republic* has still a further touch:

A Negro lay a block east on Broadway, with his face beaten in. He was not dead. An ambulance, driven by white men, dashed up.

"If you pick up that skunk we'll kill you, too," cried the crowd.

"I've got a wife and four children at home," said the white-faced ambulance man as he climbed back on the wagon.

When the fire had eaten its way that far the body was tossed into the flames. Two blocks further east lay a Negro who had been beaten until he was dying. "Let's string him up," shouted a man.

A rope was brought and the dying black in a moment was dangling from a pole. Several "good measure" shots were fired into the body and the crowd went further on.

Mr. Hurd who writes with much restraint tells how he saw a man covered with blood and half conscious, raise himself on his elbow and look feebly about, when a young man, standing directly behind him, lifted a flat stone in both hands and hurled it upon his neck. This young man was much better dressed than most of the others. He walked away unmolested.

The violence was confined not only to men. Women were in many cases the aggressors and always ready to instigate and abet.

One woman, according to the *St. Louis Globe-Democrat*, wanted to "cut the heart out" of a Negro, a man already paralyzed from a bullet wound, who was being then maltreated at the hands of a mob.

Mr. Hurd writes:

> I saw Negro women begging for mercy and pleading that they had harmed no one set upon by white women of the baser sort who laughed and answered the coarse sallies of men as they beat the Negresses' faces and breasts with fists, stones and sticks. I saw one of these furies fling herself at a militiaman who was trying to protect a Negress, and wrestle with him for his bayonetted gun, while other women attacked the refugee.
>
> "Let the girls have her," was the shout as the women attacked one young Negress. The victim's cry, "Please, please, I ain't done nothing," was stopped by a blow in the mouth with a broomstick, which one of the women swung like a baseball bat. Another woman seized the Negress' hands, and the blow was repeated as she strug-

gled helplessly. Finger nails clawed her hair and the sleeves were torn from her waist, when some of the men called, "Now let her see how fast she can run." The women did not readily leave off beating her, but they stopped short of murder, and the crying, hysterical girl ran down the street.

An older Negress, a few moments later, came along with two or three militiamen, and the same women made for her. When one of the soldiers held his gun as a barrier, the woman with the broomstick seized it with both hands, and struggled to wrest it from him, while the others, striking at the Negress, in spite of the other militiamen, frightened her thoroughly and hurt her somewhat.

To this the *St. Louis Republic* adds:

Seized with the mob spirit, two young white girls climbed on a car at Broadway and Main Street at about 4 p. m. and dragged a Negress from her seat. As they dragged the struggling Negress through the door to the street there was a great cheer from men on the sidewalk.

As the Negress attempted to break away from her assailants one of the girls—for they were only about 17 years old—pulled off her shoe and started to beat the victim over the head. The victim flinched under the blows of the girl and was bleeding when she was rescued by militiamen.

The girls were not arrested and started to walk away from the scene. There were bloodstains on their clothes and as they passed their friends they told about the part they had played in the riot.

But this sort of Negro-baiting did not make a strong enough appeal to the jaded senses of the mob. Surely there must be some other means of adding to such pleasurable excitement. Somebody suggested fire. The idea was immediately accepted. Says John T. Stewart:

The first houses were fired shortly after 5 o'clock. These were back of Main street, between Broadway and Railroad avenue. Negroes were "flushed" from the burning houses, and ran for their lives, screaming and begging for mercy. A Negro crawled into a shed and fired on the white men. Guardsmen started after him, but when they saw he was armed, turned to the mob and said:

"He's armed, boys. You can have him. A white man's life is worth the lives of a thousand Negroes."

A few minutes later matches were applied to hastily gathered debris piled about the corner of one of three small houses 100 feet from the first fired. These were back of the International Harvester Company's plant. Eight Negroes fled into the last of the houses and hid in the basement. When roof and walls were about to fall in, an aged Negro woman came out. She was permitted to walk to safety. Three Negro women followed and were not fired upon. Then came four Negro men, and 100 shots were fired at them. They fell. No one ventured out to see if they were dead, as the place had come to resemble No Man's Land, with bullets flying back and forth and sparks from the fires falling everywhere.

A Negro who crawled on hands and knees through the weeds was a target for a volley. The mob then turned back to Main street and another Negro was spied on a Main Street car. He was dragged to the street and a rioter stood over him, shooting.

The crowd then turned to Black Valley. Here the greatest fire damage was caused. Flames soon were raging and the shrieking rioters stood about in the streets, made lurid by the flames, and shot and beat Negroes as they fled from their burning homes.

This district today was a waste of smouldering debris. Firemen fought the flames all night. In this stretch were burned the Southern Railroad freight house, the Hills-Thomas Lime and Cement Company plant and the Broadway Opera House. By desperate effort, firemen saved the Public Library Building, the Bon Bon Baking Powder Company, and the J. C. Grant Chemical Company. The warehouses of the latter contained 1,000 gallons of gasoline and coal oil.

It was rumored that many Negroes were burned to death in the Broadway Opera House, an abandoned theatre structure. Bystanders claimed to have seen men, women and children seek refuge in the basement of the building.

Rioters formed in gangs and trooped through the street, chasing Negroes when they met them, and intimidating white and Negro men alike, if they attempted to offer resistance.

Here again according to the *St. Louis Globe-Democrat*, the women and children took a hand:

> They pursued the women who were driven out of the burning homes, with the idea, not of extinguishing their burning clothing, but of inflicting added pain, if possible. They stood around in groups, laughing and jeering, while they witnessed the final writhings of the terror and pain wracked wretches who crawled to the streets to die after their flesh had been cooked in their own homes.

Where was the militia? At best they stood idly about in tacit sympathy with the rioters. It was not their business to protect Negroes against white men. Richard L. Stokes makes their attitude plain in the *St. Louis Globe-Democrat*. He says:

> I wish to point out that in these riots all the antipathy toward the Negro was not confined to East St. Louis. Among the first militia to arrive from Central and Northern Illinois, were not a few who declared feelingly their understanding they were not here to protect Negroes against whites, but to guard whites against Negroes.

Subsequent testimony conflicted with this statement and showed that most of the milita, as one would suppose from the location of East St. Louis, came from Southern Illinois.

And John T. Stewart continues in the *St. Louis Star:*

> The major riot ensued at 4:30, with not a Negro in sight. A crowd of fifty young men and boys dribbling aimlessly south on Collinsville came to a pawn shop. At once there were shouts of "Get his guns," and the whites crowded through the shop doors and looted the shop of every weapon and all its ammunition. A boy not over fourteen years old emerged with a rifle and several rounds of cartridges. Another boy dragged a shotgun too big for him to carry.
>
> A detachment of militia came along and made a half-hearted effort to disarm the civilians. The only persons who gave up their arms were boys. One white man walking beside me patted a large revolver in his shirt bosom. It was fully loaded. Another handed him two

additional rounds of cartridges. Two guards passed.

"You've got nothing on me," the rioter said, and showed the militiaman his revolver and shells. When the militiaman laughed, the rioter threw his disengaged arm around the guardsman's shoulder and they disappeared around the corner.

Some of the militia were active in the fray. Miss Gruening tells of the two soldiers, members of troop L, from Olney. She passed them a few days after the riot near Cahokia Creek and entered into conversation with them. They boasted that here 'seven niggers' were thrown into the creek, "and every time the niggers came up people rocked them till they was all drowned." She imitated their vernacular. 'And how many 'niggers' did you boys actually kill?' she asked. They were modestly uncertain—they were not quite sure how many, but they had certainly shot to kill. That had been their orders.

'What!' asked Miss Gruening, 'to shoot to kill 'niggers'?'

They grinned cheerfully. 'Oh, no. Only to kill all we saw starting fires.'

'And did you see any starting fires?'

'No, all we saw was niggers flying.'

And they were to disarm every "nigger" of any kind of weapon—guns, razors, knives. They got everything away from them.

Miss Gruening wanted to know if they hadn't disarmed any whites at all.

They were doubtful. Yes, one remembered he had disarmed a drunken white man who was attacking a white woman.

Subsequently, Miss Gruening met with the Military Board of Inquiry, whose members were: Brigadier General Henry R. Hill, Brigadier General James E. Stewart, Colonel M. J. Foreman, Colonel Taylor E. Brown, Major Edward B. Tollman, Colonel William D. McChesney and Major Richard J. Abbott. She told her story and offered to identify the boys.

The Board was unenthusiastic and a trifle skeptical. Didn't Miss Gruening really suppose that the boys were joking? Doubtless they merely wanted to look big in the eyes of a lady. Yes, such jesting was in bad taste, but boys will be boys. At any rate identification was impossible because the Olney troops had been withdrawn.

Miss Gruening offered to go to Olney, to go anywhere to identify the two guardsmen.

Well, that was unnecessary, it was rather late now—on the third day of the inquiry—to institute such a complaint. Why hadn't the lady gone immediately to the commandant, who was present, and made her charge.

Miss Gruening had already been to the commandant on another matter and had been rebuffed.

As she was about to leave they laid on her a solemn charge.

> 'Young lady, as a writer, you have a heavy responsibility. If you go away and give the world the impression that the boys of the Illinois Militia or their officers failed in their duty you will be doing a serious injustice. We have gone exhaustively into the evidence. We have followed up every accusation made against Illinois guardsmen and we find not a single instance in which they misconducted themselves. On the contrary, we have found innumerable instances of the greatest heroism on the part of these young and untrained boys—instances in which Negroes were rescued from crowds of two or three hundred people. We have examined every body (Query: the burned and drowned bodies too?) and none of the wounds were made by rifles.'

Miss Gruening inquired why, in the case of so much heroism, were so many Negroes killed and only eight white men. There was no answer to that.

Many white people told Miss Gruening that the militia had done remarkable well when one considered that most of them came from towns in Southern Illinois, like Olney, for instance, at whose railway stations were placards with the inscription "Nigger, don't let the sun set on you." It was impossible, it was argued, for such men to suppose that they were being called on to protect "niggers"!

And now we come to a short list of savage deeds which most of the newspapers have failed to print. Some of them though hint at them, like the *St. Louis Globe-Democrat* for instance, when it says "enormities of savagery which would shame the jungle were committed in the presence of policemen and militiamen." All of the following statements were related by eyewitnesses to Miss Gruening and Dr. Du Bois.

Miss Gruening writing in the *Boston Journal* says succintly:

One girl was standing at a window of a white woman's house in which she worked. Her arm was shot away. A policeman and a soldier, she said, did the shooting . . . An old woman, frightfully burned, dying in the hospital, was asked if the mob had done it and replied: 'No, they jes' set fire to my house and I burned myself trying to get out' . . . One of the St. Louis reporters said that he knew exactly how people felt who had seen atrocities abroad and were trying to 'get them across' to the rest of the world, 'although,' he added, 'not even Belgium probably has anything quite as horrible to show' . . . About 10 blocks of Negro homes were burned, and the mobs stood outside and shot and stoned those who tried to escape . . . The mob seized a colored woman's baby and threw it into the fire. The woman was then shot and thrown in.

One dares not dwell too long on these horrors. There are the stories too related by Mrs. Luella Cox (white) of the Volunteers of America, a St. Louis organization. Mrs. Cox had gone over to East St. Louis on that memorable day on business connected with her society. She passed through scenes that she can never forget. She realized the storm that was brewing and tried to persuade some of the colored families living in what afterwards became the burned district to flee. They were afraid to venture out but remained hidden in their houses with what results one can shudderingly surmise.

Mrs. Cox saw a Negro beheaded with a butcher's knife by someone in a crowd standing near the Free Bridge. The crowd had to have its jest. So its members laughingly threw the head over one side of the bridge and the body over the other.

A trolley-car came along. The crowd forced its inmates to put their hands out the window. Colored people thus recognized were hauled out of the car to be beaten, trampled on, shot. A little twelve-year old colored girl fainted—her mother knelt beside her. The crowd surged in on her. When its ranks opened up again Mrs. Cox saw the mother prostrate with a hole as large as one's fist in her head.

Around a corner came a group of miners, fresh from work, their pick-axes over their shoulders. They plunged joyously into the arena. Presently Mrs. Cox caught sight of them again resting from their labors, their pick-axes slung once more over their shoulders, and on their backs dripped blood.

While Mrs. Cox was talking to Miss Gruening and Dr. Du Bois, a colored woman came up and exclaimed: "There's the lady that saved me!" The woman had spent all that terrible night crouching in a sewer pipe.

It was Mrs. Cox, too, who saw the baby snatched from its mother's arms and thrown into the flames, to be followed afterwards by the mother. This last act was the only merciful one on the part of the crowd.

This recital deals only with facts. But stop and picture for a moment Mrs. Cox's day and the memories which must haunt her and all others who spent those awful hours in St. Louis.

First the mob, always a frightful thing—lowering in dense cowardly ranks through the streets. Then the fleeing Negroes, hunted, despairing. A hoarse, sullen cry, "Get the nigger!" A shower of bullets, of bricks and stones. The flash of meat-cleavers and pickaxes. The merciless flames. And everywhere bodies, blood, hate and terrible levity.

All our hunting-songs and descriptions deal with the glory of the chase as seen and felt by the hunters. No one has visualized the psychology of the quarry, the driven, hunted thing. The Negroes of East St. Louis have in their statements supplied the world with that lack.

The following accounts are published in the somewhat disjointed fashion in which they were necessarily collected by the investigators. No interpolation whatever is added to detract from their simplicity and sincerity.

This is the testimony of Mary Edwards. She is twenty-three years old, directress of a cafeteria at Lincoln School at fifty dollars a month, has lived in East St. Louis for sixteen years:

> Knew at ten o'clock in the morning that white and colored had been fighting, but did not know seriousness of fight until five o'clock in evening when riot started at Broadway and Fourth Street. Heard shooting and yelling, saw mob pull women off street cars and beat them, but did not think rioters would come up to Eighth Street. Fires had started and were as far as Fifth Street and Broadway and swept through Fourth St., to Fifth and on to Eighth. The shooting was so violent that they were afraid to leave home. By this time rioters were on Eighth Street, shooting through homes and setting fire

to them. Daughter and father were in house dodging bullets which were coming thick. Building at corner of Eighth and Walnut was occupied by whites. Some of mob yelled, 'Save it. Whites live there.' Some of the rioters went to Eighth and Broadway and set fire to colored grocery store and colored barber shop. Man in barber shop escaped but the man and wife in store were burned up. By that time Opera House was on fire and flats on side and back of it. East end of Library Flats caught and heat was so great that father and daughter tried to escape through alley and up street to Broadway, but encountered mob at Broadway. Soldiers were in line-up on north side of street and offered no assistance. Ran across street to Westbrook's home with bullets flying all around them and rioters shouting, 'Kill him, kill him.' Here daughter lost track of father. She beat on back door of Westbrook's home but no response, ran across alley to Division Avenue, ran on white lady's porch, but the lady would not let her in. Men were shooting at her for all they were worth, but she succeeded in dodging bullets. Ran across field and got in house and crawled under bed. Mob following right behind her, but lost sight of which house she went in and set fire to each end of flat. Rather than be burned to death she ran out and mob began shooting at her again. Just at that time a man ran out of the house, and mob let girl alone and started at him. She fell in weeds and lay very quiet. Could see them beating man. About one hour afterwards she heard someone say, 'Any niggers in here?' She kept very quiet thinking them rioters. One said, 'No one does answer. Come on, boys, let's go in after them.' She then raised up not knowing they were soldiers and pleaded for her life. They picked her up and took her over the same ground she had run from the mob; put her in a machine and took her to City Hall. When she came to herself she was in the doctor's office surrounded by friends and her sister, Josephine, who had escaped with the Westbrooks. It was about one o'clock when she reached the City Hall. Mr. Edwards succeeded in getting away from mob, hid under a white man's porch until three o'clock in the morning, crawled from under there and went under side walk on Broadway and stayed there till five o'clock. (In East St. Louis, Ill., the streets are higher than the houses). He got out from under the walk and walked over where his home was still burning and stayed there till five-thirty. Started out to find girls, saw a policeman who told him he would probably find them at City Hall. On way to City Hall, he met two policemen with two colored men. One man asked him if he would send a message to his wife. Mr. Edwards said he could not do so. Policeman then arrested him charging him with being one of the rioters. He was locked up in jail and did not get out until twelve o'clock, when he was carried before Justice of Peace for trial. They found him guilty and set his trial for nine o'clock Wednesday morning and told him he would have to give bond for three hundred dollars. They would not let him have an attorney nor would they let him send for any one. He then asked the Judge to let him make a statement to the court. That was granted.

He got up and told of his experience from five o'clock Monday evening until he was arrested at 5:45 Tuesday morning. After hearing his story the Judge dismissed him.

Nathaniel Cole is twenty-two years old and worked in a steel foundry. He says:

I was on my way from Alton on an Interurban car. When the car reached East St. Louis I saw a crowd of whites hollering, 'Stop the car and get the nigger.' The car was pulled off and stopped and a Negro man pulled out and beaten. In the mean time a white child called 'There's another nigger.' I was then pulled off the car, beaten and left in the street. After the mob left, I attempted to board a car and was ejected by the conductor. Not knowing anything about East St. Louis or the mob, I ran into a white neighborhood and a woman hollered, 'Stop that nigger. Stop that nigger.' Two fellows ran out of a gangway, one with a brick and the other with a long club. I ran and was well out of the way when a Ford car came along and about twelve of the rioters got in and overtook me after I had entered an alley. They then hemmed me in a yard, where a carpenter was at work and began beating me. The carpenter then asked the rioters not to beat me up there, but turn me over to the police if I had done anything to deserve it. The rioters replied, 'The nigger takes the white man's job.' I was beaten in the face with a cane and a rubber hose. I was beaten into insensibility and when I came to they were taking stitches in my head at St. Mary's Hospital.

Observe the terseness of the statement of Nina Fleet:

Husband worked at M. & O. Round House. Was a resident of East St. Louis for ten years.

I stayed with white people in the neighborhood the night of the riot and when I returned home, Tuesday, found my house had been ransacked and burned.

My husband was killed in the riot on his way home from work.

Here follows the continued story of Mary Lewis and her sister Hattie House. Mary Lewis, who is thirty-three, speaks first. She says:

The mob gathered about my house shouting oaths, etc., and after watching and listening for a long time, I decided to try to escape. Just as I started to leave I saw them shoot a man dead, less than thirty feet from my window. The mob then went to the rear of the house and I, with my four children, slipped out the front door. I had gone but a short distance when I was spied by one of the mob and they wanted to come back, but were urged by the leader to go on as he had seen some men on another street. His remark was, 'Let her go and get the niggers running on the other street.'

I left in my house, my husband, Allen Lewis; sister, Hattie House, and a friend who was visiting Mr. McMurray.

Her sister, Hattie House, continues:

In less than twenty minutes from the time my sister left, the mob returned and began shooting and throwing bricks through the windows, while the three of us lay flat upon the floor, hoping to escape. The mob then set fire to both the front and back and when the roof began falling in we ran out through the rear door amidst the rain of bullets to the home of a Mr. Warren, white, begging him to save us. Mr. Lewis was shot just as he reached the door, and I ran into the house.

Some women who were always at the Warren house began beating me and I was compelled to leave there. I ran through a shed and seeing a big tin box, I jumped in, pulling on the lid and succeeded in concealing myself. The mob pursued, looking in every place as they thought for me, but overlooked the box. As they stood discussing the riot, one said, 'I felt sorry for that old nigger. He begged so for his life.' The answer was, 'Why should you feel sorry, Irene, you helped to kill him?' Some other person in the crowd then said, "He was such a hard nigger to kill, he was shot and then had to have his head smashed with an ax."

Lulu Suggs is twenty-four years old, and has lived in East St. Louis since April. She tells of seeing children thrown into the fire. She says:

My house was burned and all the contents. My husband was at Swifts' the night of the riot. I, with about one hundred women and children, stayed in a cellar all night, Monday night. The School for Negroes on Winstanly Avenue was burned to the ground. When there was a big fire the rioters would stop to amuse themselves, and at such time I would peep out and actually saw children thrown into the fire. Tuesday came and with that the protection of the soldiers. We escaped to St. Louis.

Chickens were of more value than Negro human lives. Mabel Randall, who is twenty-four years old, and has lived in East St. Louis for one and one-half years tells us:

Monday evening the mob broke out the windows and doors and we stayed under the bed. When dark came, we begged the white lady next door to let us get under her house and she told us that she had chickens in the yard and we could not. We then went next door and got into a coal-house piling stoves upon us until four o'clock next morning when we went to the M. & O. Railroad yards. We remained there until 5:30 and then reached the ferry.

The statement of Josephine Jones is interesting. She says:

Mrs. Jones made this statement to me, that the mob formed both times at the City Hall, May, 1917, and July 2, 1917. She also said that Mayor Mollman stood in the alley leaning on the bannister of the Justice of Peace

Building when a white man ran down the alley chasing two colored men, whom he afterwards shot and threw into the creek. When he returned to the street, Mayor Mollman was still standing there and he said, 'Fred, I shot two niggers. How do you like that?' Mayor Mollman said nothing and made no protest.

Rena Cook returned from a day's outing to horror and death. Her statement follows:

While returning from a fishing trip on an Alton St. car, we were met by a mob at Collinsville and Broadway who stopped the car and had the white people get out. The mob came in and dragged my husband and son out, beating them at the same time, threw them off the car and shot both my husband and son, killing them instantly. Two policemen stood by, but did not interfere. The mob came back in the car and ran me out and beat me into insensibility. I knew nothing more until I found myself in St. Mary's Hospital. After staying in the hospital for two days I was taken to City Hall in East St. Louis and from there the police and militia escorted me to St. Louis.

Here is a brief but comprehensive tale of treachery as told by Edward Spence:

Born in Lafayette, Alabama—came to East St. Louis five years ago. Worked in a Rolling Mill, Madison, Ill., but lived in East St. Louis. Wages $3.25 a day. He had taken his family, seven children and a wife to friends out from East St. Louis for safety. He returned to East St. Louis and walked down the street with a white man, whom he thought to be a friend. When he passed this man's gate he was shot by this same man in both arms and back. He ran one and one-half blocks and was picked up and carried to the hospital by three colored men. His address is 1208 Colas Ave., East St. Louis.

Comments are needless. Here is the testimony of Elsie L. Lothridge, twenty years old, and a resident of East St. Louis for five months. She says:

Monday, about four o'clock, mob surrounded house. My husband and I were under the bed, and the mob threw stones and broke the windows and furniture up.

The spread hid us from the people and after they broke up everything they left. Then we went to a white lady and asked could we hide in her house and she refused us, and we went in the next neighbor's house and hid in the coal-house until about four o'clock Tuesday morning. We hid in an engine until about 5:30 and then we went down to the Ferry and came across to St. Louis.

Testimony of Giles Bowmer, sixty years old, and a resident of East St. Louis for four years:

I was at my work when the rioting began. I witnessed the rioting and being so excited I could hardly realize what the trouble was. My house was not burned but it was broken into and nearly everything was destroyed, things that I have had over twenty years. I saw many homes from a short distance of Fourth Street to Seventh Street burned to the ground.

Testimony of Mose Campbell, for seven months a resident of East St. Louis:

I was attacked by the mob of about 50 or more with stones and shots, but gave chase. They shot continuously and before we reached the Southern Freight House one bullet passed through my hand, shattering the bone. The mob threatened to burn the freight house so I crawled to the other end and found safety under the trunks of a freight car. Another victim drew the mob away by this time. This man was beaten until unconscious and when he revived the soldiers who were watching him raised a cry which brought the mob back to complete the murder.

While this excitement was at its height, it gave me an opportunity to make my way to Brooklyn by back lanes. I saw the mob fire into houses the first being my own, afterwards proved to be the bier for five men and two children. Among the men were Allen Lewis, Jas. Thomas and Arbry Jones.

Testimony of twenty-year-old Vassie Randall, an employee of the Electric Sack Plant:

The mob had benches stretched across the street facing both directions that no one might escape. A Negro came along and one fellow stepped out and struck him, and then others jumped on him, kicked out his eye and when he tried to get up, they returned and killed him. They then took him to Third and Main and swung him to a telegraph pole.

I was trying to escape with my four children and the mob threatened to throw me and the children in the river. Some white people from St. Louis, Mo., came to us and then the mob let us alone and we were allowed to escape.

The testimony of William Seawood shows the attitude of the soldiers. Seawood is thirty years old and has been a resident of East St. Louis seven years. He says:

Age, thirty years old, and have been a resident of East St. Louis seven years. I left my work at 2:30 P.M., went down Fifth Street to Walnut Avenue. I then went to a lunch stand, and as there was so much shooting I was afraid to leave. The mob came very close to the stand and I ran into an alley; there I found more of the rioters. I ran out of the alley between two buildings. I met a soldier who pointed a gun at me and told me to stop and throw up my hands. One of the men hit me on the back of my neck with his fist and another hit me across the head with a stick, and I also received a glance shot. One of the rioters also put a rope around my neck and said, 'We will hang this one.'

The statement of Troy Watkins is to the same effect:

Tuesday I went to my house to get what I could. While inside a man was killed in front of my house. I thought since the soldiers were there to protect me I could go out of my house. I started out of my home and the white lady told me to go back, that they (the soldiers) had killed a man in front of my house. I went into the coal shed, got behind some tubs, when four men came in and saw me, but did not harm me. Then I went to where I was working (Kehlor Mill) where Mr. Cunningham gave us a team to go to my house and get my things. When I got there my house was burned down.

Miss Gruening told of a girl who lost her arm. Here is the girl's own account. Her name is Mineola McGee and she has been a chambermaid at $3.50 a week. She has resided in East St. Louis since February 8, 1917. She says:

Cannot locate a relative since riot, several cousins, aunt and uncle.

Tuesday morning between seven and eight o'clock, as I was on my way to work (at Mrs. Gray's) I was shot in the arm, as I was about to enter the door. The only men whom I saw on the street were a soldier and a policeman, and I think I was shot by one of the two. I fainted after being shot, and when I came to I was being taken to the hospital in a patrol wagon. At the hospital the remainder of my arm was amputated. No insurance.

And here is the testimony of Narcis Gurley, who had lived for seventy-one years to come at last to this. She says that she has lived in East St. Louis for thirty years and had earned her living by keeping roomers and as a laundress. She says:

Between five and six o'clock we noticed a house nearby burning and heard the men outside. We were afraid to come outside and remained in the house, which caught fire from the other house. When the house began falling in we ran out, terribly burned, and one white man said, "Let those old women alone." We were allowed to escape. Lost everything, clothing and household goods.

The picture shows how terribly her arms were burned.

Testimony of the Kendricks, residents of West Madison, Ill., since 1909:

Monday about 1:30 P.M. I passed through East St. Louis from Belleville on my way to West Madison and the car met the mob at State and Collinsville. The mob shouted, 'There's a Negro on the car, stop that car and get him off.' The motorman stopped the car and all the white passengers left the car, leaving myself and sister-in-law and another lady, Mrs. Arthur. At that time three of the mob ran in the car and commenced beating me. I was shot through the left arm. They dragged me to the street. I was hit in the back of the head by one white, another hit me in the mouth. When I went to make a step another hit me on the side of the head and knocked me down. After this, one shot me in the leg. They jumped on me and beat me. After this they thought me dead and left me. There were three soldiers and a policeman in this mob, but offered me no assistance. In about twenty minutes I was carried to he hospital in an ambulance.

Testimony of Mary Bell White, age fifty-nine years. She was born in East St. Louis and did laundry-work at $1.25 a day:

Saw two people burn an old man and a very old woman. They were thrown into a burning house. Monday at 4 P. M. I saw three women burned. By that time I was so excited that I ran to Tenth Street, where I met a white man who offered me and about one hundred others his protection. He had us go into an old building that had been used for a storage house. We stayed there all night. The next day I went to the City Hall and from there to St. Louis. I lost everything.

Testimony of Thomas Crittenden:

Age forty-six years and a resident of East St. Louis for five years. Worked as a laborer at $3.60 a day. Monday night his boss found out about the riot and secreted him and another fellow. The next day he found that the district in which he lived had been burned. His wife was pulled from her house by the women of the mob, who beat her into insensibility and knocked out three teeth. She was sent to Cleveland, O., where she is in a very serious condition. Through the kindness of his employer he escaped to St. Louis.

Testimony of Lulu Robinson, age 33 years, has lived in East St. Louis for eight months:

Between five and six o'clock Monday evening the mob began shooting into my home at me and my child. We backed up against the wall to dodge the shots, but I was hit three times, once through the finger, shoulder and face. My boy of twelve years was shot twice and killed. I ran away and luckily escaped the shots that were rained upon me, and found shelter in another house. My husband I have not seen or heard from since the riot.

Testimony of Frank Smith, resident of East St. Louis for about twenty-five years and employed for the last fifteen years at the Acme Cement Company:

His house was set afire by the mob, and they waited outside to shoot him, when he should emerge from the house. He waited till the last possible moment and was frightfully burned.

Family consists of a sister and brother who lived at 2136 Geyety, East St. Louis. Lost everything and will probably have to stay in hospital for six or seven weeks longer.

Testimony of Samuel J. Green, age 34 years:

I lived with my wife in East St. Louis; we have no children. I was born in Alabama and attended school through the fourth grade. I came to East St. Louis last October in search of better wages and better treatment from the white folks. I worked for the Loomin Owin Company; I received $3 for eight hours' work. I rented our home; I paid $10 a month rent. Before the riot things were fine, but on Sunday the rioting began. At night when I was going home from work I got off the car right into the thickest of the rioters. I ran and they chased me, firing at me all the time. I saw the state guards but they were helping the mob to club the Negroes. It is wonderful how I escaped unhurt. I hid in the weeds and was lost to the mob. It was about ten o'clock Monday when I saw the state guards clubbing the colored people. I shall stay here a while, then I shall go farther north.

Testimony of Salena Hubble, age 42 years:

I am a widow. I lived in East St. Louis five years. I came to wait on my sick daughter.

Before the riot the people of both races were friendly and pleasant in manners. On the evening the rioters told me to leave because they were going to burn up the whole block, as they thought I was a white woman, so they warned me to flee. I talked with a neighbor, Mrs. Clemens (a white woman) and asked her if she thought the mob would do any more harm. She said: 'I don't know, but you get ready and leave by the way of the cars over the bridge.'

Just as I started over the bridge the mob broke my windows out with rocks. I escaped because the mob didn't know I belonged to the Negro race. Before I got out of East St. Louis I saw the mob with a rope and I heard them say: 'There's a nigger. Let us hang the S—— of a B————,' and they threw the rope over the telegraph pole, but I didn't know what came of that; I saw the soldiers and they offered no assistance to the colored people. I saw the fire department come before the fire was started, but when the fire was started they did nothing to stop it. I also saw the mob throw a rope around a colored man's neck and shoot him full of holes. The soldiers offered no assistance to the man who was shot, neither did the police. I saw a crowd of soldiers go into a saloon and engage in drinking heavily of beer. The mob burned the houses in the localities where colored lived mostly. The women were as vile as the men in their vile treatment to the Negroes. I saw the soldiers driving a crowd of colored men in the streets. The men were made to hold their hands above their heads as they walked.

Testimony of Beatrice Deshong, age 26 years:

I saw the mob robbing the homes of Negroes and then set fire to them. The soldiers stood with folded arms and looked on as the houses burned. I saw a Negro man killed instantly by a member of the mob, men, small boys, and women and little girls all were trying to do something to injure the Negroes. I saw a colored woman stripped of all of her clothes except her waist. I don't know what became of her. The police and the soldiers were assisting the mob to kill Negroes and to destroy their homes. I saw the mob hang a colored man to a telegraph pole and riddle him with bullets. I saw the mob chasing a colored man who had a baby in his arms. The mob was shooting at him all of the time as long as I saw him. I ran for my life. I was nearly exhausted when a white man in the block opened the door of his warehouse and told me to go in there and hide. I went in and stayed there all night. The mob bombarded the house during the night, but I was not discovered nor hurt. The mob stole the jewelry of Negroes and used axes and hatchets to chop up pianos and furniture that belonged to them. The mob was seemingly well arranged to do their desperate work. I recognized some of the wealthy people's sons and some of the bank officials in the mob. They were as vile as they could be.

Testimony of Jerry Mayhorn:

I saw the mob running the Negroes and beating them and killing them. I saw thirty white men beating one Negro. They clubbed the Negro to death. I saw the mob shooting into the homes of Negroes and throwing stones into them. The women and children were as bad as the men. The man that worked with me in the Stock Yards swam the creek to escape the mob and they stopped to beat another Negro man to death. He escaped. I saw the mob set fire to the church and to the school; then they ran. This was about seven o'clock in the evening. I ran through the Stock Yards and down the railroad to Brooklyn, carrying my three children. I saw the soldiers, who seemed to run a little pretense, and the mob just kept on killing Negroes. The soldiers searched the colored men, but I never saw them attempt to search any of the white men.

Testimony of Robert Hersey, age 20 years:

I have lived in East St. Louis since the 25th of March, 1917. I came here because of bad treatment and poor wages. I worked in a tobacco factory in St. Louis, Mo., and received two dollars a day.

Before the riot everyone seemed friendly toward me. I never got into the thickest of the men or riot, but they hit me with clubs, bricks, and stamped me on the head. They broke my arm. But for all of that I got away from them.

I shall never return to the South whatever may happen to me here, for in the South it is always killing and burning some of our people. No let up on bad treatment and no wages either. Men must work for eighty cents a day, women for fifty cents a week, and if the whites choose not to pay that, they won't do it. I shall stay in St. Louis, Mo.

The damning statements go on and on. Among the Negroes one finds a note sometimes of blank stark despair. John T. Stewart in the *St. Louis Star* draws a pathetic picture:

One aged Negro woman passed the police station carrying in her arms all that mob spirit and fire had left of her belongings. They consisted of a worn pair of shoes —she was barefooted—an extra calico dress, an old shawl and two puppies. Tears were streaming down her face and she saw neither soldiers nor her enemies as she passed beneath the lights of the City Hall, going she knew not where.

Saddest of all is Miss Gruening's account of the old woman whom she saw poking about in the desolate ruins of what had once been her home. Her family had escaped to St. Louis, but not a fraction of their possessions remained intact. The woman was old—sixty-five—not an easy age at which to begin life anew.

"What are we to do?" she asked Miss Gruening. "We can't live South and they don't want us North. Where are we to go?"

From the statements gathered by the investigators, many of these driven people seem to feel that the example of the South in dealing with Negroes is responsible for the methods of East St. Louis. Many of them express firmly their resolve, in spite of all, never to go back South. They will stay in St. Louis, they say, or push further North.

How does East St. Louis feel? According to all accounts she is unrepentant, surly, a little afraid that her shame may hurt her business, but her head is not bowed.

In this connection Miss Gruening supplies the statement of East St. Louis Postman No. 23, who said: "The only trouble with the mob was it didn't get niggers enough. You wait and see what we do to the rest when the soldiers go. We'll get every last one of them."

And here follows a sort of composite statement of the best citizens, editors, and liberty-bond buyers of East St. Louis and its surroundings:

"Well, you see too many niggers have been coming in here. When niggers come up North they get insolent. You see they vote here and one doesn't like that. And one doesn't like their riding in the cars next to white women—and, well what are you going to do when a buck nigger pushes you off the sidewalk?"

This last pathetic question was put to Miss Gruening by three different editors on as many separate occasions.

The *St. Louis Post-Dispatch* gives the views of District Attorney Karch on the attitude of the rioters. He says:

> Those men have not left the city, and they have not repented of their excesses. They are just as bitter as they were, and the action of the Chamber of Commerce in forcing these Negroes down their throats is only inflam-

ing the men who participated in the riot.

The District Attorney told of seeing a man on a street car exhibit a revolver openly Thursday night; and remark that "it had killed niggers, and would kill some more as soon as the damned militia leaves." Other men near by expressed similar sentiments, he added. They were laboring men, apparently going home from work.

Karch emphatically confirmed the statements made to the *Post-Dispatch* Tuesday by City Clerk Whalen, who is president of the Central Trades and Labor Union of East St. Louis, to the effect that large employers of labor had given marked and continuous preference to Negroes.

"Their attitude for some time has been that they would give jobs to white men when they couldn't get any more Negroes," Karch declared. "This, as Mr. Whalen said, is because the Negroes will not unionize. Before the tenseness of this situation is relieved, these employers must convince the laboring whites that they will be given preference over imported blacks in applying for work. Instead of doing that, they are declaring they will put all the Negroes back to work, and protect them, if they have to keep troops here indefinitely. That kind of flamboyant talk only angers the men who should be quieted.

"As long as the heads of these big plants break up strikes by importing Negro strikebreakers, so long can they expect to have race riots. This is no defense for the rioters; there is no defense for them. It is just a fact that when a man's family is hungry his sense of justice doesn't operate very accurately."

Prejudice is a bad thing. But prejudice in the hands of Organized Labor in America! The Central Trades and Labor Union of East St. Louis has perpetrated a grim jest. Its motto as one may see by glancing back at page 221, is "Labor omnia vincit." Latin is apt to be a bit obscure, so we translate: "Labor conquers everything." It does. In East St. Louis it has conquered Liberty, Justice, Mercy, Law and the Democracy which is a nation's vaunt.

And what of the Federal Government?

September, 1917

THE BLACK MAN IN THE REVOLUTION
OF 1914–1918

I

As announced in the December, 1918, Crisis the National Association for the Advancement of Colored People has undertaken to see that a scientific and exhaustive history of the black man in the Great War is written. The Association wishes to duplicate no work that others may do and it is especially anxious to co-operate to the fullest extent with all persons who know the facts and are acquainted with historical methods. Already the list of those co-operating with us is of considerable size and first importance.

Preliminary to this work and with the idea of at once getting material and a point of view, I came to France. Quite by accident my trip was made on the same boat taken by Dr. R. R. Moton, of Tuskegee, who was going on a special trip arranged by Secretary of War Baker. Wherever possible Dr. Moton and I have gladly co-operated, but our missions were distinct in every respect.

After a rapid survey of the situation here I am venturing to send back a preliminary and tentative foreword to the history I hope to write. It is nothing more than a sketch—its details are lacking and some basic facts missing, but I think I have the main outlines.

The black soldier saved civilization in 1914-18. First, nearly 400,000 black men of Senegal were the troops that at the Marne and the Ourcq stopped the first onset of Germans, filled the river with their dead and made the world's greatest army recross on the dead corpses of their companions. France not only does not deny this—she is proud to acknowledge the debt.

For example, on December 29, 1918, the French Colonial League held in the Trocadéro in Paris a great celebration in honor of native troops who had come to fight for France. This celebration was sanctioned by President Poincaré and conducted in the presence of the ministers and the military Governor-General of Paris. Presiding were M. Henry Simon, Colonial Minister; M. Diagne, a Senegalese, Commissioner-General of Colonial Affairs; and M. Eugène Etienne, President of the French Colonial League.

The program, whose title page is here displayed, gives the following account of M. Diagne:[2]

> *M. Diagne, Deputy from Senegal, was made Commissioner-General of Colonial Affairs in the Cabinet of M. Clemenceau, as a result of the brilliant success of the last levy of troops in French West Africa. Under conditions calling for great tact and delicacy M. Diagne was able to render the most signal services to his country. He is administering with consummate ability his present office of Commissioner, which will involve the consideration of the numerous problems arising with respect to whatever is of special import to our black troops who throughout the war have conducted themselves with so much heroism.*
>
> *M. Diagne will give in his speech a detailed account of the loyalty of the native troops and will indicate the new obligations incumbent now on the mother country in recognition of the rights of naturalization which native troops have gained on the battle-fields which they as brothers shared with their white brothers.*

The program mentions also the decoration of M. Bakhane Diop, an African chieftain. M. Diop stood between an Arab and an Annamite and all three received the crimson badge of the Legion. That was a wonderful sight. The passage in the program reads:

> *The Cross of Chevalier of the Legion of Honor, merited in action at the front by one of these chieftains, M. Bakhane Diop, will be bestowed upon him with all the usual ceremony by one of the glorious figures in our Colonial history, General Archinard, who ranks among the most active spirits in our penetration into Africa. The*

[2] *M. Diagne*, député du Sénègal, a été nommé Commissaire Général des Effectifs Coloniaux du cabinet Clémenceau en suite de la brillante réussite du dernier recrutement en Afrique Occidentale Française. Dans des circonstances délicates, *M. Diagne*, put rendre les services les plus signalés à son pays. C'est avec la plus haute compétence qu'il administre cet important Commissariat oú se trouveront résolus les problèmes nombreux qui se posent, en ce qui concerne tout particulièrement nos troupes noires qui se sont dépensées pendant la guerre avec tant d'héroisme.

M. Diagne, dans son discours dira par le detail ce que fût la fidélité des indigènes et quels devoirs noveaux incombent maintenant à la Mére Patrie pour reconnaitre les lettres de grande naturalization que les indigènes ont gagnées sur les champs de bataille mêlés fraternellement à leurs frères blancs.

grandeur of the symbolic accolade, which will be given by General Archinard to Bakhane Diop, son of one of our most unyielding adversaries, will assuredly be one of the extremely stirring features in this celebration which is tendered by glorious France. [3]

II

America did not win the war by her fighting only. Her fighting both of colored and white troops covered less than a year of a four years' war. America's great contribution was her preparations which frightened Germany; and her sailors, engineers and laborers who made food and material available. Among these the black stevedores have won a world record. They have been the best workers in France, as is acknowledged by everybody, and their efficiency has been due in part to no small numbers of colored officers and under-officers and to colored Y. M. C. A. workers.

But America did some fighting and the most critical time of America's fighting was in the terrible days of last fall when the exhausted French had to have re-inforcements or yield. It was here that among the first units sent to aid was the Ninety-third Division. The Ninety-third was not a division. It consisted of the Eighth Illinois, the Fifteenth New York, the Separate Battalions of Maryland, the District of Columbia, and Ohio, Company L of the Sixth Massachusetts and others. It was an aggregation nobody wanted. It could not under the draft law go with its state units, or, at least, the law was so interpreted. A whole division was planned to include Colonel Young—but dark forces intervened. Yet these units were ready for work, they were eager, and they were sent to the French and have become known as the 369th, 370th, 371st and 372d Regiments of the Ninety-third Divison. Their black officers were transferred and changed considerably, but they went into battle practically with

[3]La Croix de Chevalier de la Légion d'honneur gagnée au front par un de ces chiefs: *M. Bakhane Diop* lui sera remise avec tout le cérémonial accoutumé par une des gloires de notre histoire coloniale: M. le Général *Archinard,* un des artisans les plus célèbres de notre pénétration en Afrique. La grandeur du symbole de l'accolade que donnera le Général Archinard à Backhane Diop, fils d'un de nos plus irréductibles adversaires, sera certainement une des plus émouvantes parties de cette fête de la plus grande France.

a complete roster of black officers except Colonels, a few Majors and several Captains. But most of the officers were black—for instance, the old Eighth Illinois, even after Colonel Dennison left, had a colored Lieutenant-Colonel, two colored Majors, nineteen colored Captains and ninety-eight colored First and Second Lieutenants. Colonel Hayward, of the old New York Fifteenth, succeeded in removing a larger proportion of his colored officers.

So at the most critical period of the American participation in the war these men went into action.

What was the result?

The colored Lieutenant-Colonel of the 370th, a colored Major, eight colored Captains, seventeen colored Lieutenants, eight colored under-officers and twenty-six colored privates received the *Croix de Guerre* in November.

On November 11, General Vincenden, the French Commanding Officer, said of the 370th: *"Fired by a noble ardor, they go at times even beyond the objectives given them by the higher command; they have always wished to be in the front line."* The final order of General Vincenden, December 9, said: *"In the name of France, I thank you."* He mentioned the *"hard and brilliant battles of Chavigny, Leury and the Bois de Beaumont."* He commends their *"fine appearance under arms"* like *"silk unrolling in wavy folds."* He especially mentions the exploits of three battalions (two with all colored officers and one with a white Captain) at Val St. Pierre, Aubenton and Logny, where the colored Lieutenant-Colonel distinguished himself. *"You have given us of your best and you have given it out of the fullness of your hearts. The blood of your comrades who fell on the soil of France, mixed with the blood of our soldiers, renders indissoluble the bonds of affection that unite us. We have, besides, the pride of having worked together at a magnificent task and the pride of bearing on our foreheads the ray of a common grandeur. A last time—Au Revoir!"*

The 371st and 372d Infantries were brigaded with the 157th French Division under General Goybet. On the occasion of their leaving, December 15, the General in Order No. 245 said:

"For seven months we have lived as brothers-at-arms, partaking of the same activities, sharing the same hardships and the

same dangers. Side by side we took part in the great Champagne Battle, which was to be crowned by a tremendous victory. Never will the 157th Division forget the indomitable dash, the heroic rush of the American (Negro) regiments up the observatory ridge and into the Plain of Monthois. The most powerful defenses, the most strongly organized machine gun nests, the heaviest artillery barrages—nothing could stop them. These crack regiments overcame every obstacle with a most complete contempt for danger. Through their steady devotion the Red Hand Division (157th French) for nine whole days' of severe struggle was constantly leading the way for the victorious advance of the Fourth Army. Officers, noncommissioned officers and men, I respectfully salute our glorious comrades who have fallen, and I bow to your colors—side by side with this—the flag of the 333d Regiment of Infantry (French). They have shown us the way to victory. Dear Friends from America, when you reach the other side of the ocean, do not forget the Red Hand Division. Our brotherhood has been cemented in the blood of the brave, and such bonds will never be destroyed."

The Distinguished Service Cross was given, December 16, to four colored officers, five colored privates and one colored corporal, of the 372d Regiment. On December 13, the following honors were given the 371st and 372d, *Croix de Guerre* to two colored corporals and to two colored privates. There were also seventy other citations.

On October 7, General Garnier Duplossis, of the Ninth French Army Corps *"salutes the brave American (Negro) regiments who have rivalled in intrepidity their French comrades."*

On October 8, General Goybet (General Order 234) in submitting the above transmits *"from the bottom of the heart of a chief and soldier the expression of the gratitude for the glory which you have sent to our good 157th Division."* The same day Colonel Quillet notes their *"finest qualities of bravery and daring"* in an order to the 372d Regiment. On the battlefield, October 1, General Goybet said: *"You must be proud of the courage of your officers and men and I consider it an honor to have them under my command."* The 372d Regiment was cited as a whole for bravery and four *Médailles Militaires* and four *Croix de Guerre* were given. Similar words of farewell as went to the 370th Regiment were sent to this regiment.

So much for the soldiers brigaded with the French, to whom will be added later the equally fine record of the 369th (Fifteenth New York). In fine, the universal testimony of the French army is that black officers and men did extraordinarily well.

Thus much for the Ninety-third Division.

The Ninety-second Division went through hell. It was torn and shaken in morale, seriously so by General Ballou's apparent anxiety to preserve a "Jim-Crow" régime for his officers and by the determination of men like Colonel Moss not to insist on respect to his colored officers. The Division seethed with bitterness and discontent, but it stuck to its work.

III

Meantime, anti-Negro prejudice was rampant in the American army and the officers particularly were subjected to all sorts of discrimination. Scandalous tales were spread in French towns and villages; some villages were posted "Niggers keep out!" Incidents like this continually recurred. A black chaplain with the rank of a Lieutenant reported for duty with colored stevedore regiments at Bordeaux. All the officers were white. He presented himself at the officers' mess and was refused admission. He asked for meals in his room. That was contrary to regulations. He tried the non-commissioned officers' mess. He was refused here because he was an officer. He asked them to send him meals. They refused. He tried to eat with the privates. Again regulations intervened. After a day of hunger and insult he was finally accommodated with a side table for himself in the officers' mess-room.

In the fighting units not one-third of the white soldiers saluted colored officers; they were refused at officers' clubs and in several cases openly disparaged before their men. In hospitals they were often refused admittance to officers' quarters and placed with the privates. Gossip disparaging to the black officers filled the whole American army and clashes of white and colored soldiers ended in blood-shed in a number of cases.

On top of this came subtle German propaganda.

The following was dropped from a German balloon, September 3, 1918, near St. Dié and Raon-l'Etape:

TO THE COLORED SOLDIERS OF THE UNITED STATES ARMY

Hello, boys, what are you doing over here? Fighting the Germans? Why? Have they ever done you any harm? Of course some white folks and the lying English-American papers told you that the Germans ought to be wiped out for the sake of humanity and democracy. What is democracy? Personal freedom, all citizens enjoying the same rights socially and before the law. Do you enjoy the same rights as the white people do in America, the land of freedom and democracy, or are you not rather treated over there as second-class citizens? Can you go into a restaurant where white people dine? Can you get a seat in the theatre where white people sit? Can you get a seat or a berth in the railroad car, or can you even ride in the South in the same street car with white people? And how about the law? Is lynching and the most horrible crimes connected therewith, a lawful proceeding in a democratic country? Now, all this is entirely different in Germany, where they do like colored people, where they treat them as gentlemen and as white men and quite a number of colored people have fine positions in business in Berlin and other German cities. Why, then, fight the Germans only for the benefit of the Wall Street robbers and to protect the millions they have loaned to the English, French and Italians? You have been made the tool of the egotistic and rapacious rich in England and America and there is nothing in the whole game for you but broken bones, horrible wounds, spoiled health or death. No satisfaction whatever will you get out of this unjust war. You have never seen Germany. So you are fools if you allow people to make you hate us. Come over and see for yourself. Let those do the fighting who make the profit out of this war. Don't allow them to use you as cannon-fodder. To carry a gun in this service is not an honor, but a shame. Throw it away and come over to the German lines. You will find friends who will help you along.

IV

The black men never wavered.

Why?

Because side by side with this treatment on the part of their own countrymen came the courtesy, the kindness and the utter lack of prejudice among the French. The black soldiers by their sweet-tempered consideration gained friends everywhere. They saw the wretched suffering of the French and they toiled and fought willingly for them. French officers and civilians of high social position vied with each other in doing all they could to show consideration. A Negro officer entered a café. The American white officers resented his seat at their table and started to rise—the French officers at a neighboring table very quietly and courteously nodded to the landlady and the black officer found a welcome seat with them.

Several high white southern officers of General Ballou's staff blocked nearly everything that would help or encourage the black men—the Chief of Staff repeatedly refused permissions to the photographers, with the result that the Division has almost no photographic record of its work.

But it did work and fight.

The single colored artillery brigade, 167th Field Artillery, had a General from Massachusetts, Sherburne, who believed in them. He said in General Order 11 that he desired *"to record his appreciation of the high qualitites displayed by officers and men during the recent operations in this sector. They have been zealous soldiers and skillful artillerymen. Their recompense lies in their knowledge of work well done and in the commendation of those well qualified to speak. By day and night, often under a hail of shrapnel, often through clouds of deadly gas, they have marched and fought, dragged their guns sometimes by hand into the line, kept open their lines of communication and brought up their supplies always with a cheerfulness that earned them the admiration of all."*

The Division was repeatedly under fire. It went forward in the last great drive and was preparing to take part in the great assault on Metz when the armistice came.

In one instance alone has the white soldier been able even to disparage the actual work of colored troops. In that case a battalion of the 368th Regiment was put in as support and, quite contrary to plan, was suddenly rushed forward as storm troops without equipment. Caught between the two barrages they fell back, contrary to orders, but another battalion of colored men relieved them and went forward. Where was the fault? The white officer, found skulking in the rear, said it was the cowardice of Negro officers.

So the word to acknowledge the Negro stevedore and the fighting black private has gone forth, but the American army is going to return to America determined to disparage the black officer and eliminate him from the army despite his record. And the black officer and private? They return at once bitter and exalted! They will not submit to American caste and they will ever love France!

March, 1919

AN ESSAY TOWARD A HISTORY OF THE BLACK MAN IN THE GREAT WAR

FOREWARD

The mayor of Domfront stood in the village inn, high on the hill that hovers green in the blue sky of Normandy; and he sang as we sang; *"Allons, enfants de la patrie!"* God! How we sang! How the low, grey-clouded room rang with the strong voice of the little Frenchman in the corner, swinging his arms in deep emotion; with the vibrant voices of a score of black American officers who sat round about. Their hearts were swelling—torn in sunder. Never have I seen black folk—and I have seen many —so bitter and disillusioned at the seemingly bottomless depths of American color hatred—so uplifted at the vision of real democracy dawning on them in France.

The mayor apologized gravely: if he had known of my coming, he would have received me formally at the Hotel de Ville —me whom most of my fellow-countrymen receive at naught but back doors, save with apology. But how could I explain in Domfront, that reborn feudal town of ancient memories? I could not—I did not. But I sang the Marseillaise—*"Le jour de gloire est arrivé!"*

Arrived to the world and to ever widening circles of men—but not yet to us. Up yonder hill, transported bodily from America, sits "Jim-Crow"—in a hotel for white officers only; in a Massachusetts Colonel who frankly hates "niggers" and segregates them at every opportunity; in the General from Georgia who openly and officially stigmatizes his black officers as no gentlemen by ordering them never to speak to French women in public or receive the spontaneously offered social recognition. All this ancient and American race hatred and insult in a purling sea of French sympathy and kindliness, of human uplift and giant endeavor, amid the mightiest crusade humanity ever saw for Justice!

> *Contre nous de la tyrannie,*
> *L'etendard sanglant est levé.*

This, then, is a first attempt at the story of the Hell which war in the fateful years of 1914-1919 meant to Black Folk, and particularly to American Negroes. It is only an attempt, full of the mistakes which nearness to the scene and many necessarily missing facts, such as only time can supply, combine to foil in part. And yet, written now in the heat of strong memories and in the place of skulls, it contains truth which cold delay can never alter or bring back. Later, in the light of official reports and supplementary information and with a corps of co-workers, consisting of officers and soldiers and scholars, I shall revise and expand this story into a volume for popular reading; and still later, with the passing of years, I hope to lay before historians and sociologists the documents and statistics upon which my final views are based.

SENEGALESE AND OTHERS

To everyone war is, and, thank God, must be, disillusion. This war has disillusioned millions of fighting white men—disillusioned them with its frank truth of dirt, disease, cold, wet and discomfort; murder, maiming and hatred. But the disillusion of Negro American troops was more than this, or rather it was this and more—the flat, frank realization that however high the ideals of America or however noble her tasks, her great duty as conceived by an astonishing number of able men, brave and good, as well as of other sorts of men, is to hate "niggers."

Not that this double disillusion has for a moment made black men doubt the wisdom of their wholehearted help of the Allies. Given the chance again, they would again do their duty—for have they not seen and known France? But these young men see today with opened eyes and strained faces the true and hateful visage of the Negro problem in America. When the German host—grey, grim, irresistible, poured through Belgium, out of Africa France called her sons; they came; 280,000 black Senegalese, first and last—volunteers, not drafted; they hurled the Boches back across the Ourcq and the Marne on a ghastly bridge of their own dead. It was the crisis—four long, bitter years the war wore on; but Germany was beaten at the first battle of the Marne, and by Negroes. Beside the Belgians, too, stood, first and last, 30,000 black Congolese, not to mention the 20,000 black English West Indians who fought in the East and the thousands of black troops who conquered German Africa.

STEVEDORES

But the story of stories is that of the American Negro. Here was a man who bravely let his head go where his heart at first could not follow, who for the first time as a nation within a nation did his bitter duty because it was his duty, knowing what might be expected, but scarcely foreseeing the whole truth.

We gained the right to fight for civilization at the cost of being "Jim Crowed" and insulted; we were segregated in the first officers' training camp; and we were allowed to volunteer only as servants in the Navy and as common laborers in the Army, outside of the four regular Negro regiments. The Army wanted stevedores, road builders, wood choppers, railroad hands, etc., and American Negroes were among the first to volunteer. Of the 200,000 Negroes in the American Expeditionary Force, approximately 150,000 were stevedores and laborers, doing the hardest work under, in some cases, the most trying conditions faced by any soldiers during the war. And it is the verdict of men who know that the most efficient and remarkable service has been rendered by these men. Patient, loyal, intelligent, not grouchy, knowing all that they were up against among their countrymen as well as the enemy, these American black men won the war as perhaps no other set of S. O. S. men of any other race or army won it.

Where were these men stationed? At almost every seaport in France and in some English ports; at many of the interior depots and bases; at the various assembling places where automobiles, airplanes, cars and locomotives were got ready for use; in the forests, on the mountains and in the valleys, cutting wood; building roads from ports of entry right up to the view and touch of Germans in the front-lines; burying the dead; salvaging at great risk to their own lives millions of shells and other dangerous war material, actually piling up and detonating the most deadly devices in order that French battlefields might be safe to those who walk the ways of peace.

Who commanded these thousands of black men assembled from all parts of the United States and representing in culture all the way from absolute illiterates from under-taught Southern States to well-educated men from southern private schools and colleges and even from many northern universities and colleges? By a queer twist of American reasoning on the Negro it is assumed that he is best known and best "handled" by white people from the South, who more than any other white people refuse and condemn that sort of association that would most surely acquaint the white man with the very best that is in the Negro. Therefore, when officers were to be chosen for the Negro S. O. S. men, it seems that there was a preference expressed or felt for southern white officers. Some of these were fine men, but the majority were "nigger" drivers of the most offensive type.

The big, outstanding fact about the command of these colored soldiers is that southern men of a narrow, harsh type dictated the policy and method and so forced it that it became unpopular for officers to be generous to these men. When it is considered that these soldiers were abjectly under such men, with no practical opportunity for redress, it is easy to imagine the extremes to which harsh treatment could be carried. So thoroughly understood was it that the Negro had to be "properly handled and kept in his place," even in France, large use was made even of the white non-commissioned officer so that many companies and units of Negro soldiers had no higher Negro command than corporal. This harsh method showed itself in long hours, excessive tasks, little opportunity for leaves and recreation, holding of black soldiers to barracks when in the same community white soldiers had the privilege of the town, severe punishments for slight offenses, abusive language and sometimes corporal punishment. To such extremes of "handling niggers" was this carried that Negro Y. M. C. A. secretaries were refused some units on the ground, frankly stated by officers, that it would be better to have white secretaries, and in many places separate "Y" huts were demanded for white and colored soldiers so that there would be no association or fraternizing between the races.

Worked often like slaves, twelve and fourteen hours a day, these men were well fed, poorly clad, indifferently housed, often beaten, always "Jim-Crowed" and insulted, and yet they saw the vision—they saw a nation of splendid people threatened and torn by a ruthless enemy; they saw a democracy which simply could not understand color prejudice. They received a thousand little kindnesses and half-known words of sympathy from the puzzled French, and French law and custom stepped in repeatedly to protect them, so that their only regret was the average white American. But they worked—how they worked! Everybody joins to testify to this: the white slave-drivers, the army officers, the French, the visitors—all say that the American Negro was the best laborer in France, of all the world's peoples gathered there; and if American food and materials saved France in the end from utter exhaustion, it was the Negro stevedore who made that aid effective.

THE 805TH

To illustrate the kind of work which the stevedore and pioneer regiments did, we cite the history of one of the pioneer Negro regiments: Under the act of May 18, 1917, the President ordered the formation of eight colored infantry regiments. Two of these, the 805th and 896th, were organized at Camp Funston. The 805th became a Pioneer regiment and when it left camp had 3,526 men and 99 officers. It included 25 regulars from the

25th Infantry of the Regular Army, 38 mechanics from Prairie
View, 20 horse-shoers from Tuskegee and 8 carpenters from
Howard. The regiment was drilled and had target practice. The
regiment proceeded to Camp Upton late in August, 1918, and
sailed, a part from Montreal and a part from Quebec, Canada,
early in September. Early in October the whole regiment arrived in the southern end of the Argonne forest. The men began
their work of repairing roads as follows:

A— First 2,000 meters of Clermont-Neuvilly road
from Clermont road past Apremont;

B— Second 2,000 meters of Clermont-Neuvilly road,
Charpentry cut-off road;

C— Locheres crossroad on Clermont-Neuvilly road,
north 2,000 meters, roads at Very;

D— Clermont-Neuvilly road from point 1,000 south
of Neuvilly bridge to Neuvilly, ammunition de-
tour road at Neuvilly, Charpentry roads;

E— Auzeville railhead, Varennes railhead; railhead
work at St. Juvin and Briquenay;

F— Auzeville railhead, Varennes railhead, roads at
Montblainville, roads at Landros St. George;

G— Roads at Avocourt, roads at Sommerance;

H— Roads at Avocourt, roads at Fleville;

I— Construction of ammunition dump, Neuvilly, and
railhead construction between Neuvilly and Varennes and Apremont, railroad repair work
March and St. Juvin, construction of Verdun-
Etan railroad from November 11;

K— Railhead details and road work Aubreville, road
work Varennes and Charpentry;

M— Road and railhead work Aubreville, road work
Varennes.

The outlying companies were continually in immediate sight
of the sausage balloons and witnessed many an air battle. Raids
were frequent.

A concentration had been ordered at Varennes, November
18, and several companies had taken up their abode there or at
Camp Mahout, but to carry out the salvage program, a re-
distribution over the Argonne-Meuse area had to be affected
immediately.

The area assigned the 805th Pioneer Infantry extended from

Boult-aux-Bois, almost due south to a point one kilometre west of Les Islettes; thence to Aubreville and Avocourt and Esnes; thence to Montfaucon via Bethincourt and Cuisy; thence north through Nantillois and Cunel to Bantheville; thence southwest through Romagne, Gesnes and Exermont to the main road just south of Fleville; and then north to Boultaux-Bois through Fleville, St. Juvin, Grand Pré and Briquenay.

The area comprised all of the Argonne forest, from Clermont north and the Varennes-Malancourt-Montfaucon-Romagne sections. More than five hundred square miles of battlefield was included.

A list of the articles to be salvaged would require a page. Chiefly they were Allied and enemy weapons and cannon, web and leather equipment, clothing and blankets, rolling stock, aviation electrical and engineer equipment. It was a gigantic task and did not near completion until the first week in March when more than 3,000 French carloads had been shipped.

For some weeks truck transportation was scarce and work was slow and consisted largely in getting material to roadsides.

As companies of the 805th neared the completion of their areas they were put to work at the railheads where they helped load the salvage they had gathered and that which many other organizations of the area had brought, and sent it on its way to designated depots.

With the slackening of the salvage work, the regiment found a few days when it was possible to devote time to drilling, athletics and study. School and agricultural books were obtained in large numbers and each company organized classes which, though not compulsory, were eagerly attended by the men.

Curtailment of this work was necessitated by instructions from Advance Section Headquarters to assist in every way possible the restoration of French farmlands to a point where they could be cultivated.

This meant principally the filling of trenches across fields and upon this work the regiment entered March 15 with all its strength, except what was required for the functioning of the railheads not yet closed.

There was up to this time no regimental band.

At Camp Funston instruments had been requisitioned, but

had not arrived before the regiment left. Efforts were made to enlist a colored band at Kansas City whose members wished to enter the Army as a band and be assigned to the 805th Pioneer Infantry. General Wood approved and took the matter up with the War Department. Qualified assent was obtained, but subsequent rulings prevented taking advantage of it, in view of the early date anticipated for an overseas move.

The rush of events when the regiment reached Europe precluded immediate attention being given the matter and, meanwhile, general orders had been issued against equipping bands not in the Regular Army.

Left to itself, without divisional connections, the regiment had to rely upon its own resources for diversion. The men needed music after the hard work they were doing and Colonel Humphrey sent his Adjutant to Paris to present the matter to the Y. M. C. A., Knights of Columbus and Red Cross.

The Red Cross was able to respond immediately and Captain Bliss returned January 1, 1919, with seven cornets, six clarinets, five saxophones, four slide trombones, four alto horns, two bass tubas, two baritones and a piccolo and, also, some "jazz band effects."

The band was organized on the spot and as more instruments and music were obtained, eventually reached almost its tabular strength while it reached proficiency almost over night.

The following commendation of the work of the regiment was received: "The Chief Engineer desires to express his highest appreciation to you and to your regiment for the services rendered to the 1st Army in the offensive between the Meuse and the Argonne, starting September 26, and the continuation of that offensive on November 1 and concluding with the Armistice of November 11.

"The success of the operations of the Army Engineer Troops toward constructing and maintaining supply lines, both roads and railway, of the Army was in no small measure made possible by the excellent work performed by your troops.

"It is desired that the terms of this letter be published to all the officers and enlisted men of your command at the earliest opportunity."

A soldier writes us:

"Our regiment is composed of colored and white officers.

You will find a number of complimentary things on the regiment's record in the Argonne in the history. We were, as you know, the fighting reserves of the Army and that we were right on this front from September to November 11. We kept the lines of communication going and, of course, we were raided and shelled by German long-range guns and subject to gas raids, too.

"We are now located in the Ardennes, between the Argonne and the Meuse. This is a wild and wooly forest, I assure you. We are hoping to reach our homes in May. We have spent over seven months in this section of the battle-front and we are hoping to get started home in a few weeks after you get this letter, at least. Our regiment is the best advertised regiment in the A. E. F. and its members are from all over the United States practically.

"A month or so ago we had a pay-day here and twenty thousand dollars was collected the first day and sent to relatives and banks in the United States. Every day our mail sergeant sends from one hundred to one thousand dollars per day to the United States for the men in our regiment,—savings of the small salary they receive as soldiers. As a whole they are and have learned many things by having had this great war experience."

NEGRO OFFICERS

All this was expected. America knows the value of Negro labor. Negroes knew that in this war as in every other war they would have the drudgery and the dirt, but with set teeth they determined that this should not be the end and limit of their service. They did not make the mistake of seeking to escape labor, for they knew that modern war is mostly ordinary toil; they even took without protest the lion's share of the common labor, but they insisted from the first that black men must serve as soldiers and officers.

The white Negro-hating oligarchy was willing to have some Negro soldiers—the privilege of being shot in real war being one which they were easily persuaded to share—provided these black men did not get too much notoriety out of it. But against Negro officers they set their faces like flint.

The dogged insistence of the Negroes, backed eventually by the unexpected decision of Secretary Baker, encompassed the first defeat of this oligarchy and nearly one thousand colored officers were commissioned.

Immediately a persistent campaign began:

First, was the effort to get rid of Negro officers; second, the effort to discredit Negro soldiers; third, the effort to spread race prejudice in France; and fourth, the effort to keep Negroes out of the Regular Army.

First and foremost, war is war and military organization is, and must be, tyranny. This is, perhaps, the greatest and most barbarous cost of war and the most pressing reason for its abolition from civilization. As war means tyranny, the company officer is largely at the mercy of his superior officers.

The company officers of the colored troops were mainly colored. The field officers were with very few exceptions white. The fate of the colored officers, therefore, depended almost absolutely on those placed in higher command. Moreover, American military trials and legal procedures are antiquated and may be grossly unfair. They give the accused little chance if the accuser is determined and influential.

The success, then, of the Negro troops depended first of all on their field officers; given strong, devoted men of knowledge and training there was no doubt of their being able to weed out and train company officers and organize the best body of fighters on the western front. This was precisely what the Negro-haters feared. Above all, they feared Charles Young.

CHARLES YOUNG

There was one man in the United States Army who by every consideration of justice, efficiency and long, faithful service should have been given the command of a division of colored troops. Colonel Charles Young is a graduate of West Point and by universal admission is one of the best officers in the Army. He has served in Cuba, Haiti, the Philippines, Mexico, Africa and the West with distinction. Under him the Negro division would have been the most efficient in the Army. This rightful place was denied him. For a technical physical reason ("high blood pressure") he was quickly retired from the Regular Army.

He was not allowed a minor command or even a chance to act as instructor during the war.

On the contrary, the 92d and 93d Divisions of Negro troops were given Commanding officers who with a half-dozen exceptions either distrusted Negroes or actively and persistently opposed colored officers under any circumstances. The 92d Division particularly was made a dumping ground for poor and inexperienced field officers seeking promotion. A considerable number of these white officers from the first spent more time and ingenuity in making the lot of the Negro officer hard and the chance of the Negro soldier limited than in preparing to whip the Germans.

PREJUDICE

These efforts fell under various heads: giving the colored officers no instruction in certain lines and then claiming that none were fitted for the work, as in artillery and engineering; persistently picking the poorest Negro candidates instead of the best for examinations and tests so as to make any failure conspicuous; using court martials and efficiency boards for trivial offenses and wholesale removals of the Negroes; subjecting Negro officers and men to persistent insult and discrimination by refusing salutes, "Jim-Crowing" places of accommodation and amusement, refusing leaves, etc.; by failing to supply the colored troops with proper equipment and decent clothing; and finally by a systematic attempt to poison the minds of the French against the Negroes and compel them to follow the dictates of American prejudice.

These are serious charges. The full proof of them cannot be attempted here, but a few examples will serve to indicate the nature of the proof.

At the colored Officers' Training Camp no instruction was given in artillery and a dead-line was established by which no one was commissioned higher than Captain, despite several recommendations. Certain Captains' positions, like those of the Headquarters Companies, were reserved for whites, and former non-commissioned officers were given preference with the hope that they would be more tractable than collegebred men—a hope that usually proved delusive.

The colored divisions were never assembled as units this side of the water. General Ballou, a timid, changeable white man, was put in command of the 92d Division and he antagonized it from the beginning.

General Ballou's attitude toward the men of his command, as expressed in his famous, or rather infamous, Bulletin 35, which was issued during the period of training in the United States, was manifested throughout the division during the entire time that he was in command in France. Whenever any occasion arose where trouble had occurred between white and colored soldiers, the burden of proof always rested on the colored man. All discrimination was passed unnoticed and nothing was done to protect the men who were under his command. Previous to General Bullard's suggestion that some order be issued encouraging the troops for the good work that they had done on the Vosges and Marbache fronts, there had been nothing done to encourage the men and officers, and it seemed that instead of trying to increase the morale of the division, it was General Ballou's intention to discourage the men as much as possible. His action in censuring officers in the presence of enlisted men was an act that tended toward breaking down the confidence that the men had in their officers, and he pursued this method on innumerable occasions. On one occasion he referred to his division, in talking to another officer, as the "rapist division"; he constantly cast aspersion on the work of the colored officer and permitted other officers to do the same in his presence, as is evidenced by the following incident which took place in the office of the Assistant Chief of Staff, G-3, at Bourbon-les-Bains:

The staff had just been organized and several General Headquarters officers were at Headquarters advising relative to the organization of the different offices. These officers were in conversation with General Ballou, Colonel Greer, the Chief of Staff, Major Hickox, and Brigadier-General Hay. In the course of the conversation Brigadier-General Hay made the remark that "In my opinion there is no better soldier than the Negro, but God damn a 'nigger' officer"! This remark was made in the presence of General Ballou and was the occasion for much laughter.

After the 92d Division moved from the Argonne forest to the Marbache Sector the 368th Infantry was held in reserve at Pompey. It was at this place that General Ballou ordered all of the enlisted men and officers of this unit to congregate and receive an address to be delivered to them by him. No one had any idea as to the nature of this address; but on the afternoon designated, the men and officers assembled on the ground, which was used as a drill-ground, and the officers were severely censured relative to the operation that had taken place in the Argonne forest. The General advised the officers, in the presence of the enlisted men, that in his opinion they were cowards; that they had failed; and that "they did not have the guts" that made brave men. This speech was made to the officers in the presence of all of the enlisted men of the 368th Infantry and was an act contrary to all traditions of the Army.

When Mr. Ralph Tyler, the accredited correspondent of the War Department, reached the Headquarters of the 92d Division and was presented to General Ballou, he was received with the utmost indifference and nothing was done to enable him to reach the units at the front in order to gain the information which he desired. After Mr. Tyler was presented to General Ballou, the General walked out of the office of the Chief of Staff with Mr. Tyler, came into the office of the Adjutant, where all of the enlisted men worked, and stood directly in front of the desk of the colored officer, who was seated in the office of the Adjutant, and in a loud voice said to Mr. Tyler: "I regard the colored officer as a distinct failure. He is cowardly and has none of the traits which go to make a successful officer." This expression was made in the presence of all of the enlisted personnel and in a tone of voice loud enough for all of them to hear.

General Ballou's Chief of Staff was a white Georgian and from first to last his malign influence was felt and he openly sought political influence to antagonize his own troops.

General ————————, Commanding Officer of the ———————— (92d Division), said to Major Patterson (colored), Division Judge-Advocate, that there was a concerted action on the part of the white officers throughout France to discredit the work of the colored troops in France and that everything was being done to advertise those things that would reflect discredit upon the men and officers and to withhold anything that would bring to these men praise or commendation.

On the afternoon of November 8, the Distinguished Service

Cross was awarded to Lieutenant Campbell and Private Bernard Lewis, 368th Infantry, the presentation of which was made with the prescribed ceremonies, taking place on a large field just outside of Villers-en-Haye and making a very impressive sight. The following morning a private from the 804th Pioneer Infantry was executed at Belleville, for rape. The official photographer attached to the 92d Division arose at 5 A. M. on the morning of the execution, which took place at 6 A. M., and made a moving-picture film of the hanging of this private. Although the presentation of the Distinguished Service Crosses occurred at 3 P. M. on the previous day, the official photographer did not see fit to make a picture of this and when asked if he had made a picture of the presentation, he replied that he had forgotten about it.

The campaign against Negro officers began in the cantonments. At Camp Dix every effort was made to keep competent colored artillery officers from being trained. Most of the Colonels began a campaign for wholesale removals of Negro officers from the moment of embarkation.

At first an attempt was made to have General Headquarters in France assent to the blanket proposition that white and Negro officers would not get on in the same organization; this was unsuccessful and was followed by the charge that Negroes were incompetent as officers. This charge was made wholesale and before the colored officers had had a chance to prove themselves, "Efficiency Boards" immediately began wholesale removals and as such boards could act on the mere opinion of field officers the colored company officers began to be removed wholesale and to be replaced by whites.

The court martials of Negro officers were often outrageous in their contravention of common sense and military law. The experience of one Captain will illustrate. He was a college man, with militia training, who secured a Captaincy at Des Moines —a very difficult accomplishment—and was from the first regarded as an efficient officer by his fellows; when he reached Europe, however, the Major of his battalion was from Georgia, and this Captain was too independent to suit him. The Major suddenly ordered the Captain under close arrest and after long delay preferred twenty-three charges against him. These he afterward reduced to seven, continuing meantime to heap restrictions and insults on the accused, but untried, officer. Instead of breaking arrest or resenting his treatment the Captain kept cool, hired a good colored lawyer in his division and put up so strong a fight that the court martial acquitted him and restored him to his command, and sent the Major to the stevedores.

Not every officer was able thus to preserve his calm and poise.

One colored officer turned and cursed his unfair superiors and the court martial, and revealed an astonishing story of the way in which he had been hounded.

A Lieutenant of a Machine Gun Battalion was employed at Intelligence and Personnel work. He was dismissed and reinstated three times because the white officers who succeeded him could not do the work. Finally he was under arrest for one and one-half months and was dismissed from service, but General Headquarters investigated the case and restored him to his rank.

Most of the Negro officers had no chance to fight. Some were naturally incompetent and deserved demotion or removal, but these men were not objects of attack as often as the more competent and independent men.

Here, however, as so often afterward, the French stepped in, quite unconsciously, and upset careful plans. While the American officers were convinced of the Negro officers' incompetency and were besieging General Headquarters to remove them *en masse*, the French instructors at the Gondricourt Training School, where Captains and selected Lieutenants were sent for training, reported that the Negroes were among the best Americans sent there.

Moreover, the 93d Division, which had never been assembled or even completed as a unit and stood unrecognized and unattached, was suddenly called in the desperate French need, to be brigaded with French soldiers. The Americans were thoroughly scared. Negroes and Negro officers were about to be introduced to French democracy without the watchful eye of American color hatred to guard them. Something must be done.

As the Negro troops began moving toward the Vosges sector of the battlefront, August 6, 1918, active and anti-Negro propaganda became evident. From the General Headquarters of the American Army at Chaumont the French Military Mission suddenly sent out, not simply to the French Army, but to all the Prefects and Sous-Prefects of France (corresponding to our governors and mayors), data setting forth at length the American attitude toward Negroes; warning against social recognition; stating that Negroes were prone to deeds of violence and were threatening America with degeneration, etc. The white troops backed this propaganda by warnings and tales wherever they preceded the blacks.

This misguided effort was lost on the French. In some cases peasants and villagers were scared at the approach of Negro troops, but this was but temporary and the colored troops everywhere they went soon became easily the best liked of all foreign soldiers. They were received in the best homes, and where they could speak French or their hosts understood English, there poured forth their story of injustice and wrong into deeply sympathetic ears. The impudent swagger of many white troops, with their openly expressed contempt for "Frogs" and their evident failure to understand the first principles of democracy in the most democratic of lands, finished the work thus begun.

No sounding words of President Wilson can offset in the minds of thousands of Frenchmen the impression of disloyalty and coarseness which the attempt to force color prejudice made on a people who just owed their salvation to black West Africa!

Little was published or openly said, but when the circular on American Negro prejudice was brought to the attention of the French ministry, it was quietly collected and burned. And in a thousand delicate ways the French expressed their silent disapprobation. For instance, in a provincial town a colored officer entered a full dining room; the smiling landlady hastened to seat him (how natural!) at a table with white American officers, who immediately began to show their displeasure. A French officer at a neighboring table with French officers quietly glanced at the astonished landlady. Not a word was said, no one in the dining-room took any apparent notice, but the black officer was soon seated with the courteous Frenchmen.

On the Negroes this double experience of deliberate and devilish persecution from their own countrymen, coupled with a taste of real democracy and world-old culture, was revolutionizing. They began to hate prejudice and discrimination as they had never hated it before. They began to realize its eternal meaning and complications. Far from filling them with a desire to escape from their race and country, they were filled with a bitter, dogged determination never to give up the fight for Negro equality in America. If American color prejudice counted on this war experience to break the spirit of the young Negro, it counted without its host. A new, radical Negro spirit has been born in France, which leaves us older radicals far behind. Thousands of young black men have offered their lives for the Lilies of France and they return ready to offer them again for the Sun-flowers of Afro-America.

THE 93RD DIVISION

The first American Negroes to arrive in France were the Labor Battalions, comprising all told some 150,000 men.

The Negro fighting units were the 92nd and 93rd Divisions.

The so-called 93rd Division was from the first a thorn in the flesh of the Bourbons. It consisted of Negro National Guard troops almost exclusively officered by Negroes,—the 8th Illinois, the 15th New York, and units from the District of Columbia, Maryland, Ohio, Tennessee and Massachusetts. The division was thus incomplete and never really functioned as a division. For a time it was hoped that Colonel Young might be given his chance here, but nothing came of this. Early in April when the need of the French for re-enforcements was sorest, these black troops were hurriedly transported to France and were soon brigaded with the French armies.

THE 369TH

This regiment was originally authorized by Governor Sulzer, but its formation was long prevented. Finally it was organized with but one Negro officer. Eventually the regiment sailed with colored and white officers, landing in France, January 1, 1918, and went into the second battle of the Marne in July, east of Verdun, near Ville-sur-Turbe. It was thus the first American Negro unit in battle and one of the first American units. Colored officers took part in this battle and some were cited for bravery. Nevertheless the white Colonel, Hayward, after the battle secured the transfer of every single colored officer, except the

Nevertheless the white Colonel, Hayward, after the battle secured the transfer of every single colored officer, except the bandmaster and chaplain.

The regiment was in a state of irritation many times, but it was restrained by the influnece of the non-commissioned officers—very strong in this case because the regiment was all from New York and mainly from Harlem—and especially because being brigaded with the French they were from the first treated on such terms of equality and brotherhood that they were eager to fight. There were charges that Colonel Hayward and his white officers needlessly sacrificed the lives of these men. This, of course, is hard to prove; but certainly the casualties in this regiment were heavy and in the great attack in the Champagne, in September and October, two hundred were killed and eight hundred were wounded and gassed. The regiment went into battle with the French on the left and the Morrocans on the right and got into its own barrage by advancing faster than the other units. It was in line seven and one-half days, when three to four days is usually the limit.

In all, the regiment was under fire 191 days—a record for any American unit. It received over 170 citations for the *Croix de Guerre* and Distinguished Service Cross and was the first unit of the Allied armies to reach the Rhine, November 18, with the Second French Army.

THE 371ST AND 372ND

The 371st Regiment was drafted from South Carolina and had southern white officers from the first, many of whom were arrogant and overbearing. The regiment mobilized at Camp Jackson, October 5-17, and embarked for France, April 9, from Newport News, Va. It was trained at Rembercourt-aux-Ports (Meuse) and left for the region near Bar-le-Duc, June 5. The troops arrived in the Argonne June 22. They were brigaded with the 157th French Division, 13th Army Corps, and remained in the battle-line, front and reserve, until the Armistice was signed.

There are few data at present available for the history of this regiment because there were no colored officers to preserve it. It is rumored, however, that after the first battle the number of casualties among the meanest of their officers led to some mutual understandings. The regiment received a number of citations for bravery.

As this regiment was brigaded usually with the 372nd, a part of its history follows:

The official records show that the 372nd Infantry was organized at Camp Stuart, January 1, 1918, Colonel Glendie B. Young, Infantry, U. S. N. G., commanding, and included the following National Guard units: First Separate Battalion, District of Columbia, Infantry; Ninth Battalion of Ohio, Infantry; Company L, Sixth Massachusetts, Infantry; and one company each from Maryland, Tennessee and Connecticut. To these were added later 250 men from Camp Custer; excepting the Staff, Machine Gun, Headquarters and Supply Companies, the regiment was officered by colored men.

The regiment was brigaded with the 371st into the 186th Infantry Brigade, a unit of the Provisional 93rd Division. It was understood that the 93rd Division, which was to be composed of all Negro troops, would be fully organized in France; but when the 372nd arrived at St. Nazaire, April 14, 1918, the organization was placed under command of the French. Four weeks later the brigade was dissolved and the 93rd Division ceased to be mentioned. Its four regiments were all subject to orders of the French G. Q. G., General Petain, commanding.

The regiment spent five weeks in training and re-organization at Conde-en-Barrois (Meuse), as a unit of the 13th French Army Corps. The men were trained in French methods by French officers and non-commissioned officers with French ordnance equipment. They developed so rapidly that a French Major exclaimed enthusiastically on the street: "These men are intelligent and alert. Their regiment will have a glorious career." Thus, from the beginning the worth of our troops was recognized by a veteran of the French Army.

To complete its training under actual war conditions, the regiment was sent to a "quiet sector"—sub-sector, Argonne West, on June 8, where it spent twenty days learning the organization of defensive positions and how to hold these positions under shell fire from the enemy. During this time it was a part of the 63rd French Division and during the last ten days it was a part of the 35th French Division. On July 2, the 372nd Infantry became permanently identified with the 157th French Division, commanded by General Goybet. The division consisted of two colored American regiments and one French regiment of infantry. The artillery units, engineers, sanitary train, etc., were all French. On his first inspection tour, at Vanquois, General Goybet asked one of our men if he thought the Germans could pass if they started over. The little brown private replied: "Not if the boches can't do a good job in killing all of us." That pleased the new General very much and clinched his confidence in the black troops.

On July 13 the regiment retired to a reserve position near the village of Locheres (Meuse), for temporary rest and to help sustain the coming blow. The next day Colonel Young was relieved of command by Colonel Herschel Tupes, a regular army officer. In the afternoon the regiment was assembled and prepared for action, but it later was found that it would not be needed. The attack of the Germans was launched near Rheims on the night of July 14 and the next evening the world read of the decisive defeat of the Germans by General Gourand's army.

The following Sunday found the regiment billeted in the town of Sivry-la-Perche, not very far from Verdun. After a band concert in the afternoon Colonel Tupes introduced himself to his command. In the course of his remarks, he said that he had always commanded regulars, but he had little doubt that the 372nd Infantry could become as good as any regiment in France.

On July 26 the regiment occupied sub-sector 304. The occupation of this subsector was marked by hard work and discontentment. The whole position had to be re-organized, and in doing this the men maintained their previous reputation for good work. The total stay in the sector was seven weeks. The regiment took part in two raids and several individuals distinguished themselves: one man received a *Croix de Guerre* because he held his trench mortar between his legs to continue firing when the base had been damaged by a shell; another carried a wounded French comrade from "No Man's Land" under heavy fire, and was also decorated. Several days after a raid, the Germans were retaliating by shelling the demolished village of Montzeville, situated in the valley below the Post-of-

Command and occupied by some of the reserves; Private Rufus Pinckney rushed through the heavy fire and rescued a wounded French soldier.

On another occasion, Private Kenneth Lewis of the Medical Detachment, later killed at his post, displayed such fine qualities of coolness and disdain for danger by sticking to duty until the end that two post-mortem decorations: the *Croix de Guerre* with Palm and *Medaille Militaire* were awarded. The latter is a very distinguished recognition in the French Army.

So well had the regiment worked in the Argonne that it was sent to relieve the 123rd French Infantry Regiment in the sub-sector Vanquois, on July 28. An attack by the Germans in the valley of the Aire, of which Vanquois was a key, was expected at any moment. New defenses were to be constructed and old ones strengthened. The men applied themselves with a courageous devotion, night and day, to their tasks and after two weeks of watchful working under fire, Vanquois became, a formidable defensive system.

Besides the gallantry of Private Pinckney, Montzeville must be remembered in connection with the removal of colored officers from the regiment. It was there that a board of officers (all white) requested by Colonel Young and appointed by Colonel Tupes, sat on the cases of twenty-one colored officers charged with inefficiency. Only one out of that number was acquitted: he was later killed in action. The charges of inefficiency were based on physical disability, insufficient training, unsuitability. The other colored officers who had been removed were either transferred to other units or sent to re-classification depots.

The Colonel told the Commanding General through an interpreter: "The colored officers in this regiment know as much about their duties as a child." The General was surprised and whispered to another French officer that the Colonel himself was not so brilliant and that he believed it was prejudice that caused the Colonel to make such a change. A few moments after, the Colonel told the General that he had requested that no more colored officers be sent to the regiment. In reply to this the General explained how unwise it was because the colored officers had been trained along with their men at a great expenditure of time and money by the American and French governments; and, also, he doubted if well-qualified white officers could be spared him from other American units. The General insisted that the time was at hand for the great autumn drive and that it would be a hindrance because he feared the men would not be pleased with the change. The Colonel heeded not his General and forwarded two requests for an anti-colored-officer regiment. He went so far as to tell the Lieutenant-Colonel that he believed the regiment should have white men for non-commissioned officers. Of course, the men would not have stood for this at any price. The Colonel often would tell the Adjutant to never trust a "damned black clerk" and that he considered "one white man worth a million Negroes."

About September 8 the regiment was relieved by the 129th United States Infantry and was sent to the rear for a period of rest. Twenty-four hours after arrival in the rest area, orders were received to proceed farther. The nightly marches began. The regiment marched from place to place in the Aube, the Marne and the Haute Marne until it went into the great Champagne battle on September 27.

For nine days it helped push the Hun toward the Belgian frontier. Those days were hard, but these men did their duty and came out with glory. Fortunately, all the colored officers had not left the regiment and it was they and the brave sergeants who led the men to victory and fame. The new white officers had just arrived, some of them the night before the regiment went into battle, several of whom had never been under fire in any capacity, having just come out of the training school at Langres. Nevertheless, the regiment was cited by the French and the regimental colors were decorated by Vice-Admiral Moreau at Brest, January 24, 1919.

After the relief on the battlefield, the regiment reached Somme Bionne (Marne) October 8. Congratulations came in from everywhere except American Headquarters. After a brief rest of three days the regiment was sent to a quiet sector in the Vosges, on the frontier of Alsace. The Colonel finally disposed of the remaining colored officers, except the two dentists and the two chaplains. All the officers were instructed to carry their arms at all times and virtually to shoot any soldier on the least provocation. As a consequence, a corporal of Company L was shot and killed by First Lieutenant James B. Coggins, from North Carolina, for a reason that no one has ever been able to explain. The signing of the Armistice and the cessation of hostilities, perhaps, prevented a general, armed opposition to a system of prejudice encouraged by the Commanding Officer of the Regiment.

Despite the prejudice of officers toward the men, the regiment marched from Ban-de-Laveline to Granges of Vologne, a distance of forty-five kilometers in one day and maintained such remarkable discipline that the officers themselves were compelled to accord them praise.

While stationed at Granges, individuals in the regiment were decorated on December 17 for various deeds of gallantry in the Champagne battle. General Goybet presented four military medals and seventy-two *Croix de Guerre* to enlisted men. Colonel Tupes presented four Distinguished Service Crosses to enlisted men. At the time, the regiment had just been returned to the American command, the following order was read:

Hqrs. December 15th, 1918.

157th Division
Staff.

General Order No. 246.

On the date of the 12th of December, 1918, the 371st and the 372nd R. I., U. S. have been returned to the disposal of the American Command. It is not without profound emotion that I come in the name of the 157th (French) Division and in my personal name, to say good-bye to our valiant comrades of combat.

For seven months we have lived as brothers of arms, sharing the same works the same hardships, the same dangers; side by side we have taken part in the great battle of the Champagne, that a wonderful victory has ended.

The 157th (French) Division will never forget the wonderful impetus irresistible, the rush heroic of the colored American regiments on the "Observatories Crest" and in the Plain of Menthois. The most formidable defense, the nests of machine guns, the best organized positions, the artillery barrages most crushing, could not stop them. These best regiments have gone through all with disdain of death and thanks to their courage devotedness, the "Red Hand" Division has during nine hard days of battle been ahead in the victorious advance of the Fourth (French) Army.

Officers and non-commissioned officers and privates of the 371st and 372nd Regiments Infantry, U. S., I respectfully salute your glorious dead and I bow down before your standards, which by the side of the 333rd R. I., led us to victory.

Dear Friends from America, when you have crossed back over the ocean, don't forget the "Red Hand" Division. Our fraternity of arms has been soaked in the blood of the brave. Those bonds will be indestructible.

Keep a faithful remembrance to your General, so proud to have commanded you, and remember that his thankful affection is gained to you forever.

(Signed) General Goybet, Commanding the 157th (French) Division, Infantry.

Colonel Tupes, in addressing the regiment, congratulated them on the achievements and expressed his satisfaction with their conduct. He asked the men to take a just pride in their accomplishments and their spirit of loyalty.

Can this be surpassed for eccentricity?

The seven weeks at Granges were pleasant and profitable socially. Lectures were given to the men by French officers, outdoor recreation was provided and the civilian population opened the hearts and their homes to the Negro heroes. Like previous attempts the efforts of the white officers to prevent the mingling of Negroes with the French girls of the village were futile. Every man was taken on his merits. The mayor of Granges gave the regiment an enthusiastic farewell.

On January 1, 1919, the regiment entrained for Le Mans (Sarthe). After complying with the red-tape preparatory to embarkation and the delousing process it went to Brest, arriving there January 13, 1919.

THE 370TH

Up to this point the anti-Negro propaganda is clear and fairly consistent and unopposed. General Headquarters had not only witnessed instructions in Negro prejudice to the French, but had, also, consented to wholesale removals of officers among the engineers and infantry, on the main ground of color. Even the French, in at least one case, had been persuaded that Negro officers were the cause of certain inefficiencies in Negro units.

Undoubtedly the cruel losses of the 369th Regiment were due in part to the assumption of the French at first that the American Negroes were like the Senegalese; these half-civilized troops could not in the time given them be trained in modern machine warfare, and they were rushed at the enemy almost with naked hands. The resulting slaughter was horrible. Our troops tell of great black fields of stark and crimson dead after some of these superhuman onrushes.

It was this kind of fighting that the French expected of the black Americans at first and some white American officers did not greatly care so long as white men got the glory. The French easily misunderstood the situation at first and assumed that the Negro officers were to blame, especially as this was continually suggested to them by the Americans.

It was another story, however, when the 370th Regiment came. This was the famous 8th Illinois, and it had a full quota of Negro officers, from Colonel down. It had seen service on the Mexican Border; it went to Houston, Tex., after the Thirteen had died for Freedom; and it was treated with wholesome respect. It was sent to Newport News, Va., for embarkation; once Colonel Dennison refused to embark his troops and marched them back to camp because he learned they were to be "Jim-Crowed" on the way over.

The regiment arrived at Brest, April 22, and was assigned to the 72nd French Division, remaining near Belfort until June 17. Then it went with the 34th French Division into the front-line, at St. Mihiel, for a month and later with the 36th French Division into the Argonne, where they fought. They were given a short period of rest and then they went into the front-line at Soissons, with the 59th French Division. In September and October they were fighting again.

On September 15, in the Vauxaillion area, they captured Mt. Dessinges and the adjacent woods after severe fighting. They held a sector alone afterward on the Canal L'Oise et Aisne and when attacked, repulsed the Germans and moved forward, gaining the praise of the French General. On October 24, the regiment went into the front line again, near Grand Lup, and performed excellent service; the Armistice found part of the regiment across the Belgian frontier.

The general conduct of the regiment was excellent. No case of rape was reported and only one murder. The regiment was received sixteen Distinguished Service Crosses and seventy-five *Croix de Guerre*, beside company citations.

When at first the regiment did not adopt the tactics of "shock" troops, the white Americans again took their cue and inspired a speech from the French General, which the colored men could not understand. It was not long, however, before the French General publicly apologized for his first and hasty criticism and afterward he repeatedly commended both officers and men for their bravery, intelligence and daring. This regiment received more citations than any other American regiment for bravery on the field of battle. There was, of course, the fly in the ointment,—the effort to substitute white officers was strong and continuous, notwithstanding the fact that many of the black officers of this regiment were among the most efficient in the American Army.

General Headquarters by this time had begun to change its attitude and curb the Bourbons. It announced that it was not the policy of the American Army to make wholesale removals simply on account of color and it allowed the citations for bravery of Negro troops to be approved.

Nevertheless, the pressure continued. First the colored Colonel, the ranking Negro officer in France, was sent home. The reason for this is not clear. At any rate Colonel Dennison was replaced by a white Colonel, who afterward accepted a *Croix de Guerre* for an exploit which the Negro officers to a man declare was actually performed by a Negro officer while he was sitting snugly in his tent. The men of the regiment openly jerred him, crying out: "Blue Eyes ain't our Colonel; Duncan's our Colonel!" referring to the colored Lieutenant-Colonel. But the white Colonel was diplomatic; he let the colored officers run the regiment, posed as the "Moses" of the colored race (to the open amusement of the Negroes) and quietly tried to induct white officers. "I cannot understand why they sent this white Lieutenant," he said plaintively to a colored officer. The officer at that moment had in his pocket a copy of the Colonel's telegram asking General Headquarters for white officers. But the Armistice came before the Colonel succeeded in getting but two white officers,—his brother as Major (without a battalion) and one Lieutenant.

The organization that ranked all America in distinction remained, therefore, a Negro organization, for the white Colonel was only "commanding" and Dennison was still titular head.

THE 92ND DIVISION

So much for the 93rd Division. Its troops fought magnificently in the Champagne, the Argonne and elsewhere and were given unstinted praise by the French and even commendation by the Americans. They fought well, too, despite the color of their officers—371st Regiment under white, the 369th and 372nd Regiments under white and colored, and the 370th Regiment under colored were equally brave, except that the 370th Regiment made the most conspicuous record.

One might conclude under ordinary circumstances that it was a matter of efficiency in officers and not of race, but, unfortunately, the efficient colored officer had almost no chance even to try except in the 370th Regiment and in the Champagne battle with the 372nd Regiment. With a fair chance there is no doubt that he could have led every one of these regiments just as well as the white officers. It must, too, be remembered that all the non-commissioned officers in all these regiments were Negroes.

The storm center of the Negro troops was the 92nd Division. The brigading of the 93rd Division with the French made wholesale attack and depreciation difficult, since it was continually annulled by the generous appreciation of the French. The 92nd Division, however, was planned as a complete Negro division, manned by Negro company officers. Everything depended, then, on the General and field officers as to how fair this experiment should be.

From the very first there was open and covert opposition and trouble. Instead of putting Colonel Young at the head, the white General Ballou, was chosen and surrounded by southern white officers who despised "nigger" officers.

General Ballou himself was well-meaning, but weak, vacillating, without great ability and afraid of southern criticism. He was morbidly impressed by the horror of this "experiment" and proceeded from the first to kill the morale of his troops by orders and speeches. He sought to make his Negro officers feel personal responsibility for the Houston outbreak; he tried to accuse them indirectly of German propaganda; he virtually ordered them to submit to certain personal humiliations and discriminations without protest. Thus, before the 92nd Division was fully formed, General Ballou had spread hatred and distrust among his officers and men. "That old Ballou stuff!" became a by-word in the division for anti-Negro propaganda. Ballou was finally dismissed from his command for "tactical inefficiency."

The main difficulty, however, lay in a curious misapprehension in white men of the meaning and method of race contact in America. They sought desperately to reproduce in the Negro division and in France the racial restrictions of America, on the theory that any new freedom would "spoil" the blacks. But they did not understand the fact that men of the types who became Negro officers protect themselves from continuous insult and discrimination by making and moving in a world of their own; they associate socially where they are more than welcome; they live for the most part beside neighbors who like them; they attend schools where they are not insulted; and they work where their work is appreciated. Of course, every once in a while they have to unite to resent encroachments upon their world—new discriminations in law and custom; but this is occasional and not continuous.

The world which General Ballou and his field officers tried to re-create for Negro officers was a world of continuous daily insult and discrimination to an extent that none had ever experienced, and they did this in a country where the discrimination was artificial and entirely unnecessary, arousing the liveliest astonishment and mystification.

For instance, when the Headquarters Company of the 92nd Division sailed for Brest, elaborate quarters in the best hotel were reserved for white officers, and unfinished barracks, without beds and in the cold and mud, were assigned Negro officers. The colored officers went to their quarters and then returned to the city. They found that the white Americans, unable to make themselves understood in French, had not been given their reservation, but had gone to another and poorer hotel. The black officers immediately explained and took the fine reservations.

As no Negroes had been trained in artillery, it was claimed immediately that none were competent. Nevertheless, some were finally found to qualify. Then it was claimed that technically trained privates were impossible to find. There were plenty to be had if they could be gathered from the various camps. Permission to do this was long refused, but after endless other delays and troubles, the Field Artillery finally came into being with a few colored officers. Before the artillery was ready, the division mobilized at Camp Upton, between May 28 and June 4, and was embarked by the tenth of June for France.

The entire 92nd Division arrived at Brest by June 20. A week later the whole division went to Bourbonne-les-Bains, where it stayed in training until August 6. Here a determined effort at wholesale replacement of the colored officers took place. Fifty white Lieutenants were sent to the camp to replace Negro officers. "Efficiency" boards began to weed out colored men.

Without doubt there was among colored as among white American officers much inefficiency, due to lack of adaptability, training and the hurry of preparation. But in the case of the Negro officers repeatedly the race question came to the fore and permission was asked to remove them because they were colored, while the inefficiency charge was a wholesale one against their "race and nature."

General Headquarters by this time, however, had settled down to a policy of requiring individual, rather than wholesale, accusation, and while this made a difference, yet in the army no officer can hold his position long if his superiors for any reason wish to get rid of him. While, then, many of the waiting white Lieutenants went away, the colored officers began to be systematically reduced in number.

On August 6 the division entered the front-line trenches in the Vosges sector and stayed here until September 20. It was a quiet sector, with only an occasional German raid to repel. About September 20, the division began to move to the Argonne, where the great American drive to cut off the Germans was to take place. The colored troops were not to enter the front-lines, as General Pershing himself afterward said, as they were entirely unequipped for front-line service. Nevertheless, the 368th Regiment, which arrived in the Argonne September 24, was suddenly sent into battle on the front-line on the morning of September 26. As this is a typical instance of the difficulties of Negro officers and troops, it deserves recital in detail.

It is the story of the failure of white field officers to do their duty and the partially successful and long-continued effort of company officers and men do do their duty despite this. That there was inexperience and incompetency among the colored officers is probable, but it was not confined to them; in their case the greater responsibility lay elsewhere, for it was the plain duty of the field officers: First, to see that their men were equipped for battle; second, to have the plans clearly explained, at least, step by step, to the company officers; third, to maintain liaison between battalions and between the regiment and the French and other American units.

Here follows the story as it was told to me point by point by those who were actually on the spot. They were earnest, able men, mostly Lieutenants and Captains, and one could not doubt, there in the dim, smoke-filled tents about Le Mans, their absolute conscientiousness and frankness.

THE 368TH

The 368th Regiment went into the Argonne September 24 and was put into the drive on the morning of September 26. Its duty was "combat liaison," with the French 37th Division and the 77th (white) Division of Americans. The regiment as a whole was not equipped for battle in the front-line. It had no artillery support until the sixth day of the battle; it had no grenades, no trench fires, trombones, or signal flares, no airplane panels for signaling and no shears for German wire. The wire-cutting shears given them were absolutely useless with the heavy German barbed wire and they were able to borrow only sixteen large shears, which had to serve the whole attacking battalion.* Finally, they had no maps

---

*"On advancing from the French trenches the morning of the twenty-sixth much wire was met with by organizations and owing to the fact that none had wirecutters, considerable disorganization resulted in the companies, especially in the matter of liaison.

and were at no time given definite objectives.

The Second Battalion of the 368th Regiment entered battle on the morning of September 26, with Major Elser in command; all the company officers were colored; Company F went "over the top" at 5:30 A. M.; Company H, with which the Major was, went "over" at 12:30 noon; advancing four kilometers the battalion met the enemy's fire; the Machine Gun Company silenced the fire; Major Elser, who had halted in the woods to collect souvenirs from dead German bodies, immediately withdrew part of the battalion to the rear in single file about dark without notifying the rest of the battalion. Captain Dabney and Lieutenant Powell of the Machine Gun Company led the rest of the men out in order about 10:00 P. M. When the broadside opened on September 26, Major Elser stood wringing his hands and crying: "What shall I do! What shall I do!" At night he deplored the occurrence, said it was all his fault, and the next morning Major Elser commended the Machine Gun Company for extricating the deserted part of the battalion. Moving forward again at 11 A. M., two companies went "over the top" at 4 P. M. without laison. With the rest of the battalion again, these companies went forward one and one-half kilometers. Major Elser stayed back with the Post-of-Command. Enemy fire and darkness again stopped the advancing companies and Captain Jones fell back 500 metres and sent a message about 6 A. M. on the morning of September 28 to the Major asking for reenforcements. Captain Jones stayed under snipers' fire until about 3 P. M. and when no answer to his request came from the Major, he went "over the top" again and retraced the same 500 metres. Heavy machine gun and rifle fire greeted him. He took refuge in nearby trenches, but his men began to drift away in

"As it was almost dark at this time and having no liaison with any of the other units, I decided to withdraw until I could get in touch with the Commanding Officer, 368th Infantry. The enemy searched along the trails with their artillery during our withdrawal, but none of the shells fell near us; it was pitch dark by this time and we had just reached the German's first trench. There was much confusion owing to the mass of wire we had to contend with in the dark before the companies reached the French trenches.

"Company G spent the entire day of the twenty-sixth working its way through the wire entanglements. Great difficulty was experienced in this work because of the lack of wirecutters."

—*Reports of Major M. A. Elser.*

confusion. All this time the Major was in the rear. On September 28, however, Major Elser was relieved of the command of the battalion and entered the hospital for "psycho-neurosis," or "shell shock,"—a phrase which often covers a multitude of sins. Later he was promoted to Lieutenant-Colonel and transferred to a Labor Battalion.

Meantime, on September 27, at 4:30 P. M., the Third Battalion of the 368th Infantry moved forward. It was commanded by Major B. F. Norris, a white New York lawyer, a graduate of Plattsburg, and until this battle a Headquarters Captain with no experience on the line. Three companies of the battalion advanced two and one-half kilometres and about 6:30 P. M. were fired on by enemy machine guns. The Major, who was in support with one company and a platoon of machine guns, ordered the machine guns to trenches seventy-five yards in the rear. The Major's orders were confusing and the company as well as the platoon retreated to the trenches, leaving the firing-line unsupported. Subjected to heavy artillery, grenade, machine gun and rifle fire during the whole night of September 27 and being without artillery support or grenades, the firing line broke and the men took refuge in the trench with the Major, where all spent a terrible night under rain and bombardment. Next morning, September 28, at 7:30 A. M., the firing-line was restored and an advance ordered. The men led by their colored officers responded. They swept forward two and one half kilometres and advanced beyond both French and Americans on the left and right. Their field officers failed to keep liaison with the French and American white units and even lost track of their own Second Battalion, which was dribbling away in one of the front trenches. The advancing firing-line of the Third Battalion met a withering fire of trench mortars, seventy-sevens, machine guns, etc. It still had no artillery support and being too far in advance received the German fire front, flank and rear and this they endured five hours. The line broke at 12:30 and the men retreated to the support trench, where the Major was. He reprimanded the colored officers severely. They reported the intense artillery fire and their lack of equipment, their ignorance of objectives and their lack of maps for which they had asked. They were ordered to re-form and take up positions, which they did. Many contradictory orders passed to the Company Commanders during the day: to advance, to halt, to hold, to withdraw, to leave woods as quickly as possible. Finally, at 6:30 P. M., they were definitely ordered to advance. They advanced three kilometres and met exactly the same conditions as before, —heavy artillery fire on all sides. The Company Commanders were unable to hold all their men and the Colonel ordered the Major to withdraw his battalion from the line. Utter confusion resulted,—there were many casualties and many were gassed. Major Norris withdrew, leaving a platoon under Lieutenant Dent on the line ignorant of the command to withdraw. They escaped finally unaided during the night.

The Chief of Staff said in his letter to Senator McKellar: "One of our majors commanding a battalion said: 'The men are rank cowards, there is no other words for it.' "

A colored officer writes:

"I was the only colored person present when this was uttered: It was on the 27th of last September in the second line trenches of Vienne Le Chateau in our attack in the Argonne and was uttered by Major B. F. Norris, commanding the 3rd Battalion. Major Norris, himself, was probably the biggest coward because he left his Battalion out in the front lines and came back to the Colonel's dugout a nervous wreck. I was there in a bunk alongside of the wall and this major came and laid down beside me and he moaned and groaned so terribly all night that I couldn't hardly close my eyes—he jumped and twisted worse than anything I have ever seen in my life. He was a rank coward himself and left his unit on some trifling pretext and remained back all night."

From September 26-29 the First Battalion of the 368th Infantry, under Major J. N. Merrill, was in the front-line French trenches. On the night of September 28 it prepared to advance, but after being kept standing under shell-fire for two hours it was ordered back to the trenches. A patrol was sent out to locate the Third Battalion, but being refused maps by the Colonel it was a long time on the quest and before it returned the First Battalion was ordered to advance, on the morning of September 29. By 1:00 P. M. they had advanced one mile when they were halted to find Major Merrill. Finally Major Merrill was located after two hours' search. A French Lieutenant guided them to positions in an old German trench. The Major ordered them forward 600 yards to other deserted German trenches. Terrific shellfire met them here, and there were many casualties. They stayed in the trench during the night of September 29 and at noon on September 30 were ordered to advance. They advanced three kilometres through the woods, through shell and machine gun fire and artillery barrage. They dug in and stayed all night under fire. On October 1 the French Artillery came up and put over a barrage. Unfortunately, it fell short and the battalion was caught between the German and French barrages and compelled hastily to withdraw.

The regiment was soon after relieved by a French unit and taken by train to the Marbache sector. Major Elser, of the Second Battalion, made no charges against his colored officers and verbally assumed responsibility for the failure of his battalion. There was for a time strong talk of a court martial for him. Major Merrill made no charges; but Major Norris on account of the two breaks in the line of the Third Battalion on September 28 ordered five of his colored line officers court-martialed for cowardice and abandonment of positions—a Captain, two First Lieutenants, and a Second Lieutenant were accused. Only one case,—that of the Second Lieutenant, had been decided at this writing. He was found guilty by the court-martial, but on review of his case by General Headquarters he was acquitted and restored to his command.

Colonel Greer in the letter to Senator McKellar on December 6, writes as follows: "From there we went to the Argonne and in the offensive starting there on September 26, had one regiment in the line, attached to the 38th French Corps. They failed there in all their missions, laid down and sneaked to the rear, until they were withdrawn."

This is what Colonel Durand, the French General who was in command in this action, said in a French General Order: *"L'Honneur de la prise de Binarville doit revenir au 368th R. I. U. S."*

And this is what Colonel Greer himself issued in General Order No. 38, Headquarters 92nd Division, the same day he wrote his infamous letter to this senator: "The Division Commander desires to commend in order the meritorious conduct of Private Charles E. Boykin, Company C, 326th Field Signal Battalion. On the afternoon of September 26, 1918, while the

368th Infantry was in action in the Argonne forest the Regimental Commander moved forward to establish a P. C. and came upon a number of Germans who fled to the woods which were FOUND TO BE ALIVE WITH MACHINE GUNS. The Commanding Officer ordered the woods searched to the top of the hill, the officer in charge of the scouting (2nd Lieutenant C. W. Carpenter) called for volunteers and Private Boykin, a telephone linesman, offered his services and set out with the rest of the detail. While trying to flank an enemy machine gun another opened fire killing him instantly."

This effort of the 368th Regiment was seized upon by Army gossip and widely heralded as a "failure" of Negro troops, and particularly of Negro officers. Yet the same sort of troops and many Negro officers in the Champagne and afterward in the Argonne under French leadership covered themselves with glory. The real failure in the initial Argonne drive was in American field strategy which was totally unequal to German methods and had to learn by bitter experience. It is worse than unfair to write off the first experience to the discredit of Negro troops and company officers who did all that was humanly possible under the circumstances.

OTHER UNITS

The 365th, 366th and 367th Regiments did not enter the battle-line at all in the Argonne. The whole division after the withdrawal of the 368th Regiment was, beginning with September 29, transferred to the Metz sector, preparatory to the great drive on that fortress which was begun, rather needlessly, as the civilian would judge, on the day before the signing of the Armistice, November 10.

According to plan, the 56th white American Division was on the left, the 92nd Division was in the center and the French Army was on the right. The 367th Regiment led the advance and forged ahead of the flanking units, the entire First Battalion being awarded the *Croix de Guerre;*—but this time wise field direction held them back, and for the first time they were supported by their own Negro Field Artillery. Beside the four Infantry Regiments the 92nd Division had the usual other units.

The 325th Field Signal Battalion, attached to Division Headquarters, was composed of four companies organized at Camp Sherman. It had ten colored and twenty white officers. It was in France at Bourbonne-les-Bains and then went to the Vosges, where it was split into detachments and attached to regiments under the Chief Signal Officer. While at school at Gondricourt, July 13–August 18, it made one of the best records of any unit. Many of its men were cited for bravery.

The 167th Field Artillery Brigade consisted of two regiments of Light Artillery (75s) trained at Camp Dix (the 349th and 350th) and one regiment of Heavy Artillery (the 351st) trained at Camp Meade, which used 155 howitzers. They experienced extraordinary difficulties in training. There can be no doubt but that deliberate effort was made to send up for examination in artillery not the best, but the poorest equipped candidates. Difficulty was encountered in getting colored men with the requisite technical training transferred to the artillery service. If the Commanding Officer in this case had been as prejudiced as in the case of the engineer and other units, there would have been no Negro Artillery. But Colonel Moore, although a Southerner, insisted on being fair to his men. The brigade landed in Brest June 26 and was trained at Montmorillon (Vienne). They were favorites in the town and were received into the social life on terms of perfect equality. There were five colored company officers and eight medical officers. The officers were sent to school at La Cortine and the Colonel in charge of this French school said that the work of the colored artillery brigade was better at the end of two weeks than that of any other American unit that had attended the school. The brigade went into battle in the Metz drive and did its work without a hitch, despite the fact that it had no transport facilities for their guns and had to handle them largely by hand.

The 317th Ammunition Train, which was attached to Division Headquarters, but was under the artillery in battle, was organized at Camp Funston in December, and had 1,333 officers and men, divided into two battalions, one motor and one horse, with seven companies. There were thirty-three colored and three white officers. The battalion landed in France June 27 and went to Montmorillon, and to the Artillery Training School at La Cortine, with the 167th Field Artillery. It arrived at Marbache October 18 and took part in the Metz drive. It had charge, also, of the Corps Ammunition dumps. During the drive all the officers were colored and Major Dean was in command. General Sherbourne, one of the few Commanding Officers fair to Negro troops, warmly commended the work of the artillery. No general court martial took place in the organization from the beginning and no efficiency boards sat. This was one of the very few units in which Negroes were promoted: four being made Captains, three First Lieutenants, eleven Second Lieutenants, and one a Major.

Near the close of the war thirty-five Lieutenants commissioned at Camp Taylor arrived in France and were sent to school near Nantes. They were subjected to many indignities by the American officers and were compelled to enter the classroom after the whites; they were refused leaves to town; reprimanded for conversing with the women of the city, who were anxious to be kind and sympathetic to the obviously oppressed strangers. Notwithstanding all this the men made good records and joined their command after the Armistice.

The 317th Engineers were assembled at Camp Sherman in December with 1,350 officers and men. There were two battalions and all the officers were colored, except four field officers. The Commanding Officers, however, were from the first determined to get rid of the Negroes. On May 10 the colored Captains were relieved, and sent to the 365th and 366th Regiments. The regiment came to France in June and was trained near Bourbonne-les Bains until July 20. On July 22 all the remaining colored officers, except two Lieutenants, the chaplain and the medical officers, were relieved at the repeated requests of Colonel Brown, of Georgia, and others. The regiment went to the Vosges in August, and then to the Argonne, doing excellent technical work in building and construction. All but one company were attached to the Fourth French Army Corps until December 22; only Company E remained with the 92nd Division.

The 366th Field Hospital was a colored unit with only two or three whites. It handled 10,000 cases before and during the Metz drive, four weeks, and was rated best in the American Expeditionary Force. Lieutenant Wright, the colored physician in charge, was promoted to a Captaincy.

The final engagement immediately preceding the signing of

the Armistice was fought in the Marbache sector, south of Metz, and was the most important event in which all the units of the 92nd Division actively participated. The division entered this sector October 7 and established headquarters in the village of Marbache, October 10, 1918. The several regiments were stationed in the front lines of the Division sector, with supporting units and reserves in the rear. Almost immediately upon entering this sector active operations were begun; patrols and reconnoitering parties were sent out from our lines; raiding parties were active and both sides found it necessary to be constantly on the alert. As the time for the advance of the whole Second Army grew nearer heavy shelling became more frequent, patrolling more active and raiding parties bolder. It was necessary to obtain all possible information regarding the enemy's movements and intentions before the advance began. There were many thrilling experiences in this sector during the four weeks preceding the final struggle.

On the tenth day of November came the order announcing the great drive and outlining the position of the 92nd Division in the line.

At 7 A. M. on the eleventh, the artillery broke loose with a terrific bombardment; this preparation lasted for a period of 42 minutes and was delivered upon the village of Bois Frehaut and the neighboring woods through which the infantry was to pass in its advance. In the meantime, the boys in the several companies composing the first assault line sprang from their trenches and with grim determination pushed themselves into "No Man's Land" and into the woods in the direction of the great German fortification, the city of Metz. The first objective of the 365th Infantry was Bois Frehaut (woods) three miles in depth and two miles in width. Barbed wire entanglements were everywhere and German machine guns were sputtering and large cannon were sending forth their messengers of death in all directions. The 365th Machine Gun Company, the 37-M M Platoon and our artillery and infantrymen repulsed this murderous attack and after two hours of desperate fighting Bois Frehaut was taken by the 365th and held by the Second Battalion of that organization until the bugle sounded the call to cease firing at 11 o'clock on the following morning.

The attack was led by Company H under the command of Captain William W. Green with a detachment of Company A commanded by Lieutenant Gus Mathews of Chicago with Company G and two other units in support. In fighting through the dense woods, made more difficult by large volumes of smoke from bursting shells, the attacking line in Company H became thinned and before many of the men arrived after the Company merged from the woods a flanking movement was attempted by the German machine gunners, but the timely arrival of Company G under the command of Lieutenant Walter Lyons saved Company H from this added danger. During this attack the Machine Gun Company of the 365th was active in covering the advancing infantry and kept the enemy on the run, thus making it impossible for them to deliver an effective fire against the men in the assault wave. The second assault wave was under the command of Captain Walter R. Sanders who was, also, second in command of the Second Battalion of the 365th Infantry. The second wave, under heavy shell fire and gas bombs from the artillery, moved up to occupy the position first held by the Second Battalion. While making this advance Lieutenant Walter Lowe, commanding Company A, was gassed, but he remained with his company, directing its movements until a short time before the order came to cease firing on the morning of the eleventh.

While the 365th Infantry was fighting like real heroes the units in the other battalions were doing exactly the same thing. The first objective reached by the 366th was Bois-de-Boivotte. The units in the first assault waive moved over the top at exactly seven o'clock on the morning of November 10. The artillery laid down a barrage for the advancing troops and protected their advance as far as possible, but the terrific bombardment with gas, shrapnel and machine gun fire from the German trenches made progress difficult as well as extremely dangerous. The troops, accustomed as they were by this time to bursting shells and gas bombs, ignored all personal danger and fought their way to their first objective with but few casualties. The fighting was furious during the early part of the day, but the organization was able to capture and hold much ground, varying from three to five kilometers in depth.

The 367th Infantry occupied a position on the west side of the Mosselle River. Two companies of the Second Battalion were in the first assault wave with others in support and reserve. The fighting units reached and held their objective and although the fighting was brisk the 367th did not lose a single man. With the darkness came a cessation of intensive action, the troops were reorganized and plans formulated for a renewal of the attack early the next morning.

In this general engagement the 92nd Division occupied a position a little southeast of the strong fortifications of Metz. The 165th French Division was on our right and the Seventh American Division was on our left and we kept in touch with both these divisions during the night and prepared for what subsequently proved to be the final struggle of the great world war the following morning.

At dawn the air was cool and damp; it was slightly cloudy, with a little fog in the atmosphere, just enough to give it a dull-gray color and to prevent the soldiers from seeing more than a few hundred yards in the direction of the enemy.

The keen whistling noises made by the shells from our supporting artillery as they passed over our heads on their missions of death told us that the hour was 4:30 A. M., for at that time the 351st Field Artillery Regiment began its advance upon Bois La Cote and Champey. This fire was kept up continuously until 10:45. The 350th Field Artillery Regiment, also, renewed its attack upon the woods in the neighborhood of Bois Frehaut, but ceased firing at 10 o'clock A. M., forty-five minutes earlier than the 351st. At five o'clock the First Battalion of the 350th Field Artillery laid a rolling barrage across and just north of Bouxieres-sur-Froidmont in support of the advancing infantry. Many of the same units that engaged the enemy the day before were again struggling for additional gains in the direction of Metz. Several fresh companies were brought up from the support to join those who had so gallantly repulsed the enemy on Saturday and together made a supreme effort to deliver a blow that would silence the German guns and put the Huns to flight in disorder. The only thing that saved the Kaiser's army in this sector from a crushing defeat was the order to cease firing at 11 o'clock.

At one time during the morning engagement the 56th Infantry (white) of the 7th Division, while advancing, ran into a strong barbed wire entanglement that had not been destroyed by artillery. Further advance was impossible and to retire under heavy fire from the German's big guns and merciless machine gun fire meant annihilation. Major Charles L. Appleton of the 367th Infantry, seeing the desperate situation into which the

56th Infantry had worked itself, manoeuvered several platoons to a position where they could hit the Germans from the flank and cover the retirement of the 56th. This timely act on the part of Major Appleton probably saved the 56th from complete destruction.

When the bugle sounded the call to cease firing, Company H of the 365th Infantry held 800 yards of the battle-front, five kilometers of which was taken from the Germans under the heavy guns of Metz, and held against odds five to one under intense shell and machine gun fire.

OTHER AGENCIES

So much for the 92d Division. It never had a fighting chance until the last day of the war. It was a centre of intrigue from the beginning and its weak and vacillating General spent most of his time placating the Negro haters on his staff and among his field officers, who wished nothing so much as the failure of the division as a fighting unit. How different a story if Charles Young had been let to lead his own!

Of the assisting agencies the only one that paid any attention to Negro troops was the Young Men's Christian Association. The few who came to Red Cross hospitals were, with a few exceptions, not only "Jim-Crowed" but officers were put in wards with their men. The white Young Men's Christian Association secretaries usually refused to serve Negroes in any way. Very few colored secretaries were sent and an attempt was made at first to get rid of the best of these, on the ground that their beliefs on the manhood rights and human equality of Negroes were "seditious." Matters were greatly improved when a colored man was placed in general charge of the colored work. He was never, however, furnished enough men and only three women for his vast field until after the Armistice.

On one subject the white Commanding Officers of all colored units showed more solicitude than on the organization and fighting efficiency of the troops,—that was the relations of the colored officers and men with the women of France. They began by officially stigmatizing the Negroes as rapists; they solemnly warned the troops in speeches and general orders not even to speak to women on the street; ordered the white military police to spy on the blacks and arrest them if they found them talking with French women. The white troops, taking their cue from all this senseless pother, spread tales and rumors among the peasants and villagers and sought to chastise Negroes and offending women. One officer, a high-minded gentleman, graduate and Phi Beta Kappa man of a leading American institution, was court-martialed for keeping company with a perfectly respectable girl of a family of standing in one of the towns where Negroes were quartered and while General Headquarters did not uphold the court-martial, it took occasion severly to reprimand the officer and remove him to a Labor Battalion.

The result of all this a-do was simply unnecessary bitterness among Negroes and mystification among the French. The Negroes resented being publicly stigmatized by their own countrymen as unfit for association with decent people, but the French men and women much preferred the courtesy and bonhomie of the Negroes to the impudence and swagger of many of the whites. In practically every French town where the Negro troops stayed they left close and sympathetic friends among men, women and children.

While the 92nd Division was in France there were fourteen trials for attacks on women, six of which were acquitted; of the other eight, three men were convicted of simple assault, leaving five possible cases of grave crime against women; of these, three cases are still undecided at this writing, one has been acquitted by the court, but the verdict has not been reviewed, and ONE man has been found guilty and hanged. It is only fair to add that this man belonged to a Labor Battalion and was sent to the division simply for trial. No other American division in France has a better record in this respect.

THE END

This is a partial and preliminary statement of the part the Negro played in the Great War. There is much in the tale that is missing and some mistakes, to be corrected by fuller information and reference to documents. But the main outlines are clear.

A nation with a great disease set out to rescue civilization; it took the disease with it in virulent form and that disease of race-hatred and prejudice hampered its actions and discredited its finest professions.

No adequate excuse for America's actions can be offered: Grant that many of the dismissed and transferred colored officers were incompetent, there is no possible excuse for the persistent and studied harrowing of admittedly competent men, to which every black officer testifies with a bitterness unexampled in Negro American history; there was no excuse for the persistent refusal to promote Negroes, despite their records testified to even by the French; there was no excuse for systematically refusing Negro officers and soldiers a chance to see something of greater and more beautiful France by curtailing their leaves and quartering them in the back districts.

On the other hand, there is not a black soldier but who is glad he went,—glad to fight for France, the only real white Democracy; glad to have a new, clear vision of the real, inner spirit of American prejudice. The day of camouflage is past.

This history will be enlarged and expanded, embellished with maps and pictures and with the aid of an editorial board, consisting of the leading Negro American scholars and the most distinguished of the black soldiers who fought in France, will be issued by the National Association for the Advancement of Colored People and THE CRISIS, in three volumes, in honor of the first great struggle of the modern Negro race for liberty.

May, 1919

THE BLACK MAN AND THE WOUNDED WORLD

A History of the Negro Race
in the World War and After

CHAPTER 1. INTERPRETATIONS

What is the ruling power in any given country? Speaking modernwise most would say Public Opinion. But this of course is a loose and inaccurate term. Opinion is individual. No "Public" can have an "opinion". The figure of speech is permissible but easily and crassly misleading. It is the power, wishes, opinion of certain persons which rule the world. These Dominant

Wills may rule by physical force, or superior intelligence or greater wealth or logical persuasion, and consequently may be regarded as Dominant Powers or Dominant Wishes or Dominant Intelligence or Highest Good—but always whatever rules exhibits itself as Will—action, effective deed.

To these Dominant Wills, be it the Will of One, or the Agreements of Many—of a Minority or of a Majority, and be it put in power by chance, force or reason—there must be, as long as it rules, the Submission of all individuals to its mandates. In these Current Submissions of individual men lies the core and kernel of modern ethical judgment of group action.

The effort to make these acts of submission free individual judgments is the movement toward Freedom. But Freedom is always restrained by the fear that the dethroning of the Dominant Wills at any time—that is, the refusal of a large number of persons to submit to a particular opinion or set of opinions—will result in the partial or total overthrow of civilized society, before enough submissions acknowledge, and thus enthrone, another Dominant Will. It is this fear of anarchy that leads to the persistent opposition to the right to challenge the Dominant Wills. The Right of Challenge is Democracy, and to Democracy the momentarily Dominant Wills are almost always opposed, particularly if dominion is based on force or bribery.

If the Dominant Wills are based on reason why should they fear universal Challenge—universal Democracy? Because most people are too inexperienced to get at the truth and too ignorant to reason correctly on given data. This ignorance can be corrected by universal education, but the Dominant Wills sometimes (1) do not believe in the possibility of educating all folk; (2) have desires and ambitions which can be satisfied only by the persistence of ignorance among the mass.

Thus the Dominant Wills in most periods of history have opposed the Challenge of Democracy because they desire the ignorance of most men. And they defend this desire by the assertion or even passionate belief that most men must and should be ignorant if civilization is to prevail.

Here then lies the heart and kernel of all social and political problems at any time. First we must ask whose is this Dominant Will? Then, is there any right of challenge and who can and does exercise the right? What is the attitude of the Dominant Will toward the increased intelligence and efficiency of men?

In the first quarter of the 20th century, the Dominant Wills in most lands are the wills of those persons who are seeking Incomes as distinguished from Wages and who are, by training, masters of the intricate organization of modern commerce and industry. The distinction between Income and Wage is of course not absolute, but Wage usually means a direct return for personal effort, while Income is the return which one commands by reason of his property rights or influence or social power. It is the almost universal ambition of men today to receive sufficient Income so as to make personal exertion on their part unnecessary—in other words, as we say, they desire to be "independent".

The income-receiving persons form a small but intelligent and highly specialized minority of men, while the mass of men are wage-earners or community workers in unorganized industry. So powerful and persuasive is this ruling class that most people identify its will with civilization and its industrial aims with life itself. Industry is life—commerce is government, they say openly or silently. Now modern industry requires (1) large accumulations of tools, machines, materials and transition goods and (2) regular skilled labor working over large areas of time and space synchronized with machine-like co-operation. The result is great income in goods and services which the Dominant Wills may allocate as they wish; and since the *raison d'être* of the present supporters of the Dominant Wills is the desire to share largely in this income, present government tends to support and develop the rich.

To this tendency is opposed the interest of the majority of men who are wage earners or in unorganized or primitive industry. What Right of Challenge have they before the Dominant Will? The democratic movement of the 19th century gave a few of them (the men in organized industry) a nominal right to challenge legally and at regular intervals the Dominant Wills. This Right to Vote—a mighty landmark in the advance of Man, and one which every group achieves sooner or later, or dissolves —is the beginning and not the end of democracy and meets at the outset baffling difficulties and limitations. These are chiefly (1) Ignorance (2) Propaganda (3) Law and Custom.

(1) Human society in its industrial, religious, aesthetic and other aspects is a tremendously intricate mechanism. Few even of the most intelligent grasp it thoroughly and most men have

no adequate conception of it. When now the Dominant Wills of a society form a trained group led by their selfish interests as well as their intelligence and ideals to fasten themselves in power, the ignorant mass has small chance of using their vote with enough intelligence to dislodge them without catastrophe to the State. The evident remedy for this is Education, the formal training of Children, the higher training of Youth, and the broader training of Citizens by experience, information, contacts and art—in other words the spread of Truth.

(2) But the spread of Truth is undertaken today by Propaganda. Now the dissemination of Truth presupposes normally a group of absolutely impartial Truth Bearers or Teachers or Priests or Prophets who know the Truth and who quite impartially and persistently make all free of it who will listen. But Propaganda is the effort not necessarily to spread the Truth, but to make people BELIEVE that what they hear is true; and to the propagandist any means which will accomplish this end of passionate, of unwavering and of forcible uncritical belief is justifiable. This is a dangerous but a very widespread method of public teaching today and what makes it most dangerous is the use which it makes of the Lie.

Lying is so dangerous an enemy to organized human life that usually it is regarded as an absolutely unjustifiable instrument of human advance. Yet manifestly everyone admits certain extreme cases when a deliberate Lie can be defended; and many are willing to use a partial truth to gain a good end while millions are willing without any attempt at investigation or corroboration to assume as true anything that they passionately wish to be true. Propaganda then, with large use of the deliberate Lie, the Half Truth and the Unproven Wish, has become a tremendous weapon in our day and is used particularly by the Dominant Wills to establish themselves in power by voluntary limitation of the Right of Challenge, or in other words by limiting the right to vote or the votable questions or the general field of democratic government. By this means most people today are convinced that the matters of work, wages and organized industry are quite beyond the possibility of democratic control and always will be; while a goodly number believe that the inter-relations of great nations can never be matters of open popular decision and many think that the making and interpreting of laws is not a matter for the average voter to have a voice in.

(3) Finally Law systems greatly impede democracy. Law is the attempt to reduce the logical statement the Dominant Will of the day. This is an exceedingly difficult task in itself but it is made more difficult because both the statement and the interpretation of the statement's meaning in particular cases are in the hands of technicians. These technically trained lawyers are dominated on the one hand by a mediaeval desire for perfections and consistency which makes them slaves to the precedents of dead centuries, and on the other hand they drift largely into the pay and control of the dominant income-seeking classes.

Thus ignorance, propaganda and customary law have so delimited the field of practical political democracy that it has become a very ineffective method of challenging the rule of the Dominant Wills. At the same time the rule of the Income-seekers has become peculiarly oppressive and dangerous, and for this reason the call for democratic control becomes more and more insistent. To repeat: In order to understand modern civilized life one must realize the conflict which has arisen between the Income Seekers and the Wage Earners. The great accomplishment of the 19th century was the organization of work—the far gathering of raw materials, the making of tools, machines and production goods and the synchronizing of effort. The result is a marvelous triumph of human skill and efficiency in making available a miraculous amount of consumptive goods and human services. If these goods and services had been designed for and applied to satisfying the highest wants of the mass of men our advance in culture would have been tremendous. It has been great despite the fact that the annual output of goods and services is arranged mainly to satisfy the wants of a small but powerful minority of the civilized world.

The power of this minority arises from their monopoly of finished goods, materials and production goods, which enables them largely to determine what goods shall be produced and what services paid for and at what rate, and also the ownership of the goods and services. This tremendous power—by far the greatest of modern days, and overshadowing most political power—has been successfully challenged with very great difficulty. The hindrances are: the widespread ignorance of the industrial process; the desire of most men to share this vast power rather than to curb it; the use of widespread propaganda to prove the impossibility of any fundamental change in the control of industry. In this way Democratic control has been largely kept out of industry and the owners of goods and materials have become the almost unchallenged Dominant Wills of the World.

Almost, but not quite, unchallenged, for the wage-earners have begun the challenge. The wage-earners are those whose work is determined and wages fixed by the Income Owners. There are among them a large number of Income-Seekers—i. e. those who wish not so much to curb the power of the Income Owners as to share their spoils. But gradually there has grown up among them an opinion that the wage system is right and the income system wrong, that every one should work and be paid for the work, and that the ownership of materials and productive goods should vest in the democratically controlled state. Meantime, however, before this thought became clear in their minds, their practical protest was against the amount of wages allotted them. It was too small for decent living or the rearing of children, especially when contrasted with the riches and power of the industrial world. At first they were answered that the rate of wages was not a matter of will but of natural law. Wages could not be increased save by reducing the number of laborers, by starvation, cataclysm, or voluntary restraints. This the laborers refused to believe. They tried to use political power, but were baffled by ignorance, law and propaganda.

Waters dammed in one direction burst their bounds in other and unexpected places. Democratic control, baffled in electing officials and law-making, found a new weapon in the Strike and Boycott. That is, realizing that the heart and centre of the Income-Seeker's power was his synchronizing of the industrial process over wide areas coupled with control of materials and machines, the hand workers sought to stop their coöperation and to refuse to work or refuse to buy at such critical times and places as would compel consideration of their wishes.

Propaganda and legal obstacles were for years used against the Strike, but after a century it has become a recognized weapon of offense by Wage-Earners against Employers. The open warfare of the Strike gradually softened into the parleys of the Labor Union and the Corporations; then came the shop committees and Coöperative buying, and there was foreshadowed the syndicalist control of factories and Coöperative production.

This development stimulated political democracy by educating the voters in the intricacies of industrial organization and giving them experience in group work. More political activity and more effective voting appeared so that the State itself was forced not only into some general control of Industry but even into undertaking certain lines of industrial activity. Industrial Democracy or rather Democracy in Industry seemed the swiftly approaching goal of civilization at the opening of the 20th century.

But the Dominant Wills of the Income Seekers were moving to wider conquests and had been for nearly fifty years, and the very triumphs of Industrial Democracy furnished an opportunity. Beginning with the African Slave trade a world commerce had grown up. Like national industry it began haphazard and was gradually organized and systematized. Gradually the local and national industrial systems tended to become cogs in the wheel of an international industrial organization. The basic foundations of this vaster set of enterprises were:

(A) The ownership of vast areas of "colonies" inhabited by semi-civilized people;
(B) Slave labor or peons without wage;
(C) A monopoly of valuable raw material;
(D) A monopoly of transportation facilities.

On this foundation it was proposed to build a national set of industries, and in these industries the wage earner would be pacified by high wages and even allowed some measure of democratic control. In other words the Dominant Wills proposed to share some of their economic power with the laborers in return for the political consent of the Laborer to the policy of conquest, slavery, monopoly and theft in Eastern Europe, Asia, Africa, and Central and South America.

This New Imperialism has widely prevailed and its way has been cleared by a new Propaganda. This Propaganda bases itself mainly on Race and Color—human distinctions long since discarded by Science as of little or no real significance. But this false scientific dogma which the 18th century rejected with avidity making freedom the basis of a new and world wide Humanity has been revamped by 20th century Industrialism as an Eternal Truth, so that most modern men of the masses believe the advancement of civilization necessarily involves slavery, lust and rapine in Africa.

With scarce an articulate word of protest then the world in the late 19th and early 20th centuries was hurriedly divided up among European Countries and the United States into colonies owned or controlled by white civilized nations, or "spheres of influence" dominated by them. To the casual glance of most folk this was simply a process of civilizing barbarians, "protecting" them and "developing" their resources. But its real nature is manifest when we ask, "For whose benefit is this New Imperialism of the white over the darker world?" Before 1914 the world answered with shrill accord, "For the benefit of the whites!" And they believed, thanks to organized Propaganda, that the salvation of Civilized Europe lay in the degradation of Uncivilized Africa and the subjection of the Balkans, Asia and the islands of the sea.

Since 1914, we are less assured. Since 1914 we have begun to fear lest our theory of exploitation of the semi-barbarians may not necessarily involve our own glorification. And this because in allocating the spoils of the Earth, Europe fell into a jealous quarrel that nearly overthrew Civilization and left it mortally wounded. Some there are still who see in this greatest catastrophe which the world ever knew simply a failure to agree. They argue that if Germany had not been so greedy and had been satisfied with the domination of Asia Minor, half of Portuguese Africa, and part of the Belgian Congo; and if Austria had been content with Bosnia and Herzegovina, and had not coveted Serbia, Roumania and most of the Balkans—that in this case the world industrial dominion under England, Germany, France, Italy and the United States could have been established and maintained. But is this true? On the contrary, it is a very doubtful truth. This God-defying dream had a thousand seeds of disaster: not simply a hundred recurring points of disagreement in colonial expansion and development, but the inevitable future reaction of the wage earners of Europe and the natives of the colonies.

Sooner or later Europe would learn two facts: (1) The dullest

European wage earner will gradually come to see that by upholding Imperial Aggression over the darker peoples by his political vote and his growing economic power he is but fastening tighter on himself the rule of the Rich; (2) Not even the most successful Propaganda, aided by Pseudo-Science and human hatred, can forever keep the white wage-earner from realizing that the victims of imperial greed in Asia and Africa are human beings like himself—suffering like him and from like causes, held in degradation and ignorance and like him, too, capable of infinite uplift and of ruling themselves and the world.

The Crisis then was bound to come. It did come in 1914–18. The Great War was a Scourge, an Evil, a retrogression to Barbarism, a waste, a wholesale murder. It was not necessary—it was precipitated by the will of men.

Who was to blame? Not Germany but certain Germans. Not England but certain Englishmen. Not France but certain Frenchmen. All those modern civilized citizens who submitted voluntarily to the Dominant Wills of those who ruled the leading lands in 1914 were blood guilty of the murder of the men who fell in the war. More guilty were those whose acts and thoughts made up the Dominant Wills and who were willing to increase their incomes at the expense of those who suffer in Europe and out, under the present industrial system. There is no dodging the issue. Guilt is personal. Deed is personal, Opinion and Will are personal. Systems and Nations are not to blame —individuals are to blame. Individuals caused the Great War, did its deviltry and are guilty of its endless Crime.

June, 1924

Chapter 2. The Story of the War

In 1911 the first Races Congress met in London; the object of the Congress was stated to be "to discuss, in the light of science and the modern conscience, the general relations existing between the peoples of the West and those of the East, between so-called white and so-called colored peoples, with a view to encouraging between them a fuller understanding, the most friendly feelings, and a heartier co-operation."

We urged the essential brotherhood of man in eight interesting sessions and we left filled with the hope of new world concord. Yet two knells struck on our hearts in those days, lightly but ominously. Professor Felix von Luschan, the eminent German anthropologist, insisted, despite the secretary's protest, upon ending his purely scientific and broad-minded paper on the "Anthropological View of Race" in this unexpected way:*

"The brotherhood of man is a good thing, but the struggle for life is a far better one. Athens would never have become what it was, without Sparta, and national jealousies and differences, and even the most cruel wars, have ever been the real causes of progress and mental freedom.

"As long as man is not born with wings, like the angels, he will remain subject to the eternal laws of Nature, and therefore he will always have to struggle for life and existence. No Hague Conferences, no International Tribunals, no international papers and peace societies, and no Esperanto or other international language, will ever be able to abolish war.

"The respect due by the white races to other races and by the white races to each other can never be too great, but natural law will never allow racial barriers to fall, and even national boundaries will never cease to exist.

"Nations will come and go, but racial and national antagonism will remain; and this is well, for mankind would become like a herd of sheep, if we were to lose our national ambition and cease to look with pride and delight, not only on our industries and science, but also on our splendid soldiers and our glorious ironclads. Let smallminded people whine about the horrid cost of Dreadnoughts; as long as every nation in Europe spends, year after year, much more money on wine, beer, and brandy than on her army and navy, there is no reason to dread our impoverishment by militarism.

"*Si vis pacem, para bellum;* and in reality there is no doubt that we shall be the better able to avoid war, the better we care for our armour. A nation is free only in so far as her own internal affairs are concerned. She has to respect the right of other nations as well as to defend her own, and her vital interests she will, if necessary, defend with blood and iron."

The second disquiet came from news that a German warship

*This note was appended to the paper at the request of the Secretary: "To prevent the last few paragraphs from being misinterpreted, Professor v. Luschan authorizes us to state that he regards the desire for a war between Germany and England as 'insane or dastardly.' "—EDITOR.

had sailed into Agadir, Morocco, in July, and thus announced that Germany considered herself deceived by France and England at Algeciras five years before. We sensed the shudder in the world and heard the hurrying of statesmen and the ominous speech of the Prime Minister. Then all passed, all seemed calm again for long years. We went to our world wide homes with this prayer in our hearts:

> *Save us, World Spirit from our lesser selves!*
> *Grant us that war and hatred cease,*
> *Reveal our souls in every race and hue!*
> *Help us, O Human God, in this Thy Truce*
> *To make Humanity divine!*

One year later I sat with that prematurely aged woman who wrote *"Die Waffen Nieder!"* and on whose soul the weight of the woe of war lay like lead. She spoke of Ferdinand the Warlike heir to the Austrian throne and his entourage, and shook her head sadly—"They mean war" she said, and in a little while she died and was mercifully spared the horror. Finally on June 28, in Bosnia, which Austria had seized in defiance of her solemn promise, Prinzep murdered Ferdinand and his wife. The world caught its breath for a month.

Then followed four of the most terrible years human civilization has known. So much happened and so frightful that it is difficult to see and realize the great Murder and Starvation as a whole; yet we must, and calmly seek to know it.

CAUSES

Late in July Austria, asserting the guilt of Servia for Prinzep's act and the accompanying propaganda, made demands on Servia that no independent land could be expected to yield. She was not expected to, for war had been determined in the secret councils of the Powerful. Germany said: "Either War now or no further colonial expansion and economic dominion;" Austria said: "War now or Russia will dominate the Balkans;" France said: "War now or the loss of Africa;" England said: "War now or War later with weaker allies." To this chorus there was but one effective answer: "War never, for war is Hell!" This Europe did not believe, and so between July 28, 1914, and August 28, eight of the greatest nations of the world, representing its highest and best culture, formally declared that their own best interests and the interests of religion and civilization demanded that they impose their will upon their neighbors by physical force. In 1915 Italy, Bulgaria and Turkey joined these great fighting powers, and in 1917 the United States and practically all of the rest of the world was at war. Civilization in the first half of the twentieth century of Jesus Christ declared that organized and world wide murder was the only path to salvation and peace.

Was this true? It was absolutely untrue. Each one of the contestants and every thinking human being knew it to be untrue and yet the moral and ethical problem before each human soul was baffling, almost insoluble. The situation was the culmination of world wide wrong for which millions were guilty. A world culture had arisen frankly founded on wealth; back of this wealth Germany had placed organized military force, while England had depended on domination of the seas and diplomatic intrigue, and France depended on economic efficiency and intrigue as well as military power. The decision to force changes by military power was the guilt of Germany and a deep crimson guilt. But back of it lay the age-long determination of Frenchmen, Englishmen, Russians, Austrians, Americans and practically all other modern men to monopolize the goods and services of the world for their own benefit and at the expense (a) of the undeveloped races and nations throughout the world; (b) of their own laboring classes; (c) of all foreign nations. Back here lay the blood guilt. With this greed unquestioned and unchallenged, intrigue, bribery and military force followed, and suddenly the conscience of the world faced this horrid dilemma: to fight for the greed of one's own land or submit to the greed and hate of foreigners. So we took the lesser of two awful evils and fought four long bloody years.

In 1914

War started on three fronts: Austria sought to seize Servia and failed after a month's trial. Germany determined to crush France and then turn on Russia; but Russia got ready much more quickly than anyone dreamed and by the middle of August, was pouring into East Prussia and threatening Königsberg and Danzig. German refugees began to reach Berlin. This would never do, and so with its powerful right hand on France, Germany reached over with Hindenburg on her left and inflicted a decisive defeat on the Russians late in August. Annoyed but unmoved by the Russian interlude Germany developed her main plan of crushing France by capturing Paris and defeating the main French armies.

Her plans long laid but much too rigid, were to sweep through an unresisting if not complacent Belgium and Luxembourg and fall on Paris from the north instead of from the east. The unexpected resistance of Belgium delayed the Germans two weeks, but this little respite (1) enabled the French to rearrange in part their eastward fronting forces; (2) enabled a small English force to appear in Belgium and (3) showed that fortresses could no longer resist the new siege artillery.

On came the mighty German machine in never ending columns of grey; they captured Brussels, crossed the French frontier and beat the English and French back on Paris until by September 6 they were only 25 miles away, with their seven great armies sweeping from Meaux in deep semicircle to Verdun and from Verdun to Switzerland.

Then came the first decisive battle of the war—the First Battle of the Marne, September 5–12, 1914, when the French suddenly sent an army around the right flank of the Germans and then by a series of attacks drove them back from 25 to 50 miles to the Aisne. This was the great decisive battle of the war, but alas! It did not end the fighting, it only began it; on the peak of the first onset at the Ourcq were black men fighting for France.

The great plan of the Germans for a quick crushing defeat of France had failed and the whole character of the war changed. On the sea England's already preponderating control was hardly disputed and the plan to starve Germany into submission was laid. On the Russo-Austrian frontier the Russians defeated the Austrians at Lemburg just before the Battle of the Marne, drove them out of parts of Poland and most of Galicia, and threatened the passes of the Carpathians, despite the efforts of Hindenburg to threaten Warsaw.

The Germans in France entrenched themselves along the Aisne river and it took four years to dislodge them. At first the French tried frontal attacks like that by which, the black troops helping, they recaptured Rheims. Unable to do more than dent the German line, the French and English in October and

November tried to outflank the Germans and drive them back from the sea. A terrible struggle, "The Race to the Sea", ensued. It was cold, wet, muddy and misty, and the murderous machines strewed the blood and limbs of thousands upon thousands across the black fields of Flanders. Black, brown and white men died like vermin as the French moved across the Oise, north to Lille, past Ypres and Dixmude to the mouth of the Yser where it locked itself to the sea. The Germans kept step, capturing Antwerp, which threatened their rear, and driving down the coast to Ostend. The critical battle there is known as the First Battle of Ypres and lasted from October 20 to November 17, one of the bloodiest of the war, where the suffering of human beings has seldom been surpassed; the British army was wiped out and there it was that whole battalions of black men perished and more than 200,000 corpses rotted and stank in the mud. Entrenched in deadlock, the end of the year found the great armies sinking to confused sobbing and quivering 500 miles from the Yser to the Alps, and 900 miles from Tilsit to Czernowitz.

In 1915

The second year of the war saw the Allies confident and Germans grim. The former with the expected accession of Italy, and with their sea power, proposed to end the war on the western front while the Russians were still triumphant in the east. England wished to begin with an attack along the coast. The French decided upon an attack in the Champagne and near Arras. On the other hand the Germans with Hindenburg, Ludendorff and Mackensen in the ascendency worked out a new plan of campaign which included a tremendous increase in artillery and especially the use of field howitzers with which the Russians were to be smashed while the Allies were held checkmated in the west.

The Allies began their campaign in the west by tentative French attacks in the Champagne in February and March, and also by an ambitious but ill-considered attempt in February on the part of the British to capture with white, black and brown aid the Straits of the Dardanelles. The real campaign opened with the Battle of Neuve Chapelle. This was a drive of the new British army of 500,000 in the Flanders district between March 10th and 15th.

May, 1924

RACIAL PRIDE

ASHAMED

Any colored man who complains of the treatment he receives in America is apt to be faced sooner or later by the statement that he is ashamed of his race.

The statement usually strikes him as a most astounding piece of illogical reasoning, to which a hot reply is appropriate.

And yet notice the curious logic of the persons who say such things. They argue:

White men alone are men. This Negro wants to be a man. *Ergo* he wants to be a white man.

Their attention is drawn to the efforts of colored people to be treated decently. This minor premise there attracts them. But the major premise—the question as to treating black men like white men—never enters their heads, nor can they conceive it entering the black man's head. If he wants to be a man he must want to be white, and therefore it is with peculiar complacency that a Tennessee paper says of a dark champion of Negro equality: "He bitterly resents his Negro blood."

Not so, O Blind Man. He bitterly resents your treatment of Negro blood. The prouder he is, or has a right to be, of the blood of his black fathers, the more doggedly he resists the attempt to load men of that blood with ignominy and chains. It is race pride that fights for freedom; it is the man ashamed of his blood who weakly submits and smiles.

(January, 1911, Vol. I, No. 3, p. 21)

IN BLACK

It was in Chicago. John Haynes Holmes was talking.

He said: "I met two children—one as fair as the dawn—the other as beautiful as the night." Then he paused. He had to pause for the audience guffawed in wild merriment. Why?

It was a colored audience. Many of them were black. Some black faces there were as beautiful as the night.

Why did they laugh?

Because the world had taught them to be ashamed of their color.

Because for 500 years men had hated and despised and abused black folk.

And now in strange, inexplicable transposition the rising blacks laugh at themselves in nervous, blatant, furtive merriment.

They laugh because they think they are expected to laugh—because all their poor hunted lives they have heard "black" things laughed at.

Of all the pitiful things of this pitiful race problem, this is the pitifullest. So curious a mental state tends to further subtleties. Colored folk, like all folk, love to see themselves in pictures; but they are afraid to see the types which the white world has caricatured. The whites obviously seldom picture brown and yellow folk, but for five centuries they have exhausted every ingenuity of trick, of ridicule and caricature on black folk: "grinning" Negroes, "Happy" Negroes, "gold dust twins", "Aunt Jemimas", and anything to make Negroes ridiculous. As a result if THE CRISIS puts a black face on its cover our 500,000 colored readers do not see the actual picture—they see the caricature that white folks intend when *they* make a black face. In the last few years a thoughtful, clear eyed artist, Frank Walts, has done a number of striking portraits for THE CRISIS. Mainly he has treated black faces; and regularly protests have come to us from various colored sources. His lovely portrait of the bright-eyed boy, Harry Elam, done in thoughtful sympathy, was approved by few Negroes. Our photograph of a woman of Santa Lucia, with its strength and humor and fine swing of head, was laughed at by many.

Why?

"O—er—it was not because they were black," stammer some

PAN-AFRICANISM

AFRICA

Europe had begun to look with covetous eyes toward Africa as early as 1415 when the Portuguese at the Battle Ceuta gained a foothold in Morocco. Thereafter Prince Henry of Portugal instituted the series of explorations which resulted not only in the discovery of Cape Verde, the Guinea Coast and the Cape of Good Hope, but by 1487 gave to Portugal the possession of a very fair slice of the African East Coast. This was the beginning of the Portuguese Colonies of Guinea, Angola and East Africa. Other European nations, France, Holland, Spain, England and Denmark, followed and set up trading stations along the African coast whose chief reason for existence was the fostering of the slave trade.

But the partition of Africa as we know it is much more recent and begins with the founding in 1884 of the Congo Free State whose inception was so zealously fostered by Leopold of Belgium and which in 1908 was annexed to Belgium. The scramble for African colonies was on and within a quarter of a century Africa was virtually in the hands of Europe.

In this division the British Empire gained a network of possessions extending from the Anglo-Egyptian Sudan down to South Africa, with valuable holdings on the East Coast and in Somaliland. France came next with an actually larger area, but with a smaller population. Her spoils reached from Morocco and Algeria, including the Algerian Sahara, to the French Congo, and on the Eastern Coast comprised Madagascar and French Somaliland. Germany, who was late in entering the game of colonization, contrived nonetheless to become mistress of four very valuable colonies, Togoland, Kamerun, Southwest Africa and East Africa. Italy's and Spain's possessions were relatively unimportant, embracing, for the former, Eritrea and Italian Somaliland, and for the latter, Rio de Oro and the Muni River settlements.

This was the state of affairs when the war broke out in 1914. In Africa the only independent states were the Republic of Liberia and the kingdom of Abyssinia which, according to history, has been independent since the days of Menelek, the reputed Son of Solomon and the Queen of Sheba. The number of souls thus under the rule of aliens is astounding, amounting in the case of England, France, Germany and Belgium to more than 110,000,000. During the course of the war Germany lost all four of her African colonies with a population estimated at 13,420,000. It is the question of the reapportionment of this vast number of human beings which has started the Pan-African movement. Colored America is indeed involved.

If we do not feel the chain
When it works another's pain,
Are we not base slaves indeed,
Slaves unworthy to be freed?

(February, 1919. Vol. XVII, No. 4, pp. 164-5)

RECONSTRUCTION AND AFRICA

The suggestion has been made that these colonies which Germany has lost should not be handed over to any other nation of Europe but should, under the guidance of *organized civilization*, be brought to a point of development which shall finally result in an autonomous state. This plan has met with much criticism and ridicule. Let the natives develop along their own lines and they will "go back," has been the cry. Back to what, in Heaven's name?

Is a civilization naturally backward because it is different? Outside of cannibalism, which can be matched in this country, at least, by lynching, there is no vice and no degradation in native African customs which can begin to touch the horrors thrust upon them by white masters. Drunkenness, terrible diseases, immorality, all these things have been the gifts of European civilization. There is no need to dwell on German and Belgian atrocities, the world knows them too well. Nor have France and England been blameless. But even supposing that these masters had been models of kindness and rectitude, who shall say that any civilization is in itself so superior that it must be super-imposed upon another nation without the expressed and intelligent consent of the people most concerned. The culture indigenous to a country, its folk-customs, its art, all this must have free scope or there is no such thing as freedom for the world.

The truth is, white men are merely juggling with words—or worse—when they declare that the withdrawal of Europeans from Africa will plunge that continent into chaos. What Europe, and indeed only a small group in Europe, wants in Africa is not a field for the spread of European civilization, but a field for exploitation. They covet the raw materials,—ivory, diamonds, copper and rubber in which the land abounds, and even more do they covet cheap native labor to mine and produce these things. Greed,—naked, pitiless lust for wealth and power, lie back of all of Europe's interest in Africa and the white world knows it and is not ashamed.

Any readjustment of Africa is not fair and cannot be lasting which does not consider the interest of native Africans and peoples of African descent. Prejudice, in European colonies in Africa, against the ambitious Negro is greater than in America, and that is saying much. But with the establishment of a form of government which shall be based on the concept that Africa is for Africans, there would be a chance for the colored American to emigrate and to go as a pioneer to a country which must, sentimentally at least, possess for him the same fascination as England does for Indian-born Englishmen.

(February, 1919. Vol. XVII, No. 4, pp. 165-6)

NOT "SEPARATISM"

This is not a "separatist" movement. There is no need to think that those who advocate the opening of Africa for Africans and those of African descent desire to deport any large number of colored Americans to a foreign and, in some respects, inhospitable land. Once for all, let us realize that we are Americans, that we were brought here with the earliest settlers, and that the very sort of civilization from which we came made the complete adoption of western modes and customs imperative if we were to survive at all. In brief, there is nothing so indigenous, so completely "made in America" as we. It is as absurd to talk of a return to Africa, merely because that was our home 300 years ago, as it would be to expect the members of the Caucasian race to return to the fastnesses of the Caucasus Mountains from which, it is reputed, they sprang.

But it is true that we as a people are not given to colonization, and that thereby a number of essential occupations and interests have been closed to us which the redemption of Africa would open up. The African movement means to us what the Zionist movement must mean to the Jews, the centralization of race effort and the recognition of a racial fount. To help bear the burden of Africa does not mean any lessening of effort in our own problem at home. Rather it means increased interest. For any ebullition of action and feeling that results in an ameliora-tion of the lot of Africa tends to ameliorate the condition of colored peoples throughout the world. And no man liveth to himself.

(February, 1919. Vol. XVII, No. 4, p. 166)

THE PAN-AFRICAN CONGRESS

The Pan-African Congress is an established fact. It was held February 19, 20, 21, 1919, at the Grand Hôtel, Boulevard des Capucines, Paris. The Executive Committee consisted of M. Blaise Diagne, President; Dr. W. E. Burghardt DuBois, Secre-tary; Mrs. Ida Gibbs Hunt, Assistant Secretary, and M. E. F. Fredericks. The Congress maintained an office at the Hôtel de Malte, 63 Rue Richelieu, with office hours from 10 A. M. to 6 P. M.

Fifty-seven delegates, including a number of native Africans educated abroad, were present at the Congress. In all, fifteen countries were represented, as follows:

United States of America   16
French West Indies   13
Haiti   7

France	7
Liberia	3
Spanish Colonies	2
Portuguese Colonies	1
San Domingo	1
England	1
British Africa	1
French Africa	1
Algeria	1
Egypt	1
Belgian Congo	1
Abyssinia	1
Total	57

France was represented by the Chairman of the Committee of Foreign Affairs of the French Chamber; Belgium, by M. Van Overgergh, of the Belgian Peace Commission; Portugal, by M. Freire d'Andrade, former Minister of Foreign Affairs. William English Walling and Charles Edward Russell were in attendance from the United States of America.

At the first meeting held Wednesday afternoon, February 19, M. Diagne, Deputy from Senegal to the French Chamber, opened the Congress with words of praise for French colonial rule. He expressed the hope that the ideal of racial unity would inspire all of African descent throughout the entire world.

Many interesting speeches followed, all of which struck a characteristic note. M. Candace, Deputy from Gaudeloupe, insisted with much eloquence and frankness that color should not be considered in the maintenance of human rights. That the rights of black Americans met with so little respect in the United States was, he declared, a matter for special deprecation.

Two other deputies from the French West Indies, M. Boisneuf and M. Lagrosillière, spoke with equal eloquence and expressed their inability to understand how Americans could fail to treat as equals those who in common with themselves were giving their lives for democracy and justice.

Mr. King, delegate from Liberia to the Peace Conference, gave an interesting exposition of Liberia's aims and accomplishments and expressed the hope that people of African descent everywhere would take pride in that little independent black Republic and in every way possible aid in her future development. "Let us," he concluded, "be considered a home for the darker races in Africa. It is your duty to help. We are asking for rights, but let us not, therefore, forget our duties, for remember wherever there are rights, there are also duties and responsibilities."

The Chairman of Foreign Affairs for France emphasized the fact that the sentiment of France on equality and liberty, irrespective of color, was shown by the fact that she had six colored representatives in the French Chamber, one of whom was the distinguished Chairman of the Congress, M. Diagne, who served on his Committee. Even before the Revolution France had pursued the same policy.

M. Overgergh spoke of the reforms in the Belgian colony and of an International Geographical Society which he represented.

M. d'Andrade talked of the opportunities and liberties given the natives in the Portuguese colonies.

William English Walling said that while he had to blush when America was being arraigned, he felt that changes were already going on in the United States and that in time Americans, whether willingly or not, would have to submit to the opinion of the world and accord to her colored contingent full justice and equality. She must yield or go down before the darker races of the world. If France has six colored representatives in Parliament, he said, the United States of America, considering her black population, should have at least ten colored representatives in her legislative body.

Charles Edward Russell's address stirred and inspired all. He said the old notion that one race is inferior to another is false, and this war has helped to kill that idea. This Congress, he felt, was a splendid step forward. Africa should press her claims here and now. "It is a great opportunity and yours is the duty to fulfill it," he said. "It is a duty for Africa and for world democracy, for black and white alike. Insist upon your rights!"

At the second session, Mr. Archer, ex-Mayor of Battersea, London, England, spoke of the importance of demanding one's rights, of the value of unity of purpose and effort in ameliorating the condition of people of color throughout the world, starting with the United States and England. He said that while England accords many rights to her citizens of color, she does not give them as much representation as France. "We must fight for our just rights at all times," he concluded.

Dr. George Jackson, an American, spoke of his experiences in the Belgian Congo, and explained why the natives had come to hate German Kultur. As a colored American he also had often had cause to blush for America.

Mrs. A. W. Hunton, from the United States of America, spoke of the importance of women in the world's reconstruction and regeneration of today, and of the necessity of seeking their co-operation and counsel.

At the afternoon session of the last day Mme. Jules Siefried, President of the French National Association for the Rights of Women, brought words of encouragement from the International Council, then meeting in Paris. She said that no one could appreciate better than women the struggle for broader rights and liberties.

Resolutions were passed providing for another Congress to be held in Paris during the year 1921.

The following resolutions, to be presented to the Peace Conference now in session, were unanimously adopted:

> I. The Negroes of the world in Pan-African Congress assembled demand in the interests of justice and humanity, for the purpose of strengthening the forces of Civilization, that immediate steps be taken to develop the 200,000,000 of Negroes and Negroids; to this end, they propose:
>
> > 1. That the Allied and Associated Powers establish a Code of Laws for the international protection of the Natives of Africa similar to the proposed international Code for Labor.
> >
> > 2. That the League of Nations establish a permanent Bureau charged with the special duty of overseeing the application of these laws to the political, social and economic welfare of the Natives.
>
> II. The Negroes of the world demand that hereafter the Natives of Africa and the Peoples of African descent be governed according to the following principles:
>
> > 1. *The Land:* The land and its natural resources shall be held in trust for the Natives

and at all times they shall have effective ownership of as much land as they can profitably develop.

2. *Capital:* The investment of capital and granting of concessions shall be so regulated as to prevent the exploitation of Natives and the exhaustion of the natural wealth of the country. Concessions shall always be limited in time and subject to State control. The growing social needs of the Natives must be regarded and the profits taxed for the social and material benefit of the Natives.

3. *Labor:* Slavery, forced labor and corporal punishment, except in punishment of crime, shall be abolished; and the general conditions of labor shall be prescribed and regulated by the State.

4. *Education:* It shall be the right of every Native child to learn to read and write his own language and the language of the trustee nation, at public expense, and to be given technical instruction in some branch of industry. The State shall also educate as large a number of Natives as possible in higher technical and cultural training and maintain a corps of Native teachers.

5. *Medicine and Hygiene:* It shall be recognized that human existence in the tropics calls for special safeguards and a scientific system of public hygiene. The State shall be responsible for medical care and sanitary conditions without discouraging collective and individual intiative. A service created by the State shall provide physicians and hospitals, and shall enforce rules. The State shall establish a native medical staff.

6. *The State:* The Natives of Africa must have the right to participate in the government as fast as their development permits in conformity with the principle that the government exists for the Natives and not the Natives for the government. The Natives shall have voice in the government to the

extent that their development permits, beginning at once with local and tribal government according to ancient usage, and
extending gradually as education and experience proceeds, to the higher offices of
State, to the end that, in time, Africa be
ruled by consent of the Africans.

7. *Culture and Religion:* No particular
religion shall be imposed and no particular
form of human culture. There shall be liberty
of conscience. The uplift of the Natives shall
take into consideration their present condition and shall allow the utmost scope to racial genius, social inheritance and individual
bent, so long as these are not contrary to the
best established principles of civilization.

8. *Civilized Negroes: Wherever persons of
African descent are civilized and able to meet
the tests of surrounding culture, they shall be
accorded the same rights as their fellow-citi-
zens; they shall not be denied on account of
race or color a voice in their own government, justice before the courts, and economic
and social equality according to ability and
desert.*

9. *The League of Nations:* Greater
security of life and property shall be guaran-
teed the Natives; international labor legislation shall cover Native workers as well as
whites; they shall have equitable representation in all the international institutions of
the League of Nations, and the participation
of the blacks themselves in every domain of
endeavor shall be encouraged in accordance
with the declared object of Article 19 of the
League of Nations, to wit: "The well being
and the development of these people constitute a sacred mission of civilization and it is
proper in establishing the League of Nations
to incorporate therein pledges for the accomplishment of this mission."

*Whenever it is proven that African Natives are not receiving
just treatment at the hands of any State or that any State deliber-*

ately excludes its civilized citizens or subjects of Negro descent from its body politic and cultural, it shall be the duty of the League of Nations to bring the matter to the attention of the civilized world.

BLAISE DIAGNE, *President.*
W. E. B. DU BOIS, *Secretary.*

April, 1919

MY MISSION

I went to Paris because today the destinies of mankind center there. Make no mistake as to this, my readers.

Podunk may easily persuade itself that only Podunk matters and that nothing is going on in New York. The South Sea Islander may live ignorant and careless of London. Some Americans may think that Europe does not count, and a few Negroes may argue vociferously that the Negro problem is a domestic matter, to be settled in Richmond and New Orleans.

But all these careless thinkers are wrong. The destinies of mankind for a hundred years to come are being settled today in a small room of the *Hotel Crillon* by four unobtrusive gentlemen who glance out speculatively now and then to Cleopatra's Needle on the Place de la Concorde.

You need not believe this if you do not want to. They do not care what you believe. They have the POWER. They are settling the world's problems and you can believe what you choose as long as they control the ARMIES and NAVIES, the world supply of CAPITAL and the PRESS.

Other folks of the world who think, believe and act;— THIRTY-TWO NATIONS, PEOPLES and RACES, have permanent headquarters in Paris. Not simply England, Italy and the Great Powers are there, but all the little nations; not simply little nations, but little groups who want to be nations, like the Letts and Finns, the Armenians and Jugo-Slavs, Irish and Ukrainians. Not only groups, but races have come—Jews, Indians, Arabs and All-Asia. Great churches, like the Greek Orthodox and the Roman Catholic, are watching on the ground. Great organizations, like the American Peace Society, the League to

Enforce Peace, the American Federation of Labor, the Woman's Suffrage Association and a hundred others are represented in Paris today.

In fine, not a single great, serious movement or idea in Government, Politics, Philanthropy or Industry in the civilized world has omitted to send and keep in Paris its Eyes and Ears and Fingers! And yet some American Negroes actually asked WHY I went to help represent the Negro world in Africa and America and the Islands of the Sea.

But why did I not explain my reasons and mission before going? Because I am not a fool. Because I knew perfectly well that any movement to bring the attention of the world to the Negro problem at this crisis would be stopped the moment the Great Powers heard of it. When, therefore, I was suddenly informed of a chance to go to France as a newspaper correspondent, I did not talk—I went.

What did I do when I got there? First, there were certain things that I did NOT do. I did not hold an anti-lynching meeting on the Boulevard des Italiens. I would to God I could have, but I knew that France is still under martial law,—*that no meeting can be held today in France, anywhere or at any time, without the consent of the Government; no newspaper can publish a line without the consent of the Censor and no individual can stay in France unless the French consent.*

But it did not follow that because I could not do everything I could do nothing. I first went to the Ameican Peace Commission and said frankly and openly: "I want to call a Pan-African Congress in Paris." The Captain to whom I spoke smiled and shook his head. "Impossible," he said, and added: "The French Government would not permit it." "Then," said I innocently: "It's up to me to get French consent!" "It is!" he answered, and he looked relieved.

With the American Secret Service at my heels I then turned to the French Government. There are six colored deputies in the French Parliament and one is an under-secretary in the War Department. "Of course, we can have a Pan-African Congress," he said—"I'll see Clemenceau." He saw Clemenceau, and there was a week's pause. Clemenceau saw Pichon, and there was another pause. Meantime, our State Department chuckled and announced that there would be no Congress and refused Negroes passports. England followed suit and refused to allow the Secretary of the Aborigines Protection Society even to visit Paris, while the South African natives were not allowed to sail.

But there are six Negroes in the French House and Clemenceau needs their votes. There were 280,000 black African troops in the war before whom France stands with uncovered head. The net result was that Clemenceau, Prime Minister of France, gave us permission to hold the Pan-African Congress in Paris.

What could a Pan-African Congress do? It could not agitate the Negro problem in any particular country, except in so far as that problem could be plausibly shown to be part of the problem of the future of Africa. The problem of the future of Africa was a difficult and delicate question before the Peace Conference—so difficult and so delicate that the Conference was disposed to welcome advice and co-operation.

If the Negroes of the world could have maintained in Paris during the entire sitting of the Peace Conference a central headquarters with experts, clerks and helpers, they could have settled the future of Africa at a cost of less than $10,000.

As it was the Congress cost $750. Yet with this meagre sum a Congress of fifty-eight delegates, representing sixteen different Negro groups, was assembled. This Congress passed resolutions which the entire press of the world has approved, despite the fact that these resolutions had two paragraphs of tremendous significance to us:

Wherever persons of African descent are civilized and able to meet the tests of surrounding culture, they shall be accorded the same rights as their fellow citizens; they shall not be denied on account of race or color a voice in their own Government, justice before the courts and economic and social equality according to ability and desert.

Whenever it is proven that African natives are not receiving just treatment at the hands of any State or that any State deliberately excludes its civilized citizens or subjects of Negro descent from its body politic and cultural, it shall be the duty of the League of Nations to bring the matter to the attention of the civilized world.

Precisely the same principles are being demanded today by the Jews and the Japanese. And despite the enormous significance of these demands, Colonel House of the American Peace Commission received me and assured me that he wished these resolutions presented to the Peace Conference. Lloyd George wrote me that he would give our demands "his careful consideration." The French Premier offered to arrange an audience for the President and Secretary of the Conference. Portugal and Belgium, great colonial powers, offered complete co-operation.

The League for the Rights of Man, which freed Dreyfus, appointed a special commission to hear not only of the African, but the facts as to the American Negro problem.

We got, in fact, the ear of the civilized world and if it had been possible to stay longer and organize more thoroughly and spread the truth,—what might not have been accomplished?

As it was, we have organized the "Pan-African Congress" as a permanent body, with M. Diagne as president and myself as secretary, and we plan an international quarterly BLACK RE-VIEW to be issued in English, French and possibly in Spanish and Portuguese.

The world-fight for black rights is on!

(April, 1919. Vol. XVIII, No. 1, pp. 7-9)

MANIFESTO OF THE SECOND PAN-AFRICAN CONGRESS

To The World

The absolute equality of races,—physical, political and social —is the founding stone of world peace and human advancement. No one denies great differences of gift, capacity and attainment among individuals of all races, but the voice of science, religion and practical politics is one in denying the God-appointed existence of super-races, or of races naturally and inevitably and eternally inferior.

That in the vast range of time, one group should in its industrial technique, or social organization, or spiritual vision, lag a few hundred years behind another, or forge fitfully ahead, or come to differ decidedly in thought, deed and ideal, is proof of the essential richness and variety of human nature, rather than proof of the co-existence of demi-gods and apes in human form. The doctrine of racial equality does not interfere with individual liberty, rather, it fulfils it. And of all the various criteria by which masses of men have in the past been prejudged and classified, that of the color of the skin and texture of the hair, is surely the most adventitious and idiotic.

It is the duty of the world to assist in every way the advance of the backward and suppressed groups of mankind. The rise of all men is a menace to no one and is the highest human ideal; it is not an altruistic benevolence, but the one road to world salvation.

For the purpose of raising such peoples to intelligence, self-knowledge and self-control, their intelligentsia of right ought to be recognized as the natural leaders of their groups.

The insidious and dishonorable propaganda, which, for selfish ends, so distorts and denies facts as to represent the advancement and development of certain races of men as impossible and undesirable, should be met with widespread dissemination of the truth. The experiment of making the Negro slave a free citizen in the United States is not a failure; the attempts at autonomous government in Haiti and Liberia are not proofs of the impossibility of self-government among black men; the experience of Spanish America does not prove that mulatto democracy will not eventually succeed there; the aspirations of Egypt and India are not successfully to be met by sneers at the capacity of darker races.

We who resent the attempt to treat civilized men as uncivilized, and who bring in our hearts grievance upon grievance against those who lynch the untried, disfranchise the intelligent, deny self-government to educated men, and insult the helpless, we complain; but not simply or primarily for ourselves—more especially for the millions of our fellows, blood of our blood, and flesh of our flesh, who have not even what we have—the power to complain against monstrous wrong, the power to see and to know the source of our oppression.

How far the future advance of mankind will depend upon the social contact and physical intermixture of the various strains of human blood is unknown, but the demand for the interpenetration of countries and intermingling of blood has come, in modern days, from the white race alone, and has been imposed upon brown and black folks mainly by brute force and fraud. On top of this, the resulting people of mixed race have had to endure innuendo, persecution, and insult, and the penetrated countries have been forced into semi-slavery.

If it be proven that absolute world segregation by group, color or historic affinity is best for the future, let the white race leave the dark world and the darker races will gladly leave the white. But the proposition is absurd. This is a world of men, of men whose likenesses far outweigh their differences; who mutually need each other in labor and thought and dream, but who can successfully have each other only on terms of equality, justice and mutual respect. They are the real and only peacemakers who work sincerely and peacefully to this end.

The beginning of wisdom in interracial contact is the establishment of political institutions among suppressed peoples. The habit of democracy must be made to encircle the earth. Despite the attempt to prove that its practice is the secret and divine gift of the few, no habit is more natural or more widely spread among primitive people, or more easily capable of development among masses. Local self-government with a minimum of help and oversight can be established tomorrow in Asia, in Africa, in America and in the Isles of the Sea. It will in many instances need general control and guidance, but it will fail only when that guidance seeks ignorantly and consciously its own selfish ends and not the people's liberty and good.

Surely in the 20th century of the Prince of Peace, in the millenium of Buddha and Mahmoud, and in the mightiest Age of Human Reason, there can be found in the civilized world enough of altruism, learning and benevolence to develop native institutions for the native's good, rather than continue to allow the majority of mankind to be brutalized and enslaved by ignorant and selfish agents of commercial institutions, whose one aim is profit and power for the few.

And this brings us to the crux of the matter: It is the shame of the world that today the relation between the main groups of mankind and their mutual estimate and respect is determined chiefly by the degree in which one can subject the other to its service, enslaving labor, making ignorance compulsory, uprooting ruthlessly religion and customs, and destroying government, so that the favored Few may luxuriate in the toil of the tortured Many. Science, Religion and Philanthropy have thus been made the slaves of world commerce and industry, and bodies, minds, souls of Fiji and Congo, are judged almost solely by the quotations on the Bourse.

The day of such world organization is past and whatever exuse be made for it in other ages, the 20th century must come to judge men as men and not as material and labor.

The great industrial problem which has hitherto been regarded as the domestic problem of culture lands, must be viewed far more broadly, if it is ever to reach just settlement. Labor and capital in England, France and America can never solve their problem as long as a similar and vastly greater problem of poverty and injustice marks the relations of the whiter and darker peoples. It is shameful, unreligious, unscientific and undemocratic that the estimate, which half the peoples of earth put on the other half, depends mainly on their ability to squeeze profit out of them.

If we are coming to recognize that the great modern problem is to correct maladjustment in the distribution of wealth, it must be remembered that the basic maladjustment is in the outrageously unjust distribution of world income between the dominant and suppressed peoples; in the rape of land and raw material, and monopoly of technique and culture. And in this crime white labor is *particeps criminis* with white capital. Unconsciously and consciously, carelessly and deliberately, the vast power of the white labor vote in modern democracies has been cajoled and flattered into imperialistic schemes to enslave and debauch black, brown and yellow labor, until with fatal retribution, they are themselves today bound and gagged and rendered impotent by the resulting monopoly of the world's raw material in the hands of a dominant, cruel and irresponsible few.

And, too, just as curiously, the educated and cultured of the world, the well-born and well-bred, and even the deeply pious and philanthropic, receive their training and comfort and luxury, the ministrations of delicate beauty and sensibility, on condition that they neither inquire into the real source of their income and the methods of distribution or interfere with the legal props which rest on a pitiful human foundation of writhing white and yellow and brown and black bodies.

We claim no perfectness of our own nor do we seek to escape the blame which of right falls on the backward for failure to advance, but *noblesse oblige,* and we arraign civilization and more especially the colonial powers for deliberate transgressions of our just demands and their own better conscience.

England, with her Pax Britannica, her courts of justice, established commerce and a certain apparent recognition of native law and customs, has nevertheless systematically fostered ignorance among the natives, has enslaved them and is still enslaving some of them, has usually declined even to try to train black and brown men in real self-government, to recognize civilized black folks as civilized, or to grant to colored colonies those rights of self-government which it freely gives to white men.

Belgium is a nation which has but recently assumed responsibility for her colonies, and has taken some steps to lift them from the worst abuses of the autocratic regime; but she has not confirmed to the people the possession of their land and labor, and she shows no disposition to allow the natives any voice in their own government, or to provide for their political future. Her colonial policy is still mainly dominated by the banks and great corporations. But we are glad to learn that the present government is considering a liberal program of reform for the future.

Portugal and Spain have never drawn a legal caste line against persons of culture who happen to be of Negro descent. Portugal has a humane code for the natives and has begun their education in some regions. But, unfortunately, the industrial concessions of Portuguese Africa are almost wholly in the hands of foreigners whom Portugal cannot or will not control, and who are exploiting land and re-establishing the African slave trade.

The United States of America after brutally enslaving millions of black folks suddenly emancipated them and began their education; but it acted without system or forethought, throwing the freed men upon the world penniless and landless, educating them without thoroughness and system, and subjecting them the while to lynching, lawlessness, discrimination, insult and slander, such as human beings have seldom endured and survived. To save their own government, they enfranchised the Negro and then when danger passed, allowed hundreds of thousands of educated and civilized black folk to be lawlessly disfranchised and subjected to a caste system; and, at the same time, in 1776, 1812, 1861, 1897, and 1917, they asked and allowed thousands of black men to offer up their lives as a sacrifice to the country which despised and despises them.

France alone of the great colonial powers has sought to place her cultured black citizens on a plane of absolute legal and social equality with her white and given them representation in her highest legislature. In her colonies she has a widespread but still imperfect system of state education. This splendid beginning must be completed by widening the political basis of her native government, by restoring to the indigenes the ownership of the soil, by protecting native labor against the aggression of established capital, and by asking no man, black or white, to be a soldier unless the country gives him a voice in his own government.

The independence of Abyssinia, Liberia, Haiti and San Domingo, is absolutely necessary to any sustained belief of the black folk in the sincerity and honesty of the white. These nations have earned the right to be free, they deserve the recognition of the world; notwithstanding all their faults and mistakes, and the fact that they are behind the most advanced civilization of the day, nevertheless they compare favorably with the past, and even more recent, history of most European nations, and it shames civilization that the treaty of London practically invited Italy to aggression in Abyssinia, and that free America has unjustly and cruelly seized Haiti, murdered and for a time enslaved her workmen, overthrown her free institutions by force, and has so far failed in return to give her a single bit of help, aid or sympathy.

What do those wish who see these evils of the color line and racial discrimination and who believe in the divine right of suppressed and backward peoples to learn and aspire and be free?

The Negro race through its thinking intelligentsia is demanding:

> I—The recognition of civilized men as civilized despite their race or color
>
> II—Local self government for backward groups, deliberately rising as experience and knowledge grow to complete self government under the limitations of a self governed world
>
> III—Education in self knowledge, in scientific truth and in industrial technique, undivorced from the art of beauty
>
> IV—Freedom in their own religion and social customs, and with the right to be different and non-conformist

V—Co-operation with the rest of the world in government, industry and art on the basis of Justice, Freedom and Peace

VI—The ancient common ownership of the land and its natural fruits and defence against the unrestrained greed of invested capital

VII—The establishment under the League of Nations of an international institution for the study of Negro problems

VIII—The establishment of an international section in the Labor Bureau of the League of Nations, charged with the protection of native labor.

The world must face two eventualities: either the complete assimilation of Africa with two or three of the great world states, with political, civil and social power and privileges absolutely equal for its black and white citizens, or the rise of a great black African state founded in Peace and Good Will, based on popular education, natural art and industry and freedom of trade; autonomous and sovereign in its internal policy, but from its beginning a part of a great society of peoples in which it takes its place with others as co-rulers of the world.

In some such words and thoughts as these we seek to express our will and ideal, and the end of our untiring effort. To our aid we call all men of the Earth who love Justice and Mercy. Out of the depths we have cried unto the deaf and dumb masters of the world. Out of the depths we cry to our own sleeping souls. The answer is written in the stars.

(November, 1921. Vol. XXIII, No. 1, pp. 5-10)

PAN-AFRICA AND NEW RACIAL PHILOSOPHY

During the last ten months, we have tried in the CRISIS magazine to make a re-statement of the Negro problem in certain of its aspects. We began with the question of health and disease among us. Then we took up in succession our physical rate of increase, "Karl Marx and the Negro," "The Problem of Earning a Living," "Marxism and the Negro Problem," "The Negro

Vote," "The Class Struggle Within the Race," "Negro Education," and "Our Problems of Religion."

We have considered all these matters in relation to the American Negro but our underlying thought has been continually that they can and must be seen not against any narrow, provincial or even national background, but in relation to the great problem of the colored races of the world and particularly those of African descent.

There are still large numbers of American Negroes who in all essential particulars conceive themselves as belonging to the white race. And this, not on account of their color, which may be yellow, brown or black, but on account of their history and their social surroundings. They react as white Americans. They have all the racial prejudices of white America, not only against Asiatics and Jews, but even against Mexicans and West Indians. In all questions of human interest, they would flock to white America before they would flock to the brown West Indies or to black Africa or to yellow Asia.

This, of course, is quite natural, and in a sense proves how idiotic most of our racial distinctions are. Here is a boy, born in America, of parents who were born in America, of grandparents and great grandparents born in America. He speaks the American twang; he reads American history, he gets his news from American papers, and he understands American baseball. It is impossible for that boy to think of himself as African, simply because he happens to be black. He *is* an American. But on the other hand, as he grows up and comprehends his surroundings, he is going to be made to think of himself as at least a peculiar sort of American. Against this, he is going to protest, logically and emotionally, and dwell upon the anomaly of a person being outcast and discriminated against in his own home. Gradually, however, he is going to find that this protest has only limited effect; that to most white Americans of today, Negro prejudice is something that is beyond question and will. It is a stark, true fact and little or nothing can be done about it at present. In the future, the long future, things may change. But they are not going to change in the lifetime of those now living.

So long now as this is an academic question, a matter of attitudes and thoughts and spiritual likes and dislikes, we can leave it there. But when it becomes an economic problem, a stark matter of bread and butter, then if this young, black

American is going to survive and live a life, he must calmly face the fact that however much he is an American there are interests which draw him nearer to the dark people outside of America than to his white fellow citizens.

And those interests are the same matters of color caste, of discrimination, of exploitation for the sake of profit, of public insult and oppression, against which the colored peoples of Mexico, South America, the West Indies and all Africa, and every country in Asia, complain and have long been complaining. It is, therefore, simply a matter of ordinary common sense that these people should draw together in spiritual sympathy and intellectual co-operation, to see what can be done for the freedom of the human spirit which happens to be incased in dark skin.

This was the idea that was back of the Pan-African Congresses; started in Paris directly after the war, and carried on for several years. These Congresses brought upon themselves the active enmity and disparagement of all the colony-owning powers. Englishmen, Frenchmen, Belgians and others looked upon the movement as a political movement designed to foment disaffection and strife and to correct abuse by force.

It may be that in the end nothing but force will break down the injustice of the color line. But to us who have seen and known the futility of war, the ghastly paradox of talking about Victor and Vanquished in the last world holocaust, there is a feeling that we must desperately try methods of thought and co-operation and economic re-adjustment before we yield to councils of despair. And in this program, all that has been said about economic readjustment in America for American Negroes can be said with even more emphasis concerning the Negroes of the world and concerning the darker peoples. These people raise everything necessary to satisfy human wants. They are capable of carrying on every process by which material, transported and re-made, may satisfy the needs and appetites of men. They are all of them willing and eager to work, and yet because their work is misdirected in order to make a profit for white people, these dark people must starve and be unemployed.

Here in the United States the net result of the National Recovery Act so far has been to raise wages for a small number of favored white workers and to decrease wages or push out of employment entirely the Negro. It is possible that this present result may in time be changed, and we note with interest what Secretary Ickes has said to the State Engineers and Public Works Administration:

> It is important to bear in mind that the Public Works Administration is for the benefit of all the people of the country. The established policy in the construction of public buildings and public works under its control is that in the employment of mechanics and labor, preference be given to local labor to the extent that it is available and competent, and that there be no discrimination exercised against any person because of color or religious affiliation.

Nevertheless, this we feel is going to make little difference so long as the American people believe that any white man of whatever character or education is better than any possible colored man.

It is, therefore, imperative that the colored peoples of the world, and first of all those of Negro descent, should begin to concentrate upon this problem of their economic survival, the best of their brains and education. Pan-Africa means intellectual understanding and co-operation among all groups of Negro descent in order to bring about at the earliest possible time the industrial and spiritual emancipation of the Negro peoples.

Such a movement must begin with a certain spiritual housecleaning. American Negroes, West Indians, West Africans and South Africans must proceed immediately to wipe from their minds the preconcepts of each other which they have gained through white newspapers. They must cease to think of Liberia and Haiti as failures in government; of American Negroes as being engaged principally in frequenting Harlem cabarets and Southern lynching parties; of West Indians as ineffective talkers; and of West Africans as parading around in breech-clouts.

These are the pictures of each other which white people have painted for us and which with engaging naiveté we accept, and then proceed to laugh at each other and criticize each other before we make any attempt to learn the truth. There are, for instance, in the United States today several commendable groups of young people who are proposing to take hold of Liberia and emancipate her from her difficulties, quite forgetting the fact that Liberia belongs to Liberia. They made it. They suffered and died for it. And they are not handing over their country to any group of young strangers who happen to be interested. If we want to help Liberia, our business is to see in what respect the Liberians need help, and the persons best able to give this information are the Liberians themselves.

It is a large and intricate problem but the sooner we put ourselves in position to study it with a vast and increasing area of fact and with carefully guided and momentarily tested effort, the sooner we shall find ourselves citizens of the world and not its slaves and pensioners.

November, 1933

SEGREGATION

JIM CROW

We colored folk stand at the parting of ways, and we must take counsel. The objection to segregation and "Jim Crowism" was in other days the fact that compelling Negroes to associate only with Negroes meant to exclude them from contact with the best culture of the day. How could we learn manners or get knowledge if the heritage of the past was locked away from us?

Gradually, however, conditions have changed. Culture is no longer the monopoly of the white nor is poverty and ignorance the sole heritage of the black. Many a colored man in our day called to conference with his own and dreading the contact with uncivilized people even though they were of his own blood has been astonished and deeply gratified at the kind of people he has met—at the evidence of good manners and thoughtfulness among his own.

This together with the natural human love of herding like with like has in the last decade set up a tremendous current within the colored race against any contact with whites that can be avoided. They have welcomed separate racial institutions. They have voluntarily segregated themselves and asked for more segregation. The North is full of instances of practically colored schools which colored people have demanded and, of course, the colored church and social organizations of every sort are ubiquitous.

Today both these wings of opinion are getting suspicious of each other and there are plenty of whites to help the feeling along. Whites and Blacks ask the Negro who fights separation: "Are you ashamed of your race?" Blacks and Whites ask the Negro who welcomes separation: "Do you want to give up your rights? Do you acknowledge your inferiority?"

Neither attitude is correct. Segregation is impolitic, because it is impossible. You can not build up a logical scheme of a self-sufficing, separate Negro America inside America or a Negro world with no close relations to the white world. If there are relations between races they must be based on the knowledge and sympathy that come alone from the long and intimate human contact of individuals.

On the other hand, if the Negro is to develop his own power and gifts; if he is not only to fight prejudices and oppression successfully, but also to unite for ideals higher than the world has realized in art and industry and social life, then he must unite and work with Negroes and build a new and great Negro ethos.

Here, then, we face the curious paradox and we remember contradictory facts. Unless we had fought segregation with determination, our whole race would have been pushed into an ill-lighted, unpaved, un-sewered ghetto. Unless we had built great church organizations and manned our own southern schools, we should be shepherdless sheep. Unless we had welcomed the segregation of Fort Des Moines, we would have had no officers in the National Army. Unless we had beaten open the doors of northern universities, we would have had no men fit to be officers.

Here is a dilemma calling for thought and forbearance. Not every builder of racial co-operation and solidarity is a "Jim Crow" advocate, a hater of white folk. Not every Negro who fights prejudice and segregation is ashamed of his race.

(January, 1919. Vol. XVII, No. 3, pp. 112-13)

THE RIGHT TO WORK

We have been taught to regard the industrial system today as fixed and permanent. Our problem has been looked upon as the static one of adjusting ourselves to American industry and entering it on its own terms. Our first awakening came when we found that the technique of industry changes so fast and the machine displaces and modifies human labor in so many ways, that it is practically impossible for our Negro industrial schools to equip themselves so as to train youth for current work, while the actual shops and apprentice systems are largely closed to us.

Our second lesson is to realize that the whole industrial system in the United States and in the world is changing and will change radically, either by swift evolution or here and there by revolution; and instead of our sitting like dumb and patient fools awaiting the salvation of the white industrial Lord, it is our duty now to prepare for a new organization and a new status, new modes of making a living, and a new organization of industry.

It is immaterial to us whether this change in the surrounding white world comes in ten, twenty-five or one hundred years. The fact is that the change is inevitable. No system of human culture can stand world war and industrial cataclysm repeatedly, without radical reorganization, either by reasoned reform or irrational collapse.

————————

What, then, shall we do? What can we do? Parties of reform, of socialism and communism beckon us. None of these offers us anything concrete or dependable. From Brook Farm down to the L.I.P.A., the face of reform has been set to lift the white producer and consumer, leaving the black man and his peculiar problems severely alone, with the fond hope that better white men will hate Negroes less and better white conditions make race contact more human and respectable. This has sometimes happened, but more often it has not.

Socialists and Communists assume that state control of industry by a majority of citizens or by a dictatorship of laborers, is going in some magic way to abolish race prejudice of its own accord without special effort or special study or special plan; and they want us Negroes to assume on faith that this will be the result.

Yet nothing in the history of American socialism gives us the slightest assurance on this point, and with American communism led by a group of pitiable mental equipment, who give no thought to the intricacies of the American situation, the vertical and horizontal divisions of the American working classes; and who plan simply to raise hell on any and all occasions, with Negroes as shock troops,—these offer in reality nothing to us except social equality in jail.

On the other hand, we would be idiots not to recognize the imminence of industrial change along socialistic and even communistic lines, which the American revolution sooner or later is bound to take. If we simply mill contentedly after the streaming herd, with no clear idea of our own solutions of our problem, what can we expect but the contempt of reformers and slavery to a white proletariat? If we expect to enter present or future industry upon our own terms, we must have terms; we must have power; we must learn the secret of economic organization; we must submit to leadership, not of words but of ideas; we must weld the civilized part of these 12 millions of our race into an industrial phalanx that cannot be ignored, and which America and the world will come to regard as a strong asset under any system and not merely as a weak and despicable liability.

What, then, shall we do? We cannot use the power of a State because we do not form a State. We cannot dictate as a proletariat, because we are a minority, and not, as Marxism and Socialism usually assume, an overwhelming majority with power in the reach of its outstretched arms.

On the contrary, we are a despised minority, whose social chains are not loosed, and who have the contempt of the white workers, even more than of capitalists and investors. Despite this, we are strong. Our unrealized strength is so enormous that the world wonders at our stupid apathy. We are physically able to survive slavery, lynching, debauchery, mob-rule, cheating and poverty, and yet remain the most prolific, original element in America, with good health and strength. We have brains, energy, and even taste and genius. From our depths of poverty, we have amassed some wealth. Out of charity, our schools, colleges and universities are growing to be real centers of learning, and Negro literature and art has been distilled from our blood and sweat. There is no way of keeping us in continued industrial slavery, unless we continue to enslave ourselves, and remain content to work as servants for white folk and dumb driven laborers for nothing.

What can we do? We can work for ourselves. We can consume mainly what we ourselves produce, and produce as large a proportion as possible of that which we consume.

Going back to the preaching of Robert Owen and Charles Fourier, we can by consumers and producers cooperation, by phalanstères and garden cities, establish a progressively self-supporting economy that will weld the majority of our people into an impregnable, economic phalanx.

I am aware of the gale of laughter which such a proposal produces, not only from fools, but from serious students of economics. Of course, we are told, that 1848 scotched socialism; that "labor exchanges" failed; that New Harmony died; that Proudhon's Bank of Exchange became a joke; and much else in this line. But the basic idea beneath all this did not fail, as thousands of successful co-operatives throughout the world testify; as Denmark and Russia are living witnesses; as the working men's homes of Vienna prove. Remember production is already gone co-operative with technocratic control, oligarchic ownership and built on Democratic stupidity under a plutocracy. Consumption in all America is disorganized, blind and bamboozled by lying advertising and "high-powered" selling. Why may not Negroes begin consumers' co-operation under intelligent democratic control and expand at least to the productive and consuming energy of this one group? There would be white monopoly and privilege to fight, but only stupidity and disloyalty could actually stop progress. Expell both unflinchingly.

Moreover, our strength in Negro America lies in many respects precisely where the weaknesses of former cooperation and association lurked. We have a motive such as they never had. We are fleeing, not simply from poverty, but from insult and murder and social death. We have an instinct of race and a bond of color, in place of a protective tariff for our infant industry. We have, as police power, social ostracism within to coerce a race thrown back upon itself by ostracism without; and behind us, if we will survive, is Must, not May.

Negro American consumer's cooperation will cost us something. It will mean inner subordination and obedience. It will call for inflexible discipline. It will mean years of poverty and sacrifice, but not aimless, rather to one great End. It will invite ridicule, retaliation and discrimination. All this and more. But if we succeed, we have conquered a world. No future revolution can ignore us. No nation, here or elsewhere, can oppress us. No capital can enslave us. We open the gates, not only to our own twelve millions, but to five million West Indians, and eight million black South Americans, and one hundred and fifty million and more Africans. We stretch hands and hands of strength and sinew and understanding to India and China, and all Asia. We become in truth, free.

(April, 1933. Vol. XL, No. 4, pp. 93-4)

THE NEGRO COLLEGE

It has been said many times that a Negro University is nothing more and nothing less than a university. Quite recently one of the great leaders of education in the United States, Abraham Flexner, said something of that sort concerning Howard. As President of the Board of Trustees, he said he was seeking to build not a Negro university, but a University. And by those words he brought again before our eyes the ideal of a great institution of learning which becomes a center of universal culture. With all good will toward them that say such words—it is the object of this paper to insist that there can be no college for Negroes which is not a Negro college and that while an American Negro university, just like a German or Swiss university may rightly aspire to a universal culture unhampered by limitations of race and culture, yet it must start on the earth where we sit and not in the skies whither we aspire. May I develop this thought.

In the first place, we have got to remember that here in America, in the year 1933, we have a situation which cannot be ignored. There was a time when it seemed as though we might best attack the Negro problem by ignoring its most unpleasant features. It was not and is not yet in good taste to speak generally about certain facts which characterize our situation in America. We are politically ham-strung. We have the greatest difficulty in getting suitable and remunerative work. Our education is more and more not only being confined to our own schools but to a segregated public school system far below the average of the nation with one-third of our children continuously out of school. And above all, and this we like least to mention, we suffer social ostracism which is so deadening and discouraging that we are compelled either to lie about it or to turn our faces to the red flag of revolution. It consists of studied and repeated and emphasized public insult of the sort which during all the long history of the world has led men to kill or be killed. And in the full face of any effort which any black man may make to escape this ostracism for himself, stands this flaming sword of racial doctrine which will distract his effort and energy if it does not lead him to spiritual suicide.

We boast and have right to boast of our accomplishment between the days that I studied here* and this 45th Anniversary of my graduation. It is a calm appraisal of fact to say that the history of modern civilization cannot surpass if it can parallel the advance of American Negroes in every essential line of culture in these years. And yet, when we have said this we must have the common courage honestly to admit that every step we have made forward has been greeted by a step backward on the part of the American public in caste intolerance, mob law and racial hatred.

I need but remind you that when I graduated from Fisk there was no "Jim Crow" car in Tennessee and I saw Hunter of '89 once sweep a brakeman aside at the Union Station and escort a crowd of Fisk students into the first class seats for which they had paid. There was no legal disfranchisement and a black Fiskite sat in the Legislature; and while the Chancellor of the Vanderbilt University had annually to be re-introduced to the President of Fisk, yet no white Southern group presumed to

*[Fisk University, where this address was delivered in June, 1933—ed.]

dictate the internal social life of this institution.

Manifestly with all that can be said, pro and con, and in extenuation, and by way of excuse and hope, this is the situation and we know it. There is no human way by which these facts can be ignored. We cannot do our daily work, sing a song or write a book or carry on a university and act as though these things were not.

If this is true, then no matter how much we may dislike the statement, the American Negro problem is and must be the center of the Negro American university. It has got to be. You are teaching Negroes. There is no use pretending that you are teaching Chinese or that you are teaching white Americans or that you are teaching citizens of the world. You are teaching American Negroes in 1933, and they are the subjects of a caste system in the Republic of the United States of America and their life problem is primarily this problem of caste.

Upon these foundations, therefore, your university must start and build. Nor is the thing so entirely unusual or unheard of as it sounds. A university in Spain is not simply a university. It is a Spanish university. It is a university located in Spain. It uses the Spanish language. It starts with Spanish history and makes conditions in Spain the starting point of its teaching. Its education is for Spaniards,—not for them as they may be or ought to be, but as they are with their present problems and disadvantages and opportunities.

In other words, the Spanish university is founded and grounded in Spain, just as surely as a French university is French. There are some people who have difficulty in apprehending this very clear truth. They assume, for instance, that the French university is in a singular sense universal, and is based on a comprehension and inclusion of all mankind and of their problems. But it is not so, and the assumption that it is arises simply because so much of French culture has been built into universal civilization. A French university is founded in France; it uses the French language and assumes a knowledge of French history. The present problems of the French people are its major problems and it becomes universal only so far as other peoples of the world comprehend and are at one with France in its mighty and beautiful history.

In the same way, a Negro university in the United States of America begins with Negroes. It uses that variety of the English idiom which they understand; and above all, it is founded or it should be founded on a knowledge of the history of their people in Africa and in the United States, and their present condition. Without white-washing or translating wish into fact, it begins with that; and then it asks how shall these young men and women be trained to earn a living and live a life under the circumstances in which they find themselves or with such changing of those circumstances as time and work and determination will permit.

Is this statement of the field of a Negro university a denial of aspiration or a change from older ideals? I do not think it is, although I admit in my own mind some change of thought and modification of method. The system of learning which bases itself upon the actual condition of certain classes and groups of human beings is tempted to suppress a minor premise of fatal menace. It proposes that the knowledge given and the methods pursued in such institutions of learning shall be for the definite object of perpetuating present conditions or of leaving their amelioration in the hands of and at the initiative of other forces and other folk. This was the great criticism that those of us who fought for higher education of Negroes thirty years ago, brought against the industrial school.

The industrial school founded itself and rightly upon the actual situation of American Negroes and said: "What can be done to change this situation?" And its answer was: "A training in technique and method such as would incorporate the disadvantaged group into the industrial organization of the country," and in that organization the leaders of the Negro had perfect faith. Since that day the industrial machine has cracked and groaned. Its technique has changed faster than any school could teach; the relations of capital and labor have increased in complication and it has become so clear that Negro poverty is not primarily caused by ignorance of technical knowledge that the industrial school has almost surrendered its program.

In opposition to that, the opponents of college training in those earlier years said: "What black men need is the broader and more universal training so that they can apply the general principle of knowledge to the particular circumstances of their condition."

Here again was the indubitable truth but incomplete truth. The technical problem lay in the method of teaching this broader and more universal truth and here just as in the industrial program, we must start where we are and not where we wish to be.

As I said a few years ago at Howard University, both these positions had thus something of truth and right. Because of the peculiar economic situation in our country the program of the industrial school came to grief first and has practically been given up. Starting even though we may with the actual condition of the Negro peasant and artisan, we cannot ameliorate his condition simply by learning a trade which is the technique of a passing era. More vision and knowledge is needed than that. But on the other hand, while the Negro college of a generation ago set down a defensible and true program of applying knowledge to facts, it unfortunately could not completely carry it out, and it did not carry it out, because the one thing that the industrial philosophy gave to education, the Negro college did not take and that was that the university education of black men in the United States must be grounded in the condition and work of those black men!

On the other hand, it would be of course idiotic to say, as the former industrial philosophy almost said, that so far as most black men are concerned education must stop with this. No, starting with present conditions and using the facts and the knowledge of the present situation of American Negroes, the Negro university expands toward the possession and the conquest of all knowledge. It seeks from a beginning of the history of the Negro in America and in Africa to interpret all history; from a beginning of social development among Negro slaves and freedmen in America and Negro tribes and kingdoms in Africa, to interpret and understand the social development of all mankind in all ages. It seeks to reach modern science of matter and life from the surroundings and habits and aptitudes of American Negroes and thus lead up to understanding of life and matter in the universe.

And this is a different program than a similar function would be in a white university or in a Russian university or in an English university, because it starts from a different point. It is a matter of beginnings and integrations of one group which sweep instinctive knowledge and inheritance and current reactions into a universal world of science, sociology and art. In no other way can the American Negro College function. It cannot begin with history and lead to Negro History. It cannot start with sociology and lead to Negro sociology.

Why was it that the Renaissance of literature which began among Negroes ten years ago has never taken real and lasting root? It was because it was a transplanted and exotic thing. It was a literature written for the benefit of white people and at the behest of white readers, and starting out privately from the white point of view. It never had a real Negro constituency and it did not grow out of the inmost heart and frank experience of Negroes; on such an artificial basis no real literature can grow.

On the other hand, if starting in a great Negro university you have knowledge, beginning with the particular, and going out to universal comprehension and unhampered expression, you are going to begin to realize for the American Negro the full life which is denied him now. And then after that comes a realization of the older object of our college—to bring this universal culture down and apply it to the individual life and individual conditions of living Negroes.

The university must become not simply a center of knowledge but a center of applied knowledge and guide of action. And this is all the more necessary now since we easily see that planned action especially in economic life, is going to be the watchword of civilization.

If the college does not thus root itself in the group life and afterward apply its knowledge and culture to actual living, other social organs must replace the college in this function. A strong, intelligent family life may adjust the student to higher culture; and, too, a social clan may receive the graduate and induct him into life. This has happened and is happening among a minority of privileged people. But it costs society a fatal price. It tends to hinder progress and hamper change; it makes Education, propaganda for things as they are. It leaves the mass of those without family training and without social standing misfits and rebels who despite their education are uneducated in its meaning and application. The only college which stands for the progress of all, mass as well as aristocracy, functions in root and blossom as well as in the overshadowing and heaven-filling tree. No system of learning—no university can be universal before it is German, French, Negro. Grounded in inexorable fact and condition, in Poland, Italy or elsewhere, it may seek the universal and haply it may find it—and finding it, bring it down to earth and us.

We have imbibed from the surrounding white world a childish idea of Progress. Progress means bigger and better results always and forever. But there is no such rule of Life. In 6000 years of human culture, the losses and retrogressions have been enormous. We have no assurance this twentieth century civilization will survive. We do not know that American Negroes will survive. There are sinister signs about us, antecedent to and unconnected with the Great Depression. The organized might of industry north and south is relegating the Negro to the edge of survival and using him as a labor reservoir on starvation wage. No secure professional class, no science, literature, nor art can live on such a sub-soil. It is an insistent, deep-throated cry for rescue, guidance and organized advance that greets the black leader today, and the college that trains him has got to let him know at least as much about the great black miners' strike in Alabama as about the age of Pericles.

We are on the threshold of a new era. Let us not deceive ourselves with outworn ideals of wealth and servants and luxuries, reared on a foundation of ignorance, starvation and want. Instinctively, we have absorbed these ideals from our twisted white American environment. This new economic planning is not for us unless we do it. Unless the American Negro today, led by trained university men of broad vision, sits down to work out by economics and mathematics, by physics and chemistry, by history and sociology, exactly how and where he is to earn a living and how he is to establish a reasonable Life in the United States or elsewhere—unless this is done, the university has missed its field and function and the American Negro is doomed to be a suppressed and inferior caste in the United States for incalculable time.

Here, then, is a job for the American Negro university. It cannot be successfully ignored or dodged without the growing menace of disaster. I lay the problem before you as one which you must not ignore.

To carry out this plan, two things and only two things are necessary,—teachers and students. Buildings and endowments may help, but they are not indispensable. It is necessary first to have teachers who comprehend this program and know how to make it live among their students. This is calling for a good deal, because it asks that teachers teach that which they have learned in no American school and which they never will learn until we have a Negro university of the sort that I am visioning. No teacher, black or white, who comes to a university like Fisk, filled simply with general ideas of human culture or general knowledge of disembodied science, is going to make a university of this school. Because a university is made of human beings, learning of the things they do not know from the things they do know in their own lives.

And secondly, we must have students. They must be chosen for their ability to learn. There is always the temptation to assume that the children of privileged classes, the rich, the noble, the white, are those who can best take education. One has but to express this to realize its utter futility. But perhaps the most dangerous thing among us is for us, without thought, to imitate the white world and assume that we can choose students at Fisk because of the amount of money which their parents have happened to get hold of. That basis of selection is going to give us an extraordinary aggregation. We want, by the nicest methods possible, to seek out the talented and the gifted among our constituency, quite regardless of their wealth or position, and to fill this university and similar institutions with persons who have got brains enough to take fullest advantage of what the university offers. There is no other way. With teachers who know what they are teaching and whom they are teaching, and the life that surrounds both the knowledge and the knower, and with students who have the capacity and the will to absorb this knowledge, we can build the sort of Negro university which will emancipate not simply the black folk of the United States, but those white folk who in their effort to suppress Negroes have killed their own culture.

Men in their desperate effort to replace equality with caste and to build inordinate wealth on a foundation of abject poverty have succeeded in killing democracy, art and religion.

Only a universal system of learning, rooted in the will and condition of the masses and blossoming from that manure up toward the stars is worth the name. Once builded it can only grow as it brings down sunlight and starshine and impregnates the mud.

The chief obstacle in this rich land endowed with every national resource and with the abilities of a hundred different peoples—the chief and only obstacle to the coming of that kingdom of economic equality which is the only logical end of work, is the determination of the white world to keep the black world poor and make themselves rich. The disaster which this selfish and short-sighted policy has brought, lies at the bottom of this present depression, and too, its cure lies beside it. Your clear vision of a world without wealth, of capital without profit, of income based on work alone, is the path out not only for you but for all men.

Is not this a program of segregation, emphasis of race and particularism as against national unity and universal humanity? It is and it is not by choice but by force; you do not get humanity by wishing it nor do you become American citizens simply because you want to. A Negro university, from its high ground of unfaltering facing of the Truth, from its unblinking stare at hard facts does not advocate segregation by race; it simply accepts the bald fact that we are segregated, apart, hammered into a separate unity by spiritual intolerance and legal sanction backed by mob law, and that this separation is growing in strength and fixation; that it is worse today than a half century ago and that no character, address, culture or desert is going to change it in our day or for centuries to come. Recognizing this brute fact, groups of cultured, trained and devoted men gathering in great institutions of learning proceed to ask: What are we going to do about it? It is silly to ignore the gloss of truth; it is idiotic to proceed as though we were white or yellow English or Russian. Here we stand. We are American Negroes. It is beside the point to ask whether we form a real race. Biologically we are mingled of all conceivable elements, but race is psychology, not biology; and psychologically we are a unified race with one history, one red memory and one revolt. It is not ours to argue whether we will be segregated or whether we ought to be a caste. We are segregated; we are a caste. This is our given and at present unalterable fact. Our problem is: How far and in what way can we consciously and scientifically guide our future so as to insure our physical survival, our spiritual freedom and our social growth? Either we do this or we die. There is no alternative. If America proposed the murder of this group, its moral descent into imbecility and crime and its utter loss of manhood, self-assertion and courage, the sooner we realize this the better. By that great line of McKay:

If we must die, let it not be like hogs.

But the alternative of not dying like hogs is not that of dying or killing like snarling dogs. It is rather conquering the world by thought and brain and plan; by expression and organized cultural ideals. Therefore let us not beat futile wings in impotent frenzy, but carefully plan and guide our segregated life, organize in industry and politics to protect it and expand it and above all to give it unhampered spiritual expression in art and literature. It is the counsel of fear and cowardice to say this cannot be done. What must be can be and it is only a question of Science and Sacrifice to bring the great consummation.

What that will be, no one knows. It may be a great physical segregation of the world along the Color Line; it may be an economic rebirth which ensures spiritual and group integrity amid physical diversity. It may be utter annihilation of class and race and color barriers in one ultimate mankind, differentiated by talent, susceptibility and gift—but any of these ends are matters of long centuries and not years. We live in years, swift-flying, transient years. We hold the possible future in our hands but not by wish and will, only by thought, plan, knowledge and organization. If the college can pour into the coming age an American Negro who knows himself and his plight and how to protect himself and fight race prejudice, then the world of our dream will come and not otherwise.

(August, 1933. Vol. XL, No. 4, pp. 175-7)

ON BEING ASHAMED OF ONESELF

An Essay on Race Pride

My Grandfather left a passage in his diary expressing his indignation at receiving an invitation to a "Negro" picnic. Alexander Du Bois, born in the Bahamas, son of Dr. James Du Bois of the well-known Du Bois family of Poughkeepsie, N. Y., had been trained as a gentleman in the Cheshire School of Connecticut, and the implications of a Negro picnic were anathema to his fastidious soul. It meant close association with poverty, ignorance and suppressed and disadvantaged people, dirty and with bad manners.

This was in 1856. Seventy years later, Marcus Garvey discovered that a black skin was in itself a sort of patent to nobility, and that Negroes ought to be proud of themselves and their ancestors, for the same or analogous reasons that made white folk feel superior.

Thus, within the space of three-fourths of a century, the pendulum has swung between race pride and race suicide, between attempts to build up a racial ethos and attempts to escape from ourselves. In the years between emancipation and 1900, the theory of escape was dominant. We were, by birth, law and training, American citizens. We were going to escape into the mass of Americans in the same way that the Irish and Scandinavians and even the Italians were beginning to disappear. The process was going to be slower on account of the badge of color; but then, after all, it was not so much the matter of physical assimilation as of spiritual and psychic amalgamation with the American people.

For this reason, we must oppose all segregation and all racial patriotism; we must salute the American flag and sing "Our Country 'Tis of Thee" with devotion and fervor, and we must fight for our rights with long and carefully planned campaign; uniting for this purpose with all sympathetic people, colored and white.

This is still the dominant philosophy of most American Negroes and it is back of the objection to even using a special designation like "Negro" or even "Afro-American" or any such term.

But there are certain practical difficulties connected with this program which are becoming more and more clear today. First of all comes the fact that we are still ashamed of ourselves and are thus stopped from valid objection when white folks are ashamed to call us human. The reasons of course, are not as emphatic as they were in the case of my grandfather. I remember a colored man, now ex-patriate, who made this discovery in my company, some twenty-five years ago. He was a handsome burning brown, tall, straight and well-educated, and he occupied a position which he had won, across and in spite of the color line. He did not believe in Negroes, for himself or his family, and he planned elaborately to escape the trammels of race. Yet, he had responded to a call for a meeting of colored folk which touched his interests, and he came. He found men of his own calibre and training; he found men charming and companionable. He was thoroughly delighted. I know that never before, or I doubt if ever since, he had been in such congenial company. He could not help mentioning his joy continually and reiterating it.

All colored folk had gone through the same experience, for more and more largely in the last twenty-five years, colored America has discovered itself; has discovered groups of people, association with whom is a poignant joy and despite their ideal of American assimilation, in more and more cases and with more and more determined object they seek each other.

That involves, however, a drawing of class lines inside the Negro race, and it means the emergence of a certain social aristocracy, who by reasons of looks and income, education and contact, form the sort of upper social group which the world has ong known and helped to manufacture and preserve. The early basis of this Negro group was simply color and a bald imitation of the white environment. Later, it tended, more and more, to be based on wealth and still more recently on education and social position.

This leaves a mass of untrained and uncultured colored folk and even of trained but ill-mannered people and groups of impoverished workers of whom this upper class of colored Americans are ashamed. They are ashamed both directly and indirectly, just as any richer or better sustained group in a nation is ashamed of those less fortunate and withdraws its skirts from touching them. But more than that, because the upper colored group is desperately afraid of being represented before American whites by this lower group, or being mistaken for them, or being treated as though they were part of it, they are pushed to the extreme of effort to avoid contact with the poorest classes of Negroes. This exaggerates, at once, the secret shame of being identified with such people and the anomaly of insisting that the physical characteristics of these folk which the upper class shares, are not the stigmata of degradation.

When, therefore, in offense or defense, the leading group of Negroes must make common cause with the masses of their own race, the embarrassment or hesitation becomes apparent. They are embarrassed and indignant because an educated man should be treated as a Negro, and that no Negroes receive credit for social standing. They are ashamed and embarrassed because of the compulsion of being classed with a mass of people over whom they have no real control and whose action they can influence only with difficulty and compromise and with every risk of defeat.

Especially is all natural control over this group difficult—I mean control of law and police, of economic power, of guiding standards and ideals, of news propaganda. On this comes even greater difficulty because of the incompatibility of any action which looks toward racial integrity and race action with previous ideals. What are we really aiming at? The building of a new nation or the integration of a new group into an old nation? The latter has long been our ideal. Must it be changed? Should it be changed? If we seek new group loyalty, new pride of race, new racial integrity—how, where, and by what method shall these things be attained? A new plan must be built up. It cannot be the mere rhodomontade and fatuous propaganda on which Garveyism was based. It has got to be far-sighted planning. It will involve increased segregation and perhaps migration. It will be pounced upon and aided and encouraged by every "nigger-hater" in the land.

Moreover, in further comment on all this, it may be pointed out that this is not the day for the experiment of new nations or the emphasis of racial lines. This is, or at least we thought it was, the day of the Inter-nation, of Humanity, and the disappearance of "race" from our vocabulary. Are we American Negroes seeking to move against, or into the face of this fine philosophy? Here then is the real problem, the real new dilemma between rights of American citizens and racial pride, which faces American Negroes today and which is not always or often clearly faced.

The situation is this: America, in denying equality of rights, of employment and social recognition to American Negroes, has said in the past that the Negro was so far below the average nation in social position, that he could not be recognized until he had developed further. In the answer to this, the Negro has eliminated five-sixths of his illiteracy according to official figures, and greatly increased the number of colored persons who have received education of the higher sort. They still are poor with a large number of delinquents and dependents. Nevertheless, their average situation in this respect has been greatly improved and, on the other hand, the emergence and accomplishment of colored men of ability has been undoubted. Notwithstanding this, the Negro is still a group apart, with almost no social recognition, subject to insult and discrimination, with income and wage far below the average of the nation and the most deliberately exploited industrial class in America. Even trained Negroes have increasing difficulty in making a living sufficient to sustain a civilized standard of life. Particularly in the recent vast economic changes, color discrimination as it now goes on, is going to make it increasingly difficult for the Negro to remain an integral part of the industrial machine or to increase his participation in accordance with his ability.

The integration of industry is making it more and more possible for executives to exercise their judgment in choosing for key positions, persons who can guide the industrial machine, and the exclusion of persons from such positions merely on the basis of race and color or even Negro descent is a widely recognized and easily defended prerogative. All that is necessary for any Christian American gentleman of high position and wide power to say in denying place and promotion to an eligible candidate is: "He is of Negro descent." The answer and excuse is final and all but universally accepted. For this reason, the Negro's opportunity in State directed industry and his opportunity in the great private organization of industry if not actually growing less, is certainly much smaller than his growth in education and ability. Either the industry of the nation in the future is to be conducted by private trusts or by government control. There seems in both to be little or no chance of advancement for the Negro worker, the educated artisan and the educated leader.

On the other hand, organized labor is giving Negroes less recognition today than ever. It has practically excluded them from all the higher lines of skilled work, on railroads, in machine-shops, in manufacture and in the basic industries. In agriculture, where the Negro has theoretically the largest opportunity, he is excluded from successful participation, not only by conditions common to all farmers, but by special conditions due to lynching, lawlessness, disfranchisement and social degradation.

Facing these indisputable facts, there is on the part of the leaders of public opinion in America, no effective response to our agitation or organized propaganda. Our advance in the last quarter century has been in segregated, racially integrated institutions and efforts and not in effective entrance into American national life. In Negro churches, Negro schools, Negro colleges, Negro business and Negro art and literature our advance has been determined and inspiring; but in industry, general professional careers and national life, we have fought battle after battle and lost more often than we have won. There seems no hope that America in our day will yield in its color or race hatred any substantial ground and we have no physical nor economic power, nor any alliance with other social or economic classes that will force compliance with decent civilized ideals in Church, State, industry or art.

The next step, then, is certainly one on the part of the Negro and it involves group action. It involves the organization of intelligent and earnest people of Negro descent for their preservation and advancement in America, in the West Indies and in Africa; and no sentimental distaste for racial or national unity can be allowed to hold them back from a step which sheer necessity demands.

A new organized group action along economic lines, guided by intelligence and with the express object of making it possible for Negroes to earn a better living and, therefore, more effectively to support agencies for social uplift, is without the slightest doubt the next step. It will involve no opposition from white America because they do not believe we can accomplish it. They expect always to be able to crush, insult, ignore and exploit 12,000,000 individual Negroes without intelligent organized opposition. This organization is going to involve deliberate propaganda for race pride. That is, it is going to start out by convincing American Negroes that there is no reason for their being ashamed of themselves; that their record is one which should make them proud; that their history in Africa and the world is a history of effort, success and trial, comparable with that of any other people.

Such measured statements can, and will be exaggerated. There will be those who will want to say that the black race is the first and greatest of races, that its accomplishments are most extraordinary, that its desert is most obvious and its mistakes negligible. This is the kind of talk we hear from people with the superiority complex among the white and the yellow race.

We cannot entirely escape it, since it is just as true, and just as false as such statements among other races; but we can use intelligence in modifying and restraining it. We can refuse deliberately to lie about our history, while at the same time taking just pride in Nefertari, Askia, Moshesh, Toussaint and Frederick Douglass, and testing and encouraging belief in our own ability by organized economic and social action.

There is no other way; let us not be deceived. American Negroes will be beaten into submission and degradation if they merely wait unorganized to find some place voluntarily given them in the new reconstruction of the economic world. They must themselves force their race into the new economic set-up and bring with them the millions of West Indians and Africans by peaceful organization for normative action or else drift into greater poverty, greater crime, greater helplessness until there is no resort but the last red alternative of revolt, revenge and war.

(September, 1933. Vol. XL, No. 9, pp. 199-200)

SEGREGATION

The thinking colored people of the United States must stop being stampeded by the word segregation. The opposition to racial segregation is not or should not be any distaste or unwillingness of colored people to work with each other, to cooperate with each other, to live with each other. The opposition to segregation is an opposition to discrimination. The experience in the United States has been that usually when there is racial segregation, there is also racial discrimination.

But the two things do not necessarily go together, and there should never be an opposition to segregation pure and simple unless that segregation does involve discrimination. Not only is there no objection to colored people living beside colored people if the surroundings and treatment involve no discrimination, if streets are well lighted, if there is water, sewerage and police protection, and if anybody of any color who wishes, can live in that neighborhood. The same way in schools, there is no objection to schools attended by colored pupils and taught by colored teachers. On the contrary, colored pupils can by our own contention be as fine human beings as any other sort of children, and we certainly know that there are no teachers better than trained colored teachers. But if the existence of such a school is made reason and cause for giving it worse housing, poorer facilities, poorer equipment and poorer teachers, then we do object, and the objection is not against the color of the pupils' or teachers' skins, but against the discrimination.

In the recent endeavor of the United States government to redistribute capital so that some of the disadvantaged groups may get a chance for development, the American Negro should voluntarily and insistently demand his share. Groups of communities and farms inhabited by colored folk should be voluntarily formed. In no case should there be any discrimination against white and blacks. But, at the same time, colored people should come forward, should organize and conduct enterprises, and their only insistence should be that the same provisions be made for the success of their enterprise that is being made for the success of any other enterprise. It must be remembered that in the last quarter of a century, the advance of the colored people has been mainly in the lines where they themselves working by and for themselves, have accomplished the greatest advance.

There is no doubt that numbers of white people, perhaps the majority of Americans, stand ready to take the most distinct advantage of voluntary segregation and cooperation among colored people. Just as soon as they get a group of black folk segregated, they use it as a point of attack and discrimination. Our counter-attack should be, therefore, against this discrimination; against the refusal of the South to spend the same amount of money on the black child as on the white child for its education; against the inability of black groups to use public capital; against the monopoly of credit by white groups. But never in the world should our fight be against association with ourselves because by that very token we give up the whole argument that we are worth associating with.

Doubtless, and in the long run, the greatest human development is going to take place under experiences of widest individual contact. Nevertheless, today such individual contact is made difficult and almost impossible by petty prejudice, deliberate and almost criminal propaganda and various survivals from prehistoric heathenism. It is impossible, therefore, to wait for the millennium of free and normal intercourse before we unite, to cooperate among themselves in groups of like-minded people and in groups of people suffering from the same disadvantages and the same hatreds.

It is the class-conscious working man uniting together who will eventually emancipate labor throughout the world. It is the race-conscious black man cooperating together in his own institutions and movements who will eventually emancipate the colored race, and the great step ahead today is for the American Negro to accomplish his economic emancipation through voluntary determined cooperative effort.

(January, 1934. Vol. XLI, No. 1, p. 20)

A FREE FORUM

From the day of its beginning, more than twenty-three years ago, THE CRISIS has sought to maintain a free forum for the discussion of the Negro problem. The Editor has had advantage in time and space for expressing his own opinion, but he has tried also to let other and radically antagonistic opinions have place for expression. And above all, he has sought not to make the N.A.A.C.P. responsible for his individual ideas.

To some this has seemed an anomaly. They have thought that the National Organ of an organization should always express officially what that organization thinks. But a moment of reflection will show that this is impossible. The thought of an organization is always in flux and is never definitely recorded until after long consideration. Meantime, a living periodical reflects opinions and not decisions. And it is for this reason that the editorials of THE CRISIS have always appeared as signed individual opinions of the Editor and not as the recorded decisions of the N.A.A.C.P. This has given vividness and flexibility to the magazine and at the same time has allowed differences of opinion to be thoroughly threshed out.

This policy so long continued will be carried on, we trust, even more vigorously in the year 1934. And just as in earlier years we discussed Social Equality at a time when there was no unity of opinion within or without the organization, so this year we are going to discuss Segregation and seek not dogma but enlightenment. For this purpose, we are earnestly asking not only that our readers read carefully what is going to be said, but also that they contribute their thoughts and experiences for the enlightenment of other readers. It goes without saying that we cannot publish all these contributions but we shall read them over and try honestly to reflect in these pages a new and changing philosophy concerning race segregation in the United States.

THE N.A.A.C.P. AND RACE SEGREGATION

There is a good deal of misapprehension as to the historic attitude of the National Association for the Advancement of Colored People and race segregation. As a matter of fact, the Association, while it has from time to time discussed the larger aspects of this matter, has taken no general stand and adopted no general philosophy. Of course its action, and often very effective action, has been in specific cases of segregation where the call for a definite stand was clear and decided. For instance, in the preliminary National Negro Convention which met in New York May 31st and June 1st, 1909, segregation was only mentioned in a protest against Jim Crow car laws and that because of an amendment by William M. Trotter. In the First Annual Report, January 1, 1911, the Association evolved a statement of its purpose, which said that "it seeks to uplift the colored men and women of this country by securing to them the full enjoyment of their rights as citizens, justice in all courts, and equality of opportunity everywhere." Later, this general statement was epitomized in the well-known declaration: "It conceives its mission to be the completion of the work which the great Emancipator began. It proposes to make a group of ten million Americans free from the lingering shackles of past slavery, physically free from peonage, mentally free from ignorance, politically free from disfranchisement, and socially free from insult." This phrase which I first wrote myself for the Annual Report of 1915 still expresses pregnantly the object of the N.A.A.C.P. and it has my own entire adherence.

It will be noted, however, that here again segregation comes in only by implication. Specifically, it was first spoken of in the

Second Report of the Association, January 1, 1912, when the attempt to destroy the property of Negroes in Kansas City because they had moved into a white section was taken up. This began our fight on a specific phase of segregation, namely, the attempt to establish a Negro ghetto by force of law. This phase of segregation we fought vigorously for years and often achieved notable victories in the highest courts of the land.

But it will be noted here that the N.A.A.C.P. expressed no opinion as to whether it might not be a feasible and advisable thing for colored people to establish their own residential sections, or their own towns; and certainly there was nothing expressed or implied that Negroes should not organize for promoting their own interests in industry, literature or art. Manifestly, here was opportunity for considerable difference of opinion, but the matter never was thoroughly threshed out.

The Association moved on to other matters of color discrimination: the "Full Crew" bills which led to dismissal of so many Negro railway employees; the "Jim Crow" car laws on railway trains and street cars; the segregation in government departments. In all these matters, the stand of the Association was clear and unequivocal: it held that it was a gross injustice to make special rules which discriminated against the color of employees or patrons.

In the Sixth Annual Report issued in March, 1916, the seven lines of endeavor of the Association included change of unfair laws, better administration of present laws, justice in the courts, stoppage of public slander, the investigation of facts, the encouragement of distinguished work by Negroes, and organizations.

Very soon, however, there came up a more complex question and that was the matter of Negro schools. The Association had avoided from the beginning any thoroughgoing pronouncement on this matter. In the resolutions of 1909, the conference asked: "Equal educational opportunites for all and in all the states, and that public school expenditure be the same for the Negro and white child." This of course did not touch the real problem of separate schools. Very soon, however, definite problems were presented to the Association: the exclusion of colored girls from the Oberlin dormitories in 1919; the discrimination in the School of Education at the University of Pennsylvania; and the Cincinnati fight against establishing a separate school for colored children, brought the matter squarely to the front. Later, further cases came; the Brooklyn Girls' High School, the matter of a colored High School in Indianapolis, and the celebrated Gary case.

Gradually, in these cases the attitude of the Association crystalized. It declared that further extension of segregated schools for particular races and especially for Negroes was unwise and dangerous, and the Association undertook in all possible cases to oppose such further segregation. It did not, however, for a moment feel called upon to attack the separate schools where most colored children are educated throughout the United States and it refrained from this not because it approved of separate schools, but because it was faced by a fact and not a theory. It saw no sense in tilting against windmills.

The case at Cheyney was a variation; here was an old and separate private school which became in effect though not in law a separate public normal school; and in the city of Philadelphia a partial system of elementary Negro schools was developed with no definite action on the part of the N.A.A.C.P.

It will be seen that in all these cases the Association was attacking specific instances and not attempting to lay down any general rule as to how far the advancement of the colored race in the United States was going to involve separate racial action and segregated organization of Negroes for certain ends.

To be sure, the overwhelming and underlying thought of the N.A.A.C.P. has always been that any discrimination based simply on race is fundamentally wrong, and that consequently purely racial organizations must have strong justification to be admissable. On the other hand, they faced certain unfortunate but undeniable facts. For instance, War came. The Negro was being drafted. No Negro officers were being commissioned. The N.A.A.C.P. asked for the admission of Negroes to the officers' schools. This was denied. There was only one further thing to do and that was to ask for a school for Negro officers. There arose a bitter protest among many Negroes against this movement. Nevertheless, the argument for it was absolutely unanswerable, and Joel E. Spingarn, Chairman of the Board, supported by the students of Howard University, launched a movement which resulted in the commissioning of seven hundred Negro officers in the A.E.F. In all the British Dominions, with their hundreds of millions of colored folk, there was not a single officer of known Negro blood. The American Negro scored a tremendous triumph against the Color Line by their admitted and open policy of segregation. This did not mean that Mr. Spingarn or any of the members of the N.A.A.C.P. thought it right that there should be a separate Negro camp, but they thought a separate Negro camp and Negro officers was infinitely better than no camp and no Negro officers and that was the only practical choice that lay before them.

Similarly, in the question of the Negro vote, the N.A.A.C.P. began in 1920 an attempt to organize the Negro vote and cast it in opposition to open enemies of the Negro race who were running for office. This was without doubt a species of segregation. It was appealing to voters on the grounds of race, and it brought for that reason considerable opposition. Nevertheless, it could be defended on the ground that the election of enemies of the Negro race was not only a blow to that race but to the white race and to all civilization. And while our attitude, even in the Parker case, has been criticized, it has on the whole found abundant justification.

The final problem in segregation presented to us was that of the Harlem Hospital. Here was a hospital in the center of a great Negro population which for years did not have and would not admit a single Negro physician to its staff. Finally, by agitation and by political power, Negroes obtained representation on the staff in considerable numbers and membership on the Board of Control. It was a great triumph. But it was accompanied by reaction on the part of whites and some Negroes who had opposed this movement, and an attempt to change the status of the hospital so that it would become a segregated Negro hospital, and so that presumably the other hospitals of the city would continue to exclude Negroes from their staffs. With this arose a movement to establish Negro hospitals throughout the United States.

Here was an exceedingly difficult problem. On the one hand, there is no doubt of the need of the Negro population for wider and better hospitalization; and of the demand on the part of Negro physicians for opportunities of hospital practice. This was illustrated by the celebrated Tuskegee hospital where nearly all the Negro veterans are segregated but where an efficient Negro staff has been installed. Perhaps nothing illustrates better than this the contradiction and paradox of the problem of race segregation in the United States, and the problem which the N.A.A.C.P. faced and still faces.

The N.A.A.C.P. opposed the initial establishment of the hospital at Tuskegee although it is doubtful if it would have opposed such a hospital in the North. On the other hand, once established, we fought to defend the Tuskegee hospital and give it widest opportunity.

In other words, the N.A.A.C.P. has never officially opposed separate Negro organizations—such as churches, schools and business and cultural organizations. It has never denied the recurrent necessity of united separate action on the part of Negroes for self-defense and self-development; but it has insistently and continually pointed out that such action is in any case a necessary evil involving often a recognition from within of the very color line which we are fighting without. That race pride and race loyalty, Negro ideals and Negro unity, have a place and function today, the N.A.A.C.P. never has denied and never can deny.

But all this simply touches the whole question of racial organization and initiative. No matter what we may wish or say, the vast majority of the Negroes in the United States are born in colored homes, educated in separate colored schools, attend separate colored churches, marry colored mates, and find their amusement in colored Y.M.C.A.'s and Y.W.C.A.'s. Even in their economic life, they are gradually being forced out of the place in industry which they occupied in the white world and are being compelled to seek their living among themselves. Here is segregation with a vengeance, and its problems must be met and its course guided. It would be idiotic simply to sit on the side lines and yell: "No segregation" in an increasingly segregated world.

On the other hand, the danger of easily and eagerly yielding to suggested racial segregation without reason or pressure stares us ever in the face. We segregate ourselves. We herd together. We do things such as this clipping from the *Atlanta Constitution* indicates:

> A lecture on the raising of Lazarus from the dead will be delivered at the city auditorium on Friday night. The Big Bethel choir will sing and the Graham Jackson band will give additional music. Space has been set aside for white people.

The "Jim Crow" galleries of Southern moving picture houses are filled with some of the best Negro citizens. Separate schools and other institutions have been asked by Negroes in the north when the whites had made no real demand.

Such are the flat and undeniable facts. What are we going to do about them? We can neither yell them down nor make them disappear by resolutions. We must think and act. It is this problem which THE CRISIS desires to discuss during the present year in all its phases and with ample and fair representation to all shades of opinion.

(February, 1934. Vol. XLI, No. 2, pp. 52-3)

SEPARATION AND SELF-RESPECT

What we continually face in this problem of race segregation in the United States is a paradox like this:

1. Compulsory separation of human beings by essentially artificial criteria, such as birth, nationality, language, color and race, is the cause of human hate, jealousy and war, and the destruction of talent and art.

2. Where separation of mankind into races, groups and classes is compulsory, either by law or custom, and whether that compulsion be temporary or permanent, the only effective defense that the segregated and despised group has against complete spiritual and physical disaster, is internal self-organization for self-respect and self-defense.

The dilemma is complete and there is no escape. The black man born in South Carolina has a right and a duty to complain that any public school system separated by artificial race and class lines is needlessly expensive, socially dangerous, and spiritually degrading. And yet that black man will send his child to a Negro school, and he will see to it, if he is really a man, that this Negro school is the best possible school; that it is decently housed and effectively taught by well-trained teachers. He will demand a voice in its control, finances and curriculum, and any action of his that asks for less than this will mark him as an idiot or a coward.

A black man born in Boston has a right to oppose any separation of schools by color, race or class. He has a duty to insist that the public school attended by all kinds and conditions of people, is the best and only door to true democracy and human understanding. But this black man in Boston has no right, after he has made this academic pronouncement to send his own helpless immature child into school where white children kick, cuff or abuse him, or where teachers openly and persistently neglect or hurt or dwarf its soul. If he does, he must not be surprised if the boy lands in the gutter or penitentiary. Moreover, our Boston brother has no right to sneer at the "Jim-Crow" schools of South Carolina, or at the brave teachers who guide them at starvation wage; nor can he conscientiously advise the South Carolinian to move to Boston and join the bread lines.

Let the N.A.A.C.P. and every upstanding Negro pound at the closed gates of opportunity and denounce caste and segregation; but let us not punish our own children under the curious impression that we are punishing our white oppressors. Let us not affront our own self-respect by accepting a proffered equality which is not equality, or submitting to discrimination simply because it does not involve actual and open segregation; and above all, let us not sit down and do nothing for self-defense and self-organization just because we are too stupid or too distrustful of ourselves to take vigorous and decisive action.

HISTORY OF SEGREGATION PHILOSOPHY

Race segregation in the United States too often presents itself as an individual problem; a question of my admission to this church or that theater; a question as to whether I shall live and work in Mississippi or New York for my own enjoyment, emolument or convenience.

In fact this matter of segregation is a group matter with long historic roots. When Negroes were first brought to America in any numbers, their classification was economic rather than racial. They were in law and custom classed with the laborers, most of whom were brought from Europe under a contract which made them practically serfs. In this laboring class there was at first no segregation, there was some inter-marriage and when the laborer gained his freedom, he became in numbers of cases a landholder and a voter.

The first distinction arose between laborers who had come from Europe and contracted to work for a term of years, and laborers from Africa and the West Indies who had made no contract. Both classes were often held for life, but soon there arose a distinction between servants for a term of years and servants for life. Even their admission to a Christian church organization was usually considered as emancipating a servant for life, and thus again the purely racial segregation was cut across by religious considerations.

Finally, however, slavery became a matter of racial caste, so that white laborers served for definite terms and most black workers served for life. But even here anomaly arose in the case of the small number of Negroes who were free. For a while these free Negroes were not definitely segregated from other free workers, but gradually they were forced together as a caste, holding themselves, on the one hand, strictly away from the slaves, and on the other, being excluded more and ‧ more severely from inter-course with whites of all degrees.

The result was that there grew up in the minds of the free Negro class a determination and a prejudice which has come down to our day. They fought bitterly with every means at their command against being classed with the mass of slaves. It was for this reason that they objected to being called Negroes. Negroes was synonymous with slaves. They were not slaves. They objected to being coupled with black folk by legislation or custom. Any such act threatened their own freedom. They developed, therefore, both North and South as a separate, isolated group. In large Southern cities, like New Orleans, Savannah and Charleston, they organized their own society, established schools and churches, and made themselves a complete segregated unit, except in their economic relations where they earned a living among the whites as artisans and servants, rising here and there to be semi-professional men and small merchants. The higher they rose and the more definite and effective their organization, the more they protested against being called Negroes or classed with Negroes, because Negroes were slaves.

In the North, the development differed somewhat, and yet followed mainly the same lines. The groups of free colored folk in Boston, Newport, New Haven, New York, Philadelphia, Baltimore and Cincinnati, all formed small, carefully organized groups, with their own schools and churches, with their own social life, with their own protest against being classed as Negroes. As the mass of Negroes became free in the Northern states, certain decisions were forced upon these groups. Take for instance, Philadelphia. An event happened in April, 1787, which may be called by the American Negro, the Great Decision. The free colored people of Philadelphia at that time were making a desperate fight for recognition and decent social treatment.

Two of their leaders, Richard Allen and Absalom Jones, had proffered their services during the terrible epidemic in 1792, and partly at their own expense, helped bury the deserted dead of the white folk. The Mayor properly commended them. Both these men worshipped at St. George's Methodist Church, then at 4th and Vine Streets. For years they had been made welcome; but as gradual emancipation progressed in Pennsylvania, Negroes began to pour in to the city from the surrounding country, and black Christians became too numerous at St. George's. One Sunday morning during prayer, Jones and Allen were on their knees, when they were told they must get up and go to the gallery where hereafter black folk would worship. They refused to stir until the prayer was over, and then they got up and left the church. They never went back.

Under these circumstances, what would you have done, Dear Reader of 1934? There were several possibilities. You might have been able to impress it upon the authorities of the church that you were not like other Negroes; that you were different, with more wealth and intelligence, and that while it might be quite all right and even agreeable to you that other Negroes should be sent to the gallery, that you as an old and tried member of the church should be allowed to worship as you pleased. If you had said this, it probably would have had no effect upon the deacons of St. George's.

In that case, what would you have done? You could walk out of the church but whither would you walk? There were no other white churches that wanted you. Most of them would not have allowed you to cross their threshold. The others would have segregated you in the gallery or at a separate service. You might have said with full right and reason that the action of St. George's was un-Christian and despicable, and dangerous for the future of democracy in Philadelphia and in the United States. That was all quite true, and nevertheless its statement had absolutely no effect upon St. George's.

Walking out of this church, these two men formed an organization. It was called the Free African Society. Virtually it was confined to a colored membership, although some of the Quakers visited the meetings from time to time and gave advice. Probably there was some discussion of taking the group into the fellowship of the Quakers, but liberal as the Quakers were, they were not looking for Negro proselytes. They had had a few in the West Indies but not in the United States. The excluded Negroes found themselves in a dilemma. They could do one of two things: They could ask to be admitted as a segregated group in some white organization; or they could form their own organization. It was an historic decision and they did both.

Richard Allen formed from the larger part of the group, the African Methodist Episcopal Church, which today has 750,000 members and is without doubt the most powerful single Negro organization in the United States. Absalom Jones formed St. Thomas Church as a separate Negro church in the Episcopal communion, and the church has had a continuous existence down to our day.

Which of these two methods was best will be a matter of debate. There are those who think that it was saving something of principle to remain in a white church, even as a segregated body. There are others who say that this action was simply a compromise with the devil and that having been kicked out of the Methodist Church and not allowed equality in the Episcopal Church, there was nothing for a self-respecting man to do but to establish a church of his own.

No matter which solution seems to you wisest, segregation was compulsory, and the only answer to it was internal self-organization; and the answer that was inevitable in 1787, is just as inevitable in 1934.

(March, 1934. Vol. XLI, No. 3, pp. 85-86)

SEGREGATION IN THE NORTH

I have read with interest the various criticisms on my recent discussions of segregation. Those like that of Mr. Pierce of Cleveland, do not impress me. I am not worried about being inconsistent. What worries me is the Truth. I am talking about conditions in 1934 and not in 1910. I do not care what I said in 1910 or 1810 or in B.C. 700.

The arguments of Walter White, George Schuyler and Kelly Miller have logic, but they seem to me quite beside the point. In the first place, Walter White is white. He has more white companions and friends than colored. He goes where he will in New York City and naturally meets no Color Line, for the simple and sufficient reason that he isn't "colored"; he feels his new freedom in bitter contrast to what he was born to in Georgia. This is perfectly natural and he does what anyone else of his complexion would do.

But it is fantastic to assume that this has anything to do with the color problem in the United States. It naturally makes Mr. White an extreme opponent of any segregation based on a myth of race. But this argument does not apply to Schuyler or Miller or me. Moreover, Mr. White knows this. He moved once into a white apartment house and it went black on him. He now lives in a colored apartment house with attendant limitations. He once took a friend to dine with him at the celebrated café of the Lafayette Hotel, where he had often been welcomed. The management humiliated him by refusing to serve Roland Hayes.

The attitudes of Schuyler and Kelly Miller are historically based on the amiable assumption that there is little or no segregation in the North, and that agitation and a firm stand is making this disappear; that obvious desert and accomplishment by Negroes can break down prejudice. This is a fable. I once believed it passionately. It may become true in 250 or 1,000 years. Now it is not true. No black man whatever his culture or ability is today in America regarded as a man by any considerable number of white Americans. The difference between North and South in the matter of segregation is largely a difference of degree; of wide degree certainly, but still of degree.

In the North, neither Schuyler nor Kelly Miller nor anyone with a visible admixture of Negro blood can frequent hotels or restaurants. They have difficulty in finding dwelling places in better class neighborhoods. They occupy "Lower 1" on Pullmans, and if they are wise, they do not go into dining cars when any large number of white people is there. Their children either go to colored schools or to schools nominally for both races, but actually attended almost exclusively by colored children. In other words, they are confined by unyielding public opinion to a Negro world. They earn a living on colored newspapers or in colored colleges, or other racial institutions. They treat colored patients and preach to colored pews. Not one of the 12 colored Ph.D.'s of last year, trained by highest American and European standards, is going to get a job in any white university. Even when Negroes in the North work side by side with whites, they are segregated, like the postal clerks, or refused by white unions or denied merited promotion.

No matter how much we may fulminate about "No segregation," there stand the flat facts. Moreover, this situation has in the last quarter century been steadily growing worse. Mr. Spingarn may ask judicially as to whether or not the N.A.A.C.P. should change its attitude toward segregation. The point that he does not realize is that segregation has changed its attitude toward the N.A.A.C.P. The higher the Negro climbs or tries to climb, the more pitiless and unyielding the color ban. Segregation may be just as evil today as it was in 1910, but it is more insistent, more prevalent and more unassailable by appeal or argument. The pressing problem is: What are we going to do about it?

In 1910, colored men could be entertained in the best hotels in Cleveland, Detroit and Chicago. Today, there is not a single Northern city, except New York, where a Negro can be a guest at a first-class hotel. Not even in Boston is he welcome; and in New York, the number of hotels where he can go is very small. Roland Hayes was unable to get regular hotel accommodations, and Dr. Moton only succeeds by powerful white influence and by refraining from use of the public dining room or the public lobbies.

If as Spingarn asserts, the N.A.A.C.P. has conducted a quarter-century campaign against segregation, the net result has been a little less than nothing. We have by legal action steadied the foundation so that in the future, segregation must be by wish and will and not law, but beyond that we have not made the slightest impress on the determination of the overwhelming mass of white Americans not to treat Negroes as men.

These are unpleasant facts. We do not like to voice them. The theory is that by maintaining certain fictions of law and administration, by whistling and keeping our courage up, we can stand on the "principle" of no segregation and wait until public opinion meets our position. But can we do this? When we were living in times of prosperity; when we were making post-war incomes; when our labor was in demand, we perhaps could afford to wait. But today, faced by starvation and economic upheaval, and by the question of being able to survive at all in this land in the reconstruction that is upon us, it is ridiculous not to see, and criminal not to tell, the colored people that they can not base their salvation upon the empty reiteration of a slogan.

What then can we do? The only thing that we not only can, but must do, is voluntarily and insistently to organize our economic and social power, no matter how much segregation it involves. Learn to associate with ourselves and to train ourselves for effective association. Organize our strength as consumers; learn to co-operate and use machines and power as producers; train ourselves in methods of democratic control within our own group. Run and support our own institutions.

We are doing this partially now, only we are doing it under a peculiar attitude of protest, and with only transient and distracted interest. A number of excellent young gentlemen in Washington, having formed a Negro Alliance, proceed to read me out of the congregation of the righteous because I dare even discuss segregation. But who are these young men? The products of a segregated school system; the talent selected by Negro teachers; the persons who can today, in nine cases out of ten, earn only a living through segregated Negro social institutions. These are the men who are yelling against segregation. If most of them had been educated in the mixed schools in New York instead of the segregated schools of Washington, they never would have seen college, because Washington picks out and sends ten times as many Negroes to college as New York does.

It would, of course, be full easy to deny that this voluntary association for great social and economic ends is segregation; and if I had done this in the beginning of this debate, many people would have been easily deceived, and would have yelled

"No segregation" with one side of their mouths and "Race pride and Race initiative" with the other side. No such distinction can possibly be drawn. Segregation may be compulsory by law or it may be compulsory by economic or social condition, or it may be a matter of free choice. At any rate, it is the separation of human beings and separation despite the will to humanity. Such separation is evil; it leads to jealousy, greed, nationalism and war; and yet it is today and in this world inevitable; inevitable to Jews because of Hitler; inevitable to Japanese because of white Europe; inevitable to Russia because of organized greed over all the white world; inevitable to Ethiopia because of white armies and navies; inevitable, because without it, the American Negro will suffer evils greater than any possible evil of separation: we would suffer the loss of self-respect, the lack of faith in ourselves, the lack of knowledge about ourselves, the lack of ability to make a decent living by our own efforts and not by philanthropy.

This situation has been plunged into crisis and precipitated to an open demand for thought and action by the Depression and the New Deal. The government, national and state, is helping and guiding the individual. It has entered and entered for good into the social and economic organization of life. We could wish, we could pray, that this entrance could absolutely ignore lines of race and color, but we know perfectly well it does not and will not, and with the present American opinion, it cannot. The question is then, are we going to stand out and refuse the inevitable and inescapable government aid because we first wish to abolish the Color Line? This is not simply tilting at windmills; it is, if we are not careful, committing race suicide.

"No Segregation"

Back of all slogans lies the difficulty that the meanings may change without changing the words. For instance, "no segregation" may mean two very different things:

> 1. A chance for the Negro to advance without the hindrances which arise when he is segregated from the main group, and the main social institutions upon which society depends. He becomes, thus, an outsider, a hanger on, with no chance to function properly as a man.

2. It may mean utter lack of faith of Negroes in Negroes, and the desire to escape into another group, shirking, on the other hand, all responsibility for ignorance, degradation and lack of experience among Negroes, while asking admission into the other group on terms of full equality and with full chance for individual development.

It is in the first sense that I have always believed and used the slogan: "No Segregation." On the other hand, in the second sense, I have no desire or right to hinder or stop those persons who do not want to be Negroes. But I am compelled to ask the very plain and pertinent question: Assuming for the moment that the group into which you demand admission does not want you, what are you going to do about it? Can you demand that they want you? Can you make them by law or public opinion admit you when they are supreme over this same public opinion and make these laws? Manifestly, you cannot. Manifestly your admission to the other group on the basis of your individual desert and wish, can only be accomplished if they, too, join in the wish to have you. If they do so join, all problems based mostly on race and color disappear, and there remains only the human problems of social uplift and intelligence and group action. But there is in the United States today no sign that this objection to the social and even civic recognition of persons of Negro blood is going to occur during the life of persons now living. In which case there can be only one meaning to the slogan "No Segregation;" and that is, no hindrance to my effort to be a man. If you do not wish to associate with me, I am more than willing to associate with myself. Indeed, I deem it a privilege to work with and for Negroes, only asking that my hands be not tied nor my feet hobbled.

OBJECTS OF SEGREGATION

What is the object of those persons who insist by law, custom and propaganda to keep the American Negro separate in rights and privileges from other citizens of the United States? The real object, confessed or semiconscious, is to so isolate the Negro that he will be spiritually bankrupt, physically degenerate, and economically dependent.

Against this it is the bounden duty of every Negro and every enlightened American to protest; to oppose the policy so far as it is manifest by laws; to agitate against customs by revealing facts; and to appeal to the sense of decency and justice in all American citizens.

I have never known an American Negro who did not agree that this was a proper program. Some have disagreed as to the emphasis to be put on this and that method of protest; on the efficacy of any appeal against American prejudice; but all Negroes have agreed that segregation is bad and should be opposed.

Suppose, however, that this appeal is ineffective or nearly so? What is the Negro going to do? There is one thing that he can or must do, and that is to see to it that segregation does *not* undermine his health; does *not* leave him spiritually bankrupt; and does *not* make him an economic slave; and he must do this at any cost.

If he cannot live in sanitary and decent sections of a city, he must build his own residential quarters, and raise and keep them on a plane fit for living. If he cannot educate his children in decent schools with other children, he must, nevertheless, educate his children in decent Negro schools and arrange and conduct and oversee such schools. If he cannot enter American industry at a living wage, or find work suited to his education and talent, or receive promotion and advancement according to his deserts, he must organize his own economic life so that just as far as possible these discriminations will not reduce him to abject exploitation.

Everyone of these movements on the part of colored people are not only necessary, but inevitable. And at the same time, they involve more or less active segregation and acquiescence in segregation.

Here again, if there be any number of American Negroes who have not in practical life made this fight of self-segregation and self-association against the compulsory segregation forced upon them, I am unacquainted with such persons. They may, of course, explain their compulsory retreat from a great ideal, by calling segregation by some other name. They may affirm with fierce insistency that they will never, no never, under any circumstances acquiesce in segregation. But if they live in the

United States in the year of our Lord 1934, or in any previous year since the foundation of the government, they are segregated; they accept segregation, and they segregate themselves, because they must. From this dilemma I see no issue.

(April, 1934. Vol. XLI, No. 4, pp. 115-16)

THE BOARD OF DIRECTORS ON SEGREGATION

This is the vote which was proposed to the Board of Directors by W. E. B. Du Bois:

↑"The segregation of human beings purely on a basis of race and color, is not only stupid and unjust, but positively dangerous, since it is a path that leads straight to national jealousies, racial antagonisms, and war.↑

"The N.A.A.C.P., therefore, has always opposed the underlying principle of racial segregation, and will oppose it.

↑"On the other hand, it has, with equal clearness, recognized that when a group like the American Negroes suffers continuous and systematic segregation, against which argument and appeal are either useless or very slow in effecting changes, such a group must make up its mind to associate and co-operate for its own uplift and in defense of its self-respect. ↑

"The N.A.A.C.P., therefore, has always recognized and encouraged the Negro church, the Negro college, the Negro public school, Negro business and industrial enterprises, and believes they should be made the very best and most efficient institutions of their kind judged by any standard; not with the idea of perpetuating artificial separations of mankind, but rather with the distinct object of proving Negro efficiency, showing Negro ability and discipline, and demonstrating how useless and wasteful race segregation is."

This is the modification of the Du Bois proposal, as re-written by the Committee of Administration, and placed before the Board at its April meeting:

"The National Association for the Advancement of Colored People has always opposed the segregation of human beings on the basis of race and color. We have always as a basic principle of our organization opposed such segregation and we will always continue to oppose it.

"It is true that we have always recognized and encouraged the Negro church, the Negro college, the Negro school, and Negro business and industrial enterprises, and we shall continue to encourage them, so that they may serve as proofs of Negro efficiency, ability and discipline. Not merely external necessity but our faith in the genius of the Negro race has made us do this. But this does not alter our conviction that the necessity which has brought them into being is an evil, and that this evil should be combated to the greatest extent possible.

"We reserve to ourselves complete liberty of action in any specific case that may arise, since such liberty is essential to the statesmanship necessary to carry out any ideal; but we give assurance to the white and colored peoples of the world that this organization stands where it has always stood, as the chief champion of equal rights for black and white, and as unalterably opposed to the basic principle of racial segregation."

This is the resolution passed by the Board:

> The National Association for the Advancement of Colored People is opposed both to the principle and the practice of enforced segregation of human beings on the basis of race and color.
>
> Enforced segregation by its very existence carries with it the implication of a superior and inferior group and invariably results in the imposition of a lower status on the group deemed inferior. Thus both principle and practice necessitate unyielding opposition to any and every form of enforced segregation.

These proposals and this vote will be discussed in the June issue of THE CRISIS.

It would be interesting to know what the Board means by the resolution.

Does it mean that it does not approve of the Negro Church or believe in its segregated activities in its 26,000 edifices where most branches of the N.A.A.C.P. meet and raise money to support it?

Does it mean that it lends no aid or countenance to Fisk, Atlanta, Talladega, Hampton, Howard, Wiley and a dozen other Negro Colleges?

Does it disapprove of the segregated public school system where two million Negro children are taught by 50,000 Negro teachers?

Does it believe in 200 Negro newspapers which spread N.A.A.C.P. news and propaganda?

Does it disapprove of slum clearance like the Dunbar Apartments in New York, the Rosenwald Apartments in Chicago and the $2,000,000 projects in Atlanta?

Does it believe in Negro business enterprise of any sort?

Does it believe in Negro history, Negro literature and Negro art?

Does it believe in the Negro spirituals?

And if it does believe in these things is the Board of Directors of the N.A.A.C.P., afraid to say so?

(May, 1934. Vol. XLI, No. 5, p. 149)

COUNSELS OF DESPAIR

Many persons have interpreted my reassertion of our current attitude toward segregation as a counsel of despair. We can't win, therefore, give up and accept the inevitable. Never, and nonsense. Our business in this world is to fight and fight again, and never to yield. But after all, one must fight with his brains, if he has any. He gathers strength to fight. He gathers knowledge, and he raises children who are proud to fight and who know what they are fighting about. And above all, they learn that what they are fighting for is the opportunity and the chance to know and associate with black folk. They are not fighting to escape themselves. They are fighting to say to the world: the opportunity of knowing Negroes is worth so much to us and is so appreciated, that we want you to know them too.

Negroes are not extraordinary human beings. They are just like other human beings, with all their foibles and ignorance and mistakes. But they are human beings, and human nature is always worth knowing, and withal, splendid in its manifestations. Therefore, we are fighting to keep open the avenues of human contact; but in the meantime, we are taking every advantage of what opportunities of contact are already open to us, and among those opportunities which are open, and which are splendid and inspiring, is the opportunity of Negroes to work together in the twentieth century for the uplift and development of the Negro race. It is no counsel of despair to emphasize and hail the opportunity for such work.

THE ANTI-SEGREGATION CAMPAIGN

The assumptions of the anti-segregation campaign have been all wrong. This is not our fault, but it is our misfortune. When I went to Atlanta University to teach in 1897, and to study the Negro problem, I said, confidently, that the basic problem is our racial ignorance and lack of culture. That once Negroes know civilization, and whites know Negroes, then the problem is solved. This proposition is still true, but the solution is much further away that my youth dreamed. Negroes are still ignorant, but the disconcerting thing is that white people on the whole are just as much opposed to Negroes of education and culture, as to any other kind, and perhaps more so. Not all whites, to be sure, but the overwhelming majority.

Our main method, then, falls flat. We stop training ability. We lose our manners. We swallow our pride, and beg for things. We agitate and get angry. And with all that, we face the blank fact: Negroes are not wanted; neither as scholars nor as business men; neither as clerks nor as artisans; neither as artists nor as writers. What can we do about it? We cannot use force. We cannot enforce law, even if we get it on the statute books. So long as overwhelming public opinion sanctions and justifies and defends color segregation, we are helpless, and without remedy. We are segregated. We are cast upon ourselves, to an Island Within; "To your tents, Oh Israel!"

Surely then, in this period of frustration and disappointment, we must turn from negation to affirmation, from the ever-lasting "No" to the ever-lasting "Yes". Instead of sitting, sapped of all initiative and independence; instead of drowning our originality in imitation of mediocre white folks; instead of being afraid of ourselves and cultivating the art of skulking to escape the Color Line; we have got to renounce a program that always involves humiliating self-stultifying scrambling to crawl somewhere where we are not wanted; where we crouch panting like a whipped dog. We have got to stop this and learn that on such a program they cannot build manhood. No, by God, stand erect in a mud-puddle and tell the white world to go to hell, rather than lick boots in a parlor.

Affirm, as you have a right to affirm, that the Negro race is one of the great human races, inferior to none in its accomplishment and in its ability. Different, it is true, and for most of the difference, let us reverently thank God. And this race, with its vantage grounds in modern days, can go forward of its own will, and of its own power, and its own initiative. It is led by twelve million American Negroes of average modern intelligence; three or four million educated African Negroes are their full equals, and several million Negroes in the West Indies and South America. This body of at least twenty-five million modern men are not called upon to commit suicide because somebody doesn't like their complexion or their hair. It is their opportunity and their day to stand up and make themselves heard and felt in the modern world.

Indeed, there is nothing else we can do. If you have passed your resolution, "No segregation, Never and Nowhere," what are you going to do about it? Let me tell you what you are going to do. You are going back to continue to make your living in a Jim Crow school; you are going to dwell in a segregated section of the city; you are going to pastor a Jim Crow Church; you are going to occupy political office because of Jim Crow political organizations that stand back of you and force you into office. All these things and a thousand others you are going to do because you have got to.

If you are going to do this, why not say so? What are you afraid of? Do you believe in the Negro race or do you not? If you do not, naturally, you are justified in keeping still. But if you do believe in the extraordinary accomplishment of the Negro church and the Negro college, the Negro school and the Negro newspaper, then say so and say so plainly, not only for the sake of those who have given their lives to make these things worthwhile, but for those young people whom you are teaching, by that negative attitude, that there is nothing that they can do, nobody that they can emulate, and no field worthwhile working in. Think of what Negro art and literature has yet to accomplish if it can only be free and untrammeled by the necessity of pleasing white folks! Think of the splendid moral appeal that you can make to a million children tomorrow, if once you can get them to see the possibilities of the American Negro today and now, whether he is segregated or not, or in spite of all possible segregation.

PROTEST

Some people seem to think that the fight against segregation consists merely of one damned protest after another. That the technique is to protest and wail and protest again, and to keep this thing up until the gates of public opinion and the walls of segregation fall down.

The difficulty with this program is that it is physically and psychologically impossible. It would be stopped by cold and hunger and strained voices, and it is an undignified and impossible attitude and method to maintain indefinitely. Let us, therefore, remember that this program must be modified by adding to it a positive side. Make the protest, and keep on making it, systematically and thoughtfully. Perhaps now and then even hysterically and theatrically; but at the same time, go to work to prepare methods and institutions which will supply those things and those opportunities which we lack because of segregation. Stage boycotts which will put Negro clerks in the stores which exploit Negro neighborhoods. Build a 15th Street Presbyterian Church, when the First Presbyterian would rather love Jesus without your presence. Establish and elaborate a Washington system of public schools, comparable to any set of public schools in the nation; and then when you have done this, and as you are doing it, and while in the process you are saving your voice and your temper, say softly to the world: see what a precious fool you are. Here are stores as efficiently clerked as any where you trade. Here is a church better than most of yours. Here are a set of schools where you should be proud to send your children.

THE CONSERVATION OF RACES

The Second Occasional Papers published by The American Negro Academy was "The Conservation of Races" by W. E. B. Du Bois, and was published in 1897. On page 11, I read with interest this bit:

"Here, then, is the dilemma, and it is a puzzling one, I admit.

No Negro who has given earnest thought to the situation of his people in America has failed, at some time in life, to find himself at these cross-roads; has failed to ask himself at some time: What, after all, am I? Am I an American or am I a Negro? Can I be both? Or is it my duty to cease to be a Negro as soon as possible and be an American? If I strive as a Negro, am I not perpetuating the very cleft that threatens and separates Black and White America? Is not my only possible practical aim the subduction of all that is Negro in me to the American? Does my black blood place upon me any more obligation to assert my nationality than German, or Irish or Italian blood would?

"It is such incessant self-questioning and the hesitation that arises from it, that is making the present period a time of vacillation and contradiction for the American Negro; combined race action is stifled, race responsibility is shirked, race enterprises languish, and the best blood, the best talent, the best energy of the Negro people cannot be marshalled to do the bidding of the race. They stand back to make room for every rascal and demagogue who chooses to cloak his selfish deviltry under the veil of race pride.

"Is this right? Is it rational? Is it good policy? Have we in America a distinct mission as a race—a distinct sphere of action and an opportunity for race development, or is self-obliteration the highest end to which Negro blood dare aspire?"

On the whole, I am rather pleased to find myself still so much in sympathy with myself.

METHODS OF ATTACK

When an army moves to attack, there are two methods which it may pursue. The older method, included brilliant forays with bugles and loud fanfare of trumpets, with waving swords, and shining uniforms. In Coryn's "The Black Eagle", which tells the story of Bertrand du Guesclin, one sees that kind of fighting power in the fourteenth century. It was thrilling, but messy, and on the whole rather ineffective.

The modern method of fighting, is not nearly as spectacular. It is preceded by careful, very careful planning. Soldiers are clad in drab and rather dirty khaki. Officers are not riding out in front and using their swords; they sit in the rear and use their brains. The whole army digs in and stays hidden. The advance is a slow, calculated forward mass movement. Now going forward, now advancing in the center, now running around by the flank. Often retreating to positions that can be better defended. And the whole thing depending upon G.H.Q.; that is, the thought and knowledge and calculations of the great general staff. This is not nearly as spectacular as the older method of fighting, but it is much more effective, and against the enemy of present days, it is the only effective way. It is common sense based on modern technique.

And this is the kind of method which we must use to solve the Negro problem and to win our fight against segregation. There are times when a brilliant display of eloquence and picketing and other theatrical and spectacular things are not only excusable but actually gain ground. But in practically all cases, this is true simply because of the careful thought and planning that has gone before. And it is a waste of time and effort to think that the spectacular demonstration is the real battle.

The real battle is a matter of study and thought; of the building up of loyalties; of the long training of men; of the growth of institutions; of the inculcation of racial and national ideals. It is not a publicity stunt. It is a life.

THE NEW NEGRO ALLIANCE

We find ourselves in sudden and apparently complete agreement with our young friends of Washington. It seems that the alliance fell afoul of ordinances against picketing, but that this did not result altogether in failure. Two pickets were arrested, and finally, after a month or so, the complaints were dismissed. In another case, a complaint and temporary injunction is still being fought out before the courts. This is fine. We are glad that the picketing has met with so much of success and we hope that in Washington, as in Chicago, ultimate success will come.

Further than this, the alliance explains that what it is doing, is asking for clerks whose color in the main shall correspond to neighborhoods. If there is a store in a black neighborhood, there should be at least some black clerks in the store. With this, we quite agree, and say, as we said in the Chicago case, that this is fighting segregation with segregation. If there are, for instance (and there certainly are in Washington), segregated neighborhoods, don't squat before segregation and bawl. Use segregation. Use every bit that comes your way and transmute it into power. Power that some day will smash all race separation. In the meantime, call it what you will. If the Negro Alliance wishes to say that it is not fighting segregation with segregation, it can call the thing that it is doing Transubstantiation or Willipuswallipus. Whatever they call it, that is what we both mean.

NEGRO FRATERNITIES

Nothing illustrates better our current philosophy and practice in segregation, than the rise and development of Negro fraternities in colleges. When I was a student, fraternities were not allowed in Negro colleges and in the white colleges almost no fraternity ever accepted a Negro member. For a long time, Negro students went their way accepting this situation. When given opportunity, they protested against the Color Line in fraternities, and in a few cases, where the admission to fraternities depended upon scholarship, they succeeded in breaking the Color Line.

Nevertheless, it soon became manifest that there were certain things that the college fraternity could do for a student, which colored students were not getting in the large Northern universities. They lacked very often dormitory facilities; they had no place where they could entertain visiting friends; they had no social center; they had no opportunity for companionship and conference and mutual inspiration.

At Cornell, therefore, in 1906, a group of students formed the Alpha Phi Alpha Fraternity. There were many Negro students there, and in other places, at that time and since, who have condemned this movement as segregation while others excused it as voluntary segregation. It was segregation; and nevertheless, it was necessary; and it was voluntary only in the sense that either Negroes must have their own fraternity or forego fraternal advantages. It was, therefore, as a matter of fact just as compulsory as the "Jim Crow" car.

This fraternity movement has spread all over the United States. It has resulted in colored fraternities and sororities, whose membership runs into the thousands. If anyone has any doubt as to the meaning and inspiration of these fraternities, they should attend one of their national meetings and see the type of men and women that they are bringing together: the splendid enthusiasm, the inspiration and nationwide friendship. This is the kind of segregation that is forced upon us, and it is the kind of segregation in which we glory and which we are going to make the very finest type of institution that the United States has ever seen. And moreover, this is the singular and contradictory result: more Negroes have been taken into white fraternities since Negro fraternities started than ever before. The number thus admitted is still small, but it is not, as the timid argued, smaller; it is much larger.

(June, 1934. Vol. XLI, No. 6, pp. 182-84)

LETTER OF RESIGNATION FROM THE N.A.A.C.P.

The Board of Directors of the National Association for the Advancement of Colored People at the June meeting took no action upon the resignation of Dr. DuBois, tendered as of June 11, but named a committee to confer with Dr. DuBois and see if some satisfactory settlement of differences could not be arranged.

Under date of June 26, however, Dr. DuBois addressed the following letter to the Board and released it to the press as of July 1, eight days before it came officially to the notice of the Board at its regular meeting July 9:

> In deference to your desire to postpone action on my resignation of June 11, I have allowed my nominal connection with THE CRISIS to extend to July 1, and have meantime entered into communication with the Chairman of the Board, and with your Committee on Reconciliation.
>
> I appreciate the good will and genuine desire to bridge an awkward break which your action indicated, and yet it is clear to me, and I think to the majority of the Board that under the circumstances my resignation must stand. I owe it, however, to the Board and to the public to make clear at this time the deeper reasons for my action, lest the apparent causes of my resignation seem inadequate.
>
> Many friends have truthfully asserted that the segre-

gation argument was not the main reason for my wishing to leave this organization. It was an occasion and an important occasion, but it could have been adjusted. In fact, no matter what the Board of the National Association for the Advancement of Colored People says, its action towards segregation has got to approximate, in the future as in the past, the pattern which it followed in the case of the separate camp for Negro officers during the World War and in the case of the Tuskegee Veterans' Hospital. In both instances, we protested vigorously and to the limit of our ability the segregation policy. Then, when we had failed and knew we had failed, we bent every effort toward making the colored camp at Des Moines the best officers' camp possible, and the Tuskegee Hospital, with its Negro personnel, one of the most efficient in the land. This is shown by the 8th and 14th Annual Reports of the National Association for the Advancement of Colored People.

The only thing, therefore, that remains for us is to decide whether we are openly to recognize this procedure as inevitable, or be silent about it and still pursue it. Under these circumstances, the argument must be more or less academic, but there is no essential reason that those who see different sides of this same shield should not be able to agree to live together in the same house.

The whole matter assumed, however, a serious aspect when the board peremptorily forbade all criticism of the officers and policies in THE CRISIS. I had planned to continue constructive criticism of the National Association for the Advancement of Colored People in THE CRISIS because I firmly believe that the National Association for the Advancement of Colored People faces the most gruelling of tests which come to an old organization: founded in a day when a negative program of protest was imperative and effective, it succeeded so well that the program seemed perfect and unlimited. Suddenly, by World War and chaos, we are called to formulate a positive program of construction and inspiration. We have been thus far unable to comply.

Today this organization, which has been great and effective for nearly a quarter of a century, finds itself in a time of crisis and change, without a program, without effective organization, without executive officers, who have either the ability or disposition to guide the National Association for the Advancement of Colored People in the right direction.

These are harsh and arresting charges. I make them deliberately, and after long thought, earnest effort, and with infinite writhing of spirit. To the very best of my ability, and every ounce of my strength, I have since the beginning of the Great Depression, tried to work inside the organization for its realignment and readjustment to new duties. I have been almost absolutely unsuccessful. My program for economic readjustment has been totally ignored. My demand for a change in personnel has been considered as mere petty jealousy, and my protest against our mistakes and blunders has been looked upon as disloyalty to the organization.

So long as I sit by quietly consenting, I share responsi bility. If I criticize within, my words fall on deaf ears. If I criticize openly, I seem to be washing dirty linen in public. There is but one recourse, complete and final withdrawal, not because all is hopeless nor because there are no signs of realization of the possibilities of reform and of the imperative demand for men and vision, but because evidently I personally can do nothing more.

I leave behind me in the organization many who have long thought with me, and yet hesitated at action; many persons of large ideals who see no agents at hand to realize them, and who fear that the dearth of ability and will to sacrifice within this organization, indicates a similar lack within the whole race. I know that both sets of friends are wrong, and while I desert them with deep reluctance, it is distinctly in the hope that the fact of my going may arouse to action and bring a great and gifted race to the rescue, with a re-birth of that fine idealism and devotion that founded the National Association for the Advancement of Colored People.

Under these circumstances, there is but one thing for me to do, and that is to make the supreme sacrifice of taking myself absolutely and unequivocally out of the picture, so that hereafter the leaders of the National Association for the Advancement of Colored People, without the distraction of personalities and accumulated animosities, can give their whole thought and attention to the rescuing of the greatest organization for the emancipation of Negroes that America has ever had.

I am, therefore, insisting upon my resignation, and on July 1st, whether the Board of Directors acts or does not act, I automatically cease to have any connection whatsoever in any shape or form with the National Association for the Advancement of Colored People. I do not, however, cease to wish it well, to follow it with personal and palpitating interest, and to applaud it when it is able to rescue itself from its present impossible position and reorganize itself according to the demands of the present crisis.

> Very respectfully yours,
> (Signed) W. E. B. Du Bois.

At its meeting July 9, the Board adopted the following resolution:

RESOLVED, That it is with the deepest regret that we hereby accept the resignation of Dr. W. E. B. DuBois as editor of the CRISIS, as a member of the Board of Directors, as Director of Publications and Research, as a member of the Board of the Crisis Publishing Company, and as a member of the Spingarn Medal Award Committee; and we desire at the same time to record our sense of the loss which his resignation will bring not only to the members of this Board but to every loyal member of the Association.

Dr. Du Bois joined the Association in 1910 as Director of Publications and Research. The Association was then a few months old. He was already a distinguished teacher, scholar and man of letters, Professor of Sociology in Atlanta University, and author of "Souls of Black Folk" and other works which had deeply moved the white world as well as the black. The ideas which he had propounded for a decade were the same ideas that had brought the Association into being.

He founded the CRISIS without a cent of capital, and for many years made it completely self-supporting, reaching a maximum monthly circulation at the end of the World War of 106,000. This is an unprecedented achievement in American journalism, and in itself worthy of a distinguished tribute. But the ideas which he propounded in it and in his books and essays transformed the Negro world as well as a large portion of the liberal white world, so that the whole problem of the relation of black and white races has ever since had a completely new orientation. He created, what never existed before, a Negro intelligentsia, and many who have never read a word of his writings are his spiritual disciples and descendants. Without him the Association could never have been what it was and is.

The Board has not always seen eye to eye with him in regard to various matters, and cannot subscribe to some of his criticism of the Association and its officials. But such differences in the past have in no way interfered with his usefulness, but rather the contrary. For he had been selected because of his independence of judgment, his fearlessness in expressing his convictions, and his acute and wide-reaching intelligence. A mere yes-man could not have attracted the attention of the world, could not even have stimulated the Board itself to further study of various important problems. We shall be the poorer for his loss, in intellectual stimulus, and in searching analysis of the vital problems of the American Negro; no one in the Association can fill his place with the same intellectual grasp. We therefore offer him our sincere thanks for the services he has rendered, and we wish him all happiness in all that he may now undertake.

(August, 1934. Vol. XLI, No. 8, pp. 245-6)

COMMUNISM

THE NEGRO AND RADICAL THOUGHT

Mr. Claude McKay, one of the editors of *The Liberator* and a Negro poet of distinction, writes us as follows:

> I am surprised and sorry that in your editorial, 'The Drive', published in THE CRISIS for May, you should leap out of your sphere to sneer at the Russian Revolution, the greatest event in the history of humanity; much greater than the French Revolution, which is held up as

a wonderful achievement to Negro children and students in white and black schools. For American Negroes the indisputable and outstanding fact of the Russian Revolution is that a mere handful of Jews, much less in ratio to the number of Negroes in the American population, have attained, through the Revolution, all the political and social rights that were denied to them under the regime of the Czar.

Although no thinking Negro can deny the great work that the N.A.A.C.P. is doing, it must yet be admitted that from its platform and personnel the Association cannot function as a revolutionary working class organization. And the overwhelming majority of American Negroes belong by birth, condition and repression to the working class. Your aim is to get for the American Negro the political and social rights that are his by virtue of the Constitution, the rights which are denied him by the Southern oligarchy with the active cooperation of the state governments and the tacit support of northern business interests. And your aim is a noble one, which deserves the support of all progressive Negroes.

But the Negro in politics and social life is ostracized only technically by the distinction of color; in reality the Negro is discriminated against because he is of the lowest type of worker . . . .

Obviously, this economic difference between the white and black workers manifests itself in various forms, in color prejudice, race hatred, political and social boycotting and lynching of Negroes. And all the entrenched institutions of white America,—law courts, churches, schools, the fighting forces and the Press,— condone these iniquities perpetrated upon black men; iniquities that are dismissed indifferently as the inevitable result of the social system. Still, whenever it suits the business interests controlling these institutions to mitigate the persecutions against Negroes, they do so with impunity. When organized white workers quit their jobs, Negroes, who are discouraged by the whites to organize, are sought to take their places. And these strike-breaking Negroes work under the protection of the military and the police. But as ordinary citizens and workers, Negroes are not protected by the military and the police from the mob. The ruling classes will not grant Negroes those rights which, on a lesser scale and more plausibly, are withheld from the white proletariat. The concession of these rights would immediately cause a Revolution in the economic life of this country.

We are aware that some of our friends have been disappointed with THE CRISIS during and since the war. Some have assumed that we aimed chiefly at mounting the band wagon with our cause during the madness of war; others thought that we were playing safe so as to avoid the Department of Justice; and still a third class found us curiously stupid in our attitude toward the broader matters of human reform. Such critics, and Mr. McKay is among them, must give us credit for standing to our guns in the past at no little cost in many influential quarters, and they must also remember that we have one chief cause,— the emancipation of the Negro, and to this all else must be subordinated—not because other questions are not important but because to our mind the most important social question today is recognition of the darker races.

Turning now to that marvelous set of phenomena known as the Russian Revolution, Mr. McKay is wrong in thinking that we have ever intentionally sneered at it. On the contrary, time may prove, as he believes, that the Russian Revolution is the greatest event of the nineteenth and twentieth centuries, and its leaders the most unselfish prophets. At the same time THE CRISIS does not know this to be true. Russia is incredibly vast, and the happenings there in the last five years have been intricate to a degree that must make any student pause. We sit, therefore, with waiting hands and listening ears, seeing some splendid results from Russia, like the cartoons for public education recently exhibited in America, and hearing of other things which frighten us.

We are moved neither by the superficial omniscience of Wells nor the reports in the New York *Times;* but this alone we do know: that the immediate work for the American Negro lies in America and not in Russia, and this, too, in spite of the fact that the Third Internationale has made a pronouncement which cannot but have our entire sympathy:

> The Communist Internationale once forever breaks with the traditions of the Second Internationale which in reality only recognized the white race. The Communist Internationale makes it its task to emancipate the

workers of the entire world. The ranks of the Communist Internationale fraternally unite men of all colors: white, yellow and black—the toilers of the entire world.

Despite this there come to us black men two insistent questions: What is today the right program of socialism? The editor of THE CRISIS considers himself a Socialist but he does not believe that German State Socialism or the dictatorship of the proletariat are perfect panaceas. He believes with most thinking men that the present method of creating, controlling and distributing wealth is desperately wrong; that there must come and is coming a social control of wealth; but he does not know just what form that control is going to take, and he is not prepared to dogmatize with Marx or Lenin. Further than that, and more fundamental to the duty and outlook of THE CRISIS, is this question: How far can the colored people of the world, and particularly the Negroes of the United States, trust the working classes?

Many honest thinking Negroes assume, and Mr. McKay seems to be one of these, that we have only to embrace the working class program to have the working class embrace ours; that we have only to join trade Unionism and Socialism or even Communism, as they are today expounded, to have Union Labor and Socialists and Communists believe and act on the equality of mankind and the abolition of the color line. THE CRISIS wishes that this were true, but it is forced to the conclusion that it is not.

The American Federation of Labor, as representing the trade unions in America, has been grossly unfair and discriminatory toward Negroes and still is. American Socialism has discriminated against black folk and before the war was prepared to go further with this discrimination. European Socialism has openly discriminated against Asiatics. Nor is this surprising. Why should we assume on the part of unlettered and suppressed masses of white workers, a clearness of thought, a sense of human brotherhood, that is sadly lacking in the most educated classes?

Our task, therefore, as it seems to THE CRISIS, is clear: We have to convince the working classes of the world that black men, brown men, and yellow men are human beings and suffer the same discrimination that white workers suffer. We have in addition to this to espouse the cause of the white workers, only being careful that we do not in this way allow them to jeopardize our cause. We must, for instance, have bread. If our white fellow workers drive us out of decent jobs, we are compelled to accept indecent wages even at the price of "scabbing". It is a hard choice, but whose is the blame? Finally despite public prejudice and clamour, we should examine with open mind in literature, debate and in real life the great programs of social reform that are day by day being put forward.

We have an immediate program for Negro emancipation laid down and thought out by the N.A.A.C.P. It is foolish for us to give up this practical program for mirage in Africa or by seeking to join a revolution which we do not at present understand. On the other hand, as Mr. McKay says, it would be just as foolish for us to sneer or even seem to sneer at the blood-entwined writhing of hundreds of millions of our whiter human brothers.

(July, 1921. Vol. XXII, No. 3, pp. 102-4)

THE CLASS STRUGGLE

The N.A.A.C.P. has been accused of not being a "revolutionary" body. This is quite true. We do not believe in revolution. We expect revolutionary changes in many parts of this life and this world, but we expect these changes to come mainly through reason, human sympathy and the education of children, and not by murder. We know that there have been times when organized murder seemed the way out of wrong, but we believe those times have been very few, the cost of the remedy excessive, the results as terrible as beneficent, and we gravely doubt if in the future there will be any real recurrent necessity for such upheaval.

Whether this is true or not, the N.A.A.C.P. is organized to agitate, to investigate, to expose, to defend, to reason, to appeal. This is our program and this is the whole of our program. What human reform demands today is light, more light, clear thought, accurate knowledge, careful distinctions.

How far, for instance, does the dogma of the "class struggle" apply to black folk in the United States today? Theoretically we are a part of the world proletariat in the sense that we are mainly an exploited class of cheap laborers; but practically we are not a part of the white proletariat and are not recognized by that proletariat to any great extent. We are the victims of their physical oppression, social ostracism, economic exclusion and personal hatred; and when in self-defense we seek sheer subsistence we are howled down as "scabs."

Then consider another thing: the colored group is not yet divided into capitalists and laborers. There are only the beginnings of such a division. In one hundred years if we develop along conventional lines we would have such fully separated classes, but today to a very large extent our laborers are our capitalists and our capitalists are our laborers. Our small class of well-to-do men have come to affluence largely through manual toil and have never been physically or mentally separated from the toilers. Our professional classes are sons and daughters of porters, washerwomen and laborers.

Under these circumstances how silly it would be for us to try to apply the doctrine of the class struggle without modification or thought. Let us take a particular instance. Ten years ago the Negroes of New York City lived in hired tenement houses in Harlem, having gotten possession of them by paying higher rents than white tenants. If they had tried to escape these high rents and move into quarters where white laborers lived, the white laborers would have mobbed and murdered them. On the other hand, the white capitalists raised heaven and earth either to drive them out of Harlem or keep their rents high. Now between this devil and deep sea, what ought the Negro socialist or the Negro radical or, for that matter, the Negro conservative do?

Manifestly there was only one thing for him to do, and that was to buy Harlem; but the buying of real estate calls for capital and credit, and the institutions that deal in capital and credit are capitalistic institutions. If now, the Negro had begun to fight capital in Harlem, what capital was he fighting? If he fought capital as represented by white big real estate interests, he was wise; but he was also just as wise when he fought labor which insisted on segregating him in work and in residence.

If, on the other hand, he fought the accumulating capital in his own group, which was destined in the years 1915 to 1920 to pay down $5,000,000 for real estate in Harlem, then he was slapping himself in his own face. Because either he must furnish capital for the buying of his own home, or rest naked in the slums and swamps. It is for this reason that there is today a strong movement in Harlem for a Negro bank, and a movement which is going soon to be successful. This Negro bank eventually is going to bring into cooperation and concentration the resources of fifty or sixty other Negro banks in the United States, and this aggregation of capital is going to be used to break the power of white capital in enslaving and exploiting the darker world.

Whether this is a program of socialism or capitalism does not concern us. It is the only program that means salvation to the Negro race. The main danger and the central question of the capitalistic development through which the Negro American group is forced to go is the question of the ultimate control of the capital which they must raise and use. If this capital is going to be controlled by a few men for their own benefit, then we are destined to suffer from our own capitalists exactly what we are suffering from white capitalists today. And while this is not a pleasant prospect, it is certainly no worse than the present actuality. If, on the other hand, because of our more democratic organization and our wide-spread inter-class sympathy we can introduce a more democratic control, taking advantage of what the white world is itself doing to introduce industrial democracy, then we may not only escape our present economic slavery but even guide and lead a distrait economic world.

(August, 1921. Vol. XXII, No. 4, pp. 151-2)

RUSSIA, 1926

I am writing this in Russia. I am sitting in Revolution Square opposite the Second House of the Moscow Soviets and in a hotel run by the Soviet Government. Yonder the sun pours into my window over the domes and eagles and pointed towers of the Kremlin. Here is the old Chinese wall of the inner city; there is the gilded glory of the Cathedral of Christ, the Savior. Thro' yonder gate on the vast Red Square, Lenin sleeps his last sleep, with long lines of people peering each day into his dead and speaking face. Around me roars a city of two millions—Holy Moscow.

I have been in Russia something less than two months. I did not see the Russia of war and blood and rapine. I know nothing of political prisoners, secret police and underground propaganda. My knowledge of the Russian language is sketchy and of this vast land, the largest single country on earth, I have traveled over only a small, a very small part.

But I have had certain advantages; I have seen something of Russia. I have traveled over two thousand miles and visited four of its largest cities, many of its towns, the Neva, Dneiper, Moscow and Volga of its rivers, and stretches of land and village. I have looked into the faces of its races—Jews, Tartars, Gypsies, Caucasians, Armenians and Chinese. To help my lack of language I have had personal friends, whom I knew before I came to Russia, as interpreters. They were born in Russia and speak English, French and German. This, with my English, German and French, has helped the language difficulty, but did not, of course, solve it.

I have not done my sight seeing and investigation in gangs and crowds nor according to the program of the official Foreign Bureau; but have in nearly all cases gone about with one Russian-speaking friend. In this way I have seen schools, universities, factories, stores, printing establishments, government offices, palaces, museums, summer colonies of children, libraries, churches, monasteries, boyar houses, theatres, moving-picture houses, day nurseries and co-operatives. I have seen some celebrations—self-governing children in a school house of an evening and 200,000 children and youths marching on Youth Day. I have talked with peasants and laborers, Commissars of the Republic, teachers and children.

Alone and unaccompanied I have walked the streets of Leningrad, Moscow, Nijni Novgorod and Kiev at morning, noon and night; I have trafficked on the curb and in the stores; I have watched crowds and audiences and groups. I have gathered some documents and figures, plied officials and teachers with questions and sat still and gazed at this Russia, that the spirit of its life and people might enter my veins.

I stand in astonishment and wonder at the revelation of Russia that has come to me. I may be partially deceived and half-informed. But if what I have seen with my eyes and heard with my ears in Russia is Bolshevism, I am a Bolshevik.

(November, 1926. Vol. XXXIII, No. 1, p. 8)

JUDGING RUSSIA

There is no question but that a government can carry on business. Every government does. Whether governmental industry compares in efficiency with private industry depends entirely upon what we call efficiency. And here it is and not elsewhere that the Russian experiment is astonishing and new and of fateful importance to the future civilization. What we call efficiency in America is judged primarily by the resultant profit to the rich and only secondarily by the results to the workers. The face of industrial Europe and America is set toward private wealth; that is, toward the people who have large incomes. We recognize the economic value of small incomes mainly as a means of profit for great incomes. Russia seeks another psychology. Russia is trying to make the workingman the main object of industry. His well-being and his income are deliberately set as the chief ends of organized industry directed by the state.

One can stand on the streets of Moscow or Kiev and see clearly that Russia has struck at the citadels of the power that rules modern countries. Not manhood suffrage, women's suffrage, state regulation of industry, social reform nor religious and moral teaching in any modern country have shorn organized wealth of its power as the Bolshevik Revolution has done in Russia. Is it possible to conduct a great modern government without the autocratic leadership of the rich? The answer is: this is exactly what Russia is doing today. But can she continue to do this? This is not a question of ethics or economics; it is a question of psychology. Can Russia continue to think of the State in terms of the worker? This can happen only if the Russian people believe and idealize the workingman as the chief citizen. In America we do not. The ideal of every American is the millionaire—or at least the man of "independent" income. We regard the laborers as the unfortunate part of the community and even liberal thought is directed toward "emancipating" the workingman by relieving him in part if not entirely of the necessity of work. Russia, on the contrary, is seeking to make a nation believe that work and work that is hard and in some respects disagreeable and work which is to a large extent physical is a necessity of human life at present and likely to be in any conceivable future world; that the people who do this work are the ones who should determine how the national income from their combined efforts should be distributed; in fine, that the Workingman is the State; that he makes civilization possible and should determine what civilization is to be.

For this purpose he must be a workingman of skill and intelligence and to this combined end Russian education is being organized. This is what the Russian Dictatorship of the Proletariat means. This dictatorship does not stop there. As the workingman is today neither skilled nor intelligent to any such extent as his responsibilities demand, there is within his ranks the Communist party, directing the proletariat toward their future dictatorship. This is nothing new. In this government "of the people" we have elaborate and many-sided arrangements for ruling the rulers. The test is, are we and Russia really preparing future rulers? In so far as I could see, in shop and school, in the press and on the radio, in books and lectures, in trades unions and National Congresses, Russia is. We are not.

Visioning now a real Dictatorship of the Proletariat, two questions follow: Is it possible today for a great nation to achieve such a workers' psychology? And secondly, if it does achieve it what will be its effect upon the world? The achievement of such a psychology depends partly upon Russia and partly upon Western Europe and the United States. In Russia one feels today, even on a casual visit, the beginning of a workingman's psychology. Workers are the people that fill the streets and live in the best houses, even though these houses are dilapidated; workers crowd (literally crowd) the museums and theaters, hold the high offices, do the public talking, travel in the trains.

Nowhere in modern lands can one see less of the spender and

the consumer, the rich owners and buyers of luxuries, the institutions which cater to the idle rich. One sees in Moscow, Leningrad and Kiev neither first-class hotels, nor luxurious restaurants, nor private motor cars, nor silk stockings, nor prostitutes. All these insignia of the great modern city are lacking. On the other hand, the traveler misses the courtesy and *savoir faire* which one meets in the hotel corridors of London and Paris: one misses the smart shops and well-groomed men and women who are so plentiful in Constantinople and Berlin. Does this mean that Russia has "put over" her new psychology? Not by any means. She is trying and trying hard, but there are plenty of people in Russia who still hate and despise the workingman's blouses and the peasant's straw shoes; and plenty of workers who regret the passing of the free-handed Russian nobility; who miss the splendid pageantry of the Czars and who cling doggedly to religious dogma and superstition. There must be in Russia dishonest officials and inefficient statesmen. But here Russia has no monopoly. There are those in Russia and out who say that the present effort cannot succeed for exactly the same reasons that men said the Bourgeoisie could never rule France.

But it is the organized capital of America, England, France and Germany which is chiefly instrumental in preventing the realization of the Russian workingman's psychology. It has used every modern weapon to crush Russia. It sent against Russia every scoundrel who could lead a mob and gave him money, guns and ammunition; and when Russia nearly committed suicide in crushing this civil war, modern industry began the industrial boycott, the refusal of capital and credit which is being carried on today just as far as international jealousy and greed will allow. And can we wonder? If modern capital is owned by the rich and handled for their power and benefit, can the rich be expected to hand it over to their avowed and actual enemies? On the contrary, if modern industry is really for the benefit of the people and if there is an effort to make the people the chief beneficiaries of industry, why is it that this same people is powerless today to help this experiment or at least to give it a clear way? On the other hand, so long as the most powerful nations in the world are determined that Russia must fail, there can be but a minimum of free discussion and democratic difference of opinion in Russia.

There is world struggle then in and about Russia; but it is not simply an ethical problem as to whether or not the Russian Revolution was morally right; that is a question which only history will settle. It is not simply the economic question as to whether or not Russia can conduct industry on a national scale. She is doing it today and in so doing she differs only in quantity, not in quality from every other modern country. It is not a question merely of "dictatorship." We are all subject to this form of government. The real Russian question is: Can you make the worker and not the millionaire the center of modern power and culture? If you can, the Russian Revolution will sweep the world.

(February, 1927. Vol. XXXIII, No. 4, pp. 189-90)

THE NEGRO AND COMMUNISM

The Scottsboro, Alabama, cases have brought squarely before the American Negro the question of his attitude toward Communism.

The importance of the Russian Revolution can not be gainsaid. It is easily the greatest event in the world since the French Revolution and possibly since the fall of Rome. The experiment is increasingly successful. Russia occupies the center of the world's attention today and as a state it is recognized by every civilized nation, except the United States, Spain, Portugal and some countries of South America.

The challenge to the capitalistic form of industry and to the governments which this form dominates, is more and more tremendous because of the present depression. If Socialism as a form of government and industry is on trial in Russia, capitalism as a form of industry and government is just as surely on trial throughout the world and is more and more clearly recognizing the fact.

THE AMERICAN WORKER

It has always been felt that the United States was an example of the extraordinary success of capitalistic industry, and that this was proven by the high wage paid labor and the high stand-

ard of intelligence and comfort prevalent in this country. Moreover, for many years, democratic political control of our government by the masses of the people made it possible to
envisage without violence any kind of reform in government or
industry which appealed to the people. Recently, however, the
people of the United States have begun to recognize that their
political power is curtailed by organized capital in industry and
that in this industry, democracy does not prevail; and that until
wider democracy does prevail in industry, democracy in government is seriously curtailed and often quite ineffective. Also,
because of recurring depressions the high wage is in part illu-
sory.

THE AMERICAN NEGRO

Moreover, there is in the United States one class of people who
more than any other suffer under present conditions. Because
of wholesale disfranchisement and a system of color caste, discriminatory legislation and widespread propaganda, 12,000,000
American Negroes have only a minimum of that curtailed freedom which the right to vote and influence on public opinion
gives to white Americans. And in industry Negroes are for
historic and social reasons upon the lowest round.

PROPOSED REFORM

The proposals to remedy the economic and political situation
in America range from new legislation, better administration
and government aid, offered by the Republican and Democratic
parties, on to liberal movements fathered by Progressives, the
Farmer-Labor movement and the Socialists, and finally to the
revolutionary proposals of the Communists. The Progressives
and Socialists propose in general increased government ownership of land and natural resources, state control of the larger
public services and such progressive taxation of incomes and
inheritance as shall decrease the number and power of the rich.
The Communists, on the other hand, propose an entire sweeping away of the present organization of industry; the ownership
of land, resources, machines and tools by the state, the conducting of business by the state under incomes which the state
limits. And in order to introduce this complete Socialistic

regime, Communists propose a revolutionary dictatorship by the working class, as the only sure, quick and effective path.

ADVICE TO NEGROES

With these appeals in his ears, what shall the American Negro do? In the letters from United States Senators published in this issue of THE CRISIS, we find, with all the sympathy and good-will expressed, a prevailing helplessness when it comes to advice on specific action. Reactionaries like Fess, Conservatives like Bulkley and Capper, Progressives like Borah and Norris, all can only say: "You have done as well as could be expected; you suffer many present disadvantages; there is nothing that we can do to help you, and your salvation lies in patience and further effort on your own part." The Socialist, as represented by Norman Thomas in the February CRISIS, invites the Negro as a worker to vote for the Socialist Party as the party of workers. He offers the Negro no panacea for prejudice and caste but assumes that the uplift of the white worker will automatically emancipate the yellow, brown and black.

THE SCOTTSBORO CASES

Finally, the Scottsboro cases come and put new emphasis on the appeal of the Communists. Advocating the defense of the eight Alabama black boys, who without a shadow of doubt have been wrongly accused of crime, the Communists not only asked to take charge of the defense of these victims, but they proceeded to build on this case an appeal to the American Negro to join the Communist movement as the only solution of their problem.

Immediately, these two objects bring two important problems; first, can the Negroes with their present philosophy and leadership defend the Scottsboro cases successfully? Secondly, even if they can, will such defense help them to solve their problem of poverty and caste?

If the Communistic leadership in the United States had been broadminded and far-sighted, it would have acknowledged frankly that the honesty, earnestness and intelligence of the N. A. A. C. P. during twenty years of desperate struggle proved this organization under present circumstances to be the only one, and its methods the only methods available, to defend these boys and it would have joined capitalists and laborers north and south, black and white in every endeavor to win freedom for victims threatened with judicial murder. Then beyond that and with Scottsboro as a crimson and terrible text, Communists could have proceeded to point out that legal defense alone, even if successful, will never solve the larger Negro problem but that further and more radical steps are needed.

COMMUNIST STRATEGY

Unfortunately, American Communists are neither wise nor intelligent. They sought to accomplish too much at one stroke. They tried to prove at once that the N.A.A.C.P. did not wish to defend the victims at Scottsboro and that the reason for this was that Negro leadership in the N.A.A.C.P. was allied with the capitalists. The first of these two efforts was silly and the Communists tried to accomplish it by deliberate lying and deception. They accused the N.A.A.C.P. of stealing, misuse of funds, lack of interest in the Scottsboro cases, cowardly surrender to malign forces, inefficiency and a policy of do-nothing.

Now whatever the N.A.A.C.P. has lacked, it is neither dishonest nor cowardly, and already events are proving clearly that the only effective defense of the Scottsboro boys must follow that which has been carefully organized, engineered and paid for by the N.A.A.C.P., and that the success of this defense is helped so far as the Communists cooperate by hiring bourgeois lawyers and appealing to bourgeois judges; but is hindered and made doubtful by ill-considered and foolish tactics against the powers in whose hands the fate of the Scottsboro victims lies.

If the Communists want these lads murdered, then their tactics of threatening judges and yelling for mass action on the part of white southern workers is calculated to insure this.

And, on the other hand, lying and deliberate misrepresentation of friends who are fighting for the same ideals as the Communists, are old capitalistic, bourgeois weapons of which the Communists ought to be ashamed. The final exploit at Camp Hill is worthy of the Russian Black Hundreds, whoever promoted it: black sharecroppers, half-starved and desperate were organized into a "Society for the Advancement of Colored

People" and then induced to meet and protest against Scottsboro. Sheriff and white mob killed one and imprisoned 34. If this
was instigated by Communists, it is too despicable for words;
not because the plight of the black peons does not shriek for
remedy but because this is no time to bedevil a delicate situation
by drawing a red herring across the trail of eight innocent
children.

Nevertheless, the N.A.A.C.P. will defend these 34 victims of
Southern fear and communist irresponsibility.

The ultimate object of the Communists, was naturally not
merely nor chiefly to save the boys accused at Scottsboro; it was
to make this case a center of agitation to expose the helpless
condition of Negroes, and to prove that anything less than the
radical Communist program could not emancipate them.

THE NEGRO BOURGEOISIE

The question of the honesty and efficiency of the N.A.A.C.P.
in the defense of the Scottsboro boys, just as in a dozen other
cases over the length and breadth of the United States, is entirely separate from the question as to whether or not Negro
leadership is tending toward socialism and communism or toward capitalism.

The charge of the Communists that the present set-up of
Negro America is that of the petit bourgeois minority dominating a helpless black proletariat, and surrendering to white
profiteers is simply a fantastic falsehood. The attempt to
dominate Negro Americans by purely capitalistic ideas died
with Booker T. Washington. The battle against it was begun by
the Niagara Movement and out of the Niagara Movement arose
the N.A.A.C.P. Since that time there has never been a moment
when the dominating leadership of the American Negro has
been mainly or even largely dominated by wealth or capital or
by capitalistic ideals.

There are naturally some Negro capitalists: some large land-
owners, some landlords, some industrial leaders and some
investors; but the great mass of Negro capital is not owned or
controlled by this group. Negro capital consists mainly of small
individual savings invested in homes, and in insurance, in lands
for direct cultivation and individually used tools and machines.
Even the automobiles owned by Negroes represent to a consid-

erable extent personal investments, designed to counteract the insult of the "Jim Crow" car. The Insurance business, which represents a large amount of Negro capital is for mutual co-operation rather than exploitation. Its profit is limited and its methods directed by the State. Much of the retail business is done in small stores with small stocks of goods, where the owner works side by side with one or two helpers, and makes a personal profit less than a normal American wage. Negro professional men—lawyers, physicians, nurses and teachers—represent capital invested in their education and in their office equipment, and not in commercial exploitation. There are few colored manufacturers of material who speculate on the products of hired labor. Nine-tenths of the hired Negro labor is under the control of white capitalists. There is probably no group of 12 million persons in the modern world which exhibits smaller contrasts in personal income than the American Negro group. Their emancipation will not come, as among the Jews, from an internal readjustment and ousting of exploiters; rather it will come from a wholesale emancipation from the grip of the white exploiters without.

It is, of course, always possible, with the ideals of America, that a full fledged capitalistic system may develop in the Negro group; but the dominant leadership of the Negro today, and particularly the leadership represented by the N.A.A.C.P. represents no such tendency. For two generations the social leaders of the American Negro with very few exceptions have been poor men, depending for support on their salaries, owning little or no real property; few have been business men, none have been exploiters, and while there have been wide differences of ultimate ideal these leaders on the whole, have worked unselfishly for the uplift of the masses of Negro folk.

There is no group of leaders on earth who have so largely made common cause with the lowest of their race as educated American Negroes, and it is their foresight and sacrifice and theirs alone that has saved the American freedman from annihilation and degradation.

This is the class of leaders who have directed and organized and defended black folk in America and whatever their shortcomings and mistakes—and they are legion—their one great proof of success is the survival of the American Negro as the most intelligent and effective group of colored people fighting white civilization face to face and on its own ground, on the face of the earth.

The quintessence and final expression of this leadership is the N.A.A.C.P. For twenty years it has fought a battle more desperate than any other race conflict of modern times and it has fought with honesty and courage. It deserves from Russia something better than a kick in the back from the young jackasses who are leading Communism in America today.

WHAT IS THE N.A.A.C.P.?

The N.A.A.C.P. years ago laid down a clear and distinct program. Its object was to make 12 million Americans:

> *Physically free from peonage,*
> *Mentally free from ignorance,*
> *Politically free from disfranchisement,*
> *Socially free from insult.*

Limited as this platform may seem to perfectionists, it is so far in advance of anything ever attempted before in America, that it has gained an extraordinary following. On this platform we have succeeded in uniting white and black, employers and laborers, capitalists and communists, socialists and reformers, rich and poor. The funds which support this work come mainly from poor colored people, but on the other hand, we have in 20 years of struggle, enlisted the sympathy and cooperation of the rich, the white and the powerful; and so long as this cooperation is given upon the basis of the platform we have laid down, we seek and welcome it. On the other hand, we know perfectly well that the platform of the N.A.A.C.P. is no complete program of social reform. It is a pragmatic union of certain definite problems, while far beyond its program lies the whole question of the future of the darker races and the economic emancipation of the working classes.

WHITE LABOR

Beyond the Scottsboro cases and the slurs on Negro leadership, there still remains for Negroes and Communists, the pressing major question: How shall American Negroes be emancipated from economic slavery? In answer to this both Socialists and Communists attempt to show the Negro that his interest lies with that of white labor. That kind of talk to the American Negro is like a red rag to a bull. Throughout the history of the Negro in America, white labor has been the black man's enemy, his oppressor, his red murderer. Mobs, riots and the discrimination of trade unions have been used to kill, harass and starve black men. White labor disfranchised Negro labor in the South, is keeping them out of jobs and decent living quarters in the North, and is curtailing their education and civil and social privileges throughout the nation. White laborers have formed the backbone of the Ku Klux Klan and have furnished hands and ropes to lynch 3,560 Negroes since 1882.

Since the death of Terence Powderly not a single great white labor leader in the United States has wholeheartedly and honestly espoused the cause of justice to black workers.

Socialists and Communists explain this easily: white labor in its ignorance and poverty has been misled by the propaganda of white capital, whose policy is to divide labor into classes, races and unions and pit one against the other. There is an immense amount of truth in this explanation: Newspapers, social standards, race pride, competition for jobs, all work to set white against black. But white American laborers are not fools. And with few exceptions the more intelligent they are, the higher they rise, the more efficient they become, the more determined they are to keep Negroes under their heels. It is no mere coincidence that Labor's present representative in the President's cabinet belongs to a union that will not admit a Negro, and himself was for years active in West Virginia in driving Negroes out of decent jobs. It is intelligent white labor that today keeps Negroes out of the trades, refuses them decent homes to live in and helps nullify their vote. Whatever ideals white labor today strives for in America, it would surrender nearly every one before it would recognize a Negro as a man.

Communists and the Color Line

The American Communists have made a courageous fight against the color line among the workers. They have solicited and admitted Negro members. They have insisted in their strikes and agitation to let Negroes fight with them and that the object of their fighting is for black workers as well as white workers. But in this they have gone dead against the thought and desire of the overwhelming mass of white workers, and face today a dead blank wall even in their own school in Arkansas. Thereupon instead of acknowledging defeat in their effort to make white labor abolish the color line, they turn and accuse Negroes of not sympathizing with the ideals of Labor!

Socialists have been franker. They learned that American labor would not carry the Negro and they very calmly unloaded him. They allude to him vaguely and as an afterthought in their books and platforms. The American Socialist party is out to emancipate the white worker and if this does not automatically free the colored man, he can continue in slavery. The only time that so fine a man and so logical a reasoner as Norman Thomas becomes vague and incoherent is when he touches the black man, and consequently he touches him as seldom as possible.

When, therefore, Negro leaders refuse to lay down arms and surrender their brains and action to "Nigger"-hating white workers, liberals and socialists understand exactly the reasons for this and spend what energy they can spare in pointing out to white workers the necessity of recognizing Negroes. But the Communists, younger and newer, largely of foreign extraction, and thus discounting the hell of American prejudice, easily are led to blame the Negroes and to try to explain the intolerable American situation on the basis of an imported Marxist pattern, which does not at all fit the situation.

For instance, from Moscow comes this statement to explain Scottsboro and Camp Hill:

> Again, as in the case of Sacco and Vanzetti, the American Bourgeoisie is attempting to go against proletarian social opinion. It is attempting to carry through its criminal provocation to the very end.

This is a ludicrous misapprehension of local conditions and illustrates the error into which long distance interpretation, unsupported by real knowledge, may fall. The Sacco-Vanzetti cases in Massachusetts represented the fighting of prejudiced, entrenched capital against radical propaganda; but in Jackson County, northeastern Alabama, where Scottsboro is situated, there are over 33,000 Native whites and less than 3,000 Negroes. The vast majority of these whites belong to the laboring class and they formed the white proletarian mob which is determined to kill the eight Negro boys. Such mobs of white workers demand the right to kill "niggers" whenever their passions, especially in sexual matters, are inflamed by propaganda. The capitalists are willing to curb this blood lust when it interferes with their profits. They know that the murder of 8 innocent black boys will hurt organized industry and government in Alabama; but as long as 10,000 armed white workers demand these victims they do not dare move. Into this delicate and contradictory situation, the Communists hurl themselves and pretend to speak for the workers. They not only do not speak for the white workers but they even intensify the blind prejudices of these lynchers and leave the Negro workers helpless on the one hand and the white capitalists scared to death on the other.

The persons who are killing blacks in Northern Alabama and demanding blood sacrifice are the white workers—sharecroppers, trade unionists and artisans. The capitalists are against mob-law and violence and would listen to reason and justice in the long run because industrial peace increases their profits. On the other hand, the white workers want to kill the competition of "Niggers." Thereupon, the Communists, seizing leadership of the poorest and most ignorant blacks head them toward inevitable slaughter and jail-slavery, while they hide safely in Chattanooga and Harlem.

American Negroes do not propose to be the shock troops of the Communist Revolution, driven out in front to death, cruelty and humiliation in order to win victories for white workers. They are picking no chestnuts from the fire, neither for capital nor white labor.

Negroes know perfectly well that whenever they try to lead revolution in America, the nation will unite as one fist to crush them and them alone. There is no conceivable idea that seems to the present overwhelming majority of Americans higher than keeping Negroes "in their place."

Negroes perceive clearly that the real interests of the white worker are identical with the interests of the black worker; but until the white worker recognizes this, the black worker is compelled in sheer self-defense to refuse to be made the sacrificial goat.

The Negro and the Rich

The remaining grain of truth in the Communist attack on Negro
leadership is the well-known fact that American wealth has
helped the American Negro and that without this help the
Negro could not have attained his present advancement.
American courts from the Supreme Court down are dominated
by wealth and Big Business, yet they are today the Negro's only
protection against complete disfranchisement, segregation and
the abolition of his public schools. Higher education for
Negroes is the gift of the Standard Oil, the Power Trust, the
Steel Trust and the Mail Order Chain Stores, together with the
aristocratic Christian Church; but these have given Negroes
40,000 black leaders to fight white folk on their own level and
in their own language. Big industry in the last 10 years has
opened occupations for a million Negro workers, without which
we would have starved in jails and gutters.

Socialists and Communists may sneer and say that the capitalists sought in all this profit, cheap labor, strike-breakers and
the training of conservative, reactionary leaders. They did. But
Negroes sought food, clothes, shelter and knowledge to stave
off death and slavery and only damned fools would have refused
the gift.

Moreover, we who receive education as the dole of the rich
have not all become slaves of wealth.

Meanwhile, what have white workers and radical reformers
done for Negroes? By strikes and agitation, by self-denial and
sacrifice, they have raised wages and bettered working conditions; but they did this for themselves and only shared gains
with Negroes when they had to. They have preached freedom,
political power, manhood rights and social uplift for everybody,
when nobody objected; but for "white people only" when anybody demanded it. White labor segregated Dr. Sweet in Detroit;
white laborers chased the Arkansas peons; white laborers steal
the black children's school funds in South Carolina, white laborers lynch Negroes in Alabama. Negroes owe much to white
labor but it is not all, or mostly, on the credit side of the ledger.

The Next Step

WHERE does this leave the Negro? As a practical program, it
leaves him just where he was before the Russian Revolution;

sympathetic with Russia and hopeful for its ultimate success in establishing a Socialistic state; sympathetic with the efforts of the American workingman to establish democratic control of industry in this land; absolutely certain that as a laborer his interests are the interests of all labor; but nevertheless fighting doggedly on the old battleground, led by the N.A.A.C.P. to make the Negro laborer a laborer on equal social footing with the white laborer: to maintain the Negro's right to a political vote, notwithstanding the fact that this vote means increasingly less and less to all voters; to vindicate in the courts the Negro's civil rights and American citizenship, even though he knows how the courts are prostituted to the power of wealth; and above all, determined by plain talk and agitation to show the intolerable injustice with which America and the world treats the colored peoples and to continue to insist that in this injustice, the white workers of Europe and America are just as culpable as the white owners of capital; and that these workers can gain black men as allies only and insofar as they frankly, fairly and completely abolish the Color Line.

Present organization of industry for private profit and control of government by concentrated wealth is doomed to disaster. It must change and fall if civilization survives. The foundation of its present world-wide power is the slavery and semislavery of the colored world including the American Negroes. Until the colored man, yellow, red, brown and black, becomes free, articulate, intelligent and the receiver of a decent income, white capital will use the profit derived from his degradation to keep white labor in chains.

There is no doubt, then, as to the future, or as to where the true interests of American Negroes lie. There is no doubt, too, but that the first step toward the emancipation of colored labor must come from white labor.

(September, 1931. Vol. XL, No. 9, pp. 313 ff)

KARL MARX AND THE NEGRO

Without doubt the greatest figure in the science of modern industry is Karl Marx. He has been a center of violent controversy for three-quarters of a century, and for that reason there are some people who are so afraid of his doctrines that they dare not study the man and his work. This attitude is impossible, and particularly today when the world is so largely turning toward the Marxian philosophy, it is necessary to understand the man and his thought. This little article seeks merely to bring before American Negroes the fact that Karl Marx knew and sympathized with their problem.

Heinrich Karl Marx was a German Jew, born in 1818 and died in 1883. His adult life, therefore, reached from the panic of 1837 through the administration of President Hayes. The thing about him which must be emphasized now was his encyclopedic knowledge. No modern student of industry probably ever equalled his almost unlimited reading and study.

He knew something about American Negroes from his German comrades who migrated to the United States; but these emigrants were of little help so far as his final conclusions were concerned. Kriege, a German radical, who came to the United States, said frankly in 1846, that "We feel constrained to oppose abolition with all our might." Weitling, a Communist, paid scant attention to the slavery question. The German Labor Convention at Philadelphia in 1850 was dumb on slavery. Even Weidemeyer, Marx's personal friend, said nothing about slavery in his Workingmen's League, which was founded in 1853, although the next year he opposed the Kansas-Nebraska Bill. When the League was re-organized in 1857, it still said nothing about slavery, and a powerful branch of the League which seceded in 1857 advocated widespread serfdom of blacks and Chinese.

Then came the war and Marx began to give the situation attention.

"The present struggle between the South and the North," he wrote in 1861, "is . . . nothing but a struggle between two social systems, the system of slavery and the system of free labor. Because the two systems can no longer live peaceably side by side on the North American continent, the struggle has broken out."

He was well acquainted with those splendid leaders of the English workers who kept England from recognizing the South and perhaps entering the Civil War, who employed Frederick Douglass to arouse anti-slavery sentiment, and who organized those monster mass meetings in London and Manchester late in 1862 and early in 1863. It is possible that Marx had some hand in framing the addresses sent to President Lincoln in which they congratulated the Republic and found nothing to condemn except "The Slavery and degradation of men guilty only of a colored skin or African parentage." The Manchester address congratulated the President on liberating the slaves in the District of Columbia, putting down the slave trade, and recognizing the Republics of Haiti and Liberia, and concluded that "You cannot now stop short of a complete uprooting of slavery."

It was after this, in September, 1864, that the International Workingmen's Association was formed in which Marx was a leading spirit, and his was the pen that wrote the address to Abraham Lincoln in November, 1864.

> To Abraham Lincoln, President of the United States of America.
>
> Sir:—We congratulate the American people upon your re-election by a large majority. If resistance to the Slave Power was the watchword of your first election, the triumphal war-cry of your re-election is Death to Slavery.
>
> From the commencement of the titanic American strife the workingmen of Europe felt distinctively that the Star Spangled Banner carried the destiny of their class. The contest for the territories which opened the *dire epopée,* was it not to decide whether the virgin soil of immense tracts should be wedded to the labor of the immigrant or be prostituted by the tramp of the slave-driver?
>
> When an oligarchy of 300,000 slaveholders dared to inscribe for the first time in the annals of the world 'Slavery' on the banner of armed revolt, when on the very spots where hardly a century ago the idea of one great Democratic Republic had first sprung up, whence the first declaration of the Rights of Man was issued, and the first impulse given to the European Revolution of the eighteenth century, when on those very spots counter-revolution, with systematic thoroughness, gloried in rescinding 'the ideas entertained at the time of the formation of the old constitution' and maintained 'slavery to be a beneficial institution' indeed, the only solution of the great problem of the 'relation of capital to labor,'

and cynically proclaimed property in man 'the corner-
stone of the new edifice,'—then the working classes of
Europe understood at once, even before the fanatic par-
tisanship of the upper classes, for the Confederate gen-
try had given its dismal warning, that the slaveholders'
rebellion was to sound the tocsin for a general holy war
of property against labor, and that for the men of labor,
with their hopes for the future, even their past conquests
were at stake in that tremendous conflict on the other
side of the Atlantic. Everywhere they bore therefore
patiently the hardships imposed upon them by the cotton crisis, opposed enthusiastically the pro-slavery in-
tervention-importunities of their betters—and from
most parts of Europe contributed their quota of blood to
the good of the cause.

While the workingmen, the true political power of the
North, allowed slavery to defile their own republic,
while before the Negro, mastered and sold without his
concurrence, they boasted it the highest prerogative of
the white-skinned laborer to sell himself and choose his
own master, they were unable to attain the true freedom
of labor, or to support their European brethren in their
struggle for emancipation; but this barrier to progress
has been swept off by the red sea of civil war.

The workingmen of Europe felt sure that, as the
American War of Independence initiated a new era of
ascendency for the middle class, so the American Anti-
slavery War will do for the working classes. They consider it an earnest sign of the epoch to come that it fell
to the lot of Abraham Lincoln, the single-minded son of
the working class, to lead his country through the
matchless struggle for the rescue of the enchained race
and the reconstruction of a social world.

To this the American Ambassador to London replied sympathetically. After Lincoln's assassination, Marx again drafted a
letter, May 13, 1865, in behalf of the International Association.

The demon of the 'peculiar institution,' for whose
preservation the South rose in arms, did not permit its
devotees to suffer honorable defeat on the open battlefield. What had been conceived in treason, must
necessarily end in infamy. As Philip II's war in behalf of
the Inquisition produced a Gérard, so Jefferson Davis's
rebellion a Booth . . . .

After a gigantic Civil War which, if we consider its colossal extension and its vast scene of action, seems in comparison with the Hundred Years' War and the Thirty Years' War and the Twenty-three Years' War of the Old World scarcely to have lasted ninety days, the task, Sir, devolves upon you to uproot by law what the sword has felled, and to preside over the more difficult work of political reconstruction and social regeneration. The profound consciousness of your great mission will preserve you from all weakness in the execution of your stern duties. You will never forget that the American people at the inauguration of the new era of the emancipation of labor placed the burden of leadership on the shoulders of two men of labor—Abraham Lincoln the one, and the other Andrew Johnson.

After the war had closed, in September, 1865, still another letter went to the people of the United States from the same source.

Again we felicitate you upon the removal of the cause of these years of affliction—upon the abolition of slavery. This stain upon your otherwise so shining escutcheon is forever wiped out. Never again shall the hammer of the auctioneer announce in your market-places sales of human flesh and blood and make mankind shudder at the cruel barbarism.

Your noblest blood was shed in washing away these stains, and desolation has spread its black shroud over your country in penance for the past.

Today you are free, purified through your sufferings. A brighter future is dawning upon your republic, proclaiming to the old world that a government of the people and by the people is a government for the people and not for a privileged minority.

We had the honor to express to you our sympathy in your affliction, to send you a word of encouragement in your struggles, and to congratulate you upon your success. Permit us to add a word of counsel for the future.

Injustice against a fraction of your people having been followed by such dire consequences, put an end to it. Declare your fellow citizens from this day forth free and equal, without any reserve. If you refuse them citizens' rights while you exact from them citizens' duties, you will sooner or later face a new struggle which will once more drench your country in blood.

The eyes of Europe and of the whole world are on your attempts at reconstruction, and foes are ever ready to sound the death knell of republican institutions as soon as they see their opportunity.

We therefore admonish you, as brothers in a common cause, to sunder all the chains of freedom, and your own victory will be complete.

In June of that year, a few months after Johnson had become President, Marx, writing to Engels, senses the beginnings of reaction:

I naturally see what is repulsive in the form of the Yankee movement, but I find the reason for it in the nature of a bourgeois democracy ... where swindle has been on the sovereign throne for so long. Nevertheless, the events are world-upheaving ...

Naturally, Marx stood with the Abolitionist democracy, led by Sumner and Stevens.

Mr. Wade declared in public meetings that after the abolition of slavery, a radical change in the relation of capital and of property in land is next upon the order of the day.

He was suspicious of Johnson and wrote Engels in 1865:

Johnson's policy disturbs me. Ridiculous affectation of severity against individual persons; up to now highly *vacillating* and weak in the thing itself. The reaction has already begun in America and will soon be strengthened if this spinelessness is not put an end to.

And finally, in 1877, after the Negroes had been betrayed by the Northern industrial oligarchy, he wrote:

The policy of the new president (Hayes) will make the Negroes, and the great exploitation of land in favor of the railways, mining companies, etc. . . . will make the already dissatisfied farmers, into allies of the working class.

It was a great loss to American Negroes that the great mind of Marx and his extraordinary insight into industrial conditions could not have been brought to bear at first hand upon the history of the American Negro between 1876 and the World War. Whatever he said and did concerning the uplift of the working class must, therefore, be modified so far as Negroes are concerned by the fact that he had not studied at first hand their peculiar race problem here in America. Nevertheless, he did know the plight of the working class in England, France and Germany, and American Negroes must understand what his panacea was for those folk if they would see their way clearly in the future.

(March, 1933. Vol. XL, No. 3, pp. 55-6)

MARXISM AND THE NEGRO PROBLEM

Karl Marx was a Jew born at Treves, Germany, in March, 1818. He came of an educated family and studied at the Universities of Bonn and Berlin, planning first to become a lawyer, and then to teach philosophy. But his ideas were too radical for the government. He turned to journalism, and finally gave his life to economic reform, dying in London in 1883, after having lived in Germany, Belgium, France, and, for the last thirty-five years of his life, in England. He published in 1867, the first volume of his monumental work, "Capital."

There are certain books in the world which every searcher for truth must know: the Bible, the Critique of Pure Reason, the Origin of Species, and Karl Marx' "Capital."

Yet until the Russian Revolution, Karl Marx was little known in America. He was treated condescendingly in the universities and regarded even by the intelligent public as a radical agitator whose curious and inconvenient theories it was easy to refute. Today, at last, we all know better, and we see in Karl Marx a colossal genius of infinite sacrifice and monumental industry, and with a mind of extraordinary logical keenness and grasp. We may disagree with many of the great books of truth that I have named, and with "Capital," but they can never be ignored.

At a recent dinner to Einstein, another great Jew, the story was told of a professor who was criticized as having "no sense of humor" because he tried to explain the Theory of Relativity in a few simple words. Something of the same criticism must be attached to anyone who attempts similarly to indicate the relation of Marxian philosophy and the American Negro problem. And yet, with all modesty, I am essaying the task knowing that it will be but tentative and subject to much criticism, both on my own part and that of other abler students.

The task which Karl Marx set himself was to study and interpret the organization of industry in the modern world. One of Marx's earlier works, "The Communist Manifesto," issued in 1848, on the eve of the series of democratic revolutions in Europe, laid down this fundamental proposition.

> That in every historical epoch the prevailing mode of economic production and exchange, and the social organization necessarily following from it, form the basis upon which is built up, and from which alone can be explained, the political and intellectual history of that epoch; that consequently the whole history of mankind .... has been a history of class struggles, contest between exploiting and exploited, ruling and oppressed classes; that the history of these class struggles forms a series of evolution in which, now-a-days, a stage has been reached where the exploited and oppressed class (the proletariat) cannot attain its emancipation from the sway of the exploiting and ruling class (the bourgeoisie) without, at the same time, and once and for all, emancipating society at large from all exploitation, oppression, class-distinction and class struggles.

All will notice in this manifesto, phrases which have been used so much lately and so carelessly that they have almost lost their meaning. But behind them still is living and insistent truth. The *class struggle* of exploiter and exploited is a reality. The capitalist still today owns machines, materials, and wages with which to buy labor. The laborer even in America owns little more than his ability to work. A wage contract takes place between these two and the resultant manufactured commodity or service is the property of the capitalist.

Here Marx begins his scientific analysis based on a mastery of practically all economic theory before his time and on an extraordinary, thoroughgoing personal knowledge of industrial conditions over all Europe and many other parts of the world.

His final conclusions were never all properly published. He

lived only to finish the first volume of his "Capital," and the other two volumes were completed from his papers and notes by his friend Engels. The result is an unfinished work, extraordinarily difficult to read and understand and one which the master himself would have been first to criticize as not properly representing his mature and finished thought.

Nevertheless, that first volume, together with the fairly evident meaning of the others, lay down a logical line of thought. The gist of that philosophy is that the value of products regularly exchanged in the open market depends upon the labor necessary to produce them; that capital consists of machines, materials and wages paid for labor; that out of the finished product, when materials have been paid for and the wear and tear and machinery replaced, and wages paid, there remains a surplus value. This surplus value arises from labor and is the difference between what is actually paid laborers for their wages and the market value of the commodities which the laborers produce. It represents, therefore, exploitation of the laborer, and this exploitation, inherent in the capitalistic system of production, is the cause of poverty, of industrial crises, and eventually of social revolution.

This social revolution, whether we regard it as voluntary revolt or the inevitable working of a vast cosmic law of social evolution, will be the last manifestation of the class struggle, and will come by inevitable change induced by the very nature of the conditions under which present production is carried on. It will come by the action of the great majority of men who compose the wage-earning proletariat, and it will result in common ownership of all capital, the disappearance of capitalistic exploitation, and the division of the products and services of industry according to human needs, and not according to the will of the owners of capital.

It goes without saying that every step of this reasoning and every presentation of supporting facts have been bitterly assailed. The labor theory of value has beeen denied; the theory of surplus value refuted; and inevitability of revolution scoffed at; while industrial crises—at least until this present one—have been defended as unusual exceptions proving the rule of modern industrial efficiency.

But with the Russian experiment and the World Depression most thoughtful men today are beginning to admit:

That the continued recurrence of industrial crises and wars based largely on economic rivalry, with persistent poverty, unemployment, disease and crime, are forcing the world to contemplate the possibilities of fundamental change in our economic methods; and that means thorough-going change, whether it be violent, as in France or Russia, or peaceful, as seems just as possible, and just as true to the Marxian formula, if it is fundamental change; in any case, Revolution seems bound to come.

Perhaps nothing illustrates this better than recent actions in the United States: our re-examination of the whole concept of Property; our banking moratorium; the extraordinary new agriculture bill; the plans to attack unemployment, and similar measures. Labor rather than gambling is the sure foundation of value and whatever we call it—exploitation, theft or business acumen—there is something radically wrong with an industrial system that turns out simultaneously paupers and millionaires and sets a world starving because it has too much food.

What now has all this to do with the Negro problem? First of all, it is manifest that the mass of Negroes in the United States belong distinctly to the working proletariat. Of every thousand working Negroes less than a hundred and fifty belong to any class that could possibly be considered bourgeois. And even this more educated and prosperous class has but small connection with the exploiters of wage and labor. Nevertheless, this black proletariat is not a part of the white proletariat. Black and white work together in many cases, and influence each other's rates of wages. They have similar complaints against capitalists, save that the grievances of the Negro worker are more fundamental and indefensible, ranging as they do, since the day of Karl Marx, from chattel slavery, to the worst paid, sweated, mobbed and cheated labor in any civilized land.

And while Negro labor in America suffers because of the fundamental inequities of the whole capitalistic system, the lowest and most fatal degree of its suffering comes not from the capitalists but from fellow white laborers. It is white labor that deprives the Negro of his right to vote, denies him education, denies him affiliation with trade unions, expels him from decent houses and neighborhoods, and heaps upon him the public insults of open color discrimination.

It is no sufficient answer to say that capital encourages this oppression and uses it for its own ends. This may have excused the ignorant and superstitious Russian peasants in the past and some of the poor whites of the South today. But the bulk of American white labor is neither ignorant nor fanatical. It knows exactly what it is doing and it means to do it. William Green and Matthew Woll of the A. F. of L. have no excuse of illiteracy or religion to veil their deliberate intention to keep Negroes and Mexicans and other elements of common labor, in a lower proletariat as subservient to their interests as theirs are to the interests of capital.

This large development of a petty bourgeoisie within the American laboring class is a post-Marxian phenomenon and the result of the tremendous and world-wide development of capitalism in the 20th Century. The market of capitalistic production has gained an effective world-wide organization. Industrial technique and mass production have brought possibilities in the production of goods and services which out-run even this wide market. A new class of technical engineers and managers has arisen forming a working class aristocracy between the older proletariat and the absentee owners of capital. The real owners of capital are small as well as large investors—workers who have deposits in savings banks and small holdings in stocks and bonds; families buying homes and purchasing commodities on installment; as well as the large and rich investors.

Of course, the individual laborer gets but an infinitesimal part of his income from such investments. On the other hand, such investments, in the aggregate, largely increase available capital for the exploiters, and they give investing laborers the capitalistic ideology. Between workers and owners of capital stand to-day the bankers and financiers who distribute capital and direct the engineers.

Thus the engineers and the saving better-paid workers, form a new petty bourgeois class, whose interests are bound up with those of the capitalists and antagonistic to those of common labor. On the other hand, common labor in America and white Europe far from being motivated by any vision of revolt against capitalism, has been blinded by the American vision of the possibility of layer after layer of the workers escaping into the wealthy class and becoming managers and employers of labor.

Thus in America we have seen a wild and ruthless scramble of labor groups over each other in order to climb to wealth on the backs of black labor and foreign immigrants. The Irish climbed on the Negroes. The Germans scrambled over the Negroes and emulated the Irish. The Scandinavians fought forward next to the Germans and the Italians and "Bohunks" are crowding up, leaving Negroes still at the bottom chained to helplessness, first by slavery, then by disfranchisement and always by the Color Bar.

The second influence on white labor both in America and Europe has been the fact that the extension of the world market by imperial expanding industry has established a world-wide new proletariat of colored workers, toiling under the worst conditions of 19th century capitalism, herded as slaves and serfs and furnishing by the lowest paid wage in modern history a mass of raw material for industry. With this largess the capitalists have consolidated their economic power, nullified universal suffrage and bribed the white workers by high wages, visions of wealth and the opportunity to drive "niggers." Soldiers and sailors from the white workers are used to keep "darkies" in their "places" and white foremen and engineers have been established as irresponsible satraps in China and India, Africa and the West Indies, backed by the organized and centralized ownership of machines, raw materials, finished commodities and land monopoly over the whole world.

How now does the philosophy of Karl Marx apply today to colored labor? First of all colored labor has no common ground with white labor. No soviet of technocrats would do more than exploit colored labor in order to raise the status of whites. No revolt of a white proletariat could be started if its object was to make black workers their economic, political and social equals. It is for this reason that American socialism for fifty years has been dumb on the Negro problem, and the communists cannot even get a respectful hearing in America unless they begin by expelling Negroes.

On the other hand, within the Negro groups, in the United States, in West Africa, in South America and in the West Indies, petty bourgeois groups are being evolved. In South America and the West Indies such groups drain off skill and intelligence into the white group, and leave the black labor poor, ignorant and leaderless save for an occasional demagog.

In West Africa, a Negro bourgeoisie is developing with invested capital and employment of natives and is only kept from the conventional capitalistic development by the opposition and enmity of white capital, and the white managers and engineers who represent it locally and who display bitter prejudice and tyranny; and by white European labor which furnishes armies and navies and Empire "preference." African black labor and black capital are therefore driven to seek alliance and common ground.

In the United States also a petty bourgeoisie is being developed, consisting of clergymen, teachers, farm owners, professional men and retail business men. The position of this class, however, is peculiar: they are not the chief or even large investors in Negro labor and therefore exploit it only here and there; and they bear the brunt of color prejudice because they express in word and work the aspirations of all black folk for emancipation. The revolt of any black proletariat could not, therefore, be logically directed against this class, nor could this class join either white capital, white engineers or white workers to strengthen the color bar.

Under these circumstances, what shall we say of the Marxian philosophy and of its relation to the American Negro? We can only say, as it seems to me, that the Marxian philosophy is a true diagnosis of the situation in Europe in the middle of the 19th Century despite some of its logical difficulties. But it must be modified in the United States of America and especially so far as the Negro group is concerned. The Negro is exploited to a degree that means poverty, crime, delinquency and indigence. And that exploitation comes not from a black capitalistic class but from the white capitalists and equally from the white proletariat. His only defense is such internal organization as will protect him from both parties, and such practical economic insight as will prevent inside the race group any large development of capitalistic exploitation.

Meantime, comes the Great Depression. It levels all in mighty catastrophe. The fantastic industrial structure of America is threatened with ruin. The trade unions of skilled labor are double tongued and helpless. Unskilled and common white labor is too frightened at Negro competition to attempt united action. It only begs a dole. The reformist program of Socialism meets no response from the white proletariat because it offers no escape to wealth and no effective bar to black labor, and a mud-sill of black labor is essential to white labor's standard of living. The shrill cry of a few communists is not even listened to, because and solely because it seeks to break down barriers between black and white. There is not at present the slightest indication that a Marxian revolution based on a united class-conscious proletariat is anywhere on the American far horizon. Rather race antagonism and labor group rivalry is still undisturbed by world catastrophe. In the hearts of black laborers alone, therefore, lie those ideals of democracy in politics and industry which may in time make the workers of the world effective dictators of civilization.

(May, 1933. Vol. XL, No. 5, pp. 103ff)

FOREIGN AFFAIRS

CHINA

To most folk the wonder of the Chinese revolution is not in the revolution but in the fact that Chinamen show themselves so human. There was a time when everything bizarre, curious and topsyturvy was quite as a matter of course attributed to China. When it came to rational modern thought we calmly omitted China. Histories of the world omitted China; if a Chinaman invented compass or movable type or gunpowder we promptly "forgot it" and named only their European inventors. In short, we regarded China as a sort of different and quite inconsequential planet.

Suddenly now China looms as a modern nation seeking in the bloodlust of revolution the freedom to think and be. Shall we welcome Chinese rebirth with salvos of applause? Why—er—yes; yes, of course; but say, look here: what kind of a world is this going to be, full of civilized Japs, Chinks, dagoes and darkies? Isn't it high time for Desperate Desmond Hobson to wind his golden trumpet and hail us to war for the salvation of "white" civilization?

Soberly, is not the world face to face with an enlarged, broadened, endless "race" and "color" problem, and what are those folk to do who cannot conceive a world where black, brown and white are free and equal?

(February, 1912. Vol. III, No. 4, p. 156)

HAYTI

The United States has violated the independence of a sister state. With absolutely no adequate excuse she has made a white American Admiral sole and irresponsible dictator of Hayti. The anarchy in Hayti is no worse than the anarchy in the United States at the time of our Civil War, and not as great as the anarchy today in Europe. The lynching and murder in Port-au-Prince is no worse than, if as bad, as the lynching in Georgia. Hayti can, and will, work out her destiny and is more civilized today than Texas.

Here, then, is the outrage of uninvited American intervention, the shooting and disarming of peaceful Haytian citizens, the seizure of public funds, the veiled, but deliberate design to alienate Haytian territory at the Mole St. Nicholas, and the pushing of the monopoly claims of an American corporation which holds a filched, if not a fraudulent railway charter. SHAME ON AMERICA! And what are we ten million Negroes going to do about it? Can you not at least do this? Write to President Wilson and protest; ask for a distinct, honest statement of our purposes in Hayti and an American Commission of white and colored men to point the way of Honor instead of Graft. WRITE NOW and let the Editor of THE CRISIS have a copy of your letter.

(October, 1915. Vol. X, No. 6, p. 291)

IRELAND

Few colored people know or realize what Ireland has suffered at the hands of England. On the other hand, the open dislike of Irish and colored people in the United States has given the

Irish cause little or no sympathy so far as Negroes are concerned.

It happened unfortunately that the first Irish immigration to the United States took place just as the free Negroes of the North were making their most impressive forward movement. Irishmen and black men came, therefore, in bitter industrial competition in such cities as Boston, New York and Philadelphia. Riots and street fights ensued. Irishmen hanged Negroes during the draft riots in New York City, and drove them off the streets in Philadelphia.

But all this is past. Today we must remember that the white slums of Dublin represent more bitter depths of human degradation than the black slums of Charleston and New Orleans, and where human oppression exists there the sympathy of all black hearts must go. The recent Irish revolt may have been foolish, but would to God some of us had sense enough to be fools!

(August, 1916. Vol. XII, No. 4, pp. 166-7)

TAGORE

The world in these days is beginning to listen to a great, new voice representing the colored races and speaking with the peculiar authority of a Nobel prize man. Rabindranath Tagore, the East Indian poet, and knight of the British Empire, has recently addressed the students of Tokio University, Japan. His attitude toward Europe is generous, but firm. He says:

> In Europe we have seen noble hearts who have ever stood up for the rights of man, irrespective of color and creed; who have braved calumny and insult from their own people in fighting for humanity's cause and raising their voices against the mad orgies of militarism, against the rage for brutal retaliation or rapacity that sometimes takes possession of a whole people; who are always ready to make reparation for wrongs done in the past by their own nations, and vainly attempt to stem the tide of cowardly injustice that flows unchecked because the resistance is weak and innocuous on the part of the injured.

But where Europe is too consciously busy in building up her power, defying her deeper nature and mocking it, she is heaping up her iniquities to the sky, crying for God's vengeance, and spreading the inflection of ugliness, physical and moral, over the face of the earth with her heartless commerce heedlessly outraging man's sense of the beautiful and the good.

This is his answer when asked what shall suffice for the healing of the nations:

The great problem of man's history has been the race problem. Western civilization, particularly as exemplified in Germany, has been based upon exclusiveness. It has been watchful to keep so-called 'alien' elements at arm's length; to minimize them; to exterminate them. This attitude must change, if peace is to come and endure upon the earth. We want 'a social unity with which all the different peoples could be held together, yet fully enjoying the freedom of maintaining their own differences.' Unity in difference—as the river, now hurrying along between steep banks, now loitering over the shallow meadow reaches; now flecked with foam in its swift flow, now dappled with sunbeams in its smooth and level course; now lashed to fury by the howling winds, now dimpled by the gentle summer airs still remains the river, the one—so the stream of humanity, whether expressing itself in a higher or a lower type, in white, or yellow, or black, or red, or brown man; whether rushing torrent-like through the great ways of modern commerce and industry, or sleeping in the backwaters of thought and reflection, is one.

(December, 1916. Vol. XIII, No. 2, pp. 60-1)

EGYPT AND INDIA

The sympathy of Black America must of necessity go out to colored India and colored Egypt. Their forefathers were ancient friends, cousins, blood-brothers, in the hoary ages of antiquity. The blood of yellow and white hordes has diluted the ancient black blood of India, but her eldest Buddha sits back, with kinky hair; the Negro who laid the founding stones of Egypt and furnished some of her mightiest thinkers, builders and leaders has mingled his blood with the invader on so vast a scale that the modern Egyptian mulatto hardly remembers his descent. But we are all one—we the Despised and Oppressed, the "niggers" of England and America.

We of America fight the great fight of Peace—we agitate, we petition, we expose, we plead, we argue. It is a long, slow, humiliating path, but for us War, Force, Revolution are impossible, unthinkable. For anybody the costs of bloody uprising are so vast and uncounted that they must bring pause to the wildest. Yet, who can judge others? Who sitting in America can say that Revolution is never right on the Ganges or the Nile? Who of us who suffer can judge how unbearable is the suffering of unknown friends? We bow our heads and close our aching ears. Only our hearts pray that Right may triumph and Justice and Pity over brute Force and Organized Theft and Race Prejudice, from San Francisco to Calcutta and from Cairo to New York.

(June, 1919. Vol. XVIII, No. 2, p. 62)

BLEEDING IRELAND

No people can more exactly interpret the inmost meaning of the present situation in Ireland than the American Negro. The scheme is simple. You knock a man down and then have him arrested for assault. You kill a man and then hang the corpse for murder. We black folk are only too familiar with this procedure. In a given city, a mob attacks us unprepared, unsuspecting, and kills innocent and harmless black workingmen in cold blood. The bewildered Negroes rush together and begin to defend themselves. Immediately by swift legerdemain the mob becomes the militia or a gang of "deputy sheriffs". They search, harry and kill the Negroes. They disarm them and loot their homes, and when the city awakes after the "race riot", the jail is filled with Negroes charged with rioting and fomenting crime!

So in Ireland! The Irish resist, as they have resisted for hundreds of years, various and exasperating forms of English oppression. Their resistance is called crime and under ordinary conditions would be crime; in retaliation not only the "guilty" but the innocent among them are murdered and robbed and public property is burned by English guardians of the Peace!

All this must bring mingled feelings of dismay to Irishmen. No people in the world have in the past gone with blither spirit to "kill niggers" from Kingston to Delhi and from Kumassi to Fiji. In the United States, Irish influence not only stood behind the mob in Cincinnati, Philadelphia and New York, but still stands in the American Federation of Labor to keep out Negro workingmen. All this contains no word of argument against the ultimate freedom of Ireland—which God speedily grant!—but it does make us remember how in this world it is the Oppressed who have continually been used to cow and kill the Oppressed in the interest of the Universal Oppressor.

(March, 1921. Vol. XXI, No. 5, p. 200)

LABOR

ORGANIZED LABOR

THE CRISIS believes in organized labor. It realizes that the standard of living among workers has been raised in the last half century through the efforts and sacrifice of laborers banded together in unions, and that all American labor today, white, black and yellow, benefits from this great movement.

For such reasons we carry on our front cover the printers' union label to signify that the printing and binding of this magazine is done under conditions and with wages satisfactory to the printers' union.

We do this in spite of the fact, as well known to us as to others, that the "conditions satisfactory" to labor men in this city include the deliberate exclusion from decent-paying jobs of every black man whom white workingmen can exclude on any pretense. We know, and all men know, that under ordinary circumstances no black artisan can today work as printer, baker, blacksmith, carpenter, hatter, butcher, tailor, street or railway employee, boilermaker, bookbinder, electrical worker, glass blower, machinist, plumber, telegrapher, electrotyper, textile worker, upholsterer, stone cutter, carriage maker, plasterer, mason, painter—or at any other decent trade, unless he works as a "scab," or unless in some locality he has secured such a foothold that the white union men are not able easily to oust him.

This policy is not always avowed (although there are a dozen unions affiliated with the American Federation of Labor who openly confine admission to "white" men), but it is perfectly well understood. Some unions, like the printers and the carpenters, admit a lone colored man here and there so as to enable them the more easily to turn down the rest. Others, like the masons, admit Negroes in the South where they must, and bar them in the North where they can.

Whatever the tactics, the result is the same for the mass of white workingmen in America; beat or starve the Negro out of his job if you can by keeping him out of the union; or if you must admit him, do the same thing inside union lines.

What then must be the attitude of the black man in the event of a strike like that of the white waiters of New York? The mass of them must most naturally regard the union white man as their enemy. They may not know the history of the labor movement, but they know the history of white and black waiters in New York, and when they take back the jobs out of which the white waiters have driven them, they do the natural and sensible thing, howsoever pitiable the necessity of such cutthroat policies in the labor world may be. So long as union labor fights for humanity, its mission is divine; but when it fights for a clique of Americans, Irish or German monopolists who have cornered or are trying to corner the market on a certain type of service, and are seeking to sell that service at a premium, while other competent workmen starve, they deserve themselves the starvation which they plan for their darker and poorer fellows.

(July, 1912. Vol. IV, No. 3, p. 131)

THE NEGRO AND LABOR

The usual American attitude toward Negroes in industrial countries like this is two-fold. On the one hand, the white laboring man excludes the Negro from work just as far as possible, particularly in the skilled trades; this is because, as he says, the Negro will work for lower wages and does not deserve the consideration of white labor. The employer, on the other hand, will employ Negroes when he can get them more cheaply than white men, but he considers them less efficient and their presence raises problems. They are, nevertheless, always a possible substitute when white labor becomes too exorbitant in its demands.

Neither party is apt to consider the point of view of the colored man. He needs work and being usually excluded from the union, gets his chance to labor by underbidding the white laborer; and is compelled often to regard the man who hires "scab" labor as his benefactor. On the other hand, being compelled to live somewhere, being poor and ignorant, he brings to such employers and their friends problems in housing and other social matters.

To most people these problems are a sort of perpetual American condition and show no particular change. On the contrary, this problem of Negro labor is part and parcel of the whole world problem of industry,—before, during and after the war. When there came to Europe four comparatively new crops: sugar, rice, tobacco, and later cotton, they transformed the industry and commerce of the modern world. Before that local industry had supplied the wants of the poor, but commerce was primarily to satisfy the desires and whims of the rich. It had, therefore, during the Middle Ages many of the characteristics of gambling.

When, however, there came from overseas great crops which ministered to the wants of the mass of men, then commerce became more stabilized, the demand was steadier and the amount of goods handled was much larger; so commerce expanded tremendously. Then, too, the discovery of America gave the laboring class, for the first time in modern days, free, rich land. All that was needed was labor, and labor was procured by seizing white men in Europe and black men in Africa. There was in the 15th Century no great difference between the best civilization of Africa and the best civilization of Europe; but while Africa had to protect herself against barbarians, Europe was protected by natural physical barriers, so that in Africa the slave trade came to be a defense against barbarians and therefore expanded, while in Europe certain classes of laborers began to gain political power.

There arose then in Europe the modern labor movement, and when this labor movement struck America, it found African slavery established here. At first it endured slavery because it was the slavery of an alien race; then it began to conceive that these black aliens might become laborers and free citizens, like the whites. This movement, which culminated after the Negroes had helped free America from England, was finally halted by the increase of the new cotton crop, which made slave labor more valuable than ever.

However, by the middle of the 19th Century the white laborers realized that black slavery was encroaching upon their free land and must be confined to certain limits, while the white slave owners knew that they must have more and more free land or slavery would not pay. The results were the Civil War and the legal emancipation of Negroes.

This brings us to the modern world. The situation is that the mass of European and American white laborers have gained political power and are beginning to know how to use it. They are, therefore, demanding a larger share of the profits of industry; but, on the other hand, the controllers of industry and commerce have found that by investing in tropical and semitropical lands, they have a new chance to get cheap labor and valuable raw material of the sort which is increasingly in demand in modern industry. They have induced the laboring class to vote large appropriations for armies and navies. With this they seized control of Africa, Asia and the islands of the sea.

You would think that there would have come, for this reason, revolt on the part of the yellow, brown and black laborers, and particularly of those black laborers in the United States who are legally free but still largely disfranchised both in politics and by the labor movement. Such revolt was indeed foreshadowed, but before this came the World War, which was caused by the jealousy of the nations who sought to dominate the darker world and who fell out in the division of the spoils. They fought a terrible war with each other for four years, and the result is that since the war the darker nations *are* revolting. In China, Japan and India, in Egypt and South and West Africa, in the West Indies and in America, there is a growing determination on the part of colored laborers that they are not going to remain the victims of modern industrial development. The greatest post-war problem is whether white laborers are going to recognize the demand of these dark laborers for equal consideration, or whether white capitalists and employers are going to continue to play off black and white labor against each other and thus seek to exploit and develop Asia and Africa, simply for the benefit of the privileged classes of the white world.

(April, 1923. Vol. XXV, No. 6, pp. 248-9)

POLITICS

OHIO

This fall the colored voters of Ohio have a wonderful opportunity; the 40,000 or 50,000 votes which they cast will undoubtedly decide whether women shall vote in that State and whether the last of the infamous black laws shall be swept from the statute book.

The enfranchisement of women means the doubling of the black vote at the point where that vote is needed. If woman suffrage wins in Ohio, it will sweep the Middle West and East in less than a generation. As Negroes have a larger proportion of women than the whites our relative voting importance in the North will be increased.

Moreover, we need above all classes the women's influence in politics—the influence of the mother, the wife, the teacher and the washerwoman. In the African fatherland the women stood high in counsel. We need them here again. It would be very bad, indeed, if the colored vote should be adverse to enfranchising women, even though it were not the deciding factor, for the day has gone by forever when colored men could get a respectful hearing for their protest against their own disfranchisement if, when offered the opportunity for voting for enfrancising their mothers, wives and sisters, they should fail to do so. For still another reason it will be unfortunate if the Ohio Negroes vote against votes for women; the vote will be analyzed with keen and eager intelligence, and the results studied for future use. The colored voters will turn many possible friends into critics, to put it mildly, if they inflict upon women that disfranchisement which all thinking people deplore when applied to the Negroes themselves. The general proposition that women ought to have the right to vote surely needs no argument among disfranchised colored folk:

Women are workers; workers should vote.

Women are taxpayers; taxpayers should vote.

Women have brains; voting needs brains.

Women organize, direct and largely support the family; families should vote.

Women are mothers of men; if men vote, why not women?

If politics are too nasty and rough for women voters, is it not time we asked the vote of women to cleanse them?

Is there a single argument for the right of men to vote, or for the right of black men to vote, that does not apply to the votes for women, and particularly for black women?

(August, 1912. Vol. IV, No. 4, pp. 181-2)

THE LAST WORD IN POLITICS

Before another number of THE CRISIS appears the next President of the United States will have been elected. We have, therefore, but this last word to colored voters and their friends.

Those who have scanned our advertising pages this month and last have noted an unusual phenomenon: the three great political parties have in this way been appealing to the colored vote for support. They have done this out of no love to this magazine, but because they needed the publicity which this magazine alone could give and because they knew that our news columns and editorial pages were not for sale. We commend these advertisements to our readers' notice. They are the last word of political appeal and they are undoubtedly sincere.

Taking them now and comparing and weighing them, and what is the net result? The Republican party emphasizes its past relations with the Negro, the recent appointments to office and warns against the disfranchisement and caste system of the

Democratic South. The weak point in this argument is that without the consent of Republican Presidents, Republican Congresses and a Republican Supreme Court, Southern disfranchisement could not survive a single day.*)*

The Progressive party stresses its platform of social reform, so admirable in many respects, and points to the recognition given in its party councils to the Northern Negro voter. The weak point here is the silence over the fact that Theodore Roosevelt, the perpetrator of the Brownsville outrage, has added to that blunder the Chicago disfranchisement and is appealing to the South for white votes on this platform.

The Democratic party appeals for colored votes on the ground that other parties have done and are doing precisely the things that the Democratic party is accused of doing against the Negro, and this in spite of the fact that these parties receive the bulk of the Negro vote. If, therefore, the Negro expects Democratic help and support, why does he not give the Democrats his vote? The weak point here is that the invitation is at best negative; the Negro is asked to take a leap in the dark without specific promises as to what protection he may expect after Democrats are in power.

In none of these cases, therefore, is the invitation satisfactory. Nevertheless, because the Socialists, with their manly stand for human rights irrespective of color, are at present out of the calculation, the Negro voter must choose between these three parties. He is asked virtually to vote:

1. For a party which has promised and failed.
2. For a party which has failed and promised.
3. For a party which merely promises.

We sympathize with those faithful old black voters who will always vote the Republican ticket. We respect their fidelity but not their brains. We can understand those who, despite the unspeakable Roosevelt, accept his platform which is broad on all subjects except the greatest—human rights. This we can understand, but we cannot follow.

We sincerely believe that even in the face of promises disconcertingly vague, and in the face of the solid caste-ridden South, it is better to elect Woodrow Wilson President of the United States and prove once for all if the Democratic party dares to be Democratic when it comes to black men. It has proven that it can be in many Northern States and cities. Can it be in the nation? We hope so and we are willing to risk a trial.

(November, 1912. Vol. V, No. 1. p. 29)

INTERMARRIAGE

Few groups of people are forced by their situation into such cruel dilemmas as American Negroes. Nevertheless they must not allow anger or personal resentment to dim their clear vision.

Take, for instance, the question of the intermarrying of white and black folk; it is a question that colored people seldom discuss. It is about the last of the social problems over which they are disturbed, because they so seldom face it in fact or in theory. Their problems are problems of work and wages, of the right to vote, of the right to travel decently, of the right to frequent places of public amusement, of the right to public security.

White people, on the other hand, for the most part profess to see but one problem: "Do you want your sister to marry a Nigger?" Sometimes we are led to wonder if they are lying about their solicitude on this point; and if under present laws anybody should be compelled to marry any person whom she does not wish to marry?

This brings us to the crucial question: so far as the present advisability of intermarrying between white and colored people in the United States is concerned, both races are practically in complete agreement. Colored folk marry colored folk and white marry white, and the exceptions are very few.

Why not then stop the exceptions? For three reasons: physical, social and moral.

1. For the *physical* reason that to prohibit such intermarriage would be publicly to acknowledge that black blood is a physical taint—a thing that no decent, self-respecting black man can be asked to admit.

2. For the *social* reason that if two full-grown responsible human beings of any race and color propose to live together as man and wife, it is only social decency not simply to allow, but to compel them to marry. Let those people who have yelled themselves purple in the face over Jack Johnson just sit down

and ask themselves this question: Granted that Johnson and Miss Cameron proposed to live together, was it better for them to be legally married or not? We know what the answer of the Bourbon South is. We know that they would rather uproot the foundations of decent society than to call the consorts of their brothers, sons and fathers their legal wives. We infinitely prefer the methods of Jack Johnson to those of the brother of Governor Mann of Virginia.

3. The *moral* reason for opposing laws against intermarriage is the greatest of all: such laws leave the colored girl absolutely helpless before the lust of white men. It reduces colored women in the eyes of the law to the position of dogs. Low as the white girl falls, she can compel her seducer to marry her. If it were proposed to take this last defense from poor white working girls, can you not hear the screams of the "white slave" defenders? What have these people to say to laws that propose to create in the United States 5,000,000 women, the ownership of whose bodies no white man is bound to respect?

Note these arguments, my brothers and sisters, and watch your State legislature. This winter will see a determined attempt to insult and degrade us by such non-intermarriage laws. We must kill them, not because we are anxious to marry white men's sisters, but because we are determined that white men shall let our sisters alone.

(February, 1913. Vol. V, No. 4, pp. 180-1)

THE NEGRO PARTY

There is for the future one and only one effective political move for colored voters. We have long foreseen it, but we have sought to avoid it. It is a move of segregation, it "hyphenates" us, it separates us from our fellow Americans; but self-defense knows no nice hesitations. The American Negro must either vote as a unit or continue to be politically emasculated as at present.

Miss Inez Milholland, in a recent address, outlined with singular clearness and force a Negro Party on the lines of the recently formed Woman's Party. Mr. R. R. Church, Jr., of

Tennessee, and certain leading colored men in New Jersey, Ohio and elsewhere have unconsciously and effectively followed her advice.

The situation is this: At present the Democratic party can maintain its ascendency only by the help of the Solid South. The Solid South is built on the hate and fear of Negroes; consequently it can never, as a party, effectively bid for the Negro vote. The Republican party is the party of wealth and big business and, as such, is the natural enemy of the humble working people who compose the mass of Negroes. Between these two great parties, as parties there is little to choose.

On the other hand, parties are represented by individual candidates. Negroes can have choice in the naming of these candidates and they can vote for or against them. Their only effective method in the future is to organize in every congressional district as a Negro Party to endorse those candidates, Republican, Democratic, Socialist, or what-not, whose promises and past performances give greatest hope for the remedying of the wrongs done the Negro race. If no candidate fills this bill they should nominate a candidate of their own and give that candidate their solid vote. This policy effectively and consistently carried out throughout the United States, North and South, by colored voters who refuse the bribe of petty office and money, would make the Negro vote one of the most powerful and effective of the group votes in the United States.

This is the program which we must follow. We may hesitate and argue about it, but if we are a sensible, reasonable people we will come to it and the quicker the better.

(October, 1916. Vol. XII, No. 6, pp. 268-9)

THE ARTS

THE NEGRO AND THE AMERICAN STAGE

We all know what the Negro for the most part has meant hitherto on the American stage. He has been a lay figure whose business it was usually to be funny and sometimes pathetic. He has never, with very few exceptions, been human or credible. This, of course, cannot last. The most dramatic group of people in the history of the United States is the American Negro. It would be very easy for a great artist so to interpret the history of our country as to make the plot turn entirely upon the black man. Thus two classes of dramatic situations of tremendous import arise. The inner life of this black group and the contact of black and white. It is going to be difficult to get at these facts for the drama and treat them sincerely and artistically because they are covered by a shell; or shall I say a series of concentric shells? In the first place comes the shell of what most people think the Negro ought to be and this makes everyone a self-appointed and preordained judge to say without further thought or inquiry whether this is untrue or that is wrong. Then secondly there comes the great problem of the future relations of groups and races not only in the United States but throughout the world. To some people this seems to be a tremendous and imminent problem and in their wild anxiety to settle it in the only way which seems to them the right way they are determined to destroy art, religion and good common sense in an effort to make everything that is said or shown propaganda for their ideas. These two protective shells most of us recognize; but there is a third shell that we do not so often recognize, whose sudden presence fills us with astonishment; and that is the attitude of the Negro world itself.

This Negro world which is growing in self-consciousness, economic power and literary expression is tremendously sensitive. It has sore toes, nerve filled teeth, delicate eyes and quivering ears. And it has these because during its whole conscious life it has been maligned and caricatured and lied about to an extent inconceivable to those who do not know. Any mention of Negro blood or Negro life in America for a century has been occasion for an ugly picture, a dirty allusion, a nasty comment or a pessimistic forecast. The result is that the Negro today fears any attempt of the artist to paint Negroes. He is not satisfied unless everything is perfect and proper and beautiful and joyful and hopeful. He is afraid to be painted as he is lest his human foibles and shortcomings be seized by his enemies for the purposes of the ancient and hateful propaganda.

Happy is the artist that breaks through any of these shells for his is the kingdom of eternal beauty. He will come through scarred and perhaps a little embittered, certainly astonished at the almost universal misinterpretation of his motives and aims. Eugene O'Neill is bursting through. He has my sympathy for his soul must be lame with the enthusiasm of the blows rained upon him. But it is work that must be done. No greater mine of dramatic material ever lay ready for the great artist's hands than the situation of men of Negro blood in modern America.

(June, 1924. Vol. XXVIII, No. 2, pp. 56-7)

CRITERIA OF NEGRO ART

I do not doubt but there are some in this audience who are a little disturbed at the subject of this meeting, and particularly at the subject I have chosen. Such people are thinking something like this: "How is it that an organization like this, a group of radicals trying to bring new things into the world, a fighting organization which has come up out of the blood and dust of battle, struggling for the right of black men to be ordinary human beings—how is it that an organization of this kind can turn aside to talk about Art? After all, what have we who are slaves and black to do with Art?"

Or perhaps there are others who feel a certain relief and are saying, "After all it is rather satisfactory after all this talk about rights and fighting to sit and dream of something which leaves a nice taste in the mouth".

Let me tell you that neither of these groups is right. The thing we are talking about tonight is part of the great fight we are carrying on and it represents a forward and an upward look— a pushing onward. You and I have been breasting hills; we have been climbing upward; there has been progress and we can see it day by day looking back along blood-filled paths. But as you go through the valleys and over the foothills, so long as you are climbing, the direction,—north, south, east or west,—is of less importance. But when gradually the vista widens and you begin to see the world at your feet and the far horizon, then it is time to know more precisely whither you are going and what you really want.

What do we want? What is the thing we are after? As it was phrased last night it had a certain truth: We want to be Americans, full-fledged Americans, with all the rights of other American citizens. But is that all? Do we want simply to be Americans? Once in a while through all of us there flashes some clairvoyance, some clear idea, of what America really is. We who are dark can see America in a way that white Americans can not. And seeing our country thus, are we satisfied with its present goals and ideals?

In the high school where I studied we learned most of Scott's "Lady of the Lake" by heart. In after life once it was my privilege to see the lake. It was Sunday. It was quiet. You could glimpse the deer wandering in unbroken forests; you could hear the soft ripple of romance on the waters. Around me fell the cadence of that poetry of my youth. I fell asleep full of the enchantment of the Scottish border. A new day broke and with it came a sudden rush of excursionists. They were mostly Americans and they were loud and strident. They poured upon the little pleasure boat,—men with their hats a little on one side and drooping cigars in the wet corners of their mouths; women who shared their conversation with the world. They all tried to get everywhere first. They pushed other people out of the way. They made all sorts of incoherent noises and gestures so that the quiet home folk and the visitors from other lands silently and half-wonderingly gave way before them. They struck a note not evil but wrong. They carried, perhaps, a sense of strength and accomplishment, but their hearts had no conception of the beauty which pervaded this holy place.

If you tonight suddenly should become full-fledged Americans; if your color faded, or the color line here in Chicago was miraculously forgotten; suppose, too, you became at the same time rich and powerful;—what is it that you would want? What would you immediately seek? Would you buy the most powerful of motor cars and outrace Cook County? Would you buy the most elaborate estate on the North Shore? Would you be a Rotarian or a Lion or a What-not of the very last degree? Would you wear the most striking clothes, give the richest dinners and buy the longest press notices?

Even as you visualize such ideals you know in your hearts that these are not the things you really want. You realize this sooner than the average white American because, pushed aside

as we have been in America, there has come to us not only a
certain distaste for the tawdry and flamboyant but a vision of
what the world could be if it were really a beautiful world; if we
had the true spirit; if we had the Seeing Eye, the Cunning Hand,
the Feeling Heart; if we had, to be sure, not perfect happiness,
but plenty of good hard work, the inevitable suffering that always comes with life; sacrifice and waiting, all that—but, nevertheless, lived in a world where men know, where men create,
where they realize themselves and where they enjoy life. It is
that sort of a world we want to create for ourselves and for all
America.

After all, who shall describe Beauty? What is it? I remember
tonight four beautiful things: The Cathedral at Cologne, a forest
in stone, set in light and changing shadow, echoing with sunlight and solemn song; a village of the Veys in West Africa, a
little thing of mauve and purple, quiet, lying content and shining
in the sun; a black and velvet room where on a throne rests, in
old and yellowing marble, the broken curves of the Venus of
Milo; a single phrase of music in the Southern South—utter
melody, haunting and appealing, suddenly arising out of night
and eternity, beneath the moon.

Such is Beauty. Its variety is infinite, its possibility is endless.
In normal life all may have it and have it yet again. The world
is full of it; and yet today the mass of human beings are choked
away from it, and their lives distorted and made ugly. This is
not only wrong, it is silly. Who shall right this well-nigh universal failing? Who shall let this world be beautiful? Who shall
restore to men the glory of sunsets and the peace of quiet sleep?

We black folk may help for we have within us as a race new
stirrings; stirrings of the beginning of a new appreciation of joy,
of a new desire to create, of a new will to be; as though in this
morning of group life we had awakened from some sleep that
at once dimly mourns the past and dreams a splendid future;
and there has come the conviction that the Youth that is here
today, the Negro Youth, is a different kind of Youth, because
in some new way it bears this mighty prophecy on its breast,
with a new realization of itself, with new determination for all
mankind.

What has this Beauty to do with the world? What has Beauty
to do with Truth and Goodness—with the facts of the world and
the right actions of men? "Nothing" the artists rush to answer.

They may be right. I am but an humble disciple of art and cannot presume to say. I am one who tells the truth and exposes evil and seeks with Beauty and for Beauty to set the world right. That somehow, somewhere eternal and perfect Beauty sits above Truth and Right I can conceive, but here and now and in the world in which I work they are for me unseparated and inseparable.

This is brought to us peculiarly when as artists we face our own past as a people. There has come to us—and it has come especially through the man we are going to honor tonight*—a realization of that past, of which for long years we have been ashamed, for which we have apologized. We thought nothing could come out of that past which we wanted to remember; which we wanted to hand down to our children. Suddenly, this same past is taking on form, color and reality, and in a half shamefaced way we are beginning to be proud of it. We are remembering that the romance of the world did not die and lie forgotten in the Middle Age; that if you want romance to deal with you must have it here and now and in your own hands.

I once knew a man and woman. They had two children, a daughter who was white and a daughter who was brown; the daughter who was white married a white man; and when her wedding was preparing the daughter who was brown prepared to go and celebrate. But the mother said, "No!" and the brown daughter went into her room and turned on the gas and died. Do you want Greek tragedy swifter than that?

Or again, here is a little Southern town and you are in the public square. On one side of the square is the office of a colored lawyer and on all the other sides are men who do not like colored lawyers. A white woman goes into the black man's office and points to the white-filled square and says, "I want five hundred dollars now and if I do not get it I am going to scream."

Have you heard the story of the conquest of German East Africa? Listen to the untold tale: There were 40,000 black men and 4,000 white men who talked German. There were 20,000 black men and 12,000 white men who talked English. There were 10,000 black men and 400 white men who talked French.

*Carter Godwin Woodson, 12th Spingarn Medallist.

In Africa then where the Mountains of the Moon raised their white and snow-capped heads into the mouth of the tropic sun, where Nile and Congo rise and the Great Lakes swim, these men fought; they struggled on mountain, hill and valley, in river, lake and swamp, until in masses they sickened, crawled and died; until the 4,000 white Germans had become mostly bleached bones; until nearly all the 12,000 white Englishmen had returned to South Africa, and the 400 Frenchmen to Belgium and Heaven; all except a mere handful of the white men died; but thousands of black men from East, West and South Africa, from Nigeria and the Valley of the Nile, and from the West Indies still struggled, fought and died. For four years they fought and won and lost German East Africa; and all you hear about it is that England and Belgium conquered German Africa for the allies!

Such is the true and stirring stuff of which Romance is born and from this stuff come the stirrings of men who are beginning to remember that this kind of material is theirs; and this vital life of their own kind is beckoning them on.

The question comes next as to the interpretation of these new stirrings, of this new spirit: Of what is the colored artist capable? We have had on the part of both colored and white people singular unanimity of judgment in the past. Colored people have said: "This work must be inferior because it comes from colored people." White people have said: "It is inferior because it is done by colored people." But today there is coming to both the realization that the work of the black man is not always inferior. Interesting stories come to us. A professor in the University of Chicago read to a class that had studied literature a passage of poetry and asked them to guess the author. They guessed a goodly company from Shelley and Robert Browning down to Tennyson and Masefield. The author was Countée Cullen. Or again the English critic John Drinkwater went down to a Southern seminary, one of the sort which "finishes" young white women of the South. The students sat with their wooden faces while he tried to get some response out of them. Finally he said, "Name me some of your Southern poets". They hesitated. He said finally, "I'll start out with your best: Paul Laurence Dunbar"!

With the growing recognition of Negro artists in spite of the severe handicaps, one comforting thing is occurring to both

white and black. They are whispering, "Here is a way out. Here
is the real solution of the color problem. The recognition accorded Cullen, Hughes, Fauset, White and others shows there
is no real color line. Keep quiet! Don't complain! Work! All will
be well!"

I will not say that already this chorus amounts to a conspiracy. Perhaps I am naturally too suspicious. But I will say
that there are today a surprising number of white people who
are getting great satisfaction out of these younger Negro writers
because they think it is going to stop agitation of the Negro
question. They say, "What is the use of your fighting and complaining; do the great thing and the reward is there". And many
colored people are all too eager to follow this advice; especially
those who are weary of the eternal struggle along the color line,
who are afraid to fight and to whom the money of philanthropists and the alluring publicity are subtle and deadly bribes.
They say, "What is the use of fighting? Why not show simply
what we deserve and let the reward come to us?"

And it is right here that the National Association for the
Advancement of Colored People comes upon the field, comes
with its great call to a new battle, a new fight and new things
to fight before the old things are wholly won; and to say that the
Beauty of Truth and Freedom which shall some day be our
heritage and the heritage of all civilized men is not in our hands
yet and that we ourselves must not fail to realize.

There is in New York tonight a black woman molding clay
by herself in a little bare room, because there is not a single
school of sculpture in New York where she is welcome. Surely
there are doors she might burst through, but when God makes
a sculptor He does not always make the pushing sort of person
who beats his way through doors thrust in his face. This girl is
working her hands off to get out of this country so that she can
get some sort of training.

There was Richard Brown. If he had been white he would
have been alive today instead of dead of neglect. Many helped
him when he asked but he was not the kind of boy that always
asks. He was simply one who made colors sing.

There is a colored woman in Chicago who is a great musician.
She thought she would like to study at Fontainebleau this summer where Walter Damrosch and a score of leaders of Art have
an American school of music. But the application blank of this

school says: "I am a white American and I apply for admission to the school."

We can go on the stage; we can be just as funny as white Americans wish us to be; we can play all the sordid parts that America likes to assign to Negroes; but for anything else there is still small place for us.

And so I might go on. But let me sum up with this: Suppose the only Negro who survived some centuries hence was the Negro painted by white Americans in the novels and essays they have written. What would people in a hundred years say of black Americans? Now turn it around. Suppose you were to write a story and put in it the kind of people you know and like and imagine. You might get it published and you might not. And the "might not" is still far bigger than the "might". The white publishers catering to white folk would say, "It is not interesting"—to white folk, naturally not. They want Uncle Toms, Topsies, good "darkies" and clowns. I have in my office a story with all the earmarks of truth. A young man says that he started out to write and had his stories accepted. Then he began to write about the things he knew best about, that is, about his own people. He submitted a story to a magazine which said, "We are sorry, but we cannot take it". "I sat down and revised my story, changing the color of the characters and the locale and sent it under an assumed name with a change of address and it was accepted by the same magazine that had refused it, the editor promising to take anything else I might send in providing it was good enough."

We have, to be sure, a few recognized and successful Negro artists; but they are not all those fit to survive or even a good minority. They are but the remnants of that ability and genius among us whom the accidents of education and opportunity have raised on the tidal waves of chance. We black folk are not altogether peculiar in this. After all, in the world at large, it is only the accident, the remnant, that gets the chance to make the most of itself; but if this is true of the white world it is infinitely more true of the colored world. It is not simply the great clear tenor of Roland Hayes that opened the ears of America. We have had many voices of all kinds as fine as his and America was and is as deaf as she was for years to him. Then a foreign land heard Hayes and put its imprint on him and immediately America with all its imitative snobbery woke up. We approved Hayes because London, Paris and Berlin approved him and not simply because he was a great singer.

Thus it is the bounden duty of black America to begin this great work of the creation of Beauty, of the preservation of Beauty, of the realization of Beauty, and we must use in this work all the methods that men have used before. And what have been the tools of the artist in times gone by? First of all, he has used the Truth—not for the sake of truth, not as a scientist seeking truth, but as one upon whom Truth eternally thrusts itself as the highest hand-maid of imagination, as the one great vehicle of universal understanding. Again artists have used Goodness—goodness in all its aspects of justice, honor and right —not for sake of an ethical sanction but as the one true method of gaining sympathy and human interest.

The apostle of Beauty thus becomes the apostle of Truth and Right not by choice but by inner and outer compulsion. Free he is but his freedom is ever bounded by Truth and Justice; and slavery only dogs him when he is denied the right to tell the Truth or recognize an ideal of Justice.

Thus all Art is propaganda and ever must be, despite the wailing of the purists. I stand in utter shamelessness and say that whatever art I have for writing has been used always for propaganda for gaining the right of black folk to love and enjoy. I do not care a damn for any art that is not used for propaganda. But I do care when propaganda is confined to one side while the other is stripped and silent.

In New York we have two plays: "White Cargo" and "Congo". In "White Cargo" there is a fallen woman. She is black. In "Congo" the fallen woman is white. In "White Cargo" the black woman goes down further and further and in "Congo" the white woman begins with degradation but in the end is one of the angels of the Lord.

You know the current magazine story: A young white man goes down to Central America and the most beautiful colored woman there falls in love with him. She crawls across the whole isthmus to get to him. The white man says nobly, "No". He goes back to his white sweetheart in New York.

In such cases, it is not the positive propaganda of people who believe white blood divine, infallible and holy to which I object. It is the denial of a similar right of propaganda to those who believe black blood human, lovable and inspired with new ideals for the world. White artists themselves suffer from this narrowing of their field. They cry for freedom in dealing with Negroes because they have so little freedom in dealing with whites. DuBose Heywood writes "Porgy" and writes beautifully of the black Charleston underworld. But why does he do this? Because he cannot do a similar thing for the white people of Charleston, or they would drum him out of town. The only chance he had to tell the truth of pitiful human degradation was to tell it of colored people. I should not be surprised if Octavius Roy Cohen had approached the *Saturday Evening Post* and asked permission to write about a different kind of colored folk than the monstrosities he has created; but if he has, the *Post* has replied, "No. You are getting paid to write about the kind of colored people you are writing about."

In other words, the white public today demands from its artists, literary and pictorial, racial pre-judgment which deliberately distorts Truth and Justice, as far as colored races are concerned, and it will pay for no other.

On the other hand, the young and slowly growing black public still wants its prophets almost equally unfree. We are bound by all sorts of customs that have come down as second-hand soul clothes of white patrons. We are ashamed of sex and we lower our eyes when people will talk of it. Our religion holds us in superstition. Our worst side has been so shamelessly emphasized that we are denying we have or ever had a worst side. In all sorts of ways we are hemmed in and our new young artists have got to fight their way to freedom.

The ultimate judge has got to be you and you have got to build yourselves up into that wide judgment, that catholicity of temper which is going to enable the artist to have his widest chance for freedom. We can afford the Truth. White folk today cannot. As it is now we are handing everything over to a white jury. If a colored man wants to publish a book, he has got to get a white publisher and a white newspaper to say it is great; and then you and I say so. We must come to the place where the work of art when it appears is reviewed and acclaimed by our own free and unfettered judgment. And we are going to have a real and valuable and eternal judgment only as we make ourselves free of mind, proud of body and just of soul to all men.

And then do you know what will be said? It is already saying. Just as soon as true Art emerges; just as soon as the black artist appears, someone touches the race on the shoulder and says, "He did that because he was an American, not because he was a Negro; he was born here; he was trained here; he is not a Negro—what is a Negro anyhow? He is just human; it is the kind of thing you ought to expect".

I do not doubt that the ultimate art coming from black folk is going to be just as beautiful, and beautiful largely in the same ways, as the art that comes from white folk, or yellow, or red; but the point today is that until the art of the black folk compells recognition they will not be rated as human. And when through art they compell recognition then let the world discover if it will that their art is as new as it is old and as old as new.

I had a classmate once who did three beautiful things and died. One of them was a story of a folk who found fire and then went wandering in the gloom of night seeking again the stars they had once known and lost; suddenly out of blackness they looked up and there loomed the heavens; and what was it that they said? They raised a mighty cry: "It is the stars, it is the ancient stars, it is the young and everlasting stars!"

(October, 1926. Vol. XXXII, No. 6, pp. 290-7)

TRAVEL

I GO A-TALKING

I have made a great journey to three of the four corners of this Western world, over a distance of 7,000 miles, and through thirty States; and I am overwhelmed almost to silence over the things I have seen, the persons I have known and the forces I have felt.

First, of course, and foremost, comes a sense of the vastness of this land. The sheer brute bigness of its distances is appalling. I think of the endless ride of three days and four nights from the silver beauty of Seattle to the sombre whirl of Kansas City. I think of the thousand miles of California and the empire of Texas, the grim vastness of the desert, the wideness of the blue

Pacific at San Diego—but all, is it not all typified at the Grand Canyon?

THE GRAND CANYON

It is a cruel gash in the bosom of the earth down to its very entrails—a wound where the dull titanic knife has turned and twisted in the hole, leaving its edges livid scarred, jagged and pulsing over the white and red and purple of its mighty flesh, while down below, down, down below, in black and severed vein, boils the dull and sullen flood of the Colorado.

It is awful. There can be nothing like it. It is the earth and skies gone stark and raving mad. The mountains uptwirled, disbodied and inverted stand on their peaks and throw their bowels to the skies. Their earth is air—their ether blood-red rock engreened. You stand upon their roots and fall into their pinnacles a mighty mile.

Behold this mauve and purple mocking of time and space. See yonder peak! No human foot has trod it. Into that blue shadow only the eye of God has looked. Listen to the accents of that gorge which mutters: "Before Abraham was, I am." Is yonder wall a hedge of black, or is it the rampart between Heaven and hell? I see greens—is it grass or giant pines? I see specks that may be boulders. Ever the winds sigh and drop into those sun-swept silences. Ever the gorge lies motionless, unmoved, until I fear. It is an awful thing, unholy, terrible. It is human—some mighty drama unseen, unheard, is playing there its tragedies or mocking comedy and the laugh of endless years is shrieking onward from peak to peak, unheard, unechoed and unknown.

THE TALKS

Through such a gateway I came out to the cities of men and in these I made twenty-eight talks to audiences aggregating 18,000 human souls.

What wonderful and varied audiences they were: there was the vast theatre in Los Angeles where I strained to reach the last dim gallery rows; there was the little group of a hundred or so in Stockton, and the thoughtful half thousand down in San Diego and over in Indianapolis. Most of all, perhaps, I felt the throb of personal appreciation and understanding in St. Louis and Oakland, while the stillness of a deep earnestness, almost tragedy, lay on the audiences in Fort Worth and Atlanta.

At Los Angeles I spoke again and again to audiences that did not seem to tire, while in the wonderful Northwest I met the little group at Portland, the people of Tacoma—so tireless in their thoughtful care—and crowned it all at Seattle, the wonder city that sits gleaming amid its waters with its face to the great North.

In the eighteen cities where I spoke live 500,000 Americans of Negro descent, and I cannot cease marveling at their grit and energy and alertness. They complain at themselves and criticise, but they are pulsing and alive with a new ambition and determinedness, which were to me astounding.

THE MID WEST

In Indianapolis, St. Louis and Kansas City strong groups of Negroes are uniting to fight segregation, to improve and defend the schools and to open the gate of opportunity for their children. They are not yet united or agreed, but their steps toward union and agreement in the last ten years have been most encouraging. They welcomed a gospel of fight and self-assertion.

SOUTHERN CALIFORNIA

Los Angeles was wonderful. The air was scented with orange blossoms and the beautiful homes lay low crouching on the earth as though they loved its scents and flowers. Nowhere in the United States is the Negro so well and beautifully housed, nor the average of efficiency and intelligence in the colored population so high. Here is an aggressive, hopeful group—with some wealth, large industrial opportunity and a buoyant spirit.

Down at San Diego, with its bold and beautiful coast on the great Pacific, is a smaller group, but kindly and thrifty, with pushing leaders.

THE GOLDEN GATE

The shadow of a great fear broods over San Francisco. They have not forgotten the earthquake, and the stranger realizes what it was by the awe in their tones. One misses here the buoyancy and aggressiveness of Southern California and yet the fifty-eight leaders who met me at dinner were a fine group of men, and they expect the colored world to greet them in 1915 at the exposition.

This group stands closer to the progressive whites than many others and has a chance to share in the great movements of uplift.

At Sacramento I did not speak, but a little group made my hours of waiting pleasant—an unassuming group with pleasant manners and warm hearts. I shall not forget them.

THE NORTHWEST

Up then I rushed through a rich, green valley and then through high, full-bosomed hills—through that contrast and astonishment which is California.

Portland is the older Northwest—staid and quiet, with a certain strength and bigness. The audience was small and the people were not sure of my message and purpose; but they themselves were awakening and they showed new homes and enterprises with pardonable pride.

Tacoma will always seem to me like a place of home coming. I have seldom come to a strange city with so intimate an understanding and sense of fellowship. The audience was white and black and sympathetically blended. The mayor came and spoke and ate and an old Harvard schoolmate introduced me. They gave me a loving cup and it did not seem inappropriate, so that I went away thinking not so much of a separate striving group as of a body of good friends with scant color line.

Then, as I have said, the wonderful Western pilgrimage was crowned at Seattle. The magic city of 300,000 lies on its hills above silvery waters, dream-beautiful and all but uncanny in its unexpectedness. The group of men who welcomed me were unusual in vigor and individuality. There was the lawyer who thoughtfully engineered it all; the young doctor with his cheery face; the droll politician with his reminiscences and strong opinions; the merchant from up country and his little daughter whose beautiful face of the long years ago I remembered suddenly amid the cheer of her perfect little home. There was the caterer, and the minister—it was a fine group. I have seldom seen its equal.

For one day I turned my back on the perfect memory of this golden journey and sailed out across the seas and thanked God for this the kindliest race on His green earth, for whom I had the privilege of working and to whom I had the pride of belonging.

TEXAS

Then I plunged into Texas. One day the white, drifted snows of Montana and then, in less than a week, the sound of the reaper in the golden grain of the Red River valley!

One shivers at the "Jim Crow" cars of Texas. After the luxury of the West and the public courtesy and hospitality, the dirt and impudence of a land where to travel at all meant twelve to twenty-four hours in the most primitive accommodations, was an awful change. For twenty-four hours on one journey I was able to purchase only two musty ham sandwiches to eat, and I sat up three nights in succession to keep engagements.

But what was lacking in public and white courtesy was more than compensated in private and Negro hospitality and appreciation.

At Dallas was one of the strongest, truest religious leaders I have met. At Austin were growing colleges and an audience gathered from thirty miles around. At Marshall was a group of fine men and women, and it all came to climax at Fort Worth.

"Are you going to Fort Worth?" everybody asked, knowing of the recent riot. I went. I spoke to 400 Negroes and a handful of leading whites, and I spoke the clear, plain truth as I conceive it. It was received without dissent or protest and its reception gave me deepest hope and satisfaction.

Atlanta is another story; so here let me end and, in ending, let me thank those who welcomed me, who paid my fees willingly and promptly, who were eager to listen to the message which I brought, not because it was wholly to their liking, but because it was sincere.

(July, 1913. Vol. VI, No. 3, pp. 130-2)

IN FRANCE, 1918

Toul, dim through the deepening dark of early afternoon, I saw its towers gloom dusky towards the murk of heaven. We wound in misty roads and dropped upon the city through the great throats of its walled bastions. There lay France—a strange, unknown, unfamiliar France. The city was dispossessed. Through its streets—its narrow, winding streets, old and low and dark, carven and quaint,—poured thousands upon thousands of strange feet of khaki clad foreigners, and the echoes threw back awkward syllables that were never French. Here was France beaten to her knees yet fighting as never nation fought before, calling in her death agony across the seas till her help came and with all their strut and careless braggadocio saved the worthiest nation of the world from the wickedest fate ever plotted by Fools.

Tim Brimm was playing by the town-pump. Tim Brimm and the bugles of Harlem blared in the little streets of Maron in far Lorraine. The tiny streets were seas of mud. Dank mist and rain sifted through the cold air above the blue Moselle. Soldiers—soldiers everywhere—black soldiers, boys of Washington, Alabama, Philadelphia, Mississippi. Wild and sweet and wooing leapt the strains upon the air. French children gazed in wonder—women left their washing. Up in the window stood a black Major, a Captain, a Teacher and I—with tears behind our smiling eyes. Tim Brimm was playing by the town-pump.

The audience was framed in smoke. It rose ghost-like out of memories—bitter memories of the officers near dead of pneumonia whose pain was lighted up by the nurses wanting to know whether they must be "Jim Crowed" with privates or not. Memories of that great last morning when the thunders of hell called the Ninety-second to its last great drive. Memories of bitter humiliations, determined triumphs, great victories and bugle-calls that sounded from earth to heaven. Like memories framed in the breath of God, my audience peered in upon me—good, brown faces with great, kind, beautiful eyes—black soldiers of America rescuing beloved France—and the words came in praise and benediction there in the "Y," with its little stock of cigarettes and candies and its rusty wood stove.

"Alors," said Madame, "quatres sont morts"—four dead—four tall, strong sons dead for France—sons like the sweet and blue-eyed daughter who was hiding her brave smile in the dusk. It was a tiny stone house whose front window lipped the passing side walk where ever tramped the feet of black soldiers marching home. There was a cavernous wardrobe, a great fireplace invaded by a new and jaunty iron stove. Vast, thick piles of bed rose in yonder corner. Without was the crowded kitchen and up a half-stair was our bedroom that gave upon a tiny court with arched stone staircase and green tree. We were a touching family party held together by a great sorrow and a great joy. How we laughed over the salad that got brandy instead of vinegar—how we ate the great golden pile of fried potatoes and how we poured over the post-card from the Lieutenant of the Senegalese—dear little vale of crushed and risen France, in the day when Negroes went "over the top" at Pont-à-Mousson.

Paris, Paris by purple façade of the opera, the crowd on the Boulevard des Italiens and the great swing of the Champs Elysées. But not the Paris the world knows. Paris with its soul cut to the core—feverish, crowded, nervous, hurried; full of uniforms and mourning bands, with cafés closed at 9:30—no sugar, scarce bread, and tears so intertwined with joy that there is scant difference. Paris has been dreaming a nightmare and though she awakes, the grim terror is upon her—it lies on the sandbags covering monuments, on the closed art treasures of the Louvre. Only the flowers are there, always the flowers, the Roses of England and the Lilies of France.

(March, 1919. Vol. XVII, No. 5, pp. 215-16)

THE FIELDS OF BATTLES

I have seen the wounds of France—the entrails of Rheims and the guts of Verdun, with their bare bones thrown naked to the insulting skies; villages in dust and ashes—villages that lay so low that they left no mark beneath the snow-swept landscape; walls that stood in wrecked and awful silence; rivers flowed and skies gleamed, but the trees, the land, the people were scarred and broken. Ditches darted hither and thither and wire twisted, barbed and poled, cloistered in curious, illogical places. Graves there were—everywhere and a certain breathless horror, broken by plodding soldiers and fugitive peasants.

We were at Chateau-Thierry in a room where the shrapnel had broken across the dining-table and torn a mirror and wrecked a wall; then we hastened to Rheims, that riven city where scarce a house escaped its scar and the House of Houses stood, with its laced stone and empty, piteous beauty, high and broad, about the scattered death. Then on we flew past silence and silent, broken walls to the black ridge that writhes northward like a vast grave. Its trees, like its dead, are young—broken and bent with fiery surprise—here the earth is ploughed angrily, there rise huts and blankets of wattles to hide the ways, and yonder in a hollow the Germans had built for years—concrete bungalows with electric lights, a bath-room for a Prince, and trenches and tunnels. Wide ways with German names ran in straight avenues through the trees and everywhere giant engines of death had sown the earth and cut the trees with iron. Down again we went by riven villages to the hungry towns behind the lines and up again to Verdun—the ancient fortress, with its ancient hills, where fort on fort had thundered four dream-dead years and on the plains between villages had sunk into the silent earth. The walls and moat hung gravely black and still, the city rose in clustered, drunken ruin here and in yellow ashes there, and in the narrow streets I saw my colored boys working for France.

On, on out of the destruction and the tears, down by bewildered Commercy and old Toul, where a great truck hurrying food to the starving nearly put our auto in a ditch, and up to Pont-à-Mousson where Joan of Arc on her great hill overlooks the hills of mighty Metz; then to Nancy and by the dark and winding Moselle to the snow-covered Vosges. In yonder forest day on day the Negro troops were held in leash. Then slowly they advanced, swinging a vast circle—down a valley and up again, with the singing of shells. I stood by their trenches, wattled and boarded, and saw where they rushed "over the top" to the crest, and looked on the field before Metz. Innocent it looked, but the barbed wire, thick and tough, belted it like heavy bushes and huddled in hollows lay the machine-guns, nested in concrete walls, three feet thick, squatting low on the underbrush and scattering sputtering death up that silent hillside. Such wire! Such walls! How long the great, cradling sweep of land down the valley and over the German trenches to the village beyond, beside the silent, dark Moselle!

On by the river we went to the snow-covered Vosges, where beneath the shoulder of a mountain the Ninety-second Division held a sector, with quiet death running down at intervals. The trenches circled the hills, and dug-outs nestled beneath by the battered villages.

We flew back by the hungry zone in the back-wash of war— by Epinal and Domrémy—Bourbonne-les-bains and Chaumont and so—home to Paris.

(April, 1919. Vol. XVII, No. 6, pp. 268-9)

CHAMOUNIX

I have seen the League of Nations, the Federation of the World, sitting in a little upper room and stared at by reporters, amidst streams of hopes and fears and of intrigues. After that I came to Chamounix—to cow bells and silence and trickle of waters. Above this world-on-end, lies the vast Thing of Snow, —silent, tremendous, a world apart, remembered and forgotten; a place of lights and shadows, unknown to earth. And of mists. I think the real marriage of earth and stars lies somehow in these mists. There is every preparation for it: the calm and pretty valley with its cows, with its homes, its little intrigues and tragedies, its laughter and flowers. Then gradually and gravely uplifted, the pointing pines; the fingers of the sullen, steadfast pines, pointing, always pointing. And then a space of lichen, leaf and brown gorse; and then a wide grey pause of utter rock, weirdly a waste, grim in its sense of age and strength. After that the snows, the white and blue and golden snows with their feet drabbled in the earth.

What more fitting approach to the stars, to the thoughts that lie beyond the world, enchained and hallowed? One sees this mirage of earth and skies as a mist, a grey and white uncertainty, where line and point drift, merge and dissolve into something that is just cloud and sky.

Last night in the rift of the world formed by the serried snow-broidered edge of the Alps, I saw the moon sailing in seas of sounds and tints of tawny green and hurrying waters; without the narrow rift, lifted their heads, snows of clouds and clouds of snows, mountains real and mountains spiritual, clouds of mountains and mountains of clouds, until the world, the great soiled world, was a thing so beautiful, so rare, so still and sweet that life seemed all love and wonder. I could almost hear the sound of stars raining down upon Mont Blanc: the mist of the rain was moon shine there on the dim White Mountain, and the song of the sound of it was as the voice of death calling to the victorious. It was like white age above the brutal strength of youth; it was sweet childhood which is always apart and beyond the scarred and moaning world. How singular is this ceaseless sound of waters, the dripping and dropping of snows, the roar of fallen mists, the dashing of clouds in the slow, grey and crumpled rivers of riven ice. And yet against the voice of the waters is the voice of the mountain; it is the mountain audible, the song of snows, the color of space, the feeling of things without end. The mountain is unmoveable; day and day, night after night we have flown and whirled about it, changed to city after city and ridden over hill and dale, resting and running, yet the mountain is always there, pale and calm and motionless, curiously eternal.

If I lived here long I should pray to Mont Blanc, throwing my hands in ecstacy, screaming my tears. I should heap fire against it and vow gold and jewels. It should be God. For what else can God be but a Mountain or the Sea?

In that transforming miracle of the mountain and the mist there is always sinking to earth some solemn singing as of things and of thoughts that rise above, beyond and athwart the heavy tongued earth and melt to something vaster and truer. It is midnight in the valley. I cannot sleep, for the mountain never sleeps and the moon tonight is widely awake. I sit and scribble and then ever and again creep to my window. The marvel of it, the sheer, inhuman perfectness of it all, the almost pain of its beauty and hurt of its joy! It is there still in the morning. The

White Wraith has melted into the sky, throwing earthwards one long pale finger. Its feet are at the founding stones of the universes and its head is lost with the stars. Its thoughts are the thoughts of God. The world is grey and black with purple interludes. The waters wail. At last the long shaft dies there from the topmost shoulder of the mighty hill and with its death the mist drops nearer to the black and burning earth. And always the pines point upward.

(December, 1921. Vol. XXIII, No. 2, pp. 56ff)

THE PLACE

Above everything on a Western trip looms the Place. The immensity of the thing. The mighty sweep of desert hill and mountain on a scale that dwarfs the East. From the flat Mississippi valley the earth swells slowly like the wave of some infinite ocean until we ply 7000 feet above the sea. Then mad with its awful strength the waves break with the mighty crags and snows of the Rockies. We fight for entrance and escape—Man against God. We work and run and fall and fly through cleft and seam and vale and hole, to wind to the peaceful sea. Before and beyond lies the Desert. The desert is a Color, a chameleon-like drift and turn of stark forbidding beauty—grey—gray-white to northward, buff-brown-purple-violet to south—grim, grim, grim, desolate, fateful and grim. Then come scenes—scenes so beautiful as to be indescribable: the lilies and geraniums of San Diego, the palms and roses of Los Angeles—the vines and valleys and shades of haciendas, and the Sea, the Peaceful Sea where Sun has always set and never rises.

DREAM SCENES

Wyoming had a purple carpet, black beneath the dim new moon, that lifted itself in folds as ruffled by some eternal silent wind and then dropped, pink-broidered, at the world's edge. Came Utah with ghost mountains that rose and went suddenly, silently, full draped in white; and Salt Lake City, new, old, bleak, grim, thrifty, sordid, with factories, mines and mystic cult; and then the desert, hard, dry with fantastic saw-edge mountains, empty, empty.

SHASTA AND SISKIYOU

Up we clambered from summer to spring and from spring to snow. There rose before us a pale, yellow mountain—slim and cleft with double points and its heads were veiled. It swung mysteriously and curiously before, now near and simple, now ghostly remote and terribly vast. Around it ranged the snow-swept hills, dark green with pine. But always the mountain withdrew—now right now left, now gone. But they say that behind, crowned in everlasting snow looms a vaster mountain—Almighty Shasta—but to me its face was veiled in whitened mists. Only the butte, calm sentinel stood before the awful face of the hidden mountain.

I peered and could not see. Before me rose a stretch of land and hill, rose to a black, deep and poignant blue and stopped—stopped clean cut by a cloud like a sudden knife; and Shasta was not, for God took it up to Heaven in a cloud.

Then we strained at the great flank of Siskiyou—strained and jerked and climbed, circling and scrambling until we stood a mile above the far off sea. Afar Shasta veiled its everlasting snows and round about the black and solemn hills—the bleak and ragged hills—listened and waited. Once we fell a moment down to a vale, a drab, lonesome and grim town, the last of California. But only for breath. Then double-engined, we gripped and rose above the earth, above the hills all black and white—above the clouds, above the sky—Siskiyou, Siskiyou, sang the train as sweating and gasping, we climbed into Oregon.

THE CABMAN OF FRESNO

I have forgotten his name. He was tall and lean, beautifully black, with a frank, half-bashful laugh. "I'll get you there," he said simply. And everybody echoed, "He'll get you there." How simple! I had to catch a 6:05 train in the cold, gray morning. He would get me there. I could depend upon him; I could sleep calmly. I need not fret and worry. Here was a young man on whom everyone depended. He was just a cabman with an ancient Buick. But you could depend upon him. In one simple detail of life he was perfect. In that one attribute he stood among the masters of the world. He was a god! Shakespeare could write Hamlet; Harriman could build railroads; he could start a cab on time.

THE SAN JOAQUIN VALLEY

Scarred, naked mountains, with brush and furrows, sand and boulders, rising in super-imposed triangles, with now and then a gracious swelling curve and crumbling crag above a sky—a sky so clear, so limpid and so blue, it seemed a dream of utter space and infinite beauty—a sea without shore, ship or shoal, and deep without end.

Definitely almost curtly the mountains withdrew from the level desert of cacti, weeds and white alkali. Then turning, we faced the surly mountains and climbed them—4000 feet at Tehachapi, a brown, silent cynical land of faded sage. We stormed the sullen heights in great curved swoops like a bird, and the cold mountains softened at our approach—became almost beautiful, in their naked, inhospitable way, beneath the pale sunshine. Little bleak pines begin to squat about us and rotten rocks melt into dust and sand. All is dry and parched and gasping, and the sky is blue and slightly fleeced. A road following us sliced into the hillside precariously. And then over the hill and down, the green came stealing in over the meadows and we were back to the world again. It was as though we had gasped for breath and recovered—the world had gasped for water and got at last a long, slow drink.

We wound through a rough and quarrelsome valley, with iron rocks and towering hills, a tiny stream below. As we sank lower, we knotted ourselves grotesquely above a cone-like hill, twisting above, below, in circles—with space-defying antics dropped 2000 feet.

Crickets crying a high-noon, grass and crag-tipped mountains, eager green and sunlit valley. The tang of Spring. I'm going backwards from Summer to June from June to April and ahead is December. Lovely vistas of mountain, hill and dale stretching away in the glorious sunshine, rolling in a savage, poignant beauty with a village nestling afar. Ten miles we go to drop that little mile springing and whirling, diving beneath the earth and skirting the grim precipice and diving again.

The valley is one of the world's rare hits at painting beauty whether one leaps from fertile meadow to grey and snow-gripped mountain tops, or falls from a grey and barren heaven to the beautiful bosom of earth—from Tehachapi to Calienti is a ride for singing Valkyries on iron horses wild with wings— *a-hoyia-ho! ha-ha!*

FROM THE ANGELS TO SAN DIEGO

And then the Sea—the fierce old sea—the ancient and everlasting sea spread us its wares, its silken sheen of infinite hues in blues and green—its delicately laced camisoles resting on the pale, gold bosom of the land, ghost islands and the shadow of the shades of hills—the indistinct thought of yellows, purples and browns. Silent was the sea beneath the thunder of the moving sun and sand, no word nor murmur, lying like a dream on the edge of the earth.

Then the land, the slow and mighty land, stretching from the lace-edged mountains, swept with snow, stepped down to the eyes of the sea—the land rose and stood erect toward Heaven —the brown and the velvet of its skirts torn and bedraggled and yet magnificent—above the sea it loomed and frowned. O beautiful, too beautiful world, soft La Jolla sleeping in the sun beneath Indian blankets! But still the sea—the grim old sea, the ancient and eternal sea—spread us its wares.

Silks, impalpable, imponderable, diaphanous, sheer as shine, gay as the laughter of God; velvets luscious, deep and rustling. Great sheets of beaten gold with little innocent hammer-marks, wide quilts of shimmering silver, blankets of flowing fleece and films of fire. Then—San Diego: hedges of gerania, fields of callas —star-eyed palms—dark fingers of land pointing seaward and the clustered, smoking city. The flash of white and angry teeth upon the sand gnashing, gnashing, gnashing— a slim dark finger of God beyond La Jolla touching the sea and saying: "Peace be still."

Roses and lilies, marigolds, gold mustard, yellow poppies and crimson gerania. Lead purple and grey are earth and sky and sea

—save the role and tumble of blue and silver tipped hills.

Beneath the bosom of the Peaceful Ocean, lies the Wrath of God, and underneath this wrath, the bones of the sleeping dead; white bones, and grey and black, shredded flesh and eyes that see not—bones and bones and ships and stones, layer and layer and century on century and crime on sorrow and sigh.

(May, 1923. Vol. XXVI, No. 1. pp. 9-11)

SKETCHES FROM ABROAD
Le Grand Voyage

I have taken many journeys but this is the greatest. I have seen all the states of the American Empire and something of the Western Indies. I have seen England and France many times—all parts of Germany and something of Austria, Switzerland and Italy.

But all this (save Armenia) was white, kindly on the whole—intensely interesting, but painfully white. Today I am drifting toward darkness. I have seen the skin grow sallow and the eyes darken and hair quiver, in southern France, in Spain, in Portugal, in the Canary Isles; and now I set my face toward Africa—the Eternal World of Black Folk.

There is a snow capped peak that sits in the seas. With grey mantilla about its silvered hair Teneriffe frowns on the Canaries and the Canaries smile on the waters, the waters love Africa and Africa frowns on God.

A long way—a long, long way have I come to this gate of the darkest world.

I was in England at the beginning of that singular election campaign which astonished Europe and in the end revealed the bankruptcy of traditional England. It was a cold, wet England with here and there the white sunshine of promise. It was an England on the farewell evening of the Imperial Conference. No black men were there, but brown men sat and spoke and were listened to. England fears India. Only Smuts replied. Smuts, that curious, provincial mind—German in sympathy, suspicious of France and its black armies, liberal toward all white folk but hating "niggers" and fearing East Indians. He is today the greatest leader in the British Empire. In this atmosphere Pan Africa sat and whispered. But some few listened.

I was in France when the first signs came that the hegemony of future mid-European industry, with all its inherent political power, had passed from Germany to France, with England helplessly and jealously watching. The capitalists of the Ruhr, German and French, are agreed. The world will pay. And yet there is one vast beacon of light—France is depending for her hegemony of Europe on Africa. If the rest of Europe wishes to meet her racial bid, they too must make peace—industrial and racial peace—with Africa.

At St. Etienne the most popular man in town—the head of the French and Foreign Club, the chief sportsman, the guest of a hundred hosts, and the welcomed of all business men—is one of us—Hunt, the only American Consul of Negro descent in Europe. The State Department is worried over Hunt. He deserves promotion and they dare not promote him.

Suddenly leaving all this weary world of politics and industry I plunged headlong into fairyland. I am riding down the Rhone. I see the seen and the unseen. The unseen drama of a thousand years and yet nine hundred more. The allobroges—the Dukes of Burgundy—the Kings of France, shining in the sun and river, the banks rising to mountain heights to westward, the fields and cities, eastward. The colors are pale cream, grey, pale reds, above the blues and greens and browns. The towns are solid, stolid, almost grim, with poplars sternly at attention and vines and tile and wall and tower. Yet there is a kindliness and sweetness in the air—a sense of hearth and home amid factory and swift commerce—the long black steamers, the fruit trees, the pale high hills. The scene stretches into wide plateaus before the dream-far mountains. Then comes a great shoulder of naked rock, a towered town of cream and crimson, sun fields, a mauve and white chateau in trees, the ribbon of river and its poplars; suddenly a gray town with ruined castle on the skies, a river blazing in the sun. From a hill to the right the ghost of the twelfth century stares stonily down upon us. Valence, town of the Gauls, which knew Roman, Visigoth, Lombard and Moor. Upon the right walls that in centuries gone rang with the laughter of the Lady of Poitiers— naughty, beautiful, dead Diana fair false and fortunate,—are ruins eternal above the waters of the Rhone. To the left a quiet town with one arm clasped lovingly about a hill and the other flung above the river rampart. Opposite the dream of cloudy mountains and vines, yonder a town embroidering a hillside, a solemn cypress here and there and a touch of gay color on roof and door proclaim the coming of the azure coast. Out of earth and mountain leaps on before us another town pale gray and cream, petite and beautiful with light. I see a flying buttress, the towers of a Byzantium church dominating the town and then in applause rock and boulder, rough and hard and grim. On the other side in blue and grayish purple a mighty tower and wall and city with what wonder of past hate and love and war! The ruins of a dead chateau guarding a little olden street; a lonely town of clustered grey crouching on the earth as if a part of it—with wealth of rolling tiles.

Then darkness came down, came down quickly at four and enveloped the widening plane—fell on the tower of Avignon and on the bridge where *"tout le monde y danse en ronde".* On to Arles and Mistral and his song "Have you been to Carcassonne?" But in the soft darkness my soul, free, ranged all Provence and its sweet and unseen beauty.

Avignon was shadow and dying day—the shadow of the Palace of the Shadow of the Popes somewhere down between me and the bridge.

So in the darkness we came down to where Marseilles beneath the moon shown like a jewel in a jewelled sea.

Oh but it rained in Marseilles! The waters spilled themselves across the city and under and over it all my one day and yet could not quench it, could not quite spare its laughter and charm, its satisfied provincial large-town air. The little "Cannebière" was gay and crowded and wet. The bouillabaisse at What's-his-name's (everybody knows him) was expensive and bad, but the great yellow castles that guard the mighty harbor

and the little winding sinister streets where folk pass sideways
to the seas—they were all there and they are Marseilles.

II.

I have been to Carcassonne. I have seen the city, sitting like a
tale that is told above the earth, a great grey dim and towered
thing amid a universe of purple, yellow, brown and green—a
far-flung violet heaven on earth, a clustering church quartered
town. On the plain march the great figures of France, while
yonder the Pyrenees snow-crowned look on. I have seen the sun
die on the ramparts of Carcassonne and as it died the Pyrenees
lived. They raised a song that swelled from Marseilles to Barcelona and from earth right up to the blue gold of Heaven. But
the earth empurpled died and sank and smoked a thousand
candles and cried a thousand wordless tales. The air was like
rare wine—the earth beautiful for a lover, the sky fleeced and
gilded silver and purple.

The sun falls. Smoke threads up from the nests of tiles. Goats
cry, a mist, mysterious, sweeps the purply air and on the ramparts I stand and peer.

As night rose the sky was green and black and gold above the
black ramparts fading to white and blue, while afar the grim
teeth of the Pyrenees grated on Heaven.

I rose in the night to see what the moon could do to all this.
It dripped the shadows on the scene.

Then came the drab cold morning of disillusion. After all this
grey rock stained with blood and tears was but an old machine
of murder, of desperate defense against desperate men. Its ever
winding streets were alleys where hid poverty and filth. About
the ramparts without filth still lay and within in inn and guide
lurked bold extortion. And yet Carcassonne rose above all triumphant in its crumpled beauty, its sheer and pregnant human
appeal—its hoarse voice of seven hundred years, with ghosts of
three hundred more. In the tournament range, facing the court
of Honor, there are telephone wires.

Sun and cloud, Mediterranean and Pyrenees, yellowing vines
and sheep. The vines have leaves like flowers and the purple sea
mirrors old castellated towers in yellow and red beneath the
black forbidding Pyrenees.

The Pyrenees romp with heaven, play with earth cloud and
sun until together they make superb lace work.

Black cedars, two towers of castled keeps, gold trees, grey walls, white roads and vines and vines.

Barcelona is a great city thrusting herself outside her swaddling clothes with an effort which rends her body and soul. Great avenues are shouldering aside and threading tiny, winding Old World streets and building new blocks scornful of span with rounded corners and great inner courts. One has a feeling of strident wealth and deep hidden misery, but one cannot tell. A few things I shall remember: that great cathedral of gloom at Barcelona with the lovely loneliness of its high windows, the fearsome shadow of the grave of its crypt and its singularly beautiful cloisters. The church was a sort of monumental darkness thrown against the gayety of the Pampas.

Then came a serious and savage Spain—bare nests of mountains with yellow towns creeping close to the earth.

Always and everywhere there is going on a subtle change. My brown face attracts no attention. I am darker than my neighbors but they are dark. I become, quite to my own surprise, simply a man. I cease to be specially selected for attention either elaborately pleasant or ostentatiously contemptible. Forgetting myself I study others. I feel relieved.

Madrid is disappointing. It is artificial. Its ancient soul and body have been cut away and there remain the empty Prado, the wide and ghostly park, the ranging avenues and the empty countryside. It is a city set upon a hill, but the edges of the hill are guarded from the curious. And yet I may be wrong. After all I stayed but a day at Madrid and I saw Goya writhing in oil and Goya was more than Madrid.

Lisbon is a lovely city, rising in great swelling of hills, deep creams and crimson above the sea and the calm Tagus. It is a provincial city—a city of one street and the Rocio, but a city that is happy and knows its citizens by name and is sorry for the rest of Europe. I like Lisbon. It was kind and more than hospitable. I went to the Colliseum and sat by the ringside. My neighbor explained matters carefully in polite French. He accepted a cigarette and commended its flavor. At the end he raised his hat and bowed and bade me a very good night. Imagine him in Hippodrome, New York! He would have shouldered me warily and explained on the other side the ubiquity of "damn niggers"!

Sunset at Funchal in Madeira. The little roar of the little town is softened by the mouth of bells and the curled new moon kisses the electric stars. Above glow the mountains with veils across their misty shoulders—bells, rain, and blue sky, green and white homes and the soft laughter of dark eyes—Funchal. With a great circling rainbow day dies. At dawn the fingers of God touch the hills above and they glow with green and gold.

The ship is black and white and red. It sails tomorrow and when my feet again touch earth—the earth will be Africa.

(March, 1924. Vol. XXVII, No. 5, pp. 203-5)

AFRICA

I have just come back from a journey in the world of nearly five months. I have travelled 15,000 miles. I set foot on three continents. I have visited five countries, four African islands and five African colonies. I have sailed under five flags. I have seen a black president inaugurated. I have walked in the African big bush and heard the night cry of leopards. I have traded in African markets, talked with African chiefs and been the guest of white governors. I have seen the Alhambra and the great mosque at Cordova and lunched with H. G. Wells; and I am full, very full with things that must be said.

December 16, 1923

Today I sailed from Tenerife for Africa. The night was done in broad black masses across the blue and the sun burned a great livid coal in the sky. Above rose the Peak of Tenerife, round like a woman's breast, pale with snow patches, immovable, grand.

On the boat—the *Henner* from Bremen—I am in Germany and opposite is a young man who fought four and a half years in the German army on all fronts—bitter, bitter. War is not done yet, he says. He's going to Angola.

We are six Germans in this little floating Germany: a captain, fifty or fifty-five, world roamer—San Francisco, Klondike, all Africa, gemütlich, jovial; a bull-headed, red necked first officer, stupid, good, funny; a doctor, well bred, kindly; a soldier and business man, bitter, keen, hopeful; others dumber and more uncertain. We drink Bremer beer, smoke, tell tales and the cabin rings.

December 17

On the sea—slipping lazily south, in cloud and sun and languorous air. The food is good and German. The beer is such as I have not tasted for a quarter century—golden as wine, light with almost no feel of alcohol. And I sense rather than hear a broken, beaten, but unconquered land, a spirit bruised, burned, but immortal. There is defense eager, but not apology; there is always the pointing out of the sin of all Europe.

My cabin is a dream. It is white and clean, with windows—not portholes—and pretty curtains at berth, door and window; electric light.

December 19

The languorous days are creeping lazily away. We have passed Cape Bojador of historic memory; we have passed the Tropic of Cancer, we are in the Tropics! There is a moon and by day an almost cloudless sky. I rise at eight and breakfast at eight thirty. Then I write and read until lunch at 12:30. About 1:30 I take a nap and coffee at four. Then read until 6:30 and supper. We linger at the table until nearly 9. Then reading, walking and bed by 10.

December 20

It is Thursday. Day after tomorrow I shall put my feet on the soil of Africa. As yet I have seen no land, but last night I wired to Monrovia by way of Dakar—"President King—Monrovia—Arrive Saturday, *Henner*—Du Bois." I wonder what it all will be like? Meantime it's getting hot—*hot*, and I've put on all the summer things I've got.

December 20

Tonight the sun, a dull gold ball, strange shaped and rayless sank before a purple sky into a bright green and sinking turned the sky to violet blue and grey and the sea turned dark. But the sun itself blushed from gold to shadowed burning crimson, then to red. The sky above, blue-green; the waters blackened and then the sun did not set—it died and was not. And behind gleamed the pale silver of the moon across the pink effulgence of the clouds.

December 21

Tomorrow—Africa! Inconceivable! As yet no sight of land, but it was warm and we rigged deck chairs and lay at ease. I have been reading that old novel of mine—it has points. Twice we've wired Liberia. I'm all impatience.

December 22

Waiting for the first gleam of Africa. This morning I photographed the officers and wrote an article on Germany. Then I packed my trunk and big bag. The step for descending to the boat had been made ready. Now I read and write and the little boat runs sedately on.

3:22 p. m.—I see Africa—Cape Mount in two low, pale semicircles, so pale it looks a cloud. So my great great grandfather saw it two centuries ago. Clearer and clearer it rises and now land in a long low line runs to the right and melts dimly into the mist and sea and Cape Mount begins Liberia—what a citadel for the capital of Negrodom!

When shall I forget the night I first set foot on African soil —I, the sixth generation in descent from my stolen forefathers. The moon was at the full and the waters of the Atlantic lay like a lake. All the long slow afternoon as the sun robed itself in its western scarlet with veils of misty cloud, I had seen Africa afar.

Cape Mount—that mighty headland with its twin curves, northern sentinel of the vast realm of Liberia gathered itself out of the cloud at half past three and then darkened and grew clear. On beyond flowed the dark low undulating land quaint with palm and breaking sea. The world darkened. Africa faded away, the stars stood forth curiously twisted—Orion in the zenith—the Little Bear asleep and the Southern Cross rising behind the horizon. Then afar, ahead, a lone light, straight at the ship's fore. Twinkling lights appeared below, around and rising shadows. "Monrovia" said the Captain. Suddenly we swerved to our left. The long arms of the bay enveloped us and then to the right rose the twinkling hill of Monrovia, with its crowning star. Lights flashed on the shore—here, there. Then we sensed a darker shadow in the shadows; it lay very still. "It's a boat," one said. "It's two boats." Then the shadow drifted in pieces and as the anchor roared into the deep five boats outlined themselves on the waters—great ten-oared barges black with men swung into line and glided toward us. I watched them fascinated.

Nine at Night

It was nine at night—above, the shadows, there the town, here the sweeping boats. One forged ahead with the stripes and lone star flaming behind, the ensign of the customs floating wide and bending to the long oars, the white caps of ten black sailors. Up the stairway clambered a soldier in khaki, aide-de-camp of the President of the Republic, a custom house official, the clerk of the American legation—and after them sixty-five lithe, lean black stevedores with whom the steamer would work down to Portuguese Angola and back. A few moments of formalities, greetings and goodbyes and I was in the great long boat with the President's Aide—a brown major in brown khaki. On the other side the young clerk and at the back the black, bare-legged pilot. Before us on the high thwarts were the rowers: men, boys, black, thin, trained in muscle and sinew, little larger than the oars in thickness, they bent their strength to them and swung upon them.

One in the centre gave curious little cackling cries to keep the rhythm, and for the spurts, the stroke, a bit thicker and sturdier, gave a low guttural command now and then and the boat, alive, quivering, danced beneath the moon, swept a great curve to the bar to breast its narrow teeth of foam—"t'chick-a-tickity, t'chik-a-tickity" sang the boys and we glided and raced, now between boats, now near the landing—now oars aloft at the dock. And lo! I was in Africa!

December 25

Christmas eve and Africa is singing in Monrovia. They are Krus and Fanti—men, women and children and all the night they march and sing. The music was once the music of revival hymns. But it is that music now transformed and the silly words hidden in an unknown tongue—liquid and sonorous. It is tricked and expounded with cadence and turn. And this is that same trick I heard first in Tennessee 38 years ago: The air is raised and carried by men's strong voices, while floating above in obligato, come the high mellow voices of women—it is the ancient African art of part singing so curiously and insistently different.

And so they come, gay apparelled, lit by a transparency. They enter the gate and flow over the high steps and sing and sing and sing. They saunter round the house, pick flowers, drink water and sing and sing and sing. The warm dark heat of the night steams up to meet the moon. And the night is song.

Christmas day, 1923. We walk down to the narrow, crooked wharves of Monrovia, by houses old and grey and steps like streets of stone. Before is the wide St. Paul river, double mouthed, and beyond, the sea, white, curling on the sand. Before is the isle—the tiny isle, hut-covered and guarded by a cotton tree, where the pioneers lived in 1821. We circle round —then up the river.

Great bowing trees, festoons of flowers, golden blossoms, star-faced palms and thatched huts; tall spreading trees lifting themselves like vast umbrellas, low shrubbery with grey and laced and knotted roots—the broad, black, murmuring river. Here a tree holds wide fingers out and stretches them over the water in vast incantation; bananas throw their wide green fingers to the sun. Iron villages, scarred clearings with grey, sheet-iron homes staring grim and bare at the ancient tropical flood of green.

The river sweeps wide and the shrubs bow low. Behind, Monrovia rises in clear, calm beauty. Gone are the wharves, the low and clustered houses of the port, the tight-throated business village, and up sweep the villas and the low wall, brown and cream and white, with great mango and cotton tree, with light house and spire, with porch and pillar and the green and color of shrubbery and blossom.

We climbed the upright shore to a senator's home and received his wide and kindly hospitality—curious blend of feudal lord and modern farmer—sandwiches, cake and champagne.

Again we glided up the drowsy river—five, ten, twenty miles and came to our hostess. A mansion of five generations with a compound of endless native servants and cows under the palm thatches. The daughters of the family wore, on the beautiful black skin of their necks, the exquisite pale gold chains of the Liberian artisan and the slim, black little granddaughter of the house had a wide pink ribbon on the thick curls of her dark hair, that lay like sudden sunlight on the shadows. Double porches one above the other, welcomed us to ease. A native man, gay with Christmas and a dash of gin, danced and sang and danced in the road. Children ran and played in the blazing sun. We sat at a long broad table and ate duck, chicken, beef, rice, plantain and collards, cake, tea, water and Madeira wine. Then we went and looked at the heavens, the up-twisted sky—Orion and Cassiopeia at zenith; the Little Bear beneath the horizon, new unfamiliar sights in the Milky Way—all awry, a-living—sun for snow at Christmas, and happiness and cheer.

January 1, 1924

As I look back and recall the days, which I have called great—the occasions in which I have taken part and which have had for me and others the widest significance, I can remember none like the first day of January, 1924. Once I took my bachelor's degree before a governor, a distinguished college president and others. But that was rather personal in its memory than in any way epochal. Once before the assembled races of the world I was called to speak in place of the suddenly sick Sir Harry Johnston. It was a great hour. But it was not greater than the day when I was presented to the President of the Negro Republic of Liberia.

Liberia had been resting under the shock of war. She had asked and been promised a large loan by the United States. She had conformed to every preliminary requirement and waited when waiting was almost fatal. It was not simply money, it was world prestige and high protection at a time when the little republic was sorely beset by creditors and greedy imperial powers. At the last moment, an insurgent Senate preemptorily and finally refused the request and strong recommendation of the President and his advisors and the loan was refused. The Department of State made no statement to the world and Liberia stood naked, not only well-nigh bankrupt but peculiarly defenseless amid scowling and unbelieving Powers.

It was then that the United States made a gesture of courtesy; a little thing, merely a gesture, but one so fine and so unusual that it was epochal. It sent an American Negro to Liberia. It designated him Envoy Extraordinary and Minister Plenipotentiary—the highest rank ever given by any country to a diplomatic agent in black Africa. And it named this Envoy the special representative of the President of the United States to the President of Liberia on the occasion of his inauguration, charging the envoy with a personal word of encouragement and moral support.

It was a great and significant action. It had in it nothing personal. Another appointee would have been equally significant. Liberia recognized the meaning. She showered upon the Envoy every mark of appreciation and thanks. The Commander of the Liberian Frontier Force was made his special Aide and a sergeant, his orderly. At 10 A.M. New Years morning a company of the Frontier Force, in red fez and khaki presented arms before the American Legation and escorted Solomon Porter Hood, the American Minister Resident, and myself as Envoy Extraordinary and my Aide to the Presidential Mansion —a beautiful white verandahed house waving with palms and fronting a grassy street.

Ceremonials are old and to some antiquated and yet this was done with such simplicity, grace and seriousness that none could escape its spell. The Secretary of State met us at the door, as the band played the wonderful Liberian National hymn and the soldiers saluted. He took us up a broad stairway and into a great room that stretched across the house. Here in semi-circle were ranged the foreign consuls and the cabinet—the former in white and gilt with orders and swords; the latter in solemn black. Here were England, France, Germany, Spain, Belgium,

Holland and Panama to be presented to me in order of seniority by the small brown Secretary of State with his perfect poise and ease.

The President entered—frock-coated with the star of a European order on his breast. The American Minister introduced the Envoy and the Envoy said:

YOUR EXCELLENCY:

The President of the United States has done me the great honor of designating me as his personal representative on the occasion of your inauguration. In so doing, he has had, I am sure, two things in mind. First, he wished publicly and unmistakably to express before the world the interest and solicitude which the hundred million inhabitants of the United States of America have for Liberia. Liberia is a child of the United States, and a sister Republic. Its progress and success is the progress and success of democracy everywhere and for all men; and the United States would view with sorrow and alarm any misfortune that might happen to this Republic and any obstacle that was placed in her path.

But special and peculiar bonds draw these two lands together. In America live eleven million persons of African descent, they are citizens, legally invested with every right that inheres in American citizenship. And I am sure that in this special mark of the President's favor, he has had in mind the wishes and hopes of Negro Americans. He knows how proud they are of the hundred years of independence which you have maintained by force of arms and by brawn and brain upon the edge of this mighty continent; he knows that in the great battle against color caste in America, the ability of Negroes to rule in Africa has been and ever will be a great and encouraging reinforcement. He knows that the unswerving loyalty of Negro Americans to their country is fitly accompanied by a pride in their race and lineage, a belief in the potency and promise of Negro blood which makes them eager listeners to every whisper of success from Liberia and eager helpers in every movement for your aid and comfort. The uplift and redemption of all Africa is in a special sense, the moral burden of Liberia and the advancement and integrity of Liberia is the sincere prayer of America.

May I, finally in thus expressing to your Excellency
the good wishes of my country and its President, be
permitted to add my own personal sense of the distinction put upon me in making me the humble bearer of
these messages. I have now the honor, Sir, to transmit
to you the personal word of Calvin Coolidge, President
of the United States of America by the hand of Charles
E. Hughes, Secretary of State.

(April, 1924. Vol. XXVII, No. 6, pp. 247-51)

THE PLACE, THE PEOPLE

Africa is vegetation. It is the riotous, unbridled bursting life
of leaf and limb. It is sunshine—pitiless shine of blue rising from
morning mists and sinking to hot night shadows. And then the
stars—very near are the stars to Africa, near and bright and
curiously arrayed. The tree is Africa. The strong, blinding
strength of it—the wide deep shade, the burly lavish height of
it. Animal life is there wild and abundant—perhaps in the inner
jungle I should note it more but here the herb is triumphant,
savagely sure—such beautiful shrubbery, such splendor of leaf
and gorgeousness of flower I have never seen.

And the people! Last night I went to Kru-town and saw a
Christmas masque. There were young women and men of the
color of warm ripe horse chestnuts, clothed in white robes and
turbaned. They played the Christ story with sincerity, naiveté
and verve. Conceive "Silent Night" sung in Kru by this dark
white procession with flaming candles; the little black mother
of Christ crossing with her baby, in figured⋅blue, with Joseph in
Mandingan fez and multi-colored cloak and beside them on her
worshipping knees the white wreathed figure of a solemn dark
angel. The shepherds watched their flocks by night, the angels
sang; and Simeon, raising the baby high in his black arms, sang
with my heart in English Kru-wise, *"Lord now lettest thou thy
servant depart in peace for mine eyes have seen thy salvation!"*

Liberia is gay in costume—the thrifty Krus who burst into
color of a holiday; the proud Veys always well-gowned; the
Liberian himself often in white. The children sometimes in their
own beautiful skins.

Sunday, January 13, 1924

I have walked three hours in the African bush. In the high bush mighty trees arose draped, with here and there the flash of flower and call of bird. The monkey sentinel cried and his fellows dashed down the great tree avenues. The way was marked —yonder the leopard that called last night under the moon, a bush cow's hoof; a dainty tread of antelope. We leaped the trail of driver ants and poked at the great houses of the white ants. The path rose and wound and fell now soft in green glow, now golden, now shimmery through the water as we balanced on a bare log. There was whine of monkey, scramble of timid unseen life, glide of dark snake. Then came the native farms—coffee, cocoa, plantain, cassava. Nothing is more beautiful than an African village—its harmonious colorings—its cleanliness, its dainty houses with the kitchen palaver place of entertainment, its careful delicate decorations and then the people. I believe that the African form in color and curve is the beautifulest thing on earth; the face is not so lovely—though often comely with perfect teeth and shining eyes,—but the form of the slim limbs, the muscled torso, the deep full breasts!

The bush is silence. Silence of things to be, silence vocal with infinite minor music and flutter and tremble—but silence, deep silence of the great void of Africa.

And the palms; some rose and flared like green fine work; some flared before they rose; some soared and drooped; some were stars and some were sentinels; then came the ferns—the feathery delicate things of grottos and haunts with us, leapt and sang in the sun—they thrust their virgin tracery up and out and almost to trees. Bizarre shapes of grass and shrub and leaf greeted us as though some artist all Divine was playing and laughing and trying every trick of his bewitched pencil above the mighty buildings of the ants.

I am riding on the singing heads of black boys swinging in a hammock. The smooth black bodies swing and sing, the neck set square, the hips sway. O lovely voices and sweet young souls of Africa!

Monrovia

Monrovia is a city set upon a hill. With coy African modesty her face is half turned from the bold and boisterous ocean and her wide black eyes gaze dreamfully up the Stockton and St. Paul. Her color is white and green and her head of homes rises slowly and widely in spacious shading verandah toward the great headland of Mesurado where the lighthouse screams to wandering ships. Her hair is plaited decently on mighty palm leaves and mangoes; her bare feet, stained with travel, torn with ancient cicatriced wounds drabble in the harbor waters down on Water Street and shun the mud town Plymouth Rock which is Providence Island. Her feet are ugly and old, but oh her hands, her smooth and black and flying hands are beautiful and they linger on roof and porch, in wide-throated grassy street and always they pat and smooth her hair, the green and sluggish palms of her heavy beautiful hair. And there is gold in her hair.

Africa

The spell of Africa is upon me. The ancient witchery of her medicine is burning my drowsy, dreamy blood. This is not a country, it is a world—a universe of itself and for itself, a thing Different, Immense, Menacing, Alluring. It is a great black bosom where the Spirit longs to die. It is life so burning, so fire encircled that one bursts with terrible soul inflaming life. One longs to leap against the sun and then calls, like some great hand of fate, the slow, silent crushing power of almighty sleep—of Silence, of immovable Power beyond, within, around. Then comes the calm. The dreamless beat of midday stillness at dusk, at dawn, at noon, always. Things move—black shiny bodies, perfect bodies, bodies of sleek unearthly poise and beauty. Eyes languish, black eyes—slow eyes, lovely and tender eyes in great dark formless faces. Life is slow here. Impetuous Americans quiver in impetuous graves. I saw where the ocean roars to the soul of Henry Highland Garnet. Life slows down and as it slows it deepens; it rises and descends to immense and secret places. Unknown evil appears and unknown good. Africa is the Spiritual Frontier of human kind—oh the wild and beautiful adventures of its taming! But oh! the cost thereof—the endless, endless cost! Then will come a day—an old and ever, ever young day when there will spring in Africa a civilization without coal, without noise, where machinery will sing and never rush and roar, and where men will sleep and think and dance and lie prone before the rising sons, and women will be happy.

The objects of life will be revolutionized. Our duty will not consist in getting up at seven, working furiously for six, ten and twelve hours, eating in sullen ravenousness or extraordinary repletion. No—We shall dream the day away and in cool dawns, in little swift hours, do all our work.

(April, 1924. Vol. XXVII, No. 6, pp. 273-4)

THE ALHAMBRA

What is the Alhambra? It is a fortress of pale red brick, square, stolid, forbidding, stately and severe with walled and crenelated ways, which fronts on the sun-lit river and looks on the silver-crowned Sierras beyond. Within, it smiles. Within, it is a jewel, carven with infinite care and cunning, inch on inch and line on line, pattern overlaying pattern, curve to curve and angle to angle; and then this completed whole is set like a thing of soft and simple beauty, restrained, retiring, silent, grand; of peculiar and intimate fascination in wave and circle, arc and sweep, arch and column, wall and ceiling.

We who are dark can imagine these halls in the glory of their day, shining in gold and color, carpeted with the woven loveliness of the East and South, filled with colored men and women, men of learning, bravery and finesse, who ruled land and sea and sky and spirit. "Oh, God, if I were there!" These are the people on whom today, barbarians of the West fling pennies from their profits.

On this, fell dogma, brazen misunderstanding, cruelty and toil in the name of God, and crushed and twisted it and killed it. But the ghost rises pale, grim and accusing. Spain has suffered nothing that her treatment of brown Moor and Black-a-Moor and Jew, did not let her deserve. And England shall suffer nothing that her treatment of India and Africa does not invite. The black blood of Africa was all through the builders of Moorish civilization in Spain and the impress of their spirit is over this mighty monument which we call the Alhambra.

Turn with me to it again. The color is cream, soft, old cream, never yellow, with the faintest red and brown, sometimes flow-

ering, never bursting, into faint blue and pale crimson. There is
infinite pains to achieve beauty.

In the Court of Myrtle two doves cooed and drank the waters
where dark mulatto Moors once bathed. The seven curves ride
on yonder side, the central curve taller. Seven curves above and
between them eight little grilled windows out of which the eyes
of the dead look down on an orange tree, golden with fruit. At
the other end in the golden cream of the morning sun, the seven
curves again—the great square above, the tall dome and
beyond, the shadow of the Hall of the Ambassadors and of the
World.

And the walls, the loving of the walls, the slow and careful
and endless doing and thinking, with curve and flowers; the holy
word of Islam, curling and singing and losing itself in beautiful
fancy. Carving and form and inter-lacing rise to make carving
and form and inter-lacing again and yet in all its mass and
greatness it is simply a beautiful thing.

(July, 1924. Vol. XXVIII, No. 3, pp. 105-6)

GRENADA, SPAIN

The Court of Lions—Worthy of the heaven above it and that
heaven without cloud or mist, magnificent in the morning sun;
one hundred and twenty-eight marble columns, little, lithe columns of white marble lifting sixty-eight arches, swift and slow-
curving arches, each arch an arch of arches, an endless line of
endless lines, and endless flowers and endless vines and spaces
and forms and things that droop and may not fall; and over all
and in all the word of Almighty God.

At either end two temples: fragile, complete, finely magnificent, old with eternal youth. At the corners the columns cluster
in the creamy daintiness of their beauty, then stand aside and
hand their arches one to another; arches that dream beauty to
the stars, that stand like virgins in immaculate but passionate
conception of unending forms of love.

I can conceive, from out the arches of that eastern temple and from the Hall of Kings, a splendid cortege; golden and crimson and silver in robe and sceptre; cream and black and brown and yellow of face; conquerors of worlds and rulers of men, tall and broad and splendid. They come to the Lions' Fountain with its twelve sides and twelve bronze lions and from the arched galleries round and about look out the faces of the world's great women, Candace and Semiramis and even Cleopatra.

Opposite, from the dainty temple (whose top a Spaniard ruined)—out of this still, heaven-protected beauty may walk a waiting world of evil and sin to be baptized in this sincere and simple beauty, in this beauty of unending pain.

Above and at the side, from the sheen of towered windows, north and south, look down on lion and woman and man and beautiful work of man fair faces of the dead and of them who yet may live beyond the shadow of the Sister's Hall and the world beyond.

There is nothing left unfinished, not even the brown lintels of the roofs that lean above the court. And everywhere the heaven is translated into roof, a roof of hanging holes, of faintly colored lights and creams.

The arches—the glory of that arch of the Hall of Kings that gives upon the Lion's Court. The suggestion of a point and then a curve so splendid it cannot stop on the capitals but swerves toward a hail and a kiss. And on the arch eighty-eight little points of blue, each with four curves; and back of that seven other little curves in brown and then an inset border and then a wreath of flowers and then eighty curves with blue figures; and then line and curve in black and brown and white and a ravishing inset; border and square and flower and word of God—and then—ah, who can tell all of this one arch!

The procession from the Temple turns to the right and enters the Sisters' Hall—where formerly Sultanas, black and white, poised their eager feet; a hall that rises like some great thought of God up and up—lingering to touch and paint the points of its infinite altitude—a thing of line and point and angle with every sweetness of curve and with a ceiling that is like the high Alps at Berne brought down and made human and complete.

One goes by the jewelled Mirador de Daraza—a bejewelled jewel—with glimpse of cypress, orange and myrtle.

There comes a great square hall with a roof of dark and silver stars and constellations and nine arches through which the white walls of Granada and the green mountains of Spain look in on faintly colored walls. It is all white and cream now but once it blazed in gold and crimson, blue and black—so delicately as to leave a sense of living color.

All is different—all is new—no pattern is repeated—yet it is the same, always one in style, in impression, in meaning. This afternoon the waters are surging in the Court of Lions, soft, sweet symphonies—the last sun is kissing the top of the arabesques.

Waters and cypress and hedges of box and the sound of water and great green trees and secret gardens and the splash and roar and drip of water and beyond, fields and hills and mountains and rivers and the white houses of men and above and yet beneath, high perched, ride the great snow Mountains—the ermine of the high Sierra Nevada; and olives and cacti and below the cream-brown-red of the Alhambra and above the high Sierras, ermine-mantled, ride with God.

I saw the tombs of Ferdinand and Isabella today and of the Beautiful Phillip and his wife the Fool;—I saw their tombs in Carrara marble and their coffins in ugly little iron boxes—poor, narrow fanatics to whom Columbus gave a world; religion-mad, bloodthirsty, cruel and yet pitifully, terribly in earnest. O this mad world!

(September, 1926. Vol. XXXII, No. 5. pp. 216-17)

ACROSS THE REPUBLICS

I have crossed three republics within a year—three vast imperial republics: two thousand miles in Russia from the Neva to the Volga and the Volga to the Dnieper and the Dnieper to the sea, leaving untold thousands of miles beyond. Five hundred miles through Germany and now three thousand five hundred miles from New York to Los Angeles. Everywhere I see a lonesome land, clustering with ant hills here and there in seldom ganglia for protection and companionship, for co-operation and market—huddled, crowded, fighting, snarling, hurrying, screaming things, until the huddle breaks breathless against great heights and spaces—silent rivers, silent mountains and silent stars. The huddling was least and the silence greatest and the hope tensest and most flaming in Russia. The huddling was greatest in America—New York, Philadelphia, Pittsburgh, Chicago, Denver, Los Angeles—and the silence of the plains and the Rockies, the Alleghanies and the Missouri ached in passionate protesting contrast. While in Germany the earth yearned: Black Thuringia, the lonesome Lorelei, the Wartburg of my burning Youth.

America lay washed in the blood of the Lamb—sheeted with white snow from Altoona to Ogden. Monuments gazed down upon me—William Penn the Smug; Chicago smudge; the bluffs of Council Bluffs; the infinite Rockies, naked bones of primeval earth; California flooded with rain and floating like a drowned rat with roses beneath the clouds. And then! golden gorgeous resurrection!

One strives desperately and in vain to make a meaning of it all—to give it the majesty of a unity—to grasp it in a phrase: Russia, Germany, the United States—Republics! But it eludes, baffles, and frowns. It has no eager answer. These lands of earth will not be expressed.

(April, 1927. Vol. XXXIV, No. 2, p. 70)

NEAR EAST

Constantinople flames in the morning sun. The tower of Galata, clean and high, the vast, ugly and solemn bulk of St. Sophia, the grace and bounding beauty of magnificent mosque of Sulieman!

We ride the Propontis, our sea of Marmora, in golden glory. Constantinople fades to a grey-blue of heaped buildings dwindling as the mosque of Holy Wisdom shows the vast stretch of its mighty reach. The rock islands lift dark heads to the light. Asia Minor looms and fades to white mist.

This afternoon we passed Gallipolis, merry with the sun but on the shore tenantless homes stared with dead eyes on the Sea and on the past and a white lighthouse rose on a mass of rock; beyond the drear and yellow land, sun-baked and hard, stretched back to purple hills where the dead must walk when night falls—walk and talk. Other towns lie very still with homes that live and windmills that whine and walls that bend in ruins. There is one great, round, stone windmill with shattered top.

I saw the sun set on the Hellespont. A harsh Europe stared on a greener Asia, with curve and dip of hill and dale. The world went blue and cold and up came memories on every hand. Nearer and nearer came two continents and seemed about to meet in the grey mist ahead. Then swerved—swerved and turned, turned and went down a straight and hidden passway to the left and the meeting of Europe and Asia was not, for it had not been.

It had not been and is not, although Xerxes, the second Mohammed, Constantine and Alexander tried to make it. We passed the Hellespont in the starlight. The water was dark silver, the sky a deadened blue; but the land burned black and heavy and all across the world flew Hero and Leander, Lord Byron, the Persian and the Turk, the English and the French. Above us hung the ruins of Abydos.

Then came night and brilliant stars—the Bears and the Pleiades, the joyous Milky Way; and in the night the backward turning world brought all its myths and memories:

"Sing, O Muse, the wrath of Peleus' son!"

Yonder hidden in the hills slept Troy and beyond, the snow garlands of Mount Olympus; Lemnos was on our right and on the left Tenedos and out there beyond the place where hundreds of thousands of boys were murdered by bullets and fever in 1915—out there lay Mitylene and Chios and away up yonder Samothrace. Achilles and Patroclus sleep there on the sands of Asia. All this by faith and in the night I see in the old Aegean; and now in the soft morning rises the great bulk of golden Euboaea. We sail between the Cyclades in that most beautiful world of Greece and her colonies. But all is empty; empty, barren and dead and the song and the voices, the flying boats and teaming trade—all dead, long dead.

I have seen what lives of the Glory that was Greece. Most beautiful were the lone columns of the temple of Jupiter, pale rose color, of infinite grace of form. Beyond them rose the Acropolis—that perfect building which neither the barbarism of the Turk nor the fanaticism of the Christian, nor the thefts of time and England have utterly destroyed. Forlorn it is and ragged—torn and battered, baked and burned in the savage sun. Yet through it all shines the perfection of the dream that put it there, the simple grace, the quiet restraint, the unbounded grandeur of the theme. It stands on a hill amid dark mountains with the sea behind and the city at its bare feet and all about are Salamis and Eleusis and Hymetus.

Other things are there on that World Hill—the fine strong joy of the Erechtheion, the old walls and walls within walls of the enshrining fortress; and Mars Hill, rough like Paul. In yonder little space Demosthenes talked to the Athenian citizens. In yonder little theatre Aeschylus and Euripides staged their plays.

Athens is dust, dry white dust and hot and endless street on street and proudly modern. It has been two thousand years I think since the little change began that conquered Greece: It stopped raining.

Great mountain masses escorted us through the canal and into the Gulf of Corinth. One saw the strong, heaped bulk of the Peloponnesus to the southward and to the north, the dark lands that looked beyond Athens to Delphi and Thrace. Night fell and we sailed by Ulysses and Ithaca to Italy in the morning.

(June, 1927. Vol. XXXIV, No. 4, p. 132)

SEVILLE

I see the winding of the narrow Calle Sierpes as I am tossed through it into the tower and the cathedral. The tower, Giralda of the Moors, is faintly yellow, tall and graceful, laced in Arabesque; it is simple and beautiful with its bells. The cathedral stands with the rich colors of evening pouring down upon it. In the center is the great carved choir, and through it comes the chanting of priests and boys and the faint smell of incense. There are immense and sombre shadows and the grave of the son of Christopher Columbus. Lovely are the gardens of the

Alcazar and of the palace with its great white Court of the Young Maidens and golden Hall of the Ambassadors. There are orange trees and tile benches in the park of Maria Louisa, and then one drops down to the busy Guadalquiver—the busy, hurrying Guadalquiver—filled with the shipping of Spain and the world.

(February, 1928. Vol. XXXV, No. 2, p. 61)

PERSONAL

STEVE

He was a lank puppy when he came—long and dull gold on his crinkly hair, furtive and frightened, but his eyes were the eyes of the Crucified Christ. The Girl took him in and plead for him—fed him when she thought of it and overfed him after she forgot. He was wild with the joy of a home and bounded in shooting leaps across the meadows. The Woman, who was wiser than we and knew that dogs are more than human, looked on him coldly at first, for she had loved dogs before, and love is a terrible thing.

Once he was lost and I and the Girl sought him as the sun died in the west, sought him east and west and north—calling and whistling—till at last he came darting like an arrow out of the unknown dark to leap and fawn upon us and bark triumphantly. Once he was stolen, but after two nights he crept back to us, dirty and bedraggled, with the accusing rope tied around him. Ah! but we were glad, and to celebrate we bought a collar and set his name brightly upon it.

Then of a certain Sunday morning catastrophe threatened us —two Russians stood without the gate and said, "It is our dog," and "Larrabee!" they called and he went, wagging his tail. But the Woman came quietly to the door and said, "Steve!" and he leapt back in joy and wriggled on her and kissed her. Then there was parleying and tales of his beautiful wolf-hound mother and —"But will you take him?" asked the Woman, her voice soft with fear. The Russian wife patted him tenderly and said, "No, we go back to Russia, now that Revolution has brought Freedom, and leave him with you, for he loves you and you are kind." So then the Girl left her hiding and her tears and clasped her treasure, and the Russians went back—Great God! to what?

And the dog waxed strong and mighty, golden and beautiful. Men feared his very sight, and his seldom bark was a forest of sound, but he loved the Woman with an endless love—following her every footstep, harkening to her every word, guarding her every movement. The Girl he liked next; and me he tolerated good-naturedly. To our guests he was studiously polite, with the grave courtesy of the greatly born; to all children he was humble servant—but the Woman was God!

Then came the end. After two years of delights, after the wonder of a new home, after a summer by the sounding sea and winters in snows; after great dreamful naps and terrifying forays; after evenings of strange, weird music—after all this came slow steps and pain and the great frightened look of love in his eyes grew more and more wistful as he followed the Woman whither his palsied legs could not go. So they came and took him away and gave him strange medicine to eat, but the light died in his eyes and in mercy they put him to sleep. The Woman wept.

He is gone. Last night, meseems, he slept beside the werewolves who guard the angels of the throne of God. At dawn I saw his soul flashing in golden flame across the northern skies; and now at noon behold him, leaping with mighty bounds across the broad steppes of his fathers. I hear his great voice sounding above the chaos of the beautifulest dream of two centuries, when the Christ of the Bolsheviki cried in God-begotten faith to the boiling, angry, fear-mad waters, "Peace!" and there was no peace. I feel his golden fleece bristling with almighty curses and his fangs dripping blood above the Huns who would destroy, not alone the flesh, but the spirit of a great people. On, Steve, on! rend and tear and kill and die that the sweet, good earth may live again and that Russia may not die.

All this I see (for I am Seer), but in our deserted home the Girl is silent and the Woman weeps, while I? Oh, I, always, beneath the hand of fate, write—and write—and write.

(December, 1918. Vol. XVII, No. 2, pp. 62-3)

THE HOUSE OF THE BLACK BURGHARDTS

If one slips out the Northern neck of Manhattan and flies to the left of the silver Sound, one swoops in time onto the Golden River; and dodging its shining beauty, now right, now left, one comes after a hundred miles of lake, hill and mountain, in the Old Bay State. Then at the foot of high Mt. Everett one takes a solemn decision: left is sweet, old Sheffield; but pass it stolidly by and slip gently right into tiny South Egremont which always sleeps. Then wheel right again and come to Egremont Plain and the House of the Black Burghardts.

It is the first home that I remember. There my mother was born and all her nine brothers and sisters. There perhaps my grandfather was born, although that I do not know. At any rate, on this wide and lovely plain, beneath the benediction of grey-blue mountain and the low music of rivers, lived for a hundred years the black Burghardt clan. Up and to the east of a hill of rocks was Uncle Ira; down and to the South was Uncle Harlow in a low, long, red house beside a pond—in a house of secret passages, sudden steps, low, narrow doors and unbelievable furniture. And here right in the center of the world was Uncle Tallow, as Grandfather Othello was called.

It was a delectable place—simple, square and low, with the great room of the fireplace, the flagged kitchen, half a step below, and the lower woodshed beyond. Steep, strong stairs led up to Sleep, while without was a brook, a well and a mighty elm. Almost was I born there myself but that Alfred Du Bois and Mary Burghardt honeymooned a year in town and then brought me as a baby back to Egremont Plain.

I left the home as a child to live in town again and go to school. But for furtive glimpses I did not see the house again for more than a quarter century. Then riding near on a chance journey I suddenly was homesick for that house. I came to the spot. There it stood, old, lonesome, empty. Its windowless eyes stared blindly on the broad, black highway to New York. It seemed to have shrunken timidly into itself. It had lost color and fence and grass and up to the left and down to the right its sister homes were gone—dead and gone with no stick nor stone to mark their burial.

From that day to this I desperately wanted to own that house for no earthly reason that sounded a bit like sense. It was 130 long miles from my work. It was decrepit almost beyond repair save that into its tough and sturdy timbers the Black Burghardts had built so much of their own dumb pluck that—

"Why the stairs don't even creak!" said She, climbing gingerly aloft.

But I fought the temptation away. Yachts and country estates and limousines are not adapted to my income. Oh, I inquired of course. The replies were discouraging. And once every year or so I drove by and stared sadly; and even more sadly and brokenly the House of the Black Burghardts stared back.

Then of a sudden somebody whose many names and places I do not know sent secret emissaries to me on a birthday which I had firmly resolved *not* to celebrate. Sent emissaries who showed me all the Kingdoms of this World, including something in green with a cupola; and also The House; and I smiled at the' House. And they said by telegram—"The House of the Black Burghardts is come home again—it is yours!"

Whereat in great joy I celebrated another birthday and drew plans. And from its long, hiding place I brought out an old black pair of tongs. Once my grandfather, and mayhap his, used them in the great fireplace of the House. Long years I have carried them tenderly over all the earth. The sister shovel, worn in holes, was lost. But when the old fireplace rises again from the dead on Egremont Plain, its dead eyes shall see not only the ghosts of old Tom and his son Jack and his grandson Othello and his great grandson, me—but also the real presence of these iron tongs resting again in fire worship in the House of the Black Burghardts.

(April, 1928. Vol. XXXV, No. 4, pp. 133-4)

SO THE GIRL MARRIES

The problem of marriage among our present American Negroes is a difficult one. On the one hand go conflicting philosophies: should we black folk breed children or commit biological suicide? On the other, should we seek larger sex freedom or closer conventional rules? Should we guide and mate our children like the French or leave the whole matter of sex intermingling to the chance of the street, like Americans? These are puzzling questions and all the more so because we do not often honestly face them.

I was a little startled when I became father of a girl. I scented faroff difficulties. But she became soon a round little bunch of Joy: plump and jolly, full of smiles and fun—a flash of twinkling legs and bubbling mischief. Always there on the broad campus of Atlanta University she was in scrapes and escapades—how many I never dreamed until years after: running away from her sleepy nurse; riding old Billy, the sage and dignified draft horse; climbing walls; bullying the Matron; cajoling the cooks and becoming the thoroughly spoiled and immeasurably loved Baby of the Campus. How far the spoiling had gone I became suddenly aware one summer, when we stopped a while to breathe the salt sea air at Atlantic City. This tot of four years marched beside me down the Boardwalk amid the unmoved and almost unnoticing crowd. She was puzzled. Never before in her memory had the world treated her quite so indifferently.

"Papa," she exclaimed at last, impatiently, "I guess they don't know I'm here!"

As the Girl grew so grew her problems: School; Multiplication Tables; Playmates; Latin; Clothes—Boys! No sooner had we faced one than the other loomed, the last lingered—the next threatened. She went to Kindergarten with her playmates of the Campus—kids and half-grown-ups. The half-grown-ups, Normal students, did me the special courtesy of letting the Girl dawdle and play and cut up. So when she came at the age of ten to the Ethical Culture School in New York there loomed the unlearned Multiplication Table; and a time we had! For despite all proposals of "letting the Child develop as it Will!", she must learn to read and count; and the school taught her—but at a price!

Then came the days of gawky growth; the impossible children of the street; someone to play with; wild tears at going to bed; excursions, games—and far, far in the offing, the shadow of the Fear of the Color Line.

I had a Grand Idea. Before the time loomed—before the Hurt pierced and lingered and festered, off to England she should go for high school and come back armed with manners and knowledge, cap-a-pie, to fight American race hate and insult. Off the Girl went to Bedale's, just as war thundered in the world. As a professor of Economics and History, I knew the war would be short—a few months. So away went Mother and Girl. Two mighty years rolled turbulently by and back came both through the Submarine Zone. The Girl had grown. She was a reticent stranger with whom soul-revealing converse was difficult. I found myself groping for continual introductions.

Then came Latin. The English teacher talked Latin and his class at Bedale's romped with Caesar through a living Gallia. The American teacher in the Brooklyn Girl's High did not even talk English and regarded Latin as a crossword puzzle with three inches of daily solution. "Decline Stella!"; "Conjugate Amo"; "What is the subject of 'Gallia est omnis divisa——' ". "Nonsense," said the Girl (which was quite true) "I've dropped Latin!"

"But the colleges haven't," I moaned. "Why college?" countered the Girl.

Why indeed? I tried Cicero "pro Archia Poeta". The Girl was cold. Then I pleaded for my own spiritual integrity: "I have told 12 millions to go to college—what will they say if you don't go?" The Girl admitted that that was reasonable but she said she was considering marriage and really thought she knew about all that schools could teach effectively. I, too, was reasonable and most considerate, despite the fact that I was internally aghast. This baby—married—My God!—but, of course, I said aloud: Honorable state and all that; and "Go ahead, if you like—but how about a year in college as a sort of, well, introduction to life in general and for furnishing topics of conversation in the long years to come? How about it?" "Fair enough," said the Girl and she went to college.

Boys! queer animals. Hereditary enemies of Fathers-with-daughters and Mothers! Mother had chaperoned the Girl relentlessly through High School. Most Mothers didn't bother. It was a bore and one felt like the uninvited guest or the veritable Death's Head. The Girl didn't mind much, only—"Well, really Mother you don't need to go or even to sit up." But Mother stuck to her job. I've always had the feeling that the real trick was turned in those years, by a very soft voiced and persistent Mother who was always hanging about unobtrusively. The boys liked her, the girls were goodnaturedly condescending; the Girl laughed. It was so funny. Father, of course, was busy with larger matters and weightier problems, including himself.

Clothes. In the midst of high school came sudden clothes. The problem of raiment. The astonishing transformation of the hoyden and hiker and basket ball expert into an amazing butterfly. We parents had expressed lofty disdain for the new colored beauty parlors—straightening and bleaching, the very idea! But they didn't straighten, they cleaned and curled; they didn't whiten, they delicately darkened. They did for colored girls' style of beauty what two sophisticated centuries had been doing for blonde frights. When the finished product stood forth all silked and embroidered, briefly skirted and long-limbed with impudent lip-stick and jaunty toque—well, Thrift hung its diminished head and Philosophy stammered. What shall we do about our daughter's extravagant dress? The beauty of colored girls has increased 100% in a decade because they give to it time and trouble. Can we stop it? Should we? Where shall we draw the line, with good silk stockings at $1.95 per pair?

"Girl! You take so long to dress! I can dress in fifteen minutes."

"Yes—Mamma and you look it!" came the frankly unfilial answer.

College. College was absence and premonition. Empty absence and occasional letters and abrupt pauses. One wondered uneasily what they were doing with the Girl; *who* rather than what was educating her. Four years of vague uneasiness with flashes of hectic and puzzling vacations. Once with startling abruptness there arose the Shadow of Death—acute appendicitis; the hospital—the cold, sharp knife; the horror of waiting and the namelessly sweet thrill of recovery. Of course, all the spoiling began again and it literally rained silk and gold.

Absence, too, resulted in the unexpected increase in Parent-valuation. Mother was enshrined and worshipped by the absent Girl; no longer was she merely convenient and at times in the way. She was desperately adored. Even Father took on unaccustomed importance and dignity and found new place in the scheme of things. We both felt quite set up.

Then graduation and a Woman appeared in the family. A sudden woman—sedate, self-contained, casual, grown; with a personality—with wants, expenses, plans. "There will be a caller tonight."—"Tomorrow night I'm going out."

It was a bit disconcerting, this transforming of a rubber ball of childish joy into a lady whose address was at your own house.

I acquired the habit of discussing the world with this stranger
—as impersonally and coolly as possible: teaching—travel—
reading—art—marriage. I achieved quite a detached air, letting
the domineering daddy burst through only at intervals, when it
seemed impossible not to remark—"It's midnight, my dear,"
and "when is the gentleman going? You need sleep!"

My part in Mate-selection was admittedly small but I flatter
myself not altogether negligible. We talked the young men over
—their fathers and grandfathers; their education; their ability to
earn particular sorts of living; their dispositions. All this inci-
dentally mind you—not didactically or systematically. Once or
twice I went on long letter hunts for facts; usually facts were all
too clear and only deductions necessary. What was the result?
I really don't know. Sometimes I half suspect that the Girl
arranged it all and that I was the large and solemn fly on the
wheel. At other times I flatter myself that I was astute, secret,
wise and powerful. Truth doubtless lurks between. So the Girl
marries.

I remember the Boy came to me somewhat breathlessly one
Christmas eve with a ring in his pocket. I told him as I had told
others. "Ask her—she'll settle the matter; not I." But he was a
nice boy. A rather unusual boy with the promise of fine manhood. I wished him luck. But I did not dare plead his cause. I
had learned—well, I had learned.

Thus the world grew and blossomed and changed and so the
Girl marries. It is the end of an era—a sudden break and beginning. I rub my eyes and readjust my soul. I plan frantically. It
will be a simple, quiet ceremony—

"In a church, father!"

"Oh! in a church? Of course, in a church. Well, a church
wedding would be a little larger, but——"

"With Countée's father and the Reverend Frazier Miller assisting."

"To be sure—well, that is possible and, indeed, probable."

"And there will be sixteen bridesmaids."

One has to be firm somewhere—"But my dear! who ever
heard of sixteen bridesmaids!"

"But Papa, there are eleven Moles, and five indispensables
and Margaret—"

Why argue? What has to be, must be; and this evidently had
to be. I struggled faintly but succumbed. Now with sixteen

bridesmaids and ten ushers must go at least as many invited
guests.

You who in travail of soul have struggled with the devastating
puzzle of selecting a small bridge party out of your total of
twenty-five intimate friends, lend me your sympathy! For we
faced the world-shattering problem of selecting for two only
children, the friends of a pastor with twenty-five years service
in one church; and the friends of a man who knows good people
in forty-five states and three continents. I may recover from it
but I shall never look quite the same. I shall always have a
furtive feeling in my soul. I know that at the next corner I shall
meet my Best Friend and remember that I forgot to invite him.
Never in all eternity can I explain. How can I say: "Bill, I just
forgot you!" Or "My *dear* Mrs. Blubenski, I didn't remember
where on earth you were or indeed if you were at all or ever!"
No, one can't say such things. I shall only stare at them plead-
ingly, in doubt and pain, and slink wordlessly away.

Thirteen hundred were bidden to the marriage and no human
being has one thousand three hundred friends! Five hundred
came down to greet the bride at a jolly reception which I had
originally planned for twenty-five. Of course, I was glad they
were there. I expanded and wished for a thousand. Three thousand saw the marriage and a thousand waited on the streets. It
was a great pageant; a heart-swelling throng; birds sang and
Melville Charlton let the organ roll and swell beneath his quivering hands. A sweet young voice sang of Love; and then came
the holy:

> Freudig gefeuert, Ziehet dahin!

The symbolism of that procession was tremendous. It was not
the mere marriage of a maiden. It was not simply the wedding
of a fine young poet. It was the symbolic march of young and
black America. America, because there was Harvard, Columbia, Smith, Brown, Howard, Chicago, Syracuse, Penn and
Cornell. There were three Masters of Arts and fourteen Bache-
lors. There were poets and teachers, actors, artists and students.
But it was not simply conventional America—it had a dark and
shimmering beauty all its own; a calm and high restraint and
sense of new power; it was a new race; a new thought; a new
thing rejoicing in a ceremony as old as the world. (And after it

all and before it, such a jolly, happy crowd; some of the girls even smoked cigarettes!)

Why should there have been so much of pomp and ceremony —flowers and carriages and silk hats; wedding cake and wedding music? After all marriage in its essence is and should be very simple: a clasp of friendly hands; a walking away together of Two who say: "Let us try to be One and face and fight a lonely world together!" What more? Is that not enough? Quite; and were I merely white I should have sought to make it end with this.

But it seems to me that I owe something extra to an Idea, a Tradition. We who are black and panting up hurried hills of hate and hindrance—we have got to establish new footholds on the slipping by-paths through which we come. They must at once be footholds of the free and the eternal, the new and the enthralled. With all of our just flouting of white convention and black religion, some things remain eternally so—Birth, Death, Pain, Mating, Children, Age. Ever and anon we must point to these truths and if the pointing be beautiful with music and ceremony or bare with silence and darkness—what matter? The width or narrowness of the gesture is a matter of choice. That one will have it stripped to the essence. It is still good and true. This soul wants color with bursting cords and scores of smiling eyes in happy raiment. It must be as this soul wills. The Girl wills this. So the Girl marries.

(June, 1928. Vol. XXXV, No. 6, pp. 192 ff)

VISITORS

To the hard worker in a great modern city the problem of the casual visitor is baffling. No one needs visitors more than he: he needs the enlivening and quickening contact with the world outside the office. He needs to keep human and to resist the mechanical trend of his city routine. He needs the knowledge that comes by word of mouth to correct and make real the printed page.

On the other hand, if visitors want to greet a man, it is

because he has done something—has thought, written, acted, inspired. And if a man is going to do anything today in New York, on Fifth Avenue, in a modern office, he must have periods of quiet, intensive, uninterrupted work.

Here comes the Visitor. He knows and appreciates what the Worker is doing. He wants to see him, to know him, to tell him. The Worker needs to be told. He works in a strange unmeaning silence. His voice has no echoes. No one seems to listen. No one cares—What's the use? And then—in bursts the Visitor with outstretched hand and shining eyes and joy and laughter in his voice! The world lives and moves again.

But—both Visitor and Worker must have some modicum of common sense. The Visitor blows in town on holiday. He sleeps well, eats heartily and at eleven A. M. says gaily: "Now for THE CRISIS office!" But pause, friend. Why not just go to the 'phone and say: "I'm in town. Want to see you. When are you free?" And the editor responds: "Could you come at 2? Good!" All is well. Both are happy. Both are helped.

But if the Editor is not asked and you burst in on his poised pen; if you interrupt a carefully arranged morning or a happy thought surging to be born—if you do this for no other reason but that you are too lazy to arrange a mutually convenient time —well, the Editor may be unhappy. He may think that his convenience has a right to be considered as well as yours.

———————

I was sitting in my office with a helper reading the stone-proof of the magazine: last day, last hour. It must be down at 5 or the schedule of a great printing house with 25 magazines to print would be thrown out of kilter, 800 agents would await a late magazine, and 100,000 readers would yell: "C.P.T.". We were working like hell with an hour to finish an hour and a half's work.—

"Miss Blink and Miss Blank of Seattle, to see the Editor."

Frankly I am furious. The Misses B. and B. could just as easily have called an hour later or an hour earlier. Three minutes on the telephone could have arranged a delightful visit with two intelligent and educated women whom I needed to see and question and explain. One knew Youth—mysterious, prophetic, eternal Youth. And one knew Art, subtle, intriguing trick of thought—beauty of way and mean. I could learn something of both—but not then and now—for a Ghost with dripping hands hovered above me and I had to finish that proof.

Well—I did not see them. As a result, I lost two good and helpful friends. In vain did I write next day explanation and apology. They were insulted to the last degree. Selah.

I am not altogether blameless. I often discount human facts in comparison with divine thoughts. I cannot jump readily from the understanding mind to the glad hand. And yet, frank and sympathetic comprehension of my problem and of the problem of the Visitor might bring mutual understanding.

The problem has many attempted solutions: sound proof, inner sanctums which leave the public office frankly empty— "Stepped out"; "in conference"; staring printed signs about not being at home except at such and such hours; secret bells, like Bismark's to summon oneself to mythical appointments; or alibis like that of a friend of mine. I used to find him easily ensconced in his office with smiles and open door. The public was cordially welcome, whether on business or without—crank, book agent or prophet, for a few minutes or a few hours.

"How do you do it?" I gasped, aghast.

"Just waste the day," he grinned. "Go home to dinner; take a nap, and work from Midnight to 4 A.M.!"

"H'm!" I remarked. Two years later he had a stroke of paralysis.

I have a colleague across the way. I have seen him stagger out of his office at noon with death in his eye—Death of a Big Job —murder of a fine idea. Some friend had dropped in "just for a minute" and staid an hour!

And so, let's get together on this thing. I want to see you, Visitor, I really do. But can't we compromise on the hour, if not the day? I'll go half way—honest, I will.

———

Never mind Me, but respect my Work. My Work is cold, calm, relentless. It will be done now or never. It is merciless. It glares at me cruel-kind, malignant-gracious:

"Tuesday's Work undone? Good! Here's Wednesday's!"

I shriek in vain, wring my hands—

"But Tuesday?"

The Work answers, very softly and smooth:

"There is no Tuesday. Tuesday is dead. Dead forever and forever. And Monday and last week and year 1927."

"But Tuesday's work is not done," I wail, and it echoes:

"It shall never be done. Here is Today and Wednesday and this year. They are yours. Work or die."

Sometimes I seek to fool my Master, Work. I enter stealthily Wednesday, lugging Tuesday's undone task beneath my vest. He says no word. His face is grey and grim. I know I can never deceive my Master.

And yet often, when the finished Deed stands sleek before me, clothed like a Book, an Editorial, a Speech, a Letter,—I sigh and say:

"I have bought you with my Friends—and I have but few left."

Not me, not me, Lord Visitor, craves your thoughtful sympathy and co-operation, but the Master.

If we cajole him and seek to do his will, he may nod uneasily and sleep, snore and dream! Ah, when my Work dreams, that is the Kingdom and the Power and the Glory of my friends. Then we will smoke and eat and carouse and make love and play. He will awake to find us more than ready and wild with waiting.

Happy are the workless and the Idle, who can just enjoy and need not think! But I, (woe is me!) I am the grandson of a Seventh Son, born with a Veil. From all Eternity I am sentenced to toil—and to love it.

(July, 1928. Vol. XXXV, No. 7, pp. 239-40)

"DON'T YOU REMEMBER ME?"

"Don't you remember me?" I always hear the question with an uncontrollable sinking of heart. I cannot put aside the feeling of panic. I do not remember the person and the person knows perfectly well that I do not. I am desperately trying to find some adequate answer, although I know there is none, and the person is trying, with more or less success, usually less, not to show his pique.

One of my latest experiences was in Asbury Park. I was lecturing on a warm night. There was a large audience in a low ceilinged room,—a kind audience who listened a long time, not simply to what I said, but to what many others said. It was late before I was released and I was tired. I came out on the darkened street. A man was standing in the shadow. I saw his bulk but I have not yet seen his face clearly. He was very dark and reticent.

"Don't you remember me?" he said. I wanted to say, "I have not seen your face yet," but I tried to be pleasant. "I am afraid —" I began gropingly.

He seemed surprised. "Why I was a student at Atlanta," he said. I could feel a surge of resentment boiling up in both of us. I left Atlanta exactly eighteen years before. How many years before that I had seen this boy I do not know. Whether he was a student in my class or just one of the general mass of students, I had no idea. He was a man now evidently of much less than middle-age. Twenty years ago he was a mere boy; did he realize how much he had changed in those years and how many thousands of people I had met in two decades? Did he really expect that, without any help from him, I was going instantly to recall him? If he did, he was disappointed and I was mad. Despite all my resolutions, I get thoroughly out of patience with this kind of thing, and it happens again and again.

Others have their methods of meeting the situation: there was Bishop Turner with his massive body and voice like a bull: "What? Do I know you? Of course, I know you! Now what's your name?" with a hearty thump on the back. "John Smith? Oh yes. And where are you from? Americus? Let's see. Who's your father? Yes? Yes! Yes!"

"He knew me!" says the proud and gleeful man, as he goes away.

Once or twice, tentatively and with hesitation, I have tried that plan. But it won't work—tentatively and with hesitation. Only a master blaggart can put that sort of thing over.

On the other hand, the late Booker Washington, who was Forgetfulness itself, had another method. His Secretary would hasten ahead and canvass the room. By the time Mr. Washington came in, he met him, suave and smiling.

"Mr. Washington, you remember Mr. Jones of Memphis, the President of the bank, who entertained you while you were—"

"Oh, yes, yes, Mr. Jones. So glad to see you." This plan works easily, when one can hire traveling Secretaries. Theodore Roosevelt had a natural gift for faces and names, and he cultivated it; he did almost miraculous things in the line of recalling acquaintances. But imagine the time and strength that it must have taken! Perhaps, otherwise, he might be living yet.

Personally, I am hopeless at such deeds of memory. My memory performs the most extraordinary feats. I will remember the red stripe of the table cover at San Diego, California, and utterly forget my own telephone number. And as for the names which are most illogically and inconsequently attached to human beings, I can remember few and seldom.

I do not for a moment discount the misfortune of such lack of ability to recall. Frequently, I would have been willing to pay large sums of money in cash to have been able to say:

"John Bull of Miami! I met you at 3:00 P.M., Saturday, April 4, 1903, at the corner of Beale and what-you-may-call-it Street, Memphis. You had eaten onions for dinner. How is your youngest boy who was then three?" That is what I would like. This is what I get: A dark-eyed lady looks at me reproachfully with —"I have met you three times!" While I am struggling not to blurt out: "My God, woman, you don't think I *want* to forget you, do you?" You see with modern women it is all impossible, anyway. What with a new hat, a short dress, bobbed hair and brown powder, how in the name of Tophet am I going to recognize in 1928 my charming friend of 1923? One of these floated on me at yesternight's gathering. I stood like a dumb fool. There was something familiar, of course, but who the Heck!—Los Angeles, London, Charleston, Memphis?—who, what, when? She went crimson with indignation and flew. So did I. I fell on the Village Gossip. "Who?" I gasped. "Smith!" he yelled. "Gerechtige Gott!" I murmured.

Now I ask why could she not have come up and frankly said: "I am Frances Smith of Nashville!" Why assume that anyone is happy to forget you; or if you do assume it, why speak at all? No, the fact is we colored folk are used to being snubbed and forgotten. We have the complex. We expect it. We expect that if anyone climbs a social ladder or gets notorious for any reason he will celebrate with the cheap snobbery of pretending to forget his former friends. We expect this so faithfully that we recognize it when it is not there and never was.

But what a compliment to pay a poor beggar who wants to

be decent to have such an accusation slapped full into his astonished face!

(March, 1929. Vol. XXXVI, No. 3, p. 94)

MISCELLANEOUS

THE CRISIS

The object of this publication is to set forth those facts and
arguments which show the danger of race prejudice, particularly
as manifested to-day toward colored people. It takes its name
from the fact that the editors believe that this is a critical time
in the history of the advancement of men. Catholicity and tolerance, reason and forbearance can to-day make the world-old
dream of human brotherhood approach realization; while big-
otry and prejudice, emphasized race consciousness and force
can repeat the awful history of the contact of nations and groups
in the past. We strive for this higher and broader vision of Peace
and Good Will.

The policy of THE CRISIS will be simple and well defined:

It will first and foremost be a newspaper: it will record important happenings and movements in the world which bear on the
great problem of inter-racial relations, and especially those
which affect the Negro-American.

Secondly, it will be a review of opinion and literature, recording briefly books, articles, and important expressions of opinion
in the white and colored press on the race problem.

Thirdly, it will publish a few short articles.

Finally, its editorial page will stand for the rights of men,
irrespective of color or race, for the highest ideals of American
democracy, and for reasonable but earnest and persistent attempt to gain these rights and realize these ideals. The magazine
will be the organ of no clique or party and will avoid personal
rancor of all sorts. In the absence of proof to the contrary it will
assume honesty of purpose on the part of all men, North and
South, white and black.

(November, 1910. Vol. I, No. 1, p. 10)

BUSINESS AND PHILANTHROPY

The talented, systematic, hard-headed youth of our nation are put into business. We tell them that the object of business is to make money. Our dull, soft-headed, unsystematic youth we let stray into philanthropy to work for the good of men. Then we wonder at our inability to stop stealing. This is the great American paradox.

Small wonder that we see in our world two armies: one large and successful, well dressed and prosperous. They say bluntly: "We are not in business for our health—business pays!" The other army is seedy and diffident and usually apologetic. It says: "There are things that ought to be done, and we are trying to do them—philanthropy begs." Between the business men, pure and simple and the professional philanthropists waver the world's hosts—physicians, lawyers, teachers, and servants, some regarding their work as philanthropy, most of them looking at it as business and testing its success by its pay.

Business pays.

Philanthropy begs.

Business is reality, philanthropy is dream: business first, philanthropy afterward—is this true? No, it is not. It is the foundation falsehood of our perverted social order.

In reality it is business enterprise that continually tends to defeat its own ability to pay and it is philanthropy that works to preserve a social order that will make the larger and broader and better business enterprises pay.

What is meant when we say a business pays? Simply this: that for the service rendered or the thing given, the public will to-day pay a valued equivalent in services or goods. Men do this because of their present wants. Given a people wanting certain things and corresponding business enterprises follow. Will this demand continue? That depends: if the satisfaction of these wants minister to the real health and business of the community, the demand will continue and grow; if not, eventually either the business or the nation will die. The fact then that a business pays to-day is no criterion for the future. The liquor traffic pays and so does the publishing of school books; houses of prostitution pay and so do homes for renting purposes: and yet alcoholism and prostitution mean death while education and homes mean life to this land.

The amount then that a business pays is no test of its social value. It may pay and yet gradually destroy the larger part of all business enterprise. Here enters philanthropy. Its object is to do for men not what they want done, but that which, for their own health, they ought to want done. Will such service pay? Possibly it will: possibly the people will want the service as soon as they learn of it and lo! "Philanthropy and five per cent." appears. More often, however, the people do not recognize the value of the new thing—do not want it; will not use baths or have anything to do with coffee rooms. Will they pay, then? If they perform a service necessary to human welfare and if the people are gradually learning what is really for their good, then sometimes such philanthropy pays. If it does not pay then the service offered was really unnecessary or the people to whom it was offered have ceased to advance toward betterment and are in danger of death.

The test, then, of business is philanthropy; that is, the question as to how far business enterprise is doing for men the things they ought to have done for them, when we consider not simply their present desires, but their future welfare. Just here it is that past civilizations have failed. Their economic organization catered to fatal wants and persisted in doing so, and refused to let philanthropy guide them. Just so to-day. Whenever a community seats itself helplessly before a dangerous public desire, or an ingrained prejudice, recognizing clearly its evil, but saying, "We must cater to it simply because it exists," it is final; change is impossible. Beware; the epitaph of that people is being written.

There is not a particle of ethical difference in the two callings. The legitimate object of both men is social service. The service of one is advice, inspiration and personal sympathy; the service of the other is fresh eggs and prompt delivery. Thus "from the blackening of boots to the whitening of souls" there stretches a chain of services to be done for the comfort and salvation of men.

Those who are doing these things are doing holy work, and the *work done,* not the *pay received,* is the test of the working. Pay is simply the indication of present human appreciation of the work, but most of the world's best work has been, and is being done, unappreciated.

"Ah, yes," says the cynic, "but do you expect men will work

for the sake of working?" Yes, I do. That's the reason most men work. Men want work. They love work. Only give them the work they love and they will ask no pay but their own soul's "Well done!" True it is that it is difficult to assign to each of the world's workers the work he loves; true it is that much of the world's drudgery will ever be disagreeable; but pay will never destroy inherent distaste, nor (above the starvation line) will it form a greater incentive than social service, if we were but trained to think so.

These things are true, fellow-Americans; therefore, let us, with one accord, attack the bottom lie that supports graft and greed and selfishness and race prejudice: namely, that any decent man has at any time any right to adopt any calling or profession for the sole end of personal gain.

"Surely," gasp the thrifty, "the first duty of man is to earn a living!" This means that man must at least do the world a service such as men, constituted as they are to-day, will requite with the necessities of life. This is true for some men always; perhaps for most men to-day. We pray for some sweet morning when it will be true for all men. But it was not true for Socrates, nor for Jesus Christ.

(June, 1911. Vol. II, No. 2, pp. 64-6)

OF CHILDREN

This is the Children's Number, and as it has grown and developed in the editor's hesitating hands, it has in some way come to seem a typical rather than a special number. Indeed, there is a sense in which all numbers and all words of a magazine of ideas must point to the child—to that vast immortality and wide sweep and infinite possibility which the child represents. Such thought as this it was that made men say of old as they saw baby faces like these that adorn our pages this month:

"And whosoever shall offend one of these little ones . . . it is better for him that a millstone were hanged about his neck, and he were cast into the sea."

OF THE GIVING OF LIFE

And yet the mothers and fathers and the men and women of our race must often pause and ask:

Is it worth while?

Ought children be born to us?

Have we a right to make human souls face what we face to-day?

The answer is clear: if the great battle of human right against poverty, against disease, against color prejudice is to be won, it must be won not in our day, but in the day of our children's children. Ours is the blood and dust of battle, theirs the rewards of victory. If then they are not there because we have not brought them to the world, then we have been the guiltiest factor in conquering ourselves. It is our duty then to accomplish the immortality of black blood in order that the day may come in this dark world when poverty shall be abolished, privilege based on individual desert, and the color of a man's skin be no bar to the outlook of his soul.

OF THE SHIELDING ARM

If then it is our duty as honest colored men and women battling for a great principle to bring not aimless rafts of children to the world, but as many as, with reasonable sacrifice, we can train to largest manhood, what in its inner essence shall that training be, particularly in its beginning? Our first impulse is to shield our children absolutely. Look at these happy little innocent faces: for most of them there is as yet no shadow, no thought of a color line. The world is beautiful and good, and real life is joy. But we know only too well that beyond all the disillusionment and hardening that lurk for every human soul there is that extra hurting which, even when unconscious, with fiendish refinement of cruelty waits on each corner to shadow the joy of our children; if they are backward or timid, there is the sneer; if they are forward, there is repression; the problems of playmates and amusements are infinite, and street and school and church have all that extra hazard of pain and temptation that spells hell to our babies.

The first temptation then is to shield the child; to hedge it about that it may not know and will not dream. Then, when we can no longer wholly shield, to indulge and pamper and coddle, as though in this dumb way to compensate. From this attitude comes the multitude of our spoiled, wayward, disappointed children; and we must not blame ourselves? For while the motive was pure and the outer menace undoubted, is shielding and indulgence the way to meet it?

OF THE GRIM THRUST

Some parents realizing this, leave their children to sink or swim in this sea of race prejudice. They neither shield nor explain, but thrust them forth grimly into school or street, and let them learn as they may from brutal fact. Out of this may come strength, poise, self-dependence, and out of it, too, may come bewilderment, cringing deception and self-distrust. It is, all said, a brutal, unfair method, and in its way as bad as shielding and indulgence. Why not rather face the facts and tell the truth? Your child is wiser than you think.

THE FRANK TRUTH

The truth lies ever between extremes. It is wrong to introduce the child to race consciousness prematurely. It is dangerous to let that consciousness grow spontaneously without intelligent guidance. With every step of dawning intelligence explanation —frank, free guiding explanation—must come. The day will dawn when mother must explain gently but clearly why the little girls next door do not want to play with "Niggers;" what the real cause is of the teachers' unsympathetic attitude, and how people may ride on the backs of street cars and the smoker end of trains, and still be people, honest high-minded souls.

Remember, too, that in such frank explanation you are speaking in nine cases out of ten to a good deal clearer understanding than you think, and that the child mind has what your tired soul may have lost faith in—the power and the glory.

(October, 1912. Vol. IV, No. 6, pp. 287-9)

A PHILOSOPHY FOR 1913

I am by birth and law a free black American citizen.

As such I have both rights and duties.

If I neglect my duties my rights are always in danger. If I do not maintain my rights I cannot perform my duties.

I will listen, therefore, neither to the fool who would make me neglect the things I ought to do, nor to the rascal who advises me to forget the opportunities which I and my children ought to have, and must have, and will have.

Boldly and without flinching, I will face the hard fact that in this, my fatherland, I must expect insult and discrimination from persons who call themselves philanthropists and Christians and gentlemen. I do not wish to meet this despicable attitude by blows; sometimes I cannot even protest by words; but may God forget me and mine if in time or eternity I ever weakly admit to myself or the world that wrong is not wrong, that insult is not insult, or that color discrimination is anything but an inhuman and damnable shame.

Believing this with my utmost soul, I shall fight race prejudice continually. If possible, I shall fight it openly and decidedly by word and deed. When that is not possible I will give of my money to help others to do the deed and say the word which I cannot. This contribution to the greatest of causes shall be my most sacred obligation.

Whenever I meet personal discrimination on account of my race and color I shall protest. If the discrimination is old and deep seated, and sanctioned by law, I shall deem it my duty to make my grievance known, to bring it before the organs of public opinion and to the attention of men of influence, and to urge relief in courts and legislatures.

I will not, because of inertia or timidity or even sensitiveness, allow new discriminations to become usual and habitual. To this end I will make it my duty without ostentation, but with firmness, to assert my right to vote, to frequent places of public entertainment and to appear as a man among men. I will religiously do this from time to time, even when personally I prefer the refuge of friends and family.

While thus fighting for Right and Justice, I will keep my soul clean and serene. I will not permit cruel and persistent persecution to deprive me of the luxury of friends, the enjoyment of laughter, the beauty of sunsets, or the inspiration of a well-written word. Without bitterness (but also without lies), without useless recrimination (but also without cowardly acquiescence), without unnecessary heartache (but with no self-deception), I will walk my way, with uplifted head and level eyes, respecting myself too much to endure without protest studied disrespect from others, and steadily refusing to assent to the silly exaltation of a mere tint of skin or curl of hair.

In fine, I will be a man and know myself to be one, even among those who secretly and openly deny my manhood, and I shall persistently and unwaveringly seek by every possible method to compel all men to treat me as I treat them.

(January, 1913. Vol. V, No. 3, p. 127)

THE EXPERTS

For deep insight and superb brain power commend us to Dr. Ulrich B. Phillips, of the University of Michigan.

Phillips is white and Southern, but he has a Northern job and he knows all about the Negro. He has recently been talking to the students of the University of Virginia, and he disclosed some powerful reasoning faculties. Consider this, for instance:

"To compare Negro efficiency in cotton production before and since the war, it is necessary to select districts where no great economic change has occurred except the abolition of slavery—where there has been no large introduction of commercial fertilizers, for example, and no great ravages by the bollweevil. A typical area for our purpose is the Yazoo delta in Northwestern Mississippi. In four typical counties there—Tunica, Coahonia, Bolivar and Issaquena—in which the Negro population numbers about 90 per cent of the whole, the per capita output of cotton in 1860 was two and one-third bales of 500 pounds each, while in 1910 and other average recent years it was only one and one-half bales per capita. That is to say, the efficiency of the Negroes has declined 35 per cent. A great number of other black-belt counties indicate a similar decline.

"On the other hand, the white districts throughout the cotton belt, and especially in Texas, Oklahoma and Western Arkansas, have so greatly increased their cotton output that more than half of the American cotton crop is now clearly produced by white labor. Other data of wide variety confirm this view of Negro industrial decadence and white industrial progress."

We are delighted to learn all this, for in the dark days of our college economics we were taught that it was labor *and* land, together, that made a crop; and that worn-out land and good labor would make an even poorer crop than rich land and poor labor. It seems that we were grievously in error. This is apparently true only of *white* labor. If you wish to judge *white* labor, judge it by the results on rich Texas and Oklahoma prairies, with fertilizers and modern methods; if, on the other hand, you would judge *Negro* labor, slink into the slavery-cursed Mississippi bottoms where the soil has been raped for a century; and be careful even there; pick out counties where there has been "no large introduction of commercial fertilizers," and where debt peonage is firmly planted under the benevolent guardianship of Alfred G. Stone and his kind. Then, rolling your eyes and lifting protesting hands, point out that, whereas the slave drivers of 1860 wrung 1,200 pounds of cotton from the protesting earth, the lazy blacks are able ("with no large introduction of commercial fertilizers") to get but 700 pounds for their present white masters. Hence a decline in efficiency of "35 per cent." Why, pray, 35 per cent? Why not 50 or 75 per cent? And why again are these particular counties so attractive to this expert? Is it because Issaquena County, for instance, spends $1 a year to educate each colored child enrolled in its schools, and enrolls about half its black children in schools of three months' duration or less?

Astute? Why, we confidently expect to see Phillips at the head of the Department of Agriculture if he keeps on at this rapid rate. Not that it takes brains to head our Department of Agriculture (perish the assumption!), but that it *does* call for adroitness in bolstering up bad cases.

And the bad case which the South is bolstering to-day must make the gods scream. Take this same State of Mississippi, for instance, where Negroes are so futile and inefficient: the property which they own and rent was worth $86,000,000 in 1900. In 1910 it was worth $187,000,000!

"That, of course," says the *Manufacturers' Record,* of Baltimore, being strong put to it to nullify such ugly figures, "is a merely flat statement and takes no account of the character of the holdings, whether burdened with mortgages or otherwise, and no account of what is being done with the holdings, especially land."

And then this masterly sheet bewails the fact that "Intrusion, in the guise of special care for the Negroes, of influences bitterly hostile to the whites of the South, loosened the ties of sympathy and interest of the Southern whites and the Negroes and alienated the second generation of both races from each other. In that the Negroes lost much of the advantages their fathers had had in close contact with the directing minds of the South, and the results must be considered in studying Negro progress."

The late William H. Baldwin, Jr., used to affirm that a few more generations of that "close contact with the directing minds of the South" would have left the whole South mulatoo! But the *Record* ends with this master stroke:

"Another point to be borne in mind in measuring progress is the fact that the property of nearly 12,000,000 Negroes in the United States to-day has a value less than half the value that 3,954,000 of them in slavery, or 90 per cent of their total number in the country, represented in 1860, at an average value of $600 each."

Frankly, can you beat that?

(March, 1913. Vol. V, No. 5, pp. 239-40)

PEACE

At the coming meeting of the peace societies at St. Louis the question of peace between civilized and backward peoples will not probably be considered. The secretary of the New York Peace Society writes us that "Our peace congresses have not dealt in the past with the relations of civilized and non-civilized people;" and he thinks that largely on this account "our American congresses have been more dignified and more influential than those held abroad."

We are not sure about that word "influential," but there is no doubt about the dignity of the American peace movement. It has been so dignified and aristocratic that it has been often most difficult for the humbler sort of folk to recognize it as the opponent of organized murder.

At a recent meeting of the New York Peace Society the war

in the Balkans was eulogized and applauded, and the president stated that "when we advocate peace" it is for nations "worthy of it!"

Such a peace movement belies its name. Peace today, if it means anything, means the stopping of the slaughter of the weaker by the stronger in the name of Christianity and culture. The modern lust for land and slaves in Africa, Asia and the South Seas is the greatest and almost the only cause of war between the so-called civilized peoples. For such "colonial" aggression and "imperial" expansion England, France, Germany, Russia and Austria are straining every nerve to arm themselves; against such policies Japan and China are arming desperately. And yet the American peace movement thinks it bad policy to take up this problem of machine guns, natives and rubber, and wants "constructive" work in "arbitration treaties and international law." For our part we think that a little less dignity and dollars and a little more humanity would make the peace movement in America a great democratic philanthropy instead of an aristocratic refuge.

(May, 1913. Vol. VI, No. 1, p. 26)

THE CHURCH AND THE NEGRO

The relation of the church to the Negro is, or should be, a very simple proposition. Leaving aside the supernatural significance of the church organization, we have here groups of people working for human uplift and professing the highest and most unselfish morality as exemplified by the life and teaching of Jesus of Nazareth and the Golden Rule.

By this standard all church members should treat Negroes as they themselves would wish to be treated if they were colored. They should do this and teach this and, if need be, die for this creed.

The plain facts are sadly at variance with this doctrine. The church aided and abetted the Negro slave trade; the church was the bulwark of American slavery; and the church to-day is the strongest seat of racial and color prejudice. If one hundred of the best and purest colored folk of the United States should seek to apply for membership in any white church in this land tomorrow, 999 out of every 1,000 ministers would lie to keep them out. They would not only do this, but would openly and brazenly defend their action as worthy of followers of Jesus Christ.

Yet Jesus Christ was a laborer and black men are laborers; He was poor and we are poor; He was despised of his fellow men and we are despised; He was persecuted and crucified, and we are mobbed and lynched. If Jesus Christ came to America He would associate with Negroes and Italians and working people; He would eat and pray with them, and He would seldom see the interior of the Cathedral of Saint John the Divine.

Why then are His so-called followers deaf, dumb, and blind on the Negro problem—on the human problem?

Because they think they have discovered bypaths to righteousness which do not lead to brotherhood with the poor, the dirty, the ignorant and the black. "Make them servants," they say; "we need cooks." But can a whole race be doomed to menial service in a civilization where menial service is itself doomed? And when menial service has become Service and lost its social stigma, so that white folk want to enter such service, will they welcome black folk as fellow servants? Certainly not, and the slavery argument of this cry stands revealed.

"But," cry others, "let the Negroes themselves bear their own social responsibilities for poverty, ignorance and disease. Segregate them and pile their sins upon them." Indeed! Are the poor alone responsible for poverty? And the ignorant for ignorance? Can the rich be allowed to escape with this spoil and the learned without obligation for his knowledge? If the black men in America are what they are because of slavery and oppression, how cowardly for white Christians to deny their own guilt. The real hypocrisy comes, however, when the Negro, eager to take responsibility, cries out for power with which to bear it and is denied such power. Denied higher training for his leaders, denied industrial opportunity to make a living, the self-assertion and self-defense of the ballot, denied even hospitals and common schools. Thus the church gaily tosses him stones for bread.

Even the rock of "Science" on which the white church rested with such beautiful faith, hoping to prove the majority of humanity inhuman, so that Fifth Avenue Presbyterianism would not have to dirty its dainty fingers with Fifty-third Street Baptists—and black ones at that—even this Rock of Ages is falling before honest investigation.

There is but the Golden Rule left—the despised and rejected Golden Rule. Can the church follow it? Is there common decency enough in the millions of white American church members to dare to treat Negroes as they would like to be treated if they themselves were colored?

The Negro problem is the test of the church.

(October, 1913. Vol. VI, No. 6, pp. 290-1)

THE BURDEN OF BLACK WOMEN

Dark daughter of the lotus leaves that watch
        the Southern sea,
Wan spirit of a prisoned soul a-panting to
        be free;
The muttered music of thy streams, the
        whispers of the deep
Have kissed each other in God's name and
        kissed a world to sleep.

The will of the world is a whistling wind
        sweeping a cloud-cast sky,
And not from the east and not from the west
        knelled its soul-searing cry;
But out of the past of the Past's grey past,
        it yelled from the top of the sky;
    Crying: Awake, O ancient race! Wail-
        ing: O woman arise!
    And crying and sighing and crying again
        as a voice in the midnight cries;
    But the burden of white men bore her back,
        and the white world stifled her sighs.

The White World's vermin and filth:
    All the dirt of London,
    All the scum of New York;
    Valiant spoilers of women
    And conquerors of unarmed men;
    Shameless breeders of bastards
    Drunk with the greed of gold,

Baiting their blood-stained hooks
With cant for the souls of the simple,
Bearing the White Man's Burden
Of Liquor and Lust and Lies!
Unthankful we wince in the East,
Unthankful we wail from the westward,
Unthankfully thankful we sing,
In the un-won wastes of the wild:
  I hate them, Oh!
  I hate them well,
  I hate them, Christ!
  As I hate Hell,
  If I were God
  I'd sound their knell
  This day!
Who raised the fools to their glory
But black men of Egypt and Ind?
Ethiopia's sons of the evening,
Chaldeans and Yellow Chinese?
The Hebrew children of Morning
And mongrels of Rome and Greece?
  Ah, well!

And they that raised the boasters
Shall drag them down again:
Down with the theft of their thieving
And murder and mocking of men,
Down with their barter of women
And laying and lying of creeds,
Down with their cheating of childhood,
And drunken orgies of war—

  down,

  down,

  deep down,

Till the Devil's strength be shorn,
Till some dim, darker David a-hoeing of his
  corn,

And married maiden, Mother of God,
Bid the Black Christ be born!

Then shall the burden of manhood,
Be it yellow or black or white,
And Poverty, Justice and Sorrow—
The Humble and Simple and Strong,
Shall sing with the Sons of Morning
And Daughters of Evensong:

Black mother of the iron hills that guard the
blazing sea,
Wild spirit of a storm-swept soul a-strug-
gling to be free,
Where 'neath the bloody finger marks, thy
riven bosom quakes,
Thicken the thunders of God's voice, and lo!
a world awakes!

(November, 1914. Vol. IX, No. 1, p. 31)

EASTER 1919

Easter by the sound of music tinkling up in the frozen hills
and by the burgeoning of green things all over the Earth! And
Easter, too, in our hearts! What a glorious difference between
the Easter of 1919 and that of a year ago. Last April we were
still at war,—how like a dream it seems these days—and the
future loomed dark and beyond presage. Both Africa and America were pouring forth dark hosts in response to the continued
summons to arms, and that made the hearts of some of us
heavier than ever. "It is no war of ours," said some. "And why
should we sacrifice ourselves?" asked others. But the wisest
shook their heads,—"Right is always right; this is our country.
We must save it and so doing save ourselves." So doggedly,
sullenly, gladly, splendidly, in varied manner, but always persistently, we went to war.

And we have helped save the world. And we have saved
ourselves. Not immediately, not on all sides, a little less in the

United States than elsewhere, where the actual fighting took place and others could see our valor. But the world knows us for what we are now—not cowards or traitors—our worst enemies knew better than to call us that, but a people big enough to rise above a consideration of domestic troubles—dire enough heaven knows—and to rush wholeheartedly into the business of saving the world. Suppose we had yielded to German propaganda, suppose we had refused to shoulder arms, or had wrought mischief and confusion, patterning ourselves after the I.W.W. and the pro-Germans of this country. How should we hold up our heads? But any other course than the one we have pursued, whatever our detractors may have feared and hoped, was to us unthinkable. We are not by nature traitorous. And it has been interesting and instructive to note that of those colored men who talked loudest against wholehearted co-operation with the country's cause, and who protested most vehemently against those who were outspoken in their determination to place America first,—of all those not one took an active step to prove himself willing to lay down life or even liberty for what *he* thought was right. There was talk and talk and talk. But not one played the role of Benedict Arnold. Not one was arrested even as a conscientious objector.

Which is as it should be.

For see what has happened. We are in a position to come before the world saying: "Behold us. Here we are clean-handed and with pure hearts. You must listen to us. We black people, in addition to our rights of ordinary consideration, have proven ourselves worthy of extra consideration. And so we are holding a Pan-African Congress. The whole black world is virtually represented. We shall never rest, we shall never cease to agitate, until we have received from the world what we have in such yeomanly rendered—fair play."

And all about us and our hopes rises the tide of Easter.

(April, 1919. Vol. 17, No. 6, pp. 267-8)

EVIL

We are not the only ones who are suffering. In Massachusetts two Italians[1] have been sentenced to death for a crime which has never been properly proven against them. In Leavenworth prison ninety-six white men are serving from five to twenty-year terms for no crime but simply because they belonged to an organization[2] which some people do not like. At the White House, a Children's Crusade has been inaugurated to plead for the release of hundreds of white political prisoners. In West Virginia 80,000 white men, women and children are "gaunt and pallid with hunger." Here in New York, "mothers, wives and children in your own city appeal to you for food, shelter, clothing and protection. The bread winner is in prison." Just as black people in Texas were unable to get a lawyer who dared to defend Mr. Shillady in the local courts, so in Louisiana white men cannot get a lawyer in a similar case. In Newport, Kentucky, a strike has been put down by tanks and machine guns among white men, while among black brickmakers in New York, Cossacks have done similar work. In Russia the starving are eating their own children and the melting snows disclose heaps upon heaps of the bodies of the starved dead. Five million people are starving. All the evil is not ours, my brother.

(July, 1922. Vol. XXIV, No. 3. p. 107)

AS THE CROW FLIES

Men are seeking to *fly* across the Atlantic. But this triumph over nature is half-spoiled by the fact that in most cases this is a military venture for the object of murdering men.

(June, 1927. Vol. XXXIV, No. 4.)

The *Bolsheviks* in China have been overthrown 12 times; *Boroden* has fled 9 times and the *revolution* has been over 5 times,

[1]Sacco & Vanzetti
[2]International Workers of the World

all according to English cables. Meantime, China is slowly and relentlessly kicking Europe into the sea.

(August, 1927. Vol. XXXIV, No. 6.)

Protestant churches are said to be losing a half million members a year. The wonder is that they are losing so few.

(October, 1927. Vol. XXXIV, No. 8.)

White civilization is blossoming in Indiana. One governor has just left the penitentiary; another seems to be on his way thither; and the mayor of Indianapolis is sentenced to a vacation in jail.

(November, 1927. Vol. XXXIV, No. 9.)

Isadora Duncan, a great free genius, has flown beyond the stars.

(December, 1927. Vol. XXXIV, No. 10.)

Florence Mills, bravest and finest of her craft, is dancing before God.

(*Ibid.*)

Chiang-Kai-Shek is fighting farmers and laborers in China by calling them communists.

(February, 1928. Vol. XXXV, No. 2.)

The world wants nothing so much as work. The working people of the world want nothing so much as work. Eight million people in America alone cannot find work. College professors will now explain.

(May, 1928. Vol. XXXV, No. 5.)

Persons wishing help from the Government should state their occupations in writing. Those engaged in shipping and manufactures can have practically what they want. Persons engaged in agriculture are informed that their request is unconstitutional and that further application is unnecessary.

(July, 1928. Vol. XXXV, No. 7.)

Congress has given some relief to the poor millionaires by reducing their income taxes and the taxes on corporations. This will make the nation safe for plutocracy.

(*Ibid.*)

The only difference between Republicans and Democrats is the difference between the individuals who will draw the salaries and distribute economic privileges for the next four years.

(August, 1928. Vol. XXXV, No. 8)

The liberal world that still hopes has bowed again at the bier of Nicolo Sacco and Bartolomeo Vanzetti, martyrs to Massachusetts intolerance.

(October, 1928. Vol. XXXV, No. 10)

Mussolini establishes a dictatorship in Italy. Fine! And pictures in the Sunday papers! Lenin establishes a dictatorship in Russia. Unspeakable!

(December, 1928. Vol. XXXV, No. 12)

If crime could be stopped by law we'd be angels. Yet the crime war consists of more law.

(April, 1929. Vol. XXXVI, No. 4)

King Arthur, who runs a Round Table, whenever he finds a stray Knight to knock in the head, waved his sceptre at me thoughtfully the other night and discoursed like this—"I don't get the raison d'etre of the Crow. Now, if it is meant for sophisticated people and highbrows and folks with Ph.D's and that cattle, then what does it say that they do not already know? And if it is meant for the masses, how in Tophet are they to know what it is all about?"—I was calm and stern and accepted a light from his fifteenth sceptre and replied—The Crow is designed for sophisticated people who know what happened in 1066, 1492, and in 1863. The Crow is not interested in fools and illiterates. —It fixes its calm gaze upon the Truth and particularly upon the unpleasant truth. It is cynical, sarcastic, mean and low. It leaves sugar, molasses and optimism to those who know by personal experience that God's in his Heaven.—The Crow concentrates its attention mainly on Hell.

(June, 1929. Vol. XXXVI, No. 6)

Can't you see savants of 3029 A.D. pondering the puzzle? They stuffed 5 million people into New York and then hired experts to transport them out again at a cost of a thousand million dollars; no wonder insanity increased in those ancient days!

(December, 1929. Vol. XXXVI, No. 12)

Our idea of the best joke of the season is the *New York Times* explaining how the stock crash was evidence of the essential soundness of American business.

(January, 1930. Vol. XXXVII, No. 1)

Sigmund Freud, the great psycho-analyst, greatly doubts the value of civilization. And looking the civilized countries carefully over just now we can see that he has some grounds for his argument.

(March, 1930. Vol. XXXVII, No. 3)

China was bad enough off before but now that Chiang Kai-Shek has embraced Christianity, we can confidently expect anything.

(December, 1930. Vol. XXXVII, No. 12)

If the unemployed could eat plans and promises they would be able to spend the winter on the Riviera.

(January, 1931. Vol. XXXVIII, No. 1)

Most persons can not understand why the flood of exposure concerning gang-rule, graft and stealing in the United States arouses no widespread protest or public conscience. They will be enlightened if they remember that American business, that triumphant expression of our civilization, is based fundamentally on graft, gang-rule and legalized theft.

(January, 1931. Vol. XXXVIII, No. 1)

If you are a railroad you may demand government aid; but if you are merely a starving man, doles are unconstitutional.

(February, 1931. Vol. XXXVIII, No. 2)

There are 9,000,000 persons out of work in Europe and 6,000,000 out of work in the United States. All of which shows the supreme genius of the white race for organizing industry.

(March, 1931. Vol. XXXVIII, No. 3)

The Commission of Inter-racial Co-operation has just discovered the surprising fact that the easiest way for a white man to commit crime is to use burnt cork liberally on his face. After a bath, he may then join the mob and lynch the nigger.

(March, 1931. Vol. XXXVIII, No. 3)

First, Revolution was about to destroy the Russian Revolution. Then Russians were starving. Then they were nationalizing women and spawning wolf children. Then they were cursing God and due to die in the fiery breath of Canterbury and Manning. Now comes positively the last straw: they're underselling the world wheat and oil market! Human endurance nears an end.

(April, 1931. Vol. XXXVIII, No. 4)

When is dumping not dumping? When Americans want to sell surplus wheat to Europe. When is dumping horrible, fiendish, and a threat to the foundations of the universe? When Russia wants to sell surplus wheat anywhere.

(June, 1931. Vol. XXXVIII, No. 6)

What we really would like to live to see would be the three great Races pictured in the nation's geographies, by Paul Robeson, Sun Yat Sen and Calvin Coolidge.

(June, 1931. Vol. XXXVIII, No. 6)

After all, what difference does it make to most of us whether the Star-Spangled United States Treasury is a billion dollars, or ten cents in the red?

(July, 1931. Vol. XXXVIII, No. 7)

Surely prosperity will come again but not to everybody. Every slump, every depression, like every war, leaves the dead, the wounded, the maimed and the discouraged. For them prosperity will never come again.

(August, 1931. Vol. XXXVIII, No. 8)

The United States, (which stole a large part of Mexico, invaded Nicaragua and Santo Domingo and raped Haiti, annexed the Philippines and Porto Rico and dominates Cuba, because of her economic interests and investments) is now explaining the Golden Rule to Japan.

(December, 1931. Vol. XXXVIII, No. 12)

The most hated nation on earth. We have at last achieved this peak of our ambition.

(January, 1933. Vol. XXXIX, No. 1)

The Fall of Capitalism began when it made razor blades which would get dull in a month instead of those which would easily last ten years, and at the same cost.

(Ibid.)

What joy it is to "investigate" the Negro. We don't dare study Wealth or Politics or the morals of Peachtree street; but "niggers"—Lord! any fool can make a doctor's thesis on them full of lies that universities love to publish.

(Ibid.)

America has a reputation of being quick, alert, intelligent and resourceful. Looking back on the history of the last four years, we'd like to know where in hell that reputation came from.

(May, 1933. Vol. XXXX, No. 5)

If any colored groups met as often and talked as much and accomplished as little as the white folks in the last ten years, it would be a sure sign of racial inferiority.

(August, 1933. Vol. XXXX, No. 8)

Nothing has filled us with such unholy glee as Hitler and the Nordics. When the only "inferior" peoples were "niggers" it was hard to get the attention of the *New York Times* for little matters of race, lynching and mobs. But now that the damned include the owner of the *Times*, moral indignation is perking up.

(September, 1933. Vol. XXXX, No. 9)

Hostilities have begun between Henry Ford and the United States of America. We would advise the United States to give up while the way is open. After all, it's silly not to recognize your master's voice.

(December, 1933. Vol. XXXX, No. 12)

When the Chief Justice of the United States says that our courts are corrupt, we bow to authority.

(June, 1932.)

Mr. Roosevelt's record on the Negro problem is clear. He hasn't any.

(August, 1932.)

Mr. Hoover's record on the Negro problem is not clear and in that respect it resembles his record on everything else.

(Ibid.)

Congress having done nothing but take our last cent for taxes has gone home, where we pray God it will stay awhile.

(Ibid.)

When the Governor of the Bank of England slips secretly into the U.S.A. to whisper to the Governor of the Federal Reserve, it's about time to draw out your savings account and bury it in the back yard.

(October, 1932.)

There is today in the world but one living maker of miracles, and that is Mahatma Gandhi. He stops eating, and three hundred million Indians, together with the British Empire, hold their breath until they can talk sense. All America sees in Gandhi is a joke, but the joke is America.

(November, 1932.)

It has taken just 157 years for a President of the United States to say in plain English that lynching is "a vile form of collective murder."

(January, 1934.)

THE THIRD PERIOD
1934–1948

Du Bois resigned from the NAACP over his advocacy of "voluntary segregation." He did not cease to advocate this concept once he left the organization.

The first article, "A Negro Nation Within the Nation," is a clear statement of his position.

The second article, "Does the Negro Need Separate Schools?", is one of his most trenchant essays, whose relevance has increased since it was first published thirty-five years ago.

The third essay, "Social Planning for the Negro, Past and Present," is a historical discussion of how blacks have sought to organize to solve their problems. As such, it contains an excellent history of blacks in America. Du Bois does not enter into a lengthy exposition of "voluntary segregation," though it is mentioned, but he does summarize his views on Communism and violence as weapons for blacks and why he rejects both.

A NEGRO NATION WITHIN THE NATION

June, 1935

No more critical situation ever faced the Negroes of America than that of today—not in 1830, nor in 1861, nor in 1867. More than ever the appeal of the Negro for elementary justice falls on deaf ears.

Three-fourths of us are disfranchised; yet no writer on democratic reform, no third party movement says a word about Negroes. The Bull Moose crusade in 1912 refused to notice them; the La Follette uprising in 1924 was hardly aware of them; the Socialists still keep them in the background. Negro children are systematically denied education; when the National Education Association asks for Federal aid to education it permits discrimination to be perpetuated by the present local authorities. Once or twice a month Negroes convicted of no crime are openly and publicly lynched, and even burned; yet a National Crime Convention is brought to perfunctory and unwilling notice of this only by mass picketing and all but illegal agitation. When a man with every qualification is refused a position simply because his great-grandfather was black there is not a ripple of comment or protest.

Long before the depression Negroes in the South were losing "Negro" jobs, those assigned them by common custom—poorly paid and largely undesirable toil, but nevertheless life supporting. New techniques, new enterprises, mass production, impersonal ownership and control have been largely displacing the skilled white and Negro worker in tobacco manufacturing, in iron and steel, in lumbering and mining, and in transportation. Negroes are now restricted more and more to common labor and domestic service of the lowest paid and worst kind. In textile, chemical and other manufactures Negroes were from the first nearly excluded, and just as slavery kept the poor white out of profitable agriculture, so freedom prevents the poor Negro from finding a place in manufacturing. The world-wide decline in agriculture has moreover carried the mass of black farmers, despite heroic endeavor among the few, down to the level of landless tenants and peons.

The World War and its wild aftermath seemed for a moment to open a new door; 2,000,000 black workers rushed North to work in iron and steel, make automobiles and pack meat, build houses and do the heavy toil in factories. They met first the closed trade union which excluded them from the best-paid jobs and pushed them into the low-wage gutter, denied them homes and mobbed them. Then they met the depression.

Since 1929 Negro workers, like white workers, have lost their jobs, have had mortgages foreclosed on their farms and homes, have used up their small savings. But, in the case of the Negro worker, everything has been worse in larger or smaller degree; the loss has been greater and more permanent. Technological displacement, which began before the depression, has been accelerated, while unemployment and falling wages struck black men sooner, went to lower levels and will last longer.

Negro public schools in the rural South have often disappeared, while Southern city schools are crowded to suffocation. The Booker Washington High School in Atlanta, built for 1,000 pupils, has 3,000 attending in double daily sessions. Above all, Federal and State relief holds out little promise for the Negro.

It is but human that the unemployed white man and the starving white child should be relieved first by local authorities who regard them as fellow-men, but often regard Negroes as subhuman. While the white worker has sometimes been given more than relief and been helped to his feet, the black worker has often been pauperized by being just kept from starvation. There are some plans for national rehabilitation and the rebuilding of the whole industrial system. Such plans should provide for the Negro's future relations to American industry and culture, but those provisions the country is not only unprepared to make but refuses to consider.

In the Tennessee Valley beneath the Norris Dam, where do Negroes come in? And what shall be their industrial place? In the attempt to rebuild agriculture the Southern landholder will in all probability be put on his feet, but the black tenant has been pushed to the edge of despair. In the matter of housing, no comprehensive scheme for Negro homes has been thought out and only two or three local projects planned. Nor can broad plans be made until the nation or the community decides where it wants or will permit Negroes to live. Negroes are largely excluded from subsistence homesteads because Negroes protested against segregation, and whites, anxious for cheap local labor, also protested.

The colored people of America are coming to face the fact quite calmly that most white Americans do not like them, and are planning neither for their survival, nor for their definite future if it involves free, self-assertive modern manhood. This does not mean all Americans. A saving few are worried about the Negro problem; a still larger group are not ill-disposed, but they fear prevailing public opinion. The great mass of Americans are, however, merely representatives of average humanity. They muddle along with their own affairs and scarcely can be expected to take seriously the affairs of strangers or people whom they partly fear and partly despise.

For many years it was the theory of most Negro leaders that this attitude was the insensibility of ignorance and inexperience, that white America did not know of or realize the continuing plight of the Negro. Accordingly, for the last two decades, we have striven by book and periodical, by speech and appeal, by various dramatic methods of agitation, to put the essential facts before the American people. Today there can be no doubt that Americans know the facts; and yet they remain for the most part indifferent and unmoved.

The main weakness of the Negro's position is that since emancipation he has never had an adequate economic foundation. Thaddeus Stevens recognized this and sought to transform the emancipated freedmen into peasant proprietors. If he had succeeded, he would have changed the economic history of the United States and perhaps saved the American farmer from his present plight. But to furnish 50,000,000 acres of good land to the Negroes would have cost more money than the North was willing to pay, and was regarded by the South as highway robbery.

The whole attempt to furnish land and capital for the freedmen fell through, and no comprehensive economic plan was advanced until the advent of Booker T. Washington. He had a vision of building a new economic foundation for Negroes by incorporating them into white industry. He wanted to make them skilled workers by industrial education and expected small capitalists to rise out of their ranks. Unfortunately, he assumed that the economic development of America in the twentieth century would resemble that of the nineteenth century, with free industrial opportunity, cheap land and unlimited resources under the control of small competitive capitalists. He lived to see industry more and more concentrated, land monopoly extended and industrial technique changed by wide introduction of machinery.

As a result, technology advanced more rapidly than Hampton or Tuskegee could adjust their curricula. The chance of an artisan's becoming a capitalist grew slimmer, even for white Americans, while the whole relation of labor to capital became less a matter of technical skill than of basic organization and aim.

Those of us who in that day opposed Booker Washington's plans did not foresee exactly the kind of change that was coming, but we were convinced that the Negro could succeed in industry and in life only if he had intelligent leadership and far-reaching ideals. The object of education, we declared, was not "to make men artisans but to make artisans men." The Negroes in America needed leadership so that, when change and crisis came, they could guide themselves to safety.

The educated group among American Negroes is still small, but it is large enough to begin planning for preservation through economic advancement. The first definite movement of this younger group was toward direct alliance of the Negro with the labor movement. But white labor today as in the past refuses to respond to these overtures.

For a hundred years, beginning in the Thirties and Forties of the nineteenth century, the white laborers of Ohio, Pennsylvania and New York beat, murdered and drove away fellow-workers because they were black and had to work for what they could get. Seventy years ago in New York, the centre of the new American labor movement, white laborers hanged black ones to lamp posts instead of helping to free them from the worst of modern slavery. In Chicago and St. Louis, New Orleans and San Francisco, black men still carry the scars of the bitter hatred of white laborers for them. Today it is white labor that keeps Negroes out of decent low-cost housing, that confines the protection of the best unions to "white" men, that often will not sit in the same hall with black folk who already have joined the labor movement. White labor has to hate scabs; but it hates black scabs not because they are scabs but because they are black. It mobs white scabs to force them into labor fellowship. It mobs black scabs to starve and kill them. In the present fight of the American Federation of Labor against company unions it is attacking the only unions that Negroes can join.

Thus the Negro's fight to enter organized industry has made little headway. No Negro, no matter what his ability, can be a member of any of the railway unions. He cannot be an engineer, fireman, conductor, switchman, brakeman or yardman. If he organizes separtely, he may, as in the case of the Negro Firemen's Union, be assaulted and even killed by white firemen. As in the case of the Pullman Porters' Union, he may receive empty recognition without any voice or collective help. The older group of Negro leaders recognize this and simply say it is a matter of continued striving to break down these barriers.

Such facts are, however, slowly forcing Negro thought into new channels. The interests of labor are considered rather than those of capital. No greater welcome is expected from the labor monopolist who mans armies and navies to keep Chinese, Japanese and Negroes in their places than from the captains of industry who spend large sums of money to make laborers think that the most worthless white man is better than any colored man. The Negro must prove his necessity to the labor movement and that it is a disastrous error to leave him out of the foundation of the new industrial State. He must settle beyond cavil the question of his economic efficiency as a worker, a manager and controller of capital.

The dilemma of these younger thinkers gives men like James Weldon Johnson a chance to insist that the older methods are still the best; that we can survive only by being integrated into the nation, and that we must consequently fight segregation now and always and force our way by appeal, agitation and law. This group, however, does not seem to recognize the fundamental economic bases of social growth and the changes that face American industry. Greater democratic control of production and distribution is bound to replace existing autocratic and monopolistic methods.

In this broader and more intelligent democracy we can hope for progressive softening of the asperities and anomalies of race prejudice, but we cannot hope for its early and complete disappearance. Above all, the doubt, deep-planted in the American mind, as to the Negro's ability and efficiency as worker, artisan and administrator will fade but slowly. Thus, with increased democratic control of industry and capital, the place of the Negro will be increasingly a matter of human choice, of willingness to recognize ability across the barriers of race, of putting fit Negroes in places of power and authority by public opinion. At present, on the railroads, in manufacturing, in the telephone, telegraph and radio business, and in the larger divisions of trade, it is only under exceptional circumstances that any Negro, no matter what his ability, gets an opportunity for position and power. Only in those lines where individual enterprise still counts, as in some of the professions, in a few of the trades, in a few branches of retail business and in artistic careers, can the Negro expect a narrow opening.

Negroes and other colored folk, nevertheless, exist in larger and growing numbers. Slavery, prostitution to white men, theft of their labor and goods have not killed them and cannot kill them. They are growing in intelligence and dissatisfaction. They occupy strategic positions, within nations and besides nations, amid valuable raw material and on the highways of future expansion. They will survive, but on what terms and conditions?

On this point a new school of Negro thought is arising. It believes in the ultimate uniting of mankind and in a unified American nation, with economic classes and racial barriers leveled, but it believes this is an ideal and is to be realized only by such intensified class and race consciousness as will bring irresistible force rather than mere humanitarian appeals to bear on the motives and actions of men.

The peculiar position of Negroes in America offers an opportunity. Negroes today cast probably 2,000,000 votes in a total of 40,000,000, and their vote will increase. This gives them, particularly in Northern cities, and at critical times, a chance to hold a very considerable balance of power, and the mere threat of this being used intelligently and with determination may often mean much. The consuming power of 2,800,000 Negro families has recently been estimated at $166,000,000 a month —a tremendous power when intelligently directed. Their man power as laborers probably equals that of Mexico or Yugoslavia. Their illiteracy is much lower than that of Spain or Italy. Their estimated per capita wealth about equals that of Japan.

For a nation with this start in culture and efficiency to sit down and await the salvation of a white God is idiotic. With the use of their political power, their power as consumers, and their brain power, added to that chance of personal appeal which proximity and neighborhood always give to human beings, Negroes can develop in the United States an economic nation within a nation, able to work through inner cooperation, to found its own institutions, to educate its genius, and at the same time, without mob violence or extremes of race hatred, to keep in helpful touch and cooperate with the mass of the nation. This has happened more often than most people realize, in the case of groups not so obviously separated from the mass of people as are American Negroes. It must happen in our case, or there is no hope for the Negro in America.

Any movement toward such a program is today hindered by the absurd Negro philosophy of Scatter, Suppress, Wait, Escape. There are even many of our educated young leaders who think that because the Negro problem is not in evidence where there are few or no Negroes, this indicates a way out! They think that the problem of race can be settled by ignoring it and suppressing all reference to it. They think that we have only to wait in silence for the white people to settle the problem for us;

and finally and predominantly, they think that the problem of 12,000,000 Negro people, mostly poor, ignorant workers, is going to be settled by having their more educated and wealthy classes gradually and continually escape from their race into the mass of the American people, leaving the rest to sink, suffer and die.

Proponents of this program claim, with much reason, that the plight of the masses is not the fault of the emerging classes. For the slavery and exploitation that reduced Negroes to their present level or at any rate hindered them from rising, the white world is to blame. Since the age-long process of raising a group is through the escape of its upper class into welcome fellowship with risen peoples, the Negro intelligentsia would submerge itself if it bent its back to the task of lifting the mass of people. There is logic in this answer, but futile logic.

If the leading Negro classes cannot assume and bear the uplift of their own proletariat, they are doomed for all time. It is not a case of ethics; it is a plain case of necessity. The method by which this may be done is, first, for the American Negro to achieve a new economic solidarity. There exists today a chance for the Negroes to organize a cooperative State within their own group. By letting Negro farmers feed Negro artisans, and Negro technicians guide Negro home industries, and Negro thinkers plan this integration of cooperation, while Negro artists dramatize and beautify the struggle, economic independence can be achieved. To doubt that this is possible is to doubt the essential humanity and the quality of brains of the American Negro.

No sooner is this proposed than a great fear sweeps over older Negroes. They cry "No segregation"—no further yielding to prejudice and race separation. Yet any planning for the benefit of American Negroes on the part of a Negro intelligentsia is going to involve organized and deliberate self-segregation. There are plenty of people in the United States who would be only too willing to use such a plan as a way to increase existing legal and customary segregation between the races. This threat which many Negroes see is no mere mirage. What of it? It must be faced.

If the economic and cultural salvation of the American Negro calls for an increase in segregation and prejudice, then that must come. American Negroes must plan for their economic future and the social survival of their fellows in the firm belief that this means in a real sense the survival of colored folk in the world and the building of a full humanity instead of a petty white tyranny. Control of their own education, which is the logical and inevitable end of separate schools, would not be an unmixed ill; it might prove a supreme good. Negro schools once meant poor schools. They need not today; they must not tomorrow. Separate Negro sections will increase race antagonism, but they will also increase economic cooperation, organized self-defense and necessary self-confidence.

The immediate reaction of most white and colored people to this suggestion will be that the thing cannot be done without extreme results. Negro thinkers have from time to time emphasized the fact that no nation within a nation can be built because of the attitude of the dominant majority, and because all legal and police power is out of Negro hands, and because large-scale industries, like steel and utilities, are organized on a national basis. White folk, on the other hand, simply say that, granting certain obvious exceptions, the American Negro has not the ability to engineer so delicate a social operation calling for such self-restraint, careful organization and sagacious leadership.

In reply, it may be said that this matter of a nation within a nation has already been partially accomplished in the organization of the Negro church, the Negro school and the Negro retail business, and, despite all the justly due criticism, the result has been astonishing. The great majority of American Negroes are divided not only for religious but for a large number of social purposes into self-supporting economic units, self-governed, self-directed. The greatest difficulty is that these organizations have no logical and reasonable standards and do not attract the finest, most vigorous and best educated Negroes. When all these things are taken into consideration it becomes clearer to more and more American Negroes that, through voluntary and increased segregation, by careful autonomy and planned economic organization, they may build so strong and efficient a unit that 12,000,000 men can no longer be refused fellowship and equality in the United States.

DOES THE NEGRO NEED SEPARATE SCHOOLS?

There are in the United States some 4,000,000 Negroes of school age, of whom 2,000,000 are in school, and of these, four-fifths are taught by 48,000 Negro teachers in separate schools. Less than 500,000 are in mixed schools in the North, where they are taught almost exclusively by white teachers. Besides this, there are seventy-nine Negro universities and colleges with 1,000 colored teachers, besides a number of private secondary schools.

The question which I am discussing is: Are these separate schools and institutions needed? And the answer, to my mind, is perfectly clear. They are needed just so far as they are necessary for the proper education of the Negro race. The proper education of any people includes sympathetic touch between teacher and pupil; knowledge on the part of the teacher, not simply of the individual taught, but of his surroundings and background, and the history of his class and group; such contact between pupils, and between teacher and pupil, on the basis of perfect social equality, as will increase this sympathy and knowledge; facilities for education in equipment and housing, and the promotion of such extracurricular activities as will tend to induct the child into life.

If this is true, and if we recognize the present attitude of white America toward black America, then the Negro not only needs the vast majority of these schools, but it is a grave question if, in the near future, he will not need more such schools, both to take care of his natural increase, and to defend him against the growing animosity of the whites. It is, of course, fashionable and popular to deny this; to try to deceive ourselves into thinking that race prejudice in the United States across the Color Line is gradually softening and that slowly but surely we are coming to the time when racial animosities and class lines will be so obliterated that separate schools will be anachronisms.

Certainly, I shall welcome such a time. Just as long as Negroes are taught in Negro schools and whites in white schools, the poor in the slums, and the rich in private schools; just as long as it is impracticable to welcome Negro students to Harvard, Yale, and Princeton; just as long as colleges like Williams, Amherst, and Wellesley tend to become the property of certain wealthy families, where Jews are not solicited; just so long we shall lack in America that sort of public education which will create the intelligent basis of a real democracy.

Much as I would like this, and hard as I have striven and shall strive to help realize it, I am no fool; and I know that race prejudice in the United States today is such that most Negroes cannot receive proper education in white institutions. If the public schools of Atlanta, Nashville, New Orleans, and Jacksonville were thrown open to all races tomorrow, the education that colored children would get in them would be worse than pitiable. It would not be education. And in the same way, there are many public school systems in the North where Negroes are admitted and tolerated, but they are not educated; they are crucified. There are certain Northern universities where Negro students, no matter what their ability, desert, or accomplishment, cannot get fair recognition, either in classroom or on the campus, in dining halls and student activities, or in common human courtesy. It is well known that in certain faculties of the University of Chicago, no Negro has yet received the doctorate and seldom can achieve the mastership in arts; at Harvard, Yale, and Columbia, Negroes are admitted but not welcomed; while in other institutions, like Princeton, they cannot even enroll.

Under such circumstances, there is no room for argument as to whether the Negro needs separate schools or not. The plain fact faces us, that either he will have separate schools or he will not be educated. There may be, and there is, considerable difference of opinion as to how far this separation in schools is today necessary. There can be argument as to what our attitude toward further separation should be. Suppose, for instance, that in Montclair, New Jersey, a city of wealth and culture, the Board of Education is determined to establish separate schools for Negroes; suppose that, despite the law, separate Negro schools are already established in Philadelphia, and pressure is being steadily brought to extend this separation at least to the junior high school; what must be our attitude toward this?

Manifestly, no general and inflexible rule can be laid down. If public opinion is such in Montclair that Negro children cannot receive decent and sympathetic education in the white schools, and no Negro teachers can be employed, there is for us no choice. We have got to accept Negro schools. Any agitation and action aimed at compelling a rich and powerful majority of the citizens to do what they will not do, is useless.

On the other hand, we have a right and a duty to assure ourselves of the truth concerning this attitude; by careful conferences, by public meetings, and by petitions we should convince ourselves whether this demand for separate schools is merely the agitation of a prejudiced minority, or the considered and final judgment of the town.

There are undoubtledly cases where a minority of leaders force their opinions upon a majority, and induce a community to establish separate schools, when as a matter of fact there is no general demand for it; there has been no friction in the schools; and Negro children have been decently treated. In that case, a firm and intelligent appeal to public opinion would eventually settle the matter. But the futile attempt to compel even by law a group to do what it is determined not to do, is a silly waste of money, time, and temper.

On the other hand, there are also cases where there has been no separation in schools and no movement toward it. And yet the treatment of Negro children in the schools, the kind of teaching and the kind of advice they get, is such that they ought to demand either a thoroughgoing revolution in the official attitude toward Negro students, or absolute separation in educational facilities. To endure bad schools and wrong education because the schools are "mixed" is a costly if not fatal mistake. I have long been convinced, for instance, that the Negroes in the public schools of Harlem are not getting an education that is in any sense comparable in efficiency, discipline, and human development with that which Negroes are getting in the separate public schools of Washington, D.C. And yet on its school situation, black Harlem is dumb and complacent, if not actually laudatory.

Recognizing the fact that for the vast majority of colored students in elementary, secondary, and collegiate education, there must be today separate educational institutions because of an attitude on the part of the white people which is not going materially to change in our time, our customary attitude toward these separate schools must be absolutely and definitely changed. As it is today, American Negroes almost universally disparage their own schools. They look down upon them; they often treat the Negro teachers in them with contempt; they refuse to work for their adequate support; and they refuse to join public movements to increase their efficiency.

[The reason for this is quite clear, and may be divided into two parts: (1) The fear that any movement which implies segregation even as a temporary, much less as a relatively permanent, institution in the United States, is a fatal surrender of principle, which in the end will rebound and bring more evils on the Negro than he suffers today. (2) The other reason is at bottom an utter lack of faith on the part of Negroes that their race can do anything really well. If Negroes could conceive that Negroes could establish schools quite as good as or even superior to white schools; if Negro colleges were of equal grade in accomplishment and in scientific work with white colleges, the separation would be a passing incident and not a permanent evil; but as long as American Negroes believe that their race is constitutionally and permanently inferior to white people, they necessarily disbelieve in every possible Negro institution.]

The first argument is more or less metaphysical and cannot be decided a priori for every case. There are times when one must stand up for principle at the cost of discomfort, harm, and death. But in the case of the education of the young, you must consider not simply yourself but the children and the relation of children to life. It is difficult to think of anything more important for the development of a people than proper training for their children; and yet I have repeatedly seen wise and loving colored parents take infinite pains to force their little children into schools where the white children, white teachers, and white parents despised and resented the dark child, made mock of it, neglected or bullied it, and literally rendered its life a living hell. Such parents want their child to "fight" this thing out—but, dear God, at what a cost! Sometimes, to be sure, the child triumphs and teaches the school community a lesson; but even in such cases the cost may be high, and the child's whole life turned into an effort to win cheap applause at the expense of healthy individuality. In other cases, the result of the experiment may be complete ruin of character, gift, and ability, and ingrained hatred of schools and men. For the kind of battle thus indicated, most children are under no circumstances suited. It is the refinement of cruelty to require it of them. Therefore, in evaluating the advantage and disadvantage of accepting race hatred as a brutal but real fact, or of using a little child as a battering ram upon which its nastiness can be thrust, we must give greater value and greater emphasis to the rights of the child's own soul. We shall get a finer, better balance of spirit; an infinitely more capable and rounded personality by putting children in schools where they are wanted, and where they are happy and inspired, than in thrusting them into hells where they are ridiculed and hated.

Beyond this, lies the deeper, broader fact. If the American Negro really believed in himself; if he believed that Negro teachers can educate children according to the best standards of modern training; if he believed that Negro colleges transmit and add to science, as well as or better than other colleges, then he would bend his energies, not to escaping inescapable association with his own group, but to seeing that his group had every opportunity for its best and highest development. He would insist that his teachers be decently paid; that his schools were properly housed and equipped; that his colleges be supplied with scholarship and research funds; and he would be far more interested in the efficiency of these institutions of learning, than in forcing himself into other institutions where he is not wanted.

As long as the Negro student wishes to graduate from Columbia, not because Columbia is an institution of learning but because it is attended by white students; as long as a Negro student is ashamed to attend Fisk or Howard because these institutions are largely run by black folk, just so long the main problem of Negro education will not be segregation but self-knowledge and self-respect.

There are not many teachers in Negro schools who would not esteem it an unparalleled honor and boast of it to their dying day if, instead of teaching black folk, they could get a chance to teach poor whites, Irishmen, Italians or Chinese in a "white" institution. This is not unnatural. This is to them a sort of acid test of their worth. It is but the logical result of the "white" propaganda which has swept civilization for the last thousand years, and which is now bolstered and defended by brave words, high wages, and monopoly of opportunities. But this state of mind is suicidal and must be fought, and fought doggedly and bitterly: First, by giving Negro teachers decent wages, decent schoolhouses and equipment, and reasonable chances for advancement; and then by kicking out and leaving to the mercy of the white world those who do not and cannot believe in their own.

Lack of faith in Negro enterprise leads to singular results:

Negroes will fight frenziedly to prevent segregated schools; but if segregation is forced upon them by dominant white public opinion, they will suddenly lose interest and scarcely raise a finger to see that the resultant Negro schools get a fair share of the public funds so as to have adequate equipment and housing; to see that real teachers are appointed, and that they are paid as much as white teachers doing the same work. Today, when the Negro public school system gets from half to one-tenth of the amount of money spent on white schools, and is often consequently poorly run and poorly taught, colored people tacitly if not openly join with white people in assuming that Negroes cannot run Negro enterprises, and cannot educate themselves, and that the very establishment of a Negro school means starting an inferior school.

The N.A.A.C.P. and other Negro organizations have spent thousands of dollars to prevent the establishment of segregated Negro schools, but scarcely a single cent to see that the division of funds between white and Negro schools, North and South, is carried out with some faint approximation of justice. There can be no doubt that if the Supreme Court were overwhelmed with cases where the blatant and impudent discrimination against Negro education is openly acknowledged, it would be compelled to hand down decisions which would make this discrimination impossible. We Negroes do not dare to press this point and force these decisions because, forsooth, it would acknowledge the fact of separate schools, a fact that does not need to be acknowledged, and will not need to be for two centuries.

Howard, Fisk, and Atlanta are naturally unable to do the type and grade of graduate work which is done at Columbia, Chicago, and Harvard; but why attribute this to a defect in the Negro race, and not to the fact that the large white colleges have from one hundred to one thousand times the funds for equipment and research that Negro colleges can command? To this, it may logically be answered, all the more reason that Negroes should try to get into better-equipped schools, and who, pray, denies this? But the opportunity for such entrance is becoming more and more difficult, and the training offered less and less suited to the American Negro of today. Conceive a Negro teaching in a Southern school the economics which he learned at the Harvard Business School! Conceive a Negro teacher of history retailing to his black students the sort of history that is taught at the University of Chicago! Imagine the history of Reconstruction being handed by a college professor from the lips of Columbia professors to the ears of the black belts! The results of this kind of thing are often fantastic, and call for Negro history and sociology, and even physical science taught by men who understand their audience, and are not afraid of the truth.

There was a time when the ability of Negro brains to do first-class work had to be proven by facts and figures, and I was a part of the movement that sought to set the accomplishments of Negro ability before the world. But the world before which I was setting this proof was a disbelieving world. I did not need the proof for myself. I did not dream that my fellow Negroes needed it; but in the last few years, I have become curiously convinced that until American Negroes believe in their own power and ability they are going to be helpless before the white world, and the white world, realizing this inner paralysis and lack of self-confidence, is going to persist in its insane determination to rule the universe for its own selfish advantage.

Does the Negro need separate schools? God knows he does. But what he needs more than separate schools is a firm and unshakable belief that 12,000,000 American Negroes have the inborn capacity to accomplish just as much as any nation of 12,000,000 anywhere in the world ever accomplished, and that this is not because they are Negroes but because they are human.

So far, I have noted chiefly negative arguments for separate Negro institutions of learning based on the fact that in the majority of cases Negroes are not welcomed in public schools and universities nor treated as fellow human beings. But beyond this, there are certain positive reasons due to the fact that American Negroes have, because of their history, group experiences and memories, a distinct entity, whose spirit and reaction demand a certain type of education for its development.

In the past, this fact has been noted and misused for selfish purposes. On the ground that Negroes needed a type of education "suited" to them, we have an attempt to train them as menials and dependents; or in the case of West Indians, an attempt to perpetuate their use as low-paid laborers by limiting their knowledge; or in the case of African natives, efforts to deprive them of modern languages and modern science in order to seal their subordination to outworn mores, reactionary native rulers, industrialization.

What I have in mind is nothing like this. It is rather an honest development of the premises from which this plea for special education starts. It is illustrated by these facts: Negroes must know the history of the Negro race in America, and this they will seldom get in white institutions. Their children ought to study textbooks like Brawley's *Short History,* the first edition of Woodson's *Negro in Our History,* and Cromwell, Turner, and Dykes's *Readings from Negro Authors.* Negroes who celebrate the birthdays of Washington and Lincoln, and the worthy, but colorless and relatively unimportant "founders" of various Negro colleges, ought not to forget the fifth of March—that first national holiday of this country—which commemorates the martyrdom of Crispus Attucks. They ought to celebrate Negro Health Week and Negro History Week. They ought to study intelligently, and from their own point of view, the slave trade, slavery, emancipation, Reconstruction, and present economic development.

Beyond this, Negro colleges ought to be studying anthropology, psychology, and the social sciences from the point of view of the colored races. Today, the anthropology that is being taught, and the expeditions financed for archeological and ethnographical explorations, are for the most part straining every nerve to erase the history of black folk from the record. One has only to remember that the majority of anthropologists have peopled the continent of Africa itself with almost no Negroes, while men like Sayce* and Reisner have even declared that the Ethiopians have no Negro blood! All this has been done by the legerdemain and metaphysics of nomenclature, and in the face of the great and important history of black blood in the world.

Recently, something has been done by colored scholars to correct the extraordinary propaganda of postwar psychology which sent men like Brigham** and McDougall† rushing into scientific proof of Negro congenital inferiority. But much more is necessary and demanded of Negro scholarship. In history and the social sciences the Negro school and college have an

*Archibald Henry Sayce (1845–1933), historian of antiquity.
**William T. Brigham (1841–1926), American scientist.—M.W.
†William McDougall (1871–1938), psychologist.

unusual opportunity and role. It does not consist simply in trying to parallel the history of white folk with similar boasting about black and brown folk, but rather an honest evaluation of human effort and accomplishment, without color blindness, and without transforming history into a record of dynasties and prodigies.

Here, we have in America, a working class which in our day has achieved physical freedom, and mental clarity. An economic battle has just begun. It can be studied and guided; it can teach consumers' co-operation, democracy, and socialism, and be made not simply a record and pattern for the Negro race, but a guide for the rise of the working classes throughout the world, just at the critical time when these classes are about to assume their just political domination, which is destined to become the redemption of mankind.

Much has been said of the special aesthetic ability of the Negro race. Naturally, it has been exaggerated. Naturally, it is not a racial characteristic in the sense of hereditary, inborn, and heritable difference; but there is no doubt but what the tremendous psychic history of the American and West Indian groups has made it possible for the present generation to accumulate a wealth of material which, with encouragement and training, could find expression in the drama, in color and form, and in music. And nowhere could this training better be pursued than in separate Negro schools under competent and intelligent teachers. What little has already been done in this line is scarcely a beginning of what is possible, provided the object is not simple entertainment or bizarre efforts at money raising.

In biology, the pioneering work of Carolyn Bond Day could be extended indefinitely in Negro laboratories; and in the purely physical and chemical sciences, the need of Negroes familiar with the intricate technical basis of modern civilization would not only help them to find their place in the industrial scene for their own organization, but also enable them to help Abyssinia, India, China, and the colored world to maintain their racial integrity, and their economic independence. It could easily be the mission and duty of American Negroes to master this scientific basis of modern invention, and give it to all mankind.

Thus, instead of our schools being simply separate schools, forced on us by grim necessity, they can become centers of a new and beautiful effort at human education, which may easily lead and guide the world in many important and valuable aspects. It is for this reason that when our schools are separate, the control of the teaching force, the expenditure of money, the choice of textbooks, the discipline and other administrative matters of the sort ought, also, to come into our hands, and be incessantly demanded and guarded.

I remember once, in Texas, reading in a high school textbook for colored students, the one anecdote given concerning Abramam Lincoln: He was pictured as chasing Negro thieves all night through the woods from his Mississippi flatboat! Children could read that history in vain to learn any word of what had been accomplished in American history by Benjamin Banneker, Jan Matseliger, Elijah McCoy, Frederick Douglass, or James Dunn. In fact, one of the peculiar tragedies of the smaller Southern colleges is that they hire as teachers of history, economics, and sociology colored men trained in Northern institutions, where not a word of any information concerning these disciplines, so far as Negroes are concerned, has ever been imparted to them. I speak from experience, because I came to Atlanta University to teach history in 1897 without the slightest idea from my Harvard tuition that Negroes ever had any history!

I know that this article will forthwith be interpreted by certain illiterate "nitwits" as a plea for segregated Negro schools and colleges. It is not. It is simply calling a spade a spade. It is saying in plain English that a separate Negro school, where children are treated like human beings, trained by teachers of their own race, who know what it means to be black in the year of salvation 1935, is infinitely better than making our boys and girls doormats to be spit and trampled upon and lied to by ignorant social climbers, whose sole claim to superiority is ability to kick "niggers" when they are down. I say, too, that certain studies and discipline necessary to Negroes can seldom be found in white schools.

It means this, and nothing more. To sum up this: Theoretically, the Negro needs neither segregated schools nor mixed schools. What he needs is Education. What he must remember is that there is no magic, either in mixed schools or in segregated schools. A mixed school with poor and unsympathetic teachers, with hostile public opinion, and no teaching of truth concerning black folk, is bad. A segregated school with ignorant placeholders, inadequate equipment, poor salaries, and wretched housing is equally bad. Other things being equal, the mixed school is the broader, more natural basis for the education of all youth. It gives wider contacts; it inspires greater self-confidence; and suppresses the inferiority complex. But other things seldom are equal, and in that case Sympathy, Knowledge, and the Truth, outweigh all that the mixed school can offer.

SOCIAL PLANNING FOR THE NEGRO, PAST AND PRESENT

VIOLENCE AND REBELLION

From the day of the Negro's landing in the United States down to the present, there have been four well-defined plans of emancipation and social uplift. The first plan was naturally that of violence; the individual and organized resistance to slavery. The extent of this is usually misapprehended in the United States because the plan began in Africa and the West Indies and only its last efforts were extended to the mainland. Henry M. Stanley estimates that in the African slave raids for every slave captured, at least four persons were left dead in the villages; and where the cause of Negro slavery was inter-tribal war, the toll of death was even greater. On the middle passage to America there were repeated efforts at mutiny in the 18th and 19th centuries, down to the celebrated cases of the "Amistad" and the "Creole."

The Negroes once landed in the Western world were for many years a cause of turmoil. Ovando solicited that no Negro slaves be sent to Haiti for they "fled among the Indians and taught them bad customs and could never be captured." The story of the fugitive Maroons in South American and Jamaica is one of the sagas of modern history. They fought the English government for a hundred years; they resisted the Spanish and Portuguese and they achieved freedom which continues to our day in Haiti and Guiana.

The fear of slave violence on the American mainland is suffi- ciently proven by the legislation. The laws of South Carolina in

1712 were defended as necessary "to restrain the disorders, rapiness and inhumanity to which they are naturally prone and inclined." The law of 1740 declared that "many late, horrible and barbarous massacres have actually been committed and many more designed on the white inhabitants of this province by Negro slaves." Harsh and pitiless legislation based on these promises continued during slavery and especially was revived and increased after the attempts of Vesey and Nat Turner.

We must not forget that the last effective act of violence which the slaves used was their mass movement during the Civil War which added 200,000 soldiers and even larger numbers of servants and laborers to the Union Army. It was this actual adherence of slaves to the Union casue and the threat that it would be extended indefinitely that made the Civil War hopeless for the South and led to its sudden cessation.

FUGITIVE SLAVES

The third plan which acted as the safety valve for slavery was that of the fugitive; it was by far the most successful attack on slavery, and began a real social reorganization for the Negro. In a comparatively empty country, the individual slave who could not and would not endure the system would not have to wait until he got the assent and support of a large number of his fellows. He could steal away to the swamps of Florida and Virginia and along the Appalachian Mountains and the Mississippi Valley into the North. This running away of slaves was first an individual enterprise; then it became organized and systematized under Negro leaders and finally gained the cooperation and active help of whites during the era of the Underground Railroad.

The Underground Railroad led to the Civil War. It meant that the capital invested in slaves was continually suffering losses, and the slave owners demanded, more and more peremptorily, the enactment of severe fugitive slave laws. The last one, which they secured on the eve of the Civil War, not only interfered with individual rights, but state rights. It led to retaliatory nullification in the North, intensified the bitterness between the sections, and eventually resulted in Civil War.

It is difficult to say how many slaves escaped, but the black population of the North increased from 130,000 in 1820 to

345,000 in 1860; this is a considerably larger increase than that of the total Negro population, and if we remember that this Northern group was composed of poor emigrants with broken family life and insecure economic basis suddenly transferred from city to town, it seems certain that at least 100,000 of them were fugitives from slavery and represented a loss of at least $25,000,000 in invested capital, and perhaps much more than that. It was this economic loss that spurred secession.

Meantime, there were especial centers of runaway slaves. There were the fugitive slaves at the time of the Revolutionary War who not only took part in the hostilities, but caused infinite difficulties in peace negotiations. There were the 1,000 Negroes, who in 1815 manned a former British port in Georgia and resisted the power of the United States. And finally there were the so-called Seminole wars which were simply slave raids for runaway property.

MASS MIGRATION

Besides these efforts, there were more far-reaching efforts to settle the Negro problem by mass migration. A proposal to leave this country for Africa seemed logical in the 18th century when so many Negroes were newly come to the country. This plan was not simply a plan of white folk. Paul Cuffe was actually the first person who successfully transported emigrants, taking 38 Negroes to Africa at his own expense. Later, came the American Colonization Society, but their plan for wholesale migration was spoiled by the effort of the radical South to turn this migration into an attempt to bolster slavery by getting rid of free Negroes. Nevertheless, out of that effort, together with the attempt to enforce the slave trade laws, came the settlement at Liberia.

Among the free Negroes of the North, plans for social amelioration began about 1830 when the Nat Turner insurrection in the South and the new foreign immigration to the North, made the economic situation of the free Negroes difficult. Riots and discriminatory laws in Ohio and Pennsylvania led to the Conventions of 1830 and 1831 and to a well thought-out plan of migration. The British government was approached and offered asylum, at first in Canada and later, after the West Indian emancipation, in the West Indies. The Canadian migration was financed by Negroes themselves and large numbers went to Ontario where they built up successful settlements. Their influence on American Negroes has been great. They were headquarters of the Underground Railroad. It was here that John Brown went to perfect his plans for the Harper's Ferry raids; and it was here that Richard B. Harrison was born.

Between 1830 and 1860, the situation of American Negroes became increasingly difficult because of the spread of the abolition controversy and the rise of the cotton kingdom. An increasing number of Negroes in the 50's began to consider that wholesale migration was the only escape. They saw no chance of emancipation in the United States. Even Frederick Douglass placed his whole hope on war and blood, but, nevertheless, steadfastly opposed migration.

In 1854, a remarkable convention met in Cleveland, Ohio. They made three proposals: Martin R. Delaney proposed migration to the Niger Valley of Africa; James M. Whitfield proposed to go to Central America; and Theodore Holly, to Haiti. They not only made these propositions, but they actually made the necessary investigation and at the next colonization convention in Canada in 1856, Holly made a report which resulted, eventually, in 2,000 Negro emigrants going to Haiti. Delaney concluded eight treaties with African kings and brought evidences of land concessions and welcome. Whitfield did not actually get to Central American before the Civil War broke out.

The war stopped migration schemes, until black fugitives began to pour into the Union armies. For a while, Lincoln did not realize the significance of this tremendous secession of power to the North and withdrawal of labor force from the South. The first problem, and an irritating problem it was, was what was going to be done to get rid of the Negroes. If some plan of mass migration could be devised there was the possibility not simply of withdrawing these slaves from work in the South, but of inducing the border states to give up slavery. Lincoln had long been an advocate of colonization. He said frankly that he could not conceive Negroes and white people living together in the United States as equals. He, therefore, secured in 1861 an appropriation of $100,000 from Congress and a further appropriation of $500,000 in 1862. He consulted delegations of Negroes and made contacts with foreign countries, but before he went further, he suddenly saw just what the significance of Negro soldiers and laborers was. He saw that without their help, the war against the South could not be won, while with their help and the threat of increased accessions from the slaves, the opposition in the South was doomed. Moreover, he became convinced that mass migration of the Negroes could not be carried on with their consent nor at a price which the United States was willing to pay. His one venture with 500 Negro settlers on a little island near Haiti was a disastrous failure and nearly half of the victims died of disease and were cheated outrageously by their white manager.

[Then came the era of Reconstruction and with the thrill of political power in the minds of the Negro and his friends, social reconstruction by migration was practically given up, except that Negroes moved in considerable groups from place to place in the South, in order to find free land and better working conditions.] When, however, the revolution of 1876 came and the Negro by force and fraud was disfranchised, a great migration movement to the West was conceived by Henry Adams in Louisiana and Benjamin Singleton in Tennessee. Some 50,000 Negroes actually migrated to Kansas and the West and it took conciliation and violence in the South to stop the stream. Its more effectual stoppage, however, was due to poverty and cold welcome in the West. Nevertheless, a Negro population was planted in Kansas and its descendants remain there. Later, Bishop Turner and Congressman Morgan of Alabama tried to revive the project of migration to Africa, but its only result was one shipload of 200 Negroes in 1885.

On the other hand, [the migration of Negroes from South to North has gone on continually since the Civil War. Between 1880 and 1900, some 10,000 to 20,000 a year went into the North, while from 1910 to 1930, between 1,000,000 and 1,500,000 moved in one of the great mass movements of the history of migration.]

POLITICAL ENFRANCHISEMENT

Meantime, the fourth great plan for the social emancipation of Negroes began with the Reconstruction efforts in the Civil War. [From 1867–1876, the Negroes placed their whole hope of full emancipation and economic security upon their vote and this forms one of the most interesting episodes in American history. It was not simply the enfranchisement of black folk, it was the attempt to reconstruct the basis of American democracy and to put the political power in the hands of the lowest working group. The bottom economic rail was put on top.]If this group had had leadership and a greater chance for industrial development, there might have ensued in the South a dictatorship of the proletariat which might have led the modern world. But, of course, no such rapid transition from feudal slavery to industrial democracy could be expected. These laborers were themselves under the direction and ideology of a capitalistic form of industry. Their idea of emancipation was the rise of an exploiting class of black capitalists. Nevertheless, their realistic grasp of the situation led them to preliminary efforts not to exploit labor but to make the situation of the emancipated workers as advantageous as possible. They tried cooperative farming in Louisiana and state division of large plantations in South Carolina. They advocated and made actual free public school education in every Southern state. They gave opportunity for the poor man, not only to vote, but to represent his class in the legislature and the greatest charge against Reconstruction— that the legislature was filled by people who did not pay taxes —was really its greatest glory. The non-taxpaying laborer was the man who for a long time dominated the legislature with both white and black representatives.

There were, however, two unconquerable centers of opposition: one was the white landholder, who despite the fortunes of war, was enabled to continue his monopoly of the land through the determination of Andrew Johnson. It was one of the ironies of fate that the poor white who was the author of the legislation which distributed free land to the peasants of Europe and the North, was also the man who succeeded in keeping the emancipated Negroes of the South as landless serfs.

The second unconquerable center of opposition was the new capitalism of the North which was rising to tremendous and ruthless power. This new capitalism looked upon the South not as a center of new democracy, but as a center of exploitation. So long as the Southern land monopolist threatened the power and career of the Northern industrialists, he was perfectly willing to let black and white labor have its way in the South. But when Southern labor began to increase its demands and power, and on the other hand, the Southern landholder showed himself willing to unite with the Northern capitalists in new exploitation, the bargain of 1876 was made and the laborers, white and black, were disfranchised. What ensued in the South after emancipation was not at all the classical bourgeois revolution but something far more complicated and reactionary.

However, the plan for Negro emancipation by political means did not end in 1876. The Negro held on to vestiges of his political power, first, by black congressmen, up until the beginning of the 20th century, by a few members of Southern legislatures, and especially by their power inside the Republican Party. This latter power was gradually undermined by the fact that it had back of it less and less of real democratic control and, therefore, could more easily be seduced by bribery and manipulation.

Appointments of Negroes to federal office also became less in number, as Reconstruction receded. Nevertheless, there were certain compensations in the North. Negroes appeared in the legislature of 11 or 12 Northern states and sometimes played a conspicuous part. They were elevated to the judicial bench in the District of Columbia and three other states, and in cities, particularly like Chicago and New York, they occupied from time to time positions of real power.

The result of this political influence can be shown in many ways. Between 1884 and 1897, 25 civil rights laws, in addition to the national civil rights law, were passed in 16 Northern states. Many of them, including the national law, were emasculated by judicial interpretation, but others, like the Massachussetts and New York laws, are effective today. Federal appropriations for Negro education in the case of Howard University and the land grant colleges have been secured. On the other hand, further discriminatory legislation has been held up. Jim-Crow cars have been kept out of Delaware, West Virginia, and Missouri, and partially out of Maryland. A flood of anti-racial intermarriage laws introduced in 1913 in Congress and 12 different states were defeated in every instance but one.

On the other hand, in the South, Jim-Crow legislation and disfranchisement laws between 1881 and 1910 swept through with little opposition.

It became clearer and clearer, as the plan of political power to emancipate the American Negro was followed, that something was lacking; that the poverty and inexperience of the Negro made it impossible for him to exercise his political power in full, and that as a minority, even then, he could not succeed unless he could make some alliance with the majority. There ensued, therefore, two plans which both explain and supplement the plan of political power from 1867–1930.

One of these movements came in 1896–1920 and it sought firmly to integrate the American Negro into American industry as a farmer, laborer, skilled artisan, and capitalist. The other movement, sought by agitation and legal defense, to clear away race discrimination and allow untrammeled advancement of black folk according to ability. These two latter movements fell into bitter controversy. The economic movement ended with the World War and the anti-discrimination movement declined with the depression.

THE WASHINGTON PLAN

The plan of social Reconstruction advocated by Booker T. Washington was not simply a plan for the uplift of labor as is so often assumed, and it can be only understood as we consider its immediate background. The late William H. Baldwin, President of the Long Island Railroad and slated to be President of the Pennsylvania, was a young man trained in Southern industry. He was one of the first to conceive of the training of black laborers who should share work with white laborers and at the same time keep the white labor movement from too strong and insistent demands in its fight with capital.

This idea began in the day when the "one big union" of the Knights of Labor had changed to the craft unionism of the American Federation of Labor. The strength of the labor movement was growing but almost without exception it excluded black skilled labor. However, black skilled labor was valuable and could be trained in the South. It was the idea of Mr. Baldwin and gradually of many others that you would not only do a service to and open opportunity for black folk, but you would in this same way serve capital and hold white labor in check.

About this time, Booker T. Washington took charge of Tuskegee in Alabama. He was an opportunist with high ideals. He believed in political rights for people who could exercise them, but in the case of Southern Negroes, he knew that they could not exercise them without the consent of the white South. He took the position, therefore, that the Negro must gain an economic status before he could use his political rights and in this he was undoubtedly right; but on the other hand, his idea of the economic status which Negroes must gain was based unquestionably on the capitalistic organization of the United States.

Mr. Washington's program included a temporary acquiescence in giving up Negro political rights and agitation for civil rights and insistence upon training young Negroes for farming and industry. Up from a thrifty solid class of black landlords and artisans, Washington expected a class of Negro capitalists to arise and employ Negro workers. The plan was launched by the Atlanta Speech in 1896 and was triumphant from that date until about 1910. It included alliance with white capital and was rewarded by large contributions toward Negro education, especially such schools as conformed to the Hampton-Tuskegee type.

As a first step toward this new Negro capitalism, Mr. Washington especially stressed landholding, widespread peasant proprietorship, and even large farms among Negroes; and then a training of Negro laborers and artisans for use in industry at a wage if necessary less than that demanded by union labor. The result of this compromise was a new understanding between leading elements, North and South, with regard to the Negro. The Negro college, while not entirely discouraged, was looked upon with some suspicion, and positions for Negro college graduates became difficult. To some extent, appointments and opportunities for young Negroes were carefully censored and referred for approval to Tuskegee, over a very wide extent of country. Negro newspapers were brought in line by judicious advertising and other means of control. This was really regarded as a clever and farsighted compromise, which, if it did not solve, would at least peacefully postpone the solutions of a baffling, intricate problem of race contact until more favorable times. Between 1900–1910, Mr. Washington became one of the most popular men in America, in constant demand North and South as a speaker, adviser, and referee.

As the current opinion of the land became unified, Mr. Washington's program began to become increasingly suspicious in the eyes of Negroes. A wave of Jim-Crow legislation and disfranchising bills swept over the South and the border states. Already separation of the races in travel had been made compulsory in eight Southern states before 1891, but had paused. Now, a new wave of legislation began in 1898 and covered South Carolina, North Carolina, Virginia, Maryland and Oklahoma. Determined and repeated efforts were made in Missouri, West Virginia, and Delaware. Disfranchising laws swept over the South and border statates, from 1890–1910, at the very time when Negro politcial power and agitation had been lulled to its lowest by the Washington compromise. This triumph of the radical, anti-Negro South and the continued prevalence of lynching which went on at the rate of one to two a week during most of Mr. Washington's career, greatly embarrassed him. He hated caste and lawlessness as much as any man. He wanted the best for his people, but he implicitly believed that once his economic program could be put through all else would follow. He made the fatal mistake of trying to forestall criticism from Negroes and of acquiescing in the neglect if not the suppression of Negro colleges.

The result was the outburst of wrath and criticism led by the younger college-bred Negro group, an outburst which eventually split the Negro group in twain. But it was not that criticism that doomed the Washington program. It was plain failure of the economic rebuilding which I emphasized. This is shown by the trend of Negro employment. Despite the effort of both Hampton and Tuskegee to train farmers and servants, both of these decreased in number. Farmers, instead of forming 57 per cent of workers, as in 1890, now formed 37 per cent. Servants had decreased from 31 per cent in 1890 to 22 per cent in 1920. Since then, they have increased to 29 per cent. Manifestly, then, there were forces at work to drive the Negroes off the farm and out of the servant quarters. On the other hand, the number of Negroes in commerce and transportation and in the manufacturing and mechanical industries, increased largely from 10 per cent in 1890 to 29 per cent in 1930, but it was not at all the kind of increase that Mr. Washington had in mind. The newcomers were mainly laborers. They made some headway into the semi-skilled industries, but were kept out by the trade unions. The trade unions held against them as an excuse the fact that they had been trained and that the plan had been to train them as strikebreakers and low-cost laborers. The caste system in the South increased the whole ideology of caste throughout the United States until laboring men felt themselves degraded to work with black men. Moreover, the attempt of Negroes to enter the employing class as merchants and land-holders was made impossible by severe competition and monopoly. The attempt to teach Negroes the skill of modern industry was also frustrated by the changing of skill, mass production, and use of machinery. While, therefore, land ownership among Negroes and the accumulation of property increased until 1910, it then began to decrease and the increase in Negro property, while a creditable index of thrift, was dwarfed by the immense piling up of capital in the hands of whites. Without doubt, the Washington program improved the economic status of the Negro, but on the other hand, and just as surely, it did not show a way out because it fastened the chains of exploitation on Negro labor and increased labor antagonism in the laboring classes.

This was particularly shown in the new development in the South where white labor used its political and social influence to replace black labor and eliminate the so-called Negro jobs. At the time of the depression, therefore, the status of Negro labor, both North and South, was precarious, through the opposition of unions and the discrimination of employers in the North and the competition of poor white labor in the South.

LEGAL DEFENSE

The next plan for social reorganization was that of agitation of legal defense. It was a first a part of the plan for political power and not a demand for fixing the unconstitutionality of disfranchisement legislation and the enforcing of war amendments. One of the earliest group movements to agitate for this was the National League formed in Boston in 1885. It was local in its membership but had some influence.

In 1887, T. Thomas Fortune, Editor of what is now the *New York Age*, issued an appeal for a national organization, and repeated this in 1889. The so-called Afro-American League, afterward changed to Afro-American Council, met in Chicago with 21 states represented in Jaunuary, 1890. J. C. Price was president, and Mr. Fortune, secretary. The League held another meeting in Tennessee and then died, until Bishop Walters revived it in 1898. It met that year in September at Rochester and later in November in Washington. The object of the organization was to investigate lynching, to test the constitutionality of discriminatory laws, to secure civil-rights legislation, to promote migration from the South and to encourage organization. It met for several years and practically died with a final meeting in St. Paul, Minnesota, about 1900. Its weekness was that it consisted simply of an annual meeting without a continuous working organization. The result was that it did little more than meet, organize, and pass resolutions. In the year 1905, a new aspect came over the plans for American Negroes for social reconstruction.

The new disfranchisement laws and the wave of discriminatory legislation, coupled with Mr. Washington's concessions, alarmed the colored people. Particularly the young colored college man began to fear the dictatorship of the Tuskegee machine and the difficulty of expressing even legitimate criticism. This opposition was crystalized by the jailing of Monroe Trotter in Boston for trying to heckle Mr. Washington during a speech at the colored church. It seems to me that this was going too far, and that while Trotter was much more bitter and outspoken than was necessary, yet he did have a right to talk even though he criticized Mr. Washington. The result was that a call was issued in June, 1905, signed by 59 men from 17 states. In July, 1905, 29 of these men, representing 14 states, met at Niagara Falls and formed the Niagara Movement. The Movement grew, and in 1906 held a significant meeting at Harper's Ferry. The manifesto which it sent out was plain and bitter.

The Niagara Movement, however, had certain inherent difficulties. First, it was a racial movement of men entirely unknown outside their group and with no means of contact by which they could easily reach influential persons in the white group. And secondly, Mr. Trotter, who owned and edited the one organization journal, was not an organization man. He was an extreme individualist. When, therefore, in 1909 there was held a conference in New York with practically the same program that the Niagara Movement had, practically all of the leading members of the Niagara Movement went into the N.A.A.C.P., seven of them going upon its Board of Directors, and thus to a large measure the work of the Niagara Movement became merged with that of the N.A.A.C.P. The N.A.A.C.P. said in its first report:

The National Association for the Advancement of Colored People seeks to uplift the colored men and women of this country by securing to them the full enjoyment of their rights as citizens, justice in all courts, and equality of opportunity everywhere. It favors and aims to aid, every kind of education among them save that which teaches special privileges or prerogative, class or caste. It recognizes the national character of the Negro problem and no sectionalism. It believes in the holding of the Constitution of the United States and its amendments, in the spirit of Abraham Lincoln. It upholds the doctrine of "all men up and no man down." It abhors Negro crime, but still more the conditions which breed crime, and most of all the crimes committed by mobs in the mockery of the law, by individuals in the name of the law.

It believes that the scientific truths of the Negro problem must be available before the country can see its way wholly clear to right existing wrongs. It has no other belief than that the best way to uplift the colored man and the best way to aid the white man to peace is social content; it has no other desire than exacting justice, and no other motive than patriotism. (First Annual Report, January 1, 1911. N.A.A.C.P.)

The work of the N.A.A.C.P. is too well-known to call for review here. I need only point out that its greatest triumph was in the matter of legal defense. Practically, it made the Supreme Court for the first time in the history of the country affirm the validity of the 15th Amendment, outlaw the Grandfather Clauses, and curtail the segregation ordinances. It also secured some protection for accused Negroes from mob violence and made the most effective anti-lynching campaign in the history of the country.

The first sign of change that faced the N.A.A.C.P., was the falling off of its income and the decrease in the circulation of *The Crisis*. This was not due to the fact that the American Negro did not want to fight discrimination and lynching and was not willing to pursue cases in legal defense which should build up the foundation of the whole caste system in marriage, in travel and education. But it did come from the fact that the colored people, economically, were unable to stand the expense. It had been the proud boast of the N.A.A.C.P. that beginning as a quasi-philanthropic institution, expecting to rely upon funds furnished mainly by rich white friends, it had become during its best years supported in the main by the mass of colored workers and that *The Crisis* had been made financially independent by the same kind of support. The amounts of money which it received from rich white people were small and their withdrawal would have made no particular difference in its program. The falling off now of this income meant that the colored people were financially unable to sustain this program and especially to back its expansion. We realized this before the depression and the causes lay in a new industrial development, North and South. In the South, the Negro was losing the monopoly of certain jobs which he had had. The machine was displacing semi-skilled and skilled labor among both Negroes and whites. A new monopoly of capital and materials was so changing the face of industry that the Negro was becoming a reservoir of casual labor and the general causes of the collapse of agriculture throughout the world were at work in increased degree among Negro farmers.

The mass migration of Negroes to the North alleviated but did not change the basic trouble. They found themselves in the midst of difficulties connected with housing, difficulties connected with unions, difficulties connected with the casual character of their labor and the low wage for which they were obliged to work. This should have taught the Negroes of the United States that a change of tactic was absolutely necessary. Agitation and legal defense must be kept up so far as possible but that possibility at present has its limitations. Before them, and of more importance and of fundamental influence even to the campaign against race discrimination itself, was a new plan of social security.

THE PRESENT DILEMMA

I began to advocate, therefore, for the N.A.A.C.P. a new social program as early as 1928. I was by no means clear in my own thinking, but was groping for light and for that reason had visited Russia, had begun the study of Karl Marx and had voted the Socialist ticket since 1912. My efforts brought little reaction; no particular opposition and at the same time no emphasis of agreement until the wave of depression overwhelmed us. Then, suddenly, there came to the fore, a peculiar situation made by the fact that the problem of race discrimination always cuts across and hinders the settlement of other problems, and we are repeatedly forced to give up direct attack upon it in order to save our very lives.

It happened in the Civil War. In the midst of a fight for physical freedom, civil and political rights, the Negro was suddenly faced with the problem of fighting when the outcome was by no means clear nor was it altogether certain just where his interest lay. He was compelled for a time to lay aside his racial demands to become Union soldiers and laborers and afterward was rewarded by receiving a greater measure of political power and civil rights than he had dreamed of. The same kind of dilemma came at the time of the World War.

We had no choice between war and peace—the nation was rushing headlong. We had no allies save a small group of thinkers who for the most part were not interested in Negroes. Labor was near unanimous for war and so were most socialists here and abroad. We were in a raging flood and our only real choice was to fight swimming with the current or to be drowned in impotent opposition. I said then and under similar circumstances would say again, close ranks and fight for our own liberty while the world was committing suicide.

The victim of mob violence, lynching and residential segregation for a time had to concentrate his efforts toward securing decent treatment of his segregated regiments, an opportunity for men to become officers even if they were black and permission to fight at the front instead of work blindly in the rear. After the World War, the Negro was able to return to his attack upon prejudice with increased power and efficiency. The years from 1919 to 1929 represent a high water mark of our organized striving for increased political power, the suppression of lynching and legal defense.

The irony of the situation, however, proved to be the fact that the cause for which we were verbally compelled to fight itself failed in its very victory and cast us with all men, workers and owners, in the maelstrom of world depression. Today, then, our original paradox again appears with wider ramification and vaster perils.

We are in the midst of a national and world movement to reconstruct the basis of industry. In order to be efficient coworkers in this reconstruction, we have got to escape the present threat of starvation, to conserve our schools and social organizations and to get regular, decently paid work. With that foundation settled, even in a reasonable degree, we can begin again to fight discrimination. But until unemployment among American Negroes is decreased and a decent standard of living reestablished, we have no resources upon which the battle against discrimination can effectively be carried.

Here, then, is the dilemma and how has it been met? Briefly put, there have been three moves: (1) toward invoking the protection of restored capitalism, (2) a movement toward alliance with organized labor, and (3) a movement toward socialism.

In the first category may be placed practically all of the older organizations: the Urban League, the Federation of Churches, the N.A.A.C.P. Nearly all of these organizations have, to be sure, shown signs of uneasiness at their position. The Urban League organized a National Economic Council, which through an executive committee and workers' council was designed to guide the Negro through the crisis. Apparently, this never functioned. The N.A.A.C.P. sought to adopt an economic program but was unable to agree on anything definite. The Federation of Churches had adopted a liberal labor program, but has not applied it to Negroes. Gradually, most of these and many other organizations under the guidance of the Joint Committee on Recovery, fell back upon a drive on the administration to secure justice for the Negro in relief and reorganization; but the difficulty was in determining just what economic justice for the Negro involved and how it could best be secured. The organizations themselves had scant common ground. Ten of them were religious. Four were academic fraternities and sororities, one is a fraternal order, one an organization for agitation and reform, four organizations of professional men, one designed for club work, and three are industrial organizations. The only thing upon which this conglomerate body could wholeheartedly unite was the matter of race discrimination.

Of the fact of discrimination, the Joint Committee has

unearthed ample proof, but as to what we are going to do about
it, the Joint Committee, quite naturally, has nothing to say and
nothing to think.

Indeed, everything that has happened in the NRA and the
New Deal might easily have been foretold before the NRA was
established.

If the United States government comes in to the depression
picture to administer local relief, that relief must be directly
carried out by local people and these local people in the places
where Negroes are most numerous are going to be prejudiced
and narrow.

If the government is going to relieve the farmer by a scaricity
program or bonuses, the people who are going to reap the benefit from that program are going to be the white people who
own the land. If the government is going to establish a great
power organization with towns and industries, in these towns
and industries there is going to be repeated the same pattern of
discrimination and segregation that is current in the nation. If
we are going to have housing projects, subsistence homesteads,
farm credit and credit unions, we are going to find in the carrying out of these plans the same American prejudice against
color that we find everywhere. What, then, are we to do? Are
we to starve to death until we settle color discrimination in
America or are we first to secure the power to fight before we
enter battle? The one thing that we are bound to do in self-
defense is to see that in the midst of all this whirlpool we make
sure of such beginnings of economic security that in the future
we shall have power to work out our destiny; and to this, everything else is subordinate.

If segregated homesteads and segregated land will give us
more secure employment and higher wage, we cannot for a
moment hesitate. If segregated schools will give us better education, then we must have segregated schools. If segregated housing will give us decent homes, we have no right to choose for
our children and our families slums for the sake of herding with
the white unfit. Our first business in the midst of the great
economic revolution, which is going on, is to secure a place for
ourselves.

To this, the advocates of labor alliance answer: There is only
one haven of refuge for the American Negro. He must recognize that his attempt to enter the ranks of capital as an exploiter

came too late, if it were ever a worthy ideal for a group of workers. He is now forever excluded by the extraordinary monopoly which white capital and credit have upon the machines and materials of the world. Moreover, that solution after all was possible only for the few. The great mass of Negroes belong to the laboring class. They have the same interests that white laborers have. They must join the white labor movement.

This, however, is not nearly as easy as it might seem. Not only has the attempt of American Negroes to join the ranks of the white labor movement been discouraging for more than a century, but even today, the welcome which they are accorded is questionable. In the first place, the farmers and servants who compose the mass of workers among colored people are not organized. If we take the 30,000,000 of organizable laborers, less than 7,000,000 are organized, even if we include the company unions. If we take the less than 5,000,000 who are organized, the overwhelming majority of them will not allow the Negroes to join their ranks under any circumstances, and most of the rest have only allowed Negroes to intrude when the power of Negro labor was such that they did not dare to oppose its competition. There are undoubtedly today a number of unions which are disposed to welcome Negro members and who recognize something of the real solidarity of labor interests; but their total number must be less than half a million. With such workers, Negro labor ought by all means to unite; but to say that the union of American Negro labor with a half million out of 5,000,000 organized laborers is a labor alliance, is seriously to overstate the case.

Suppose, now, that the Negro turns to the promise of socialism whither I have long looked for salvation. I was once a member of the celebrated Local No. 1 in New York. I am convinced of the essential truth of the Marxian philosophy and believe that eventually land, machines and materials must belong to the state; that private profit must be abolished; that the system of exploiting labor must disappear; that people who work must have essentially equal income; and that in their hands the political rulership of the state must eventually rest.

Notwithstanding the fact that I believe this is the truth and that this truth is being gradually exemplified by the Russian experiment, I must, nevertheless, ask myself seriously; how far can American Negroes forward this eventual end? What part can they expect to have in a socialistic state and what can they do now to bring about this realization? And my answer to this has long been clear. There is no automatic power in socialism to override and suppress race prejudice. This has been proven in America, it was true in Germany before Hitler and the analogy of the Jews in Russia is for our case entirely false and misleading. One of the worst things that Negroes could do today would be to join the American Communist Party or any of its many branches. The Communists of America have become dogmatic exponents of the inspired word of Karl Marx as they read it. They believe, apparently, in immediate, violent and bloody revolution, and they are willing to try any and all means of raising hell anywhere and under any circumstances. This is a silly program even for white men. For American colored men, it is suicide. In the first place, its logical basis is by no means sound. The great and fundamental change in the organization of industry which Karl Marx with his splendid mind and untiring sacrifice visualized must, to be sure, be brought about by revolution, but whether in all times and places and under all circumstances that revolution is going to involve war and bloodshed, is a question which every sincere follower of Marx has a right to doubt.

The most baffling paradox today is the attitude of men toward war. On the one hand, we have the advocates of radical reform in our fundamental, economic and political structure, insisting that the only path to this era of peace and justice is through violent revolution. On the other hand, we have the advocates of the present system insisting that they can only insure peace by worldwide preparation for the same kind of war which recently took the lives of ten million men.

The ordinary man seeking peace, has, then, apparently not a choice between peace and war, but only a choice of the kind of war in which he will fight and the object for which he will fight, and apparently he must strive to make this last great murder of the West, this new War to end War, as peaceful and reasonable as possible.

Leaving for a moment the question as to how inevitable this dilemma is, we American Negroes under the race hate now prevalent, will in any case stand between the two armies as buffer and victim, pawn and peon. And we can only take this attitude: We abhor violence and bloodshed; we will join no movement that advocates a program of violence, except as the last defense against aggression.

We see togay as the chief aggressor and threatener of violence, not indeed communisum, but greed and reaction, masquerading as patriotism and fascism, armed to the teeth, intolerant and ready to kill and repress not only those who oppose them, but those who dare to express opposing thoughts.

Such discrimination, represented in the United States by various patriotic women's organizations, by war veterans' leagues, by the army and navy and its friends, are the most dangerous advocates of war and murder; and it is foolish for those who believe in world peace and economic justice to be so misled by this reaction as to burst into wild words and futile deeds and thus give greed a chance to kill the innocent.

Granted that the Marxian dialectic is a masterful statement of a great truth, yet the revolution which it sets down as inevitable, may logically, even if not probably, come by votes without violence, by restricted violence, or if with widespread violence, not with cruelty and unnecessary bloodshed. They are fools who think that successful and beneficial revolution consists primarily in raising the devil, and it is very doubtful if such persons will ever lead America to peace and justice. It may well be that in the awful and fundamental changes to come, calm, silent and compassionate men may be compelled to lead the world to peace through irresistible force but never through irresponsible deviltry.

In any real revolution, every step that saves violence is to the glory of the great end. We may not save all, but we may never forget that revolution is not the object of socialism or communism rightly conceived; that their object is justice and if haply the world can find that justice without blood, the world is the infinite gainer. Persistent and dominant denial of this possibility may be made and may be true, but wise men will never cease to seek it. We black men say, therefore, we do not believe in violence. Our object is justice not violence, and we will fight only when there is no better way.

The proletariat which stands for violence is that proletariat which becomes the tool to carry out capitalistic violence. The first study of workers is not to fight but to convince themselves that union of workers, class solidarity, is better than force and a substitute for it.

The real problem, then, is this concert of the workers. The real emphasis today is not on revolution but on class consciousness and this is the job of socialism and the first proof of conversion is the abolition of race prejudice.

It is the duty of socialism to battle the war psychologically and not to promote it. Early Christianity with its battle hymns and war metaphors made the same ghastly mistake—"Its blood-red banner streams afar" down to our own day.

If, now, reaction toward capitalism can no more save Negroes today than it could in the past; and if the opportunity to ally the Negro with white labor has been limited in the past and while wider today is still too limited for effective action, and if a program of avowed violence is out of the question, what can the Negro do? This brings me really to the end of my part of this program, but I may say for the benefit and attack of my good friend, Mr. Harris, to my mind, this is our program; so to organize the vast consumers' power of this group as to secure wide economic independence through the exchange of services and the exchange and manufacture of goods. Through these methods, to train the American Negroes so that they will realize in their own group and realize at first, the kind of social reformation which the whole world is bound to come to some day. And above all to stop this great people from being ashamed of itself, of its color and history; of living together and working together and to realize that race segregation is the white man's loss and not the black man's damnation.

Black Reconstruction is one of Du Bois' most well-known and most important books. It was the first attempt to present the Reconstruction era from the black point of view. The selection reprinted here is Chapter IV, "The General Strike," in which Du Bois shows that black slaves, by running away to Union lines during the Civil War, in effect, went on strike against the South, thereby depriving the South of its necessary labor force.

(*Black Reconstruction in America: 1860-1880*, World Publishing Co., New York, 1935, pp. 55-83.)

THE GENERAL STRIKE

How the Civil War meant emancipation and how the black worker won the war by a general strike which transferred his labor from the Confederate planter to the Northern invader, in whose army lines workers began to be organized as a new labor force

When Edwin Ruffin, white-haired and mad, fired the first gun at Fort Sumter, he freed the slaves. It was the last thing he meant to do but that was because he was so typically a Southern oligarch. He did not know the real world about him. He was provinicial and lived apart on his plantation with his servants, his books and his thoughts. Outside of agriculture, he jumped at conclusions instead of testing them by careful research. He knew, for instance, that the North would not fight. He knew that Negroes would never revolt.

And so war came. War is murder, force, anarchy and debt. Its end is evil, despite all incidental good. Neither North nor South had before 1861 the slightest intention of going to war. The thought was in many respects ridiculous. They were not prepared for war. The national army was small, poorly equipped and without experience. There was no file from which someone might draw plans of subjugation.

When Northern armies entered the South they became armies of emancipation. It was the last thing they planned to be. The North did not propose to attack property. It did not propose to free slaves. This was to be a white man's war to preserve the Union, and the Union must be preserved.

Nothing that concerned the amelioration of the Negro touched the heart of the mass of Americans nor could the common run of men realize the political and economic cost of Negro slavery. When, therefore, the Southern radicals, backed by political oligarchy and economic dictatorship in the most extreme form in which the world had seen it for five hundred years, precipitated secession, that part of the North that opposed the plan had to hunt for a rallying slogan to unite the majority in the North and in the West, and if possible, bring the Border States into an opposing phalanx.

Freedom for slaves furnished no such slogan. Not one-tenth of the Northern white population would have fought for any such purpose. Free soil was a much stronger motive, but it had no cogency in this contest because the Free Soilers did not dream of asking free soil in the South, since that involved the competition of slaves, or what seemed worse than that, of free Negroes. On the other hand, the tremendous economic ideal of keeping this great market for goods, the United States, together with all its possibilities of agriculture, manufacture, trade and profit, appealed to both the West and the North; and what was then much more significant, it appealed to the Border States.

> To the flag we are pledged, all its foes we abhor,
> And we ain't for the nigger, but we are for the war.

The Border States wanted the cotton belt in the Union so that they could sell it their surplus slaves; but they also wanted to be in the same union with the North and West, where the profit of trade was large and increasing. The duty then of saving the Union became the great rallying cry of a war which for a long time made the Border States hesitate and confine secession to the far South. And yet they all knew that the only thing that really threatened the Union was slavery and the only remedy was Abolition.

If, now, the far South had had trained and astute leadership, a compromise could have been made which, so far as slavery was concerned, would have held the abnormal political power of the South intact, made the slave system impregnable for generations, and even given slavery practical rights throughout the nation.

Both North and South ignored in differing degrees the interests of the laboring classes. The North expected patriotism and union to make white labor fight; the South expected all white men to defend the slaveholders' property. Both North and South expected at most a sharp, quick fight and victory; more probably the South expected to secede peaceably, and then outside the Union, to impose terms which would include national recognition of slavery, a new slave territory and new cheap slaves. The North expected that after a threat and demonstration to appease its "honor," the South would return with the right of slave property recognized and protected but geographically limited.

Both sections ignored the Negro. To the Northern masses the Negro was a curiosity, a sub-human minstrel, willingly and naturally a slave, and treated as well as he deserved to be. He had not sense enough to revolt and help Northern armies, even if Northern armies were trying to emancipate him, which they were not. The North shrank at the very thought of encouraging servile insurrection against the whites. Above all it did not propose to interfere with property. Negroes on the whole were considered cowards and inferior beings whose very presence in America was unfortunate. The abolitionists, it was true, expected action on the part of the Negro, but how much, they could not say. Only John Brown knew just how revolt had come and would come and he was dead.

Thus the Negro himself was not seriously considered by the majority of men, North or South. And yet from the very beginning, the Negro occupied the center of the stage because of very simple physical reasons: the war was in the South and in the South were 3,953,740 black slaves and 261,918 free Negroes. What was to be the relation of this mass of workers to the war? What did the war mean to the Negroes, and what did the Negroes mean to the war? There are two theories, both rather over-elaborated: the one that the Negro did nothing but faithfully serve his master until emancipation was thrust upon him; the other that the Negro immediately, just as quickly as the presence of Northern soldiers made it possible, left serfdom and took his stand with the army of freedom.

It must be borne in mind that nine-tenths of the four million black slaves could neither read nor write, and that the overwhelming majority of them were isolated on country plantations. Any mass movement under such circumstances must materialize slowly and painfully. What the Negro did was to wait, look and listen and try to see where his interest lay. There was no use in seeking refuge in an army which was not an army of freedom; and there was no sense in revolting against armed masters who were conquering the world. As soon, however, as it became clear that the Union armies would not or could not return fugitive slaves, and that the masters with all their fume and fury were uncertain of victory, the slave entered upon a general strike against slavery by the same methods that he had used during the period of the fugitive slave. He ran away to the first place of safety and offered his services to the Federal Army. So that in this way it was really true that he served his former master and served the emancipating army; and it was also true that this withdrawal and bestowal of his labor decided the war.

The South counted on Negroes as laborers to raise food and money crops for civilians and for the army, and even in a crisis, to be used for military purposes. Slave revolt was an ever-present risk, but there was no reason to think that a short war with the North would greatly increase this danger. Publicly, the South repudiated the thought of its slaves even wanting to be rescued. The New Orleans *Crescent* showed "the absurdity of the assertion of a general stampede of our Negroes." The London *Dispatch* was convinced that Negroes did not want to be free. "As for the slaves themselves, crushed with the wrongs of Dred Scott and Uncle Tom—most provoking—they cannot be brought to 'burn with revenge.' They are spies for their master. They obstinately refuse to run away to liberty, outrage and starvation. They work in the fields as usual when the planter and overseer are away and only the white women are left at home."

Early in the war, the South had made careful calculation of the military value of slaves. The Alabama *Advertiser* in 1861 discussed the slaves as a "Military Element in the South." It said that "The total white population of the eleven states now comprising the Confederacy is 5,000,000, and, therefore, to fill up the ranks of the proposed army, 600,000, about ten per cent of the entire white population, will be required. In any other country than our own such a draft could not be met, but the Southern states can furnish that number of men, and still not leave the material interest of the country in a suffering condition."

The editor, with fatuous faith, did not for a moment contemplate any mass movement against this program on the part of the slaves. "Those who are incapacitated for bearing arms can oversee the plantations, and the Negroes can go on undisturbed in their usual labors. In the North, the case is different; the men who join the army of subjugation are the laborers, the producers and the factory operatives. Nearly every man from that section, especially those from the rural districts, leaves some branch of industry to suffer during his absence. The institution of slavery in the South alone enables her to place in the field a force much larger in proportion to her white population than the North, or indeed any country which is dependent entirely on free labor. The institution is a tower of strength to the South, particularly at the present crisis, and our enemies will be likely to find that the 'Moral Cancer' about which their orators are so fond of prating, is really one of the most effective weapons employed against the Union by the South."

Soon the South of necessity was moving out beyond this plan. It was no longer simply a question of using the Negroes at home on the plantation to raise food. They could be of even more immediate use, as military labor, to throw up breastworks, transport and prepare food and act as servants in camp. In the Charleston *Courier* of November 22, able-bodied hands were asked to be sent by their masters to work upon the defenses. "They would be fed and properly cared for."

In 1862, in Charleston, after a proclamation of martial law, the governor and counsel authorized the procuring of Negro slaves either by the planter's consent or by impressment "to work on the fortifications and defenses of Charleston harbor."

In Mississippi in 1862, permission was granted the Governor to impress slaves to work in New Iberia for salt, which was becoming the Confederacy's most pressing necessity. In Texas, a thousand Negroes were offered by planters for work on the public defenses.

By 1864, the matter had passed beyond the demand for slaves as military laborers and had come to the place where the South was seriously considering and openly demanding the use of Negroes as soldiers. Distincly and inevitably, the rigor of the slave system in the South softened as war proceeded. Slavery showed in many if not all respects its best side. The harshness and the cruelty, in part, had to disappear, since there were left on the plantations mainly women and children, with only a few men, and there was a certain feeling and apprehension in the air on the part of the whites which led them to capitalize all the friendship and kindness which had existed between them and the slaves. No race could have responded to this so quickly and thoroughly as the Negroes. They felt pity and responsibility and also a certain new undercurrent of independence. Negroes were still being sold rather ostentatiously in Charleston and New Orleans, but the long lines of Virginia Negroes were not marching to the Southwest. In a certain sense, after the first few months everybody knew that slavery was done with; that no matter who won, the condition of the slave could never be the same after this disaster of war. And it was, perhaps, these considerations, more than anything else, that held the poised arm of the black man; for no one knew better than the South what a Negro crazed with cruelty and oppression and beaten back to the last stand could do to his oppressor.

The Southerners, therefore, were careful. Those who had been kind to their slaves assured them of the bad character of the Yankee and of their own good intentions.

Thus while the Negroes knew there were Abolitionists in the North, they did not know their growth, their power or their intentions and they did hear on every side that the South was overwhelmingly victorious on the battlefield. On the other hand, some of the Negroes sensed what was beginning to happen. The Negroes of the cities, the Negroes who were being hired out, the Negroes of intelligence who could read and write, all began carefully to watch the unfolding of the situation. At the first gun of Sumter, the black mass began not to move but to heave with nervous tension and watchful waiting. Even before war was declared, a movement began across the border. Just before the war large numbers of fugitive slaves and free Negroes rushed into the North. It was estimated that two thousand left North Carolina alone because of rumors of war.

When W. T. Sherman occupied Port Royal in October, 1861, he had no idea that he was beginning emancipation at one of its strategic points. On the contrary, he was very polite and said that he had no idea of interfering with slaves. In the same way, Major General Dix, on seizing two counties of Virginia, was careful to order that slavery was not to be interfered with or slaves to be received into the line. Burnside went further, and as he brought his Rhode Island regiment through Baltimore in June, he courteously returned two Negroes who tried to run away with him. They were "supposed to be slaves," although they may have been free Negroes. On the 4th of July, Colonel Pryor of Ohio delivered an address to the people of Virginia in which he repudiated the accusation that the Northern army were Abolitionists.

"I desire to assure you that the relation of master and servant as recognized in your state shall be respected. Your authority over that species of property shall not in the least be interfered with. To this end, I assure you that those under my command have peremptory orders to take up and hold any Negroes found running about the camp without passes from their masters."

Halleck in Missouri in 1862 refused to let fugitive slaves enter his lines. Burnside, Buell, Hooker, Thomas Williams and McClellan himself, all warned their soldiers against receiving slaves and most of them permitted masters to come and remove slaves found within the lines.

The constant charge of Southern newspapers, Southern politicans and their Northern sympathizers, that the war was an abolition war, met with constant and indignant denial. Loyal newspapers, orators and preachers, with few exceptions, while advocating stringent measures for putting down the Rebellion, carefully disclaimed any intention of disturbing the "peculiar institution" of the South. The Secretary of State informed foreign governments, through our ministers abroad, that this was not our purpose. President Lincoln, in his earlier messages, substantially reiterated the statement. Leading generals, on entering Southern territory, issued proclamations to the same effect. One even promised to put down any slave insurrection "with an iron hand," while others took vigorous measures to send back the fugitives who sought refuge within their lines.

"In the early years of the war, if accounts do not err, during the entire period McClellan commanded the Army of the Potomac, 'John Brown's Body' was a forbidden air among the regimental bands. The Hutchinsons were driven from Union camps for singing abolition songs, and in so far as the Northern army interested itself at all in the slavery question, it was by the use of force to return to their Southern masters fugitives seeking shelter in the Union lines. While the information they possessed, especially respecting the roads and means of communication, should have been of inestimable service to the Federals, they were not to be employed as laborers or armed as soldiers. The North avoided the appearance of a desire to raise the Negroes from the plane of chattels to the rank of human beings."

Here was no bid for the cooperation of either slaves or free Negroes. In the North, Negroes were not allowed to enlist and often refused with indignation. "Thus the weakness of the South temporarily became her strength. Her servile population, repulsed by Northern proslavery sentiment, remained at home engaged in agriculture, thus releasing her entire white population for active service in the field; while, on the other hand, the military resources of the North were necessarily diminished by the demands of labor."

It was as Frederick Douglass said in Boston in 1865, that the Civil War was begun "in the interests of slavery on both sides. The South was fighting to take slavery out of the Union, and the North fighting to keep it in the Union; the South fighting to get it beyond the limits of the United States Constitution, and the

North fighting for the old guarantees;—both despising the Negro, both insulting the Negro."

It was, therefore, at first by no means clear to most of the four million Negroes in slavery what this war might mean to them. They crouched consciously and moved silently, listening, hoping and hesitating. The watchfulness of the South was redoubled. They spread propaganda: the Yankees were not only not thinking of setting them free, but if they did anything, they would sell them into worse slavery in the West Indies. They would drive them from even the scant comfort of the plantations into the highways and purlieus. Moreover, if they tried to emancipate the slaves, they would fail because they could not do this without conquest of the South. The South was unconquerable.

The South was not slow to spread propaganda and point to the wretched condition of fugitive Negroes in order to keep the loyalty of its indispensable labor force. The Charleston *Daily Courier* said February 18, 1863: "A company of volunteers having left Fayette County for the field of action, Mr. Nance sent two Negro boys along to aid the company. Their imaginations became dazzled with the visions of Elysian fields in Yankeedom and they went to find them. But Paradise was nowhere there, and they again sighed for home. The Yanks, however, detained them and cut off their ears close to their heads. These Negroes finally made their escape and are now at home with Mr. Nance in Pickens. They are violent haters of Yankees and their adventures and experiences are a terror to Negroes of the region, who learned a lesson from their brethren whose ears are left in Lincolndom!"

The Charleston *Mercury,* May 8, 1862, said: "The Yankees are fortifying Fernandina (Florida) and have a large number of Negroes engaged on their works. Whenever the Negroes have an opportunity, they escape from their oppressors. They report that they are worked hard, get little rest and food and no pay."

The Savannah *Daily News* reports in 1862 that many stolen Negroes had been recaptured: "The Yankees had married a number of the women and were taking them home with them. I have seen some who refused to go and others who had been forced off at other times who had returned."

It was a lovely dress parade of Alphonse and Gaston until the Negro spoiled it and in a perfectly logical way. So long as the Union stood still and talked, the Negro kept quiet and worked.

The moment the Union army moved into slave territory, the Negro joined it. Despite all argument and calculation and in the face of refusals and commands, wherever the Union armies marched, appeared the fugitive slaves. It made no difference what the obstacles were, or the attitudes of the commanders. It was "like thrusting a walking stick into an anthill," says one writer. And yet the army chiefs at first tried to regard it as an exceptional and temporary matter, a thing which they could control, when as a matter of fact it was the meat and kernel of the war.

Thus as the war went on and the invading armies came on, the way suddenly cleared for the onlooking Negro, for his spokesmen in the North, and for his silent listeners in the South. Each step, thereafter, came with curious, logical and inevitable fate. First there were the fugitive slaves. Slaves had always been running away to the North, and when the North grew hostile, on to Canada. It was the safety valve that kept down the chance of insurrection in the South to the lowest point. Suddenly, now, the chance to run away not only increased, but after preliminary repulse and hesitation, there was actual encouragement.

Not that the government planned or foresaw this eventuality; on the contrary, having repeatedly declared the object of the war as the preservation of the Union and that it did not propose to fight for slaves or touch slavery, it faced a stampede of fugitive slaves.

Every step the Northern armies took then meant fugitive slaves. They crossed the Potomac, and the slaves of northern Virginia began to pour into the army and into Washington. They captured Fortress Monroe, and slaves from Virginia and even North Carolina poured into the army. They captured Port Royal, and the masters ran away leaving droves of black fugitives in the hands of the Northern army. They moved down the Mississippi Valley, and if the slaves did not rush to the army, the army marched to the slaves. They captured New Orleans, and captured a great black city and a state full of slaves.

What was to be done? They tried to send the slaves back, and even used the soldiers for recapturing them. This was all well enough as long as the war was a dress parade. But when it became real war, and slaves were captured or received, they could be used as much-needed laborers and servants by the Northern army.

This but emphasized and made clearer a truth which ought

to have been recognized from the very beginning: The Southern worker, black and white, held the key to the war; and of the two groups, the black worker raising food and raw materials held an even more strategic place than the white. This was so clear a fact that both sides should have known it. Fremont in Missouri took the logical action of freeing slaves of the enemy round about him by proclamation, and President Lincoln just as promptly repudiated what he had done. Even before that, General Butler in Virginia, commander of the Union forces at Fortress Monroe, met three slaves walking into his camp from the Confederate fortifications where they had been at work. Butler immediately declared these men "contraband of war" and put them to work in his own camp. More slaves followed, accompanied by their wives and children. The situation here was not quite so logical. Nevertheless, Butler kept the fugitives and freed them and let them do what work they could; and his action was approved by the Secretary of War.

"On May twenty-sixth, only two days after the one slave appeared before Butler, eight Negroes appeared; on the next day, forty-seven, of all ages and both sexes. Each day they continued to come by twenties, thirties and forties until by July 30th the number had reached nine hundred. In a very short while the number ran up into the thousands. The renowned Fortress took the name of the 'freedom fort' to which the blacks came by means of a 'mysterious spiritual telegraph.' "

In December, 1861, the Secretary of the Treasury, Simon Cameron, had written, printed and put into the mails his first report as Secretary of War without consultation with the President. Possibly he knew that his recommendations would not be approved, but "he recommended the general arming of Negroes, declaring that the Federals had as clear a right to employ slaves taken from the enemy as to use captured gunpowder." This report was recalled by the President by telegraph and the statements of the Secretary were modified. The incident aroused some unpleasantness in the cabinet.

The published report finally said:

"Persons held by rebels, under such laws, to service as slaves, may, however, be justly liberated from their constraint, and made more valuable in various employments, through voluntary and compensated service, than if confiscated as subjects of property."

Transforming itself suddenly from a problem of abandoned plantations and slaves captured while being used by the enemy for military purposes, the movement became a general strike against the slave system on the part of all who could find opportunity. The trickling streams of fugitives swelled to a flood. Once begun, the general strike of black and white went madly and relentlessly on like some great saga.

"Imagine, if you will, a slave population, springing from antecedent barbarism, rising up and leaving its ancient bondage, forsaking its local traditions and all the associations and attractions of the old plantation life, coming garbed in rags or in silks, with feet shod or bleeding, individually or in families and larger groups,—an army of slaves and fugitives, pushing its way irresistibly toward an army of fighting men, perpetually on the defensive and perpetually ready to attack. The arrival among us of these hordes was like the oncoming of cities. There was no plan in this exodus, no Moses to lead it. Unlettered reason or the mere inarticulate decision of instinct brought them to us. Often the slaves met prejudices against their color more bitter than any they had left behind. But their own interests were identical, they felt, with the objects of our armies; a blind terror stung them, an equally blind hope allured them, and to us they come."

"Even before the close of 1862, many thousands of blacks of all ages, ragged, with no possessions, except the bundles which they carried, had assembled at Norfolk, Hampton, Alexandria and Washington. Others, landless, homeless, helpless, in families and in multitudes, including a considerable number of wretched white people, flocked North from Tennessee, Kentucky, Arkansas and Missouri. All these were relieved in part by army rations, irregularly issued, and by volunteer societies of the North, which gained their money from churches and individuals in this country and abroad. In the spring of 1863, there were swarming crowds of Negroes and white refugees along the line of defense made between the armies of the North and South and reaching from Maryland to Virginia, along the coast from Norfolk to New Orleans. Soldiers and missionaries told of their virtues and vices, their joy and extreme suffering. The North was moved to an extraordinary degree, and endless bodies of workers and missionaries were organized and collected funds for materials.

"Rude barracks were erected at different points for the temporary shelter of the freedmen; but as soon as possible the colonies thus formed were broken up and the people encouraged to make individual contracts for labor upon neighboring plantations. In connection with the colonies, farms were cultivated which aided to meet the expenses. Hospitals were established at various points for the sick, of whom there were great numbers. The separation of families by the war, and illegitimate birth in consequence of slavery, left a great number of children practically in a state of orphanage."

This was the beginning of the swarming of the slaves, of the quiet but unswerving determination of increasing numbers no longer to work on Confederate plantations, and to seek the freedom of the Northern armies. Wherever the army marched and in spite of all obstacles came the rising tide of slaves seeking freedom. For a long time, their treatment was left largely to the discretion of the department managers; some welcomed them, some drove them away, some organized them for work. Gradually, the fugitives became organized and formed a great labor force for the army. Several thousand were employed as laborers, servants, and spies.

A special war correspondent of the New York *Tribune* writes: " 'God bless the Negroes,' say I, with earnest lips. During our entire captivity, and after our escape, they were ever our firm, brave, unflinching friends. We never made an appeal to them they did not answer. They never hesitated to do us a service at the risk even of life, and under the most trying circumstances revealed a devotion and a spirit of self-sacrifice that was heroic. The magic word 'Yankee' opened all their hearts, and elicited the loftiest virtues. They were ignorant, oppressed, enslaved; but they always cherished a simple and a beautiful faith in the cause of the Union and its ultimate triumph, and never abandoned or turned aside from a man who sought food or shelter on his way to Freedom."

This whole move was not dramatic or hysterical, rather it was like the great unbroken swell of the ocean before it dashed on the reefs. The Negroes showed no disposition to strike the one terrible blow which brought black men freedom in Haiti and which in all history has been used by all slaves and justified. There were some plans for insurrection made by Union officers:

"The plan is to induce the blacks to make a simultaneous

movement of rising, on the night of the 1st of August next, over the entire States in rebellion, to arm themselves with any and every kind of weapon that may come to hand, and commence operations by burning all the railroad and country bridges, and tear up railroad tracks, and to destroy telegraph lines, etc., and then take to the woods, swamps, or the mountains, where they may emerge as occasion may offer for provisions and for further depredations. No blood is to be shed except in self-defense. The corn will be ripe about the 1st of August and with this and hogs running in the woods, and by foraging upon the plantations by night, they can subsist. This is the plan in substance, and if we can obtain a concerted movement at the time named it will doubtless be successful."

Such plans came to naught for the simple reason that there was an easier way involving freedom with less risk.

The South preened itself on the absence of slave violence. Governor Walker of Florida said in his inaugural in 1865: "Where, in all the records of the past, does history present such an instance of steadfast devotion, unwavering attachment and constancy as was exhibited by the slaves of the South throughout the fearful contest that has just ended? The country invaded, homes desolated, the master absent in the army or forced to seek safety in flight and leave the mistress and her helpless infants unprotected, with every incitement to insubordination and instigation, to rapine and murder, no instance of insurrection, and scarcely one of voluntary desertion has been recorded."

The changes upon this theme have been rung by Southern orators many times since. The statement, of course, is not quite true. Hundreds of thousands of slaves were very evidently leaving their masters' homes and plantations. They did not wreak vengeance on unprotected women. They found an easier, more effective and more decent way to freedom. Men go wild and fight for freedom with bestial ferocity when they must—where there is no other way; but human nature does not deliberately choose blood—at least not black human nature. On the other hand, for every slave that escaped to the Union army, there were ten left on the untouched and inaccessible plantations.

Another step was logical and inevitable. The men who handled a spade for the Northern armies, the men who fed them, and as spies brought in information, could also handle a gun and

shoot. Without legal authority and in spite of it, suddenly the
Negro became a soldier. Later his services as soldier were not
only permitted but were demanded to replace the tired and
rebellious white men of the North. But as a soldier, the Negro
must be free.

The North started out with the idea of fighting the war without touching slavery. They faced the fact, after severe fighting,
that Negroes seemed a valuable asset as laborers, and they
therefore declared them "contraband of war." It was but a step
from that to attract and induce Negro labor to help the Northern armies. Slaves were urged and invited into the Northern
armies; they became military laborers and spies; not simply
military laborers, but laborers on the plantations, where the
crops went to help the Federal army or were sold North. Thus
wherever Northern armies appeared, Negro laborers came, and
the North found itself actually freeing slaves before it had the
slightest intention of doing so, indeed when it had every intention not to.

The experience of the army with the refugees and the rise of
the departments of Negro affairs were a most interesting, but
unfortunately little studied, phase of Reconstruction. Yet it
contained in a sense the key to the understanding of the whole
situation. At first, the rush of the Negroes from the plantations
came as a surprise and was variously interpreted. The easiest
thing to say was that Negroes were tired of work and wanted
to live at the expense of the government; wanted to travel and
see things and places. But in contradiction to this was the extent
of the movement and the terrible suffering of the refugees. If
they were seeking peace and quiet, they were much better off
on the plantations than trailing in the footsteps of the army or
squatting miserably in the camps. They were mistreated by the
soldiers; ridiculed; driven away, and yet they came. They increased with every campaign, and as a final gesture, they
marched with Sherman from Atlanta to the sea, and met the
refugees and abandoned human property on the Sea Islands and
the Carolina Coast.

This was not merely the desire to stop work. It was a strike
on a wide basis against the conditions of work. It was a general
strike that involved directly in the end perhaps a half million
people. They wanted to stop the economy of the plantation
system, and to do that they left the plantations. At first, the

commanders were disposed to drive them away, or to give them away, or to give them quasi-freedom and let them do as they pleased with the nothing that they possessed. This did not work. Then the commanders organized relief and afterward, work. This came to the attention of the country first in Pierce's "Ten Thousand Clients." Pierce of Boston had worked with the refugees in Virginia under Butler, provided them with food and places to live, and given them jobs and land to cultivate. He was successful. He came from there, and, in conjunction with the Treasury Department, began the work on a vaster scale at Port Royal. Here he found the key to the situation. The Negroes were willing to work and did work, but they wanted land to work, and they wanted to see and own the results of their toil. It was here and in the West and the South that a new vista opened. Here was a chance to establish an agrarian democracy in the South: peasant holders of small properties, eager to work and raise crops, amenable to suggestion and general direction. All they needed was honesty in treatment, and education. Wherever these conditions were fulfilled, the result was little less than phenomenal. This was testified to by Pierce in the Carolinas, by Butler's agents in North Carolina, by the experiment of the Sea Islands, by Grant's department of Negro affairs under Eaton, and by Banks' direction of Negro labor in Louisiana. It is astonishing how this army of striking labor furnished in time 200,000 Federal soldiers whose evident ability to fight decided the war.

General Butler went from Virginia to New Orleans to take charge of the city newly captured in April, 1862. Here was a whole city half filled with blacks and mulattoes, some of them wealthy free Negroes and soldiers who came over from the Confederate side and joined the Federals.

Perhaps the greatest and most systematic organizing of fugitives took place in New Orleans. At first, Butler had issued orders that no slaves would be received in New Orleans. Many planters were unable to make slaves work or to support them, and sent them back of the Federal lines, planning to reclaim them after the war was over. Butler emancipated these slaves in spite of the fact that he knew this was against Lincoln's policy. As the flood kept coming, he seized abandoned sugar plantations and began to work them with Negro labor for the benefit of the government.

By permission of the War Department, and under the authority of the Confiscation Act, Butler organized colonies of fugitives, and regulated employment. His brother, Colonel Butler, and others worked plantations, hiring the Negro labor. The Negroes stood at Butler's right hand during the trying time of his administration, and particularly the well-to-do free Negro group were his strongest allies. He was entertained at their tables and brought down on himself the wrath and contempt, not simply of the South, but even of the North. He received the black regiment, and kept their black officers, who never forgot him. Whatever else he might have been before the war, or proved to be afterwards, "the colored people of Louisiana under the proper sense of the good you have done to the African race in the United States, beg leave to express to you their gratitude."

From 1862 to 1865, many different systems of caring for the escaped slaves and their families in this area were tried. Butler and his successor, Banks, each sought to provide for the thousands of destitute freemen with medicine, rations and clothing. When General Banks took command, there was suffering, disease and death among the 150,000 Negroes. On January 30, 1863, he issued a general order making labor on public works and elsewhere compulsory for Negroes who had no means of support.

Just as soon, however, as Banks tried to drive the freedmen back to the plantations and have them work under a half-military slave régime, the plan failed. It failed, not because the Negroes did not want to work, but because they were striking against these particular conditions of work. When, because of wide protest, he began to look into the matter, he saw a clear way. He selected Negroes to go out and look into conditions and to report on what was needed, and they made a faithful survey. He set up a little state with its department of education, with its landholding and organized work, and after experiment it ran itself. More and more here and up the Mississippi Valley, under other commanders and agents, experiments extended and were successful.

Further up the Mississippi, a different system was begun under General Grant. Grant's army in the West occupied Grand Junction, Mississippi, by November, 1862. The usual irregular host of slaves then swarmed in from the surrounding country.

They begged for protection against recapture, and they, of course, needed food, clothing and shelter. They could not now be reenslaved through army aid, yet no provision had been made by anybody for their sustenance. A few were employed as teamsters, servants, cooks and scouts, yet it seemed as though the vast majority must be left to freeze and starve, for when the storms came with the winter months, the weather was of great severity.

Grant determined that Negroes should perform many of the camp duties ordinarily done by soldiers; that they should serve as fatigue men in the departments of the surgeon general, quartermaster, and commissary, and that they should help in building roads and earthworks. The women worked in the camp kitchens and as nurses in the hospitals. Grant said, "It was at this point where the first idea of the Freedmen's Bureau took its origin."

Grant selected as head of his Department of Negro Affairs, John Eaton, chaplain of the Twenty-Seventh Ohio Volunteers, who was soon promoted to the colonelcy of a colored regiment, and later for many years was a Commissioner of the United States Bureau of Education. He was then constituted Chief of Negro Affairs for the entire district under Grant's jurisdiction.

"I hope I may never be called on again to witness the horrible scenes I saw in those first days of the history of the freedmen in the Mississippi Valley. Assistants were hard to get, especially the kind that would do any good in our camps. A detailed soldier in each camp of a thousand people was the best that could be done. His duties were so onerous that he ended by doing nothing. . . . In reviewing the condition of the people at that time, I am not surprised at the marvelous stories told by visitors who caught an occasional glimpse of the misery and wretchedness in these camps. . . . Our efforts to do anything for these people, as they herded together in masses, when founded on any expectation that they would help themselves, often failed; they had become so completely broken down in spirit, through suffering, that it was almost impossible to arouse them.

"Their condition was appalling. There were men, women and children in every stage of disease or decrepitude, often nearly naked, with flesh torn by the terrible experiences of their escapes. Sometimes they were intelligent and eager to help themselves; often they were bewildered or stupid or possessed by the

wildest notions of what liberty might mean—expecting to exchange labor, and obedience to the will of another, for idleness
and freedom from restraint. Such ignorance and perverted notions produced a veritable moral choas. Cringing deceit, theft,
licentiousness—all the vices which slavery inevitably fosters—
were hideous companions of nakedness, famine, and disease. A
few had profited by the misfortunes of the master and were
jubilant in their unwonted ease and luxury, but these stood in
lurid contrast to the grimmer aspects of the tragedy—the
women in travail, the helplessness of childhood and of old age,
the horrors of sickness and of frequent death. Small wonder that
men paused in bewilderment and panic, foreseeing the demoralization and infection of the Union soldier and the downfall of
the Union cause."

There were new and strange problems of social contact. The
white soldiers, for the most part, were opposed to serving
Negroes in any manner, and were even unwilling to guard the
camps where they were segregated or protect them against violence. "To undertake any form of work for the contrabands, at
that time, was to be forsaken by one's friends and to pass under
a cloud."

There was, however, a clear economic basis upon which the
whole work of relief and order and subsistence could be placed.
All around Grand Junction were large crops of ungathered corn
and cotton. These were harvested and sold North and the re-
ceipts were placed to the credit of the government. The army
of fugitives were soon willing to go to work; men, women and
children. Wood was needed by the river steamers and woodcut-
ters were set at work. Eaton fixed the wages for this industry
and kept accounts with the workers. He saw to it that all of them
had sufficient food and clothing, and rough shelter was built for
them. Citizens round about who had not abandoned their plantations were allowed to hire labor on the same terms as the
government was using it. Very soon the freedmen became self-
sustaining and gave little trouble. They began to build themselves comfortable cabins, and the government constructed
hospitals for the sick. In the case of the sick and dependent, a
tax was laid on the wages of workers. At first it was thought the
laborers would object, but, on the contrary, they were perfectly
willing and the imposition of the tax compelled the government
to see that wages were promptly paid. The freedmen freely

acknowledged that they ought to assist in helping bear the burden of the poor, and were flattered by having the government ask their help. It was the reaction of a new labor group, who, for the first time in their lives, were receiving money in payment for their work. Five thousand dollars was raised by this tax for hospitals, and with this money tools and property were bought. By wholesale purchase, clothes, household goods and other articles were secured by the freedmen at a cost of one-third of what they might have paid the stores. There was a rigid system of accounts and monthly reports through army officials.

In 1864, July 5, Eaton reports: "These freedmen are now disposed of as follows: In military service as soldiers, laundresses, cooks, officers' servants, and laborers in the various staff departments, 41,150; in cities on plantations and in freemen's villages and cared for, 72,500. Of these 62,300 were entirely self-supporting—the same as any industrial class anywhere else—as planters, mechanics, barbers, hackmen,' draymen, etc., conducting enterprises on their own responsibility or working as hired laborers. The remaining 10,200 receive subsistence from the government, 3,000 of them are members of families whose heads are carrying on plantations and have under cultivation 4,000 acres of cotton. They are to pay the government for their sustenance from the first income of the crop. The other 7,200 include the paupers—that is to say, all Negroes over and under the self-supporting age, the crippled and sick in hospital, of the 113,650 and those engaged in their care. Instead of being unproductive, this class has now under cultivation 500 acres of corn, 790 acres of vegetables and 1,500 acres of cotton, besides working at wood-chopping and other industries. There are reported in the aggregate over 100,000 acres of cotton under cultivation. Of these about 7,000 acres are leased and cultivated by blacks. Some Negroes are managing as high as 300 or 400 acres."

The experiment at Davis Bend, Mississippi, was of especial interest. The place was occupied in November and December, 1864, and private interests were displaced and an interesting socialistic effort made with all the property under the control of the government. The Bend was divided into districts with Negro sheriffs and judges who were allowed to exercise authority under the general control of the military officers. Petty theft and idleness were soon reduced to a minimum and "the community

distinctly demonstrated the capacity of the Negro to take care
of himself and exercise under honest and competent direction
the functions of self-government."

When General Butler returned from Louisiana and resumed
command in Virginia and North Carolina, he established there
a Department of Negro Affairs, with the territory divided into
districts under superintendents and assistants. Negroes were
encouraged to buy land, build cabins and form settlements, and
a system of education was established. In North Carolina, under
Chaplain Horace James, the poor, both black and white, were
helped; the refugees were grouped in small villages and their
work systematized, and enlisted men taught in the schools,
followed by women teachers from the North. Outside of New
Bern, North Carolina, about two thousand freedmen were settled and 800 houses erected. The department at Port Royal
continued. The Negroes showed their capacity to organize labor
and even to save and employ a little capital. The government
built 21 houses for the people on Edisto Island. The carpenters
were Negroes under a Negro foreman. There was another village of improved houses near Hilton Head.

"Next as to the development of manhood: this has been
shown in the first place in the prevalent disposition to acquire
land. It did not appear upon our first introduction to these
people, and they did not seem to understand us when we used
to tell them that we wanted them to own land. But it is now an
active desire. At the recent tax sales, six out of forty-seven
plantations sold were bought by them, comprising two thousand
five hundred and ninety-five acres, sold for twenty-one hundred
and forty-five dollars. In other cases, the Negroes had authorized the superintendent to bid for them, but the land was reserved by the United States. One of the purchases was that
made by Harry, noted above. The other five were made by the
Negroes on the plantations, combining the funds they had saved
from the sale of their pigs, chickens and eggs, and from the
payments made to them for work—they then dividing off the
tract peaceably among themselves. On one of these, where Kit,
before mentioned, is the leading spirit, there are twenty-three
fieldhands. They have planted and are cultivating sixty-three
acres of cotton, fifty of corn, six of potatoes, with as many more
to be planted, four and a half of cowpeas, three of peanuts, and
one and a half of rice. These facts are most significant."

Under General Saxton in South Carolina, the Negroes began to buy land which was sold for non-payment of taxes. Saxton established regulations for the cultivation of several abandoned Sea Islands and appointed local superintendents.

"By the payment of moderate wages, and just and fair dealing with them, I produced for the government over a half million dollars' worth of cotton, besides a large amount of food beyond the needs of the laborers. These island lands were cultivated in this way for two years, 1862 and 1863, under my supervision, and during that time I had about 15,000 colored freedmen of all ages in my charge. About 9,000 of these were engaged on productive labor which relieved the government of the support of all except newly-arrived refugees from the enemy's lines and the old and infirm who had no relations to depend upon. The increase of industry and thrift of the freedmen was illustrated by their conduct in South Carolina before the organization of the Freedmen's Bureau by the decreasing government expenditure for their support. The expense in the department of the South in 1863 was $41,544, but the monthly expense of that year was steadily reduced, until in December it was less than $1,000."[14]

Into this fairly successful land and labor control was precipitated a vast and unexpected flood of refugees from previously untouched strongholds of slavery. Sherman made his march to the sea from Atlanta, cutting the cotton kingdom in two as Grant had invaded it along the Mississippi.

"The first intimation given me that many of the freedmen would be brought hither from Savannah came in the form of a request from the General that I would 'call at once to plan the reception of seven hundred who would be at the wharf in an hour.' This was Christmas day, and at 4 P.M., we had seven hundred—mainly women, old men and children before us. A canvass since made shows that half of them had traveled from Macon, Atlanta and even Chattanooga. They were all utterly destitute of blankets, stockings or shoes; and among the seven hundred there were not fifty articles in the shape of pots or kettles, or other utensils for cooking, no axes, very few coverings for many heads, and children wrapped in the only article

[14] *Testimony Before Reconstruction Committee,* February 21, 1866, Part II, p. 221.

not worn in some form by the parents." Frantic appeals went out for the mass of Negro refugees who followed him.

A few days after Sherman entered Savannah, Secretary of War Stanton came in person from Washington. He examined the condition of the liberated Negroes found in that city. He assembled twenty of those who were deemed their leaders. Among them were barbers, pilots and sailors, some ministers, and others who had been overseers on cotton and rice plantations. Mr. Stanton and General Sherman gave them a hearing.

As a result of this investigation into the perplexing problems as to what to do with the growing masses of unemployed Negroes and their families, General Sherman issued his epoch-making Sea Island Circular, January 18, 1865. In this paper, the islands from Charleston south, the abandoned rice fields along the rivers for thirty miles back from the sea and the country bordering the St. John's River, Florida, were reserved for the settlement of the Negroes made free by the acts of war and the Proclamation of the President.

General Rufus Saxton was appointed Inspector of Settlements and Plantations and was required to make proper allotments and give possessory titles and defend them until Congress should confirm his actions. It was a bold move. Thousands of Negro families were distributed under this circular, and the freed people regarded themselves for more than six months as in permanent possession of these abandoned lands. Taxes on the freedmen furnished most of the funds to run these first experiments. On all plantations, whether owned or leased, where freedmen were employed, a tax of one cent per pound on cotton and a proportional amount on all other products was to be collected as a contribution in support of the helpless among the freed people. A similar tax, varying with the value of the property, was levied by the government upon all leased plantations in lieu of rent.

Saxton testified: "General Shermans' Special Field Order No. 15 ordered their colonization on forty-acre tracts, and in accordance with which it is estimated some forty thousand were provided with homes. Public meetings were held, and every exertion used by those whose duty it was to execute this order to encourage emigration to the Sea Islands, and the faith of the government was solemnly pledged to maintain them in possession. The greatest success attended the experiment, and although the planting season was very far advanced before the transportation to carry the colonists to the Sea Islands could be obtained, and the people were destitute of animals and had but few agricultural implements and the greatest difficulty in procuring seeds, yet they went out, worked with energy and diligence to clear up the ground run to waste by three years' neglect; and thousands of acres were planted and provisions enough were raised for those who were located in season to plant, besides a large amount of sea island cotton for market. The seizure of some 549,000 acres of abandoned land, in accordance with the act of Congress and orders from the head of the bureau for the freedman and refugees, still further strengthened these ignorant people in the conviction that they were to have the lands of their late masters; and, with the other reasons before stated, caused a great unwillingness on the part of the freedmen to make any contracts whatever. But this refusal arises from no desire on their part to avoid labor, but from the causes above stated. . . .

"To test the question of their forethought and prove that some of the race at least thought of the future, I established in October, 1864, a savings bank for the freedmen of Beaufort district and vicinity. More than $240,000 had been deposited in this bank by freedmen since its establishment. I consider that the industrial problem has been satisfactorily solved at Port Royal, and that, in common with other races, the Negro has industry, prudence, forethought, and ability to calculate results. Many of them have managed plantations for themselves, and show an industry and sagacity that will compare favorably in their results—making due allowances—with those of white men."

Eventually, General Saxton settled nearly 30,000 Negroes on the Sea Islands and adjacent plantations and 17,000 were self-supporting within a year. While 12,000 or 13,000 were still receiving rations, it was distinctly understood that they and their farms would be held responsible for the payment. In other such cases, the government had found that such a debt was a "safe and short one."

Negroes worked fewer hours and had more time for self-expression. Exports were less than during slavery. At that time the Negroes were mere machines run with as little loss as possible to the single end of making money for their masters. Now, as it was in the West Indies, emancipation had enlarged the Negro's purchasing power, but instead of producing solely for export, he was producing to consume. His standard of living was rising.

Along with this work of the army, the Treasury Department of the United States Government was bestirring itself. The Secretary of the Treasury, Salmon P. Chase, early in 1862, had his attention called to the accumulation of cotton on the abandoned Sea Islands and plantations, and was sure there was an opportunity to raise more. He, therefore, began the organization of freedmen for cotton raising, and his successor, William Pitt Fessenden, inaugurated more extensive plans for the freedmen in all parts of the South, appointing agents and organizing freedmen's home colonies.

On June 7, 1862, Congress held portions of the states in rebellion responsible for a direct tax upon the lands of the nation, and in addition Congress passed an act authorizing the Secretary of the Treasury to appoint special agents to take charge of captured and abandoned property. Military officers turned over to the Treasury Department such property, and the plantations around Port Royal and Beaufort were disposed of at tax sales. Some were purchased by Negroes, but the greater number went to Northerners. In the same way in North Carolina, some turpentine farms were let to Negroes, who managed them, or to whites who employed Negroes. In 1863, September 11, the whole Southern region was divided by the Treasury Department into five special agencies, each with a supervising agent for the supervision of abandoned property and labor.

Early in 1863, General Lorenzo Thomas, the adjutant general of the army, was organizing colored troops along the Mississippi River. After consulting various treasury agents and department commanders, including General Grant, and having also the approval of Mr. Lincoln, he issued from Milliken's Bend, Louisiana, April 15th, a lengthy series of instruction covering the territory bordering the Mississippi and including all the inhabitants.

He appointed three commissioners, Messrs. Field, Shickle and Livermore, to lease plantations and care for the employees. He sought to encourage private enterprises instead of government colonies; but he fixed the wages of able-bodied men over fifteen years of age at $7 per month, for able-bodied women $5 per month, for children twelve to fifteen years, half price. He laid a tax for revenue of $2 per 400 pounds on cotton, and five cents per bushel on corn and potatoes.

This plan naturally did not work well, for the lessees of plantations proved to be for the most part adventurers and speculators. Of course such men took advantage of the ignorant people. The commissioners themselves seem to have done more for the lessees than for the laborers; and, in fact, the wages were from the beginning so fixed as to benefit and enrich the employer. Two dollars per month was charged against each of the employed, ostensibly for medical attendance, but to most plantations thus leased no physician or medicine ever came, and there were other attendant cruelties which avarice contrived.

On fifteen plantations leased by the Negroes themselves in this region there was notable success, and also a few other instances in which humanity and good sense reigned; the contracts were generally able to lay by small gains. This plantation arrangement along the Mississippi under the commissioners as well as the management of numerous infirmary camps passed, about the close of 1863, from the War to the Treasury Department. A new commission or agency with Mr. W. P. Mellon of the treasury at the head established more careful and complete regulations than those of General Thomas. This time it was done decidedly in the interest of the laborers.

July 2, 1864, an Act of Congress authorized the treasury agents to seize and lease for one year all captured and abandoned estates and to provide for the welfare of former slaves. Property was declared abandoned when the lawful owner was opposed to paying the revenue. The Secretary of the Treasury, Fessenden, therefore issued a new series of regulations relating to freedmen and abandoned property. The rebellious States were divided into seven districts, with a general agent and special agents. Certain tracts of land in each district were set apart for the exclusive use and working of the freedmen. These reservations were called Freedmen Labor Colonies, and were under the direction of the superintendents. Schools were established, both in the Home Colonies and in the labor colonies. This new system went into operation the winter of 1864-1865, and worked well along the Atlantic Coast and Mississippi Valley. In the Department of the Gulf, however, there was discord between the treasury agents and the military authorities, in many cases, became corrupt, but these regulations remained in force until the Freedmen's Bureau was organized in 1865.

By 1865, there was strong testimony as to the efficiency of the Negro worker. "The question of the freedmen being self-supporting no longer agitated the minds of careful observers."

Carl Schurz felt warranted in 1865 in asserting: "Many freedmen—not single individuals, but whole 'plantation gangs'—are working well; others are not. The difference in their efficiency coincides in a great measure with a certain difference in the conditions under which they live. The conclusion lies near, that if the conditions under which they work well become general, their efficiency as free laborers will become general also, aside from individual exceptions. Certain it is, that by far the larger portion of the work done in the South is done by freedmen!"

Whitelaw Reid said in 1865: "Whoever has read what I have written about the cotton fields of St. Helena will need no assurance that another cardinal sin of the slave, his laziness—'inborn and ineradicable,' as we were always told by his masters—is likewise disappearing under the stimulus of freedom and necessity. Dishonesty and indolence, then, were the creation of slavery, not the necessary and constitutional faults of the Negro character."

"Returning from St. Helena in 1865, Doctor Richard Fuller was asked what he thought of the experiment of free labor, as exhibited among his former slaves, and how it contrasted with the old order of things. 'I never saw St. Helena look so well,' was his instant reply; 'never saw as much land there under cultivation—never saw the same general evidences of prosperity, and never saw Negroes themselves appearing so well or so contented.' Others noticed, however, that the islands about Beaufort were in a better condition than those nearer the encampments of the United States soldiers. Wherever poultry could be profitably peddled in the camps, cotton had not been grown, nor had the Negroes developed, so readily, into industrious and orderly communities." Similar testimony came from the Mississippi Valley and the West, and from Border States like Virginia and North Carolina.

To the aid of the government, and even before the government took definite organized hold, came religious and benevolent organizations. The first was the American Missionary Association, which grew out of the organization for the defense of the Negroes who rebelled and captured the slave ship *Amis-*

tad and brought it into Connecticut in 1837. When this association heard from Butler and Pierce, it responded promptly and had several representatives at Hampton and South Carolina before the end of the year 1861. They extended their work in 1862-1863, establishing missions down the Atlantic Coast, and in Missouri, and along the Mississippi. By 1864, they had reached the Negroes in nearly all the Southern States. The reports of Pierce, Dupont and Sherman aroused the whole North. Churches and missionary societies responded. The Friends contributed. The work of the Northern benevolent societies began to be felt, and money, clothing and, finally, men and women as helpers and teachers came to the various centers.

"The scope of our work was greatly enlarged by the arrival of white refugees—a movement which later assumed very large proportions. As time went on Cairo (Illinois) became the center of our activities in this direction. It was the most northerly of any of our camps, and served as the portal through which thousands of poor whites and Negroes were sent into the loyal states as fast as opportunities offered for providing them with homes and employment. Many of these became permanent residents; some were sent home by Union soldiers to carry on the work in the shop or on the farm which the war had interrupted. It became necessary to have a superintendent at Cairo and facilities for organizing the bands of refugees who were sent North by the army. There was an increasing demand for work."

New organizations arose, and an educational commission was organized in Boston, suggested by the reports of Pierce, and worked chiefly in South Carolina. Afterward, it became the New England Freedmen's Aid Society and worked in all the Southern States. February 22, 1862, the National Freedmen's Relief Association was formed in New York City. During the first year, it worked on the Atlantic Coast, and then broadened to the whole South. The Port Royal Relief Committee of Philadelphia, later known as the Pennsylvania Freedmen's Relief Association, the National Freedmen's Relief Association of the District of Columbia, the Contraband Relief Association of Cincinnati, afterward called the Western Freedmen's Commission, the Women's Aid Association of Philadelphia and the Friends' Associations, all arose and worked. The number increased and extended into the Northwest. The Christian Commission, organized for the benefit of soldiers, turned its attention to Negroes.

In England, at Manchester and London, were Freedmen's Aid Societies which raised funds; and funds were received from France and Ireland.

Naturally, there was much rivalry and duplication of work. A union of effort was suggested in 1862 by the Secretary of the Treasury and accomplished March 22, 1865, when the American Freedmen's Union Commission was incorporated, with branches in the chief cities. Among its officers were Chief Justice Chase and William Lloyd Garrison. In 1861, two large voluntary organizations to reduce suffering and mortality among the freedmen were formed. The Western Sanitary Commission at St. Louis, and the United States Sanitary Commission at Washington, with branches in leading cities, then began to relieve the distress of the freedmen. Hospitals were improved, supplies distributed, and Yeatman's plan for labor devised. Destitute white refugees were helped to a large extent. But even then, all of these efforts reached but a small portion of the mass of people freed from slavery.

Late in 1863, President Yeatman of the Western Sanitary Commission visited the freedmen in the Mississippi Valley. He saw the abuses of the leasing system and suggested a plan for organizing free labor and leasing plantations. It provided for a bureau established by the government to take charge of leasing land, to secure justice and freedom to the freedmen; hospital farms and homes for the young and aged were to be established; schools with compulsory attendance were to be opened. Yeatman accompanied Mellon, the agent of the department, to Vicksburg in order to inaugurate the plan and carry it into effect. His plan was adopted by Mellon, and was, on the whole, the most satisfactory.

Thus, confusion and lack of system were the natural result of the general strike. Yet, the Negroes had accomplished their first aim in those parts of the South dominated by the Federal army. They had largely escaped from the plantation discipline, were receiving wages as free laborers, and had protection from violence and justice in some sort of court.

About 20,000 of them were in the District of Columbia; 100,-000 in Virginia, 50,000 in North Carolina; 50,000 in South Carolina, and as many more each in Georgia and Louisiana. The Valley of the Mississippi was filled with settlers under the Treasury Department and the army. Here were nearly 500,000 former slaves. But there were 3,500,000 more. These Negroes needed only the assurance that they would be freed and the opportunity of joining the Northern army. In larger and larger numbers, they filtered into the armies of the North. And in just the proportion that the Northern armies became in earnest, and proposed actually to force the South to stay in the Union, and not to make simply a demonstration, in just such proportion the Negroes became valuable as laborers, and doubly valuable as withdrawing labor from the South. After the first foolish year when the South woke up to the fact that there was going to be a real, long war, and the North realized just what war meant in blood and money, the whole relation of the North to the Negro and the Negro to the North changed.

The position of the Negro was strategic. His was the only appeal which would bring sympathy from Europe, despite strong economic bonds with the South, and prevent recognition of a Southern nation built on slavery. The free Negroes in the North, together with the Abolitionists, were clamoring. To them a war against the South simply had to be a war against slavery. Gradually, Abolitionists no longer needed fear the mob. Disgruntled leaders of church and state began to talk of freedom. Slowly but surely an economic dispute and a political test of strength took on the aspects of a great moral crusade.

The Negro became in the first year contraband of war; that is, property belonging to the enemy and valuable to the invader. And in addition to that, he became, as the South quickly saw, the key to Southern resistance. Either these four million laborers remained quietly at work to raise food for the fighters, or the fighter starved. Simultaneously, when the dream of the North for man-power produced riots, the only additional troops that the North could depend on were 200,000 Negroes, for without them, as Lincoln said, the North could not have won the war.

But this slow, stubborn mutiny of the Negro slave was not merely a matter of 200,000 black soldiers and perhaps 300,000 other black laborers, servants, spies and helpers. Back of this half million stood 3½ million more. Without their labor the South would starve. With arms in their hands, Negroes would form a fighting force which could replace every single Northern white soldier fighting listlessly and against his will with a black man fighting for freedom.

This action of the slaves was followed by the disaffection of the poor whites. So long as the planters' war seemed successful, "there was little active opposition by the poorer whites; but the conscription and other burdens to support a slaveowners' war became very severe; the whites not interested in that cause became recalcitrant, some went into active opposition; and at last it was more desertion and disunion than anything else that brought about the final overthrow."

Phillips says that white mechanics in 1861 demanded that the permanent Confederate Constitution exclude Negroes from employment "except agricultural domestic service, so as to reserve the trades for white artisans." Beyond this, of course, was a more subtle reason that, as the years went on, very carefully developed and encouraged for a time the racial aspect of slavery. Before the war, there had been intermingling of white and black blood and some white planters openly recognized their colored sons, daughters and cousins and took them under their special protection. As slavery hardened, the racial basis was emphasized; but it was not until war time that it became the fashion to pat the disfranchised poor white man on the back and tell him after all he was white and that he and the planters had a common object in keeping the white man superior. This virus increased bitterness and relentless hatred, and after the war it became a chief ingredient in the division of the working class in the Southern States.

At the same time during the war even the race argument did not keep the Southern fighters from noticing with anger that the big slaveholders were escaping military service; that it was a "rich man's war and the poor man's fight." The exemption of owners of twenty Negroes from military service especially rankled; and the wholesale withdrawal of the slaveholding class from actual fighting which this rule made possible, gave rise to intense and growing dissatisfaction.

It was necessary during these critical times to insist more than usual that slavery was a fine thing for the poor white. Except for slavery, it was said: " 'The poor would occupy the position in society that the slaves do—as the poor in the North and in Europe do,' for there must be a menial class in society and in 'every civilized country on the globe, besides the Confederate states, the poor are the inferiors and menials of the rich.' Slavery was a greater blessing to the non-slaveholding poor than to the owners of slaves, and since it gave the poor a start in society that it would take them generations to work out, they should thank God for it and fight and die for it as they would for their 'own liberty and the dearest birthright of freemen.' "

But the poor whites were losing faith. They saw that poverty was fighting the war, not wealth.

"Those who could stay out of the army under color of the law were likely to be advocates of a more numerous and powerful army. . . . Not so with many of those who were not favored with position and wealth. They grudgingly took up arms and condemned the law which had snatched them from their homes. . . . The only difference was the circumstance of position and wealth, and perhaps these were just the things that had caused heartburnings in more peaceful times.

"The sentiments of thousands in the upland countries, who had little interest in the war and who were not accustomed to rigid centralized control, was probably well expressed in the following epistle addressed to President Davis by a conscript. . . .

". . . 'It is with intense and multifariously proud satisfaction that he [the conscript] gazes for the last time upon our holy flag —that symbol and sign of an adored trinity, cotton, niggers and chivalry.' "

This attitude of the poor whites had in it as much fear and jealousy of Negroes as disaffection with slave barons. Economic rivalry with blacks became a new and living threat as the blacks became laborers and soldiers in a conquering Northern army. If the Negro was to be free where would the poor white be? Why should he fight against the blacks and his victorious friends? The poor white not only began to desert and run away; but thousands followed the Negro into the Northern camps.

Meantime, with perplexed and laggard steps, the United States Government followed the footsteps of the black slave. It made no difference how much Abraham Lincoln might protest that this was not a war against slavery, or ask General McDowell "if it would not be well to allow the armies to bring back those fugitive slaves which have crossed the Potomac with our troops" (a communication which was marked "secret"). It was in vain that Lincoln rushed entreaties and then commands to Frémont in Missouri, not to emancipate the slaves of rebels, and then had to hasten similar orders to Hunter in South Carolina. The slave, despite every effort, was becoming the center of war. Lincoln, with his uncanny insight, began to see it. He began to talk about compensation for emancipated slaves, and Congress, following almost too quickly, passed the Confiscation Act in August, 1861, freeing slaves which were actually used in war by the enemy. Lincoln then suggested that provision be made for colonization of such slaves. He simply could not envisage free Negroes in the United States. What would become of them? What would they do? Meantime, the slave kept looming. New Orleans was captured and the whole black population of Louisiana began streaming toward it. When Vicksburg fell, the center of perhaps the vastest Negro population in North America was tapped. They rushed into the Union lines. Still Lincoln held off and watched symptoms. Greeley's "Prayer of Twenty Millions" received the curt answer, less than a year before Emancipation, that the war was not to abolish slavery, and if Lincoln could hold the country together and keep slavery, he would do it.

But he could not, and he had no sooner said this than he began to realize that he could not. In June, 1862, slavery was abolished in the territories. Compensation with possible colonization was planned for the District of Columbia. Representatives and Senators from the Border States were brought together to talk about extending this plan to their states, but they hesitated.

In August, Lincoln faced the truth, front forward; and that truth was not simply that Negroes ought to be free; it was that thousands of them were already free, and that either the power which slaves put into the hands of the South was to be taken from it or the North could not win the war. Either the Negro was to be allowed to fight, or the draft itself would not bring enough white men into the army to keep up the war.

More than that, unless the North faced the world with the moral strength of declaring openly that they were fighting for the emancipation of slaves, they would probably find that the world would recognize the South as a separate nation; that ports would be opened; that trade would begin, and that despite all the military advantage of the North, the war would be lost.

In August, 1862, Lincoln discussed Emancipation as a military measure; in September, he issued his preliminary proclamation; on January 1, 1863, he declared that the slaves of all persons in rebellion were "henceforward and forever free."

The guns at Sumter, the marching armies, the fugitive slaves, the fugitives as "contrabands," spies, servants and laborers; the Negro as soldier, as citizen, as voter—these steps came from

1861 to 1868 with regular beat that was almost rhythmic. It was the price of the disaster of war, and it was a price that few Americans at first dreamed of paying or wanted to pay. The North was not Abolitionist. It was overwhelmingly in favor of Negro slavery, so long as this did not interfere with Northern moneymaking. But, on the other hand, there was a minority of the North who hated slavery with perfect hatred; who wanted no union with slaveholders; who fought for freedom and treated Negroes as men. As the Abolition-democracy gained in prestige and power, they appeared as prophets, and led by statesmen, they began to guide the nation out of the morass into which it had fallen. They and their black friends and the new freedmen became gradually the leaders of a Reconstruction of Democracy in the United States, while marching millions sang the noblest war-song of the ages to the tune of "John Brown's Body":

Mine eyes have seen the glory of the coming of the Lord,
He is trampling out the vintage where the grapes of wrath are stored,
He hath loosed the fateful lightning of his terrible swift sword,
His Truth is marching on!

Black Folk: Then and Now *was Du Bois' second work on Africa. It incorporates much of his first work,* The Negro, *but with the introduction of new material it becomes a new and separate work. It is also better written than the previous volume.*
The selection here is the seventh chapter, "The Trade in Men."

(*Black Folk: Then and Now,* Henry Holt and Company, New York, 1939, pp. 126-44)

THE TRADE IN MEN

The new thing in the Renaissance was not simply freedom of spirit and body, but a new freedom to destroy freedom; freedom for eager merchants to exploit labor; freedom for white men to make black slaves. The ancient world knew slaves and knew them well; but they were slaves who worked in private and personal service, or in public service like the building of pyramids and making of roads. When such slaves made goods, the goods made them free because men knew the worker and the value of his work and treated him accordingly. But when, in the later fifteenth century, there came slaves, and mainly black slaves, they performed an indirect service. That service became for the most part not personal but labor which made crops, and crops which sold widely in unknown places and in the end promised vaster personal services than previous laborers could directly give.

This then was not mere labor but capitalized labor; labor transmitted to goods and back to services; and the slaves were not laborers of the older sort but a kind of capital goods; and capital, whether in labor or in goods, in men or in crops, was impersonal, inhuman, and a dumb means to mighty ends.

Immediately black slaves became not men but things; and were valued as things are valued, by the demand and supply of their labor force as represented by their bodies. They belonged, it happened, to a race apart, unknown, unfamiliar, because the available supply of people of that race was for the moment cheaper; because religious feuds and political conquest in Africa rendered masses of men homeless and defenseless, while state-building in feudal Europe conserved and protected the peasants. Hence arose a doctrine of race based really on economic gain but frantically rationalized in every possible direction. The ancient world knew no races; only families, clans, nations; and degrees and contrasts of culture. The medieval world evolved an ideal of personal worth and freedom for wide groups of men and a dawning belief in humanity as such. Suddenly comes America; the sale of men as goods in Africa; the crops these goodsmen grew; the revolution in industry and commerce, in manufacture and transport; in trade and transformation of goods for magnificent service and power. "The Commercial Revolution of the sixteenth century through the opening of new trade routes to India and America, the development of world markets, and the increased output of silver from the German, Austrian and Mexican mines, made possible the productive use of capital which had heretofore been employed chiefly in military operations, and which resulted in its rapid increase. Great companies flourished and a new class of wealthy merchants arose to vie in luxury not only with the great landed proprietors but even with princes and kings. Many parallels are to be found between this and the Industrial Revolution three centuries later."

It was not a mere case of parallelism but of cause and effect: the African slave trade of the sixteenth and seventeenth centuries gave birth to the Industrial Revolution of the eighteenth and nineteenth. The cry for the freedom of man's spirit became a shriek for freedom in trade and profit. The rise and expansion of the liberal spirit were arrested and diverted by the theory of race, so that black men became black devils or imbeciles to be consumed like cotton and sugar and tobacco, so as to make whiter and nobler men happier.

There are two reasons why the history of Africa is peculiar. Color of skin is not one that was regarded as important before the eighteenth century. "I am black but comely, O ye daughters of Jerusalem," cries the old Hebrew love song. Cultural backwardness was no reason—Africa, as compared with Europe, Asia, and America, was not backward before the seventeenth century. It was different, because its problems were different. At times Africa was in advance of the world. But *climate:* hot sun and flooding rains made Africa a land of desert, jungle, and disease, where culture could indeed start even earlier than in ice-bound Europe, but where, unaided by recent discoveries of science, its survival and advance was a hard fight. And finally, and above all, beginning with the fifteenth century and culminating in the eighteenth and nineteenth, *mankind in Africa became goods*—became merchandise, became even real estate. Men were bought and sold for private profit and on that profit Europe, by the use of every device of modern science and technique, began to dominate the world.

How did Africans become goods? Why did they submit? Why did the white world fight and scheme and steal to own them? Negroes were physically no weaker than others, if as weak; they were no more submissive. Slavery as an institution is as old as humanity; but never before the Renaissance was the wealth and well-being of so many powerful and intelligent men made squarely dependent not on labor itself but on the buying of labor power. And never before nor since have so many million workers been so helpless before the mass might and concentrated power of greed, helped on by that Industrial Revolution which black slavery began in the sixteenth century and helped to culmination in the nineteenth.

A new and masterful control of the forces of nature evoked a Frankenstein, which Christianity could not guide. But the Renaissance also gave birth to an idea of individual freedom in Europe and emphasized the Christian ideal of the worth of the common man. The new industry, therefore, which was as eager to buy and sell white labor as black, was canalized off toward the slavery of blacks, because the beginnings of the democratic ideal acted so as to protect the white workers. To dam this philanthropy and keep it from flooding into black slavery, the theory of the innate and eternal inferiority of black folk was invented and diffused. It was not until the nineteenth century that the floods of human sympathy began to burst through this artificial protection of slavery and in the abolition movement start to free the black worker.

Fortunately, as Gobineau rationalized this subjection of men, Marx saw the virus of labor exploitation, of labor regarded and treated as goods, poisoning Europe. He saw the social revolution; revolution in ideas which traffic in labor force for power and personal enjoyment brought; and he saw this becoming the object of that very industrial revolution to which black slavery gave birth. Freedom then became freedom to enslave all working classes and soon the emancipation of the new wage slaves, arising out of the hell of the Industrial Revolution, was hindered by chattel slavery and then men began dimly to see slavery as it really was.

Then chattel slavery of black folk fell, but immediately and in its very falling it was rebuilt on African soil, in the image and pattern of European wage slavery of the eighteenth and nineteenth centuries, which at the time was yielding before a new labor movement. The abolitionists, however, did not realize where the real difference between white and black workers had entered. Initially the goods which the white workers made had made them free; because they began to get their share; but the goods which black slaves made did not make them free. It long kept them slaves with a minimum share, because these workers were isolated in far and wild America. The eaters and wearers and smokers of their crops, even the owners of their crops and bodies, did not see them working or know their misery or realize the injustice of their economic situation. They were workers isolated from the consumer and consumers bargained only with those who owned the fruit of their stolen toil, often fine, honest, educated men.

Those then who in the dying nineteenth century and dawning twentieth saw the gleam of the new freedom were too busy to realize how land monopoly and wage slavery and forced labor in present Africa were threatening Europe of the twentieth century, re-establishing the worst aspects of the factory system and dehumanizing capital in the world, at the time when the system was diligently attacked in cultured lands. They did not see that here was the cause of that new blossoming of world wars which instead of being wars of personal enmity, of dynastic ambition, or of national defense, became wars for income and income on so vast a scale that its realization meant the enslavement of the majority of men. They therefore did not finish the task, and today in the twentieth century, as the white worker struggles toward a democratization of industry, there is the same damming and curtailment of human sympathy to keep the movement from touching workers of the darker races. On their exploitation is being built a new fascist capitalism. Hence the significance of that slave trade which we now study.

Greece and Rome had their chief supplies of slaves from Europe and Asia. Egypt enslaved races of all colors, and if there were more blacks than others among her slaves, there were also more blacks among her nobles and Pharaohs, and both facts are explained by her racial origin and geographical position. The fall of Rome led to a cessation of the slave trade, but after a long interval came the white slave trade of the Saracens and Moors, and finally the modern trade in Negroes.

Slavery as it exists universally among primitive people is a system whereby captives in war are put to tasks about the homes and in the fields, thus releasing the warriors for systematic fighting and the women for leisure. Such slavery has been common among all people and was widespread in Africa. The relative number of African slaves under these conditions varied according to tribe and locality, but usually the labor was not hard; and slaves were recognized members of the family and might and did often rise to high position in the tribe.

Remembering that in the fifteenth century there was no great disparity between the civilization of Negroland and that of Europe, what made the striking difference in subsequent devel-

opment? European civilization, cut off by physical barriers from
further incursions of barbaric races, settled more and more to
systematic industry and to the domination of one religion; African culture and industry were not only threatened by powerful
African barbarians from the west and central regions of the
continent, but also by invading Arabs with a new religion
precipitating from the eleventh to the sixteenth centuries a
devastating duel of cultures and faiths.

When, therefore, a demand for workmen arose in America,
European exportation was limited by unity of religious ties and
economic stability. African exportation was encouraged not
simply by the Christian attitude toward heathen, but also by the
Moslem enmity toward the unconverted. Two great modern
religions, therefore, agreed at least in the policy of enslaving
heathen blacks; while the conquest of Egypt, the overthrow of
the black Askias by the Moors at Tondibi, brought economic
chaos among the advanced Negro peoples. Finally the duel
between Islam and Fetish left West Africa naked to the slave-
trader.

The modern slave trade began with the Mohammedan conquests in Africa, when heathen Negroes were seized to supply
the harems, and as soldiers and servants. They were bought
from the masters and seized in war, until the growing wealth
and luxury of the conquerors demanded larger numbers. Then
Negroes from the Egyptian Sudan, Abyssinia, and Zanzibar
began to pass into Arabia, Persia, and India in increased numbers. As Negro kingdoms and tribes rose to power they found
the slave trade lucrative and natural, since the raids in which
slaves were captured were ordinary inter-tribal wars. It was not
until the eighteenth and nineteenth centuries that the demand
for slaves made slaves the object, and not the incident, of African wars.

There was, however, between the Mohammedan and American slave trade one fundamental difference which has not
heretofore been stressed. The demand for slaves in Mohammedan countries was to a large extent a luxury demand. Black
slaves were imported as soldiers and servants or as porters of
gold and ivory rather than industrial workers. The demand,
therefore, was limited by the wealth of a leisure class or the
ambitions of conquest and not by the prospect of gain on the
part of a commercial class. Even where the idle rich did not
support slavery in Africa, other conditions favored its continu-

ance, as Cooley points out, when he speaks of the desert as a cause of the African slave trade.

"It is impossible to deny the advancement of civilization in that zone of the African continent which has formed the field of our inquiry. Yet barbarism is there supported by natural circumstances with which it is vain to think of coping. It may be doubted whether, if mankind had inhabited the earth only in populous and adjoining communities, slavery would have ever existed. The Desert, if it be not absolutely the root of the evil, has, at least, been from the earliest times the great nursery of slave hunters. The demoralization of the towns on the southern borders of the desert has been pointed out, and if the vast extent be considered of the region in which man has no riches but slaves, no enjoyment but slaves, no article of trade but slaves, and where the hearts of wandering thousands are closed against pity by the falling misery of life, it will be difficult to resist the conviction that the solid buttress on which slavery rests in Africa, is—The Desert."

In Mohammedan countries there were gleams of hope in slavery. In fiction and in truth the black slave had a chance. Once converted to Islam, he became a brother to the best, and the brotherhood of the faith was not the sort of idle lie that Christian slave masters made it. In Arabia black leaders arose like Antar; in India black slaves carved out principalities where their descendants still rule.

Some Negro slaves were brought to Europe by the Spaniards in the fourteenth century, and a small trade was continued by the Portuguese, who conquered territory from the "tawny" Moors of North Africa in the early fifteenth century. Later, after their severe repulse at Al Kasr Al Kebir, the Portuguese swept farther down the West Coast in quest of trade with Negroland, a new route to India and the realm of Prester John. As early as 1441, they reached the River of Gold, and their story is that their leader seized certain free Moors and the next year exchanged them for ten black slaves, a target of hide, ostrich eggs, and some gold dust. The trade was easily justified on the ground that the Moors were Mohammedans and refused to be converted to Christianity, while heathen Negroes would be better subjects for conversion and stronger laborers.

In the next few years a small number of Negroes continued to be imported into Spain and Portugal as servants. We find, for instance, in 1474, that Negro slaves were common in Seville.

There is a letter from Ferdinand and Isabella in the year 1474 to a celebrated Negro, Juan de Valladolid, commonly called the "Negro Count" (El Conde Negro), nominating him to the office of "mayoral of the Negroes" in Seville. The slaves were apparently treated kindly, allowed to keep their own dances and festivals, and to have their own chief, who represented them in the courts, as against their own masters, and settled their private quarrels.

In Portugal, "the decline of the population, in general, and the labor supply, in particular, was especially felt in the southern provinces, which were largely stripped of population. This resulted in the establishment there of a new industrial system. The rural lands were converted into extensive estates held by absentee landlords, and worked by large armies of black bondmen recently brought from Africa. Soon the population of Algarve was almost completely Negro; and by the middle of the Sixteenth century, blacks outnumbered whites in Lisbon itself. As intermarriage between the two races went on from the beginning, within a few generations Ethiopian blood was generally diffused throughout the nation, but it was notably pronounced in the south and among the lower classes."

Between 1455 and 1492 little mention is made of slaves in the trade with Africa. Columbus is said to have suggested Negroes for America, but Ferdinand and Isabella refused. Nevertheless, by 1501, we have the first incidental mention of Negroes going to America in a declaration that Negro slaves "born in the power of Christians were to be allowed to pass to the Indies, and the officers of the royal revenue were to receive the money to be paid for their permits."

About 1504 Ovando, Governor of Spanish America, was objecting to Negro slaves and "solicited that no Negro slaves should be sent to Hispaniola, for they fled amongst the Indians and taught them bad customs, and never could be captured." Nevertheless a letter from the king to Ovando, dated Segovia, in September, 1505, says, "I will send more Negro slaves as you request; I think there may be a hundred. At each time a trustworthy person will go with them who may have some share in the gold they may collect and may promise them ease if they work well." There is a record of a hundred slaves being sent out this very year, and Diego Columbus was notified of fifty to be sent from Seville for the mines in 1510.

After this time frequent notices show that Negroes were common in the New World. When Pizarro, for instance, had been slain in Peru, his body was dragged to the cathedral by two Negroes. After the battle of Anaquito, the head of the viceroy was cut off by a Negro; and during the great earthquake in Guatemala a most remarkable figure was a gigantic Negro seen in various parts of the city. Núñez had thirty Negroes with him on the top of the Sierras, and there was rumor of an aboriginal tribe of Negroes in South America. One of the last acts of King Ferdinand was to urge that no more Negroes be sent to the West Indies, but, under Charles V, Bishop Las Casas drew up a plan of assisted migration to America and asked in 1517 the right for immigrants to import twelve Negro slaves each, in return for which the Indians were to be freed.

Las Casas, writing in his old age, owns his error: "This advice that license should be given to bring Negro slaves to these lands, the Clerigo Casas first gave, not considering the injustice with which the Portuguese take them and make them slaves; which advice, after he had apprehended the nature of the thing, he would not have given for all he had in the world. For he always held that they had been made slaves unjustly and tyrannically; for the same reason holds good of them as of the Indians."

As soon as the plan was broached, a Savoyard, Lorens de Gomenot, Governor of Bresa, obtained a monopoly of this proposed trade and shrewdly sold it to the Genoese for twenty-five thousand ducats. Other monopolies were granted in 1523, 1527, and 1528. Thus the American trade became established and gradually grew, passing successively into the hands of the Portuguese, the Dutch, the French, and the English.

At first the slave trade was of the same kind and volume as that already passing northward over the desert routes. Soon, however, the American trade developed. A strong, unchecked demand for brute labor in the West Indies and on the continent of America grew, until it culminated in the eighteenth century, when Negro slaves were crossing the Atlantic at the rate of fifty to one hundred thousand a year. This called for slave raiding on a scale that drew slaves from most parts of Africa, although centering on the West Coast, from the Senegal to St. Paul de Loanda. The Mohammedan trade continued along the East Coast and the Nile Valley.

Carleton Beals says: "This vast labor army, conscripted for developing the Americas, represented a force of many millions of man power. It was taken from all parts of Africa; from Angola and from the deep Congo, from Bonny River and the central Niger and Hausaland, from Lagos, Dahomey, Old Calabar; from Madagascar and Ethiopia and Gabun. The Portuguese, Spanish, Flemish, Dutch, English, French recruiting agents with their platoons of soldiers reached far above Stanley Pool to the Mozambique, clear south of Kunene River. Portuguese Guinea and the Gold Coast poured forth their contingents. Not only the Yoruba, Egba, Jebu, Sokoto, the Mandingo, but the Hottentots and Bushmen gave up forced levies.

"Mohammedan Negro settlements are found in Brazil, the Guianas and elsewhere. Some of them still speak and use Arabic."

Herskovits believes: "From contemporary documentary evidence that the region from which the slaves brought to the New World were derived, has limits that are less vast than stereotyped belief would have them. . . .That some, perhaps in the aggregate, even impressive numbers of slaves, came from the deep interior, or from East or South Africa, does not make less valid the historical evidence that by far the major portion of the slaves brought to the New World came from a region that comprises only a fraction of the vast bulk of the African continent."

There was thus begun in modern days a new slavery and slave trade. It was different from that of the past, because more and more it came in time to be founded on racial caste, and this caste was made the foundation of a new industrial system. For four hundred years, from 1450 to 1850, European civilization carried on a systematic trade in human beings of such tremendous proportions that the physical, economic, and moral effects are still plainly to be remarked throughout the world. To this must be added the large slave trade of Mussulman lands, which began with the seventh century and raged almost unchecked until the end of the nineteenth century.

These were not days of decadence, but a period that gave the world Shakespeare, Martin Luther, Raphael, Haroun-al-Raschid and Abraham Lincoln. It was the day of the greatest expansion of two of the world's most pretentious religions, and of the beginnings of modern organization of industry. In the midst of this advance and uplift, this slave trade and slavery spread more human misery, inculcated more disrespect for and neglect of humanity, a greater callousness to suffering, and more petty, cruel, human hatred than can well be calculated. We may excuse and palliate it, and write history so as to let men forget it; it remains a most inexcusable and despicable blot on modern history.

The Portuguese built the first slave-trading fort at Elmina, on the Gold Coast, in 1482, and extended their trade down the West Coast and up the East Coast. Under them the abominable traffic grew larger and larger, until it became far the most important in money value of all the commerce of the Zambesi basin. There could be no extension of agriculture, no mining, no progress of any kind where it was so extensively carried on.

It was the Dutch, however, who launched the overseas slave trade as a regular institution. They began their fight for freedom from Spain in 1579; in 1595, as a war measure against Spain, which at that time was dominating Portugal, they made their fight for slaves in their first vogage to Guinea. By 1621 they had captured Portugal's various slave forts on the West Coast and hey proceeded to open sixteen forts along the coast of the Gulf of Guinea. Ships sailed from Holland to Africa, got slaves in exchange for their goods, carried the slaves to the West Indies or Brazil, and returned home laden with New World produce. In 1621 the private companies trading in the west were all merged into the Dutch West India Company, which sent in four years fifteen thousand four hundred and thirty Negroes to Brazil, carried on war with Spain, supplied even the English plantations, and gradually became the great slave carrier of the day.

The commercial supremacy of the Dutch early excited the envy and emulation of the English. The Navigation Ordinance of 1651 was aimed at them, and two wars were necessary to wrest the slave trade from the Dutch and place it in the hands of the English. The final terms of peace, among other things, surrendered New Netherlands to England and opened the way for England to become henceforth the world's greatest slave trader.

The English trade began with Sir John Hawkins' voyages in 1562 and later, in which "the Jesus, our chiefe shippe," played a leading part. Desultory trade was kept up by the English until the middle of the seventeenth century, when English chartered slave-trading companies began to appear. In 1662 the "Royal Adventurers," including the king, the queen dowager, and the Duke of York, invested in the trade, and finally the Royal

African Company, which became the world's chief slave trader, was formed in 1672 and carried on a growing trade for a quarter of a century. Jamaica had finally been captured and held by Oliver Cromwell in 1655 and formed the West Indian base for the trade in men.

The chief contract for trade in Negroes was the celebrated "Asiento" or agreement of the King of Spain to the importation of slaves into Spanish domains. The Pope's Bull of Demarcation, 1493, debarred Spain from African possessions, and compelled her to contract with other nations for slaves. This contract was in the hands of the Portuguese in 1600; in 1640 the Dutch received it, and in 1701, the French. The War of the Spanish Succession was motivated not so much by royal rivalries as to bring this slave trade monopoly to England.

This Asiento of 1713 was an agreement between England and Spain by which the latter granted the former a monopoly of the Spanish colonial slave trade for thirty years; and England engaged to supply the colonies within that time with at least one hundred and forty-four thousand slaves at the rate of forty-eight hundred per year. The English counted this prize as the greatest result of the Treaty of Utrecht (1713), which ended the mighty struggle against the power of Louis XIV. The English held the monopoly for thirty-five years until the Treaty of Aix-la-Chapelle, although they had to go to war over it in 1739.

It has been shown by a recent study made at Howard University that the development of England as a great capitalist power was based directly and mainly upon the slave trade. English industry and commerce underwent a vast expansion in the early seventeenth century, based on the shipment of English goods to Africa, of African slaves to the West Indies, and of West Indian products back to England. About 1700 Bristol became an important center of the slave trade, followed by London and Liverpool. Liverpool soon overtook both Bristol and London. In 1709 it sent out one slaver of thirty tons burden; encouraged by Parliamentary subsidies which amounted to nearly a half million dollars between 1729 and 1750, the trade increased to fifty-three ships in 1751; eighty-six in 1765, and at the beginning of the nineteenth century, one hundred and eighty-five, which carried forty-nine thousand two hundred and thirteen slaves in one year. In 1764 a quarter of the shipping of Liverpool was in the African trade and Liverpool merchants conducted one half of England's trade with Africa. The value of all English goods sent to Africa was 464,000 pounds sterling of which three-fourths was of English manufactures.

This growth of Liverpool indicated the evolution of the capitalist economy in England. Liverpool did not grow because it was near the Lancaster manufacturing district, but, on the contrary, Lancaster manufacturers grew because they were near the Liverpool slave trade and largely invested in it. Thus Liverpool made Manchester.

Karl Marx emphasized the importance of slavery as the foundation of the capitalist order. He said, "Slavery is an economic category just as any other. Direct slavery is the pivot of bourgeois industry, just as are machinery and credit, etc. Without slavery there is no cotton; without cotton, there is no modern industry. It is slavery that has given value to universal commerce, and it is world trade which is the condition of large scale industry. Thus, slavery is an economic category of the first importance."

The tremendous economic stake of Great Britain in the African and West Indian trade is shown by these figures, after Bryan Edwards: from 1701 to 1787 British ships took to Africa goods to the value of twenty-three million pounds sterling. Of these, fourteen million pounds sterling were of British manufacture. Slaves, gold and other products were purchased with these goods. The slaves were transported to the West Indies. From the West Indies in the century from 1698 to 1798 Great Britain imported goods to the value of over two hundred million pounds.

The basis of the English trade, on which capitalism was erected, was Negro labor. This labor was cheap and was treated as capital goods and not as human beings. The purchase of slaves furnished a large market for British manufacture, especially textiles. African gold became the medium of exchange which rising capitalism and the profits of African trade demanded. The large fortunes which were turned to industrial investment, and especially to the African trade, stimulated industries like ship building, which helped make England mistress of the seas. The West Indies too as a seat of slavery furnished an outlet for British manufacture and a source of raw materials. From this again large fortunes arose which were transferred to the mother country and invested.

All this spelled revolution: world-wide revolution starting in Europe; sinister and fatal revolution in West Africa. The city-state represented by Yoruban civilization had fought with the empire builders of the Sudan and retreated toward the Gulf of Guinea. Here they came in contact with the new western slave trade. It stimulated trade and industry; but the trade was not only in gold and oil and ivory, it was in men; and those nations that could furnish slaves were encouraged and prospered. The ruder culture of Ashanti and Dahomey outstripped Yoruba. Benin was changed. Blood lust was encouraged and the human culture which the slave trade helped build up for Europe, tore down and debauched West Africa.

The culture of Yoruba, Benin, Mossiland and Nupe had exhausted itself in a desperate attempt to stem the on-coming flood of Sudanese expansion. It had succeeded in maintaining its small, loosely federated city-states suited to trade, industry, and art. It had developed strong resistance toward the Sudan state builders toward the north, as in the case of the fighting Mossi; but behind this warlike resistance lay the peaceful city life which gave industrial ideas to Byzantium and shared something of Ethiopian and Mediterranean culture.

The first advent of the slave traders increased and encouraged native industry, as is evidenced by the bronze work of Benin; but soon this was pushed into the background, for it was not bronze metal but bronze flesh that Europe wanted. A new state-building tyranny, ingenious, well organized but cruel, and built on war, forced itself forward in the Niger Delta. The powerful state of Dahomey arose early in the eighteenth century. Ashanti, a similar kingdom, began its conquests in 1719 and grew with the slave trade because the profits of the trade and the insatiable demands of the Europeans disrupted and changed the older native economy.

Thus state building in West Africa began to replace the city economy; but it was a state built on war and on war supported and encouraged largely for the sake of trade in human flesh. The native industries were changed and disorganized. Family ties and government were weakened. Far into the heart of Africa this devilish disintegration, coupled with Christian rum and Mohammedan raiding, penetrated.

Few detailed studies have been made of the Mohammedan slave trade. Slave raiding was known in the Nile Valley from the time of the Egyptians and with the advent of Islam it continued, but it was incidental to conquest and proselytism. Later, however, it began to be commercialized; it was systematically organized with raiders, factories, markets, and contractors. By the nineteenth century African slaves were regularly supplied to Egypt, Turkey, Arabia, and Persia; and also to Morocco there came from the Western Sudan and Timbuktu about four thousand annually.

Egyptians in the nineteenth century tried to stop this slave trade, but they encountered vested interests making large profits. The trade continued to exist as late as 1890. The English charge that under the Madhi in the Egyptian Sudan, slavery and slave raiding were widespread; but this was the result of the very misrule and chaos which caused the Madhist movement and for which it was not responsible. Doubtless many of the Madhist followers were enslaved and robbed under cover of religious frenzy; but the Madhi could not in the midst of war curb an evil which forced recognition even from Chinese Gordon. From the East African coast and especially the lake districts a stream of slaves went to the coast cities, whence they were sent to Madagascar, Arabia and Persia. In 1862, nineteen thousand slaves a year were passing from the regions about Lake Nysasa to Zanzibar. Minor trade in slaves took place in and about Abyssinia and Somaliland. Turkey began to check the slave traffic between 1860 and 1890. In Morocco it continued longer.

The face of Africa was turned south and west toward these slave traders instead of northward toward the Mediterranean, where for two thousand years and more Europe and Africa had met in legitimate trade and mutual respect. The full significance of the battle at Tondibi, which overthrew the Askias, was now clear. Hereafter Africa for centuries was to appear before the world, not as the land of gold and ivory, of Gongo Mussa and Meroe, but as a bound and captive slave, dumb and degraded.

The natural desire to avoid a painful subject has led historians to gloss over the details of the slave trade and leave the impression that it was a local African West Coast phenomenon and confined to a few years. It was, on the contrary, continent wide and centuries long; an economic, social, and political catastrophe probably unparalleled in human history.

Usually the slave trade has been thought of from its sentimental and moral point of view; but it is its economic significance that is of greatest moment. Whenever the human element in industry is degraded, society must suffer accordingly. In the case of the African slave trade the human element reached its nadir of degradation. Great and significant as was the contribution of black labor to the seventeenth, eighteenth, and nineteenth centuries, its compensation approached zero, falling distinctly and designedly below the cost of human reproduction; and yet on this system was built the wealth and power of modern civilization. One can conceive no more dangerous foundation; because even when the worst aspects were changed and the slave trade limited and the slave given certain legal rights of freedom, nevertheless the possibilities of low wages for the sake of high profits remained an ideal in industry, which made the African slave trade the father of industrial imperalism, and of the persistence of poverty in the richest lands.

As Marx declared: "Under the influence of the colonial system, commerce and navigation ripened like hot-house fruit. Chartered companies were powerful instruments in promoting the concentration of capital. The colonies provided a market for the rising manufactures, and the monopoly of this market intensified accumulation. The treasures obtained outside Europe by direct looting, enslavement, and murder, flowed to the motherland in streams, and were there turned into capital."

The exact proportions of the slave trade can be estimated only approximately. From 1680 to 1688 we know that the English African Company alone sent two hundred forty-nine ships to Africa, shipped there sixty thousand, seven hundred eighty-three Negro slaves, and after losing fourteen thousand, three hundred eighty-seven on the middle passage, delivered forty-six thousand, three hundred ninety-six in America.

It seems probable that 25,000 Negroes a year arrived in America between 1698 and 1707. After the Asiento of 1713 this number rose to 30,000 annually, and before the Revolutionary War it had reached at least 40,000 and perhaps 100,000 slaves a year.

The total number of slaves imported is not known. Dunbar estimates that nearly 900,000 came to America in the sixteenth century, 2,750,000 in the seventeenth, 7,000,000 in the eighteenth, and over 4,000,000 in the nineteenth, perhaps 15,000,000 in all. Certainly it seems that at least 10,000,000 Negroes were expatriated. The Mohammedan slave trade meant the expatriation or forcible migration in Africa of millions more.

(Many other millions were left dead in the wake of the raiders.) It would be conservative, then, to say that the slave trade cost Negro Africa from a fourth to a third of its population. And yet people ask today the cause of the stagnation of culture in that land since 1600! Such a large number of slaves could be supplied only by organized slave raiding. The African continent gradually became revolutionized. Whole regions were depopulated, whole tribes disappeared; the character of people developed excesses of cruelty instead of the flourishing arts of peace. The dark, irresistible grasp of fetish took firmer hold on men's minds. Advances toward higher civilization became more difficult. It was a rape of a continent to an extent seldom if ever paralleled in ancient or modern times.

In the American trade, there were not only the horrors of the slave raid, which lined the winding paths of the African jungles with bleached bones, but there were also the horrors of what was called the "middle passage," that is the voyage across the Atlantic. As Sir William Dolben said, "The Negroes were chained to each other hand and foot, and stowed so close that they were not allowed above a foot and a half for each in breadth. Thus crammed together like herrings in a barrel, they contracted putrid and fatal disorders; so that they who came to inspect them in a morning had occasionally to pick dead slaves out of their rows, and to unchain their carcases from the bodies of their wretched fellow-sufferers to whom they had been fastened."

It was estimated that out of every one hundred lot shipped from Africa only about fifty lived to be effective laborers across the sea; and among the whites more seamen died in that trade in one year than in the whole remaining trade of England in two. The full realization of the horrors of the slave trade was slow in reaching the ears and conscience of the modern world, just as today the treatment of natives in European colonies is brought to publicity with the greatest difficulty. The first move against the slave trade in England came in Parliament in 1776, but it was not until thirty-one years later, in 1807, that the trade was banned through the arduous labors of Clarkson, Wilberforce, Sharpe, and others.

Denmark had already abolished the trade, and the United States attempted to do so the following year. Portugal and Spain were induced to abolish the trade between 1815 and 1830. Not withstanding these laws, the contraband trade went on until the beginning of the Civil War in America. The reasons for this were the enormous profit of the trade and the continued demand of the American slave barons, who had no sympathy with the efforts to stop their source of cheap labor supply.

However, philanthropy was not working alone to overthrow Negro slavery and the slave trade. It was seen, first in England and later in other countries, that slavery as an industrial system could not be made to work satisfactorily in modern times. Its cost tended to become too great, as the sources of supply of slaves dried up, on the other hand, the slave insurrections from the very beginning threatened the system, as modern labor strikes have threatened capitalism, from the time when the slaves rose on the plantation of Diego Columbus down to the Civil War in America. Actual and potential slave insurrections in the West Indies, in North and South America, kept the slave owners in apprehension and turmoil, or called for a police system difficult to maintain.

The red revolt of Haiti struck the knell of the slave trade. In North America revolt finally took the form of organized running away to the North. All this with the growing scarcity of suitable land led to the abolition of the slave trade, the American Civil War and the disappearance of the American slave system. Further effort stopped the Mohammedan slave raider, but slowly because its philanthropic objects were clouded and hindered by the new Colonial Imperialism of Christian lands, which sought not wholly to abolish slavery but rather to reestablish it under new names, with a restricted slave trade.

Such is the story of the Rape of Ethiopia—a sordid, pitiful, cruel tale. Raphael painted, Luther preached, Corneille wrote, and Milton sang; and through it all, for four hundred years, the dark captives wound to the sea amid the bleaching bones of the dead; for four hundred years the sharks followed the scurrying ships; for four hundred years America was strewn with the living and dying millions of a transplanted race; for four hundred years Ethiopia stretched forth her hands unto God.

Dusk of Dawn was Du Bois' first autobiography. Published in 1940 when he was 72, it is less an autobiography than it is an attempt at "elucidating the inner meaning of significance of [the] race problem by explaining it in terms of the one human life that I know best." Thus, his concern is less the story of his own life as it is in using his life as the basis for an "autobiography of a concept of race."

Two selections are reprinted here. The first is from Chapter V., "The Concept of Race." In this excerpt Du Bois discusses his feelings about Africa, which were always very intense. Given his New England background, he himself found it difficult to understand completely from where his strong feelings for Africa had come. He concludes: "My African racial feeling was then purely a matter of my own later learning and reaction; my recoil from the assumptions of the whites; my experience in the South at Fisk. But it was none the less real and a large determinant of my life and character. I felt myself African by 'race' and by that token was African and an integral member of the group of dark Americans who were called Negroes."

The second excerpt is Chapter 6, "The White World." In it he examines the prevalent attitudes, personal and historical, which whites have toward blacks.

(*Dusk of Dawn: An Essay Toward An Autiobiography of a Race Concept*, Schocken Books, New York, 1968, originally published 1940, pp. 116-130, pp. 134-72.)

THE CONCEPT OF RACE

Feelings About Africa

Africa is, of course, my fatherland. Yet neither my father nor my father's father ever saw Africa or knew its meaning or cared overmuch for it. My mother's folk were closer and yet their direct connection, in culture and race, became tenuous; still, my tie to Africa is strong. On this vast continent were born and lived a large portion of my direct ancestors going back a thousand years or more. The mark of their heritage is upon me in color and hair. These are obvious things, but of little meaning in themselves; only important as they stand for real and more subtle differences from other men. Whether they do or not, I do not know nor does science know today.

But one thing is sure and that is the fact that since the fifteenth century these ancestors of mine and their other descendants have had a common history; have suffered a common disaster and have one long memory. The actual ties of heritage between the individuals of this group, vary with the ancestors that they have in common and many others: Europeans and Semites, perhaps Mongolians, certainly American Indians. But the physical bond is least and the badge of color relatively unimportant save as a badge; the real essence of this kinship is its social heritage of slavery; the discrimination and insult; and this heritage binds together not simply the children of Africa, but extends through yellow Asia and into the South Seas. It is this unity that draws me to Africa.

When shall I forget the night I first set foot on African soil? I am the sixth generation in descent from forefathers who left this land. The moon was at the full and the waters of the Atlantic lay like a lake. All the long slow afternoon as the sun robed herself in her western scarlet with veils of misty cloud, I had seen Africa afar. Cape Mount—that mighty headland with its twin curves, northern sentinel of the realm of Liberia—gathered itself out of the cloud at half past three and then darkened and grew clear. On beyond flowed the dark low undulating land quaint with palm and breaking sea. The world grew black. Africa faded away, the stars stood forth curiously twisted—Orion in the zenith—the Little Bear asleep and the Southern Cross rising behind the horizon. Then afar, ahead, a lone light shone, straight at the ship's fore. Twinkling lights appeared below, around, and rising shadows. "Monrovia," said the Captain.

Suddenly we swerved to our left. The long arms of the bay enveloped us and then to the right rose the twinkling hill of Monrovia, with its crowning star. Lights flashed on the shore—here, there. Then we sensed a darker shading in the shadows; it lay very still. "It's a boat," one said. "It's two boats!" Then the shadow drifted in pieces and as the anchor roared into the deep, five boats outlined themselves on the waters—great ten-oared barges with men swung into line and glided toward us.

It was nine at night—above, the shadows, there the town, here the sweeping boats. One forged ahead with the flag—stripes and a lone star flaming behind, the ensign of the customs floating wide; and bending to the long oars, the white caps of ten black sailors. Up the stairway clambered a soldier in khaki, aide-de-camp of the President of the Republic, a customhouse official, the clerk of the American legation—and after them sixty-five lithe, lean black stevedores with whom the steamer would work down to Portuguese Angola and back. A few moments of formalities, greetings and good-bys and I was in the great long boat with the President's aide—a brown major in brown khaki. On the other side, the young clerk and at the back, the black barelegged pilot. Before us on the high thwarts were the rowers: men, boys, black, thin, trained in muscle and sinew, little larger than the oars in thickness, they bent their strength to them and swung upon them.

One in the center gave curious little cackling cries to keep up the rhythm, and for the spurts and the stroke, a call a bit thicker and sturdier; he gave a low guttural command now and then; the boat, alive, quivering, danced beneath the moon, swept a great curve to the bar to breast its narrow teeth of foam—"t'chick-a-tickity, t'chick-a-tickity," sang the boys, and we glided and raced, now between boats, now near the landing—now cast aloft at the cock. And lo! I was in Africa.

Christmas Eve, and Africa is singing in Monrovia. They are Krus and Fanti—men, women and children, and all the night they march and sing. The music was once the music of mission revival hymns. But it is that music now transformed and the silly words hidden in an unknown tongue—liquid and sonorous. It is tricked out and expounded with cadence and turn. And this is that same rhythm I heard first in Tennessee forty years ago: the air is raised and carried by men's strong voices, while floating above in obbligato, come the high mellow voices of women—it is the ancient African art of part singing, so curiously and insistently different.

So they come, gay appareled, lit by transparency. They enter the gate and flow over the high steps and sing and sing and sing. They saunter around the house, pick flowers, drink water and sing and sing and sing. The warm dark heat of the night steams up to meet the moon. And the night is song.

On Christmas Day, 1923, we walk down to the narrow,

crooked wharves of Monrovia, by houses old and gray and step-like streets of stone. Before is the wide St. Paul River, double-mouthed, and beyond, the sea, white, curling on the sand. Before us is the isle—the tiny isle, hut-covered and guarded by a cotton tree, where the pioneers lived in 1821. We board the boat, then circle round—then up the river. Great bowing trees, festoons of flowers, golden blossoms, star-faced palms and thatched huts; tall spreading trees lifting themselves like vast umbrellas, low shrubbery with gray and laced and knotted roots—the broad, black, murmuring river. Here a tree holds wide fingers out and stretches them over the water in vast incantation; bananas throw their wide green fingers to the sun. Iron villages, scarred clearings with gray, sheet-iron homes staring, grim and bare, at the ancient tropical flood of green.

The river sweeps wide and the shrubs bow low. Behind, Monrovia rises in clear, calm beauty. Gone are the wharves, the low and clustered houses of the port, the tight-throated business village, and up sweep the villas and the low wall, brown and cream and white, with great mango and cotton trees, with lighthouse and spire, with porch and pillar and the color of shrubbery and blossom.

We climbed the upright shore to a senator's home and received his wide and kindly hospitality—curious blend of feudal lord and modern farmer—sandwiches, cake, and champagne. Again we glided up the drowsy river—five, ten, twenty miles and came to our hostess, a mansion of five generations with a compound of endless native servants and cows under the palm thatches. The daughters of the family wore, on the beautiful black skin of their necks, the exquisite pale gold chains of the Liberian artisan and the slim, black little granddaughter of the house had a wide pink ribbon on the thick curls of her dark hair, that lay like sudden sunlight on the shadows. Double porches, one above the other, welcomed us to ease. A native man, gay with Christmas and a dash of gin, sang and danced in the road. Children ran and played in the blazing sun. We sat at a long broad table and ate duck, chicken, beef, rice, plantain, collards, cake, tea, water and Madeira wine, Then we went and looked at the heavens, the uptwisted sky—Orion and Cassiopeia at zenith; the Little Bear beneath the horizon, now unfamiliar sights in the Milky Way—all awry, a-living—sun for snow at Christmas, and happiness and cheer.

The shores were lined with old sugar plantations, the buildings rotting and falling. I looked upon the desolation with a certain pain. What had happened, I asked? The owners and planters had deserted these homes and come down to Monrovia, but why? After all, Monrovia had not much to offer in the way of income and occupation. Was this African laziness and inefficiency? No, it was a specimen of the way in which the waves of modern industry broke over the shores of far-off Africa. Here during our Civil War, men hastened to raise sugar and supply New York. They built their own boats and filled the river and sailed the sea. But afterwards, Louisiana came back into the Union, colored Rillieux invented the vacuum pan; the sugar plantations began to spread in Cuba and the Sugar Trust monopoly of refining machinery, together with the new beet sugar industry, drove Liberia quickly from the market. What all this did not do, the freight rates finished. So sugar did not pay in Liberia and other crops rose and fell in the same way.

As I look back and recall the days, which I have called great —the occasions in which I have taken part and which have had for me and others the widest significance, I can remember none like the first of January, 1924. Once I took my bachelor's degree before a governor, a great college president, and a bishop of New England. But that was rather personal in its memory than in any way epochal. Once before the assembled races of the world I was called to speak in London in place of the suddenly sick Sir Harry Johnston. It was a great hour. But it was not greater than the day when I was presented to the President of the Negro Republic of Liberia.

Liberia had been resting under the shock of world war into which the Allies forced her. She had asked and been promised a loan by the United States to bolster and replace her stricken trade. She had conformed to every preliminary requirement and waited when waiting was almost fatal. It was not simply money, it was world prestige and protection at a time when the little republic was sorely beset by creditors and greedy imperial powers. At the last moment, an insurgent Senate peremptorily and finally refused the request and strong recommendation of President Wilson and his advisers, and the loan was refused. The Department of State made no statement to the world, and Liberia stood naked, not only well-nigh bankrupt, but peculiarly defenseless amid scowling and unbelieving powers.

It was then that the United States made a gesture of courtesy; a little thing, and merely a gesture, but one so unusual that it was epochal. President Coolidge, at the suggestion of William H. Lewis, a leading colored lawyer of Boston, named me, an American Negro traveler, Envoy Extraordinary and Minister Plenipotentiary to Liberia—the highest rank ever given by any country to a diplomatic agent in black Africa. And it named this Envoy the special representative of the President of the United States to the President of Liberia, on the occasion of his inauguration; charging the Envoy with a personal word of encouragement and moral support. It was a significant action. It had in it nothing personal. Another appointee would have been equally significant. But Liberia recognized the meaning. She showered upon the Envoy every mark of appreciation and thanks. The Commander of the Liberian Frontier Force was made his special aide, and a sergeant, his orderly. At ten A.M. New Year's morning, 1924, a company of the Frontier Force, in red fez and khaki, presented arms before the American Legation and escorted Solomon Porter Hood, the American Minister Resident, and myself as Envoy Extraordinary and my aide to the Presidential Mansion—a beautiful white, verandaed house, waving with palms and fronting a grassy street.

Ceremonials are old and to some antiquated and yet this was done with such simplicity, grace and seriousness that none could escape its spell. The Secretary of State met us at the door, as the band played the impressive Liberian National hymn, and soldiers saluted:

> All hail! Liberia, hail!
> In union strong, success is sure.
> We cannot fail.
> With God above,
> Our rights to prove,
> We will the world assail.

We mounted a broad stairway and into a great room that stretched across the house. Here in semi-circle were ranged the foreign consuls and the cabinet—the former in white, gilt with orders and swords; the latter in solemn black. Present were England, France, Germany, Spain, Belgium, Holland, and Panama, to be presented to me in order of seniority by the small brown Secretary of State with his perfect poise and ease. The President entered—frock-coated with the star and ribbon of a Spanish order on his breast. The American Minister introduced me, and I said:

"The President of the United States has done me the great honor of designating me as his personal representative on the occasion of your inauguration. In so doing, he has had, I am sure, two things in mind. First, he wished publicly and unmistakably to express before the world the interest and solicitude which the hundred million inhabitants of the United States of America have for Liberia. Liberia is a child of the United States, and a sister Republic. Its progress and success is the progress and success of democracy everywhere and for all men; and the United States would view with sorrow and alarm any misfortune which might happen to this Republic and any obstacle that was placed in her path.

"But special and peculiar bonds draw these two lands together. In America live eleven million persons of African descent; they are citizens, legally invested with every right that inheres in American citizenship. And I am sure that in this special mark of the President's favor, he has had in mind the wishes and hopes of Negro Americans. He knows how proud they are of the hundred years of independence which you have maintained by force of arms and by brawn and brain upon the edge of this mighty continent; he knows that in the great battle against color caste in America, the ability of Negroes to rule in Africa has been and ever will be a great and encouraging reenforcement. He knows that the unswerving loyalty of Negro Americans to their country is fitly accompanied by a pride in their race and lineage, a belief in the potency and promise of Negro blood which makes them eager listeners to every whisper of success from Liberia, and eager helpers in every movement for your aid and comfort. In a special sense, the moral burden of Liberia and the advancement and integrity of Liberia is the sincere prayer of America."

And now a word about the African himself—about this primitive black man: I began to notice a truth as I entered southern France. I formulated it in Portugal. I knew it as a great truth one Sunday in Liberia. And the Great Truth was this: efficiency and happiness do not go together in modern culture. Going south from London, as the world darkens it gets happier. Portugal is deliciously dark. Many leading citizens would have difficulty keeping off a Georgia "Jim Crow" car. But, oh, how lovely a land and how happy a people! And so leisurely. Little use of trying to shop seriously in Lisbon before eleven. It isn't done. Nor at noon; the world is lunching or lolling in the sun. Even after four P.M. one takes chances, for the world is in the Rocio. And the banks are so careless and the hotels so leisurely. How delightfully angry Englishmen get at the "damned, lazy" Portuguese!

But if this of Portugal, what of Africa? Here darkness descends and rests on lovely skins until brown seems lucious and natural. There is sunlight in great gold globules and soft, heavy-scented heat that wraps you like a garment. And laziness; divine, eternal, languor is right and good and true. I remember the morning; it was Sunday, and the night before we heard the leopards crying down there. Today beneath the streaming sun we went down into the gold-green forest. It was silence—silence the more mysterious because life abundant and palpitating pulsed all about us and held us drowsy captives to the day. Ahead the gaunt missionary strode, alert, afire, with his gun. He apologized for the gun, but he did not need to, for I saw the print of a leopard's hind foot. A monkey sentinel screamed, and I heard the whir of the horde as they ran.

Then we came to the village; how can I describe it? Neither London, nor Paris, nor New York has anything of its delicate, precious beauty. It was a town of the Veys and done in cream and pale purple—still, clean, restrained, tiny, complete. It was no selfish place, but the central abode of fire and hospitality, clean-swept for wayfarers, and best seats were bare. They quite expected visitors, morning, noon, and night; and they gave our hands a quick, soft grasp and talked easily. Their manners were better than those of Park Lane or Park Avenue. Oh, much better and more natural. They showed breeding. The chief's son—tall and slight and speaking good English—had served under the late Colonel Young. He made a little speech of welcome. Long is the history of the Veys and comes down from the Eastern Roman Empire, the great struggle of Islam and the black empires of the Sudan.

We went on to other villages—dun-colored, not so beautiful, but neat and hospitable. In one sat a visiting chief of perhaps fifty years in a derby hat and a robe, and beside him stood a shy young wife done in ebony and soft brown, whose liquid eyes would not meet ours. The chief was taciturn until we spoke of schools. Then he woke suddenly—he had children to "give" to a school. I see the last village fading away; they are plastering the wall of a home, leisurely and carefully. They smiled a good-by—not effusively, with no eagerness, with a simple friendship, as we glided under the cocoa trees and into the silent forest, the gold and silent forest.

And there and elsewhere in two long months I began to learn: primitive men are not following us afar, frantically waving and seeking our goals; primitive men are not behind us in some swift foot-race. Primitive men have already arrived. They are abreast, and in places ahead of us; in others behind. But all their curving advance line is contemporary, not prehistoric. They have used other paths and these paths have led them by scenes sometimes fairer, sometimes uglier than ours, but always toward the Pools of Happiness. Or, to put it otherwise, these folk have the leisure of true aristocracy—leisure for thought and courtesy, leisure for sleep and laughter. They have time for their children—such well-trained, beautiful children with perfect, unhidden bodies. Have you ever met a crowd of children in the east of London or New York, or even on the Avenue at Forty-second or One Hundred and Forty-second Street, and fled to avoid their impudence and utter ignorance of courtesy? Come to Africa, and see well-bred and courteous children, playing happily and never sniffling and whining.

I have read everywhere that Africa means sexual license. Perhaps it does. Most folk who talk sex frantically have all too seldom revealed their source material. I was in West Africa only two months, but with both eyes wide. I saw children quite naked and women usually naked to the waist—with bare bosom and limbs. And in those sixty days I saw less of sex dalliance and appeal than I see daily on Fifth Avenue. This does not mean much, but it is an interesting fact.

The primitive black man is courteous and dignified. If the platforms of Western cities had swarmed with humanity as I have seen the platforms swarm in Senegal, the police would have a busy time. I did not see one respectable quarrel. Therefore shall we all take to the Big Bush? No. I prefer New York. But my point is that New York and London and Paris must learn of West Africa and may learn.

The one great lack in Africa is communication—communication as represented by human contact, movement of goods, dissemination of knowledge. All these things we have—we have in such crushing abundance that they have mastered us and defeated their real good. We meet human beings in such throngs that we cannot know or even understand them—they become to us inhuman, mechanical, hateful. We are choked and suffocated, tempted and killed by goods accumulated from the ends of the earth; our newspapers and magazines so overwhelm us with knowledge—knowledge of all sorts and kinds from particulars as to our neighbors' underwear to Einstein's mathematics that one of the great and glorious joys of the African bush is to escape from "news."

On the other hand, African life with its isolation has deeper knowledge of human souls. The village life, the forest ways, the teeming markets, bring an intimate human knowledge that the West misses, sinking the individual in the social. Africans know fewer folk, but know them infinitely better. Their intertwined communal souls, therefore, brook no poverty nor prostitution—these things are to them un-understandable. On the other hand, they are vastly ignorant of what the world is doing and thinking, and of what is known of its physical forces. They suffer terribly from preventable disease, from unnecessary hunger, from the freaks of the weather.

Here, then, is something for Africa and Europe both to learn; and Africa is eager, breathless, to learn—while Europe? Europe laughs with loud guffaws. Learn of Africa? Nonsense. Poverty cannot be abolished. Democracy and firm government are incompatible. Prostitution is world old and inevitable. And Europe proceeds to use Africa as a means and not as an end; as a hired tool and welter of raw materials and not as a land of human beings.

I think it was in Africa that I came more clearly to see the close connection between race and wealth. The fact that even in the minds of the most dogmatic supporters of race theories and believers in the inferiority of colored folk to white, there was a conscious or unconscious determination to increase their incomes by taking full advantage of this belief. And then gradually this thought was metamorphosed into a realization that the income-bearing value of race prejudice was the cause and not the result of theories of race inferiority; that particularly in the

United States the income of the Cotton Kingdom based on black slavery caused the passionate belief in Negro inferiority and the determination to enforce it even by arms.

THE WHITE WORLD

The majority of men resent and always have resented the idea of equality with most of their fellow men. This has had physical, economic, and cultural reasons: the physical fear of attack; the economic strife to avert starvation and secure protection and shelter; but more especially I presume the cultural and spiritual desire to be one's self without interference from others; to enjoy that anarchy of the spirit which is inevitably the goal of all consciousness. It is only in highly civilized times and places that the conception arises of an individual freedom and develop-ment, and even that was conceived of as the right of a privileged minority, and was based on the degradation, the exclusion, the slavery of most others. The history of tribes and clans, of social classes and all nations, and of race antipathies in our own world, is an exemplification of this fight against equality and inability even to picture its possibility.

The result is that men are conditioned and their actions forced not simply by their physical environment, powerful as mountains and rain, heat and cold, forest and desert always have been and will be. When we modify the effects of this environment by what we call the social environment, we have conceived a great and important truth. But even this needs further revision. A man lives today not only in his physical environment and in the social environment of ideas and cus-toms, laws and ideals; but that total environment is subjected to a new socio-physical environment of other groups, whose social environment he shares but in part.

A man in the European sixteenth century was born not sim-ply in the valley of the Thames or Seine, but in a certain social class and the environment of that class made and limited his world. He was then, consciously or not, not fully a man; he was an artisan and until he complied with the limitations of that class he was continually knocking his hands, head and heart against an environment, composed of other classes, which limi-ted what he could and could not do and what he must do; and this greater group environment was not a matter of mere ideas and thought; it was embodied in muscles and armed men, in scowling faces, in the majesty of judge and police and in human law which became divine.

Much as I knew of this class structure of the world, I should never have realized it vividly and fully if I had not been born into its modern counterpart, racial segregation; first into a world composed of people with colored skins who remembered slavery and endured discrimination; and who had to a degree their own habits, customs, and ideals; but in addition to this I lived in an environment which I came to call the white world. I was not an American; I was not a man; I was by long education and continual compulsion and daily reminder, a colored man in a white world; and that white world often existed primarily, so far as I was concerned, to see with sleepless vigilance that I was kept within bounds. All this made me limited in physical movement and provincial in thought and dream. I could not stir, I could not act, I could not live, without taking into careful daily account the reaction of my white environing world. How I traveled and where, what work I did, what income I received, where I ate, where I slept, with whom I talked, where I sought recreation, where I studied, what I wrote and what I could get published—all this depended and depended primarily upon an overwhelming mass of my fellow citizens in the United States, from whose society I was largely excluded.

Of course, there was no real wall between us. I knew from the days of my childhood and in the elementary school, on through my walks in the Harvard yard and my lectures in Germany, that in all things in general, white people were just the same as I: their physical possibilities, their mental processes were no different from mine; even the difference in skin color was vastly overemphasized and intrinsically trivial. And yet this fact of racial distinction based on color was the greatest thing in my life and absolutely determined it, because this surrounding group, in alliance and agreement with the white European world, was settled and determined upon the fact that I was and must be a thing apart.

It was impossible to gainsay this. It was impossible for any time and to any distance to withdraw myself and look down upon these absurd assumptions with philosophical calm and humorous self-control. If, as happened to a friend of mine, a lady in a Pullman car ordered me to bring her a glass of water, mistaking me for a porter, the incident in its essence was a joke to be chuckled over; but in its hard, cruel significance and its unending inescapable sign of slavery, it was something to drive a man mad.

For long years it seemed to me that this imprisonment of a human group with chains in hands of an environing group, was a singularly unusual characteristic of the Negro in the United States in the nineteenth century. But since then it has been easy for me to realize that the majority of mankind has struggled through this inner spiritual slavery and that while a dream which we have easily and jauntily called democracy envisages a day when the environing group looses the chains and compulsion, and is willing and even eager to grant families, nations, sub-races, and races equality of opportunity among larger groups, that even this grand equality has not come; and until it does, individual equality and the free soul is impossible. All our present frustration in trying to realize individual equality through communism, fascism, and democracy arises from our continual unwillingness to break the intellectual bonds of group and racial exclusiveness.

Thus it is easy to see that scientific definition of race is impossible; it is easy to prove that physical characteristics are not so inherited as to make it possible to divide the world into races; that ability is the monopoly of no known aristocracy; that the possibilities of human development cannot be circumscribed by color, nationality, or any conceivable definition of race; all this has nothing to do with the plain fact that throughout the world today organized groups of men by monopoly of economic and physical power, legal enactment and intellectual training are limiting with determination and unflagging zeal the development of other groups; and that the concentration particularly of economic power today puts the majority of mankind into a slavery to the rest.

There has been an understandable determination in the United States among both Negro and white thinkers to minimize and deny the realities of racial difference. The race problem has been rationalized in every way. It has been called the natural result of slavery; the effect of poverty and ignorance; the situation consequent upon lack of effort and thought on the part of Americans and of other races. But all this reasoning has its logical pitfalls: granted that poverty causes color prejudice, color prejudice certainly is a cause of poverty. Ignorance leads to exploitation and mistreatment, but the black child is more often forced into ignorance and kept there than the white child. Thus it is impossible for the clear-headed student of human action in the United States and in the world, to avoid facing the fact of a white world which is today dominating human culture and working for the continued subordination of the colored races.

It may be objected here that so general a statement is not fair; that there are many white folk who feel the unfairness and crime of color and race prejudice and have toiled and sacrificed to counteract it. This brings up the whole question of social guilt. When, for instance, one says that the action of England toward the darker races has been a course of hypocrisy, force and greed covering four hundred years it does not mean to include in that guilt many persons of the type of William Wilberforce and Granville Sharpe. On the other hand because British history has not involved the guilt of all Britons we cannot jump to the opposite and equally fallacious conclusion that there has been no guilt; that the development of the British Empire is a sort of cosmic process with no individual human being at fault. In the history of England, France, America, Germany and Italy, we have villains who have selfishly and criminally desired and accomplished what made for the suffering and degradation of mankind. We have had others who desired the uplift and worked for the uplift of all men. And we have had a middle class of people who sometimes ignorantly and sometimes consciously shifted the balance now here, and now there; and when, in the end, this balance of public opinion, this effective social action, has made for the degradation of mankind or in so far as it has done this, that part of England which has allowed this or made it possible is blood-guilty of the result. So in America, not the philosophy of Jefferson nor the crusade of Garrison nor the reason of Sumner was able to counterbalance the race superiority doctrines of Calhoun, the imperialism of Jefferson Davis, nor the race hate of Ben Tillman. As a result white America has crucified, enslaved, and oppressed the Negro group and holds them still, especially in the South, in a legalized position of inferior caste.

With the best will the factual outline of a life misses the

essence of its spirit. Thus in my life the chief fact has been race
—not so much scientific race, as that deep conviction of myriads of men that congenital differences among the main masses
of human beings absolutely condition the individual destiny of
every member of a group. Into the spiritual provincialism of this
belief I have been born and this fact has guided, embittered,
illuminated and enshrouded my life. Yet, how shall I explain
and clarify its meaning for a soul? Description fails—I have
tried that. Yet, lest I omit the most important thing in the life
of an American Negro today and the only thing that adequately
explains his success, failures and foibles, let me attempt its
exposition by personifying my white and colored environment.

When, for example, the obsession of his race consciousness
leaves him, my white friend, Roger Van Dieman (who, I hasten
to add, is an abstraction and integration and never existed), is
quite companionable; otherwise he is impossible. He has a way
of putting an excessive amount of pity in his look and of stating
as a general and incontrovertible fact that it is "horrible" to be
an Exception. By this he means me. He is more than certain that
I prove the rule. He is not a bright person, but of that famous
average, standardized and astonished at anything that even
seems original. His thesis is simple: the world is composed of
Race superimposed on Race; classes superimposed on classes;
beneath the whole thing is "Our Family" in capitals, and under
that is God. God seems to be a cousin, or at least a blood
relative, of the Van Diemans.

"Of course," he says, "you know Negroes are inferior."

I admit nothing of the sort, I maintain. In fact, having known
with some considerable intimacy both male and female, the
people of the British Isles, of Scandinavia, of Russia, of Germany, north and south, of the three ends of France and the two
ends of Italy; specimens from the Balkans and black and white
Spain; the three great races of Asia and the melange of Africa,
without mentioning America, I sit here and maintain that black
folk are much superior to white.

"You are either joking or mad," he says.

Both and neither. This race talk is, of course, a joke, and
frequently it has driven me insane and probably will permanently in the future; and yet, seriously and soberly, we black
folk are the salvation of mankind.

He regards me with puzzled astonishment and says confidentially:

"Do you know that sometimes I am half afraid that you really believe this? At other times I see clearly the inferiority complex."

The former after lunch, I reply, and the latter before.

"Very well," he says, "let's lunch."

Where? I ask quizzically, we being at the time in the Roaring Forties.

"Why—oh, well—their refusal to serve you lunch at least does not prove your superiority."

Nor yet theirs, I answer; but never mind, come with me to Second Avenue, where Labor lives and food is bad.

We start again with the salad.

"Now, superiority consists of what?" he argues.

Life is, I remark, (1) Beauty and health of body. (2) Mental clearness and creative genius. (3) Spiritual goodness and receptivity. (4) Social adaptability and constructiveness.

"Not bad," he answers. "Not bad at all. Now I contend that the white race conspicuously excells in beauty, genius, and construction, and is well abreast even in goodness."

And I maintain that the black race excels in beauty, goodness, and adaptability, and is well abreast in genius.

"Sheer nonsense and pure balderdash. Compare the Venus of Milo and the Apollo Belvedere with a Harlem or Beale Street couple."

I retort: in short, compare humanity at its worst with the Ideal, and humanity suffers. But black folk in most attributes of physical beauty, in line and height and curve, have the same norms as whites and differ only in small details of color, hair and curve of countenance. Now can there be any question but that as colors, bronze, mahogany, coffee and gold are far lovlier than pink, gray, and marble? Hair is a matter of taste. Some will have it drab and stringy and others in a gray, woven, unmoving mass. Most of us like it somewhere between, in tiny tendrils, smoking curls and sweeping curves. I have loved all these varieties in my day. I prefer the crinkly kind, almost wavy, in black, brown, and glistening gold. In faces, I hate straight features; needles and razors may be sharp—but beautiful, never.

"All that is personal opinion. I prefer the colors of heaven and day: sunlight hair and sky-blue eyes; straight noses and thin lips, and that incomparable air of haughty aloofness and aristocracy."

And I, on the contrary, am the child of twilight and night, and choose intricately curly hair, black eyes, full and luscious features; and that air of humility and wonder which streams from moonlight. Add to this voices that caress instead of rasp, glances that appeal rather than repel, and a sinuous litheness of movement to replace Anglo-Saxon stalking—there you have my ideal. Of course, you can bury any human body in dirt and misery and make it horrible. I have seen the East End of London.

"Beauty seems to be simply opinion, if you put it that way."

To be sure. But whose opinion?

"Bother beauty. Here we shall never agree. But, after all, I doubt if it makes much difference. The real point is Brains: clear thinking, pure reason, mathematical precision and creative genius. Now, without plague, stand and acknowledge that here the white race is supreme."

Quite the contrary. I know no attribute in which the white race has more conspicuously failed. This is white and European civilization; and as a system of culture it is idiotic, addle-brained, unreasoning, topsy-turvy, without precision; and its genius chiefly runs to marvelous contrivances for enslaving the many, and enriching the few, and murdering both. I see absolutely no proof that the average ability of the white man's brain to think clearly is any greater than that of the yellow man or of the black man. If we take even that doubtful but widely heralded test, the frequency of individual creative genius (when a real racial test should be the frequency of ordinary common sense) —if we take the Genius as the savior of mankind, it is only possible for the white race to prove its own incontestable superiority by appointing both judge and jury and summoning its own witnesses.

I freely admit that, according to white writers, white teachers, white historians, and white molders of public opinion, nothing ever happened in the world of any importance that could not or should not be labeled "white." How silly. I place black iron-welding and village democracy, and yellow printing and state building, side by side with white representative government and the steam engine, and unhesitatingly give the palm to the first. I hand the first vast conception of the solar system to the Africanized Egyptians, the creation of Art to the Chinese, the highest conception of Religion to the Asiatic Semites, and then let Europe rave over the Factory system.

"But is not well-being more widely diffused among white folk than among yellow and black, and general intelligence more common?"

True, and why? Ask the geography of Europe, the African Slave Trade and the industrial technique of the nineteenth-century white man. Turn the thing around, and let a single tradition of culture suddenly have thrust into its hands the power to bleed the world of its brawn and wealth, and the willingness to do this, and you will have exactly what we have today, under another name and color.

"Precisely. Then, at least, the white race is more advanced and no more blameworthy than others because, as I insist, its native intelligence is greater. It is germ plasm, seed, that I am talking about. Do you believe in heredity?"

Not blindly; but I should be mildly surprised to see a dog born of a cat.

"Exactly; or a genius born of a fool."

No, no; on the contrary, I rather expect fools of geniuses and geniuses of fools. And while I stoutly maintain that cattiness and dogginess are as far apart as the East from the West, on the other hand, I just as strongly believe that the human ass and the superman have much in common and can often, if not always, spawn each other.

"Is it possible that you have never heard of the Jukes, or of the plain results of hereditary degeneration and the possibilities of careful breeding?"

It is not possible; they have been served up to me ad infinitum. But they are nothing. I know greater wonders: Lincoln from Nancy Hanks, Dumas from a black beast of burden, Kant from a saddler, and Jesus Christ from a manger.

"All of which, instead of disproving, is exact and definite proof of the persistence of good blood."

Precisely, and of the catholicity of its tastes; the method of proof is this: when anything good occurs, it is proof of good blood; when anything bad occurs, it is proof of bad blood. Very well. Now good and bad, native endowment and native deficiency, do not follow racial lines. There is good stock in all races and the outcropping of bad individuals, too; and there has been absolutely no proof that the white race has any larger share of the gifted strains of human heritage than the black race or the yellow race. To be sure, good seed proves itself in the flower and the fruit, but the failure of seed to sprout is no proof that it is not good. It may be proof simply of the absence of manure— or its excessive presence.

Granted, that when time began, there was hidden in a Seed that tiny speck that spelled the world's salvation, do you think today it would manifest itself crudely and baldly in a dash of skin color and a crinkle of hair? Is the subtle mystery of life and consciousness and of ability portrayed in any such slapdash and obvious marks of difference?

"Go out upon the street; choose ten white men and ten colored men. Which can carry on and preserve American civilization?"

The whites.

"Well, then."

You evidently consider that a compliment. Let it pass. Go out upon the street and choose ten men and ten women. Which could best run a Ford car? The men, of course; but hold. Fly out into the sky and look down upon ten children of Podunk and ten children of Chicago. Which would know most about elevated railroads, baseball, zoology, and movies?

"The point is visible, but beyond that, outside of mere experience and education, and harking back to native gift and intelligence, on your honor, which has most, white folk or black folk?"

There you have me deep in the shadows, beyond the benign guidance of words. Just what is gift and intelligence, especially of the native sort? And when we compare the gift of one human soul with that of another, are we not seeking to measure incommensurable things; trying to lump things like sunlight and music and love? And if a certain shadowy Over-soul can really compare the incomparable with some transcendental yardstick, may we not here emerge into a super-equality of man? At least this I can quite believe.

"But it is a pious belief, not more."

Not more; but a pious belief outweighs an impious unbelief.

Admitting that the problem of native human endowment is obscure, there is no corresponding obscurity in spiritual values. Goodness and unselfishness; simplicity and honor; tolerance, susceptibility to beauty in form, color, and music; courage to look truth in the face; courage to live and suffer in patience and humility, in forgiveness and in hope; eagerness to turn, not simply the other cheek, but the face and the bowed back; capacity to love. In all these mighty things, the greatest things in the world, where do black folk and white folk stand?

Why, man of mine, you would not have the courage to live one hour as a black man in America, or as a Negro in the whole wide world. Ah, yes, I know what you whisper to such accusation. You say dryly that if we had good sense, we would not live either; and that the fact that we do submit to life as it is and yet laugh and dance and dream, is but another proof that we are idiots.

This is the truly marvelous way in which you prove your superiority by admitting that our love of life can only be intelligently explained on the hypothesis of inferiority. What finer tribute is possible to our courage?

What great works of Art have we made? Very few. The Pyramids, Luxor, the Bronzes of Benin, the Spears of the Bongo, "When Malinda Sings" and the Sorrow Song she is always singing. Oh, yes, and the love of her dancing.

But art is not simply works of art; it is the spirit that knows Beauty, that has music in its soul and the color of sunsets in its headkerchiefs; that can dance on a flaming world and make the world dance, too. Such is the soul of the Negro.

Why, do you know the two finest things in the industry of the West, finer than factory, shop or ship? One is the black laborer's Saturday off. Neither the whip of the driver, nor the starvation wage, nor the disgust of the Yankee, nor the call of the cotton crop, has yet convinced the common black variety of plantation laborer that one day in the week is enough for rest and play. He wants two days. And, from California to Texas, from Florida to Trinidad, he takes two days while the planter screams and curses. They have beaten the English slavery, the French and German peasants, and the North Italian contadini into twelve-hour, six-day slaves. They crushed the Chinese and Indian coolie into a twenty-four-hour beast of burden; they have even made the American, free, white and twenty-one, believe that daily toil is one of the Ten Commandments. But not the Negro. From Monday to Friday the field hand is a slave; then for forty-eight hours he is free, and through these same forty-eight hours he may yet free the dumb, driven cattle of the world.

Then the second thing, laughter. This race has the greatest of the gifts of God, laughter. It dances and sings; it is humble; it longs to learn; it loves men; it loves women. It is frankly, baldly, deliciously human in an artificial and hypocritical land. If you will hear men laugh, go to Guinea, "Black Bottom," "Niggertown," Harlem. If you want to feel humor too exquisite and subtle for translation, sit invisibly among a gang of Negro workers. The white world has its gibes and cruel caricatures; it has its loud guffaws; but to the black world alone belongs the delicious chuckle.

"But the State; the modern industrial State. Wealth of work, wealth of commerce, factory and mine, skyscrapers; New York, Chicago, Johannesburg, London and Buenos Aires!"

This is the best expression of the civilization in which the white race finds itself today. This is what the white world means by culture.

"Does it not excel the black and yellow race here?"

It does. But the excellence here raises no envy; only regrets. If this vast Frankenstein monster really served its makers; if it were their minister and not their master, god and king; if their machines gave us rest and leisure, instead of the drab uniformity of uninteresting drudgery; if their factories gave us gracious community of thought and feeling; beauty enshrined, free and joyous; if their work veiled them with tender sympathy at human distress and wide tolerance and understanding—then, all hail, White Imperial Industry! But it does not. It is a Beast! Its creators even do not understand it, cannot curb or guide it. They themselves are but hideous, groping hired Hands, doing their bit to oil the raging devastating machinery which kills men to make cloth, prostitutes women to rear buildings and eats little children.

Is this superiority? It is madness. We are the supermen who sit idly by and laugh and look at civilization. We, who frankly want the bodies of our mates and conjure no blush to our bronze cheeks when we own it. We, who exalt the Lynched above the Lyncher, and the Worker above the Owner, and the Crucified above Imperial Rome.

"But why have you black and yellow men done nothing better or even as good in the history of the world?"

We have, often.

"I never heard of it."

Lions have no historians.

"It is idiotic even to discuss it. Look around and see the

pageantry of the world. It belongs to white men; it is the expression of white power; it is the product of white brains. Who can have the effrontery to stand for a moment and compare with this white triumph, yellow and brown anarchy and black savagery?"

You are obsessed by the swiftness of the gliding of the sled at the bottom of the hill. You say: what tremendous power must have caused its speed, and how wonderful is Speed. You think of the rider as the originator and inventor of that vast power. You admire his poise and *sang-froid,* his utter self-absorption. You say: surely here is the son of God and he shall reign forever and forever.

You are wrong, quite wrong. Away back on the level stretches of the mountain tops in the forests, amid drifts and driftwood, this sled was slowly and painfully pushed on its little hesitating start. It took power, but the power of sweating, courageous men, not of demigods. As the sled slowly started and gained momentum, it was the Law of Being that gave it speed, and the grace of God that steered its lone, scared passengers. Those passengers, white, black, red and yellow, deserve credit for their balance and pluck. But many times it was sheer luck that made the road not land the white man in the gutter, as it had others so many times before, and as it may him yet. He has gone farther than others because of others whose very falling made hard ways iced and smooth for him to traverse. His triumph is a triumph not of himself alone, but of humankind, from the pusher in the primeval forests to the last flier through the winds of the twentieth century.

And so to leave our parable and come to reality. Great as has been the human advance in the last one thousand years, it is, so far as native human ability, so far as intellectual gift and moral courage are concerned, nothing as compared with any one of ten and more millenniums before, far back in the forests of tropical Africa and in hot India, where brown and black humanity first fought climate and disease and bugs and beasts; where man dared simply to live and propagate himself. There was the hardest and greatest struggle in all the human world. If in sheer exhaustion or in desperate self-defense during this last moment of civilization he has rested, half inert and blinded with the sweat of his efforts, it is only the silly onlooker who sees but the passing moment of time, who can think of him as subhuman and inferior.

All this is Truth, but unknown, unapprehended Truth. Indeed, the greatest and most immediate danger of white culture, perhaps least sensed, is its fear of the Truth, its childish belief in the efficacy of lies as a method of human uplift. The lie is defensible; it has been used widely and often profitably among humankind. But it may be doubted if ever before in the world so many intelligent people believed in it so deeply. We deliberately and continuously deceive not simply others, but ourselves as to the truth about them, us, and the world. We have raised Propaganda to a capital "P" and elaborated an art, almost a science, of how one may make the world believe what is not true, provided the untruth is a widely wished-for thing like the probable extermination of Negroes, the failure of Japanese Imperialism, the incapacity of India for self-rule, collapse of the Russian Revolution. When in other days the world lied, it was a world that expected lies and consciously defended them; when the world lies today it is to a world that pretends to love truth.

"In other words, according to you, white folk are about the meanest and lowest on earth."

They are human, even as you and I.

"Why don't you leave them, then? Get out, go to Africa or to the North Pole; shake the dust of their hospitality from off your feet?"

There are abundant reasons. First, they have annexed the earth and hold it by transient but real power. Thus, by running away, I shall not only not escape them, but succeed in hiding myself in out of the way places where they can work their deviltry on me without photograph, telegraph, or mail service. But even more important than this: I am as bad as they are. In fact, I am related to them and they have much that belongs to me—this land, for instance, for which my fathers starved and fought; I share their sins; in fine, I am related to them.

"By blood?"

By Blood.

"Then you are railing at yourself. You are not black; you are no Negro."

And you? Yellow blood and black has deluged Europe in days past even more than America yesterday. You are not white, as the measurements of your head will show.

"What then becomes of all your argument, if there are no races and we are all so horribly mixed as you maliciously charge?"

Oh, my friend, can you not see that I am laughing at you? Do you suppose this world of men is simply a great layer cake with superimposed slices of inferior and superior races, interlaid with mud?

No, no. Human beings are infinite in variety, and when they are agglutinated in groups, great and small, the groups differ as though they, too, had integrating souls. But they have not. The soul is still individual if it is free. Race is a cultural, sometimes an historical fact. And all that I really have been trying to say is that a certain group that I know and to which I belong, as contrasted with the group you know and to which you belong, and in which you fanatically and glorifyingly believe, bears in its bosom just now the spiritual hope of this land because of the persons who compose it and not by divine command.

"But what is this group; and how do you differentiate it; and how can you call it 'black' when you admit it is not black?"

I recognize it quite easily and with full legal sanction; the black man is a person who must ride "Jim Crow" in Georgia.

My mythical friend Van Dieman is not my only white companion. I have others—many others; one and one especially I want to bring to your attention not because of his attitude toward me but rather because of his attitude toward himself. He represents the way in which my environing white group distorts and frustrates itself even as it strives toward Justice and all because of me. In other words, because of the Negro problem. The average reasonable, conscientious, and fairly intelligent white American faces continuing paradox.

This other friend of mine is free, white, and twenty-one. Which is to say—he is as free as the law and his income, his family and friends, and his formal and informal education allow. He is "white" so far as the records show and as tradition tells; he is not simply twenty-one—he is fifty-one. He is respectable, that is, he belongs to the Episcopal Church, the Union League and Harvard Clubs, and the Republican Party. He is educated, in the sense that he can read if he will, he can write in case his stenographer is absent and he has the privilege of listening to Metropolitan Opera on Tuesdays. He is a Son of the American Revolution, a reserve officer and a member of the American Legion. He reads the *Times* and the *Evening Post* (Saturday); he subscribes for the *Atlantic* and last year he read two books. He also began "Man the Unknown." He owns a home in Westchester assessed at fifty thousand; he drives a Buick. He associates quite often with a wife and a child of fifteen and more often with his fellow employees of the wholesale house which pays him ten thousand a year.

Frankly, my friend faces a dilemma. It is this: his pastor, the Reverend J. Simpson Stodges, D.D., preaches to him Sundays (except July, August and September) a doctrine that sounds like this (I say "sounds" because Dr. Stodges has explanations which mitigate the extremities of his ex cathedra statements): The Doctor asserts in sermons that Peace on Earth is the message of Christ, the Divine leader of men; that this means Good Will to all human beings; that it means Freedom, Toleration of the mistakes, sins and shortcomings of not only your friends but of your enemies. That the Golden Rule of Christianity is to treat others as you want to be treated and that finally you should be willing to sacrifice your comfort, your convenience, your wealth and even your life for mankind; in other words, that Poverty is better than riches and that the meek shall inherit the earth.

Stated thus plainly, this is to my friend's mind pretty stiff doctrine for an ordinary human being in A.D. 1940; and while he believes it in a sense (having been reared in a Godly and Presbyterian household and by a father who spared no rods and spoiled no children), yet, as he puts it to Dr. Stodges in his own parlor, Could a man live up to all that today?

Now, Dr. Stodges out of the pulpit is a most companionable fellow; excellent family, good manners, Oxford accent and Brooks Brothers to-order clothes. He plays keen golf, smokes a rare weed and knows a Bronx cocktail from a Manhattan. Well, the Doctor explained things rather satisfactorily. This Christian business of Peace, Good Will, the Golden Rule, Liberty and Poverty, was, of course, the Ideal. But, bless your soul, man, we can't all always attain the heights, much less live in their rarefied atmosphere. Aim at 'em—that's the point, and in fact, at least live a Gentleman with the "G" capitalized.

Now my friend is exceedingly anxious to be a gentleman. His father, to be sure, sneered at gentlemen and his grandfather for certain obscure reasons both hated them and denied their existence. His great-great-great-grandfather, whose existence the Media Research Bureau had discovered, was, however, highbred enough to shoulder a pitchfork against England. But at college, at his club, and with his daily companions it appeared altogether desirable to be genteel—to have manners, an "air," and a tailor. As there was no one to preach gentility in plain words, my friend has gathered this rather vague definition: a Gentleman relies on the Police and Law for protection and self-assertion; he is sustained by a fine sense of Justice for himself and his Family, past and present; he is always courteous in public with "ladies first" and precedence to "gray hairs"; and even in private, he minds his manners and dignity and resists his neighbor's wife; he is charitable, giving to the needy and deserving, to the poor and proud, to inexplicable artists and to the Church. He certainly does not believe in the WPA or other alphabetical ways of encouraging laziness and waste and increasing his taxes. And finally, without ostentation, he is exclusive; picking his associates with care and fine discrimination and appearing socially only where the Best People appear. All this calls for money and a good deal of it. He does not want to be vulgarly and ostentatiously rich. As millionaires go, he is relatively poor, which is poverty as he understands it.

Now my friend knows that this conception lets one in for a certain snobbishness and tendency toward "climbing." And yet it does furnish atmosphere, comfort and a reasonable rule of life for a modern man of position. It is not, of course, the Christianity of the Gospels, nor the career of the Knight Errant; but it is a good, honest, middle path suited to good, honest, middle-aged men.

If the matter halted here, my friend might be vaguely disappointed, but fairly well satisfied. After all, in the workaday life we can't expect moral heroes in quantity. But the trouble is, my friend saw the edges of the Great War (from a swivel chair in America) and he belongs to the American Legion. Also he reads the papers and converses in club lobbies. From this he has assimilated a new and alarming code of action. As Americans we've got to be "prepared" for "defense." Well enough to think of a world of peace, but we haven't got it. Not only that, but the world is not preparing for peace. Everywhere and all over it is not only preparing for war—it is fighting. What is the sense of man, even though he be big, strong, well, sitting down empty-handed while around him are grouped a dozen men armed to the teeth with every device that brains and money can furnish? No, no, this will never do. We've got to have an army and a big army for a big country. We need a militia and a universal draft; we need several big seventy-five million dollar battle-ships with cruisers, airplane carriers and submersibles. We must play expensively at war with elaborate maneuvers. Defense, Preparedness—that's the word.

America must be prepared for all eventualities. England wants her trade, France wants her gold, Germany wants her markets, Russia wants her laborers remade into Bolsheviks. Italy wants her raw material; and above all—Japan! Japan is about to conquer the world for the yellow race and then she'll be ready to swallow America. We must, therefore, be prepared to defend ourselves.

In order to defend America and make an efficient, desirable country, we must have authority and discipline. This may not sound like the Good Will of the Christian but at bottom, it is. There is no use pretending any longer that all men are equal. We know perfectly well that Negroes, Chinamen, Mexicans and a lot of others who are presuming to exercise authority in this country are not our equals. Human beings should be considered as facts and not as possibilities and most of them have no possibilities. Unless, therefore, we have Efficiency—Ability at the top and submission and thrift at the bottom—we are going to come a cropper. Critics may sneer at this and call it caste or fascism, but a country and a world governed by gentlemen for gentlemen is after all the only one worth living in.

There may come some argument as to who should belong to this ruling caste of the Efficient. My friend does not want to be snobbish nor assume too much. Ability will rise. On the whole it would seem that well-bred persons of English descent and New England nurture are the kernel and hope of the land. There will, of course, be modifications in the membership of this group. Without doubt remnants of the Southern slave-holding aristocracy and some of the Mid-Western agrarian stock belong. But we have got to have the best at the top and we know pretty well who the best are.

This hierarchy we should defend vigorously. For this, deliberate propaganda is necessary and permissible; propaganda assists the truth and hurries it on; it may at times exaggerate and distort but all this is for a defensible end and newspapers, radio channels, and news distribution agencies should be owned and used for this end. Here comes the necessity of smoking out radicals. Radicals are insidious intellectuals, themselves usually unsuccessful misfits, envious of success and misled by cranks. They not only advocate impossible panaceas but they undermine the safety of the state. If honest and able, they are even more dangerous. They should be sternly dealt with.

Having thus established a country worth saving, patriotism comes next; and patriotism means standing by your country, thick and thin. It means not simply being an American but feeling proud of America and publicly asserting the fact from time to time. Also, it means seeing to it that other people are patriotic; looking about carefully when the "Star-Spangled Banner" is played to see who is sitting down and why; keeping a watchful eye on the flag. Americans traveling abroad, or at any rate white Americans, should, like the English, have such a panoply thrown about them that street urchins will be afraid to make faces and throw stones.

Finally, my friend learned that a nation must not only be powerful; that power must expand; more territory; more commerce; widened influence and that sort of thing. America must no longer be provincial. It must sit among the great powers of the earth, consulted for all world movements. In fact, it is not too much to think of this marvelous country as a sort of superpower, umpire of humanity, tremendous, irresistible.

Now all these things intrigue my friend. On his trip to Europe last summer he was made to feel more strongly his Americanism, partly in protest against the outrageous misunderstanding and apparent jealousy of America which he met, and partly from the complacency which swelled his breast when he noted what a great country America was in the eyes of Europe and how everybody was hanging on her lightest whisper. Would she please call a peace conference? Would she please restore the gold standard? Would she kindly sell her raw materials cheap? Would she please lend a helping hand in China and Africa? Would she forbear from completely swallowing South America? And so forth and so on.

But there was one difficulty about this code of Americanism which my friend learned; and that was that it led directly and inevitably to another code to which, theoretically, he was definitely opposed, but which, logically, he could not see his way to resist. It was not stated as clearly as any of the other codes; it certainly did not echo in Sunday sermons, although he sometimes suspected it lurked there. It did not enter into his definition of "gentleman" and seemed in fact opposed to it. And yet, somehow, all the gentlemen that he knew were strongly for it. It did seem bound up with his Americanism and yet there again, he resented the logical imputation.

The statement of this fourth code of action was found in unfinished assumption rather than plain words; in unfinished sentences, in novels, in editorials written for country papers by city scriveners; in organizations like the Ku Klux Klan which he thought was extremely silly; or the Security League, which was very respectable. This code rested upon the fact that he was a White Man. Now until my friend had reached the age of thirty he had not known that he was a white man, or at least he had not realized it. Certainly, so far as his skin was concerned, he knew that he was not black, brown, or very yellow. But it never occurred to him that there was any divine significance in that rather negative fact. But lately he had come to realize that his whiteness was fraught with tremendous responsibilities, age-old and infinite in future possibilities. It would seem that colored folks were a threat to the world. They were going to overthrow white folk by sheer weight of numbers, destroy their homes and marry their daughters.

It was this last point that particularly got upon his nerves. He had, as I've said, a girl of fifteen, rather pretty and fragile; and he and his wife were planning already certain advantageous family and economic alliances for the young miss. Much of their social life was already being guided to this end. Now, imagine a world where she would have to repel the advances of Japanese or Negroes!

He had noticed with some disturbed feeling that Negroes in particular were not nearly as agreeable and happy as they used to be. He had not for years been able to get a cheap, good colored cook and the last black yard man asked quite exorbitant wages. He now had white help. They were expensive but in fashion. He had had only last year to join in a neighborhood association to keep a Negro from buying a lot right in the next block!

Now all this led him to understand, if not to sympathize with, a code which began with War. Not only preparedness nor simply defense, but war against the darker races, carried out now and without too nice discrimination as to who were dark: war against the Riff, the Turk, Chinese, Japanese, Indians, Negroes, Mulattoes, Italians and South Americans. Recently this fact, which he knew perfectly well himself, has been confirmed by that great authority, Charles Lindbergh, who flew into wealth and omniscience through one trip to Paris. War and all that goes to implement war: We must hate our enemies. That sounds heathenish; but there can be no effective war, no determination to fight evil to the death, without full-bellied Hate! We need to lay emphasis upon "white": acting like a "White" man, doing things "white"; "white" angels, etc.; efforts to boost novels which paint white heroes, black devils and brown scoundrels with yellow souls; efforts to use the theater and the movies for the same reason; emphasis upon the race element in crime.

In this matter, too, there cannot unfortunately be too nice an honesty. Self-preservation is a First Law; the crimes and short-comings of white people, while unfortunate, are incidental; news of them must be ignored or suppressed; crimes of colored people are characteristic and must be advertised as stern warnings. He had noted with surprise and satisfaction that the only place in the movies where Negroes were in special evidence was in jails. That was the only way to make that true which ought to be true and which was true but hidden. War, righteous Hate and then Suspicion. It was very easy to be deceived by other races; to think of the Negro as good-natured; of the Chinaman as simply "queer"; of the Japanese as "imitative." No. Look for low subtle methods and death-dealing ideals. Meet them by full-blooded contempt for other races. Teach this to children so that it will become instinctive. Then they won't get into trouble by playing artlessly with colored children or even with colored dolls unless, of course, they are attired as servants.

Next, Exploitation. No use wincing at the word. No sense in letting Roosevelt and the "New Deal" mislead you. The poor must be poor so that the Rich may be Rich. That's clear and true. It merely means using the world for the good of the world and those who own it; bringing out its wealth and abundance; making the lazy and shiftless and ignorant work for their soul's good and for the profit of their betters, who alone are capable of using Wealth to promote Culture.

And finally, Empire: the white race as ruler of all the world and the world working for it, and the world's wealth piled up for the white man's use. This may seem harsh and selfish and yet, of course, it was perfectly natural. Naturally white men would and must rule and any question of their ruling should be met and settled promptly. My friend had not thought that there was any question of this, and there was not before the first World War. There we made the wretched mistake of letting the colored folk dip in, and it turned their weak heads. They almost thought they won the war. He remembered his own disgust at seeing American Negroes actually tricked up as officers—shoulder-straps, Sam Browne belts, and all. He could not conceive of a world where white people did not rule colored people, and certainly if the matter actually came to a trial of force, would he not naturally have to stand for War, Hate, Suspicion and Exploitation in order to put over the Empire of the Whites?

The trouble was, however, that when my friend tabulated all of the codes which he at once and apparently simultaneously was to put in action, he found a most astonishing result, and here it is:

Christian	*Gentleman*	*American*	*White Man*
Peace	Justice	Defense	War
Good Will	Manners	Caste	Hate
Golden Rule	Exclusiveness	Propaganda	Suspicion
Liberty	Police	Patriotism	Exploitation
Poverty	Wealth	Power	Empire

Looking them over, he doesn't know what on earth to do. It is not only dilemma, it is almost quadri-lemma. Perhaps he might put a line between "Christian Gentleman" on the one hand and the "American White Man" on the other, and so arrange a very tremendous and puzzling dilemma.

My friend comes and sits down with me and asks me frankly what to do about it. And I? Why, I appeal to you, Gentle Reader. What should he do about it?

My friend's fault is that he is logical. His reasoning is a clean, simple process like two plus two equal four. This is the cause of his present unrest. Other folk are deliciously impervious to reason. They are pacifists with the help of the police and backed by careful preparation for war. They are filled with Good Will for all men, provided these men are in their places and certain of them kept there by severe discountenance. In that case courtesy smooths human relations. They certainly aim to treat others as they want to be treated themselves, so far as this is

consistent with their own necessarily exclusive position. This
position must be maintained by propaganda inculcating a perfectly defensible contempt for inferiors and suspicion of strangers and radicals. They believe in liberty under a firm police
system backed by patriotism and an organization of work which
will yield profit to capital. And, of course, they believe in poverty so long as they have sufficient wealth. This they are certain
is the way to make America the greatest country on earth for
white supremacy.

This makes my friend tear his pale hair. "How can they do
it?" he yells. "It ain't reasonable." I explained patiently: possibly they are playing acrostics. See how they might arrange their
meanings?

Peace

       Manners

             Propaganda

                    Exploitation

Good Will

       Exclusiveness

            Patriotism

                Empire
                Hate

            Propaganda

       Police

Poverty

                War

           Caste

       Exclusiveness

Liberty

"Fact is," I add, "I've heard them singing in St. Thomas's:

> The Prince of *Peace* goes forth to *War*
> A *Kingly Crown* to ga-a-ain!
> His *blood-red banner* floats afar.
> Who follows *in his Name!*"

"Your quotation is not exact," responds my literal friend.
"Perhaps not, but it comes to the same thing: they combine

Peace, War, Empire, Bolshevism and Jesus Christ in one happy family."

My friend waves all this aside. "Outside of spoofing and horse-play," he insists, "it's all both reasonable and impossible. Take each column alone and it is to me absolutely convincing. I believe in it. Think of a world with Peace, Good Will, Freedom, the Golden Rule and Poverty! My God, what a Paradise, despite death and accident, cold and heat—what? That fellow Gandhi is the only human leader today with the right idea. It's magnificent. It's tremendous."

"Plain living and high thinking," I suggest.

"Of course," he responds, "only—well, one wants some Beauty—travel, gowns, palaces, diamonds, and Grand Opera —"

I intervene, "But don't forget the preceding lines: 'never to blend our pleasure or our pride, with sorrow of the meanest thing that feels.' "

"But—well, that brings me down out of the clouds," he complains. "This can't be a world of saints. We have got to have wealth and servants. Servants must be cheap and willing and the mean ought not to be so sensitive. Perhaps they are not. But why not have a world of gentlemen—well-policed, everybody in his place; all the rich, courteous and generous and all the poor appreciative; propaganda for the right, love of country and prosperous business; White World leading the Colored as far as the darkies can go. Certainly despite all your democracy, blood will tell. Now that seems to be *practical.* They've got something like that in England. Or at least, they think they have.

"But if I put this thing to the club, as man to man, no sooner have I mentioned England than they're in arms. England, dammit, has a bigger navy and merchant marine than we, with which she monopolizes the world-carrying trade; she patronizes and despises us, and then pats us on the back when her chestnuts are red-hot; she rules a bigger empire. And France won't pay us and has a big black army; and Russia is stirring up Revolution with a big Red army; and Germany! Good Lord! Hitler is anti-Christ. I tell you what, we got to watch out. America is the greatest nation on earth and the world is jealous of her. We got to be prepared if it takes a billion a year for powder and guns. We've got to be disciplined; a stern, severe code for the lazy and criminal; training for boy scouts and militia. We must put patriotism before everything—make 'em salute the flag, stop radical treason, keep out the dirty foreigners, disfranchise niggers and make America a Power!

"Well, I like America. Darn it! I *love* it. My father died for it, although not in war—and I am reasonably willing to. There's no doubt about it, lambs have got no business prowling about lions and—oh, Hell! Honest to God, what do you think Asia and Africa would do to us, if they got a chance?"

"Skin us alive," I answer cheerfully, loving the "us."

"Well, then! Skin them and skin 'em first and keep 'em skinned. I'm a He-White-Man, get me?

"Then, look at these other columns. Suppose they are not logical, correct, compelling. We cannot run this world without the police and courts of Justice. We must not be discourteous even to the pushing, careless, impudent American fellow-citizen, but something is due our own self-respect. Can we get on without being exclusive? I don't mean downright snobbishness, but be careful, nice, 'aristocratic' in the best meaning of the term. Finally, we of the upper class must have money. We must have it, no matter how we get it, or civilization is lost.

"Well, now, if we cannot do without these things, then, they must become our rule of life. But no sooner have you settled it this way than there comes that business of being an American. Can we give that up? Can we go in for Humanity and the Internation? Lord knows I'd like to but somehow, I can't see it. Suppose America disarmed like Denmark, gave up poison gas, big battleships and dinky little officers in khaki? Suppose we continue to neglect discipline for the mob and stop teaching thick and thin patriotism? I admit it isn't exactly honest business; America isn't so wonderful as nations go, but must we not make Americans believe it wonderful? Can we emphasize the fact that Lincoln told smutty stories and Washington held slaves and Jefferson begat bastards, and Webster drank more than was good for him? Suppose we did not become powerful as well as big? What is going to happen to us? Well, there you are. We've got to be Americans even if we give up being Christians and Gentlemen."

Or again, and here my friend gets a bit embarrassed and red in the face: "You see," he says to me confidentially, "I've got a little daughter, young yet, but a nice little thing. Probably she is going to be pretty, certainly is going to have some money from her aunt as well as a bit from me. She is being educated, and I may say rather expensively educated, in a private school. She may go in for art or some high class profession, or she may not; but certainly, I hope she will marry and marry well. There will be children and grandchildren and great-grandchildren and so on ad infinitum. Now, I tell you frankly, I want them all white. Even if she were a son, while the case wouldn't be so bad, still I don't want to think of colored folk sharing my blood. Can you for a moment conceive a world where brown men and dagoes were giving orders to white men and women? It would spell the end of civilization. Of course, there may be a few exceptions, but the mass of the colored world can't think, they can't rule, they can't direct, and we mustn't let them try. And to keep them from trying we've got to pound them back into their places every time they show their heads above the ramparts!"

Then my friend stopped. He turned red and grew apologetic. "Of course," he stammered, "I don't exactly mean you—you are an Exception, at least in some respects—"

"In some respects?" I rejoin helplessly. But my friend stiffened. Suddenly he ceased speaking and stared at the headlines in the evening paper. The world had gone to war again to defend Democracy!

The democracy which the white world seeks to defend does not exist. It has been splendidly conceived and discussed, but not realized. If it ever is to grow strong enough for self-defense and for embracing the world and developing human culture to its highest, it must include not simply the lower classes among the whites now excluded from voice in the control of industry; but in addition to that it must include the colored peoples of Asia and Africa, now hopelessly imprisoned by poverty and ignorance. Unless these latter are included and in so far as they are not, democracy is a mockery and contains within itself the seeds of its own destruction.

Hitler is the late crude but logical exponent of white world race philosophy since the Conference of Berlin in 1884. Europe had followed the high, ethical dream of a young Jew but twisted that ethic beyond recognition to any end that Europe wanted. If that end was murder, the "Son of God went forth to war!" If that end was slavery, God thundered, "Cursed be Canaan," and Paul echoed "Servants obey your masters!" If poverty was widespread and seemingly inevitable, Christ was poor and alms praiseworthy.

There persisted the mud-sill theory of society that civilization not only permitted but must have the poor, the diseased, the wretched, the criminal upon which to build its temples of light. Western Europe did not and does not want democracy, never believed in it, never practiced it and never without fundamental and basic revolution will accept it. Not the keen, the bold, the brave and the enlightened are the ones which modern individual struggle throws to the fore but rather the lucky and the strong.

How now, not so much in the judgment of the common man, but in the light of science, can the racial attitude of the white world be explained and rationalized and removed from the harsh judgment put upon it by the darker races today? Negroes in Africa, Indians in Asia, mulattoes and mestizoes in the West Indies, Central and South America, all explain the attitude of the white world as sheer malevolence; while the white people of the leading European countries honestly regard themselves as among the great benefactors of mankind and especially of colored mankind.

In this dilemma sociologists of earlier years took refuge in inventing a new entity, the group, which had action, guilt, praise and blame quite apart from the persons composing the group. It was of course a metaphysical hypothesis which had its uses in reasoning, but could not be regarded as corresponding to exact truth. No such group over-soul has been proven to exist.

The facts of the situation however as science today conceives it, are clear. The individual may act consciously and rationally and be responsible for what he does; but on the other hand many of his actions, and indeed, as we are coming to believe, most of his actions, are not rational and many of them arise from subconscious urges. It is our duty to assess praise and blame for the rational and conscious acts of men, but to regard the vast area of the subconscious and the irrational and especially of habit and convention which also produce significant action, as an area where we must apply other remedies and judgments if we would get justice and right to prevail in the world. Above all we must survey these vague and uncharted lands and measure their limits.

Looking at this whole matter of the white race as it confronts the world today, what can be done to make its attitudes rational and consistent and calculated to advance the best interests of the whole world of men? The first point of attack is undoubtedly the economic. The progress of the white world must cease to rest upon the poverty and the ignorance of its own proletariat and of the colored world. Thus industrial imperialism must lose its reason for being and in that way alone can the great racial groups of the world come into normal and helpful relation to each other. The present attitude and action of the white world is not based solely upon rational, deliberate intent. It is a matter of conditioned reflexes; of long followed habits, customs and folkways; of subconscious trains of reasoning and unconscious nervous reflexes. To attack and better all this calls for more than appeal and argument. It needs carefully planned and scientific propaganda; the vision of a world of intelligent men with sufficient income to live decently and with the will to build a beautiful world. It will not be easy to accomplish all this, but the quickest way to bring the reason of the world face to face with this major problem of human progress is to listen to the complaint of those human beings today who are suffering most from white attitudes, from white habits, from the conscious and unconscious wrongs which white folk are today inflicting on their victims. The colored world therefore must be seen as existing not simply for itself but as a group whose insistent cry may yet become the warning which awakens the world to its truer self and its wider destiny.

Du Bois' immense contribution to an understanding of international affairs was his insistence on viewing the world from a racial perspective. At the beginning of the twentieth century he had recognized the overwhelming importance of race as a point of conflict in the coming years and events bore him out.

In "Prospect of a World without Race Conflict" he viewed the world as it would be after World War II. His prognosis was that racial conflict would persist for many years. In this article, he set forth a program for the minimization of international racial conflict.

(*American Journal of Sociology*, March 1944.)

PROSPECT OF A WORLD WITHOUT RACE CONFLICT

Abstract

The philosophy of biological race differences which divide the world into superior and inferior people will persist after this war. This is shown in the persecution of Jews, the refusal to emancipate India, the relations between Asia and Europe, and the attitude toward South America and the Caribbean. To leave out discussions of race in post-war planning enables Europe and America to fight for democracy and the abolition of poverty while ignoring the fact that race prejudice makes this fight consistent with compulsory poverty, disease, and repression of most of the workers of the world.

It is with great regret that I do not see after this war, or within any reasonable time, the possibility of a world without race conflict; and this is true despite the fact that race conflict is playing a fatal role in the modern world. The supertragedy of this war is the treatment of the Jews in Germany. There has been nothing comparable to this in modern history. Yet its technique and its reasoning have been based upon a race philosophy similar to that which has dominated both Great Britain and the United States in relation to colored people.

This philosophy postulates a fundamental difference among the greater groups of people in the world, which makes it necessary that the superior peoples hold the inferior in check and rule them in accordance with the best interest of these superiors. Of course, many of the usual characteristics were missing in this outbreak of race hate in Germany. There was in reality little of physical difference between German and Jew. No one has been able to accuse the Jews of inferiority; rather it was the superiority of the Jews in certain respects which was the real cause of conflict. Nevertheless, the ideological basis of this attack was that of fundamental biological difference showing itself in spiritual and cultural incompatibility. Another difference distinguishes this race war. Usually the cure for race persecution and subordination has been thought to be segregation, but in this case the chance to segregate the Jews, at least partially in Palestine, has practically been vetoed by the British government.

In other parts of the world the results of race conflict are clear. The representative of Prime Minister Churchill presiding over the British war cabinet has been the prime minister of the Union of South Africa. Yet South Africa has without doubt the worst race problem of the modern world. The natives have been systematically deprived of their land, reduced to the status of a laboring class with the lowest of wages, disfranchised, living and working under caste conditions with only a modicum of education, and exposed to systematic public and private insult. There is a large population of mixed-bloods, and the poverty, disease, and crime throughout the Union of South Africa are appalling. Here in a land which furnishes gold and diamonds and copper, the insignia of the luxury and technique of modern civilization, this race hate has flourished and is flourishing. Smuts himself, as political leader of the Union of South Africa, has carried out much of the legislation upon which this race conflict is based; and, although from time to time he has expressed liberal ideas, he has not tried or succeeded in basically ameliorating the fundamental race war in that part of the world.

The situation in India is another case of racial conflict. The mass of people there are in the bondage of poverty, disfranchisement, and social caste. Despite eminent and widely known leadership, there has not come on the part of the British any effective attempt fundamentally to change the attitude of the governing country toward the subject peoples. The basic reason for this, openly or by inference, is the physical difference of race which makes it, according to British thought, impossible that these peoples should within any reasonable space of time become autonomous or self-governing. There have been promises, to be sure, from time to time, and promises are pending; but no one can doubt that if these people were white and of English descent, a way out of the present impasse would have long since been found.

There is no doubt but that India is a congeries of ignorant, poverty-stricken, antagonistic groups who are destined to go through all the hell of internal strife before they emancipate themselves. But it is just as true that Europe of the sixteenth century was no more ready for freedom and autonomy than India. But Europe was not faced and coerced by a powerful overlord who did not believe Europeans were men and was determined to treat them as serfs to minister to his own comfort and luxury.

In India we have the first thoroughgoing case of modern colonial imperialism. With the capitalism built on the African slave trade and on the sugar, tobacco, and cotton crops of America, investment in India grew and spread for three hundred years, until there exists the greatest modern case of the exploitation of one people by another. This exploitation has been modified in various ways: some education has been furnished the Indians, a great system of railroads has been installed, and industrialism has been begun. But nothing has been done to loosen to any appreciable degree the strangle hold of the British Empire on the destinies of four hundred million human beings. The prestige and profit of the control of India have made it impossible for the British to conceive of India as an autonomous land.

The greatest and most dangerous race problem today is the problem of relations between Asia and Europe: the question as to how far "East is East and West is West" and of how long they are going to retain the relation of master and serf. There is in reality no difference between the reaction to this European idea on the parts of Japan and China. It is a question simply of method of eliminating it. The idea of Japan was to invoke war and force—to drive Europe out of Asia and substitute the domination of a weak Asia by a strong Japan. The answer of China was co-operation and gradual understanding between Great Britain, France, America, and China. Chinese leaders are under no illusions whatever as to the past attitude of Europe toward Chinese. The impudence, browbeating, robbery, rape, and insult is one long trail of blood and tears, from the Opium War to the kowtowing before the emperor in Berlin. Even in this present war and alliance there has occurred little to reassure China: certain courtesies from the British and belated and meager justice on the part of the United States, after the Soong sister had swept in on us with her retinue, jade, and jewels. There has not only been silence concerning Hong Kong, Burma, and Singapore but there is the continued assumption that the subjugation of Japan is in the interest of Europe and America and not of Asia. American military leaders have insisted that we must have in the Pacific after this war American bases for armed force. But why? If Asia is going to develop as a self-governing, autonomous part of the world, equal to other parts, why is policing by foreigners necessary? Why cannot Asia police itself? Only because of the deep-seated belief among Europeans and Americans that yellow people are the biological inferiors to the whites and not fit for self-government.

Not only does Western Europe believe that most of the rest of the world is biologically different but it believes that in this difference lies congenital inferiority; that the black and brown and yellow people are not simply untrained in certain ways of doing and methods of civilization; that they are naturally inferior and inefficient; that they are a danger to civilization as civilization is understood in Europe. This belief is so fundamental that it enters into the very reforms that we have in mind for the post-war world.

In the United States the race problem is peculiarly important just now. We see today a combination of northern investors and southern Bourbons desiring not simply to overthrow the New Deal but to plunge the United States into fatal reaction. The power of the southerners arises from the suppression of the Negro and poor-white vote, which gives the rotten borough of Mississippi four times the political power of Massachusetts and enables the South through the rule of seniority to pack the committees of Congress and to dominate it. Nothing can be done about this situation until we face fairly the question of color discrimination in the South; until the social, political, and economic equality of civilized men is recognized, despite race, color, and poverty.

In the Caribbean area, in Central and South America, there has been for four hundred years wide intermixture of European, African, and Red Indian races. The result in one respect is widely different from that of Europe and North America; the social equality of Negroes, Indians, and mulattoes who were civilized was recognized without question. But the full results of this cultural liberalism were largely nullified by the economic control which Western Europe and North America held over these lands. The exploitation of cheap colored labor through poverty and low prices for materials was connived at as usual in the civilized world and the spoils shared with local white politicians. Economic and social prestige favored the whites and hindered the colored. A legend that the alleged backwardness of the South Americans was due to race mixture was so far stressed in the world that South America feared it and catered to it; it became the habit to send only white Brazilians, Bolivians, and Mexicans abroad to represent their countries; to encourage white immigration at all costs, even to loss of autonomy; to draw color lines in the management of industry dominated by Europe and in society where foreigners were entertained. In short, to pretend that South America hated and distrusted dark blood as much as the rest of the world, often even when the leaders of this policy were known themselves to be of Negro and Indian descent.

Thus the race problem of South and Central America, and especially of the islands of the Caribbean, became closely allied with European and North American practice. Only in the past few decades are there signs of an insurgent native culture, striking across the color line toward economic freedom, political self-rule, and more complete social equality between races.

There still is a residual sense of racial difference among parts of Europe; a certain contemptuous attitude toward Italy has been manifest for a long time, and the Balkans have been a byword for inefficiency and muddle. The pretensions of the Greeks to represent ancient Greek culture and of the Rumanians to be Roman have been laughed at by Western Europe. The remainder of the Balkans and Russia have been looked upon as Asiatic barbarism, aping civilization. As quasi-Asiatic, they have come in for the racial contempt poured upon the yellow peoples. This attitude greeted the Russian revolution and staged almost a race war to uphold tottering capitalism, built on racial contempt. But in Eastern Europe today are a mass of awakening men. They know and see what Russia has done for her debased masses in a single generation, cutting across lines not only between Jew and Gentile but between White Russians, Ukrainians, Tartars, Turks, Kurds, and Kalmuks. As Sidney and Beatrice Webb declared:

> All sections of the community—apart from those legally deprived of citizenship on grounds unconnected with either race or nationality—enjoy, throughout the USSR, according to law, equal rights and duties, equal privileges and equal opportunities. Nor is this merely a formal equality under the law and the federal constitution. Nowhere in the world do habit and custom and

public opinion approach nearer to a like equality in fact. Over the whole area between the Arctic Ocean and the Black Sea and the Central Asian mountains, containing vastly differing races and nationalities, men and women, irrespective of conformation of skull or pigmentation of skin, even including the occasional African Negro admitted from the United States, may associate freely with whom they please; travel in the same public vehicles and frequent the same restaurants and hotels; sit next to each other in the same colleges and places of amusement; marry wherever there is mutual liking; engage on equal terms in any craft or profession for which they are qualified; join the same churches or other societies; pay the same taxes and be elected or appointed to any office or position without exception.

This, Eastern Europe knows, while Western Europe is still determined to build its culture on race discrimination and expects Russia to help her. But how far can Russia be depended upon to defend, in world war, British and American investments in Asia and Africa?

The attitude of America and Britain toward De Gaulle is puzzling until we remember that, since Gobineau, racial assumptions have entered into the relations between France and the Nordic world. During the first World War the United States was incensed at the social equality attitudes of the "frogs," while Britain as well as Germany resented the open dependence of France on her black colonial soldiers. One present great liberal statesman, Smuts, led a crusade against arming blacks in any future European war. Yet De Gaulle not only uses Senegalese soldiers but recognizes the Negro governor of a strategic French colonial province; while Burman, writing of the history of the Free French, exclaims: "I am witnessing a miracle, the rebirth of France in the jungles of Africa!" Racial caste and profitable investment after the war indicate a halt in our support of De Gaulle. France since the eighteenth century has insisted on recognizing the social equality of civilized men despite race. She has for this reason been regarded as traitor to the white colonial front, in government and in society, despite her investors who have supported British methods. Hitler is not the only modern statesman who has sneered at "mongrel" France.

These are some but by no means all of the race problems

which face the world; yet they are not being disucssed except indirectly. The Atlantic Charter as well as the agreements in Moscow and Teheran have been practically silent on the subject of race. It is assumed that certain fundamental matters and more immediate issues must be met and settled before this difficult question of race can be faced. Let us now ask ourselves if this is ture. What *are* the fundamental questions before the world at war?

If we measure the important matters by current discussion, we may range them somewhat as follows: (1) defense against aggression; (2) full employment after the war; (3) eventual fair distribution of both raw materials and manufactured goods; (4) abolition of poverty; and (5) health.

To anyone giving thought to these problems, it must be clear that each of them, with all of its own peculiar difficulties, tends to break asunder along the lesions of race difference and race hate. Among the primary factors entering into the discussion is the folklore and supersitition which lurks in the mind of modern men and makes them thoroughly believe, in accord with inherited prejudice and unconscious cerebration, that the peoples of the world are divided into fundamentally different groups with differences that are eternal and cannot be forgotten and cannot be removed. This philosophy says that the majority of the people of the world are impossible.

Therefore, when we discuss any of the listed problems, we usually see the solution within the frame of race and race difference. When we think of defense against aggression, we are thinking particularly of Europe, and the aggregation which we have in mind is not simply another Hitler but a vaster Japan, if not all Asia and the South Sea Islands. The "Yellow peril" as envisaged by the German Emperor William II has by no means passed from the subconscious reactions of Western Europe. That is the meaning of world police and "our way of life."

When we think of the problem of unemployment, we mean especially unemployment in the developed countries of Western Europe and America. We do not have in mind any fundamental change so far as the labor of the darker world is concerned. We do not think of full employment and a living wage for the East Indian, the Chinese coolie, and the Negro of South Africa or even the Negro of our own South. We want the white laborer in England and in America to receive a living wage and economic security without periodic unemployment.

In such case we can depend on the political power of white labor to maintain the present industrial organization,. But we have little or no thought of colored labor, because it is disfranchised and kept in serfdom by the power of our present governments.

This means, of course, that the industrial organization of these countries must be standardized; they must not clog their own avenues of trade by tariff restrictions and cartels. But these plans have very seldom gone far enough to envisage any change in the relations of Europe and America to the raw material of Africa and Asia or to accepting any idea of so raising the prices of this raw material and the wages of the laborers who produce it that this mass of labor will begin to approach the level of white labor. In fact, any such prospect the white laborers with votes in their hands would in vast majorities oppose.

In both the United States and the Union of South Africa it has been the organized white laborers who have systematically by vote and mob opposed the training of the black worker and the provision of decent wages for him. In this respect they have ranged themselves with exploiting investors and disseminators of race hatred like Hitler. When recently in the United States the President's Fair Employment Practices Commission sought to secure some steps of elementary justice for black railway workers, the railway unions refused even to attend the hearings. Only the Communists and some of the C.I.O. unions have ignored the color line—a significant fact.

Our attitude toward poverty represents the constant lesion of race thinking. We have with difficulty reached a place in the modern white world where we can contemplate the abolition of poverty; where we can think of an industrial organization with no part of its essential co-operators deprived of income which will give them sufficient food and shelter, along with necessary education and some of the comforts of life. But this conception is confined almost entirely to the white race. Not only do we refuse to think of similar possibilities for the colored races but we are convinced that, even though it were possible, it would be a bad thing for the world. We must keep the Negroes, West Indians, and Indonesions poor. Otherwise they will get ambitious: they will seek strength and organization; they will demand to be treated as men, despite the fact that we know they are not men; and they will ask social equality for civilized human beings the world over.

There is a similar attitude with regard to health; we want

white people to be well and strong, to "multiply and replenish the earth"; but we are interested in the health of colored people only in so far as it may threaten the health and wealth of whites. Thus in colonies where white men reside as masters, they segregate themselves in the most healthful parts of the country, and let the natives fester and die in the swamps and lowlands. It is for this reason that Englishmen and South Africans have seized the high land of Kenya and driven the most splendid of races of East Africa into the worst parts of the lowland, to the parts which are infested by the tsetse fly, where their cattle die and they are forced laborers on white farms.

Perhaps in no area of modern civilized endeavor is the matter of race revealed more startlingly than in the question of education. We have doubts as to the policy of so educating the colored races that they will be able to take part in modern civilization. We are willing to educate them so that they can help in our industrial development and we want them to become good workmen so long as they are unorganized. But when it comes to a question of real acquaintanceship with what the more advanced part of the world has done and is doing, we try to keep the backward races as ignorant as possible. We limit their schools, their travel, and their knowledge of modern tongues.

There are, of course, notable exceptions: the Negro colleges of the southern United States, the Indian universities, and some advance even in university training in South Africa and in East and West Africa. But this advance is hindered by the fact that popular education is so backward that the number of persons who can qualify for higher training is very small, especially the number who can enter the professions necessary to protect the economic status of the natives and to guide the natives in avoidance of disease. In all these matters race interferes with education.

Beyond this we have only to mention religion. There is no denying that certain missionaries have done fine work in ameliorating the lot of backward people, but at the same time there is not a ghost of a doubt that today the organized Christian church is unfavorable toward race equality. It is split into racial sections and is not disposed to disturb to any great degree the attitude of civilization toward the Chinese, the Indians, and the Negroes. The recent pronouncement of the Federation of Churches of Christ was a fine and forward-looking document, but it has aroused no attention, much less enthusiasm, among the mass of Christians and will not. The Catholic church never champions the political or economic rights of subject peoples.

This insistent clinging to the older patterns of race thought has had extraordinary influence upon modern life. In the first place, it has for years held back the progress of the social sciences. The social sciences from the beginning were deliberately used as instruments to prove the inferiority of the majority of the people of the world, who were being used as slaves for the comfort and culture of the masters. The social sciences long looked upon this as one of their major duties. History declared that the Negro had no history. Biology exaggerated the physical differences among men. Economics even today cannot talk straight on colonial imperialism. Psychology has not yet recovered from the shame of its "intelligence" tests and its record of "conclusions" during the first World War.

Granted, therefore, that this is the basic attitude of the majority of civilized people, despite exceptions and individual differences, what must we expect after this war? In the first place, the British Empire is going to continue, if Mr. Churchill has his way, without "liquidation"; and there is slight chance that the English Labour party or any other democratic elements in England are going to be able to get past the suspensory veto of the House of Lords and the overwhelming social power of the British aristocracy. In America the control of wealth over our democracy is going to be reinforced by the action of the oligarchic South. A war-weary nation is going to ignore reform and going to work to make money. If, of course, the greedy industrial machine breaks down in 1950 as it did in 1929, there will be trouble; but the Negroes will be its chief victims and sufferers. Belgium has held its Congo empire with rare profit during the war, and the home land will recoup its losses in Europe by more systematic rape of Africa. So Holland will batten down again upon the South Seas, unless the Japanese interlude forces some slight change of heart. South America will become an even more closely integrated part of British and American industry, and the West Indies will work cheaply or starve, while tourists throw them pennies.

The only large cause for disquiet on the part of Western Europe and North America is the case of Russia. There they are reassured as to the attitude of Stalin toward the working people of the Western world. Evidently he has decided that the Western European and American workers with votes in their hands are capable of deciding their own destiny; and, if they are not, it is their own fault. But what is going to be the attitude of Russia toward colonial peoples? How far and where and when is Russia going to protect and restore British and American investments and control in Asia and Africa? Certainly her attitude toward the Chinese has shown in the past and still shows that she has the greatest sympathy with coolie labor and no love for Chiang Kai-shek. Will she have a similar attitude toward the other peoples of Asia, of Africa, and of the South Seas? If so, smooth restoration of colonial imperialism is not going to be easy.

What now can be done by intelligent men who are aware of the continuing danger of present racial attitudes in the world? We may appeal to two groups of men: first, to those leaders of white culture who are willing to take action and, second, to the leaders of races which are victims of present conditions. White leaders and thinkers have a duty to perform in making known the conclusions of science on the subject of biological race. It takes science long to percolate to the mass unless definite effort is made. Public health is still handicapped by superstitions long disproved by science; and race fiction is still taught in schools, in newspapers, and in novels. This careless ignorance of the facts of race is precisely the refuge where antisocial economic reaction flourishes.

We must then, first, have wide dissemination of truth. But this is not all: we need deliberate and organized action on the front where race fiction is being used to prolong economic inequality and injustice in the world. Here is a chance for a modern missionary movement, not in the interest of religious dogma, but to dissipate the economic illiteracy which clouds modern thought. Organized industry has today made the teaching of the elementary principles of economic thought almost impossible in our schools and rare in our colleges; by outlawing "Communistic" propaganda, it has effectually in press and on platform almost stopped efforts at clear thinking on economic reform. Protest and revelation fall on deaf ears, because the public does not know the basic facts of the distribution of property and income today among individuals; accurate details of the sources of income and conditions of production and distribution of goods and use of human services, in order that we may know who profits by investment in Asia and Africa as well as in America and Europe, and why and how they profit.

Next we need organized effort to release the colored laborer from the domination of the investor. This can best be accomplished by the organization of the labor of the world as consumers, replacing the producer attitude by knowledge of consumer needs. Here the victims of race prejudice can play their great role. They need no longer be confined to two paths; appeal to a white world ruled by investors in colored degradation or war and revolt. There is a third path: the extrication of the poverty-stricken, ignorant laborer and consumer from his bondage by his own efforts as a worker and consumer, united to increase the price of his toil and reduce the cost of the necessities of life. This is being done here and there, but the news of it is suppressed, the difficulties of united action deliberately increased, and law and government united in colonial areas to prevent organization, manipulate prices, and stifle thought by force. Here colored leaders must act; but, before they act, they must know. Today, naturally, they are for the most part as economically illiterate as their masters. Thus Indian moneylenders are the willing instruments of European economic oppression in India; and many American and West Indian Negroes regard as economic progress the chance to share in the exploitation of their race by whites.

A union of economic liberals across the race line, with the object of driving exploiting investors from their hideout behind race discrimination, by freeing thought and action in colonial areas is the only realistic path to permanent peace today.

A great step toward this would be an international mandates commission with native representation, with power to investigate and report, and with jurisdiction over all areas where the natives have no effective voice in government.

Color and Democracy *was written as Du Bois' response to the preliminary founding conference of the United Nations in 1944 at Dumbarton Oaks. At the end of World War I it had been his hope that Western society would begin to take steps to insure the self-determination of the colored world. Increased exploitation of that world was the only result. As World War II neared its end,*

Du Bois saw even more clearly that unless Western society ceased its exploitation of the colored world, the eventual result would be international race war. As an associate delegate to the founding conference of the United Nations in San Francisco the following year, Du Bois saw that the United Nations would not be the instrument for the cessation of colonial exploitation as he had hoped.

The following selection from the second chapter of Color and Democracy, *"The Disfranchised Colonies," describes the colonial world.*

(*Color and Democracy,* Harcourt, Bruce & World Co., New York, 1945, pp. 17-25.)

THE DISFRANCHISED COLONIES

COLONIES AND THE COLONIAL SYSTEM MAKE THE COLONIAL PEOPLES IN A SENSE THE SLUMS OF THE WORLD, DISFRANCHISED AND HELD IN POVERTY AND DISEASE.

Colonies are the slums of the world. They are today the places of greatest concentration of poverty, disease, and ignorance of what the human mind has come to know. They are centers of helplessness, of discouragement of initiative, of forced labor, and of legal suppression of all activities or thoughts which the master country fears or dislikes.

They resemble in some ways the municipal slums of the nineteenth century in cultured lands. In those days men thought of slums as inevitable, as being caused in a sense by the wretched people who inhabited them, as yielding to no remedial action in any conceivable time. If abolished, the dregs of humanity would re-create them. Then we were jerked back to our senses by the realization that slums were investments where housing, sanitation, education, and spiritual freedom were lacking, and where for this reason the profits of the landlords, the merchants, and the exploiters were enormous.

To most people this characterization of colonies will seem overdrawn, and of course in one major respect colonies differ radically from slums. Municipal slums are mainly festering sores drawing their substance from the surrounding city and sharing the blood and the culture of that city. Colonies on the other hand, are for the most part quite separate in race and culture from the peoples who control them. Their culture is often ancient and historically fine and valuable spoiled too often by misfortune and conquest and misunderstanding. This sense of separation, therefore, makes colonies usually an integral entity beyond the sympathy and the comprehension of the ruling world. But in both city and colony, labor is forced by poverty, and crime is largely disease.

What then are colonies? Leaving analogies, in this case none too good, we look to facts, and find them also elusive. It is difficult to define a colony precisely. There are the dry bones of statistics; but the essential facts are neither well measured nor logically articulated. After all, an imperial power is not interested primarily in censuses, health surveys, or historical research. Consequently we know only approximately and with wide margins of error, the colonial population, the number of the sick and the dead, and just what happened before the colony was conquered.

For the most part, today the colonial peoples are colored of skin; this was not true of colonies in other days, but it is mainly true today. And to most minds, this is of fatal significance: coupled with Negro slavery, Chinese coolies, and doctrines of race inferiority, it proves to most white folk the logic of the modern colonial system: Colonies are filled with peoples who never were abreast with civilization and never can be.

This rationalization is very satisfactory to empire-builders and investors, but it does not satisfy science today, no matter how much it did yesterday. Skin color is a matter of climate and colonies today are mainly in the hot, moist tropics and semi-tropics. Naturally, here skins are colored. But historically these lands also were seats of ancient cultures among normal men. Here human civilization began, in Africa, Asia and Central America. What has happened to these folks across the ages? They have been conquered, enslaved, oppressed, and exploited by stronger invaders. But was this invading force invariably stronger in body, keener in mind, and higher in culture? Not necessarily, but always stronger in offensive technique, even though often lower in culture and only average in mind.

Offensive technique drew the conquerors down upon the conquered, because the conquered had the fertile lands, the needed materials, the arts of processing goods for human needs. With the conquerors concentrating time and thought on these aspects of culture, usually the conquered could not oppose the barbarians with muscle, clubs, spears, gunpowder, and capital. In time, the invaders actually surpassed, and far surpassed, the weaker peoples in wealth, technique, and variety of culture patterns, and made them slaves to industry and servants to white men's ease.

But what of the future? Have the present masters of the world such an eternal lien on civilization as to ensure unending control? By no means; their very absorption in war and wealth has so weakened their moral fiber that the end of their rule is in sight. Also, the day of the colonial conquered peoples dawns, obscurely but surely.

Today, then, the colonial areas lie inert or sullenly resentful or seething with hate and unrest. With unlimited possibilities, they have but scraps of understanding of modern accumulations of knowledge; but they are pressing toward education with bitter determination. The conquerors, on the other hand, are giving them only the passing attention which preoccupation with problems of wealth and power at home leaves for colonial "problems."

What then, do modern colonies look like, feel like? It is difficult to draw any universal picture. Superficial impressions are common: black boys diving for pennies; human horses hitched to rickshaws; menial service in plethora for a wage near nothing; absolute rule over slaves, even to life and death; fawning, crawling obeisance; high salaries, palaces, and luxury coupled with abject, nauseating, diseased poverty—this in a vague, imperfect way paints the present colonial world.

It is not nearly so easy as it would appear to fill in this outline and make it precise and scientific. Empires do not want nosy busybodies snooping into their territories and business. Visitors to colonies are, to be sure, allowed and even encouraged; but their tours are arranged, officials guide them in space and in thought, and they see usually what the colonial power wants them to see and little more. Dangerous "radicals" are rigorously excluded. My own visits to colonies have been rare and unsatisfactory. Several times I have tried in vain to visit South Africa. No visas were obtainable. I have been in British and French West Africa and in Jamaica.

In Sierra Leone I landed at Freetown in 1923. I was passed through the customs without difficulty, as my papers were in order. Then for some reason the authorities became suspicious. With scant courtesy, I was summoned peremptorily down to headquarters, to a room off the common jail, with pictures of escaped criminals decorating the walls. What did I want in Sierra Leone? I handed in my passport, showing that I was United States Minister Plenipotentiary to Liberia, stopping simply to visit on my way home. The commissioner unbent and dismissed me. That afternoon I was invited to a tea party at the governor's mansion! What would have happened to me if I had not had a diplomatic passport, or if I had been merely a colored man seeking to study a British colony?

The same year I visited Senegal and Conakry. I was received with great courtesy, but into the ruling caste; I had no contact with the mass of the colonial people. I lodged with the American consul; the French consul had me at dinner and the English consul at tea in his palatial mansion. But little did I see or learn of the millions of Negroes who formed the overwhelming mass of the colonial population.

In 1915, I visited Jamaica. I landed at Kingston and then, being tired and on vacation, did the unconventional thing of walking across the island to Mantego Bay. I immediately became an object of suspicion. It was wartime. I was in a sense, albeit unconsciously, intruding into Jamaica's backyard. I had proper visas, but I was not following the beaten path of the tourist. I was soon warned by a furtive black man that the police were on my track. My only recourse was to look up a long-time friend, principal of the local school. He ostentatiously drove me downtown, seated with him high in his surrey behind prancing horses. Thus was I properly introduced and vouched for. The point is that in all these cases one saw the possibility of arbitrary power without appeal and of a race and class situation unknown in free countries.

In the main, colonial peoples are living abnormally, save those of the untouched or inert mass of natives. Where the whites form a small ruling group, they are most abnormal and are not, as is assumed, replicas of the home group. They consist chiefly of representatives of commercial concerns whose first object is to make money for themselves and the corporations they represent. They are in the main hard-boiled, often ruthless businessmen, unrestrained by the inhibitions of home in either law or custom. Next come the colonial officials, either identical with the commercial men or more or less under their domination, especially through home influence. Colonials and businessmen clash, but business usually wins. Sometimes philanthropic career officials get the upper hand; but they are in danger of being replaced or losing promotion. The official class—heads, assistants, clerks, wives, and children—are apt to be arrogant, raised above their natural position and feeling their brief authority; they lord it over despised natives and demand swift and exemplary punishment for any affront to their dignity. The courts presided over by whites are usually even-handed in native quarrels, but through fear are strict, harsh, and even cruel in cases between natives and whites. White prestige must be maintained at any cost. There is usually a considerable group of white derelicts, hangers-on, sadistic representatives of the "superior race," banished to colonies by relatives who are ashamed to keep them at home.

This whole group of whites forms a caste apart, lives in segregated, salubrious, and protected areas, seldom speaks the vernacular or knows the masses except officially. Their regular income from colonial services is liberal according to home standards and often fantastic according to the standard of living in colonies. Conceive of an income of $10,000 a year for a colonial governor over people whose average income is $25 a year! The officials get frequent vacations with pay, and are pensioned after comparatively short service. The pensions are paid for life by colonial taxation, and the pensioners are regarded as experts on colonial matters the rest of their lives.

Where the white resident contingent is relatively large, as in South Africa and Kenya, the caste conditions are aggravated and the whites become the colony while the natives are ignored and neglected except as low-paid labor largely without rights that the colonists need respect.

Below this group of white overlords are the millions of natives. Their normal and traditional life has been more or less disrupted and changed in work, property, family life, recreation, health habits, food, religion, and other cultural matters. Their initiative, education, freedom of action, have been interfered with to a greater or less extent. Authority has been almost entirely withdrawn from their control and the white man's word is law in most cases. Their native standards of life have been destroyed and the new standards cannot be met by a poverty that is the worst in the world. The mass of natives sink into careless, inert, or sullen indifference, making their contact with whites as rare as possible, and incurring repeated punishment for laziness and infraction of arbitrary or inexplicable rules.

Up from these rise two groups: the toadies or "white folks niggers," who use flattery and talebearing to curry favor; and the resentful, bitter, and ambitious who seek by opposition or education to achieve the emancipation of their land and people. The educated and the half-educated, in particular, are the object of attack and dislike by the whites and are endlessly slandered in all testimony given visitors and scientists.

The missionaries form another class. They have been of all sorts of persons: unworldly visionaries, former pastors out of a job, social workers with and without social science, theologians, crackpots, and humanitarians. Their vocation is so unconventional that it is almost without standards of training or set norms of effort. Yet missionaries have spent tens of millions of dollars and influenced hundreds of millions of men with results that literally vary from heaven to hell. Missionaries represent the oldest invasion of whites, and incur at first the enmity of business and the friendship of natives. Colonial officials, on pressure from home, compromise differences, and the keener natives thereupon come to suspect missionary motives and the native toadies rush to get converted and cash in on benefits. The total result varies tremendously according to the pressure of these elements.

Despite a vast literature on colonial peoples, there is to day no sound scientific basis for comprehensive study. What we have are reports of officials who set out to make a case for the imperial power in control; reports of missionaries, of all degrees of reliability and object; reports of travelers swayed by every conceivable motive and fitted or unfitted for testimony by widely varying education, ideals, and reliability. When science tries to study colonial systems in Africa and Asia, it meets all sorts of hindrances and incomplete statements of fact. In few cases is there testimony from the colonial peoples themselves, or impartial scientific surveys conducted by persons free of compulsion from imperial control and dictation.

The studies we have of colonial peoples and conditions are

therefore unsatisfactory. Even the great *African Survey* edited by Lord Hailey is mainly based on the testimony and the figures of colonial officials; that is, of men who represent the colonial organization, who are appointed on recommendation of persons whose fortunes are tied up with colonial profits, and who are naturally desirous of making the best-possible picture of colonial conditions. This does not mean that there is in this report, or in many others, deliberate and conscious deception; but there is the desire to make a case for the vested interests of a large and powerful part of the world's property-owners.

Other studies are made by visitors and outsiders who can get the facts only as the government officials give them opportunity. Many opportunities have been afforded such students in the past, but the opportunities fall far short of what complete and scientific knowledge demands. Moreover, such visitors arrive more or less unconsciously biased by their previous education and contacts, which lead them to regard the natives as on the whole a low order of humanity, and especially to distrust more or less completely the efforts of educated and aspiring Natives. The native elite, when through education and contact they get opportunity to study and tell of conditions, often, and naturally, defeat their own cause before a prejudiced audience by their bitterness and frustration and their inability to speak with recognized authority.

Thus, unfortunately, it is not possible to present or refer to any complete and documented body of knowledge which can give an undisputed picture of colonies today. This does not mean that we have no knowledge of colonial conditions; on the contrary, we have a vast amount of testimony and study; but practically every word of it can be and is disputed by interested parties, so that the truth can be reached only by the laborious interpretation of careful students. Nearly every assertion of students of colonial peoples is disputed today by colonial officials, many travelers, and a host of theorists. Despite this, greater unanimity of opinion is growing, but it is far from complete....

The World and Africa *was Du Bois' final book about Africa and not only is it his best on this particular subject, but it is one of his most well-written books.*

The first selection is the second chapter, "The White Masters of the World." In it he describes what white domination "over the world has meant to mankind and especially to Africans in the nineteenth and twentieth centuries."

The second selection is the seventh chapter, "Atlantis," which describes the history of the west coast of Africa.

(*The World and Africa,* New York, International Publishers, 1965, pp. 16-43, pp. 148-63.)

THE WHITE MASTERS OF THE WORLD

What are the real causes back of the collapse of Europe in the twentieth century? What was the real European imperialism pictured in the Paris Exposition of 1900? France did not stand purely for art. There was much imitation, convention, suppression, and sale of genius; and France wanted wealth and power at any price. Germany did not stand solely for science. I remember when the German professor at whose home I was staying in 1890 expressed his contempt for the rising businessmen. He had heard them conversing as he drank in a *Bierstube* at Eisenach beneath the shade of Luther's Wartburg. Their conversation, he sneered, was *lauter Geschäft!* He did not realize that a new Germany was rising which wanted German science for one main purpose—wealth and power. America wanted freedom, but freedom to get rich by any method short of anarchy; and freedom to get rid of the democracy which allowed laborers to dictate to managers and investors.

All these centers of civilization envied England the wealth and power built upon her imperial colonial system. One looking at European imperialism in 1900 therefore should have looked first at the depressed peoples. One would have found them also among the laboring classes in Europe and America, living in slums behind a façade of democracy, nourished on a false education which lauded the triumphs of the industrial undertaker, made the millionaire the hero of modern life, and taught youth that success was wealth. The slums of England emphasized class differences; slum dwellers and British aristocracy spoke different tongues, had different manners and ideals. The goal of human life was illustrated in the nineteenth-century English novel: the aristocrat of independent income surrounded by a herd of obsequious and carefully trained servants. Even today the British butler is a personage in the literary world.

Out of this emerged the doctrine of the Superior Race: the theory that a minority of the people of Europe are by birth and natural gift the rulers of mankind; rulers of their own suppressed labor classes and, without doubt, heaven-sent rulers of yellow, brown, and black people.

This way of thinking gave rise to many paradoxes, and it was characteristic of the era that men did not face paradoxes with any plan to solve them. There was the religious paradox: the contradiction between the Golden Rule and the use of force to keep human beings in their appointed places; the doctrine of the White Man's Burden and the conversion of the heathen, faced by the actuality of famine, pestilence, and caste. There was the assumption of the absolute necessity of poverty for the majority of men in order to save civilization for the minority, for that aristocracy of mankind which was at the same time the chief beneficiary of culture.

There was the frustration of democracy: lip service was paid to the idea of the rule of the people; but at the same time the mass of people were kept so poor, and through their poverty so diseased and ignorant, that they could not carry on successfully a modern state or modern industry. There was the paradox of peace: I remember before World War I stopping in at the Hotel Astor to hear Andrew Carnegie talk to his peace society. War had begun between Italy and Turkey but, said Mr. Carnegie blandly, we are not talking about peace among unimportant people; we are talking about peace among the great states of the world. I walked out. Here I knew lay tragedy, and the events proved it; for the great states went to war in jealousy over the ownership of the little people.

The paradox of the peace movement of the nineteenth century is a baffling comment on European civilization. There was not a single year during the nineteenth century when the world was not at war. Chiefly, but not entirely, these wars were waged to subjugate colonial peoples. They were carried on by Europeans, and at least one hundred and fifty separate wars can be counted during the heyday of the peace movement. What the peace movement really meant was peace in Europe and between Europeans, while for the conquest of the world and because of the suspicion which they held toward each other, every nation maintained a standing army which steadily grew in cost and menace.

One of the chief causes which thus distorted the development of Europe was the African slave trade, and we have tried to rewrite its history and meaning and to make it occupy a much less important place in the world's history than it deserves.

The result of the African slave trade and slavery on the European mind and culture was to degrade the position of labor and the respect for humanity as such. Not, God knows, that the ancient world honored labor. With exceptions here and there, it despised, enslaved, and crucified human toil. But there were counter currents, and with the Renaissance in Europe—that new light with which Asia and Africa illumined the Dark Ages of Europe—came new hope for mankind. A new religion of personal sacrifice had been building on five hundred years of the self-effacement of Buddha before the birth of Christ, and the equalitarianism of Mohammed which followed six hundred years after Christ's birth. A new world, seeking birth in Europe, was also being discovered beyond the sunset.

With this new world came fatally the African slave trade and Negro slavery in the Americas. There were new cruelties, new hatreds of human beings, and new degradations of human labor. The temptation to degrade human labor was made vaster and deeper by the incredible accumulation of wealth based on slave labor, by the boundless growth of greed, and by world-wide organization for new agricultural crops, new techniques in industry, and world-wide trade.

Just as Europe lurched forward to a new realization of beauty, a new freedom of thought and religious belief, a new demand by laborers to choose their work and enjoy its fruit, uncurbed greed rose to seize and monopolize the uncounted treasure of the fruit of labor. Labor was degraded, humanity was despised, the theory of "race" arose. There came a new doctrine of universal labor: mankind were of two sorts—the superior and the inferior; the inferior toiled for the superior; and the superior were the real men, the inferior half men or less. Among the white lords of creation there were "lower classes" resembling the inferior darker folk. Where possible they were to be raised to equality with the master class. But no equality was possible or desirable for "darkies." In line with this conviction, the Christian Church, Catholic and Protestant, at first damned the heathen blacks with the "curse of Canaan," then held out hope of freedom through "conversion," and finally acquiesced in a permanent status of human slavery.

Despite the fact that the nineteenth century saw an upsurge in the power of laboring classes and a fight toward economic equality and political democracy, this movement and battle was made fiercer and less successful and lagged far behind the accumulation of wealth, because in popular opinion labor was fundamentally degrading and the just burden of inferior peoples. Luxury and plenty for the few and poverty for the many was looked upon as inevitable in the course of nature. In addition to this, it went without saying that the white people of Europe had a right to live upon the labor and property of the colored peoples of the world.

In order to establish the righteousness of this point of view, science and religion, government and industry, were wheeled into line. The word "Negro" was used for the first time in the world's history to tie color to race and blackness to slavery and degradation. The white race was pictured as "pure" and superior; the black race as dirty, stupid, and inevitably inferior; the yellow race as sharing, in deception and cowardice, much of this color inferiority; while mixture of races was considered the prime cause of degradation and failure in civilization. Everything great, everything fine, everything really successful in human culture, was white.

In order to prove this, even black people in India and Africa were labeled as "white" if they showed any trace of progress; and, on the other hand, any progress by colored people was attributed to some intermixture, ancient or modern, of white blood or some influence of white civilization.

This logical contradiction influenced and misled science. The same person declared that mulattoes were inferior and warned against miscegenation, and yet attributed the pre-eminence of a Dumas, a Frederick Douglass, a Booker Washington, to their white blood.

A system at first conscious and then unconscious of lying about history and distorting it to the disadvantage of the Negroids became so widespread that the history of Africa ceased to be taught, the color of Memnon was forgotten, and every effort was made in archaeology, history, and biography, in biology, psychology, and sociology, to prove the all but universal assumption that the color line had a scientific basis.

Without the winking of an eye, printing, gunpowder, the smelting of iron, the beginnings of social organization, not to mention political life and democracy, were attributed exclusively to the white race and to Nordic Europe. Religion sighed with relief when it could base its denial of the ethics of Christ and the brotherhood of men upon the science of Darwin, Gobineau, and Reisner.

It was bad enough in all conscience to have the consequences of this thought, these scientific conclusions and ethical sanctions, fall upon colored people the world over; but in the end it was even worse when one considers what this attitude did to the European worker. His aim and ideal was distorted. He did not wish to become efficient but rich. He began to want not comfort for all men, but power over other men for himself. He did not love humanity and he hated "niggers." When our High Commissioner after the Spanish War appealed to America on behalf of "our little brown brother," the white workers replied,

> He may be a brother of William H. Taft,
> But he ain't no brother of mine.

Following the early Christian communism and sense of human brotherhood which began to grow in the Dark Ages and to blossom in the Renaissance there came to white workers in England, France, and Germany the iron law of wages, the population doctrines of Malthus, and the bitter fight against the early trade unions. The first efforts at education, and particularly the trend toward political democracy, aroused an antagonism of which the French Revolution did not dream. It was this bitter fight that exacerbated the class struggle and resulted in the first furious expression of Communism and the attempt at revolution. The unity of apprentice and master, the Christian sympathy between rich and poor, the communism of medieval charity, all were thrust into the new strait jacket of thought: poverty was the result of sloth and crime; wealth was the reward of virtue and work. The degraded yellow and black peoples were in the places which the world of necessity assigned to the inferior; and toward these lower ranks the working classes of all countries tended to sink save as they were raised and supported by the rich, the investors, the captains of industry.

In some parts of the world, notably in the Southern states of America, the argument went further than this: frank slavery of black folk was a better economic system than factory exploitation of whites. It was the natural arrangement of industry. It ought to be extended, certainly where colored people were in the majority. For half a century before 1861 the bolder minds of the South dreamed of a slave empire embracing the American tropics and extending eventually around the world. While their thought did not go to a final appraisement of white laboring classes, they certainly had in mind that these classes must rise or fall; must be forced into the class of employers with political power, or, like the poor whites of the South, be pushed down beside or even below the working slaves.

This philosophy had sympathizers in Europe. Without doubt, a large majority of influential public opinion in England, and possibly in both France and Germany, favored the South at the outbreak of the Civil War and sternly set its face against allowing any maudlin sympathy with "darkies," half monkeys and half men, in the stern fight for the extension of European domination of the world. Widespread insensibility to cruelty and suffering spread in the white world, and to guard against too much emotional sympathy with the distressed, every effort was made to keep women and children and the more sensitive men deceived as to what was going on, not only in the slums of white countries, but also all over Asia, Africa, and the islands of the sea. Elaborate writing, disguised as interpretation, and the testimony of so-called "experts," made it impossible for charming people in Europe to realize what their comforts and luxuries cost in sweat, blood, death, and despair, not only in the remoter parts of the world, but even on their own doorsteps.

A gracious culture was built up; a delicately poised literature treated the little intellectual problems of the rich and well-born, discussed small matters of manners and convention, and omitted the weightier ones of law, mercy, justice, and truth. Even the evidence of the eyes and senses was denied by the mere weight of reiteration. The race that produced the ugly features of a Darwin or a Winston Churchill was always "beautiful," while a Toussaint and a Menelik were ugly because they were black.

The concept of the European "gentleman" was evolved: a man well bred and of meticulous grooming, of knightly sportsmanship and invincible courage even in the face of death; but one who did not hesitate to use machine guns against assagais and to cheat "niggers"; an ideal of sportsmanship which reflected the Golden Rule and yet contradicted it—not only in business and in industry within white countries, but all over Asia and Africa—by indulging in lying, murder, theft, rape, deception, and degradation, of the same sort and kind which has left the world aghast at the accounts of what the Nazis did in Poland and Russia.

There was no Nazi atrocity—concentration camps, wholesale maiming and murder, defilement of women or ghastly blasphemy of childhood—which the Christian civilization of Europe had not long been practicing against colored folk in all parts of the world in the name of and for the defense of a Superior Race born to rule the world.

Together with the idea of a Superior Race there grew up in Europe and America an astonishing ideal of wealth and luxury: the man of "independent" income who did not have to "work for a living," who could indulge his whims and fantasies, who was free from all compulsion either of ethics or hunger, became the hero of novels, of drama and of fairy tale. This wealth was built, in Africa especially, upon diamonds and gold, copper and tin, ivory and mahogany, palm oil and cocoa, seeds extracted and grown, beaten out of the blood-stained bodies of the natives, transported to Europe, processed by wage slaves who were not receiving, and as Ricardo assured them they could never receive, enough to become educated and healthy human beings, and then distributed among prostitutes and gamblers as well as among well-bred followers of art, literature, and drama.

Cities were built, ugly and horrible, with regions for the culture of crime, disease, and suffering, but characterized in popular myth and blindness by wide and beautiful avenues where the rich and fortunate lived, laughed, and drank tea. National heroes were created by lopping off their sins and canonizing their virtues, so that Gladstone had no connection with slavery,

Chinese Gordon did not get drunk, William Pitt was a great patriot and not an international thief. Education was so arranged that the young learned not necessarily the truth, but that aspect and interpretation of the truth which the rules of the world wished them to know and follow.

In other words, we had progress by poverty in the face of accumulating wealth, and that poverty was not simply the poverty of the slaves of Africa and the peons of Asia, but the poverty of the mass of workers in England, France, Germany, and the United States. Art, in building, painting, and literature, became cynical and decadent. Literature became realistic and therefore pessimistic. Religion became organized in social clubs where well-bred people met in luxurious churches and gave alms to the poor. On Sunday they listened to sermons—"Blessed are the meek"; "Do unto others even as you would have others do unto you"; "If thine enemy smite thee, turn the other cheek"; "It is more blessed to give then to receive"—listened and acted as though they had read, as in very truth they ought to have read—"Might is right"; "Do others before they do you"; "Kill your enemies or be killed"; "Make profits by any methods and at any cost so long as you can escape the lenient law." This is a fair picture of the decadence of that Europe which led human civilization during the nineteenth century and looked unmoved on the writhing of Asia and of Africa.

Nothing has been more puzzling than the European attitude toward sex. With professed reverence for female chastity, white folk have brought paid prostitution to its highest development; their lauding of motherhood has accompanied a lessening of births through late marriage and contraception, and this has stopped the growth of population in France and threatened it in all Europe. Indeed, along with the present rate of divorce, the future of the whole white race is problematical. Finally, the treatment of colored women by white men has been a worldwide disgrace. American planters, including some of the highest personages in the nation, left broods of colored children who were sometimes sold into slavery.

William Howitt (1792-1879), an English Quaker, visited Australia and the East early in the nineteenth century and has left us a record of what he saw. Of the treatment of women in India he wrote: "The treatment of the females could not be described. Dragged from the inmost recesses of their houses, which the religion of the country had made so many sanctuaries, they were exposed naked to public view. The virgins were carried to the Court of Justice, where they might naturally have looked for protection, but they now looked for it in vain; for in the face of the ministers of justice, in the face of the spectators, in the face of the sun, those tender and modest virgins were brutally violated. The only difference between their treatment and that of their mothers was that the former were dishonoured in the face of day, the latter in the gloomy recesses of their dungeon. Other females had the nipples of their breasts put in a cleft bamboo and torn off. What follows is too shocking and indecent to transcribe! It is almost impossible, in reading of these frightful and savage enormities, to believe that we are reading of a country under the British government, and that these unmanly deeds were perpetrated by British agents, and for the purpose of extorting the British revenue."

It would be unfair to paint the total picture of Europe as decadent. There have been souls that revolted and voices that cried aloud. Men arraigned poverty, ignorance, and disease as unnecessary. The public school and the ballot fought for uplift and freedom. Suffrage for women and laborers and freedom for the Negro were extended. But this forward-looking vision had but partial and limited success. Race tyranny, aristocratic pretense, monopolized wealth, still continued to prevail and triumphed widely. The Church fled uptown to escape the poor and black. Jesus laughed—and wept.

The dawn of the twentieth century found white Europe master of the world and the white peoples almost universally recognized as the rulers for whose benefit the rest of the world existed. Never before in the history of civilization had self-worship of a people's accomplishment attained the heights that the worship of white Europe by Europeans reached.

Our poets in the "Foremost Ranks of Time," became dithyrambic: "Better fifty years of Europe than a cycle of Cathay!" In home and school the legend grew of this strong, masterful giant with mighty intellect, clear brain, and unrivaled moral stamina, who was conducting the world to the last heights of human culture. Yet within less than half a century this magnificent self-worshiping structure had crashed to the earth.

Why was this? It was from no lack of power. The power of white Europe and North America was unquestionable. Their science dominated the scientific thought of the world. The only writing called literature was that of English and French writers, of Germans and Italians, with some recognition of writers in Spain and the United States. The Christian religion, as represented by the Catholic Church and the leading Protestant denominations, was the only system of belief recognized as real religion. Mohammedans, Buddhists, Shintoists, and others were all considered heathen.

The most tremendous expression of power was economic; the powerful industrial organization and integration of modern industry in management and work, in trade and manufacture, was concentrated in England, France, Germany, and the United States. All Asia and Eastern Europe was an appendage; all Africa, China, India, and the islands of the sea, Central and South America and the Caribbean area were dominated by Europe, while Scandinavia, Holland, and Belgium were silent copartners in this domination.

The domination showed itself in its final form in political power either through direct rulership, as in the case of colonies, or indirect economic power backed by military pressure exercised over the backward nations. It was rather definitely assumed in the latter part of the nineteenth century that this economic domination was but a passing phase which in time would lead to colonial absorption.

Particularly was this true with regard to Asia. India was already a part of the British Empire, and Burma. Indonesia was Dutch and Indo-China, French. The future of China depended upon how Europe would divide the land among the British Empire and the Germans, American trade, Italy, France, and Russia. It was a matter simply of time and agreement. General consent had long since decided that China should no longer rule itself.

With regard to the South American countries there was the determination that they must obey the economic rule of the European and North American system. The world looked forward to political and economic domination by Europe and North America and to a more or less complete approach to colonial status for the rest of the earth. Africa of course must remain in absolute thrall, save its white immigrants, who would rule the blacks.

The reason for this world mastery of Europe was rationalized as the natural and inborn superiority of white peoples, showing itself not only in the loftiest of religions, but in a technical mastery of the forces of nature—all this in contrast to the low mentality and natural immorality of the darker races living in lovely lands, "Where every prospect pleases, and only Man is vile!"—as the high-minded Christians sang piously. But they forgot or never were told just how white superiority wielded its power or accomplished this dominion. There were exceptions, of course, but for the most part they went unheard. Howitt, for instance, wrote from personal knowledge as well as research on the colonial question and described some phases of the pressure of Europe on the rest of the world in the centuries preceding the nineteenth. Speaking of the Indians of America, Howitt said: "All the murders and desolation of the most pitiless tyrants that ever diverted themselves with the pangs and convulsions of their fellow creatures, fall infinitely short of the bloody enormities committed by the Spanish nation in the conquest of the New World, a conquest on a low estimate, effected by the murder of ten millions of the species! After reading these accounts, who can help forming an indignant wish that the hand of Heaven, by some miraculous interposition, had swept these European tyrants from the face of the earth, who like so many beasts of prey, roamed round the world only to desolate and destroy; and more remorseless than the fiercest savage, thirsted for human blood without having the impulse of natural appetite to plead in their defence!"

Howitt turned to the Portuguese in India: "The celebrated Alphonso Albuquerque made the most rapid strides, and extended the conquests of the Portuguese there beyond any other commander. He narrowly escaped with his life in endeavouring to sack and plunder Calicut. He seized on Goa, which thenceforward became the metropolis of all the Portuguese settlements in India. He conquered Molucca, and gave it up to the plunder of his soldiers. The fifth part of the wealth thus thievishly acquired was reserved for the king, and was purchased on the spot by the merchants for two hundred thousand pieces of gold. Having established a garrison in the conquered city, he made a traitor Indian, who had deserted from the king of Molucca and had been an instrument in the winning of a place, supreme magistrate; but again finding Utimut, the renegade, as faithless to himself, he had him and his son put to death, even though a hundred thousand pieces of gold, a bait that was not easily resisted by these Christian marauders, was offered for their lives. He then proceeded to Ormuz in the Persian Gulph, which was a great harbour for the Arabian merchants; reduced it, placed a garrison in it, seized on fifteen princes of the blood, and carried them off to Goa. Such were some of the deeds of this celebrated general, whom the historians in the same breath in which they record these unwarrantable acts of violence, robbery, and treachery, term an excellent and truly glorious commander! He made a descent on the isle of Ceylon, and detached a fleet to the Moluccas, which established a settlement in those delightful regions of the cacao, the sago-tree, the nutmeg, and the clove. The kings of Persia, of Siam, Pegu, and others, alarmed at his triumphant progress, sought his friendship; and he completed the conquest of the Malabar coast. With less than forty thousand troops, the Portuguese struck terror into the empire of Morocco, the barbarous nations of Africa, the Mamelucs, the Arabians, and all the eastern countries from the island of Ormuz to China."

Turning to the Dutch, Howitt continued:

"To secure the dominion of these, they compelled the princes of Ternate and Tidore to consent to the rooting up of all the clove and nutmeg trees in the islands not entirely under the jealous safeguard of Dutch keeping. For this they utterly exterminated the inhabitants of Banda, because they would not submit passively to their yoke. Their lands were divided amongst the white people, who got slaves from other islands to cultivate them. For this Malacca was besieged, its territory ravaged, and its navigation interrupted by pirates; Negapatan was twice attacked; Cochin was engaged in resisting the kings of Calicut and Travancore, and Ceylon and Java were made scenes of perpetual disturbances. These notorious dissensions have been followed by as odious oppressions, which have been practiced at Japan, China, Cambodia, Arracan on the banks of the Ganges, at Achen, Coromandel, Surat, in Persia, at Bassora, Mocha, and other places. For this they encouraged and established in Celebes a system of kidnapping the inhabitatns for slaves which converted that island into a hell."

Howitt then turned to England in India: "Unfortunately, we all know what human nature is. Unfortunately, the power, the wealth, and the patronage brought home to them by the very violation of their own wishes and maxims were of such an overwhelming and seducing nature that it was in vain to resist them. Nay, in such colours does the modern philosophy of conquest and diplomacy disguise the worst transactions between one state and another, that it is not for plain men very readily to penetrate to the naked enormity beneath."

"But if there ever was one system more Machiavelian—more appropriative of the shew of justice where the basest injustice was attempted—more cold, cruel, haughty, and unrelenting than another—it is the system by which the government of the different states of India has been wrested from the hands of their respective princes and collected into the grasp of the British power."

"The first step in the English friendship with the native princes, has generally been to assist them against their neighbours with troops, or to locate troops with them to protect them from aggression. For these services such enormous recompense was stipulated for, that the unwary princes, entrapped by their fears of their native foes rather than of their pretended friends, soon found that they were utterly unable to discharge them. Dreadful exactions were made on their subjects, but in vain. Whole provinces, or the revenues of them, were soon obliged to be made over to their grasping *friends;* but they did not suffice for their demands. In order to pay them their debts or their interest, the princes were obliged to borrow large sums at an extravagant rate. These sums were eagerly advanced by the English in their private and individual capacities, and securities again taken on lands or revenues. At every step the unhappy princes became more and more embarrassed, and as the embarrassment increased, the claims of the Company became proportionably pressing. In the technical phraseology of money-lenders, 'the screw was then turned,' till there was no longer any enduring it."

We may turn now to the conquest of Africa. The Portuguese, Dutch, and British decimated the West Coast with the slave trade. The Arabs depopulated the East Coast. For centuries the native Bantu, unable to penetrate the close-knit city-states of the Gulf of Guinea, had slowly been moving south, seeking pasture for their herds and protecting their culture from the encroachment of the empire-building in the black Sudan.

In the nineteenth century black folk and white—Hottentot,

Bushman and Bantu, French, Dutch, and British—met at the Cape miscalled "Good Hope." There ensued a devil's dance seldom paralleled in human history. The Dutch murdered, raped, and enslaved the Hottentots and Bushmen; the French were driven away or died out; the British stole the land of the Dutch and their slaves and the Dutch fled inland. The incoming Bantu, led by Chaka, the great Zulu chieftain, fell on both Dutch and English with a military genius unique in history.

The black Bantu had almost won the wars when a mulatto native discovered diamonds. Then English and Dutch laid bare that cache of gold, the largest in the world, which the ocean thrust above the dark waters of the south five million years ago. Enough; the greed of white Europe, backed by the British Navy, fought with frenzied determination, world-wide organization, and every trick of trade, until the blacks were either dead or reduced to the most degrading wage bondage in the modern world; and the Dutch became vassals of England, to be repaid by the land and labor of eight million blacks.

Frankel, the complacent servant of capitalists and their defender, has written: "The wealth accruing from the production of diamonds in South Africa has probably been greater than that which has ever been obtained from any other commodity in the same time anywhere in the world."

This was but a side enterprise of Britain. By means of its long leadership in the African slave trade to America, Great Britain in the nineteenth century began to seize control of land and labor all over Africa. Slowly the British pushed into the West and East coasts. They overthrew Benin and Ashanti. A British governor of Ashanti later admitted: "The earliest beginnings, which had their inception in the dark days of the slave trade, cannot but hold many things that modern Englishmen must recall with mingled shame and horror. The reader will find much to deplore in the public and private acts of many of the white men who, in their time, made history on the Coast; and some deeds were done which must forever remain among the most bitter and humiliating memories of every Britisher who loves his country and is jealous of its fair name."

The French conquered Dahomey and the remains of the Mandingo, Haussa, and other kingdoms. The British pitted Christianity against Islam in East Africa and let them fight it out until at last Uganda became a British protectorate.

In Abyssinia the natives drove back British, Egyptians, and Italians, and the Mahdi with his black Mohammedan hordes came in from the west and drove England and Egypt out of the Sudan. The threat of the French and their possible alliance with Abyssinia brought the British back with machine guns.

It is said that Kitchener's warfare against the followers of the Mahdi was so brutal that even the British Tories were revolted. His own brother-in-law said of him: "Well, if you do not bring down a curse on the British Empire for what you have been doing there is no truth in Christianity." His desecration of the Mahdi's tomb even Winston Churchill called a "foul deed." And when Kitchener found that even the promoters of the inexcusable war could not swallow this last, he tried to put the blame of the desecration onto Gordon's nephew by making absolutely false accusations. Everywhere is this sordid tale of deception, force, murder, and final subjection. We need hardly recall the Opium War in China, which the British, followed by the Americans and French, made excuse for further aggression.

The singular thing about this European movement of aggression and dominance was the rationalization for it. Missionary effort during the nineteenth and early twentieth century was widespread. Millions of pounds and dollars went into the "conversion of the heathen" to Christianity and the education of the natives. Some few efforts, as in Liberia and Sierra Leone, were made early in the nineteenth century to establish independent Negro countries, but this was before it was realized that political domination was necessary to full exploitation.

Slowly the Sudan from the Atlantic to the Nile was conquered. Slowly Egypt itself and the Egyptian Sudan passed under the control of Europe. The resistance of Nubia and Ethiopia was almost in vain down into the twentieth century. West Africa fought brilliantly and continuously. But in all this development the idea persisted in European minds that no matter what the cost in cruelty, lying, and blood, the triumph of Europe was to the glory of God and the untrammeled power of the only people on earth who deserved to rule; that the right and justice of their rule was proved by their own success and particularly by their great cities, their enormous technical mastery over the power of nature, their gigantic manufacture of goods and systems of transportation over the world. Production for production's sake, without inquiry as to how the wealth and services were distributed, was the watchword of the day.

For years the British imperial government avoided direct responsibility for colonial exploitation. It was all at first "free enterprise" and "individual initiative." When the scandal of murder and loot could no longer be ignored, exploitation became socialized with imperialism. Thus, for a century or more the West India Company, the Niger Company, the South and East Africa Companies, robbed and murdered as they pleased with no public accounting. At length, when these companies had stolen, killed, and cheated to such an extent that the facts could not be suppressed, governments themselves came into control, curbing the more outrageous excesses and rationalizing the whole system.

Science was called to help. Students of Africa, especially since the ivory-sugar-cotton-Negro complex of the nineteenth century, became hag-ridden by the obsession that nothing civilized is Negroid and every evidence of high culture in Africa must be white or at least yellow. The very vocabulary of civilization expressed this idea; the Spanish word "Negro," from being a descriptive adjective, was raised to the substantive name of a race and then deprived of its capital letter.

Then came efforts to bring harmony and co-operation and unity—among the exploiters. A newspaper correspondent who had received world-wide publicity because of his travels in Africa was hired by the shrewd and unscrupulous Leopold II of Belgium to establish an international country in central Africa "to peacefully conquer and subdue it, to remold it in harmony with modern ideas into National States, within whose limits the European merchant shall go hand in hand with the dark African trader, and justice and law and order shall prevail, and murder and lawlessness and the cruel barter of slaves shall be overcome."

Thus arose the Congo Free State, and by balancing the secret designs of German, French, and British against each other, this state became the worst center of African exploitation and started the partition of Africa among European powers. It was designed to form a pattern for similar partition of Asia and the South Sea islands. The Berlin Congress and Conference followed. The products of Africa began to be shared and distributed around the world. The dependence of civilized life upon products from the ends of the world tied the everyday citizen more and more firmly to the exploitation of each colonial area: tea and coffee, diamonds and gold, ivory and copper, vegetable oils, nuts and dates, pepper and spices, olives and cocoa, rubber, hemp, silk, fibers of all sorts, rare metals, valuable lumber, fruit, sugar. All these things and a hundred others became necessary to modern life, and modern life thus was built around colonial ownership and exploitation.

The cost of this exploitation was enormous. The colonial system caused ten times more deaths than actual war. In the first twenty-five years of the nineteenth century famines in India starved a million men, and famine was bound up with exploitation. Widespread monopoly of land to deprive all men of primary sources of support was carried out either through direct ownership or indirect mortgage and exorbitant interest. Disease could not be checked: tuberculosis in the mines of South Africa, syphilis in all colonial regions, cholera, leprosy, malaria.

One of the worst things that happened was the complete and deliberate breaking-down of cultural patterns among the suppressed peoples. "Europe was staggered at the Leopoldian atrocities, and they were terrible indeed; but what we, who were behind the scenes, felt most keenly was the fact that the real catastrophe in the Congo was desolation and murder in the larger sense. The invasion of family life, the ruthless destruction of every social barrier, the shattering of every tribal law, the introduction of criminal practices which struck the chiefs of the people dumb with horror—in a word, a veritable avalanche of filth and immorality overwhelmed the Congo tribes."

The moral humiliation forced on proud black people was illustrated in the British conquest of Ashanti. The reigning Asantahene had never been conquered. His armies had repeatedly driven back the British, but the British finally triumphed after five wars by breaking their word and overwhelming him by numbers and superior weapons. They promised him peace and honor, but they demanded a public act of submission.

"This, of course, was a terrible blow to Prempi's pride. It was a thing that no Ashanti king had ever done before, except when Mensa voluntarily made his submission by deputy in 1881; and was the one thing above all others that he would have avoided if he could. For a few moments he sat irresolute, nervously toying with his ornaments and looking almost ready to cry with shame and annoyance; but Albert Ansa came up and held a whispered conversation with him, and he then slipped off his sandals and, laying aside the golden circlet he wore on his head, stood up with his mother and walked reluctantly across the square to where the Governor was sitting. Then, halting before him, they prostrated themselves and embraced his feet and those of Sir Francis Scott and Colonel Kempster.

"The scene was a most striking one. The heavy masses of foliage, that solid square of red coats and glistening bayonets, the artillery drawn up ready for any emergency, the black bodies of the Native Levies, resting on their long guns in the background, while inside the square the Ashantis sat as if turned to stone, as Mother and Son, whose word was a matter of life and death, and whose slightest move constituted a command which all obeyed, were thus forced to humble themselves in sight of the assembled thousands."

Perhaps the worst thing about the colonial system was the contradiction which arose and had to arise in Europe with regard to the whole situation. Extreme poverty in colonies was a main cause of wealth and luxury in Europe. The results of this poverty were disease, ignorance, and crime. Yet these had to be represented as natural characteristics of backward peoples. Education for colonial people must inevitably mean unrest and revolt; education, therefore, had to be limited and used to inculcate obedience and servility lest the whole colonial system be overthrown.

Ability, self-assertion, resentment, among colonial peoples must be represented as irrational efforts of "agitators"—folk trying to attain that for which they were not by nature fitted. To prove the unfitness of most human beings for self-rule and self-expression, every device of science was used: evolution was made to prove that Negroes and Asiatics were less developed human beings than whites; history was so written as to make all civilization the development of white people; economics was so taught as to make all wealth due mainly to the technical accomplishment of white folks supplemented only by the brute toil of colored peoples; brain weights and intelligence tests were used and distorted to prove the superiority of white folk. The result was complete domination of the world by Europe and North America and a culmination and tempo of civilization singularly satisfactory to the majority of writers and thinkers at the beginning of the twentieth century. But it was a result that was hollow, contradictory, and fatal, as the next few years quickly showed.

The proof of this came first from the colonial peoples themselves. Almost unnoticed, certainly unlistened to, there came from the colonial world reiterated protest, prayers, and appeals against the suppression of human beings, against the exclusion of the majority of mankind from the vaunted progress of the world. The world knows of such protests from the National Congress of India, but little has been written of the protests of Africa. For instance, on the Gold Coast, British West Africa, in 1871, some of the kings and chiefs and a number of educated natives met at Mankesim and drew up a constitution for self-government. These members of the Fanti tribe were in alliance with England and had supported the British against the Ashanti in the five long wars. They now proposed an alliance with Britian to establish self-government. This constitution, the Mfantsi Amanbuhu Fekuw or Fanti Confederation, agitated in 1865, organized in 1867, and adopted in 1871, consisted of forty-seven articles, many of which were subdivided into several sections. Some of the principal articles were as follows:

> Article 8. That it be the object of the Confederation
> § 1. To promote friendly intercourse between all the Kings and Chiefs of Fanti, and to unite them for offensive and defensive purposes against their common enemy.
> § 2. To direct the labours of the Confederation towards the improvement of the country at large.
> § 3. To make good and substantial roads through-out all the interior districts included in the Confederation.
> § 4. To erect school-houses and establish schools for the education of all children within the Confederation and to obtain the service of efficient schoolmasters.
> § 5. To promote agricultural and industrial pursuits, and to endeavour to introduce such new plants as may hereafter become sources of profitable commerce to the country.
> § 6. To develop and facilitate the working of

the mineral and other resources of the country.

Article 12. That this Representative Assembly shall have the power of preparing laws, ordinances, bills, etc., of using proper means for effectually carrying out the resolutions, etc., of the Government, of examining any questions laid before it by the ministry, and by any of the Kings and Chiefs, and, in fact, of exercising all the functions of a legislative body.

Articles 21 to 25 deal with education.

Article 26. That main roads be made connecting various provinces or districts with one another and with the sea coast. . . .

Article 37. That in each province or district provincial courts be established, to be presided over by the provincial assessors.

Article 43. That the officers of the Confederation shall render assistance as directed by the executive in carrying out the wishes of the British Government.

Article 44. That it be competent to the Representative Assembly, for the purpose of carrying on the administration of the Government, to pass laws, etc., for the levying of such taxes as it may seem necessary.

This was the so-called Fanti Federation, and in punishment for daring to propose such a movement for the government of an African British colony, the participants were promptly thrown in jail and charged with treason.

This attitude toward native rights and initiative has continued right down to our day. In 1945 the colored people of South Africa, speaking for eight million Negroes, Indians, and mixed groups, sent out this declaration to the proposed United Nations:

The non-European is debarred from education. He is denied access to the professions and skilled trades; he is denied the right to buy land and property; he is denied the right to trade or to serve in the army—except as a stretcher-bearer or servant; he is prohibited from entering places of entertainment and culture. But still more, he is not allowed to live in the towns. And if it was a crime in Nazi Germany for an "Aryan" to mix with or marry a non-Aryan, it is equally a criminal offence in South Africa for a member of the Herrenvolk to mix with or marry with the slave race. . . . In the majority of instances there is a separate law for Europeans and a separate law for non-Europeans; in those rare cases where one Act legislates for both, there are separate clauses discriminating against the non-Europeans. While it is true that there are no Buchenwald concentration camps in South Africa, it is equally true that the prisons of South Africa are full to overflowing with non-Europeans whose criminality lies solely in the fact that they are unable to pay the poll-tax, a special racial tax imposed upon them. But this law does not apply to the Aryan; for him there is a different law which makes the nonpayment of taxes not a criminal, but a civil, offence for which he cannot be imprisoned.

But if there is no Buchenwald in South Africa, the sadistic fury with which the Herrenvolk policemen belabour the non-European victim, guilty or not guilty, is comparable only to the brutality of the S.S. Guards. Moreover, the treatment meted out to the non-European in the Law Courts is comparable only to the fate of the non-Aryan in the Nazi Law Courts. But the fundamental difference in law and morality is not only expressed in different paragraphs of the Legal Statutes, it lies in the fundamentally different concept of the value of the life of a non-European as compared with the value placed upon the life of a European. The life of a non-European is very cheap in South Africa, as cheap as the life of a Jew in Nazi Germany.

From the foregoing it is clear that the non-Europeans of South Africa live and suffer under a tyranny very little different from Nazism. And if we accept the premise—as we hope the Nations of the World do—that peace is indivisible, if we accept that there can be no peace as long as the scourge of Nazism exists in any corner of the globe, then it follows that the defeat of German Nazism is not the final chapter of the struggle against tyranny. There must be many more chapters before the peoples of the world will be able to make a new beginning. To us in South Africa it is indisputable that there can be no peace as long as this system of tyranny remains. To us it is ludicrous that this same South African Herrenvolk

should speak abroad of a new beginning, of shaping a
new world order, whereas in actuality all they wish is the
retention of the present tyranny in South Africa, and its
extension to new territories. Already they speak of new
mandates and new trusteeships, which can only mean
the extension of their Nazi-like domination over still
wider terrain. It is impossible to make a new start as long
as the representatives of this Herrenvolk take any part
in the shaping of it. For of what value can it be when the
very same people who speak so grandiosely abroad of
the inviolability of human rights, at home trample ruthlessly underfoot those same inalienable rights? It is the
grossest of insults not only to the eight million non-
Europeans of South Africa, but to all those who are
honestly striving to shape a world on new foundations,
when the highest representative of the Herrenvolk of
South Africa, Field-Marshal Smuts, who has devoted
his whole life to the entrenchment of this Nazi-like
domination, brazenly speaks to the Nations of the
World of the "sanctity and ultimate value of human
personality" and "the equal rights of men and women."

This does not say that all European civilization is oppression,
theft, and hypocrisy; there has been evidence of selfless religious faith; of philanthropic effort for social uplift; of individual
honesty and sacrifice. But this, far from answering the indictment I have made, shows even more clearly the moral plight of
present European culture and what capitalistic investment and
imperialism have done to it.

Because of the stretch in time and space between the deed
and the result, between the work and the product, it is not only
usually impossible for the worker to know the consumer; or the
investor, the source of his profit, but also it is often made impossible by law to inquire into the facts. Moral judgment of the
industrial process is therefore difficult, and the crime is more
often a matter of ignorance rather than of deliberate murder and
theft; but ignorance is a colossal crime in itself. When a culture
consents to any economic result, no matter how monstrous its
cause, rather than demand the facts concerning work, wages,
and the conditions of life whose results make the life of the
consumer comfortable, pleasant, and even luxurious, it is an
indication of a collapsing civilization.

Here for instance is a lovely British home, with green lawns,
appropriate furnishings and a retinue of well-trained servants.

Within is a young woman, well trained and well dressed, intelligent and high-minded. She is fingering the ivory keys of a grand piano and pondering the problem of her summer vacation, whether in Switzerland or among the Italian lakes; her family is not wealthy, but it has a sufficient "independent" income from investments to enjoy life without hard work. How far is such a person responsible for the crimes of colonialism?

It will in all probability not occur to her that she has any responsibility whatsoever, and that may well be true. Equally, it may be true that her income is the result of starvation, theft, and murder; that it involves ignorance, disease, and crime on the part of thousands; that the system which sustains the security, leisure, and comfort she enjoys is based on the suppression, exploitation, and slavery of the majority of mankind. Yet just because she does not know this, just because she could get the facts only after research and investigation—made difficult by laws that forbid the revealing of ownership of property, source of income, and methods of business—she is content to remain in ignorance of the source of her wealth and its cost in human toil and suffering.

The frightful paradox that is the indictment of modern civilization and the cause of its moral collapse is that a blameless, cultured, beautiful young woman in a London suburb may be the foundation on which is built the poverty and degradation of the world. For this someone is guilty as hell. Who?

This is the modern paradox of Sin before which the Puritan stands open-mouthed and mute. A group, a nation, or a race commits murder and rape, steals and destroys, yet no individual is guilty, no one is to blame, no one can be punished!

The black world squirms beneath the feet of the white in impotent fury or sullen hate:

> I hate them, O I hate them well!
> I hate them, Christ, as I hate hell!
> If I were God, I'd sound their knell,
> This day!

The whole world emerges into the Syllogism of the Satisfied: "This cannot be true. This is not true. If it were true I would not believe it. If it is true I do not believe it. Therefore it is false!" Only an Emerson could see the paradox:

O all you virtues, methods, mights;
Means, appliances, delights;
Reputed wrongs, and braggart rights;
Smug routine, and things allowed;
Minorities, things under cloud,
Hither take me, use me, fill me,
Vein and artery, though ye kill me.

In 1945 Jan Smuts, Prime Minister of South Africa, who had
once declared that every white man in South Africa believes in
the suppression of the Negro except those who are "mad, quite
mad," stood before the assembled peoples of the world and
pleaded for an article on "human rights" in the United Nations
Charter. Nothing so vividly illustrates the twisted contradiction
of thought in the minds of white men. What brought it about?
What caused this paradox? I believe that the trade in human
beings between Africa and America, which flourished between
the Renaissance and the American Civil War, is the prime and
effective cause of the contradictions in European civilization
and the illogic in modern thought and the collapse of human
culture. For this reason I am turning to a history of the African
slave trade in support of this thesis.

ATLANTIS

*This is the story of the West Coast of Africa and its relation to
the development of the world from A.D. 500 to 1500.*

It has long been the belief of modern men that the history of
Europe covers the essential history of civilization, with unimportant exceptions; that the progress of the white race has been
along the one natural, normal path to the highest possible human culture. Even in its collapse today, the dominant opinion
is that this is but an unfortunate halting on the way; the same
march must and will be resumed after a breathing space for
recovery.
On the other hand, we know that the history of modern

Europe is very short; scarcely a moment of time as compared with that of eternal Egypt. The British Empire is not more than two hundred and fifty years old; France in her present stature dates back three hundred years; the United States was born only a hundred and seventy years ago; and Germany less than one hundred years. When, therefore, we compare modern Europe with the great empires which have died, it is not far different in length of days from the empires of Persia, Assyria, the Hittites, and Babylon. Ethiopia ruled the world longer than England has.

It is surely a wider world of infinitely more peoples that Europe has ruled; but does this reveal eternal length of rule and inherent superiority in European manhood, or merely the temporary possession of a miraculously greater brute force? Mechanical power, not deep human emotion nor creative genius nor ethical concepts of justice, has made Europe ruler of the world. Man for man, the modern world marks no advance over the ancient; but man for gun, hand for electricity, muscle for atomic fission, these show what our culture means and how the machine has conquered and holds modern mankind in thrall. What in our civilization is distinctly British or American? Nothing. Science was built on Africa and Religion on Asia.

Was there no other way for the advance of mankind? Were there no other cultural patterns, ways of action, goals of progress, which might and may lead man to something finer and higher? Africa saw the stars of God; Asia saw the soul of man; Europe saw and sees only man's body, which it feeds and polishes until it is fat, gross, and cruel.

Let us turn to West Africa, where man tried a different way for a thousand years. First we face the query: how do we know what man did in West Africa, since black Africa has no written history? This brings the curious assumption that lack of written record means lack of matter and deed worth recording. The deeds of men that have been clearly and accurately written down are as pinpoints to the oceans of human experience. To recall that experience we must rely on written record, varying from direct narrative to indirect allusion and confirmation; we must rely also on memory—the memory of contemporary onlookers, of those who heard their word, of those who over a lapse of years interpreted it and handed it on; we must rely on the mute but powerful testimony of habits, customs, and ideals, which echo and reflect vast stretches of past time. Finally, we agree upon as true history and actual fact any interpretation of past action which we today believe and want to believe is true. The relation of this last historical truth to real truth may vary from fact to falsehood.

Climate, with sun and ice, gave Europe opportunity to expand vastly the Asiatic and African invention of written records. Heat and rain made written record in West Africa almost impossible and forced that land to rely on the memories of men, developed over the centuries to a marvelous system of folklore and tradition. But back of both methods lay real human history recorded in cultural patterns, industry, religion, and art.

One of the extraordinary developments of civilization in Africa was on the West Coast around the great Gulf of Guinea. Frobenius has fancifully called this "Atlantis" and regards it as possibly a development of the culture of that fabled island in the Atlantic. Whatever its origin, there grew up on the West Coast of Africa a peculiarly African state. How far back its development extends, no man knows. We have a fairly authentic history from the seventeenth century on, creditable but discontinuous reports in the sixteenth and fifteenth, and before that only customs, tradition, and legend.

On a coast protected from inland by mountain, forest, and desert, and on the west by the ocean, there grew up an agricultural culture centering in the village. On this was developed in time, industry and art. Industry discovered division of labor between cities; each town had its own peculiar industry and then traded its surplus with the other towns. The towns were united in a loose confederacy with councils and chiefs.

Six hundred years before Christ, Phoenicians traded on the West Coast of Africa and a century later the Carthaginians. From prehistoric times this coast was peopled by the black West African type of Negro. The center of their culture lay above the Bight of Benin, along the slave coast, and reached east and north. It can be traced in stone monuments, architecture, works of art, and especially patterns of culture.

The fabrication of cloth and tools was widespread and leisurely, as befitted a tropical sun. For there was here the fierce fight with the mosquito, just as in the Congo, and east there was the duel with the tsetse fly; and this battle with malaria, sleeping-sickness, and a dozen enemies of man was as much a part of the struggle for life and happiness as any of man's activities. Despite this, not only the making of cloth, the fashioning of garments, and the welding of iron reached a high development but there grew up also an art, primitive but of exceptional power, which has influenced the modern world and deserves to be called one of the three or four original art forms of this earth. Agriculture and fishing, manufacturing and pottery, the welding and processing of metal, the development of painting and art, characterize this Negro culture.

In Ashanti weaving was done with simple tools, calling for great skill, and resulted in cloth artistically beautiful. There was wood-carving, divided into many separate branches; carvers made fetishes and drums and figures which were individual and original. "Regarded in the light of certain modern aesthetic tendencies, they possess an individuality and peculiar merit which astonish many people who see them for the first time. Love and appreciation of what is artistic and beautiful are attributes which cannot be said to be the prerogative of all of us. In Ashanti, however, such traits seem to be possessed by what we should call 'the uneducated masses.' There is hardly any object capable of artistic treatment which is not made the medium for some ornamental design which gives aesthetic delight to the African's mind and eye; such as stools, spoons, combs, wooden plates, calabashes, doors, sticks, staves of office, canoes, *wari* boards, knives, mortars, drums, ivory tusks, pots, pipes, weights and scales, metal work of every description, walls of temples and dwellings, and textiles of every kind. Even the tools and appliances used to obtain these effects, the forge itself, the shuttle, the mesher used for making nets, are ornamental, being decorated with artistic effects, which, however crude, are never vulgar and inartistic."

The true West African showed great skill in plastic art; he carved ivory and wood, and the bronzes of Benin are among the most noteworthy remains of artistic effort in the world. When the state was seized by the British in 1897, they found carved elephant tusks, bronzes cast by the *cire-perdue* process, including the well-known bronze head of a Negress, now in the British Museum, a masterpiece of art.

A bronze head was discovered by Frobenius in Nigeria in 1910–1912. In this remarkable figure we have what is perhaps the finest known example of African achievement in the realm of the plastic arts. In the words of its discoverer, "the setting of the lips, the shape of the ears, the contour of the face, all prove, if separately examined, the perfection of a work of true art which the whole of it obviously is. . . . It is cast in what we call the *cire-perdue,* or the hollow cast, and is very finely chased, indeed like the best Roman examples."

Considerations growing out of the study of this and terracotta specimens, supplemented by many other findings reported by previous investigators, led Frobenius to the daring conclusion that this art belongs to the old order of Central African civilization whose beginnings go back perhaps to the second millennium before Christ. He was also of the opinion that there is sufficient evidence to warrant the assumption that there were important links between this ancient culture and some of those famous and widely heralded civilizations which flourished along the banks of the Nile and in the Mediterranean Basin in the Classical and pre-Classical Ages.

The oldest art is that of pottery, of which there are endless remains in West Africa. Traces of pottery-making go back certainly five hundred years and possibly a thousand years on the West Coast. It is done chiefly by women and is a hereditary craft handed down from mother to daughter.

It may well be that the West Coast Negroes first gave to civilization the art of welding iron which spread over all Africa and then eventually into Europe and Asia. It is of course possible that iron welding was discovered on other continents independently of Africa, but no continent had so wide a use of iron in earliest times.

According to Boas: "It seems likely that at times when the European was still satisfied with rude stone tools, the African had invented or adopted the art of smelting iron. Consider for a moment what this invention has meant for the advance of the human race. As long as the hammer, knife, drill, the spade, and the hoe had to be chipped out of stone, or had to be made of shell or hard wood, effective industrial work was not impossible, but difficult. A great progress was made when copper found in large nuggets was hammered out into tools and later on shaped by melting; and when bronze was introduced; but the true advancement of industrial life did not begin until the hard iron was discovered. It seems not unlikely that the people who made the marvelous discovery of reducing iron ores by smelting were the

African Negroes. Neither ancient Europe, not ancient western Asia, nor ancient China knew iron, and everything points to its introduction from Africa. At the time of the great African discoveries toward the end of the past century, blacksmiths were found all over Africa from north to south and from east to west. With his simple bellows and a charcoal fire he reduced the ore that is found in many parts of the continent and forged implements of great usefulness and beauty."

Torday has argued: "I feel convinced by certain arguments that seem to prove to my satisfaction that we are indebted to the Negro for the very keystone of our modern civilization and that we owe him the discovery of iron." Togoland is perhaps the oldest and most famous iron-working area in Africa.

According to Reclus, "The smelting and working of iron, most useful of all metallurgic discoveries, has been attributed to the Negroes as well as to the Chalybes of Asia Minor; and the Bongos of the White Nile, as well as some other African tribes, have constructed furnaces of a very ingenious type. Their smelters and forgers are, for the most part, satisfied with rude and primitive implements, in the use of which they, however, display marvellous skill. The Fangs of the Ogowe basin produce excellent iron, whose quality is scarcely equalled by Europeans themselves. In most of the native tribes the smiths constitute a special caste, much respected and even dreaded for their reputed knowledge of the magic arts."

Concerning West African art in general, Sir Michael Sadler said: "West Africa has made its own characteristic contribution to the artistic treasures of the world." Sir William Rothenstein added: "I know nothing of the culture which produced these noble pieces, nor what influences, native or alien, inspired them. I know only that they are superb works of art, worthy to be set beside the best examples of sculpture of any period." According to J. J. Sweeney, the American critic: "As a sculptural tradition, African art has had no rival."

Professor Roger Fry, distinguished British art critic, said: "We have the habit of thinking that the power to create expressive plastic form is one of the greatest of human achievements, and the names of great sculptures are handed down from generation to generation, so that it seems unfair to be forced to admit that certain nameless savages have possessed this power not only in a higher degree than we at this moment, but than we as a nation have ever possessed it. And yet that is where I find myself. I have to admit that some of these things are great sculpture, greater, I think, than anything we produced even in the Middle Ages. Certainly they have the special qualities of sculpture in a higher degree. They have indeed complete plastic freedom; that is to say, these African artists really conceive form in three dimensions. Now this is rare in sculpture."

In drum and strings African music reached a high degree of originality and perfection. The development of the drum language by intricate rhythms enabled the natives not only to lead in dance and ceremony, but to telegraph all over the continent with a swiftness and precision hardly rivaled by the electric telegraph. Von Hornbostel said of African music, particularly in Togo: "The African Negroes are uncommonly gifted for music, probably, on an average, more so than the white race. This is clear not only from the high development of African music, especially as regards polyphony and rhythm, but a very curious fact, unparalleled, perhaps, in history, makes it even more evident; namely, the fact that Negro slaves in America and their descendants, abandoning their original music style, have adapted themselves to that of their white masters and produced a new kind of folk music in that style. Presumably no other people would have accomplished this. In fact, the plantation songs and spirituals and also the blues and ragtimes which have launched or helped to launch our modern dance music, are the only remarkable kinds of music brought forth in America by immigrants."

Professor von Luschan considered the craftsmanship of Benin workers equal to the best that was ever produced by Cellini. Yet at the time they were creating, "in 1550, not a single peasant's house in Scandinavia had a window; and as late as 1773 Dr. Johnson and Boswell entered during their tour of the Hebrides, a hovel which 'for a window had only a small hole, which was stopped with a piece of turf, that was taken out occasionally to let in light.' In Berlin at the time of the Great Elector (1681), many houses in the capital had pigsties immediately below the front windows."

Frobenius wrote of West African cultures: "What these old captains recounted, these chiefs of expeditions—Delbes, Marchais, Pigafetta, and all the others, what they recounted is true. It can be verified. In the old Royal Kunstkammer of Dresden, in the Weydemann collection of Ulm, in many another 'cabinet of curiosities' of Europe, we still find West African collections dating from this epoch. Marvellous plush velvets of an extreme softness, made of the tenderest leaves of a certain kind of banana plant; stuffs soft and supple, brilliant and delicate, like silks, woven with the fibre of a raffia, well prepared; powerful javelins with points encrusted with copper in the most elegant fashion; bows so graceful in form and so beautifully ornamented that they would do honor to any museum of arms whatsoever; calabashes decorated with the greatest taste; sculpture in ivory and wood of which the work shows a very great deal of application and style.

"And all that came from the countries of the African periphery, delivered over after that to slave merchants. . . .

"But when the pioneers of the last century pierced this zone of 'European civilization' and the wall of protection which had, for the time being raised behind it—the wall of protection of the Negro still 'intact'—they found everywhere the same marvels which the captains had found on the coast.

"In 1906 when I penetrated into the territory of Kassai-Sankuru, I found still, villages of which the principal streets were bordered on each side, for leagues, with rows of palm trees, and of which the houses, decorated each one in charming fashion, were works of art as well.

"No man who did not carry sumptuous arms of iron or of copper, with inlaid blades and handles covered with serpent skin. Everywhere velvets and silken stuffs. Each cup, each pipe, each spoon was an object of art perfectly worthy to be compared to the creations of the Roman European style. But all this was only the particularly tender and iridescent bloom which adorns a ripe and marvellous fruit; the gestures, the manners, the moral code of the entire people, from the little child to the old man, although they remained within absolutely natural limits, were imprinted with dignity and grace, in the families of the princes and the rich as in the vassals and slaves. I know of no northern people who can be compared with these primitives for unity of civilization. Alas these last 'Happy Isles'! They, also, were submerged by the tidal wave of European civilization. And the peaceful beauty was carried away by the floods.

"But many men had this experience: the explorers who left the savage and warrior plateau of the East and the South and the North to descend into the plains of the Congo, of Lake Victoria, of the Ubangi: men such as Speke and Grant, Livingstone, Cameron, Stanley, Schweinfurth, Junker, de Brazza—all of them—made the same statements: they came from countries dominated by the rigid laws of the African Ares, and from then on they penetrated into the countries where peace reigned, and joy in adornment and in beauty; countries of old civilization, of ancient styles, of harmonious styles."

All this industry in West Africa was developed around the Africans' ideas of religion: the worship of souls of trees and plants, of animals; the use of the fetish; the belief in fairies and monsters. Along with this went training for medicine men and chiefs, and careful rules for birth, marriages, and funerals.

Of religion Frobenius said: "There is, among the deities possessed by all the other dark-skinned African nations combined, not one who can equal Shango, the [West African] Yoruban God of Thunder, in significance. This country's first royal ruler sprang, as its people believe, from his loins. His posterity still have the right to give the country its kings.

"Myth relates that Shango was born of the All-Mother, Yemaya. Powerful, warlike, and mighty, he was as great a God as was ever created in the minds of a nation striving for self-expression. He was the Hurler of Thunderbolts, Lord of the Storm; a God who burns down cities and rends trees. He is cruel and savage, yet splendid and beneficent.

"The floods which he pours give life to the soil and gladden the fields. Mankind fears him, yet loves him. Terrified by his wrath, they pray for his presence. They picture him riding a ram. They represent him with his hands full of thunderbolts, surrounded by his wives, the Lakes and the Rivers. He lives in a palace of brass, which is dazzlingly bright, and whence lightning shoots forth. He has a mighty 'medicine,' which he takes through his mouth, and fire comes out when he opens it."

The architecture of the West Coast was strikingly integrated with climate, physiography, and culture. The lovely buildings of Benin and Ashanti have been described. A traveler in 1835 described the palace of a chief in Togoland: "Glele's palace was enormous—it had housed in its time more than two thousand people—but the greater part is falling into ruins. . . . This palace is by far the largest and most elaborate piece of Negro architecture I have seen; it was with that of Great Benin I imagine the most important in West Africa."

In 1787 the Chevalier de Boufflers, writing to the Comtesse de Sabran, spoke of his enthusiastic admiration of the beauty and cleanness of the townships in the Senegal.

The climate and physical surroundings conditioned much of this human development. There was lacking here the stone and dry climate which made it easy to preserve records in the Nile valley. Material on the West Coast disappeared before the dampness and the hosts of insects. This made the art of memory recording, of tradition handed down, of unusual importance, and here it was developed to an astonishing extent. The population invented systems of writing of which at least two on the Guinea Coast and the Cameroons have come down to our day. There were probably others. Thus alphabets which were never invented in Europe came to the world through Asia and Africa.

Certain states on the West Coast were politically noteworthy. Among these were the Mossi states, two of which still exist. Each state consisted of several kingdoms of which one had the leadership. According to Delafosse: "This organization, which still functions in our day at Wagadugu and at Yatenga, strangely resembles that which, according to what has been told us by Arab authors and the writers of Timbuktu, existed at Ghana, at Diara, at Gao, and at Mandingo, as well as what could formerly be observed at Coomassie, at Bonney, in certain states of subequatorial Africa, and also what can be studied in some of the little kingdoms of the Senegal, principally the Jolof, and elsewhere."

This seems to constitute the type, perhaps more perfected at Mossi than elsewhere, of all the states worthy of that name, great or small, that have been developed all across Negro Africa since the most remote antiquity. "If the Mandingo empire, founded and directed by Negroes of probably pure race, could nevertheless have benefited by some foreign influence through the canal of Islamism, if the kingdoms of Ashanti and Dahomey, as those of the Senegal and of the Congo, might have received some inspiration from the Europeans, it seems very certain that the Mossi empires have always been sheltered from all non-Negro interference as well as non-Negro influence, and consequently the political institutions which characterize them and which are found almost all over Negro Africa are of indigenous origin."

The Mossi state did not make territorial conquests and always constituted a rampart against the extension of Mohammedanism. In its integrity it represented a civilization uniquely and really Negro.

Secret societies have always played an important part in West

Africa. They include a large variety of associations, of which the majority are mutual benefit clubs. Membership confers social distinction and are methods of bestowing charity. Some have six or seven grades and judicial functions, with execution for recalcitrants. One which was perhaps known to Ptolemy, the geographer of the second century, is associated with the leopard and has made difficulties for administrators in modern times. The secret societies used masks and ceremonies and are peculiarly West African.

The whole culture complex of the African West Coast is native and original. It is a picture of the development of human institutions unique in the history of mankind, and we can only lament that we know so little of it and have studied it so imperfectly. This body of culture grew up strong and self-contained upon the West Coast and met in time the sudden impact of two outer forces: Islam from the north and Christianity from the west.

"West Africans are still today in the period of integral collectivism, known to our ancestors before the Middle Ages, while we have arrived at individualism. The question which presents itself is to know whether indeed we have made definitive progress in this line, since many of our thinkers, of the so-called advance guard, demand, as a benefit, the return to collectivism, although of a somewhat different form. This proves that the peoples of Negro Africa have not marched at the same rate of speed as the peoples of Europe, but in nowise proves that the former are inferior to the latter. Who knows, indeed, whether the latter have not gone too fast?"

Among the groups which showed striking intellectual development were the Abron, whose state dates from the fifteenth century; the Akan people, including the Ashanti, whose known history goes back beyond 1600. In addition there were the Ewe, Yoruba, people of Benin, Dahomey, and Nubia. Benin was among the oldest of the states and has a legendary history going back to A.D. 880 or perhaps earlier. It was a carefully organized state with a remarkable native culture. It was with Benin that the Portuguese made contact in the fifteenth century and traded in slaves and other produce. The people of Yoruba, with a notable culture, moved westward as the kingdoms of the Sudan began to expand, and attacked Dahomey.

Dahomey has a known history that dates from before the sixteenth century; it had a well-organized state with farmers and artisans, but they became middlemen in the slave trade. In the nineteenth century they made a treaty with the French, but finally war broke out and the country became a French protectorate.

The Ashanti played a notable part in West Africa. They conquered the Fanti people and fought six wars with England between 1803 and 1874; they were finally subdued in 1894. Their king, Osai Tutu Quamina, was a man of intelligence and character who would have made advantageous contact between whites and Negroes if he had been treated fairly. But the English during these days were wavering between two ideas: between the suppression of the slave trade to America and emancipation of the slaves in the West Indies, and the newer idea of reducing West Africa to colonial status. For a time they hesitated, even setting up the Negro state of Sierra Leone to be ruled by free slaves, and co-operating with the similar American experiment in Liberia. Finally, however, when the clear meaning of colonial imperialism began to be understood, they turned to definite conquest. The Fanti people who had helped the English conquer the Ashanti attempted to organize their relation to England by a federation, but the constitution that they adopted was regarded as treasonable and those who drafted it were put in jail, although afterward released by the Home Secretary.

The whole European situation was changing in the late nineteenth century. The Franco-Prussian war had been fought, Germany was a great power, and England was consolidating a wide colonial empire. The native culture on the West Coast underwent various consecutive changes. The powerful states of earlier days had been pressed back by the developments in the Sudan and even in the Nile valley. They found prosperity and encouragement in the new trade to the West, which developed and degenerated into man-hunting; most of the black kingdoms on the coast became intermediaries. The slaves and prisoners captured during the internal wars became no longer incidents of these wars, but the wars became deliberate efforts to gather slaves for trade and export.

The character of culture on the slave coasts slowly changed; an element of cruelty crept into states like Benin and Ḍahomey, although other states, like that of the Yoruba, seem to have resisted to some extent. But the ancient culture of the Atlantic coast was ruined by the trade in slaves, by the importation of gin, and by the European trade; European goods drove out native art and artistic industry.

Of all this West African cultural development our knowledge is fragmentary and incomplete, jumbled up with the African slave trade. There has been no systematic, general study of the history of humanity on this coast. Nearly all has disappeared in the frantic effort to paint Negroes as apes fit only for slavery and then to forget the whole discreditable episode, wipe it out of history, and emphasize the glory and philanthropy of Europe. The invaluable art treasure which Britain stole from Benin has never been properly classified or exhibited, but lies in the British Museum.

Yet on the West Coast was perhaps the greatest attempt in human history before the twentieth century to build a culture based on peace and beauty, to establish a communism of industry and of distribution of goods and services according to human need. It was crucified by greed, and its very memory blasphemed by the modern historical method.

There can be no doubt but that the level of culture among the masses of Negroes in West Africa in the fifteenth century was higher than that of northern Europe, by any standard of measurement—homes, clothes, artistic creation and appreciation, political organization and religious consistency. "Throughout the whole of the Middle Ages, West Africa had a more solid politico-social organization, attained a greater degree of internal cohesion and was more conscious of the social function of science than Europe." What stopped and degraded this development? The slave trade; that modern change from regarding wealth as being for the benefit of human beings, to that of regarding human beings as wealth. This utter reversal of attitude which marked the day of a new barter in human flesh did not die with the slave, but persists and dominates the thought of Europe today and during the fatal era when Europe by force ruled mankind.

The Southern Negro Youth Congress was a radical black organization of southern black youth which was organized in 1937. At what was to be its last meeting, October 20, 1946, Du Bois gave the keynote address. "Behold the Land" has come to be considered a classic speech in the history of blacks in America.

BEHOLD THE LAND

The future of American Negroes is in the South. Here three hundred and twenty-seven years ago, they began to enter what is now the United States of America; here they have made their greatest contribution to American culture; and here they have suffered the damnation of slavery, the frustration of reconstruction and the lynching of emancipation. I trust then that an organization like yours is going to regard the South as the battle-ground of a great crusade. Here is the magnificent climate; here is the fruitful earth under the beauty of the Southern sun; and here if anywhere on earth, is the need of the thinker, the worker and the dreamer. This is the firing line not simply for the emancipation of the American Negro but for the emancipation of the African Negro and the Negroes of the West Indies; for the emancipation of the colored races; and for the emancipation of the white slaves of modern capitalistic monopoly.

ALLIES IN THE WHITE SOUTH

Remember here, too, that you do not stand alone. It may seem like a failing fight when the newspapers ignore you; when every effort is made by white people in the South to count you out of citizenship and to act as though you did not exist as human beings while all the time they are profiting by your labor; gleaning wealth from your sacrifices and trying to build a nation and a civilization upon your degradation. You must remember that despite all this, you have allies and allies even in the white South. First and greatest of these possible allies are the white working classes about you. The poor whites whom you have been taught to despise and who in turn have learned to fear and hate you. This must not deter you from efforts to make them understand, because in the past in their ignorance and suffering they have been led foolishly to look upon you as the cause of most of their distress. You must remember that this attitude is hereditary from slavery and that it has been deliberately cultivated ever since emancipation.

Slowly but surely the working people of the South, white and black, must come to remember that their emancipation depends upon their mutual cooperation; upon their acquaintanceship with each other; upon their friendship; upon their social intermingling. Unless this happens each is going to be made the football to break the heads and hearts of the other.

WHITE YOUTH IS FRUSTRATED

White youth in the South is peculiarly frustrated. There is not a single great ideal which they can express or aspire to, that does not bring them into flat contradiction with the Negro problem. The more they try to escape it, the more they land into hypocrisy, lying and double-dealing; the more they become, what they least wish to become, the oppressors and despisers of human beings. Some of them, in larger and larger numbers, are bound to turn toward the truth and to recognize you as brothers and sisters, as fellow travellers toward the dawn.

"JAMES BYRNES, THE FAVORITE SON OF THIS COMMONWEALTH"

There has always been in the South that intellectual elite who saw the Negro problem clearly. They have always lacked and some still lack the courage to stand up for what they know is right. Nevertheless they can be depended on in the long run to follow their own clear thinking and their own decent choice. Finally even the politicians must eventually recognize the trend in the world, in this country, and in the South. James Byrnes, that favorite son of this commonwealth, and Secretary of State of the United States, is today occupying an indefensible and impossible position; and if he survives in the memory of men, he must begin to help establish in his own South Carolina something of that democracy which he has been recently so loudly preaching to Russia. He is the end of a long series of men whose eternal damnation is the fact that they looked *truth* in the face and did not see it; John C. Calhoun, Wade Hampton, Ben Tillman are men whose names must ever be besmirched by the fact that they fought against freedom and democracy in a land which was founded upon Democracy and Freedom.

Eventually this class of men must yield to the writing in the stars. That great hypocrite, Jan Smuts, who today is talking of humanity and standing beside Byrnes for a United Nations, is at the same time, oppressing the black people of Africa to an extent which makes their two countries, South Africa and the Southern South, the most reactionary peoples on earth. Peoples whose exploitation of the poor and helpless reaches the last degree of shame. They must in the long run yield to the forward march of civilization or die.

What Does the Fight Mean

If now you young people instead of running away from the battle here in Carolina, Georgia, Alabama, Louisiana and Mississippi, instead of seeking freedom and opportunity in Chicago and New York—which do spell opportunity—nevertheless grit your teeth and make up your minds to fight it out right here if it takes every day of your lives and the lives of your children's children; if you do this, you must in meetings like this ask yourselves what does the fight mean? How can it be carried on? What are the best tools, arms, and methods? And where does it lead?

I should be the last to insist that the uplift of mankind never calls for force and death. There are times, as both you and I know, when

> "Tho' love repine and reason chafe,
> There came a voice without reply,
> 'Tis man's perdition to be safe
> When for the truth he ought to die."

At the same time and even more clearly in a day like this, after the millions of mass murders that have been done in the world since 1914, we ought to be the last to believe that force is ever the final word. We cannot escape the clear fact that what is going to win in this world is reason if this ever becomes a reasonable world. The careful reasoning of the human mind backed by the facts of science is the one salvation of man. The world, if it resumes its march toward civilization, cannot ignore reason. This has been the tragedy of the South in the past; it is still its awful and unforgivable sin that it has set its face against reason and against the fact. It tried to build slavery upon freedom; it tried to build tyranny upon democracy; it tried to build mob violence on law and law on lynching and in all that despicable endeavor, the state of South Carolina has led the South for a century. It began not the Civil War—not the War between the States—but the War to Preserve Slavery; it began mob violence and lynching and today it stands in the front rank of those defying the Supreme Court on disfranchisement.

Nevertheless reason can and will prevail; but of course it can only prevail with publicity—pitiless, blatant publicity. You have got to make the people of the United States and of the world know what is going on in the South. You have got to use every field of publicity to force the truth into their ears, and before their eyes. You have got to make it impossible for any human being to live in the South and not realize the barbarities that prevail here. You may be condemned for flamboyant methods; for calling a congress like this; for waving your grievances under the noses and in the faces of men. That makes no difference; it is your duty to do it. It is your duty to do more of this sort of thing than you have done in the past. As a result of this you are going to be called upon for sacrifice. It is no easy thing for a young black man or a young black woman to live in the South today and to plan to continue to live here; to marry and raise children; to establish a home. They are in the midst of legal caste and customary insults; they are in continuous danger of mob violence; they are mistreated by the officers of the law and they have no hearing before the courts and the churches and public opinion commensurate with the attention which they ought to receive. But that sacrifice is only the Beginning of Battle, you must re-build this South.

There are enormous opportunities here for a new nation, a new Economy, a new culture in a South really new and not a mere renewal of an old South of slavery, monopoly and race hate. There is a chance for a new cooperative agriculture on renewed land owned by the State with capital furnished by the State, mechanized and coordinated with city life. There is chance for strong, virile Trade Unions without race discrimination, with high wage, closed shop and decent conditions of work, to beat back and hold in check the swarm of landlords, monopolists and profiteers who are today sucking the blood out of this land. There is chance for cooperative industry, built on the cheap power of T.V.A. and its future extensions. There is opportunity to organize and mechanize domestic service with decent hours, and high wage and dignified training.

"BEHOLD THE LAND"

There is a vast field for consumers cooperation, building business on public service and not on private profit as the mainspring of industry. There is chance for a broad, sunny, healthy home life, shorn of the fear of mobs and liquor, and rescued from lying, stealing politicians, who build their deviltry on race prejudice.

Here in this South is the gateway to the colored millions of the West Indies, Central and South America. Here is the straight path to Africa, the Indies, China and the South Seas. Here is the Path to the Greater, Freer truer World. It would be shame and cowardice to surrender this glorious land and its opportunities for civilization and humanity to the thugs and lynchers, the mobs and profiteers, the monopolists and gamblers who today choke its soul and steal its resources. The oil and sulphur; the coal and iron; the cotton and corn; the lumber and cattle belong to you the workers, black and white, and not to the thieves who hold them and use them to enslave you. They can be rescued and restored to the people if you have the guts to strive for the real right to vote, the right to real education, the right to happiness and health and the total abolition of the father of these scourges of mankind, *poverty.*

The Great Sacrifice

"Behold the beautiful land which the Lord thy God hath given thee." Behold the land, the rich and resourceful land, from which for a hundred years its best elements have been running away, its youth and hope, black and white, scurrying North because they are afraid of each other, and dare not face a future of equal, independent, upstanding human beings, in a real and not a sham democracy.

To rescue this land, in this way, calls for the *Great Sacrifice.* This is the thing that you are called upon to do because it is the right thing to do. Because you are embarked upon a great and holy crusade, the emancipation of mankind black and white; the upbuilding of democracy; the breaking down, particularly here in the South, of forces of evil represented by race prejudice in South Carolina; by Lynching in Georgia; by disfranchisement in Mississippi; by ignorance in Louisiana and by all these and monopoly of wealth in the whole South.

There could be no more splendid vocation beckoning to the youth of the twentieth century, after the flat failures of white civilization, after the flamboyant establishment of an industrial system which creates poverty and the children of poverty which are ignorance and disease and crime; after the crazy boasting of a white culture that finally ended in wars which ruined civilization in the whole world; in the midst of allied peoples who have yelled about democracy and never practised it either in the British Empire or in the American Commonwealth or in South Carolina.

Here is the chance for young women and young men of devotion to lift again the banner of humanity and to walk toward a civilization which will be free and intelligent; which will be healthy and unafraid; and build in the world a culture led by black folk and joined by peoples of all colors and all races—without poverty, ignorance and disease! Once a great German poet cried: "Selig der den Er in Sieges Glanze findet."

"Happy man whom Death shall find in Victory's splendor."

But I know a happier one: he who fights in despair and in defeat still fights. Singing with Arna Bontemps the quiet, determined philosophy of undefeatable men:

> I thought I saw an angel flying low,
> I thought I saw the flicker of a wing
> Above the mulberry trees; but not again,
> Bethesda sleeps. This ancient pool that healed
> A Host of bearded Jews does not awake.
> This pool that once the angels troubled does not move.
> No angel stirs it now, no Saviour comes
> With healing in His hands to raise the sick
> and bid the lame man leap upon the ground.
>
> The golden days are gone. Why do we wait
> So long upon the marble steps, blood
> Falling from our open wounds? and why
> Do our black faces search the empty sky?
> Is there something we have forgotten? Some precious thing
> We have lost, wandering in strange lands?
>
> There was a day, I remember now,
> I beat my breast and cried, "Wash me God,"
> Wash me with a wave of wind upon
> The barley; O quiet one, draw near, draw near!
> Walk upon the hills with lovely feet
> And in the waterfall stand and speak!

W.E.B. DU BOIS

"From McKinley to Wallace," an autobiographical essay in which Du Bois discusses his involvement in politics from 1896 to 1948.

(*Masses & Mainstream,* August, 1948.)

FROM MCKINLEY TO WALLACE

My fifty years as a
political independent

Johnny Morgan used to keep a newsstand in the front part of the Post Office in my hometown. Through the displays of literature there I got my first idea of national politics. I was fascinated by Keppler's cartoons of BLAINE—THE TATTOOED MAN, in the campaign of 1880, when I was twelve years of age. Blaine was a Republican and our Lawyer Joyner, who was a Democrat, was looked upon with a certain suspicion. So that, perhaps, I got something of an independent twist in politics by having it impressed upon me at an early age that a leading Republican was a grafter, while all the respectable people that I knew were Republicans.

There was little of what could be called politics in the local situation. The selectmen and the few other officers elected at the town meeting received no salary, and probably very few perquisites; it was chiefly a matter of honor. Perhaps, of course, there was something beneath all of this which I did not know. However, on the whole, our town did not consider that politics was an altogether decent occupation. The less government the better was our motto, and no respectable man ever offered himself for public office. He always had it "thrust" upon him. We did not take any interest at all, so far as I can remember, in state politics; but the national election did call for some attention and action.

Garfield's assassination took place while I was in high school; Arthur became President. I cannot remember that I had any particular attitude toward either of them, or any political judgment. But when Cleveland was elected in 1885, I had graduated from high school and was at Fisk University in Tennessee. There I began to see national politics from the viewpoint of the South.

I remember the alarm that was felt when we realized that for the first time since the Civil War a Democrat was in office. Around me was a fierce and brutal political life. I remember going downtown and staring fascinated at the marks of bullets in the door of a public building where a politician had been shot to death the day before. Politics was associated with disorder. My schoolmates, most of them older than I, frequently carried pistols. On the whole, however, Cleveland pleased me because of certain political appointments of colored men, like Matthews and Trotter, and because nothing happened to indicate any attempt at re-enslavement of Negroes.

It was here that my first political activity took place, when I made several speeches in favor of prohibition. This was a subject upon which I felt expert: in my Massachusetts hometown, drunkenness was the great curse and temptation. I spoke two or three times, before, violently in favor of laws to curb it. I was about nineteen at the time.

I was at Harvard when Harrison was inaugurated in 1889. My main thought was on my studies and I can remember very little that I thought or said concerning the new President. So, too, when Cleveland came to power again in 1893, I was in Germany, and felt no great interest. I missed knowledge of Mark Hanna until much later.

By the time of the next election, the McKinley campaign of '96, I found myself in the midst of political controversy. First of all, I was just finishing two years' teaching at Wilberforce in McKinley's own state of Ohio. Then, before McKinley was inaugurated, I had gone to Philadelphia to make my first sociological study; and from there to Georgia to begin my career as a teacher. There I was disfranchised.

I saw the rise of the Free Silver movement, and the beginning of Populism. I was wrong in most of my judgments. My Harvard training made me stand staunchly for the Gold Standard, and I was suspicious of the Populist "Radicals." At the same time, I had seen face-to-face something of the social-democratic movement in Germany. I had gone to their meetings; and by the time McKinley got to work on his high tariff and showed his

evident kinship to big business, I began to awaken. Certain of
my earlier teachings now came into conflict. I had been trained
to believe in Free Trade, which the new McKinley high tariff
contradicted. I began to realize something of the meaning of the
new Populist movement in its economic aspects.

When Theodore Roosevelt began the first of his two terms in
1901, I was teaching in the South and trying to study and
measure its currents. I began to see the situation more clearly.
I was attracted to Roosevelt by his attitude toward my folk in
the appointing of Crum to the port collectorship in South
Carolina and his defense of the little black postmistress at In-
dianola, Mississippi. Also, I knew he was right in his fight
against the trusts. His luncheon with Booker T. Washington
raised such a row in the South that it made me a strong Roosevelt partisan. Then came reaction. I believed in the "muckrak-
ers" whom Roosevelt eventually attacked; they were revealing
the graft and dishonesty in American political life. Roosevelt
was hedging.

I was particularly incensed when he punished, with needless
severity, the colored soldiers who were accused of having revolted under the gravest provocation at Brownsville, Texas, in
1906. On the whole, by the time he went out of office, I held
him under deep suspicion. Then, in 1910, I came to New York
to help organize the National Association for the Advancement
of Colored People, and there my first real step toward independence in politics took place.

I was bitterly opposed to Taft, who followed Roosevelt in
office. Taft, without doubt, catered to the South and did little
or nothing for the American Negro. I wrote in June, 1908:

> When all is said and done, the flat fact remains that
> William Taft represents that class of Americans who
> believe that Negroes are less than men; few of them
> ought to vote; their education should be restricted; their
> opportunities should be limited; their fate must be left
> to the white South; their "value" is their money value
> to their neighbors; and on occasion they may be treated
> like dogs (*vide* Brownsville).

I felt that the announced policies of the Democratic party—
its antimonopoly stand, its denunciation of imperialism, especially as this affected the brown and black people of the West

Indies and the Philippines, its pledge to support organized labor
—merited the Negro's support. I pointed out:

> Throughout the South great corporations are more
> and more grasping and grinding, and crushing Negro
> labor in mines, mills, lumber camps and brickyards, and
> then posing for praise in giving them work at rates
> twenty-five per cent below decent living. If this nation
> does not assume control of corporations, corporations
> will assume control of this nation. Have you no interest
> in this, Mr. Black Worker?

Taft triumphed, though it was unquestionably true that more
Negroes voted against him than ever before voted against a
Republican candidate.

In the critical election of 1912, I at first saw salvation in the
new "Bull Moose" movement under Theodore Roosevelt. I
even went so far as to offer a plank on the Negro problem to the
Bull Moose convention. Joel Spingarn took it to the convention,
but Theodore Roosevelt told him he must beware of "that man
Du Bois."

This proffered plank demanded the cutting of Southern congressional representation in proportion to the disfranchisement
of the Southern masses, an end to lynching, the abolition of
segregation, the elimination of peonage, the equalization of education, the democratization of the armed forces, and the prohibition of restrictive covenants. The plank was never so much as
discussed. Most Negro delegates were refused seats at the convention and Roosevelt tried to woo the Bourbon South through
his teammate, Parker of Louisiana.

I decided then that our best policy in politics was to support
Wilson and the Democratic party. Wilson was a scholar whose
works I had used in my classes, and although a Southerner, he
certainly appeared to be a liberal one. I, therefore, joined forces
with Bishop Walters of the Zion Methodist Church, who was
already openly a Democrat, and tried to see how many Negro
voters could be induced to vote the Democratic ticket. It was
a pretty difficult job in 1912 for a Negro to be a Democrat. He
was considered as either deliberately disloyal to his people, or
a plain grafter. It was difficult to get a Negro audience to listen
patiently to any advocacy of the party which once stood for
slavery, and against the party of Abraham Lincoln.

In the resulting election the Negro vote did something for the election of Woodrow Wilson; how much it was impossible to say. Certainly more Negroes voted for Wilson than had ever before voted for a Democratic Presidential candidate since the Civil War.

We extracted from Wilson certain clear promises for justice toward the American Negro, and at a time when lynching was rampant, we hoped to get a clear statement against it. The result was bitterly disappointing. There has been no time in the history of the United States when so much legislation calculated to infringe the political and civil rights of Negroes was proposed in Congress and state legislatures. They tried to repeal the Fifteenth Amendment; sought at Federal ban on intermarriage; and attacked Negro office-holding. Many of the Southerners looked upon Wilson's election as a field day for a permanent caste status for Negroes. This was a severe blow to my attempt at political leadership; but at the same time there was very little that my opponents could say in favor of the Republican party.

In 1911, I joined the Socialist Party. I became a member of that celebrated Chapter No. 1, in which several of my colleagues were already enrolled—Mary White Ovington, William English Walling and Charles Edward Russell. The N.A.A.C.P. at the time was definitely tending towards the left, although naturally Villard was on the right, and Spingarn rather in the middle.

I had hardly joined the party, however, when the question of the next election came up; and, as I have shown, first I tried to back Roosevelt, and then did what I could to support Wilson. I quickly became aware that I was going contrary to the party line; that a member of the Socialist Party must vote for the Socialist candidate under all circumstances. For me to do this seemed a betrayal of the best interests of the Negro people. They could not afford to have a man in the White House whose election was not due, at least in part, to their vote. The situation was critical. Therefore, I resigned from the Socialists and never since have joined a political party. For registration purposes I usually have enrolled as a Socialist, and lately as American Labor.

This incident illustrates perhaps one fair criticism that could be made of my independence in politics. My tendency was to stand outside of party and think, explain and choose. At the

same time, I am quite aware that practical democratic government calls for party organization and action, and party organization implies the subordination of individual will to the party
platform. Unless this is done, democratic government tends
toward anarchy.

It is this necessity, however, that makes the role of the politician and statesman approach hypocrisy and condonation of
wrong so often. It was this, of course, that explained the fact
that Franklin D. Roosevelt depended upon bosses like Hague
and Kelly. It must always be a difficult point of decision as to
how far a citizen can be a loyal party man and an independent
voter. With my particular type of thinking and impulse to action, it was impossible for me to be a party man.

In October, 1916, I wrote:

> The Negro voter enters the present campaign with no
> enthusiasm. Four years ago the intelligent Negro voter
> tried a great and important experiment. He knew that
> the rank and file of the Bourbon democracy was without
> sense or reason, based on provincial ignorance and es-
> sentially uncivilized, but he saw called to its leadership
> a man of high type and one who promised specifically
> to American Negroes justice—"Not mere grudging jus-
> tice, but justice executed with liberality and cordial
> good feeling." They have lived to learn that this state-
> ment was a lie, a peculiarly miserable campaign decep-
> tion. They are forced, therefore, to vote for the
> Republican candidate, Mr. Hughes, and they find there
> little that is attractive.

We tried to get some reassuring statements out of Hughes,
but were unable to do so. He was practically silent on the Negro.
Nevertheless, we felt there was almost nothing that we could do
except to vote Republican during that campaign and that was
the advice I gave. Wilson was re-elected, narrowly, and the war
came and our participation in it.

We were then brought into politics by the demand for decent
treatment in the draft and in the training centers, particularly
in the South; and especially by a demand for Negro officers. The
Wilson administration became conscious of the political and
social power of Negroes and was scared for a time of possible
German influence. It yielded in the matter of Negro officers,

after we had campaigned widely. Eventually, 700 officers were commissioned. Wilson also promised Villard a Race Commission of Inquiry, but did not keep his word. Then came the scandal of the treatment of Negro soldiers in Europe. The result was, naturally, to turn most Negroes definitely toward support of Harding in 1920.

I did, then, point out:

> The Republican party has for twenty-five years joined the white South in disfranchising us; it has permitted us to be Jim Crowed, deprived of schools and segregated. It has partially disfranchised us in its party councils and proposed practically to eliminate us as soon as this campaign is over. It has encouraged and recognized the "Lily-White" factions, and nearly driven us from public office. In addition to this, the Republicans represent reaction and privilege, the abolition of freedom of speech, the punishment of thinkers, the suppression of the labor movement, the encouragement and protection of trusts, and a new protective tariff to tax the poor for the benefit of the rich.
>
> The Democratic party stands for exactly the same things as the Republicans. Between their professed and their actual policies there is no difference worth noting. To be sure, the Northern wing of the party has tendencies toward some recognition of the laborers' demands and the needs of a stricken war-cursed world, but this is more than neutralized by the Solid South.

Harding's death brought Coolidge to the White House. Coolidge was as colorless toward the race problem as toward other things. But at the suggestion of Bill Lewis, a leading colored Democrat of Boston, he went out of his way to appoint me special Minister Plentipotentiary to Liberia to attend the inauguration of President King. I was at the time already on a visit there, so my appointment was purely a gesture of courtesy.

I remember on my return making a detailed report to Mr. Coolidge and recommending things that really would have been of advantage to Africa. He listened very patiently; I was not at all sure that he understood anything I was saying. He certainly paid no heed to it.

In 1924, my support went to La Follette's Progressive Party

for it seemed clear that he and his party were infinitely superior
to the Coolidge-Davis alternative.

Of the two million Negro votes that year about a million went
to Coolidge, and probably as many as 500,000 to La Follette,
the latter a splendid tribute to the developing independence of
the Negro voter.

The election of 1928 probably represented the lowest point
to which the influence of the Negro in politics ever fell in the
United States since enfranchisement. Indeed, in all respects it
was probably the most disgraceful of all our political campaigns,
bringing in not simply anti-Negro hate, but religious intolerance, the question of sumptuary liquor laws, and a general bitterness and antagonism.

The campaign went so badly that I succeeded in October,
1928, in getting colored leaders representing all phases of
thought to join me in a statement, one of the most important,
perhaps, in the history of the Negro since the Civil War. It said
in part:

> All of us are at this moment united in the solemn
> conviction that in the Presidential campaign of 1928,
> more than in previous campaigns since the Civil War,
> the American Negro is being treated in a manner which
> is unfair and discouraging. We accuse the political lead-
> ers of this campaign of permitting without protest, pub-
> lic and repeated assertions on the platform, in the press,
> and by word of mouth, that color and race constitute in
> themselves an imputation of guilt and crime. . . .
>
> We are asking in this appeal for a public repudiation
> of this campaign of racial hatred. Silence and whispering
> in this case are worse than in matters of personal charac-
> ter and religion. Will white America make no protest?
> Will the candidates continue to remain silent? Will the
> church say nothing? Is there any truth, any issue in this
> campaign, either religious tolerance, liquor, water
> power, tariff or farm relief, that touches in weight the
> transcendent and fundamental question of the open,
> loyal and unchallenged recognition of the essential
> humanity of twelve million Americans who happen to
> be dark-skinned?

This was signed by R. R. Moton, of Tuskegee; John Hope, of
Morehouse; Mordecai W. Johnson, of Howard; C. C. Spaulding,

of the North Carolina Mutual Insurance Company; James Weldon Johnson, Secretary of the N.A.A.C.P.; Eugene K. Jones, of the National Urban League; Mary McLeod Bethune; Monroe N. Work; Reverdy C. Randsom, bishop in the A.M.E. Church; Channing H. Tobias, of the Y.M.C.A.; Carl Murphy, editor of the *Afro-American;* L. K. Williams, president of the National Baptist Convention, and others. It represented practical unanimity among the Negro leaders.

I wrote in November, 1928:

> Many Americans place their hopes of political reform in the United States on the rise of a Third Party which will register the fact that the present Republican and Democratic parties no longer differ in any essential respect; that both represent the rule of organized wealth, and neither of them has been willing to take radical ground with regard to the tariff, the farmer, labor, or the Negro.
>
> The efforts, however, to organize a Third Party movement have not been successful. The Populists failed. The Socialists failed. The Progressives failed. The Farmer-Labor movement failed. Many reasons have been advanced for these failures, but by common consent the real effect reason has seldom been discussed and that reason is in the Solid South: the fact is that no party in American politics can disappear if it is sure of 136 Southern electoral votes.

Hoover, who was inaugurated in 1929, furnished every reason for the final driving of the Negro out of the Republican party. The Negro was not mentioned in his message to Congress. My indictment of Herbert Hoover was written in 1932. I accused him of consorting with the "Lily-Whites" of the South and helping to disfranchise Negroes in the councils of the Republican Party. He nominated known enemies of the Negro for public office, as in the case of Parker of North Carolina for the Supreme Court. He was unfriendly to Haiti and Liberia, and permitted outrageous discrimination in government, especially in the case of Red Cross relief following the Mississippi flood in 1927. In a Tennessee speech in 1928, he promised to appoint to office no person to whom white Southerners objected. Not only was Hoover antagonistic to the Negroes in particular, but in the great national problems of industrial depression, the international debt and the tariff; "in all these President Hoover had been either wrong or helplessly inadequate and each of these failures affected us."

That meant that with the advent of Franklin Roosevelt, President from 1933 to 1945, the Negroes went largely into the ranks of the Democratic party for various reasons: as a rebound from the policies of Taft and Hoover; in gratitude to Roosevelt because of his recognition of Negroes as an integral part of the nation needing relief and work, and capable of bearing their burden in the Great Depression.

The support of Roosevelt by Negroes was not unanimous nor continuous. He made concessions to the South in the matter of wages; and the National Recovery Administration (N.R.A.) aroused much complaint of discrimination. He was often ill-advised by Southerners. But nevertheless, under no recent President have Negroes felt that they received as much justice as under Franklin Roosevelt. I supported him in all four of his terms.

Truman's accession in 1945 brought in a border state politician of apparent good will but narrow training and small vision. His final advocacy of civil rights, his appointment of a Negro Territorial Governor, and other actions during the Second World War brought him a considerable measure of Negro support, so that the Democratic party still probably has a larger Negro following than the Republican. But unfortunately, with the true Truman method he has already begun to talk soft on civil rights. He had not a word to say about them on his recent barnstorming trip to the West and Southwest. This, plus his action in the case of Palestine, and his attitude toward Russia, have made it probable that in the next election the majority of Negroes are going to vote for either a Republican or for Wallace.

My own influence, wherever it can be exercised, and the area is small, has been distinctly in favor of Wallace. Not simply because of his attitude toward Negroes, which is unusually liberal, but even more because of his advocacy of peace, and because of his friendship for and understanding of Russia. I cannot escape the feeling that the attempt of Russia to change the economic foundation of modern life is an even greater phenomenon than the French Revolution.

As I look back upon these fifty years of political activity I can see first, of course, that they occupied a comparatively small part of my thought and work. They were incidental to my main object in studying the Negro problem and interpreting the Negro people to the world. Yet they were important to me in changing my early attitude, which sought completely to divorce politics from the mass of social activity, and brought me to the much truer idea that a basis of political life is and must be economic.

THE FOURTH PERIOD
1948–1963

In 1950, Du Bois was persuaded to run for Senator from New York on the American Labor Party ticket. His campaign consisted of ten speeches and several radio appearances. The following is one of those speeches.

SPEECH BY DR. WILLIAM E. B. DU BOIS, A.L.P. CANDIDATE FOR U.S. SENATOR AT A.L.P. RALLY, GOLDEN GATE BALLROOM

Thursday, October 5, 1950

Harlem is one of the most widely known localities on earth. In Europe, Asia, and Africa the average man has heard of Harlem and has some idea of its significance as a center, not simply of Negro expression but of a new concept of democratic power. Naturally the meaning of Harlem has greatly changed in the course of time. At the close of the Civil War there were only 15,000 Negroes in the whole city of New York and none in the empty farming district to the north of 14th Street.

By the beginning of the century the center of New York's Negro population lay at 53rd Street. It was there that the music and drama which afterward made Harlem famous began; and between 1900 and 1910, Phil Peyton the Negro real estate man, began the opening of Harlem to the crowded Negro population then living on the West Side below 53rd Street.

It was the First World War, with its stoppage of foreign immigration and new opportunities for work, that brought the great influx of Negroes into this area of New York. The black community of 60,000 which had gathered here by 1910, became a hundred thousand by 1920 and doubled each decade to 200,000 in 1930 and 400,000 in 1940. Probably today Harlem and adjacent areas contain more than a half million persons of Negro descent, perhaps the largest Negro city community in the western world.

In its earlier years, from 1900 to 1920, Harlem connoted Negro art in music and theater, with Williams and Walker, Cole and Johnson, Will Marion Cook, Sissle and Blake and Florence Mills; hither came the Blues from Memphis and Jazz with Jim Europe. The world looked on Harlem as a playground and slum, which the rich and curious visited and which sent its singers and dancers around the world. But beyond and beneath this Harlem, was a crowded labyrinth of homes and workers; with poverty, disease and crowding; with all that swell and pulse of living that makes life in a great city. Out of this came, in the twenties, attempts at expression, at writing and acting; poets, novelists and play-wrights began to appear and a Negro literature which was a part and important part of American literature. Also there came crime with gambling and prostitution, assault and theft and this made an ideal stamping ground for politics in the lower sense of that term. Here among the poor and depressed, votes could be bought cheaply and both Tammany and the Republican machines soon began to disburse considerable funds to control the Harlem vote. This was paid for in cash and followed by a few offices and jobs and sale of the right to sell liquor and women and the numbers.

Then came the depression of the thirties and Harlem sank in poverty, relief, destitution and crime; the literary renaissance disappeared in a grim fight to live and survive; and by the advent of the forties there came to Harlem a new sense of the power and meaning of life in this section; born of struggle and of a growth of intelligence and planning. Politics took on new meaning and no longer meant simply pay for votes or for the privilege of breaking the law. The Harlem Negro began to demand representation in government and representation by men of his own choosing and not simply by those chosen and thrust over him. Political machinery began to pass into his hands and he entered the city government, the police force, the civil service, the State Legislature and the national Congress. But he was content still to share power and not yet ready to use it for new ends.

During this time Harlem thought of itself as a Negro Community dealing mainly with the problems of the American Negro. Although a community of workers, it did not conceive itself as part of the labor problem of the city or nation. Harlem did not ask to guide democracy, only to share it on the same terms as other folk shared it.

Although a part of the American expression of democracy, it wanted to be a part of that democracy, for which others did the thinking and guiding. This was natural for a group brought up with a slave psychology; whose highest ambition quite naturally was to share and not to guide; to be recognized and not to dictate. But Harlem lived in a changing age; in an age when the burden of governing was shifting from the privileged to the mass; from the owner of property to the creator of value. This meant often, as men feared it would, transfer of power from intelligence to ignorance and from experience to uncertainty; yet at the same time, it was bringing a new thing into the world: a broad sense of unselfish care for the mass of humanity, instead of the fierce struggle of the smart to survive at any cost; and a feeling of the unity of mankind across lines of race as well as class. Thus the Harlem voter gradually began to feel himself not simply as symbol of a race, but as part of a people; not simply as a center for entertaining the rich, but much more as a community of citizens whose duty it was to help make a new nation and a new world.

To illustrate my meaning, I remember how a quarter of a century ago, I started a Little Theater in the basement of the 135th Street Library, to let Harlem portray and entertain and express itself. Young Aaron Douglas painted the scenery. The so-called Krigwa Players wrote their own plays and acted the parts and furnished their own audiences. After hesitation we entered a nationwide contest of Little Theatres downtown and won second prize. That ruined us; Broadway beckoned to our actors and they fled to money-making and show-off, instead of sticking to the far finer task of building a community which through drama, could take its rightful place in the building of a nation. Then the depression finished our venture and now a new world looks at Harlem in this crisis of modern civilization. It sees it not simply as an entertainment center but as one of the world's great testing grounds for modern democracy where the representatives of a great people have a chance to guide the world in a day when as perhaps never before the world needs guidance.

And it is a battle, make no mistake about it—the last Great Battle of the West: centered about a new development of the grave and unanswered question: where in the State—in the Organized Community—does the real ultimate Power lie: the power of police control; of the organization of Work and Wage? Of the content and range of education? Of the ownership and distribution of property? In these matters of universal power, where and whose is the ultimate control?

We know how historically this power at first rested naturally in the Father of the family; then as the family multiplied, it was shared by a Council of Elders and the King who stood at their head by choice or self-assertion. But as families and clans grew to tribes and nations, the powers and identity of rulers varied by chance and strength, until the right to rule became tangled, hidden and often incapable of any clear explanation or understanding. Then men had to clear away the underbrush and rationalize government; first into royal rule "by the Grace of God" until kings mistook themselves for God and were beheaded; until certain citizens, distinguished by birth, ability or wealth monopolized the right to rule the state. This often degenerated into a rule of self-interest and privilege and in Europe in the 18th and early 19th centuries, men grown rich by reason of new discoveries and inventions, took over the powers of government, yielding the working class some limited rights to share their power. In the latter part of the 19th century this rule of the Rich and property-holding classes with increased numbers of workers sharing political power, brought the whole world under the control of Europe through a new science and technique and reduced to subservience the workers of the world outside Europe. This was scarcely accomplished when in the 20th century the world burst into flame, in a confused and rapidly changing series of wars; first a war to redistribute the Colonies of Asia and Africa among the empires of Europe; then to prevent by force the working classes from controlling the property and curtailing the powers of the rich; and finally the attempt of the colonial people themselves wholly to escape the control of Europe and North America.

This is the muddled world in which we find ourselves today: its basic problems of property, wage, power and privilege are increasingly clear: the answer to these problems is not War; and the interests involved are not simply nor mainly the interests of the rich, nor of industry in itself. A new era of power, held and exercised by the working classes the world over, is dawning and while its eventual form is not yet clear, its progress can not be held back by any power of man. It is facing this problem that Harlem stands today and in its light, we must act and vote. First then Peace and Civil Rights; then Study, Education and Public

Information in a press free from the control of Big Business is our program.

It may seem nonsense to a proverbially modest group to conceive that they who have always followed, listened and asked, should today with a certain suddenness be ordered to lead, to inform and speak out in clear, firm tones. Yet this is far more true than you think. The majority of the people of the world are today watching Harlem and American Negroes with fascinated interest. Today in China and India; in Indonesia and the Philippines; through the length and breadth of Africa; in the Caribbean and the South Seas, in the Near East and South America, men are asking—many have asked me personally— what is this dark group of 15 million Americans thinking and advising; the group which has fought and faced Europe and America hand to hand for three awful centuries until today, while not yet free; they yet stand with 2 million ballots in their hands and brains in their heads to vote as modern men and not as purchased slaves: What do they think and advise in this crisis of the modern world. Where does Harlem stand in the battle for Peace and Civil Rights?

Your answer should be calm and clear: Harlem stands for Peace and Civil Rights; for Peace among all nations, before and behind the Iron Curtain; for Civil Rights for all men, Chinese, and Koreans, Russians and Poles, black, brown and yellow peoples, as well as for Englishmen and Americans.

There was a day when most men believed that progress depended on war; that by war and mainly by war had modern men gained Freedom, Religion and Democracy. We believed this because we were taught this in our literature and science, in church and school, on platform and in newspaper. It was always a lie and as war has become universal and so horrible and destructive that everybody recognizes it as Murder, crippling, insanity and stark death of human culture, we realize that there is scarce a victory formerly claimed by war, which mankind might not have gained more cheaply and more decently and even more completely by methods of peace. If that was true in the past, it is so clear and indisputable today that no sane being denies it. And yet of all nations of earth today the United States alone wants War, prepares for war, forces other nations to fight and asks you and me to impoverish ourselves, give up health and schools, sacrifice our sons and daughters to a Jim-crow army and commit suicide for a world war that nobody wants but the rich Americans who profit by it. This is the reason for this meeting; for this campaign, for my candidacy for the United States Senate: I want progress; I want education; I want social medicine; I want a living wage and Old Age Security; I want Employment for all and Relief for the Unemployed and Sick; I want Public Works, Public Services and Public Improvement; and because I know and you know that we cannot have these things and at the same time fight, destroy and kill all around the world in order to make huge profits for Big Business, for that reason, I take my stand beside the millions in every continent and nation and cry Peace—No More War; end the rule of Brass Hats in our government and investments. Let us stop the antics of the Wild Man of Tokyo, who is determined of his own will to fight China and Russia, and the Eisenhowers who declare openly in public hearing, "We can lick the World!"

If war were a matter of careful study and grave decision; of prayerful thought and solemn deliberation, we might take its fearful outbreak as at least no more than human error, soon to be stopped by decency and common sense. But when did you even vote for war? You who have spent most of your lives in a fighting, murdering world? When did you ever have a chance to decide this matter of maiming and murder? Never and you never will as long as an executive on his own initiative can start a little 'police action' which costs the lives and health of 20,000 American boys in order that Big Business can interfere into the governments of Asia and reap millions. A pretty batch of scoundrels we are supporting in order to make money for persons who already have more then they can spend: Chiang Kai-Shek and Syngman Rhee; Quirino, Bao-Dai, the rulers of Persia and Greece; Budenz and Bentley, Anders; and a host of allied and associated spies, thieves and liars. The people of communities like Harlem foot the bill and sacrifice our children for this precious privilege.

In order to stop you from discussing or voting on war, we have erected again in America, a Slave State; just as a century ago we made the discussion of Negro Slavery illegal. It is possible today that an honest American, without committing a crime or an illegal act, can be jailed and impoverished if he talks peace, higher wage or civil rights; this may be done even without trial or hearing; and any public discussion of the case can be absolutely stopped. I am a candidate for public office today, because only in a campaign like this can I discuss peace and civil rights on the platform, over the radio or in the public press. This is Liberty, this is America. One right is left to us and that is the ballot, outside of Mississippi, Georgia and their sister states, who because of disfranchisement hold all positions of power in Congress.

Here in New York, you can vote for Peace, provided of course your employer does not know it. And he need not know it. Legally it is none of his business how you vote. Your vote is secret. It may not be tomorrow, but it is today. Only three nights ago, Governor Dewey turned the old Abraham Lincoln stop on this platform and told his audience what must have been real news to them, how he and the Republican Party had bought and paid for your votes. He told you how he favored the F.E.P.C. but forgot to remind you how long he stalled on it and ducked until he had to yield. He rightly charged Truman with failing to keep his civil rights promises but did not mention that Republican leader Vandenburg was his right-hand man to clinch the job. He mentioned housing but not in Stuyvesant Town. He deplored failure to pass anti-poll tax and anti-lynching legislature by Democratic Congresses which acted exactly like Republican Congresses. Indeed any attempt of Republicans or Democrats to assess guilt for anti-Negro bias is merely exercise in the Pot calling the Kettle black. I ask Harlem to vote overwhelmingly for Peace and Civil Rights against Dewey and Lynch.

The United States Senate is probably the most powerful legislative body on earth. Senators are elected by the people for six year terms and they represent in theory all the people; but in fact the chief interest of certain people. These interests are not equally distributed: Business and Banking, Law and Manufacturing, Commerce and the learned Professions are over-represented by trained and talented men; but labor and servants, farmers and women, the poor and unfortunate, have small voice or thought in this body; and 15 million Negroes, have no voice at all. In November, New York will choose a senator from three candidates: One is a respectable citizen, who speaks for property and investment and the military forces, and who expressed this week his fear of Peace. These interests are already over-represented in the Senate; they do not need more Lehmans.

Another candidate is a hack politician who represents New York public life at its lowest. He has no business in the United States Senate, where he would stand shoulder to shoulder with war-mongers and profiteers. I am a third candidate: think the matter over carefully: Which of these three men would best voice the interests of the people represented here today?

STATEMENT ISSUED BY W.E.B. DU BOIS BEFORE HE WAS ARRAIGNED ON CHARGES OF BEING AN "AGENT OF A FOREIGN PRINCIPLE"

September, 1951

It is a curious thing that today I am called upon to defend myself against criminal charges for openly advocating the one thing all people want—peace. For 38 years I have worked and studied hoping that in some way I might help my people and my fellow men to a better way of life, free of poverty and injustice.

My interest in world affairs is long standing. For two years, from 1892 to 1894, I studied at the University of Berlin and traveled in Germany, Austria-Hungary, Italy and France. I attended the World Races Congress in 1911 in London. I organized Pan-African Congresses in Paris, London, Brussels and Lisbon in 1919, 1921, and 1923.

I was on consultation in 1919 and 1921 with the founders of the League of Nations. I attended the first meeting of the League Assembly in Geneva and met with the directors of the Commission of Mandates and the International Labor Organization in 1928. I had the honor of serving as special minister from the United States to Liberia.

In 1936, as a fellow of the Carl Shurz Foundation, I spent five months in Germany and then went on to China, Japan, Manchuria and Russia.

I was appointed special consultant and attended the founding conference in San Francisco of the United Nations. Later, in 1945, I attended the Pan-African Congress in London.

I cite these facts simply to indicate that my personal concern and activities for peace these last few years are fully consonant with my entire life interest in the cause of promoting peace through understanding among the peoples of the world.

With me today are three of my co-workers in the Peace Information Center, persons of integrity and principle who share with me the deep moral conviction that differences between nations must not be allowed to bring about destruction of the human race.

It is a sad commentary that we must enter a courtroom today to plead not guilty to something that cannot be a crime—advocating peace and friendship between the American people and the peoples of the world. These indictments are a shameful proclamation to the world that our government considers peace alien, and its advocacy criminal. In a world which has barely emerged from the horrors of the second World War and which trembles on the brink of atomic catastrophe, can it be criminal to hope and work for peace?

We feel now as we have always felt that our activities for peace, and, in particular, the outlawing of atomic warfare cannot conceivably fall within the purview of a statute such as the Foreign Agents Registration Act. As chairman of the Peace Information Center during its existence, I can categorically state that we are an entirely American organization whose sole objective as Americans was to secure peace and prevent a third world war.

It is revealing that the Justice Department can find no statute which provides protection for the Negro people from such outrages as the execution of the Martinsville Seven, yet, it displays great ingenuity in distorting legislation to make it apply to advocates of peace.

A great demand for peace is being voiced throughout our country. Men and women everywhere are questioning our tragic military adventures in Korea and the prospect of war with China. There is deep apprehension at the thought that an atomic war may be unleashed. In the light of this, the shabby trick of branding those who seek peace as "aliens" and "criminals" will not stem this tide. I am confident that every American who desires peace, Negro and white, Catholic, Jew and Protestant, the three million signers of the World Peace Appeal and the tens of millions more will join us in our fight to vindicate our right to speak for peace.

SPEECH OF DR. W.E.B. DU BOIS AT A SAVE THE ROSENBERGS RALLY UNDER THE AUSPICES OF THE CIVIL RIGHTS CONGRESS

The Rosenbergs are not accused of betraying military secrets to an enemy of their country. At the time the alleged deed was perpetrated, we were friends and allies with the Soviet Union. It could not be alleged that the Rosenbergs were dealing with an enemy. Later, when they were actually arrested and charged with treason, friction had arisen over Korea and other matters, and the Korean war had begun. Although the Soviet Union was not a direct party, nevertheless it was fear of the Soviets and a growing vision of a war between the United States and Russia which furnished the atmosphere in which this trial was held.

Under such circumstances, in this case as in many other cases in the past, accusation itself spelled conviction.

How fortunate it would have been for us and for the world if at the time the Rosenbergs were accused we had in fact freely given to the Soviet Union and to the whole world the secret of the atom bomb. That would have been a gesture toward peace which would have convinced mankind of our real desire for a free world and for true democracy, and our abhorrence of imperial exploitation. It would have saved the nation enough funds for social medicine and the cure of cancer and infantile paralysis; for the harnessing of our great, destroying river systems; and watering of our deserts; and especially the restoration and development of our educational systems. But we did not do this; on the contrary, we set ourselves to conquer not only the Soviet Union but the world.

Turning then from this spoiled dream of peace, let us consider the facts of the relations between the United States and the Soviet Union before, during and after the second world war.

For many years there was unquestioned friendship between the United States and Russia. My high-school textbooks used to praise the cession of Alaska as binding the two nations together. Much was said in my youth of the splendid court of the Czars, and no American ambassadorship was more sought for than the embassy to Russia.

There were some criticisms. For instance, as a high school student, I remember reading in the *Century Magazine* a series of articles by George Kennan, father of the present man with the same name. He criticized severely the cruelty of the Czars, the repression of freedom, and the exile to Siberia. Afterward we heard much about Russian anarchy, revolt and assassination, mitigated in part by the emancipation of the serfs which came about the same time that American Negro slaves were emancipated.

In 1917 it is fair to say that the overwhelming liberal public opinion in the United States was with the revolutionists. Great liberal leaders and thinkers who in 1918 hailed the Russian Revolution as greater than the French and as fulfilling the dream of the American, need not today be ashamed of their enthusiasm, for it was echoed around the forward-thinking world. I remember the visit of Katherine Breshkovskaya, mother of the revolution, to America. I was present when Jane Adams entertained her at Hull House.

Then because of the British attempt to beat back the revolution, came the attack on Russia of fourteen nations, including America, followed by an extraordinary propaganda which has persisted to our day. Especially did the expulsion of Leon Trotsky and his exile to Mexico impress liberals and set them against Stalin before they knew the whole truth.

But above all came the propaganda of Hitler. No matter how much we were frightened by fascism in Italy and Nazism in Germany, many influential Americans admired both Hitler and Mussolini, and went along with Great Britain in an all-out attempt to appease them. It was for this reason that we refused to invite the Soviet Union to alliance against the Nazi attack on Western Europe. Along with Great Britain we steadfastly refused to negotiate with Russia, sending second-rank negotiators and putting off decision, until at last the Soviet Union in self-defense made alliance with Hitler.

Then as France and England tottered on the brink and Hitler turned from the finishing blow to overthrow the Soviet Union, we regained our senses in part, and with reluctance made alliance with the Soviet Union and Great Britain against the Nazis. But we were certain that the Soviet Union was going to be overthrown in a short time. It was, therefore, our belief that if we could prolong the conflict as much as possible, Hitler might be so much weakened by the Russian resistance that both communism and Nazism would overthrow themselves.

There is no doubt that this was the reason behind our delay

in furnishing a second front against the Nazis. Although hard pressed, the Soviets were putting up fierce resistance against the mighty *wehrmacht.* We therefore promised the Russians help, but we followed the lead of Churchill and Britain, and that was to wait until the Russians were overthrown, and meantime to conserve our strength and attack through Southern Europe so as to preserve the western European highway to Asia and the control of the Mediterranean. Then when Hitler's armies returned from Russia, even if victorious, they would find it difficult to overthrow Great Britain and France, with the Allies firmly entrenched in southern Europe and northern Africa.

The unexpected and incredible happened. The Russians at the cost of over 15 million lives and one hundred billions of property, smashed Hitler and the German armies and did this without the help of American or Western European soldiers. Some material and munitions we furnished the Soviets, but it formed about 5 percent of their total needs. We sent many trucks and jeeps, but not as many as the Soviets captured from the Germans. This small supply was stopped too early, and after the war we refused to loan the Soviets a dollar, while we gave 90 millions to the Union of South Africa.

When this entirely new situation faced us at Potsdam and Yalta, we came to an understanding with Russia, and did it gladly, yielding control over the territory which bordered on the Soviet territory which we had tried to preserve as a *cordon sanitaire* from which the west planned to attack and reconquer the Soviets. We could not in decency nor in armed might refuse to yield the Baltic states which had been Russian territory; nor Poland which the West had armed against the Soviets; nor could we compel Czechoslovakia to follow western dictatorship. Our appreciation of the Soviet effort was ecstatic. Our Secretary of State, Cordell Hull, praised "the epic quality of their patriotic fervor." General Douglas MacArthur said of the Red Army: "The world situation at the present time indicates that the hopes of civilization rest on the worthy banners of the courageous Russian army. During my lifetime I have participated in a number of wars and have witnessed others, as well as studying in great detail the campaigns of outstanding leaders of the past. In none have I observed such effective resistance to the heaviest blows of a hitherto undefeated enemy, followed by a smashing counter-attack which is driving the enemy back to his own land. The scale and grandeur of the effort make it the greatest military achievement in all history."

At Quebec, on August 31, 1943, Prime Minister Winston Churchill declared concerning the Soviet Government and its leadership:

> No government ever formed among men has been capable of surviving injuries so grave and cruel as those inflicted by Hitler on Russia . . . Russia has not only survived and recovered from those frightful injuries but has inflicted, as no other force in the world could have inflicted, mortal damage on the German army machine.

Colonel Raymond Robins, head of the American Red Cross in Russia, said:

> Soviet Russia has always wanted international peace. Lenin knew that his great domestic program would be deflected if not destroyed by war. The Russian people have always wanted peace, education, production, exploitation of a vast and rich territory engage all their thoughts and energies and hopes.
>
> Soviet Russia exploits no colonies, seeks to exploit none. Soviet Russia operates no foreign trade cartels, seeks none to exploit. Stalin's policies have wiped out racial, religious, national and class antagonisms within the Soviet territories. This unity and harmony of the Soviet peoples point the path to international peace.

In return we needed Soviet alliance against the still powerful army and navy of Japan; and particularly we expected to develop China as our ally, not only against Japan but in the industrial empire which we hoped to build in Asia after the war, in our role as successor to the British empire.

To our astonishment this failed, when the Communists drove out our ally, Chiang Kai-shek, and took the arms and ammunition which we had given him. There remained only, to the mind of most Americans, the protection of the newly discovered atom bomb. It is easy to see how during this almost hysterical change and reaction charges or even rumors that the secret of the atom bomb had been revealed to Russia alarmed the nation.

In September, 1949, the President announced that the Soviet Union knew the secret of the atom bomb, and from that many concluded that this secret had been betrayed to the Soviet Union by Americans, and that eventually a third world war between the United States and the Soviet Union must follow.

Widespread and deliberate propaganda induced most Americans, even liberals and radicals, to accept this belief. When Fuchs was convicted as a spy in 1950, and Judith Coplon accused, atomic traitors were scented everywhere, and in 1951 the Rosenbergs were accused.

Here is the background of the kind of public opinion in which they were tried. It is doubtful if anyone in this room, under these circumstances, would have escaped grave danger of conviction. The case against the Rosenbergs was sworn to by a confessed spy, who received immunity even though it has never been proven that he possessed any atomic secret which he could reveal. The Rosenbergs were tried in an atmosphere of race prejudice, during the attempt to establish universal military service, and the crusade of the National Association of Manufacturers to make the United States fight the Soviet Union for possession of markets of Asia and the world.

It is for this reason that the Rosenbergs were convicted, and most Americans who are not carried away by the hysteria of the Korean war cannot believe that the Rosenbergs committed a crime or had a just trial. This meeting tonight is a protest to try and see that in the end justice will prevail.

The significance of the Rosenberg case, therefore, reaches beyond the fate of two individuals, tragic as that may be. It becomes a part of the great peace crusade. In the midst of war and fear of war we do unbelievable things, we rush to lying, slander and hate because we fear what war will do to us and to ours. In blind recoil from mass murder we do anything which in our fevered imagination seems likely to save us from war. This is the reason why here in a nation born in peace and justice, we are almost without protest committing crimes against humanity, against elementary civil rights, against every ideal of democracy. The public opinion which crucifies a father and mother in the prime of life is based on the abject fear of disaster to the whole nation. But fear is not fact, and ignorantly to commit an unforgiveable crime in the name of a greater crime is no excuse. First we must know beyond all doubt that the Rosenbergs were spies. It is no accident that the law of civilization has always declared it far better that ten guilty escape rather than one innocent person be punished for a crime he never committed.

In this case the greater reason for pause is our rush to war, to which this nation has yielded without cause and without reason. The blood guilt is upon us Americans who, alone in the world, demand mass murder and force and continued slaughter of helpless Korea.

A quarter of a century ago, in the midst of war hysteria and postwar inflation, we committed in this nation a judicial crime as great as that which we now contemplate, because of the hate born of the first World War; because of race prejudice in New England against Irish and the newly-come Italians; and particularly because booming industry feared radicals—we murdered Sacco and Vanzetti. We murdered two workers of high ideals and steadfast faith. No man today doubts the frightful miscarriage of justice in this case. Yet at the time some of the most influential Americans refused to say a word or raise a hand of protest. Vanzetti, addressing the court, April 9, 1927, said (and with these same words he speaks again to us tonight):

> The jury did not understand the difference between a man who is against war because he believes war is unjust and because he hates no country, and a man who hates war because he is in favor of the country which is fighting the land in which he lives; such a man is a spy and commits a crime against his country in order to serve its enemy. We are not men of that kind. Nobody can say that we are German spies. We were against the war because we did not believe in the purpose for which they say the war was fought. We believe that war is wrong and we believe this more after the ten years in which we have studied and observed day by day. And I am glad to be on the scaffold of doom if I can say to mankind: Look out! You are in the tomb of the flower of mankind. For what? All that they said to you, all that they have promised you, it was a lie, it was a fraud, it was a crime. They promised you liberty; where is liberty? They promised you prosperity; where is prosperity?

Sacco and Vanzetti are dead; but you live. And may you live to prevent another such crime as this.

In his last years, Du Bois could not get published except in radical journals. Prominent among these was the weekly news-paper the National Guardian, *for which Du Bois wrote 115 articles.*

The following articles are from the pages of the National Guardian *and provide a good picture of Du Bois' concerns and thoughts during the 1950's to his death.*

THE HARD-BIT MAN IN THE LOUD SHIRTS

January 22, 1953

The President whose exit we celebrate is a perplexing human being. He had no broad educational background. He had an inferiority complex natural after succeeding Roosevelt, which was followed by an inflated overestimate of himself, his power and his place in history. He imagines himself as stepping down from a most successful administration; in fact he was emphatically repudiated by the largest poll in American history, having ruined Stevenson's chances by imposing his own policy on him.

Truman's contradictions in character have frightened the nation. He blends homely likeableness with human insensibility and stubbornness which has no regard for the truth. When he saw himself defeated in 1948, he deliberately lied to liberals and Negroes with no intention of even trying to fulfill promises he knew his own party would repudiate. He was quite prepared to assent to whatever course they took. He defends Margaret's voice with low invective, and stands by his friends no matter whether they are honest men or thieves; but once his stubborn mind is made up he fights McCarran and McCarthy.

Deeper down in his hard-bit soul, he ranks with Adolf Hitler as one of the greatest killers of our day. Without expressing a word of public regret he killed 150,000 Japanese men, women and children and was surprised when his flippant threat to do it again sent a shudder around the world. He forced the nation into the Korean War and tried to scare it into universal military service. His last word to the nation is a threat of universal doom such as no other sane ruler ever uttered.

Truman's truculence, his loud clothes and terrible shirts, are bad enough; his distortion of history and ignorance of literature are even worse. Read his last grotesque story of our relations with the Soviet Union.

These can be nothing less than deliberate misstatements on Truman's part. He proposes to make the nation believe what he stubbornly wants to believe. He and his whole administration are propaganda, which his Bright Boys in Washington furnish at command. He, his cabinet, his generals, his ambassadors summon their ghost-writers as they do their cooks. They distort the Truth and the Right so completely, that the nation last November said in vast despair:

"Anything but Truman—even Eisenhower."

DR. DU BOIS ON STALIN: "HE KNEW THE COMMON MAN . . . FOLLOWED HIS FATE"

March 16, 1953

Joseph Stalin was a great man; few other men of the 20th century approach his stature. He was simple, calm and courageous. He seldom lost his poise; pondered his problems slowly, made his decisions clearly and firmly; never yielded to ostentation nor coyly refrained from holding his rightful place with dignity. He was the son of a serf, but stood calmly before the great without hesitation or nerves. But also—and this was the highest proof of his greatness—he knew the common man, felt his problems, followed his fate.

Stalin was not a man of conventional learning; he was much more than that: he was a man who thought deeply, read understandingly and listened to wisdom, no matter whence it came. He was attacked and slandered as few men of power have been; yet he seldom lost his courtesy and balance; nor did he let attack drive him from his convictions nor induce him to surrender positions which he knew were correct. As one of the despised minorities of man, he first set Russia on the road to conquer race prejudice and make one nation out of its 140 groups without destroying their individuality.

His judgment of men was profound. He early saw through the flamboyance and exhibitionism of Trotsky, who fooled the world, and especially America. The whole ill-bred and insulting attitude of Liberals in the U.S. today began with our naive acceptance of Trotsky's magnificent lying propaganda, which he carried around the world. Against it, Stalin stood like a rock and moved neither right nor left, as he continued to advance toward a real socialism instead of the sham Trotsky offered.

Three great decisions faced Stalin in power and he met them magnificently: first, the problem of the peasants, then the West European attack, and last the Second World War. The poor Russian peasant was the lowest victim of tsarism, capitalism and the Orthodox Church. He surrendered the Little White Father easily; he turned less readily but perceptibly from his ikons; but his kulaks clung tenaciously to capitalism and were near wrecking the revolution when Stalin risked a second revolution and drove out the rural bloodsuckers.

Then came intervention, the continuing threat of attack by all nations, halted by the Depression, only to be re-opened by Hitlerism. It was Stalin who steered the Soviet Union between Scylla and Charybdis: Western Europe and the U.S. were willing to betray her to fascism, and then had to beg her aid in the Second World War. A lesser man than Stalin would have demanded vengeance for Munich, but he had the wisdom to ask only justice for his fatherland. This Roosevelt granted but Churchill held back. The British Empire proposed first to save itself in Africa and southern Europe, while Hitler smashed the Soviets.

The Second Front dawdled, but Stalin pressed unfalteringly ahead. He risked the utter ruin of socialism in order to smash the dictatorship of Hitler and Mussolini. After Stalingrad the Western World did not know whether to weep or applaud. The cost of victory to the Soviet Union was frightful. To this day the outside world has no dream of the hurt, the loss and the sacrifices. For his calm, stern leadership here, if nowhere else, arises the deep worship of Stalin by the people of all the Russias.

Then came the problem of Peace. Hard as this was to Europe and America, it was far harder to Stalin and the Soviets. The conventional rulers of the world hated and feared them and would have been only too willing to see the utter failure of this attempt at socialism. At the same time the fear of Japan and Asia was also real. Diplomacy therefore took hold and Stalin was picked as the victim. He was called in conference with British Imperialism represented by its trained and well-fed aristocracy; and with the vast wealth and potential power of America represented by its most liberal leader in half a century.

Here Stalin showed his real greatness. He neither cringed nor strutted. He never presumed, he never surrendered. He gained the friendship of Roosevelt and the respect of Churchill. He asked neither adulation nor vengeance. He was reasonable and conciliatory. But on what he deemed essential, he was inflexible. He was willing to resurrect the League of Nations, which had insulted the Soviets. He was willing to fight Japan, even though Japan was then no menace to the Soviet Union, and might be death to the British Empire and to American trade. But on two points Stalin was adamant: Clemenceau's "Cordon Sanitaire" must be returned to the Soviets, whence it had been stolen as a threat. The Balkans were not to be left helpless before Western exploitation for the benefit of land monopoly. The workers and peasants there must have their say.

Such was the man who lies dead, still the butt of noisy jackals and of the ill-bred men of some parts of the distempered West. In life he suffered under continuous and studied insult; he was forced to make bitter decisions on his own lone responsibility. His reward comes as the common man stands in solemn acclaim.

AMERICAN NEGROES AND AFRICA

February 14, 1955

One of the curious results of current fear and hysteria is the breaking of ties between Africa and American Negroes. When we think of the hell which Irish Americans have given Ireland, and how Scandinavia, Italy, Germany, Poland and China have been aided by their emigrants in the United States, it is tragic that American Negroes today are not only doing little to help

Africa in its hour of supreme need, but have no way of really knowing what is happening in Africa.

When the Cotton Kingdom of the 19th century built on black slavery led to a campaign in church and society to discount Africa, its culture and history, American Negroes shrank from any ties with Africa and accepted in part the color line. By the 20th century, however, knowledge of Africa and its history spread in Negroes' schools and literature. Negro churches helped Africa, African students appeared here and movements looking toward closer ties with Africa spread. From the First World War to 1945 the Pan-African movement held international conferences to unite the Negro race in mutual aid, information and planning.

A Council on African Affairs was formed in 1939 under the leadership of Paul Robeson, returning from his first visit to Africa. It soon had a membership of 2,000 whites and blacks. It collected a library and some specimens of African art; entertained visiting Africans and students, raised relief funds for starving Negroes in South Africa, issued a monthly bulletin and arranged lectures.

Then in 1949, without hearing or chance for defense, the Council was listed on the Attorney-General's "subversive" list. It remained under attack and most of its support faded away.

In the industrial world the significance of Africa increased. Today out of Africa come 95 per cent of the world's diamonds; 80 per cent of the cobalt; 60 per cent of the gold; 75 per cent of the sisal hemp; 70 per cent of the palm oil; 70 per cent of the cocoa; 35 per cent of the phosphates; 30 per cent of the chrome and manganese; 20 per cent of the copper; 15 per cent of the coffee; an increasing part of the uranium and radium, and large amounts of tin, iron and spices.

Naturally, American investment in Africa has increased: in the first half of the century it rose from $500 million to $1,500 million; South Africa asked us in 1949 for a loan of $50 million, eventually got nearly twice as much. the Morgan, Rockefeller and Ford interests have been investing in South Africa; General Motors, Firestone, General Electric have followed suit. General Lucius Clay, who headed the "Freedom Crusade" among us, once also headed a mining company in South Africa which netted $9 million profit in three years.

In 1950 the U.S. Consul General to South Africa said: "This

country has a greater future than almost any young country in the world." The vice president of the largest U.S. railway equipment manufacturer said South Africa had unlimited potentiality for development: "I can see it going ahead with great speed for it is so rich in so many kinds of raw materials. The South Africans are a great people."

The result of exploitation of Africa in the first half of the 20th century was revolt in the second half, from Tunis to the Cape of Good Hope. There has been demand for independence in Egypt and for autonomy in the Sudan; bloody rebellion goes on in Kenya; unrest and threats exist in Uganda; Ethiopia has regained independence and recovery of her sea coast; West Africa revolted in 1948 and today approaches dominion status in the British Empire for there are as many blacks in the Gold Coast and Nigeria as there are whites in England. Both France and Portugal are slowly admitting a black intelligentsia to full civil rights, while even the Belgian Congo which restrained Negro education will open a Negro university.

But in the Union of South Africa a white nation has determined on race subordination as a policy, and 2,600,000 whites are attempting to rule and exploit ten million blacks and colored. The Rhodesias are attempting to follow this policy in part. The looming struggle is of vast portent.

Meantime this current story gets small space in the Afro-American press with its 150 weekly newspapers circulating among two million readers. Four of the leading papers have from 100,000 to 300,000 readers each and are in the realm of big business, subject to the control of finance capital in advertising, allotment of newsprint and political influence. Political party funds are often available to swell income during elections, and their main support comes from readers who must not offend the Department of Justice and the FBI or they will lose their jobs. Meantime since the Second World War, 15 million American Negroes have sent less than $10,000 to help the struggles of 200,000,000 Africans.

On the other hand the Negro press discusses race relations in the United States, reports news of the Negro group and personal items. Its chief demand for 150 years has been political, civil and social equality with white Americans.

Here they are advancing rapidly, and today it is clear that they have a chance to trade wide breaks in the American color line for acquiescence in American and West European control of the world's colored peoples. This is shown by the pressure on them to keep silence on Africa and Asia and on white working-class movements, and in return to accept more power to vote; abolition of separation in education; dropping of "jim-crow" units in our military forces and gradual disappearance of the Negro ghetto in work and housing. To this is added much long-delayed recognition of Negro ability and desert.

It is fair to admit that most American Negroes, even those of intelligence and courage, do not yet fully realize that they are being bribed to trade equal status in the United States for the slavery of the majority of men. When this is clear, especially to black youth, the race must be aroused to thought and action and will see that the price asked for their cooperation is far higher than need be paid, since race and color equality is bound to come in any event.

THE BELGIAN CONGO: COPPER CAULDRON

March 27, 1955

The great Congo River, third longest in the world, curls around the center of Africa where in the past extraordinary human development in handicraft and political organization has taken place. A kingdom of Congo had existed for centuries when the Portuguese arrived in the 15th century. They induced the Mfumu or king to accept Christianity, and his son was educated in Portugal. One of his successors traveled in Europe in 1600. In intricate political organization and weaving of velvets, satins and damasks the Congolese became noted.

Then came centuries of invasion from west and northeast, and finally this valley fell into the claws of Leopold II of Belgium, with Stanley as his press agent. The two inveigled the Congress of Berlin to let Leopold hold the Congo as a sort of great Christian enterprise where "Peace and Religion" would march hand in hand.

The result in theft and sheer cruelty astounded even Europe, more especially as both France and Germany, and Britain hiding behind Portugal, stood ready to show Belgium how and were at the time content with cutting off the coastline. But the Belgian state took over, staggering under this colony 14 times the size of Belgium itself and with many more inhabitants.

Belgium was at that time under socialist leadership, but that did not curb colonial imperialism. First Belgium confiscated all native rights to land ownership. Then they subsidized all chiefs and put labor under vast corporations in which Britain and America invested. They curbed education to elementary instruction under Catholics, with a few exceptions. They gave the natives training in skills of a higher grade than in South Africa or the Rhodesias, but kept wages low and did not give enough education to permit training even for physicians; and for a long time they refused to let Negroes enter Belgian higher schools at home.

Then came demands in Brussels at the Second Pan-African Congress. Immediately black students who were not too radical began to be received in Belgian schools. An official report says in 1954: "In 1947 a school for administrative and commercial training was opened. In the same year the Centre Universitaire Congolais Lovanium was organized with the intention to group the existing schools together and lay the foundations for an institute of higher education."

Meantime the Belgian Congo had become a center of vast investment and profit. The colony raised palm oil and palm nuts, cotton, coffee, rubber, cocoa and ivory. It became one of the greatest copper-producing countries in the world. Also gold, tin, cobalt and silver were exported. It became the largest producer of industrial diamonds, and nearly 60 per cent of the world supply of uranium ore was produced and now goes chiefly to the United States.

There has arisen bitter strife in the copper mines, with the natives organizing a union and seeking higher wages. There is one Negro newspaper representing the intelligentsia but influenced or actually subsidized by the Belgian masters. Perhaps more than in any other African colony the Belgians are making desperate efforts to see that no organized opposition to their ownership of the Congo develops among educated Negroes. Colored West Indian clerks have long been hired, and propaganda against Negro organization is carefully spread. Indeed, as the Council on African Affairs says:

The Belgian delegate will support his contention by citing the fact that in 1953 the Belgian Chamber of Representatives approved a revision of Article I, Paragraph 4 of the Belgian Constitution to make it clear that Belgium and the Congo together form a single sovereign state.

Belgian officials have for some time been exasperated by what they regard as the over-zealous concern of the UN for the welfare of the Congolese. The British and French have, of course, also squirmed when their colonial policies were under review, but the Belgian representatives, M. Pierre Ryckmans, has been particularly perverse in rejecting any and all UN efforts toward the political and social advancement of colonial peoples, sometimes casting the lone negative vote on such issues. That is why we say—do not be surprised if Belgium employs the above-mentioned technical excuse to try to end, once and for all, UN "meddling" with the Congo.

The present Belgian Minister of Colonies puts the matter as follows:

On a political and administrative plane, it is necessary to create the psychological conditions for harmonious co-existence and peaceful collaboration between natives and whites. With the birth of a true native middle class —with interests common to those of the whites—these conditions tend to become closer and closer.

So save in the copper-mine unions, rebellion in the Congo has not yet developed. It is still possible, and if black French Africa bordering on the Congo for 1,600 miles goes socialist, as it may; and if Uganda, Kenya and Tanganyika to the east continue to surge with protest as they do now, the Belgian Congo may yet join the ideology of Black West Africa.

KENYA: THE WAR THAT CAN'T BE WON

April 3, 1955

I saw Jomo Kenyatta in 1945 at the Fifth Pan-African Congress in Manchester, England. He was a big man, yellow in

color, intelligent. Today he is in jail convicted of planning the
rebellion in Kenya against British oppression. Whether or not
he actually planned this rebellion, I do not know; but never in
modern history was a nation more justified in revolution than
the five million black people of Kenya.

Kenya is a fertile island set in a desert sea. Kenya mountain
rises from its northeastern corner, exactly on the Equator, covered with eternal snow. Of the 225,000 square miles in Kenya
over half is desert. Of the rest, 3,000 white settlers own 16,700
square miles of the most fertile land and 5,250,000 Africans
occupy, without ownership rights, 52,000 square miles of the
poorest.

This land originally belonged to cattle-herding tribes without
permanent settlements. English missionaries, inspired by Livingstone's appeal, first entered followed by explorers seeking
the source of the Nile. Then came the colonial imperialists,
England seeking to outrun the Germans. Finally England seized
the territory, confiscated all the land and sold it to whites at two
cents an acre in baronies of 10 to 100 thousand acres.

Of the good land held by whites, only six per cent is under
cultivation. On the native reserves the density of inhabitants per
square mile is 674, and half this land is unsuitable for cultivation. Driven from their land, the Africans began to enter the
towns, where many thousands of them lived without shelter in
conditions of near-starvation. Laborers and servants are paid an
average of $5.18 a month, clerks and artisans from $11 to $42.

In the legislature the 29,000 whites have 14 elected representatives; the 90,000 Asiatics have six, and the 24,000 Arabs
one elected and one appointed; the 5,251,120 Negroes have no
elected representatives but the Governor nominates six to speak
for them. The natives pay three different kinds of direct taxes,
and indirect taxes are placed on their necessities instead of on
luxuries. They have been in the past subjected continually to
forced labor, legal and illegal; the successors of the missionaries,
including Anglican bishops, once insisted that the settlers
should have the right to force the natives to work.

In the last 25 years the policy of England has vacillated.
Commission after commission has made proposals, but the basic
situation has not been changed. Of the Negro children 7 to 11
years old, a third are in school, and Kenya spends about $6 a
year on their education. The black folk of Kenya made every

effort to obtain relief. They built and ran thousands of schools of their own. They made close contact with the British Labour Party but got nothing from them. They organized the Kenya African Union and held a conference attended by delegates from all Kenya. They declared in 1947:

> That the political objective of the Africans of Kenya must be self-government by Africans for Africans, the rights of all racial minorities being safeguarded.
>
> That more land must be made available both in the Crown Lands and in the highlands for settlement by Africans.
>
> That free compulsory education for Africans, as is given to the children of other races, is overdue.
>
> That the deplorable wages, housing and other conditions of African laborers must be substantially improved and that the principle of equal pay for equal work be recognized.

The Union grew to 10,000 members. Patriotic songs were written and seven weekly newspapers established. Two representatives were sent to England to plead with the British people, but no substantial relief came. As a resident white said: "We are going to stay here for the good of Africa, and as long as we stay we rule!"

At last in 1952 open rebellion flared in Kenya with secret organization, murder and arson. As to just how far this went, how many were killed and how the economy was disrupted, there has been no official report; but clearly the whites were frightened. A state of "emergency" was declared on October 20, 1952. By June 1954, $22,500,000 had been spent to suppress the rebellion and the fight is now costing $2,800,000 a month.

The Royal Air Force has dropped 220 tons of bombs in nine months. British troops and police have killed 130 Africans for every European killed in the Kenya war, without counting the number of Africans killed by RAF bombs. The Kenya African Union has been suppressed and its leaders jailed. Jomo Kenyatta said when sentenced to seven years in jail: "What we shall continue to object to is discrimination in the government of this country, and we shall not accept that, in jail or out of it ... What we have done and shall continue to do is to demand rights for the African people as human beings."

As D. N. Pritt, the great British lawyer, says: "A cruel and brutal war has been raging for nearly two and a half years to hold the Africans in subjection and maintain the settlers as masters of the best land in the country. This war cannot be won by the British in a military sense. If it could be, it would still leave unresolved, and indeed untouched, every agrarian, economic and national grievance, and would thus inevitably lead to a new war in the near future."

THE NEGRO IN AMERICA TODAY

January 16, 1956

There is curious and puzzling contradiction in current reports on the status of the Negro in the United States. It is said on the one hand that his progress is marvellous and his present status so encouraging that time and patience will soon see the Negro recognized in law and custom as an American, with all the rights enjoyed by other Americans.

In support of this view are cited the increasing number of Negro voters and officeholders; the recent decisions of the Supreme Court against segregation; and a general disposition in the nation to recognize the Negro as a citizen.

Contradicting this view is the fact that Negro suffrage is progressing but slowly and the Negro vote is still practically suppressed in many states; that in the South the Negro fills almost no public offices; and that murder, lawlessness, economic oppression and injustice in the courts are still the lot of millions of Negroes; that segregation in schools still remains in most of the South, and complete nullification of the Supreme Court decision is bitterly advocated.

The solution of this contradiction lies in the fact that it is true that the emergence of American Negroes from slavery in 1863 to partial freedom 90 years later is remarkable and hopeful. But it is equally true that American Negroes are not free compared with the working classes of the Western world or of the Soviet Union and China; that white color caste in some groups and places, especially in the North and West, has largely disappeared, yet in general it still prevails widely in the South; and it is true that as a group the Negro is poor, ignorant and sick, despite his struggles. He has difficulty in getting work and his wage is invariably substandard. In considerable portions of the United States, it is no exaggeration to say that a Negro still gets less consideration than a dog.

Just what the total situation is, reduced to actual facts and figures nobody knows exactly and everybody guesses broadly. The United States as a nation has doggedly refused to conduct or encourage a scientific and complete study of the Negro population, because it feared to face the facts, whether favorable or discouraging. The national census deliberately hides the total picture. Twice Atlanta University has proposed and begun such a study: in 1896 to 1914, and again in 1941 to 44. In neither case could adequate support and cooperation be secured.

Many individual and group studies have been made, culminating in the Gunnar Myrdal report in 1944; nevertheless, today, no one can say with accuracy how far and how fast the Negro is escaping color caste. This is to the shame of American social science. Faced with an unusual opportunity for a laboratory test of human development; with a great group, so segregated by color and social conditions as to be easily made the object of observation and measurement, the opportunity has been deliberately and continuously neglected.

Negroes themselves do not know their condition. They live in widely differing localities and social environments. Wherever they live and under whatever circumstances, they make desperate effort, by protective isolation and careful compliance with public opinion, to achieve security and comfort.

A Negro in Atlanta sends his children to separate schools, attends a separate church, lives largely in sections of the city separate from whites. He pursues limited and largely separated occupations, and is paid lower wages for the same kind of work than whites get. He buys at stores, but is careful to frequent those stores where he knows his patronage is wanted, and where he will be fairly treated. Even in these he will not attempt to eat lunch or try on shoes or hats. He does not frequent parks or theaters except in very special circumstances. In fact, he lives in a world largely Negro; but there he is unmolested and may have a comfortable and successful life. If asked, he declares that he meets little or no race friction, which is true.

The city group of Negroes is recruited increasingly by influx from the rural districts. This migration is so large and continous that while 77% of the Negro population was rural in 1900, in 1950 only 38% were in the country districts. This brings new city problems of crime and delinquency. In the rural communities and the small towns in the lower South, six million Negroes are still near slavery in many districts. They are running away to cities at the rate of tens of thousands a year. Discrimination in housing, North and South, by law and covenant, has been widespread and still prevails despite court decisions.

In the North, Negroes are mainly in the large cities. There the limitations are fewer, but they exist. In New York their chances to earn a living have increased since World War II but still are limited; there are certain jobs for which they do not apply; in the jobs they hold they can seldom expect high pay or promotion. The mass of ordinary workers keep largely to themselves; they do not in any large numbers go to downtown theaters, restaurants or places of amusement; they seldom go to a white church; they join few public organizations. They live largely in a colored world.

The well-to-do Negroes move more freely, but not widely; they can enter the more expensive hotels; they can be served at most restaurants but they are not always welcome and realize it; they are invariably refused at summer resorts, at recreation centers and usually at automobile camps; and are not too welcome at many public assemblies. Not a single Negro in New York City has ever become a member of a recognized social club, despite the fact that Negroes have often gained high political position and many have wealth and culture.

They have recently gained high political office—a federal judge; three colonial governors; Congressmen and ministers to foreign lands; state senators; City Councilmen, city judges, Borough President in New York City, etc. Still, in most cases, they are careful not to appear at social functions where their presence might be unwelcome. There have been several instructors in the large universities and a few professors, but not many.

Negroes have advanced in art, especially music; less in literature; considerably in science and the professions, although in the latter case they are largely confined to practice among Negroes.

HOW UNITED ARE NEGROES?

January 23, 1956

The outstanding fact about the Negro group in America, which has but lately gained notice, is that it is flying apart into opposition economic classes. This was to be expected. But most people, including myself, long assumed that the American Negro, forced into social unity by color caste, would achieve economic unity as a result, and rise as a mass of laborers led by intelligent planning to a higher unity with the laboring classes of the world.

This has not happened. On the contrary, and quite logically, the American Negro is today developing a distinct bourgeoisie bound to and aping American acquisitive society and developing an employing and a laboring class. This division is only in embryo, but it can be sensed.

In New York the Negro families receiving an income of $5,000 and more a year form about 10 per cent of the Negro population. That means that they have an income of at least $30,000,000 a year which puts some of them into the capitalist class. On the other hand, there are at least 50,000 Negro families in the city whose income is less than $1,000 a year, which is near pauperism. They are open to exploitation and crime.

THE NEGRO BUSINESSMAN

In the 18th century, the Negro slaves and freedmen were guided within by Negro religious preachers in church units. Then, in the 19th century, they developed leaders in the Abolition movement. After emancipation they had the intelligent leadership of preachers, teachers and artists who, together with philanthropic black men of affairs, guided and advised the group.

But from 1910 until after the First World War, Negro businessmen forged to the front and today they form the most powerful class among Negroes and dominate their thought and action. This class bases its ideals on American business methods and aims. They spend conspicuously, organize for widespread social enjoyment and extravagance and regard the private profit motive as the end of thought and life.

The 300 or more Negro newspapers, with few exceptions, are mouthpieces of this bourgeoisie and bow to the dictates of big business which monopolizes newsprint, world news and credit facilities. Franklin Frazier, a leading American sociologist, once president of the American Sociological Society, has recently emphasized the significance of this development in his *Bourgeoisie Noire*, published in French in the Librairie Plon, in Paris.

THE NEGRO WORKER

Negro public opinion is thus tied to current American thought either by reasons of security or sometimes by direct money bribery, especially during political campaigns. The dream among the intelligentsia of an independent Negro vote devoted to Negro progress, has therefore largely disappeared except under stress of some particular outrage like the Till murder.

Class differentiation in Negro organizations is developing more slowly than in general life. In the church organizations there is a distinction between the churches of the very poor and ignorant and those of the well-to-do. But in the latter the main support comes from the workers; and in control the physician often shares office and power with the janitor and porter.

In the mass organization like the NAACP, the bulk of support from the beginning has come from the working class. Recently the well-to-do and rich have notably increased their contributions. It is still the dollars of the poor which support the organization and keep it a popular movement, except in some localities. The Negro control of the organization also is still the domain of the Negro intelligentsia rather than the businessman.

Opposite the small Negro bourgeoisie is the great mass of black labor. It is at present only vaguely aware of its conflict of interest with the Negro businessman. This businessman employs a considerable number of Negroes and exploits them quite as much and often more than whites because of the limited jobs open to Negroes. As, however, the Negro laborer joins the white unions, he is drawn into the great labor movement and begins to recognize black business exploitation. But the main mass of American labor is at present in conservative unions under reactionaries like Meany. So far as these unions admit Negroes, the Negroes follow the reactionary philosophy of the white.

Here the black, like the white, is restrained by charges of subversion and fear of loss of jobs.

THEY ARE A MIXTURE

It must, of course, be realized by Americans as well as by foreigners that the 15,000,000 American Negroes are not a mass of persons belonging to one race. They are a mixture of African and European peoples and American Indians. They are of all colors of skin from white to black and every degree of economic situation and culture. Much of the Negro problem stems from these facts. Their unity heretofore has been spiritual as much as physical and today they can scarcely be distinguished from Sicilians, Egyptians or Berbers; not even entirely from Asians.

Of the total result of the forces thus tabulated, no one can be sure today, but the situation needs careful watching. The liberal and radical American forces cannot count on Negro following so long as Negroes get jobs and make money and continue to be satisfied with their present status as half or three-quarters free. But conservative and industrial Americans also cannot count on Negro following if caste allows disfranchisement and results in unpunished murder.

Meantime the Negro intelligentsia must reassert its influence on the mass of Negro labor and wheel it into step with the world labor movement, especially in Asia and Africa; of which today Black America dare not talk.

THE THEORY OF A THIRD PARTY

March 26, 1956

We are about to enter a political campaign with no chance to express our opinions freely on the most important problems that face us and the civilized world. It was precisely to meet such situations that political parties were first suggested. A state without permitted differences of thought is a state with no freedom of action. To obtain concert of action men unite into parties. Unless there is freedom for such union, there can be no real freedom of action.

There is, however, nothing sacred about the number of political parties in a state. Logically there can be as many parties as there are differences of opinion. We Americans have come to think that a two-party system is a part of holy writ. Nothing of the sort. One party, two parties, three parties or seven parties may work. If a nation is in substantial agreement, one political party is enough; if not, ten parties may arise. The crucial question is how far the distribution of parties is effective in allowing public opinion to express itself and to direct the state.

ONE PARTY—TWO NAMES

When the United States was formed, political opinion fell naturally into two parties: conservatism of the old aristocratic methods of English history, and advance toward the new, broader democracy set on change. Then the situation altered. The age of Jackson pushed America toward wider democracy, but we found within democracy itself many differences of opinion: should persons vote, or property? Could labor be property? Should land be free to its tillers? Should labor unions be recognized?

Public opinion varied in every way, and the two dominant parties dodged and ignored these questions. So long as public opinion was satisfied with one party under two names, the question of slavery, land and labor could be ignored in politics. But when the South demanded the right to use slave labor anywhere in the nation, and Abolitionists demanded abolition of slavery everywhere, then a third party arose, demanding at least no spread of present slave territory. On this platform offered by a third party, a majority of voters united—and the Whig-Democracy was beaten.

FOR WHOM DO YOU VOTE?

Today, most Americans want peace, lower taxes; less preparation for war and more for social progress. Shall we vote for Republicans when no Republican candidate opposes war? Shall we vote for Democrats when no Democrat stands for peace? If for neither Democrat nor Republican, then for whom?

Increasing difficulties have been put in the path of persons who wish to vote for any but the two dominant parties. Can we support the Republican or Democratic ticket when neither will support education, water control for the public benefit, or adequate security for sickness and old age? And when both these parties are trying to kill public enterprises like the TVA and give over public resources like oil, gas and water sites to private profiteers and public grafters?

If no conscientious, intelligent American can vote for either of the present parties, then for whom can he vote? Increasing difficulties face anyone who tries to form a third party. Examine the laws of states, made by collusion between Republicans and Democrats, which keep a third party off the ballot in any election; which threaten any advocate of a third party with disgrace, jail, or loss of occupation.

WHY SO MUCH MONEY?

In most places no one but a Republican-Democrat can hire a convenient hall or hotel for stating his views; radio and television are open only to the dominant parties on equal time, and the theoretical custom of giving equal time to a third party is going to be absolutely forbidden as quietly as possible, by the Senate committee which is pretending to investigate bribery of Senators.

Moreover, why is so much money needed to support a candidate or carry on the election of a President? Why must a Presidential candidate have ten millions of dollars for the 1956 election? Why, if not for buying the support of lawmakers, courts and voters?

Finally, in one vast and fatal field, foreign affairs, we are today confronted by a demand which has become a pre-emptory order that we give up all vestige of difference of opinion and vote blindfolded as an inner government clique, in the employ of Big Business, orders us to vote. In our decision on war we must be "bi-partisan," which means we must follow the muddled greed of Dulles and Hoover or be blasted as "subversive."

Whither, in God's name, democracy in the United States?

THE CHANCE IN 1948

In 1948, we had a chance to put the Progressive Party in power. Had we done so, we would have had no Korean War, nor would we find ourselves as we are today, hated and feared by the vast majority of the human race. We used laws and lies to drive voters from daring to vote for Wallace; we even induced Wallace to fear the Soviet Union so abjectly that he lost faith in his own principles and we put into power the man who gave the signals for the killing of more innocent human beings than any other man in modern history.

It thus today becomes unpatriotic for honest Americans to vote for anybody but a warmonger. The voter is at the mercy of the organized political bosses of two parties, with huge funds and special privileges granted by Big Business. The election becomes a farce.

The nation should demand the right to put a third party on the ballot, under reasonable and equitable conditions. All enrolled parties should have equal access to organs of propaganda. Expenses really necessary for any party to take part in elections should be paid by government, and not by private contributions of those who use the government for private profit—and thus can give billions to control education, instead of making it a government duty. The exact sums spent on elections should be known to the public.

Go Down The List

There is another possibility which personally I am considering: that is, not to vote at all.

Eisenhower is not a person for whom I can possibly vote: he turned his back on the Rosenbergs and sent them to a shameful death; he has done nothing about murder in Mississippi or Alabama. He can catch bank robbers in New York in 24 hours. He has done nothing to implement the Supreme Court decision on education. He took an excellent stand at Geneva, but reversed it forthwith as soon as his boys got hold of him. He will not stop preparation for war nor reduce war taxes. I cannot vote for him.

I regard Nixon and Knowland as untrustworthy politicians of the lowest order.

I am glad that Stevenson can talk English. But what does he say? He is not opposed to war with the Soviet Union; he cannot open his mouth without slurring "communism"; he is fundamentally an anti-Negro Southerner like his grandfather.

I do not know what Kefauver favors, and I doubt if he does.

Harriman is a colonial imperialist who hates the Soviet Union as only a Big Business man can, and is ready to buy his way to the White House.

Dewey is utterly unscrupulous and responsible for the unspeakable burden of Dulles and Brownell. And so on.

REFUSAL TO CONDONE

There is no chance for any third party candidate on any platform to get his beliefs before the people. No first-class newspaper will give even a fair report of the opinions of anyone who does not hate "communists," attack socialism, ridicule liberals and praise our "foreign policy."

What then can I do? What can you do? I can stay home and let rich tyrants rule, who now hold the power. The result of the election I cannot change, but I can at least refuse to condone it. I can stay home and let fools traipse to the polls. I call this sit-down strike the only recourse of honest men today so far as the Presidency is concerned.

THE SAGA OF NKRUMAH

July 30, 1956

Kwame Nkrumah was a black boy of Accra, a peasant and not of chieftain rank. He went to the mission school and then to work. He saw the looting of the United Africa Company when, during the depression, this vast monopoly was starving people of the Gold Coast to death. Britain summoned her warships from Gibraltar and alerted her black troops of the West Coast and for the first time these troops refused to budge. England paused. Here was trouble in sight.

Young Nkrumah went to America and to England. He went to Moscow. He was in Paris when the trade unions met after World War II. He helped call the Fifth Pan-African Congress in England in 1945. There I first saw him and Kenyatta of Kenya and Johnson of Sierra Leone. Nkrumah was shabby, kindly, but earnest, and he and others called for justice in the cocoa market and freedom for the Gold Coast. I did not then dream that Nkrumah had the stamina and patience for this task.

That cocoa story was a fairy tale. Spaniards raised cocoa in Fernando Po with slaves; Britain and Holland processed it into chocolate and sold it in New York. Then the Quaker Cadburys of England had a scheme. They induced the world to boycott Spanish slavery so as to bring the cocoa crop to British West African plantations. But Tettie Quarsie balked them. He was a little black cocoa laborer on the island of Principe. He smuggled cocoa plants to the Gold Coast. Soon more cocoa was growing on the Gold Coast than in all the rest of the world and it was growing on little one-acre Negro farms and not on British-owned plantations.

The buyers from London, Amsterdam and New York thus could not control production, but they combined to control buying and bid so low that the growers struck. The cocoa market was thrown into confusion and, with war looming, England was forced to take over all cocoa buying. They offered the farmers the same low price but promised to refund any profit. They made $5,000,000 profit and then reneged on their promise. The Gold Coast seethed and the Fifth Pan-African Congress complained. Nkrumah returned to the Gold Coast determined on independence. He laid out a plan for home rule on socialist lines and the government threw him in jail as a "communist." But the uproar was so great that they had to release him. Quietly and effectively he went into organization.

He worked not from the Chiefs down; not from the black British-educated intelligentia over, but from the working masses up. He lived, ate and slept with them. He traveled among them all over the land; he talked and pled in proud Ashanti, in Togoland, in the dark, crowded cities of the Coast. In the ensuing election his Convention People's Party won a clear majority.

Nkrumah then told Britain in effect that either it would grant independence to the Gold Coast or the Coast would take it. South Africa threatened, but Britain was reasonable. If Nkrumah could secure a steady democratic majority; if Nkrumah could secure the home talent to rule; if Nkrumah could insure the economic stability of the Gold Coast—in such unlikely case the Gold Coast would be recognized as an independent dominion of the British Commonwealth.

Nkrumah took over the sale of cocoa as a government

monopoly. He planned an electric power dam on the Volta River with British and foreign capital, but so fenced it in by government supervision that its "free enterprise" was under strict social control. Slowly but surely Nkrumah spread education, and secured educated black civil servants to man the ship of state. In the 1954 election he increased his popular majority. The British began to yield. Some of their best officials on the Gold Coast cooperated whole-heartedly with Nkrumah.

But the Colonial Office in England played its last hand. It sowed seeds of internal dissent; it encouraged tribalism and provincialism; especially among the Ashanti whom the British had conquered in the 19th century after six wars. Now Ashanti chiefs were encouraged to resent the domination of a peasant from the coast. They demanded autonomy for Ashanti and the "Federation" of the many provinces of the Gold Coast, with its total population of only five million.

Nkrumah called for a conference and a British Commission appeared. The Ashanti refused to take part. One of the black Oxford-educated leaders, married to the daughter of Sir Stafford Cripps, leaped to the aid of the dissidents. But cool Nkrumah gave rein to the commission, compromised and kept power in the hands of the central government while recognizing the right of provincial debate and suggestion.

Togoland voted to stand by Nkrumah. Then Nkrumah offered to appeal to the people in a final election. After that he demanded independence with or without British consent. Moreover, he insisted that the new nation be called "Ghana" after that black nation which flourished in Africa one thousand years ago before white slave drivers named the shores of Guinea, "Gold" and "Slave" and "Grain."

Last week Nkrumah increased his majority in a nation-wide election: he secured 71 Legislative Assembly delegates out of a total of 104. I cabled him my congratulations.

Following is the address by Dr. W.E.B. DuBois at the National Guardian's *eighth birthday dinner in New York on November 15.*

NATIONAL GUARDIANSHIP

December 3, 1956

These are days of disappointment and even frustration for those who have seen a world marching forward toward the welfare state and then hesitating and partially retreating before counter-revolution.

In human history there is nothing unusual in this situation. Progress is seldom continuous. Time and again in the history of mankind it has faltered, and we have only to remember that the progress of men, which is not to be doubted in the long run, is never a straight march but is always a lurching forward and a falling back, and we only keep up hope as we see that progress has continued and will continue.

Nevertheless in these days of uncertainty, we have to live and here in the United States, where for many it is difficult to earn a living without selling one's soul to falsehood and greed; where it is not always safe to speak or write frankly unless one agrees with current public opinion, this is the time of all times when the wise man falls back on clear thinking which is still possible, and real knowledge, which is still obtainable, in order at least in his own soul to know the truth and to build a future on it.

Let me venture to recall some pertinent things which have happened in the fifty-sixth year of the last five centuries. In the year 1456 the Turks had just captured Constantinople and Mohammedanism and Christianity stared each other full in the face. Gutenberg had published the Bible from movable type. Prince Henry the Navigator had opened an unknown world, while a little ragged boy of five, Christopher Columbus, was racing through the streets of Genoa and watching the great ships sail away. In China the Ming dynasty reigned and scholars were publishing dictionaries. The people, the great masses of all people, were dumb, driven cattle. But among the leading few of Europe a curiosity to know the past arose; a yearning stirred in their hearts for the "fair face of beauty all too fair to see." Michelangelo painted and carved in the Vatican. Cathedrals blossomed in stone. This was the age of Renaissance. But what were the people doing and thinking—the ordinary people who work and slave to feed and clothe the world? We know little of them. They toiled under rod and whip; they died like flies when the Black Death swept from Constantinople to London, where alone 68,000 died. They walked in dirt, rags and lice.

Four hundred years ago in 1556, three men were destined to remake our conception of the world as center of the universe: Copernicus who was dying; Galileo who was being born; and Francis Bacon, father of modern science, who was five years old. Suleiman the Magnificent had his foot on the heart of Europe, and the great Emperor Akbar ruled in India.

In Europe, the masses of awakening men tried to believe in good. They fought and killed to believe. Luther died in 1546; in the mad throes of Reformation which followed, millions were crippled, burned, and killed. On one wild night of 1572, 50,000 Christians murdered each other and reddened the streets of France.

The punishment of crime was based on revenge, exquisite pain, and protection of property. Criminals were to be killed, not cured. In the throes of religion from the beginning of the fifteenth century with Joan of Arc to the end of the eighteenth, 300,000 witches were tortured, hanged, and burned alive. The Mongols swept over the toiling masses of India.

Three hundred years ago, in 1656, Shakespeare had sung his song and played his part and was forty years dead at fifty years of age. The Thirty Years War, perhaps the most horrible of modern times, was eight years ended, but its misery and filth still lived. John Bunyan was in jail writing "Pilgrim's Progress," Milton was recording the loss of Paradise, and Moliere was amusing the court of Louis XIV. In India the Taj Mahal was standing in sheer beauty. The Chinese had issued an encyclopedia in 24,000 volumes.

The year 1756 was in the center of the age of science. Johnson's dictionary was published, but symbolically cutting across it, this year saw the Black Hole of Calcutta as Asiatic protest against European intrusion and Lisbon had an earthquake which killed tens of thousands. In Africa the black Mandingo empires were spreading Mohammedanism west and south, and the heathen Bantu peoples began marching south where a century later they met the Boers. In between the slowly retreating millions and the state-building intruders, western Christianity thrust with trade in gold, pepper, and slaves. On the slavery of Negroe., Britain founded her wealth, commerce, and empire. Capitalistic production was built on her slave trade. As Karl

Marx wrote in a celebrated passage: "If money comes into the world with a congenital bloodstain on one cheek, capital comes dripping from head to foot, from every pore, with blood and dirt." England seized India at Plassey, George III resigned, and later lost America; Robert Owen and William Godwin argued the matter of income for the poor; William Pitt and Benjamin Franklin guided politics and science, and exactly two hundred years ago this year, the Seven Years War began colonial imperialism of the white European world over the darker nations of the earth, an adventure which still fights at Suez this very day.

Exploitation of labor: that is the inborn idea that most men are born to work for the support, ease, and luxury of the few for various reasons like superior merit, color of skin, or progress of culture. This idea, beginning in slavery and developing through serfdom to wage labor and military might, still exists today in the minds of most folk to poison every effort to raise the mass of men to real and effective equality.

A hundred years ago in 1856, Darwin was working on his Origin of Species and the Negroid Dumas was writing his novels. The Bessemer process of making steel was transforming industry into dictatorship, and the Communist Manifesto, then eight years old, was beginning to ferment in the minds of discontented men. The labor movement, with strikes and unions, began to spread in Europe. The Cotton Kingdom arose in America. The Russian serfs were emancipated in 1861, but in the United States the Supreme Court heard the arguments in the Dred Scott case, and its decision in 1857 tried to fasten slavery on American Negroes forever: while John Brown raided the slave-owners in Kansas. The Crimean War was fought to conquer the Balkans, including Hungary, and the war of England against China aimed at complete European domination of the entire East. The West fought bitterly against popular education, for the continued subjection of women, and against votes for the mass of laborers. The Reform Bill and our Civil War heralded change!

With this background there was left a weird task for the twentieth century. We can scarcely be surprised if we have not in 1956 even begun to clean up the mess—neither surprised nor discouraged. We see a head-on collision between social progress and incorporated wealth, striving to save scientific knowledge from the monopoly of private wealth and build a state which would exist for the benefit of those who have made and need it and not for those who by chance or legal chicanery claim to own it. On the whole the progress toward such states has succeeded to a marked degree in most nations. In Russia, Eastern Europe, and China, its success is the wonder of our age which nothing can disparage, even if we know that the path has not been straight nor the goal yet wholly attained.

In the United States we have far from failed. We have moved decisively toward the welfare state by mass education and a standard of living above most of the world; roads, state housing, and federal flood control; recognition of labor unions; scientific research and marvellous technique helped by the government; and a growing recognition of the right even of black folk to live as equals of whites. All this has lulled the nation to acquiescence in our great losses: the failure of democratic control of our government; the increasing rule of private wealth and the use of that wealth for war on socialism, for control of colonial labor and materials. To support this dictatorship of the rich we have tried to stop our bold and wise men from thinking and expressing their thought, and from pointing out our mistakes and danger. The counter-revolution of private wealth against social welfare has put many of our leaders in jail; has scared most of our scientists into silence, has choked literature, hamstrung newsgathering, and made our colleges beggars for the dole of corporations and our teachers of youth the mouthpieces of private industry, set on marking millions of the peoples of the earth the serfs of the white West. For this end even our organized white labor has been bribed and misled, and our civilization has become spending income for show, indulgence, and world war, rather than for further conquest of poverty, disease, and ignorance.

This is the battle we must yet win, because looking on the past we know that American Big Business is fighting the very stars in their courses, that the welfare state is bound to win. Toward this victory the *National Guardian*, with your help, leads.

We sing with Whitman:

> *That is nothing that is quell'd by one or two failures,*
> *or by any number of failures,*
> *Or by the indifference or ingratitude of the people or*
> *by any unfaithfulness,*

> *Or the show of the tushes of power, soldiers, cannon,*
>   *penal statutes.*
> *What we believe in waits latent forever through all the*
>   *continents,*
> *Invites no one, promises nothing, sits in calmness and*
>   *light, is positive and composed, knows no*
>   *discouragement,*
> *Waiting patiently, waiting its time.*

NEGRO HISTORY CENTENARIES

January 14, 1957

I am venturing to write several leading men and organizations within the Negro race to remind them that the year 1957 will usher in a series of centenaries which deeply affect the history of the Negro race and of this country. May I point out a few:

> 1957:–One hundredth anniversary of the Dred Scott decision.
> 1959: One hundredth anniversary of the death of John Brown.
> 1963: One hundredth anniversary of the Emancipation Proclamation.
> 1961 to 1965: One hundredth anniversary of the participation of American Negroes in the Civil War.
> 1968: One hundredth anniversary of the death of Thaddeus Stevens, of the enfranchisement of the Freedmen, and of the Freedmen's Bureau.
> 1972: One hundredth anniversary of the birth of Paul Laurence Dunbar.
> 1976: One hundredth anniversary of the Bargain of 1876.

There are many other significant anniversaries which recall Negro history and the cultural tie of the black man with American history. If we neglect to mark this history, it may be distorted or forgotten. Already repeated efforts are being made to prove that slavery was not the cause of the Civil War; to minimize the part of Negroes in the slavery controversy and the war;

to slander friends of the Negro, and to represent his enfranchisement as a serious mistake.

It would be wrong to make these celebrations occasions for controversies or exacerbation of race hate. Rather they should be occasions for calm and scientific inquiry into the past, participated in by persons of authority, white and black, Northern and Southern. We must only be sure that every point of view has adequate and worthy representation.

I suggest that these celebrations be varied in character and place and in sponsorship; we have only to be sure that no important event or person is forgotten in these centenaries of the first participation of the Negro masses as free citizens in the civilization of the United States. Colleges might celebrate jointly or singly the birthdays of distinguished men; newspapers might issue special editions to recall great events; organizations might hold special meetings or alert their branches and fraternities might offer prizes for essays or even books on certain subjects.

WILL THE GREAT GANDHI LIVE AGAIN?

February 11, 1957

The greatest philosopher of our era pointed out the inherent contradictions in many of our universal beliefs; and he sought eventual reconciliation of these paradoxes. We realize this today. Our newly inaugurated President asks the largest expenditure for war in human history made by a nation, and proclaims this as a step toward peace! We have larger endowments devoted to peace activity than any other nation on earth, and less activity for abolishing war.

As I look back on my own attitude toward war during the last 70 years, I see repeated contradiction. In my youth, nourished as I was on fairy tales, including some called History, I quite naturally regarded war as a necessary step toward progress. I believed that if my people ever gained freedom and equality, it would be by killing white people.

Then, as a young man in the great afflatus of the late nineteenth century, I came to believe in peace. No more war. I

signed the current pledge never to take part in war. Yet during
the First World War, "the war to stop war," I was swept into
the national maelstrom.

After the depression I sensed recurring contradictions. I saw
Gandhi's non-violence gain freedom for India, only to be followed by violence in all the world; I realized that the hundred
years of peace from Waterloo to 1914 was not peace at all, but
war of Europe on Africa and Asia, with troubled peace only
between the colonial conquerors. I saw Britain, France, and
America trying to continue to force the world to serve them by
using their monopoly of land, technique, and machinery,
backed by gunpowder, and then threatening atomic power.

Then Montgomery in Alabama tried to show the world the
synthesis of this antithesis. And not the white Montgomery of
the Slave Power; not even the black Montgomery of the Negro
professional men, merchants, and teachers; but the black workers: the scrubbers and cleaners; the porters and seamstresses.
They turned to a struggle not for great principles and noble
truths, but just asked to be let alone after a tiring day's work;
to be free of petty insult after hard and humble toil. These folk,
led by a man who had read Hegel, knew of Karl Marx, and had
followed Mohandas Karamchand Gandhi, preached: "Not by
Might, nor by Power, but by My Spirit," saith the Lord. Did this
doctrine and practice of non-violence bring solution of the race
problem in Alabama? It did not. Black workers, many if not all,
are still walking to work, and it is possible any day that their
leader will be killed by hoodlums perfectly well known to the
white police and the city administration, egged on by white
councils of war, while most white people of the city say nothing
and do nothing.

All over the lower South this situation prevails. Despite law,
in the face of drooling religion and unctuous prayer, while the
nation dances and yells and prepares to fight for peace and
freedom, there is race war, jails full of the innocent, and ten
times more money spent for mass murder than for education of
children. Where are we, then, and whither are we going? What
is the synthesis of this paradox of eternal and world-wide war
and the coming of the Prince of Peace?

It lies, I think, not in the method but in the people concerned.
Among normal human beings, with the education customary

today in most civilized nations, non-violence is the answer to the temptation to force. When threat is met by fist; when blow follows blow, violence becomes customary. But no normal human being of trained intelligence is going to fight the man who will not fight back. In such cases, peace begins and grows just because it is. But suppose they are wild beasts or wild men? To yield to the rush of the tiger is death, nothing less. The wildness of beasts is nature; but the wildness of men is neglect and, often, our personal neglect. This is the reason beneath our present paradox of peace and war.

For now near a century this nation has trained the South in lies, hate, and murder. We are emphasizing today that when Robert E. Lee swore to serve the nation and then broke his word to serve his clan, his social class, and his private property—that this made him a hero; that although he did not believe in human slavery, he fought four long years, with consummate skill, over thousands of dead bodies, to make it legal for the South to continue to hold four million black folk as chattel bondsmen— that this makes him a great American and candidate for the Hall of Fame.

We have for 80 years as a nation widely refused to regard the killing of a Negro in the South as murder, or the violation of a black girl as rape. We have let white folk steal millions of black folks' hard-earned wages, and openly defended this as natural for a "superior" race. As a result of this, we have today in the South millions of persons who are pathological cases. They cannot be reasoned with in matters of race. They are not normal and cannot be treated as normal. They are ignorant and their schools are poor because they cannot afford a double school system and would rather themselves remain ignorant than let Negroes learn.

Remedy for this abnormal situation would be education for all children and education all together, so as to let them grow up knowing each other as human. Precisely this path these abnormal regions refuse to follow. Here, then, is no possible synthesis. So long as a people insult, murders and hates by hereditary teaching, non-violence can bring no peace. It will bring migration until that fails, and then attempts at bloody revenge. It will spread war and murder. Can we then by effort make the average white person in states like South Carolina,

Georgia, Alabama, Mississippi, and Louisiana normal, intelligent human beings?

If we can, we solve our antithesis; great Gandhi lives again. If we cannot civilize the South, or will not even try, we continue in contradiction and riddle.

A FUTURE FOR PAN-AFRICA: FREEDOM, PEACE, SOCIALISM

March 11, 1957

On March 6, 1957, the Gold Coast, British colony on the West Coast of Africa, will become a Dominion of the British Commonwealth, ranking with Canada, Australia and the Union of South Africa. This former center of the slave trade to America will assume the name of Ghana, an ancient Negro kingdom of northwest Africa which, between the 5th and 15th centuries, included much of the present territory of the Gold Coast.

Ghana will occupy an area about as large as the United Kingdom, with 4,125,000 inhabitants, nearly all of whom are black Africans. Within its borders will lie the ancient kingdom of the Ashanti, which fought six wars against England and, despite insult and humiliation, never surrendered the golden stool of its sovereignty. Ghana will be independent and self-governing and the inauguration of this state will be witnessed by officials from many of the world's leading nations. including the Vice President of the United States.

I have just sent the Prime Minister, Dr. Kwame Nkrumah, the following greetings:

I have your kind invitation of January 22, 1957. In behalf of myself and of my wife, Shirley Graham, I thank you for it and want to say how great was our desire to accept it. But since the U.S. government refused to issue as passports, we must with deep regret inform you of our inability to accept. I have recently also, and for the same reason, been compelled to my sorrow to decline a trip to China for lectures and participation in the celebration of the 250th anniversary of the birth of Benjamin Franklin.

However, because of the fact that I am now entering the 90th year of my life, and because of my acquaintanceship with you during the last 12 years, which cover the years of your imprisonment, vindication and political triumph, I trust you will allow me a few words of advice for the future of Ghana and Africa.

I venture the more readily to do this because, 40 years ago at the end of the First World War, I tried to establish some means of cooperation between the peoples of African descent throughout the world. Since then five Pan-African Congresses have met and, at the last one in England in 1945, I had the pleasure of meeting you.

Today, when Ghana arises from the dead and faces this modern world, it must no longer be merely a part of the British Commonwealth or a representative of the world of West Europe, Canada and the United States. Ghana must on the contrary be the representative of Africa, and not only that, but of Black Africa below the Sahara desert. As such, her first duty should be to come into close acquaintanceship and cooperation with her fellow areas of British West Africa and Liberia; with the great areas of black folk in French West and Equatorial Africa; with the Sudan, Ethiopia, and Somaliland; with Uganda, Kenya and Tanganyika; with the Belgian Congo and all Portuguese Africa; with the Rhodesias and Bechuanaland; with Southwest Africa, the Union of South Africa and Madagascar; and with all other parts of Africa and with peoples who want to cooperate. All the former barriers of language, culture, religion and political control should bow before the essential unity of race and descent, the common suffering of slavery and the slave trade and the modern color bar.

Ignoring the old sources of division and lack of knowledge of and sympathy for each other, Ghana should lead a movement of black men for Pan-Africanism, including periodic conferences and personal contacts of black men from the Sahara to the Indian Ocean. With a program of peace and with no thought of force, political control or underground subversion, a new series of Pan-African Congresses should be held; they should include delegates from all groups and especially from the African congresses which already exist in many parts of Africa and which got their inspiration in most cases from the first Pan-African Congress in Paris in 1919.

The new series of Pan-African Congresses would seek common aims of progress for Black Africa, including types of political control, economic cooperation, cultural development, universal education and freedom from religious dogma and dictation.

The consequent Pan-Africa, working together through its independent units, should seek to develop a new African economy and cultural center standing between Europe and Asia, taking from and contributing to both. It should stress peace and join no military alliance and refuse to fight for settling European quarrels. It should avoid subjection to and ownership by foreign capitalists who seek to get rich on African labor and raw material, and should try to build a socialism founded on old African communal life; rejecting on the one hand the exaggerated private initiative of the West, and seeking to ally itself with the social program of the progressive nations; with British and Scandinavian socialism, with the progress toward the welfare state of India, Germany, France and the United States; and with the Communist states like the Soviet Union and China, in peaceful cooperation and without presuming to dictate as to how socialism must or can be attained at particular times and places.

Pan-African socialism seeks the welfare state in Black Africa. It will refuse to be exploited by people of other continents for their own benefit and not for the benefit of the peoples of Africa. It will no longer consent to permitting the African majority of any African country to be governed against its will by a minority of invaders who claim racial superiority or the right to get rich at African expense. It will seek not only to raise but to process its raw material and to trade it freely with all the world on just and equal terms and prices.

Pan-Africa will seek to preserve its own past history, and write the present account, erasing from literature the lies and distortions about black folk which have disgraced the last centuries of European and American literature; above all, the new Pan-Africa will seek the education of all its youth on the broadest possible basis without religious dogma and in all hospitable lands as well as in Africa and for the end of making Africans not simply profitable workers for industry nor stoolpigeons for propaganda, but for making them modern, intelligent, responsible men of vision and character.

I pray you, my dear Mr. Nkrumah, to use all your power to

put a Pan-Africa along these lines into working order at the earliest possible date. Seek to save the great cultural past of the Ashanti and Fanti peoples, not by inner division but by outer cultural and economic expansion toward the outmost bounds of the great African peoples, so that they may be free to live, grow and expand; and to teach mankind what non-violence and courtesy, literature and art, music and dancing, can do for this greedy, selfish and war-stricken world.

I hereby put into your hands, Mr. Prime Minister, my empty but still significant title of "President of the Pan-African Congress," to be bestowed on my duly-elected successor who will preside over a Pan-African Congress due, I trust, to meet soon and for the first time on African soil, at the call of the independent state of Ghana.

NEGROES AND SOCIALISM

April 29, 1957

The one hope of American Negroes is Socialism. Otherwise, under the corporate rule of monopolized wealth, they will be confined to the lowest wage group. This most Negroes do not realize. I myself long stressed Negro private business enterprise, but I soon saw a "group economy" was necessary for protection.

Then I fell back on Consumers' Co-operation as defense and at one time helped to start 50 experiments scattered throughout the nation with especial success in Memphis. These failed, as Consumers' Co-operation throughout the nation has failed or is failing because, without the support of the state, it cannot succeed. Or, in other words, co-operation calls for Socialism, and Socialism today is using co-operation in production and consumption.

That is why Socialism is spreading and even moving toward its ideal, Communism—to each according to his needs; from each according to his ability.

American Negroes have been taught from the day of the Freedmen's Savings Bank that Work, Thrift, Saving, private capitalism and exploitation of the worker was the straight and only path to economic salvation. That the world has discovered

the pitfalls in this path, and has increasingly turned toward
Socialism is not taught today to Negro children or adults. On
the contrary, they are being asked to believe that Communism
is a crime; and that Socialism is its misleading shadow.

Most Negroes do not realize how Socialism has advanced in
the world and even in the United States. Nearly all civilized
nations now own their railroads and means of communications;
furnish homes and housing, parks and recreation; light and
power; schools and hospitals. Half the world goes further than
this and owns all capital, having abolished private profit. This
plan of work and income has been difficult to achieve because
of human ignorance and fallibility and because the attempt to
socialize industry has been met by opposition and disagreement
from the former most powerful nations of the world.

Nevertheless the United States itself has taken increased
supervision of its railroads, telegraphs and telephones; has increased its ownership of public power, controls large areas of
education and owns increasing blocks of capital. Were it not for
war and preparations for war which take 78 per cent of our
heavy taxation, Socialism and uplift in education, health and
decent living would rise by leaps and bounds.

Negroes have long been taught that their political interests lie
in appointments to relatively minor political positions. On the
contrary, our main interest lies in stopping this senseless fear of
Socialism and Communism and the crazy idea that we can
control human thought and effort by endless war. Vote to cut
military expense to the bone and triple our outlay for education,
health and happiness!

We suffer discrimination in the right to vote, in education, in
helps to health and in jobs and wages. But it is in voting that
we can beat back discrimination and enable ourselves to overcome all other hurts by our own efforts—and not simply by the
good will of our fellows or the fear of foreign censure. That is,
by voting for all measures which advance Socialism and against
all surrender to the rule of wealth.

We should vote against giving public power to private corporations. We should vote for more public ownership, and not less.
We should vote for raising the income of the poor. Our vote
should no longer be sold for office-holding, but for the advancement of the welfare state.

WATCHWORD FOR NEGROES: REGISTER AND VOTE!

July 8, 1957

It was no easy matter for American Negroes to bring 27,000 representatives to Washington to protest against lawlessness and discrimination. The meeting might have become an hysterical and bitter demonstration, which the police—if not the army—would have been only too ready to suppress. On the other hand the meeting might have been so calm and moderate as to be meaningless. This the paid Red-baiters tried to ensure. The result lay between these extremes. The feeling of tremendous self-repression pulsed in the air and was held in check by long-imposed religious custom. The music and the shouting were not there in a throng which could have sung like the thunder of cataracts and groaned with memories that few peoples could match. It was wise that all this emotion was held in check, but it passes understanding how, on the other hand, the President of the United States could sit silent through this meeting and "never say a mumblin' word!"

But these pilgrims expressed themselves, not only in thousands of personal and group conferences, but in some clear words of the speakers. The clearest advice to the persons present were: "Register and Vote!" If to those present and listening this advice meant nothing more than it has since 1876, it had little significance. But it must have meant more; it had to mean more. The American people as a mass have little faith in voting. It is seldom that more than half of the eligible voters go to the polls. Few voters expect or try to better conditions, secure more equitable laws or higher type of officials by elections. A letter to a congressman may help, if he ever sees it; but a ballot? Who trusts it, whether it is cast for the Republican or Democratic party, or for a "Third Party" which "endorses" either?

But the advice at the Washington Pilgrimage to register and vote touched a new note. It did not refer to the great parties. Every person who listened knew that right there in Washington, looking on and listening in, lay the whole power and the vast machinery of government. The Republicans cannot return to power without the Negro vote; the Democrats cannot assume power without it. Congress was in session and over the way sat the Supreme Court. Was the Pilgrimage appealing to these repositories of power? No. These folk were thinking of Montgomery, Alabama, where recently a boycott of house servants and lowpaid laborers was able to rid them partially of petty discrimination in their transportation to work, based on race and color.

The boycott did not keep a good many of them from losing their jobs; from lower wages; from illegal arrest and, above all, from the deliberate refusal of officials to stop mob violence or even attempted murder against black folk and their leaders. These leaders in Washington told them to register and vote in Montgomery, and in a thousand counties, cities and towns in Mississippi, Louisiana, Georgia, Florida and South Carolina, where local government has sunk to bribery, cheating, mob violence and anarchy under local dictators like "Senator" Eastland, chairman of the Senate Committee on the "Judiciary."

If the Pilgrims and their people will follow this advice, and if the U. S. government will make democratic government—which it recommends to Hungary—possible in the rural South, the government of that section of the U. S. will be revolutionized. That is why the white South and its new industry will never allow eligible Negroes this right to vote, if they can help it. That is why President Eisenhower's advice to the States to assume more power of taxation and administration will never be implemented so long as the two great parties can rule the nation from Washington in defiance of democratic procedures. If the people take back control of local government, freedom and democracy will rule the nation as they once did until the Slave Power seized control of the Federal Government.

Of course, for the localities and their voters to seize and hold government, they must be free to vote; they must know the facts as to laws, officials and elections; they must have the whole undergrowth of rank weed and noisome swamp cleaned from the local governments of the southern South. There must be public schools run by each community; there must be a free local press and lecturers from all over the land and the world to teach Mississippi what civilization is and may be.

And then must come Social Reform; and it can start right in the Negro Church where the boycott started.

THE INDEPENDOCRAT AT THE DINNER TABLE

July 7, 1958

Friend wife regards me disparagingly as she serves the soup; it is split pea from a can, but reinforced and encouraged with home genius.

"So you're entering politics again."

I nod dissent. The soup is very tasty.

"But you are advocating a third party."

"Yes."

"What chance has a third party?"

"Small, I fear."

"Then why on earth do you support it?"

"I must—one never can tell when the change will come."

"Also, one never can tell when brambles will bear berries."

"Or shrimps whistle; but one can guess when third parties must come in order to avert disaster. I somehow sense the critical time. I cannot believe that the American people are stupid enough to bow much longer to the rule of the idiots now in Washington or to confine their choice in Albany to an heir of the Robber Barons or of the Rockefeller Oil Trust whose victims at Caracas yesterday spit in our faces."

"You can't imagine this? You who saw the Communists jailed, the Rosenbergs crucified, Sobell persecuted, Saypol and Kaufman promoted, and you, yourself handcuffed for talking peace."

With the roast, which has delicious gravy, I hasten to admit that I am naturally credulous.

"To live is to try. To try is often to fail. To fail is to try again. What else? That is life. A third party is due either by vote or by violence. I prefer a vote."

The Lawyer, after a second helping, butts in. As a rule I avoid lawyers; but this one helped keep me out of jail. I like him.

"But the guys that you got about you—can you trust them?"

"Yes."

"Why?"

"Because we agree."

"Entirely?"

"Oh, no—naturally not being human; but in essentials. We

agree on seven points: No more war; cease preparation for war and atomic bomb testing; stop universal military service; justice to labor with fair taxation; abolish the racial and color line; peaceful co-existence with socialist states; recognition of a citizen's right to vote for Socialism."

"Is that all these fellows believe in."

"Oh, no—each one believes in this and much more. For instance, the Socialist reveres Trotsky, hates Stalin and declares that the Soviet Union is not really a socialist state."

"And you agree with him?"

"Oh, no. I say: 'Trotsky and Stalin are dead, and will in all probability remain so. Call the U.S.S.R. what you will, it has given the world the best educational system today in existence; it has established social medicine for 200,000,000 people; it has abolished unemployment; it has broken the grip on a nation of one of the worst systems of superstition and religious dogmatism the world has seen; it has planned industry successfully and advanced science miraculously. It should be our aim to do as well as this and to do it if we can in less time and less cost. But at whatever time and cost, do it we must'."

The Lawyer returns to the fray. "And do you lean on Liberals?" he wants to know.

"As little as possible, yet we must lean somewhere. Liberals are avowed enemies of socialism, but firm friends of progress. They mean well and usually that is about all they mean. Nevertheless, the good intentions which pave Hell are better than no pavement at all."

I manage to avoid the green salad, but the dessert is rhumbaba and delicious. Friend Wife is ominously silent, while I sip and muse aloud, as the others politely pretend to listen.

"The free democracies of the West are disintegrating, Socialism increases, Communism spreads, France falls and we seem to follow. Our Senators are old and frightened, and ordered about by a pro-slavery South, owned by Texan oil millionaires and led by Eastland and Byrd. Our Congressmen are spry and active representatives of their own private business interests, while well-paid lobbies with the best brains in the land attend to public business. Big Business is buying up our educational system and telling us what to teach. The news agencies tell us what we may hear. The Department of Justice tries to limit what we may say; and the Department of State, where we may go.

We just don't know how to use our freedom; so we gamble and take dope."

The teacher who is nice but timid puts down her spoon and sighs:

"You are impossible."

"True," I beam. "And that is because I live in an Impossible World. Despite that, I refuse to commit suicide. I face Hoover and his secret police resurrected from the Medieval Inquisition. The FBI gathers gossip, tittle-tattle guesses, and lies, in secret dossiers which scare the bravest. It can detect in hours treason against Big Business but is unable to discover the Ku Klux Klan in years. Congress lets itself be blackmailed into giving endless money to snoop and hire liars at wages far higher than we pay teachers and artists—and without Civil Service rules.

"All this is frightening and I am far from serene, but somehow I cannot believe that the United States of America, once the greatest democracy on earth, will forever remain unseeing enough to bow to this unreason."

I happen here to look across the table and see stark Fear. It lies behind the eyes of the Man who is always Silent. I suddenly realize why he is afraid, for his wife, his child, his job; for his own soul, now lost, which once dared poetry, satire and sketched cartoons; he is afraid for me. Yet he says no word and I make no reply. I continue to talk.

"The nation may awake this fall. It may not. If not, we fail and try again—What?"

I'm not sure who spoke—it might have been me—or even Friend Wife:

"You ask a definition of a Fool?"

Friend Wife smiles and herds us upstairs for coffee.

Approaching 91 years of age at the time, and in ill health, Dr. Du Bois was advised by his doctors against making the journey to Accra in Africa's hottest season. In his place, the Address was read by his wife, Mrs. Shirley Graham Du Bois.

THE FUTURE OF AFRICA

ADDRESS TO THE ALL-AFRICAN PEOPLE'S CONFERENCE, ACCRA

December 22, 1958

Fellow Africans: About 1735, my great-great grandfather was kidnapped on this coast of West Africa and taken by the Dutch to the colony of New York in America, where he was sold in slavery. About the same time a French Huguenot, Jacques Du Bois, migrated from France to America and his great-grandson, born in the West Indies and with Negro blood, married the great-great granddaughter of my black ancestor. I am the son of this couple, born in 1868, hence my French name and my African loyalty.

As a boy I knew little of Africa save legends and some music in my family. The books which we studied in the public school had almost no information about Africa, save of Egypt, which we were told was not Negroid. I heard of few great men of Negro blood, but I built up in my mind a dream of what Negroes would do in the future even though they had no past.

Then happened a series of events: In the last decade of the 19th century, I studied two years in Europe, and often heard Africa mentioned with respect. Then, as a teacher in America, I had a few African students. Later at Atlanta University a visiting professor, Franz Boas, addressed the students and told them of the history of the Black Sudan. I was utterly amazed and began to study Africa for myself. I attended the Paris Exposition in 1900, and met with West Indians in London in a Pan-African Conference. This movement died, but in 1911 I attended a Races Congress in London which tried to bring together representatives from all races of the world. I met distinguished Africans and was thrilled. However, World War I killed this movement.

We held a small meeting in 1919 in Paris. After peace was declared, in 1921, we called a much larger Pan-African Congress in London, Paris and Brussels. The 200 delegates at this congress aroused the fury of the colonial powers and all our efforts for third, fourth and fifth congresses were only partially successful because of their opposition. We tried in vain to convene a congress in Africa itself.

The great depression of the thirties then stopped our efforts for 15 years. Finally in 1945 black trade union delegates to the Paris meeting of trade unions called for another Pan-African Congress. This George Padmore organized and, at his request, I came from America to attend the meeting at Manchester, England. Here I met Kwame Nkrumah, Jomo Kenyatta, Johnson of Liberia and a dozen other young leaders.

The program of Pan-Africa as I have outlined it was not a plan of action, but of periodical conferences and free discussion. And this was a necessary preliminary to any future plan of united or separate action. However, in the resolutions adopted by the successive Congresses were many statements urging united action, particularly in the matter of race discrimination. Also, there were other men and movements urging specific work.

World financial depression interfered with all these efforts and suspended the Pan-African Congresses until the meeting in Manchester in 1945. Then, it was reborn and this meeting now in Accra is the sixth effort to bring this great movement before the world and to translate its experience into action.

My only role in this meeting is one of advice from one who has lived long, who has studied Africa and has seen the modern world.

In this great crisis of the world's history, when standing on the highest peaks of human accomplishment we look forward to Peace and backward to War, when we look up to Heaven and down to Hell, let us mince no words. We face triumph or tragedy without alternative.

Africa, ancient Africa, has been called by the world and has lifted up her hands! Africa has no choice between private capitalism and socialism. The whole world, including capitalist countries, is moving toward socialism, inevitably, inexorably. You can choose between blocs of military alliance, you can choose between groups of political union; you cannot choose between socialism and private capitalism because private capitalism is doomed!

But what is socialism? It is a disciplined economy and political organization to which the first duty of a citizen is to serve the state; and the state is not a selected aristocracy, or a group of self-seeking oligarchs who have seized wealth and power. No! The mass of workers with hand and brain are the ones whose collective destiny is the chief object of all effort.

Gradually, every state is coming to this concept of its aim. The great Communist states like the Soviet Union and China have surrendered completely to this idea. The Scandinavian states have yielded partially; Britain has yielded in some respects, France in part, and even the United States adopted the New Deal which was largely socialism; though today further American socialism is held at bay by 60 great groups of corporations who control individual capitalists and the trade union leaders.

On the other hand, the African tribe, whence all of you sprung, was communistic in its very beginnings. No tribesman was free. All were servants of the tribe of whom the chief was father and voice.

When now, with a certain suddenness, Africa is whirled by the bitter struggle of dying private capitalism into the last great battleground of its death throes, you are being tempted to adopt at least a passing private capitalism as a step to some partial socialism. This would be a grave mistake.

For 400 years Europe and North America have built their civilization and comfort on theft of colored labor and the land and materials which rightfully belong to these colonial peoples.

The dominant exploiting nations are willing to yield more to the demands of the mass of men than were their fathers. But their yielding takes the form of sharing the loot—not of stopping the looting. It takes the form of stopping socialism by force and not of surrendering the fatal mistakes of private capitalism. Either capital belongs to all or power is denied all.

Here then, my Brothers, you face your great decision: Will you for temporary advantage—for automobiles, refrigerators and Paris gowns—spend your income in paying interest on borrowed funds; or will you sacrifice your present comfort and the chance to shine before your neighbors, in order to educate your children, develop such industry as best serves the great mass of people and make your country strong in ability, self-support and self-defense? Such union of effort for strength calls for sacrifice and self-denial, while the capital offered you at high price by the colonial powers like France, Britain, Holland, Belgium and the United States, will prolong fatal colonial imperialism, from which you have suffered slavery, serfdom and colonialism.

You are not helpless. You are the buyers and to continue existence as sellers of capital, these great nations, former owners of the world, must sell or face bankruptcy. You are not compelled to buy all they offer now. You can wait. You can starve a while longer rather than sell your great heritage for a mess of Western capitalist pottage. You can not only beat down the price of capital as offered by the united and monopolized Western private capitalists, but at last today you can compare their offers with those of socialist countries like the Soviet Union and China, which with infinite sacrifice and pouring out of blood and tears, are at last able to offer weak nations needed capital on better terms than the West.

The supply which socialist nations can at present spare is small as compared with that of the bloated monopolies of the West, but it is large and rapidly growing. Its acceptance involves no bonds which a free Africa may not safely assume. It certainly does not involve slavery and colonial control which the West has demanded and still demands. Today she offers a compromise, but one of which you must beware:

She offers to let some of your smarter and less scrupulous leaders become fellow capitalists with the white exploiters if in turn they induce the nation's masses to pay the awful costs. This happened in the West Indies and in South America. This may yet happen in the Middle East and Eastern Asia. Strive against it with every fibre of your bodies and souls. A body of local private capitalists, even if they are black, can never free Africa; they will simply sell it into new slavery to old masters overseas.

As I have said, this is a call for sacrifice. Great Goethe sang, *"Entbehren sollst du, sollst entbehren"*—"Thou shalt forego, shalt do without." If Africa unites, it will be because each part, each nation, each tribe gives up a part of its heritage for the good of the whole. That is what union means; that is what Pan-Africa means: When the child is born into the tribe the price of his growing up is giving a part of his freedom to the tribe. This he soon learns or dies. When the tribe becomes a union of tribes, the individual tribe surrenders some part of its freedom to the paramount tribe.

When the nation arises, the constituent tribes, clans and

groups must each yield power and some freedom to the demands of the nation or the nation dies before it is born. Your local tribal, much-loved languages must yield to the few world tongues which serve the largest number of people and promote understanding and world literature.

This is the great dilemma which faces Africans today, faces one and all: Give up individual rights for the needs of Mother Africa; give up tribal independence for the needs of the nation.

Forget nothing, but set everything in its rightful place; the glory of the six Ashanti wars against Britain; the wisdom of the Fanti Confederation; the growth of Nigeria; the song of the Songhay and Hausa; the rebellion of the Mahdi and the hands of Ethiopia; the greatness of the Basuto and the fighting of Chaka; the revenge of Mutessi, and many other happenings and men; but above all—Africa, Mother of Men.

Your nearest friends and neighbors are the colored people of China and India, the rest of Asia, the Middle East and the sea isles, once close bound to the heart of Africa and now long severed by the greed of Europe. Your bond is not mere color of skin but the deeper experience of wage slavery and contempt. So too, your bond with the white world is closest to those who support and defend China and help India and not those who exploit the Middle East and South America.

Awake, awake, put on thy strength, O Zion! Reject the weakness of missionaries who teach neither love nor brotherhood, but chiefly the virtues of private profit from capital, stolen from your land and labor. Africa, awake! Put on the beautiful robes of Pan-African socialism.

You have nothing to lose but your chains! You have a continent to regain! You have freedom and human dignity to attain!

THE VAST MIRACLE OF CHINA TODAY

June 8, 1959

I have traveled widely on this earth since my first trip to Europe 67 years ago. Save South America and India, I have seen most of the civilized world and much of its backward regions. Many leading nations I have visited repeatedly. But I have never seen a nation which so amazed and touched me as China in 1959.

I have seen more impressive buildings but no more pleasing architecture; I have seen greater display of wealth, and more massive power; I have seen better equipped railways and boats and vastly more showy automobiles; but I have never seen a nation where human nature was so abreast of scientific knowledge; where daily life of everyday people was so outstripping mechanical power and love of life so triumphing over human greed and envy and selfishness as I see in China today.

It is not a matter of mere numbers and size; of wealth and power; of beauty and style. It is a sense of human nature free of its most hurtful and terrible meannesses and of a people full of joy and faith and marching on in a unison unexampled in Holland, Belgium, Britain and France; and simply inconceivable in the United States.

A typical, ignorant American put it this way in Moscow: "But how can you make it go without niggers?" In China he would have said: "But see them work:" dragging, hauling, lifting, pulling—and yet smiling at each other, greeting neighbors who ride by in autos, helping strangers even if they are "niggers"; seeking knowledge, following leaders and believing in themselves and their certain destiny. Whence comes this miracle of human nature, which I never saw before or believed possible?

I was ten weeks in China. There they celebrated my 91st birthday with a thoughtfulness and sincerity that would simply be impossible in America even among my own colored people. Ministers of state were there, writers and artists, actors and professional men; singers and children playing fairy tales. Anna Louise Strong came looking happy, busy and secure. There was a whole table of other Americans, exiled for daring to visit China; integrated for their skills and loyalty.

I traveled 5,000 miles, by railway, boat, plane and auto. I saw all the great cities: Peking, Shanghai, Hankow and its sisters; Canton, Chungking, Chengtu, Kunming and Nanking. I rode its vast rivers tearing through mighty gorges; passed through its villages and sat in its communes. I visited its schools and colleges, lectured and broadcast to the world. I visited its minority groups. I was on the borders of Tibet when the revolt occurred. I spent four hours with Mao Tse-tung and dined twice with

Chou En-lai, the tireless Prime Minister of this nation of 680 million souls.

The people of the land I saw; the workers, the factory hands, the farmers and laborers, scrubwomen and servants. I went to theaters and restaurants, sat in the homes of the high and the low; and always I saw a happy people; people with faith that need no church nor priest and laughs gaily when the Monkey King fools the hosts of Heaven and overthrows the angels.

In all my wandering, I never felt the touch or breath of insult or even dislike—I who for 90 years in America scarcely ever saw a day without some expression of hate for "niggers."

What is the secret of China in the second half of the 20th Century? It is that the vast majority of a billion human beings have been convinced that human nature in some of its darkest recesses can be changed, if change is necessary. China knows, as no other people know, to what depths human meanness can go.

I used to weep for American Negroes, as I saw through what indignities and repressions and cruelties they had passed; but as I have read Chinese history in these last months and had it explained to me stripped of Anglo Saxon lies, I know that no depths of Negro slavery in America have plumbed such abysses as the Chinese have seen for 2,000 years and more.

They have seen starvation and murder; rape and prostitution; sale and slavery of children; and religion cloaked in opium and gin, for converting the "Heathen." This oppression and contempt came not only from Tartars, Mongolians, British, French, Germans and Americans, but from the Chinese themselves: Mandarins and warlords, capitalists and murdering thieves like Chiang Kai-shek; Kuomintang socialists and intellectuals educated abroad.

Despite all this, China lives, and has been transformed and marches on. She is not ignored by the United States. She ignores the United States and leaps forward. What did it? What furnished the motive power and how was it applied?

First it was the belief in himself and in his people by a man like Sun Yatsen. He plunged on, blind and unaided, repulsed by Britain and America, but welcomed by Russia. Then efforts toward socialism, which wobbled forward, erred and lost, and at last was bribed by America and Britain and betrayed by

Chiang Kai-shek, with its leaders murdered and its aims misunderstood, when not deliberately lied about.

Then came the Long March from feudalism, past capitalism and socialism to communism in our day. Mao Tse-tung, Chou En-lai, Chu Teh and a half dozen others undertook to lead a nation by example, by starving and fighting; by infinite patience and above all by making a nation believe that the people and not merely the elite—the workers in factory, street, and field—composed the real nation. Others have said this often, but no nation has tried it like the Soviet Union and China.

And on the staggering and bitter effort of the Soviets, beleagured by all Western civilization, and yet far-seeing enough to help weaker China even before a still weak Russia was safe—on this vast pyramid has arisen the saving nation of this stumbling, murdering, hating world.

In China the people—the laboring people, the people who in most lands are the doormats on which the reigning thieves and murdering rulers walk, leading their painted and jeweled prostitutes—the people walk and boast. These people of the slums and gutters and kitchens are the Chinese nation today. This the Chinese believe and on this belief they toil and sweat and cheer.

They believe this and for the last ten years their belief has been strengthened until today they follow their leaders because these leaders have never deceived them. Their officials are incorruptible, their merchants are honest, their artisans are reliable, their workers who dig and haul and lift do an honest days work and even work overtime if their state asks it, for they are the State; they are China.

A kindergarten, meeting in the once Forbidden City, was shown the magnificence of this palace and told: "Your fathers built this, but now it is yours; preserve it." And then, pointing across the Ten An Men square to the vast building of the new Halls of Assembly, the speaker added: "Your fathers are building new palaces for you; enjoy them and guard them for yourselves and your children. They belong to you!"

China has no rank nor classes; her universities grant no degrees; her government awards no medals. She has no blue book of "society." But she has leaders of learning and genius, scientists of renown, artisans of skill and millions who know and believe this and follow where these men lead. This is the joy of this nation, its high belief and its unfaltering hope.

China is no utopia. Fifth Avenue has better shops where the rich can buy and the whores parade. Detroit has more and better cars. The best American housing outstrips the Chinese and Chinese women are not nearly as well-dressed as the guests of the Waldorf-Astoria. But the Chinese worker is happy.

He has exorcised the Great Fear that haunts the West: the fear of losing his job; the fear of falling sick; the fear of accident; the fear of inability to educate his children; the fear of daring to take a vacation. To guard against such catastrophe Americans skimp and save, cheat and steal, gamble and arm for murder.

The Soviet citizen, the Czech, the Pole, the Hungarian have kicked out the stooges of America and the hoodlums set to exploit the peasants. They and the East Germans no longer fear these disasters; and above all the Chinese sit high above these fears and laugh with joy.

They will not be rich in old age. They will not enjoy sickness but they will be healed. They will not starve as thousands of Chinese did only a generation ago. They fear neither flood nor epidemic. They do not even fear war, as Mao Tse-tung told me. War for China is a "Paper Tiger." China can defend itself and back of China stands the unassailable might of the Soviet Union.

Envy and class hate is disappearing in China. Does your neighbor have better pay and higher position than you? He has this because of greater ability or better education, and more education is open to you and compulsory for your children.

The young married couple do not fear children. The mother has pre-natal care. Her wage and job are safe. Nursery and kindergarten take care of the child and it is welcome, not to pampered luxury but to good food, constant medical care and education for his highest ability.

All this is not yet perfect. Here and there it fails, falls short and falters; but it is so often and so widely true, that China believes, lives on realized hope, follows its leaders and sings:

"O, Mourner, get up offa your knees."

The women of China are free. They wear pants so that they can walk, climb and dig; and climb and dig they do. They are not dressed simply for sex indulgence or beauty parades. They occupy positions from ministers of state to locomotive engineers, lawyers, doctors, clerks and laborers. They are escaping "household drudgery"; they are strong and healthy and beautiful not simply of leg and false bosom but of real brain and brawn.

In Wuhan, I stood in one of the greatest steelworks of the world. A crane which moved a hundred tons loomed above. I said, "My God, Shirley, look up there!" Alone in the engine-room sat a girl with ribboned braids, running the vast machine.

You won't believe this, because you never saw anything like it; and if the State Department has its way, you never will. Let *Life* lie about communes; and the State Department shed crocodile tears over ancestral tombs. Let Hong Kong wire its lies abroad. Let "Divine Slavery" persist in Tibet until China kills it. The truth is there and I saw it.

America makes or can make no article that China is not either making or can make, and make better and cheaper. I saw its export exposition in Canton: a whole building of watches, radios, electric apparatus, cloth in silk and wool and cotton; embroidery, pottery, dishes, shoes, telephone sets. There were five floors of goods which the world needs and is buying in increasing quantities, except the ostrich United States, whose ships rot.

Fifteen times I have crossed the Atlantic and once the Pacific. I have seen the world. But never so vast and glorious a miracle as China.

THE LIE OF HISTORY AS IT IS TAUGHT TODAY

February 15, 1960

One hundred years ago next year this nation began a war more horrible than most wars, and all wars stink. From 1861 to 1865 Americans fought Americans, North fought South, brothers fought brothers. All trampled on the faces of four million black folk cowering beneath their feet in mud and blood. Some Americans hated slavery but were unwilling to fight. They would let the "erring sisters depart in peace," with their elegant luxury, cringing service and home-grown concubines. Free Negroes and their white friends organized the escape of slaves and fugitive slaves became a main cause of war. One man John Brown, fought slavery with bare fists and was crucified three years before the flash of Sumter.

So the nation reeled into murder, hate, hurt and destruction until they killed 493,273 human beings in battle, left a million more in pain, and nearly bankrupted the whole nation. "We are not fighting slavery," cried the North. "We are fighting for independence," cried the South. "We are not fighting with Negroes," insisted the North as it returned black fugitives. "Negroes do not want to be free," jeered the South; Negroes whispered: "Let us fight for freedom." The Northerners hated the struggle and nearly all who could bought immunity, while some laborers rioted and hanged Negroes to lamp posts. Most workers refused to volunteer and thousands of soldiers deserted from the ranks.

The South yelled and rushed to war, ran the Northerners home again and again, ranted and blustered and tried to frighten victory out of impossible odds, while their soldiers deserted in increasing droves.

Louder and louder rose voices in the North: "Free the slaves!" It was the only real reason for war. Lincoln was firm: "I am not fighting to free slaves but only for Union"—union to planting, manufacture and trade. Still voices arose led by Frederick Douglass: "Arm the slaves." Lincoln said: "It would be giving arms to the enemy."

The Northern armies began to use the slaves as servants, stevedores and spies; already the Southerners were using the slaves to guard their families and to raise food and clothes for themselves as they fought the fight for slavery. The world looked in amazement on this new free democracy as it staggered, killed and destroyed, both sides appealing for help.

Slowly in the gloom thousands of black slaves began silently to move from plantation to the camps of the Northern armies. Slowly the nation joined the cry of black and white abolitionists: "Free the slaves!" And the bleeding trenches added: "Arm them. The slaves are already armed with muscles if not with guns. They will feed the slave power unless we use them." Black regiments appeared in Kansas, South Carolina and Louisiana. Finally Lincoln saw the truth and dared to change his mind. He offered compensated emancipation and colonization of blacks abroad. The South refused. The war reached bloody stalemate and the nation trembled. Volunteers ceased to offer and corpses clogged the rivers of Virginia. Lee started North, and Lincoln threatened. "Surrender or I abolish slavery," he cried in September, 1862, beneath the smoke of Antietam. He armed eventually two hundred thousand slaves and a million awaited his call.

The Negroes fought like the damned, two hundred thousand of them; led by two hundred black officers and subalterns, they tore into a hundred and more battles and left seventy thousand dead and dying on the fields. They served in every arm of service and in every area of struggle. They were slaughtered at Fort Wagner to hold Carolina. They committed suicide at Port Hudson so that the Father of Waters should flow "unvexed to the sea." They were buried in the Crater to help Grant capture Richmond, the capitol of the Confederacy, and a black regiment led Abraham Lincoln through the city singing,

> John Brown's body lies a' moldering in the grave
> But his soul goes marching on . . .

The South cursed them and treated them as outlaws; Forest murdered and burned them at Fort Pillow. But Lincoln testified that without these black soldiers and the hundreds of thousands of Negro laborers, guards, informers and spies we could not have won the war. On January 1, 1863, Lincoln declared the slaves in rebel territory "then, thenceforward and forever free." The South saw hell in the blazing heavens and with one last gasp tried themselves openly to arm the slaves. They failed and Lee surrendered.

Such was the sordid tale of the war which has been called the "Rebellion," the "Civil War" and the "War Between the States," but whose real name was the "War to Preserve Slavery." That was the only name which made sense to those who fought the war and those who supported it. It sang in their songs and chanted in their poetry:

> In the beauty of the lilies
> Christ was born across the sea.
> As he died to make men holy,
> Let us die to make men free.

Then we turned from the abolition of slavery to our muttons: to making money. Some Americans stepped forward with alms and teachers for the black freed men. Some rushed South to make money with cheap labor and high cotton. But most of the nation tried to forget the Negro. He was free, what more did he want? He asked for a Freedmen's Bureau and got a small one paid for mainly with the unclaimed bounties of dead black soldiers. Philanthropists gave him a bank and cheated him out of most of his savings when it failed. Votes? Nonsense, unless planters demand a lower tariff, payment for the Confederate debt and compensation for freed slaves.

We refused to let the horrible mistake of war teach our children anything. We gave it less and less space in our textbooks, until today slavery gets a paragraph and the Civil War a page.

Moreover, the whole cause and meaning of the war is distorted in 10,000 books which falsify the real story. Now in weighty tome, gaudy magazine and television the war was merely an unfortunate misunderstanding. It seems nobody wanted slavery and the South, having had it forced upon her, was about to abolish it but for senseless, impatient agitation. All of our history from the Missouri Compromise through the Compromise of 1850 to the secession of South Carolina is being thus rewritten and the Negro painted as a contented slave, a lazy freedman, a thieving voter and today as happily integrated into American life.

Thereupon with no guidance from the past the nation marched on with officers strutting, bands playing and flags flying to secure colonial empire and new cheap slave labor and land monopoly in Asia, Africa and the islands of the seas. We fought two World Wars killing nearly 500,000 American youth, and added 50,000 more dead by "police action" in Korea. In all we destroyed more wealth than we have since been able to count. We are now wasting $40,000,000,000 a year for more wars and we owe $284,000,000,000 for past wars. In sixty years we have spent only $14 billion for education.

So now comes the time to celebrate the War to Preserve Slavery. The South, which for a century has insisted that theirs was a just war fought with the highest motives by the noblest of men, is pouring forth books and pamphlets to prove this. This all Southern white children have been taught to believe until it is to most of them a matter of absolute and indisputable truth. Historians, North and South, have spread the story and artists have depicted it, so that most Southern states next year will celebrate as a triumph in human effort this despicable struggle to keep black Americans in slavery.

The North, on the other hand, sees little reason to remember or celebrate this war. It would prefer to forget it, but most Northern states will stage some sort of celebration to recall the keeping of this nation united for producing more millionaires than any other people and for proving what philanthropists we are. We gave and are still giving alms to Negroes.

The South will preen itself. What a courageous folk, lynching singlehanded since the Civil War 5,000 helpless Negroes and disfranchising millions. Virginia will lead the rejoicing with a $1,750,000 centennial budget and Mississippi is following with $500,000. Arkansas will join in with Faubus, and Georgia will sing the Jubilee, but not with "Marching Through Georgia." Colored citizens will be asked to attest how loyally they protected old master's family while he fought for slavery.

The whole United States will stage a mighty pageant to cost at first $200,000 and millions later. Big Business, including the Stock Exchange and travel bureaus, will play a major part, but the emancipation of slaves will be ignored. So says the head of the Centennial committee, a nice old white gentleman with a black mammy who serves under an army general, called deservedly the Third Ulysses S. Grant.

Listen America! Hear that we will not celebrate the freeing of four million slaves! O dark Potomac where looms the gloom of the Lincoln Memorial. Father Abraham, unlimber those great limbs; let the bronze blaze with blood and the eyes of sorrow again see. Stand and summon out of the past the woman whose eyes saw "the glory of the coming of the Lord"; the Seer who said: "For what avail the plough or sail or land or life if freedom fail?" The abolitionist who cried: "I will not retreat a single inch and I will be heard!" Arouse Phillips and Sumner, Stevens and Birney and the whole legion who hated slavery and let them march to Capitol Hill. Warn them again, that this nation must have a "new birth of freedom" even if "all the wealth piled up by the bondsmen's two hundred and fifty years of unrequited toil shall be sunk" and if "every drop of blood drawn by the lash, be paid by another drawn by the sword." As was said three thousand years ago, so still it must be said that "the judgments of the Lord are true and righteous altogether."

This is but the raving of an old man who has long dreamed that American Negroes could be men and look white America in the face without blinking. Not only dreamed but saw in 1913 the Negroes of six states celebrate the Jubilee of Emancipation

without apology. Here in New York we inaugurated an abolition celebration securing a state appropriation of $10,000 and
a Negro Board of Control. We spent the money honestly and
effectively and centred it on recalling the part which Negroes
played in the war. We pictured the progress of American
Negroes and the forgotten history of their motherland, Africa.
For a week beginning October 21, 1913, in the 11th Regiment
Armory, Ninth Avenue and 62nd Street, 30,000 persons attended the celebration and 350 actors took part. Few who saw
ever forgot the Egyptian Temple, the Migration of the Bantu
and the March of the Black Soldiers. Three times later in Washington, Philadelphia and Los Angeles the pageant was repeated.
James Weldon Johnson and I went further and planned for 1918
a Jubilee of the 14th Amendment, but the First World War
killed that dream.

Today no Negro leader who holds a good government appointment, or is favored of the great benevolent foundations or
has a job in Big Business, or is financed by the State Department
to travel abroad, will dare dream of celebrating in any way the
role which Negroes played in the Civil War. It would be "racist"
for an "integrated" Negro American to recall the Emancipation
of black slaves in the United States. And any Negro school or
college would risk its income if it staged a celebration.

Possibly the main moral of all this is the failure of history as
it is taught today even to attempt to tell the exact truth or learn
it. Rather, so many historians conceive it their duty to teach as
truth what they or those who pay their salaries believe to have
been true. Thus we train generations of men who do not know
the past, or believe a false picture of the past, to have no trustworthy guide for living and to stumble doggedly on, through
mistake after mistake, to fatal ends. Our history becomes "lies
agreed upon" and stark ignorance guides our future.

A PROGRAM OF REASON, RIGHT AND JUSTICE FOR TODAY

May 23, 1960

Daily lately as I read the morning news, I find myself asking
if age is driving me a bit crazy or if I'm living in a crazy nation.

I have lived through much history and read far more, but I can remember no situation which parallels the present. Governments and rulers have always lied. But never with the quick, bland, easy assurance such as our transformation of a spying trip which failed into a weather exploration—and then blaming the Soviet Union for "propaganda." We have only to scan our magazines to see how the United States is being transformed from an unsophisticated people of original Tinkers and Thinkers to a nation of Liars and Buyers.

President Eisenhower continues to astonish me. Yesterday this Delphic oracle came from the golf links: "We never enslaved anyone." Today we learn that Turkey is not our spy base but a "bastion of Freedom," where the NATO of the "Free World" dares not stay long enough to hear the President's welcome, because Prime Minister Menderes is trying to outrun angry students threatening his life.

Right here I draw a breath of relief. Students at last to the rescue, even in the West. I had lost faith in them as during the McCarthy nightmare I spoke at a few institutions and looked into their blank faces. But today young seekers after knowledge live again despite a woeful lack of teachers. Not only in Turkey, which we have purchased, but in Japan where they defy Prime Minister Kishi's plan to tie Nippon to the Pentagon; and in South Korea where they have driven a demagogue out of power.

Of course I am especially uplifted by the revolt of Negro students in America. With neither leadership nor encouragement from their own people (despite all the declarations of the johnnie-come-latelies frantically scrambling abroad the bandwagon), alone and unaided they put their finger on a vital spot and acted. Our Negro Problem is not simply disfranchisement, lynching, mob-law, court injustice and widespread serfdom with poverty and disease: it is a daily, unending series of petty, senseless insults carried out almost everywhere, and always by civilized people of religion and culture for no earthly reason except senseless meanness and neglect.

In the South a Negro goes downtown to buy a few necessities, and can't buy a bite to eat; he can't get a drink; he can't go to a movie; sometimes he can't sit in a park; and of course he can't bathe in the ocean, as in Biloxi, in the most ignorant state of the Union, where there are 26 miles of beach. Black students—not agitators, not even radicals, since little economics or social science is taught in Southern schools—just honest, clear-headed youth who one day say: "We buy our school books and paper at Woolworth's; why not buy a sandwich?"

Then the proud, cultured South goes berserk. Boys and girls are arrested, clubbed and jailed. Churches sing, pray and send Billy Graham to Africa. Still students "sit down." Then Big Business moves in. It threatens colored college presidents. Some, like Wright of Fisk, refuse to yield. Some, like Trenholm of Alabama, crawl. Then Big Business squeezes parents and some parents, to save their jobs, plead with their children; but at least at one colored college 4,000 students withdraw while their president skulks. They threaten to put a white president in at Lincoln who will teach Negroes their place. They may try this at Howard. They may starve Fisk. What will result? Will the students fall back into line? I think not. Some white students feel the glorious possibilities of this day; but the nation is silent and dumb.

Are we happy at all this? No, America is scared to death. Asia has arisen. Africa arises. The Soviet Union marches on. East Europe is triumphant. Cuba is free. Panama and Latin America follow. But the United States is stubborn.

We lie about China and support a man on her borders to attack her whom we ourselves have called a scoundrel. We invest six hundred million dollars in slave labor and stolen gold, diamonds and uranium in South Africa where our Boer allies have 18,000 Negroes in jail and ten million more fated to be hammered into slavery. We woo Adenauer to preserve a Germany which our army, with the help of the leader of the AFL-CIO, fashioned as a threat for a Third World War to conquer the Soviets. We bribe Franco, cajole Italy and, as long as possible, we will hang on to Trujillo. We are intriguing in Viet-Nam and Laos and praying for war between India and China, which fails to occur.

Signs of disaster gather about our heads. We are unable to sell enough abroad to pay for what we buy and have been compelled to spend four billions in the last two years out of our hoard of gold to pay the deficit. Our cost of living rises continuously and unemployment spreads, despite our ingenious efforts to deceive the public. The gamblers of the stock market are sweating in vain to unload on the suckers the inflated values of our monopolized industry. We are soaking the sick with high-priced medicines and hospital fees beyond the reach of the poor. We are bribing our skilled labor with high wages paid out of the hides of exploited Negro and Mexican labor and from the poverty and disease of poor whites.

Our justice is showered with injustice. Our jails seethe with the revolts of the wretched and the innocent and of thousands whose only crime is being black. We murder Chessman for no crime we can prove; we jail Uphaus and Sobell, torture Winston and drive Heikkila to death. Why? The bomb-proof shelters of the editorial offices of the New York Times hear a rumor that our judges often actually pay two years' salary for nomination.

We are deliberately distorting history—not simply United States history—so as to excuse Negro slavery and deify slave owners, to praise the traitors who solemnly swore to support their country and then fought desperately to betray it and preserve Negro slavery; but especially to twist and distort the world wars and the triumph of socialism.

We started with propaganda which out-Hitlered Hitler. Big Business monopolized news-gathering, newspapers, periodicals and publishing. The nation was led to believe that communism was a conspiracy and crime, and socialism its handmaid. We were told that the communist states were failures, their citizens serfs and prisoners, seething with revolt; their women prostitutes and their education only "brain-washing" propaganda. Many wanted to use our atom bomb immediately on Moscow, but when we found the Soviets already had it we accused them of stealing it from us, as they were certainly too dumb to have invented it.

We planned for war. Our State Department and national leaders cooperated with Collier's magazine in 1951. The nation was primed to conquer the Soviet Union in 1960. This is 1960. This was to be the year of conquest. Collier's (of blessed memory) foretold the event in 130 pages, written by Allan Nevins, our "leading" historian; Stuart Chase, our "leading" economist; Edward R. Murrow, our "great" news interpreter; Margaret Chase Smith, our woman Senator; Robert Sherwood and J. B. Priestley. Our Senator wrote of "Russia Reborn" under American soldiers, presumably armed with flaming napalm and disease germs. This victory had to be postponed, but our propaganda continued.

We continued to sneer at education and progress in the Soviet Union. I once heard Conant of Harvard, formerly High Commissioner of Germany, tell the Harvard Club of New York that Soviet leaders repeatedly refused to tell him what examinations were given high school students for entrance into college. He finally learned (here in America) that "the Communist Party would not allow any examinations!" This proved Soviet education a farce. A few years later came Sputnik and the photographing of the back of the moon. We had to acknowledge the superiority of Soviet education, the progress of her science and the fact that her industrial development might soon equal or even outstrip ours.

Khrushchev dared to visit us and, while Congress went into hiding, he made the finest speech for world peace which has been heard here since Lincoln at Gettysburg. We then photographed Russian fortifications and lied about it. Why? Because Allen Dulles and our military rulers are still determined to smash the Summit conference and plunge the world into war.

Meantime we want to help the world. We remember how American charity has often fed the hungry and healed the sick. Taking every advantage of this memory, Big Business has used it to the hilt. The Marshall Plan was to help war-torn Europe. In reality it helped American business to buy into European industry, beat back socialist labor, bribe skilled labor and pay soldiers. In fact with most of the funds we are arming all foreigners we can bribe or scare to help us fight Communists, and with what's left we are using our public tax funds to give rich American investors private capital, or to bribe native quislings in India and Africa to betray their countries to American industry. Already in New York alone we have four "African" organizations, financed by Big Business, and officered by Negroes supposed to give "information" on Africa. Pious churchmen are furnishing the requisite religious background. For all of this Eisenhower is now demanding four billions of our dollars which ought to be used for social medicine, education and housing.

However, my friends note, an election is coming up. So what? There is, to be sure, a President soon to be chosen. The expenditure of all candidates for the office in 1956 was said to have been $100,000,000. This year it may be $500,000,000. Only Big Business, well-heeled stock gamblers and the China Lobby can bid. Whether a Democrat or Republican wins, it will be the same gang. You will have no chance to vote for a meaningful third party. You will have no chance to vote for peace or war; for social medicine, housing or decent education. Why?

We know the reason. It is because the United States is no longer a democracy. Most citizens know this well and do not waste time going to the polls. If it were true that we have what we want in this nation, we could sit still and wait on reason. But it is not true. We are ruled by a minority armed with wealth and power. This usurpation we must fight. We must first demand the right to have a third party on the ballot. This the politicians prevent and these politicians must go.

Here is a program for those who have not lost hope and who yet believe in America. Forget the Presidency. It will make not a jot of difference whether Nixon and Chiang Kai-shek, or Kennedy and Cardinal Spellman, win the office. Concentrate on Senators and Congressmen, legislators and city councilmen and ward heelers.

Insist on a chance to vote for peace, for the total abolition of the color line; for no family income above $25,000 or below $5,000; for free education from kindergarten through college; for housing on a nation-wide scale; for training of all for the work they can do in so far as such work is needed for the best interests of all. Insist on discipline for this work. Allow no laborer to be paid less than his product is worth; and let no employer take what he does not make. Curb corporations by putting most of them under government ownership.

Heal the sick as a privilege, not as a charity. Make private ownership of natural resources a crime. Stop interference with private and personal belief by religious hypocrites. Preserve the utmost freedom for dream of beauty, creative art and joy of living. Call this socialism, communism, reformed capitalism or holy rolling. Call it anything—but get it done!

Perhaps this is insane, but to me it is Reason, Right and Justice. As Bert Williams once said: "I may be crazy, but I ain't no Fool!"

At a time when Dr. Du Bois' life and work are being cele-brated, his advice to younger people, as given in an address (printed below) at the memorial meeting for the late Louis E. Burnham of the (National) Guardian *staff, is especially appro-priate.*

ON THE VAST AND RECKLESS WASTE OF HUMAN LIFE

June 20, 1960

I knew Louis Burnham for about 25 years. There are many matters of which I might speak concerning him; of the work he did; of the work he was doing at the time of his death; and of what he might yet have done had he lived. I might refer, as all of you must, to the future of his family and the education of his children. And above all none can forget his honesty and utter sacrifice.

I speak, however, only of one matter which seems to me of greatest moment to this audience. What I want to say has to do with the saving of lives like that of Louis Burnham; the stopping of the vast and reckless waste which goes on each year in this country and others, and deprives the world of irreplaceable help for the tasks which we have to do.

Here was a man of 44 at the beginning of what we regard as the prime of life. His education and apprenticeship had ended and his full life begun. Suddenly he is dead. Why? Let us take refuge in no mystical fatalism. He is dead because in his busy life he did not find sufficient time to attend to the needs of his body. He had a good body, not weak nor deformed, comely and normal. He had work to do, work of great moment but some of that work was neglected. The neglected work had to do with the preservation of the working mechanism which was his body.

This often is the fault of the individual. Some men abuse their bodies; others neglect them. But Louis Burnham was not that sort. If he neglected his health or overworked, it was unconscious and because of his own absorption in what he saw as his duty, and because his friends neglected to warn him, and the state of which he was citizen furnished no adequate code of health.

Happy the child that starts with a healthy rhythm of life. But when once he's grown, the responsibility for preserving health falls on himself, his friends and the state. These three. But today increasingly the greatest responsibility is that of the state. We easily forget this. We blame a busy man for not resting, but how can he rest when his work is not done, when his family may be in danger of starvation and when his friends do not sense this or warn him, and the state does not furnish him facilities for good health?

We fall into the habit of going to a physician when we're sick, which is putting the cart before the horse. We should go to the physician before we are sick so as not to become sick. Our friends should feel it their duty to warn us when we are driving too hard and in the wrong direction. But above all the modern state should see to it that its workers rest, that they have recreation, that their work is done under healthy conditions and that there is an abundance of trained physicians and nurses, ten times as many hospitals as we have, and services and medicines within easy reach of all.

Two years ago I was in London and was taken violently ill. I was treated for a week or ten days by an excellent physician and when I was well and asked for my bill I was told that there was no bill, that the British government paid for the physician's services and the cost of my medicines was less than five dollars. This was British social medicine which the American Medical Association has spent millions of dollars to prove is a failure.

About fifty years ago a group of physicians in the State of New York organized the Life Extension Institute whose duty it would be for a small annual fee to advise clients just what the state of their health was and what they ought to do about it. I joined the organization in 1918, but gradually the organized physicians of the State of New York so limited the work and functions of the Life Extension Institute as to curtail most of its usefulness. They told me at last frankly: "Unless you have some specific ailment we really have no right nor facilities to advise you." And I had to reply: "It is just because I have no particular disease nor complaint that I want the services of an organization like this."

The provisions for vacation, treatment, operations and hospitalization in the socialist and communist lands of the world go beyond that of social medicine in Britain. It is here in America, one of the wealthiest nations in the world, that health is grievously neglected, that there are far too few nurses and physicians and that the loss of life because of neglect and poverty is far greater than is necessary.

Most people give little thought to the health of their bodies. They are sure that the body's health is natural and they go on enjoying it. If they are taken ill they go to a physician. But to rush in upon any strange physician with a body already out of order is a crazy thing to do. The physician must learn what is the matter and that is not easy. He must become acquainted with the peculiarities of your particular body and that calls for time.

The physician to whom you go should be your physician who already knows the condition of your body and the character of your work; and his business is not simply to see that you recover from a temporary illness, but rather to see that you do not get it. Physicians should direct eating by advice, and above all direct drinking. The present use of alcohol is not only unnecessary; it is idiotic. Alcohol is a useful and pleasant beverage, but it is not designed for continuous guzzling. Refraining from drinking liquids is, if anything, more dangerous. And the directing of a continual flow of smoke and gas over sensitive mucuous membranes is neither reasonable nor in the end pleasant. I suppose that more than anything else, one has to ask normal people today to stop trying to turn night into day and day into night in their work and play.

The greatest tribute that we can now pay to the life of Louis Burnham is to look around at our friends who are doing the world's work and pick out, as we easily can, those who are working too hard and trying to do too much and not getting enough rest nor medical advice of the right kind. Then we can take a further step, which is so needed today, and try to build up in the United States health services paid for by the states from our taxes and servants of health trained and paid by the state which will bring social medicine to the United States; not simply to the young, not simply to the old, but especially to the great mass of people who are doing the world's work.

We should vote for administrators and legislators who see this as their duty and against those who for any reason neglect this duty. We should try to bring to this nation something of the health services which can be found in the Soviet Union, in China and in all socialist and communist states. There is no reason why the average normal human being should not live at least seventy years in happy useful life doing his share of work and being a joy and help for his fellows and not a burden.

For this is a beautiful world. We know its hurt and evil all too well. Yet we must never forget its beauty and possibilities. I have seen the high Alps blazing above Berne; the royal palms swaying in West Africa; the golden rain of Hawaii. I have seen a crowd of 500,000 working people filling the Red Square before the Kremlin, and thousands singing the Marsellaise and dancing in the Place de la Concorde. I have heard the babies laughing in the nurseries of Peking below the Great Wall of China. This beauty can grow and men can see it if we but let them live.

> And by contagion of the sun we may
> Catch at a spark from that primeval fire.
> And learn that we are better than our clay.
> And equal to the peaks of our desire.

THE BELGIAN CONGO

The World Must Soon Awake to Bar War in Congo

September 26, 1960

Congo was a tragic miscalculation. Little Belgium had inherited El Durado. Hundreds of millions of dollars poured into this land annually from a great territory 40 times its size. In this empire was one of the world's greatest deposits of copper to carry electric power over sea and land; elephant tusks to furnish piano keys for lovely music, palm oil, fruit, rare woods, fibers and lately uranium for bombs to raise hell.

Nobody knows how vast a horde of wealth Congo has poured into Belgium, Europe and North America in the last century, for this is a secret of individual initiative in the capitalist world of Nordic supremacy. But all men including Pope and Protestant hierarchy and learned colleges know how many cheap laborers were slaves of white Europe to make Belgians clean, comfortable and learned and leaders of civilization. Once the atrocities of the Congo aroused the world and the Belgian folk took Congo out of the private purse of Leopold to rule themselves.

I remember talking to the first Belgian Socialist premier in the 'twenties, and his firm promise to institute reform and stop cutting off the hands of lagging black workers. I remember the legends of the King of Congo whom the Portuguese met in the 15th century and whose royal son was educated in Lisbon. I had read as a boy Stanley's flamboyant and lying proclamation of the great new Christian Kingdom of Congo which civilization was about to rear in the Dark Continent, to lead the natives to God.

Centuries passed: The 16th with its great flowering of imperial black Africa south of the Sahara; the 17th with the duel of Fetish and Moslem, and the Long March of Bantu from Niger to Zambesi; the 18th century and the British trade in slaves from Africa to America; and the 19th century when Europe stole the world and built its culture on the degradation of Asia and Africa.

Out of this wreched past was naturally born this century of war and destruction, with the West stubbornly determined to restore its domination of mankind, and with the East—in Europe, Asia and Africa—increasingly set on freedom and independence. Belgium, despite its baptism in war and rapine, because it lay in the crossing paths of greedy empires, made peace with all, and came to understanding with the wheeling buzzards of the West.

If you want to make money invest in the Congo enterprises: profitable, respectable private enterprise, paying high and regular dividends, and no questions asked. Moreover the natives were happy, their tribal rule was intact and their chiefs happy so long as the black slaves toiled for their white masters, and the wealth rolled into Europe.

When in 1921 I held a session of the Pan-African Congress in Brussels, and one young Congolese, Panda, ventured to join us in criticism of Belgian rule, the Belgian press raged: "Bolsheviks," spies and revolutionists they called us, the natives were content and the Holy Catholic Church was giving them enough education for their good; not too much, not enough to make them unhappy and demanding more than their few brains could use.

Congo had no such unhappy intelligentsia as the British had nursed in West Africa and the French in Senegal. Even if Belgium did not have enough trained Congolese to educate as physicians, at least Black Congo did not want to vote. So Belgium crowed even as late at the World Exposition of 1958.

And then in 1960 the bubble burst and black Congo demanded not only a share in government but independence. It was inconceivable. It was unbelievable. Even when my wife, Shirley Graham, who read my message to the Sixth Pan-African Congress, meeting as the All-African Conference in Accra in 1958, told me of Lumumba there demanding independence for Congo, I thought he was an unthinking fanatic.

But I pride myself on ability to learn; on seeing what appears before my eyes. Yesterday, I was paying farewell to the President of Ghana, just as he was taking leave of Lumumba, Prime Minister of Congo, who was on his way home from a meeting of the Security Council which had ordered Belgium out of Congo because it dare not to do otherwise. After Lumumba flew home in a Russian jet plane, President Nkrumah and I talked for a few moments.

We knew that the trials of Congo had not ended but just begun. The luxury-loving West, which was parading and yachting, gambling and horse-racing, dressing and dancing and keeping darkies out of highly paid unions, was not going to give up Congo millions without a desperate struggle even if it involved world war. Ghana, the Soviet Union and China must furnish capital and technical skill to keep the great wheels of Congo enterprise running; but running not for profit of white skilled labor and the idle rich, but for the starving, sick and ignorant Africans.

From me the President asked but one service: the starting again of the *Encyclopedia Africana* which I tried desperately to begin back in 1900. We must unite Africa, he said, and know its history and culture. Against all dreams of an independent black Congo stand arrayed today forces of terrible strength: the organized business enterprise of the Western world; incorporated monopoly, with secret concealed, anonymous personalities, ruled by dictators, amenable to no laws of morality whose only object is gain of wealth, at any cost of life, liberty or of human happiness.

This faceless, conscienceless power is today armed to the teeth and spending for force and violence more money than for anything else on earth and hiring all the ability and genius of the world which is for sale, for the murder, rape, destruction and degradation of man, which big business wants accomplished; and hiding this from common knowledge by every device available to man.

Ranged therefore against free and independent Congo is the Oppenheimer gold and diamond trust, the Lever Brothers world monopolies under its legion of names; the oil trusts, Standard, Shell and others, the French, Swiss and West German cartels, and that part of the Christian church and Moslem religion which is dependent on the charity of the rich.

But the truth is winning; socialism is spreading, communism is becoming more and more possible to increasing millions:

> Fear not, O little flock the foe,
> That madly seeks thine overthrow
> Fear not its rage and Power!

Finally down toward Land's End, on the Cape of Evil Omen, are some three million whites in the Union of South Africa, the Rhodesias and Southwest Africa, who are determined to rule 20 or more million blacks as slaves and servants. They say this brazenly and openly in the face of the world and none do anything, save black Africa. And here the next world war will begin unless the world wakes up and wakes soon.

NIGERIA BECOMES PART OF THE MODERN WORLD

January 16, 1961

I have just spent two weeks in Nigeria. I hesitate to record even briefly the tremendous impression which this land made on me because my stay was so short and because the meaning of this nation is so momentous to the modern world. Nigeria, as large as France and Italy combined, with as many people as England, is a portion of the Middle Ages set suddenly into the last half of our century. It brings in Benin and Ife, an art form which already has tranformed modern art and a technique of casting bronze and copper which has amazed historians of technology. It flatly contradicts modern history as received today and makes morals and religion in Europe and America largely hypocrisy.

The black people of Nigeria stride into this modern world with no dream that their color is a disgraceful insignia of inferiority. I sat, November 12, in the dining room of an air conditioned modern hotel in Lagos, when suddenly the black waiters stood at attention; there arose the whistling cry "Zeek!" by which for 25 years Nigeria has hailed Nnamdi Azikiwe as he agitated for independence; out of a private dining room at the far end strode a six-foot black man robed in flowing white and crowned in embroidered velvet. He was the Governor-elect of this nation; he had left his dinner guest, the retiring British Governor, to come greet me and my wife to Nigeria.

Why was this man being made the first black Governor of a British colony? Because Britain in a last subtle move had decided to yield to Nigeria's irrestible demand for independence by granting to a Nigerian the formerly powerful office of Governor-general, now shorn of its power to make laws and dictate policy, but still robed in the tinsel of pomp and circumstance. One hundred thousand people witnessed this inauguration. I had traveled 6,000 miles at Azikiwe's invitation to be sure that socialism would be represented on this occasion. For this the Governor-elect greeted me. And I had come to learn just how powerless the new Governor would be. I knew that already Britain had been disappointed in failing to keep Northern Nigeria out of federation with the south and how Moral Rearmament, financed by big business, had been working on Azikiwe.

America was discovered and Guinea and India invaded by Europe in the same decade and then there began a phantasmagoria which for 300 years transformed the modern world. A British Protestant Christian, William Howitt (*Colonization and Christianity*, London, 1838), recorded the truth:

> The barbarities and desperate outrages of the so-called Christian race, throughout every region of the world, and upon every people that they have been able to subdue, are not to be paralleled by those of any other

race, however fierce, however untaught, and however reckless of mercy and of shame, in any age of the earth.

Out of this tragic past the Nigerians of today march, largely ignorant of the significance of what has happened to them. They have never been conquered by Europeans, but, through bribery and deception, were so manipulated by the British Empire as to regard the British mainly as benefactors.

Nigerians through the lore of their fathers look back on a mighty past. They remember the empire of the Songhay where in the early 16th century the black Mohammed Askia ruled an Empire as large as all Europe; and as the Arab chronicle says: "There reigned everywhere great plenty and absolute peace!" Their University of Sankoré was a world center of learning among the peoples of the Mediterranean.

What happened? European traders came to barter with a trading people in spices and gold. Domestic slaves furnished labor and gradually became themselves material for labor exported to Spain and Portugal long decimated by war. Then in America came a wider demand for labor promising fabulous wealth. Britain, starting with white indentured servants, seized and dominated a vast and profitable black slave trade. Africa lost a hundred million souls from the middle of the 16th to the middle of the 19th centuries. Slave raids became tribal wars, and slave labor changed the face of commerce and industry in Europe. Industrial Revolution built a new world based on wealth in private hands. Whence came this wealth?

Karl Marx tells us:

> The discovery of gold and silver in America, the extirpation, enslavement and entombment in mines of the aboriginal population, the beginning of the conquest and looting of the East Indies, the turning of Africa into a warren for the commercial hunting of black-skins, signalised the rosy dawn of the era of capitalist production . . .
>
> *Tantae molis erat,* to establish the "eternal laws of Nature" of the capitalist mode of production, to complete the process of separation between laborers and conditions of labor, to transform at one pole the social means of production and subsistence into capital, at the opposite pole, the mass of the population into wage-laborers, into "free laboring poor," that artificial product

of modern society. If money, according to Augier, "comes into the world with a congenital bloodstain on one cheek," capital comes dripping from head to foot, from every pore, with blood and dirt.

But the Nigerians knew little of the wider meaning of this. They only felt the impact of black invaders from the East like the Haussa and later the Fulani; and the push of the Ibos and Yoruba from western Atlantis. War raged among these African peoples, wars which changed their folkways and art; which built their economy on far-off slavery and tempted missionaries from Europe to uplift their morals, bring them primary schools, but often interfere ignorantly with their folkways. Traders like Goldie and his Niger company sailed up the Niger and gradually turned the face of Nigeria from the Mediterranean to the slave-trading Atlantic. The coast of the Gulf of Guinea was annexed by force and by treaties with chiefs which made them pensioners of England and by bribery expanded the empire.

Thus arose modern Nigeria, untouched by color caste, proud and masterful but living in an unknown world. The vast territory, which stretched north and west from the island of Lagos, became loosely unified under British administrators and was called Nigeria after the fabulous river, which for 2,500 miles flowing north, east and south puzzled and misled the world, until it poured into the Atlantic through a hundred mouths forming a delta twice the size of the state of New Jersey. A freebooter, Frederick Lugard, after fighting in China and India and killing Christians and Moslems in Uganda, was recognized by the British government as an "empire builder" and raised to the peerage. By skillful bribery called "indirect rule" he annexed all Nigeria to the British Empire.

A black man who later became Bishop Crowther helped explore the Niger in 1841. But the coasts of the Gulf of Guinea became restless under this pressure of Europe. The Slave Coast, the Grain Coast, the Gold Coast agitated for greater voice in government. Crowther's grandson, Herbert Macauley, agitated for voice in government and was jailed in 1928. Young Nnamdi Azikiwe, educated in the United States, founded the *West African Pilot* in 1937, followed by a string of other protesting papers. Before World War I, the British ruled all Northern Nigeria by a Governor-general and the rest of Nigeria through a council on which the Governor had a majority composed of officials and merchants. The West African Congress, inspired by and following the First Pan-African Congress, secured some elected members to this council.

There followed the participation of Nigerians in World War II by which the Allies drove Germany out of Africa and then came the rise of trade unions. These unions met with the world unions in Paris in 1945, struggled for and won their right to speak for themselves, and joined in calling the Fifth Pan-African Congress that year in England.

The agitation of Azikiwe and others in Nigeria increased until the wiser Britishers advised yielding, but the die-hards tried to hold Northern Nigeria from joining the South. They failed. Northern Nigeria joined the Federation and with the Governor-generalship stripped of power, Azikiwe was nominated to the place, after escaping a charge of misusing funds in organizing his bank. It was hoped his good will had been secured and could be made certain by a privy councilorship and a possible knighthood later.

There came disquieting difficulties. I do not know all the facts, but these seem true. Using British social contacts with the proud Sultans and Emirs of Northern Nigeria it had been planned that the son of the Sultan of Sokoto would be educated at Oxford and become leader of Northern Nigeria. However, the Sultan could not stomach the idea of his son being educated at a Christian college. He therefore substituted a young Nigerian of lower rank, Abubakar Tafawa Balewa, a teacher trained at the University of London. Knighted by the Queen, he became Prime Minister of a Federated Nigeria and the most powerful official in the nation. But curiously, Balewa is a friend of Azikiwe and working amicably with him. He is no socialist in the modern sense, but he is not frightened of communism, because he knows the ancient communal African family and state. Azikiwe also is no communist, but I have talked socialism with him and found him most interested.

Power of directing legislation and proposing policy lies in the hands of the Prime Minister of Nigeria; the Prime Minister of the Federation, and the three Prime Ministers of Northern, Eastern and Western Nigeria. But these must all consult the Governor. He cannot force their decisions, but he is by far the most popular man in Nigeria and his word is influential.

WHAT FUTURE FOR NIGERIA?

January 23, 1961

Nigeria is a rich land. By this the West means that it has an abundance of cheap labor; immense areas of rich land and forests; and stores of coal, oil, lead, tin, zinc and other metals. It can produce palm oil, raise cocoa and fruit, and has vast potential water power. If developed by Western capital and technique as colonies have been, Nigeria could be a vast source of wealth and power to the world.

When, on the other hand, Nigerians call their country rich, they mean that there can be raised in this land enough to feed, clothe and shelter the people, and surplus to sell abroad for machinery and skills and comforts. In the past, Nigerians have by their folkways in family and clan life avoided extreme poverty and hunger; settled the problem of women so as to support widows, take care of orphans and avoid prostitution; they have fought disease and crime and been on the whole a contented people. But contact with the modern world has shown them the possibility of greater happiness. They see the necessity of education in modern knowledge, the possibilities of more comfort in living, better fighting of disease, larger production of goods with less work and a broader life. How can this be attained?

The British teach that if Nigerians accept their leadership and advice, all will be well, but the Nigerians, looking back on the past, are beginning to realize the slave trade, the cheating in commerce and exploiting in work. They remind the British that only agitation, punished often by jail, has forced the British to yield the blacks a voice in government. They are glad to make the transfer of authority from white to black in peace and harmony but are determined to be watchful in the future. They are, however, not disposed to question the usual investment procedure of business and individual initiative and are willing that a Nigerian bourgeoisie should share profit arising from foreign exploiting of land and labor.

Americans, on the other hand, announced at the summer meeting of NATO a plan to drive both Britain and France from Africa and to put American capital in full charge. They would be willing to associate American Negro capitalists with them and such Nigerian businessmen as are willing to let white

Americans lead. This NATO meeting was considerably upset when an American Negro present dissented from their plans.

Facing these plans are two kinds of thinking. There is a trend toward socialism, not dominant but strong and Azikiwe is in sympathy with this. It believes in raising capital as much as possible at home, and in borrowing from communist countries rather than from Britain or the United States. It does not welcome American Negroes unless they are thoroughly African in sympathy and suspicious of the West.

There is, however, a third force which must be watched: that is the ancient faith in communal family and clan. This method of protecting the masses is distinctly socialist. In the past no member of the tribe need go hungry while any had food. Widows married the dead man's brother. Orphans were adopted in the family. Capital was raised by the tribe and profits belonged to the tribe. Land could not be sold and all had land to use. Trade was carried on by small distributors, chiefly women, in vast markets where the consumer came in direct contact with producer.

These old folkways and this economic organization have changed by the breaking up of families, by some rise of mass industry and the growth of cities. A new and pushing bourgeoisie is gaining power and foreigners with capital are widely in evidence. British, Swiss and Lebanese corporations do large business and in America lately there are 12 organizations which profess great interest in Africa or knowledge of it. They are called variously "American Committee on Africa," "African Studies Association," "African-American Institute," "Society of African Culture," "African Defense Aid," etc. They are mainly financed by the government or by big business.

These organizations and other persons almost without exception dub any return to African communalism as "communism" and sternly warn Africans against it. This does not please men like Azikiwe or the Federal Prime Minister. While Britain advises Nigeria to advance by installing private capitalism and individual initiative, a growing number of educated Nigerians are beginning to ask if their country cannot step directly from communalism to socialism and avoid the catastrophe of modern private capitalism. The investors and the native bourgeois are still in the lead but the race is not to the swift.

This puts a hard strain on Northern Nigeria. Here is the

stronghold of hereditary power, restrained by ancient custom and the domination of women and now pushed by the demands of democracy. The chiefs are yielding by accepting election as local councilors, but the House of Chiefs is still of great influence and the Sultans and Emirs will long rank as more than ordinary citizens. They are yielding in hospitals and schools but how far will they yield in trade and industry? It was an inspiration to see the University College at Ibadan and the new University at Enugu, built by the joint effort of Nigerian and British but now turned over to black administration.

Lagos and lower Nigeria were always centers of town life. I rode through Ibadan, a city of a million inhabitants. There the bourgeois merchant and civil servant are powerful but so also is the consumers' market. At Onitsha I saw one of the largest markets in Africa, selling cotton and velvet, dishes and tools, food and drink and all manner of materials stretched over acres, dominated by women and seething with activity.

We paid our respects before to the Asantahene in Kumasi, and now to the Obi of Onitsha in Nigeria, a mild man of dignity and education before whom thousands still prostrate themselves. We rode by the throngs at the palace of the Aleko of Abeokuta. Such kings have reigned longer than any European dynasty and they feel it. But they despise the rule of the mob and the assumption of the tinker and the shopkeeper. Here they draw close to British aristocracy and British aristocracy cultivates them almost obsequiously. At the State Ball of the new black Governor, British ladies (and not barmaids) sat with and danced in the arms of robed and crowned black Emirs. How will democracy fare in this fight?

On the other hand where lie the interests of the Western world?

There are in the world today at least 25 giant corporations which are international empires and interlocked centers of vast wealth and power. British Unilever alone has a billion dollars in capital and a new annual income of more than a quarter of a billion and trade in every corner of the Western and colonial worlds. These corporations control armies, navies and nuclear weapons, screen news and direct public opinion, and make the laws which curb or let them. They rule Western Europe and all America. They have lost most of Asia but they are now set to dominate Africa. Nigeria has its own 40,000,000 and is tied by blood and custom to at least 60,000,000 other blacks in the Sudan, Uganda, Kenya and other regions.

If Western capital can put into world industry and commerce this cheap black labor working on rare raw materials, it can by modern methods leave in the hands of capitalists as profit incalculable power to control mankind. On the other hand, if this profit can be kept in the hands of the workers, socialism can triumph tomorrow in a world devoid of poverty, ignorance and unnecessary disease.

AMERICAN NEGROES AND AFRICA'S RISE TO FREEDOM

February 13, 1961

In the United States in 1960 there were some 17,000,000 persons of African descent. In the 18th century they had regarded Africa as their home to which they would eventually return when free. They named their institutions "African" and started migration to Africa as early as 1815. But the American Negroes were soon sadly disillusioned: first their immigrants to Liberia found that Africans did not regard them as Africans; and then it became clear by 1830 that colonization schemes were a device to rid America of free Africans so as to fasten slavery more firmly to support the cotton kingdom.

Negroes therefore slowly turned to a new ideal: to strive for equality as American citizens, determined that when Africa needed them they would be equipped to lead them into civilization. Meantime, however, American Negroes learned from their environment to think less and less of their fatherland and its folk. They learned little of its history or its present conditions. They began to despise the colored races along with white Americans and to acquiesce in color prejudice.

From 1825 to 1860 the American Negro went through hell. He yelled in desperation as the slave power tried to make the whole union a slave nation and then to extend its power over the West Indies; he became the backbone of the Abolition movement; he led thousands of fugitives to freedom; he died with John Brown and made the North victorious in the Civil

War. For a few years he led democracy in the South until a new and powerful capitalism disfranchised him by 1876.

Meantime a great change was sweeping the earth. Socialism was spreading; first in theory and experiment for a half century and then at last in 1917 in Russia where a communist state was founded. The world was startled and frightened. The United States joined 16 other nations to prevent this experiment which all wise men said would fail miserably in a short time. But it did not fail. It defended its right to try a new life, and staggering on slowly but surely began to prove to all who would look that communism could exist and prosper.

What effect did this have on American Negroes? By this time their leaders had become patriotic Americans, imitating white Americans almost without criticism. If Americans said that communism had failed, then it had failed. And this of course Americans did say and repeat. Big business declared communism a crime and communists and socialists criminals. Some Americans and some Negroes did not believe this; but they lost employment or went to jail.

Meantime, many thoughtful white Americans, fearing the advance of socialism and communism not only in Europe but in America under the "New Deal," conceived a new tack. They said the American color line cannot be held in the face of communism. It is quite possible that we can help beat communism if in America we begin to loosen if not break the color line.

The movement started and culminated in a Supreme Court decision which was a body blow to color discrimination, and certainly if enforced would take the wind out of the sails of critics of American democracy.

To the Negroes the government said, it will be a fine thing now if you tell foreigners that our Negro problem is settled; and in such case we can help with your expenses of travel. A remarkable number of Negroes of education and standing found themselves able to travel and testify that American Negroes now had no complaints.

Then came three disturbing facts: (1) The Soviet Union was forging ahead in education and science and it drew no color line. (2) Outside the Soviet Union, in England, France and all West Europe, especially Scandinavia, socialism was spreading: state housing, state ownership of railroads, telegraphs and telephones, subways, buses and other public facilities; social medicine, higher education, old age care, insurance and many other sorts of relief; even in the United States, the New Deal was socialism no matter what it was called. (3) The former slave South had no intention of obeying the Supreme Court. To the Bourbon South it was said: don't worry, the law will not be enforced for a decade if not a century. Most Negroes still cannot vote, their schools are poor and the black workers are exploited, diseased and at the bottom of the economic pile. Trade unions north as well as south still discriminate against black labor. But finally a new and astonishing event was the sudden rise of Africa.

My own study had for a long time turned toward Africa. I planned a series of charts in 1900 for the Paris Exposition, which gained a Grand Prize. I attended a Pan-African conference in London and was made secretary of the meeting and drafted its resolutions.

In 1911 the Ethical Culture Societies of the world called a races congress in London and made Felix Adler and me secretaries for America. In 1915 I published my first book on African history and there was much interest and discussion. In 1919 I planned a Pan-African Congress, but got little support. Blaise Diagne of Senegal, whose volunteers had saved France from the first onslaught of the Germans in World War I, induced Clemenceau to allow the Congress despite the opposition of the United States and Britain. It was a small meeting, but it aroused a West African Congress the next year which was the beginning of independence for Ghana and Nigeria.

In 1921 I called a second Pan-African Congress to meet in London, Paris and Brussels. This proved a large and influential meeting, with delegates from the whole Negro world. The wide publicity it gained led to the organization of congresses in many parts of Africa by the natives. Our attempt to form a permanent organization located in Paris was betrayed but I succeeded in assembling a small meeting in London and Lisbon in 1923. I tried a fourth congress in Tunis but France forbade it. At last in 1927 I called the Fourth Pan-African Congress in New York. It was fairly well attended by American Negroes but by few Africans. Then the Second World War approached and the work was interrupted.

Meanwhile methods changed and ideas expanded. Africans themselves began to demand more voice in colonial government and the Second World War had made their cooperation so necessary to Europe that at the end actual and unexpected freedom for African colonies was in sight.

Moreover there miraculously appeared Africans able to take charge of these governments. American Negroes of former generations had always calculated that when Africa was ready for freedom, American Negroes would be ready to lead them. But the event was quite opposite. The African leaders proved to be Africans, some indeed educated in the United States, but most of them trained in Europe and in Africa itself. American Negroes for the most part showed neither the education nor the aptitude for the magnificent opportunity which was suddenly offered. Indeed, it now seems that Africans may have to show American Negroes the way to freedom.

The rise of Africa in the last 15 years has astonished the world. Even the most doubting of American Negroes have suddenly become aware of Africa and its possibilities and particularly of the relation of Africa to the American Negro. The first reaction was typically American. Since 1910 American Negroes had been fighting for equal opportunity in the United States. Indeed, Negroes soon faced a curious paradox.

Now equality began to be offered; but in return for equality, Negroes must join American business in its domination of African cheap labor and free raw materials. The educated and well-to-do Negroes would have a better chance to make money if they would testify that Negroes were not discriminated against and join in American red-baiting.

American Negroes began to appear in Africa, seeking chances to make money and testifying to Negro progress. In many cases their expenses were paid by the State Department. Meantime Negro American colleges ceased to teach socialism and the Negro masses believed with the white masses that communism is a crime and all socialists conspirators.

Africans know better. They have not yet all made up their minds what side to take in the power contest between East and West but they recognize the accomplishments of the Soviet Union and the rise of China.

Meantime American Negroes in their segregated schools and with lack of leadership have no idea of this world trend. The effort to give them equality has been overemphasized and some of our best scholars and civil servants have been bribed by the

State Department to testify abroad and especially in Africa to the success of capitalism in making the American Negro free. Yet it was British capitalism which made the African slave trade the greatest commercial venture in the world; and it was American slavery that raised capitalism to its domination in the 19th century and gave birth to the Sugar Empire and the Cotton Kingdom. It was new capitalism which nullified Abolition and keeps us in serfdom.

The Africans know this. They have in many cases lived in America. They have in other cases been educated in the Soviet Union and even in China. They will make up their own minds on communism and not listen solely to American lies. The latest voice to reach them is from Cuba.

Would it not be wise for American Negroes themselves to read a few books and do a little thinking for themselves? It is not that I would persuade Negroes to become communists, capitalists or holy rollers; but whatever belief they reach, let it for God's sake be a matter of reason and not of ignorance, fear, and selling their souls to the devil.

A LOGICAL PROGRAM FOR A FREE CONGO

May 15, 1961

The Congo is a mighty valley which is—without its artificial political boundaries—half the size of the United States outside Alaska. It is rich in known and undeveloped resources: copper, gold, silver, industrial diamonds, uranium and many other metals. It has vast forests of hardwoods, and palms of all sorts. Its elephants furnish ivory, its people grow fruits, fibers and vegetable oils. There is unbounded water power from nearly 3,000 miles of the vast and curving Congo and its tributaries.

For this wealth and for the cheap labor of its 15,000,000 of peoples, the Western world today is staging one of its greatest and most ruthless battles. Corporate industry today is making a last and desperate stand to control Africa. It is not merely little Belgium or Tshombe of Katanga; it is the organized wealth of North America, the British Commonwealth, France, West Germany, Switzerland and Italy. The West still believes that it can buy the world with money, own it and live on it in ease and luxury. To this end, the citizens of the United States alone are spending $50,000,000,000 a year and more.

Because of the increased and world-wide use of electricity which demands copper for transmission, because of the use of ivory in modern art and industry and because of the increasing use of atomic energy, the Congo has become a center of African development, and the reason for the desperate determination of America and Western Europe to control this part of Africa.

The Congo valley is not, as currently painted, a nest of howling savages with a few half-educated leaders filled with crazy and impossible ambitions. The history of this territory today is confused, disjointed and deliberately misinterpreted. But history there is, and it must be studied and understood.

All this story cannot yet be united into one continuous and scientifically provable history, but there are parts of it well known and of great fascination. The culture of the Bushongo, who were part of the Ba-Luba family, is noteworthy. The Luba-lunda people founded Katanga and other states, and in the 16th century came the larger and more ambitious realm of the Mwata Yanvo.

The last of the 14 rulers of this line was a feudal lord of about 300 chiefs, who paid him tribute in ivory, skins, corn, cloth and salt. This included about 100,000 square miles and 2,000,000 or more inhabitants. The use of the loom in Africa reached the coast after its use inland had become general. Velvets, brocades, satins, taffetas and damasks were imported to Congo by those great traders, the Bateke.

During the last 20 centuries the Congo saw a series of cultural developments which rose, spread and fell before the oncoming Bantu of the north, or the western rush of the Zeng of Zanzibar, and, perhaps, because of the northern march of the empire of the Monomotapa. There arose the manufacture of brocades and velvets, iron-making spread, and work in copper and bronze. The art of West Africa spread through parts of the Valley and the extraordinary political organization of the Bushongo—with its organization of government with representatives of arts and crafts, where every chief represented not only a territory but an industry.

Then, with the imperial expansion of the Sudan southward and the westward growth of Atlantis came the thousand-year march of the Bantu from the Sahara to the Cape. Across all this struck the slave trade, from Africa to America, for 100 fatal years; and on that rose the Industrial Revolution. Europe seized Africa; France in the north; Britain in the east and south; and Germany, at long last forcing herself into east, south and west Africa; and, finally, Leopold of Belgium, slipping craftily in between the rivalries of France, Britain and Germany, helped by an American explorer, Henry M. Stanley, organized the so-called Congo Free State. The great powers allowed him to proceed, though curbing his boundaries, each planning eventual seizure.

But Leopold was crafty. He called religion and trade to his aid and flamboyantly announced a great development of the African peoples. The Congo Free State, however, instead of becoming a center of civilization and religion, sank to such cruelty and exploitation that the world screamed in protest. Leopold was forced to surrender control of the Congo to the State of Belgium.

Once I talked with Vandervelde, a Socialist Minister of Belgium, concerning the future of the Congo. He planned much and tried hard, but the industry which Leopold had begun in the Congo was now in the hands of great corporations owned by Britain, France, Germany, Switzerland and the United States. Despite Socialist plans, they seized the land, exploited the labor and began to make huge profit from ivory, copper, diamonds and uranium.

They planned to avoid the mistakes of France and Britain in developing a class of educated natives who might aspire to share rule with the colonial power. On the other hand, they tried to appease the native. They left much home rule in the hands of recognized tribal chiefs paid by the State. They gave skilled work and wages larger than customary to an increasing group of workers. They allowed the Catholic Church and a few Protestant sects to give primary education to numbers of children. But they kept the natives from attending Belgian higher schools or establishing such schools in the Congo.

For a time this seemed an ideal plan. Peace reigned and profits soared. In the end the plan failed and somewhat suddenly. Instead of Negro ambition being confined and drained off slowly into an intelligentsia such as both France and Britain had produced, the Congolese movement swelled within almost silently and then suddenly burst into a demand for complete independence—a demand led by young men like Patrice Lumumba. The demand was so unexpected that the Belgians were at first at a loss as to how to meet it.

Then they turned swiftly. They planned a small introduction of higher learning to supply the Congolese with the professional help which they so desperately needed, physicians, dentists, social workers, and even lawyers. On the industrial side they encouraged a Congolese bourgeoisie, skilled workers, and even managers, who would be paid enough to join the Belgians in exploiting the masses. Thus arose Kasavubu and Tshombe.

Notwithstanding their efforts the Belgians could not win the battle. A young man, Patrice Lumumba, led a movement for a Congo State completely independent of Belgium. He had a fair education although never allowed to attend an institution of higher learning. But he was honest and sincere and had an increasing following. The Belgians first attacked him as all colonial powers attack native leaders. He was accused of dishonesty in his position in the Post Office. He was sent to jail, just as all colonials have been like Nehru, Ghandhi, Nkrumah and Macauley. Later he was even accused of debauchery and drug taking.

These were all lies, just as other Western tales about Soviet women and Chinese workers. My wife has seen and heard and talked with Lumumba. I have seen him. He was a clean and frank young man, nervous, excitable, but no criminal, no drunkard. The Belgians saw that they could not keep him from gaining a majority of the new Congolese parliament and so they maneuvered to have Kasavubu, a man whom they could control, made president, with Lumumba's consent, so long as Lumumba was Prime Minister. By all rules of modern politics the executive power of the country lay in Lumumba's hands while the majority of parliament supported him. But Kasavuba, after being made an officer in the Belgian army, usurped power and dismissed Lumumba without a parliamentary vote.

In addition to this, a further and more desperate effort was resorted to. Katanga, in southeast Congo, bordering the Rhodesias and Portuguese Angola, was rising to fantastic prosperity through the mining and sale of copper. The profits to Europeans and North America in 1960 were the largest in the history of the Congo. The need of this colonial foundation to support Western industry was greater than ever; and it was not difficult to bribe a black man to throw in his efforts with the Belgians and their allies.

Tshombe was the son of a bourgeois Congolese. In the All-African Congress held in Accra in 1958 he had pledged himself to work for African independence. But, on the other hand, he had seen what European industry and wealth could mean. The Belgians had flattered him and pushed him forward, and he conceived that the independence of Katanga from the rest of the Congo would mean the rise of black men like himself. He therefore led a movement of secession to take the prosperous and industrial Katanga out of the new, black, independent state. This was just what Western Europe and North America wanted: fragmentation of this vast center of cheap labor and valuable material.

But this plan could not be realized so long as Lumumba held a majority in parliament. The conspirators did not dare to reassemble parliament and they silently agreed upon a bloody and revolting deed which curiously illustrates the difference between what we call "backward" and "modern" civilization. To Congolese of the Tshombe type, evil is done away with by a direct, decisive blow. The West does the same thing but pauses in the execution, so as to avoid or postpone criticism. They use hypocrisy and deceit. The West was going to displace Lumumba, but by imprisonment or deportation or "accident," simply by denying him protection. Tshombe, or his men, on the other hand, murdered him in cold blood. The West then hastened to cash in on the new Madagascar which had just slipped out of colonial hell. They got together a hurried meeting. But the world shuddered at murder and hesitated. The Belgian ministry fell. The British Commonwealth split. The United States gagged.

Here, then, we stand today, and the chief object of our periodicals and literary writers, of our industrial leaders and great corporations, is to make America believe that African freedom depends upon the transforming of the Congo Republic into a series of small, antagonistic states whose chief function is to furnish profits for Western capitalism.

A logical program for an independent Congo State is clear. Let the people of the Congo recede from catering almost solely to the wants of the Western world and begin working for their own simple needs. Let them decrease the amount of copper mined and of uranium exported. The copper will not spoil if it lies longer in the ground. The present need for atomic energy does not call for continued Congo effort.

The people of the Congo should till the soil, raise the food they need, the fiber they wear and material for their homes. To do this effectively they need education, especially in agriculture. A wide and desperate effort to educate the people of the Congo should be started. They must learn to read, write and count; and also they must have nurses, physicians and dentists, and above all, teachers, but not flunkies screened by the FBI.

Much of this education they can do for themselves; help can be obtained from neighboring African states, and the money which the West is furnishing for investment and bombs could be loaned the Congo for schools. Ancient African barter can be restored in the marketplace; simple industry for local needs can be established with modern methods. Trade with their African neighbors can increase and also such European trade as the Congo needs, and not solely for Western profit. In this way a united people could become self-supporting, intelligent and healthy, and take their place among the nations of the world.

On June 4, 1957, Du Bois was interviewed on Channel 5 in New York City by Al Morgan. The following is a transcript of that interview.

INTERVIEW WITH DR. W.E.B. DU BOIS

MORGAN: Our first guest is William Edward Burghardt Du Bois. An economical biographer would say: He was born in Massachusetts 89 years ago of a family that had been in this country since the seventeenth century. Educated at Harvard, his research and writing about the Negro people have brought him acclaim as a distinguished historian, and his international crusade for world peace through such devices as the Stockholm Peace Appeal and the Peace Information Center. These have earned him the censure of many Americans, who have branded him a fellow-traveller. Other high points of Dr. Du Bois' resume include helping to organize the NAACP in 1909, editing its magazine *The Crisis* for more than twenty years, and running as the New York candidate of the American Labor Party for the United States Senate in 1950, polling a quarter of a million votes. Among his recent works are *Black Reconstruction in America,* just re-issued by Russell Publishers which the *New York Times* called the most painstakingly thorough study ever made on the subject, and this novel, *The Ordeal of Mansart,* the first of a trilogy he is now writing.

First of all, Dr. Du Bois, let's turn to your most current controversy. Though you have made at least fourteen trips abroad during your life, the passport office at Washington, D. C., told us this afternoon that ever since 1952 you have not been granted a passport. They say that this is due to your refusal to fill out an application blank and all the questions contained in all passport requests. Those questions read: "Are you now a member of the Communist Party? Have you ever been a member? If so, state the period of your membership." Why did you refuse to sign this blank?

DU BOIS: I refused to sign that as a matter of principle. I am not a member of the Communist Party but I think that the government has no right to ask a person to say anything about his religious views or his political views, that that is an invasion of his private life. Moreover, the passport division refused me a passport before they had this question on the application at all. I wanted to go to the Peace Conference at Montevideo and they refused it because they said they didn't think that my trip there would be to the best interests of the United States. The next time that I applied again, the Communist matter wasn't on the application, and they simply waited a long time and before they got through waiting this statement appeared on the application.

MORGAN: But you refuse to answer it now on the basis of principle?

DU BOIS: On the basis of principle.

MORGAN: Dr. Du Bois, you say you are not a Communist. How would you describe yourself? Are you a Socialist, a conservative?

DU BOIS: I am certainly not a conservative. I should call myself a Socialist, although that isn't a very definite term. But

I mean I believe in the welfare state. I believe that business should be carried on not for private profit but for public welfare. I believe in many of the steps which are usually associated with socialism.

MORGAN: On page 163 of your book which was published six years ago, *In Battle for Peace,* you speak of Soviet Russia in this fashion: "I regard that land as today the most hopeful nation on earth." That was six years ago. Do you still feel that way, Doctor?

DU BOIS: I still feel that way.

MORGAN: Does Russia come closest to the kind of socialism you subscribe to?

DU BOIS: I think it does. Russia and China.

MORGAN: Last Sunday, Nikita Khrushschev in his CBS interview predicted that the United States of America would be a socialist state within two generations. Do you agree with that?

DU BOIS: I don't know about the two generations, but certainly the United States will become a socialist state. There is nothing else for it to become. We can't go on becoming a state which is ruled by business for businessmen and for private profit. We have already taken many steps toward socialism. We will take more. Eventually we shall come to be a Communist state. But how long that is going to take, I don't pretend to say.

MORGAN: How will that come about?

DU BOIS: It will come about by the increase of socialism, by the change in our attitude toward each other, by making an individual American think of the progress of America and the welfare of America rather than thinking of his own advantage over his fellows, by ceasing to make the butt of our jokes the person who has suffered injury, by doing away with what the Germans call schadenfreude, by the extension of sacrifice and of love and of sympathy for our fellow beings.

MORGAN: Now you are talking philosophically, Dr. Du Bois. I would like to have your answer specifically. Will it come about through violence and force, or democratically, or through elections—exactly how?

DU BOIS: I think it will come about democratically, not by violence. There was a time when I thought that the only way in which progress could be made in the world was by violence. I thought that the only way that the darker people were going to get recognition was by killing a large number of white people.

But I think that most of us are beginning to realize that that is not true, that the violence that accompanies revolution is not the revolution. The revolution is the reform, is the change of thought, is the change of attitude on the people who are affected by it.

MORGAN: All right, Dr. Du Bois, let's turn to Russia. I have read your writing and much of it praises the Russian system. But before we move on to what you consider to be its virtues, I'd like to ask you what major criticisms, if any, you have of Russia today.

DU BOIS: Well, the criticism would be of the difficulty of carrying out a welfare state on so large a scale, the number of bureaucrats, the power that must be put in their hands. But I think that that is a difficulty which occurs in every state. In every state which is making progress there is always the difficulty of saying how much freedom the individual can have in consonance with the best interests of the state. I think that when you consider what Russia was before the twentieth century, that the progress which the people have made there since has been simply phenomenal, and that that is the thing that brings my great admiration. I don't want you to think I pretend that I am a specialist on Russia. After all, Russia is a very large country. I have seen only parts of it. I have been there three times—in 1926, in 1936, and in 1949. Enough to make comparisons, but I haven't been all over the country and I do not speak Russian. So that it might be that if I knew more than I do today I would change my conclusions. But from what I have seen and what I have read, I think my conclusion stands as it did six years ago, and it's the most hopeful country on earth.

MORGAN: Well, let me take you back to last October. The Hungarian Republic was over-run by Soviet tanks and guns in an obviously unfair battle which has been called in less polite terms a bloodbath. Do you approve of Russia's action?

DU BOIS: I do not know just what Russia's action was. I do know that the United States of America gave the Hungarians every reason to think that if they started a revolution that they were going to get help. They spent a great deal of money on it, and they spent a good deal of time. In addition to that, there are a great many business interests of the United States who had investments in Hungary and who expected to have more investments if they could change the form of government. Now, whether the Russian intervention was an intervention that was called for by the mass of the Hungarian people or whether it was intervention that was not called for, that I do not know. I am not an expert on Hungary although I have seen it twice.

MORGAN: Well, Milovan Djilas, the deposed Yugoslav Vice-President, now imprisoned by Tito, wrote in the *New Leader* magazine for November 19 last year: "The world has rarely witnessed such unprecedented unity of the popular masses. The heroic intoxication was so high that bare-handed boys and girls were stopping the tanks of the interventionists, who like the Cossacks of Nicholas I of 1848 tried to suppress their liberty and enslave their country." And almost every observer who has reported on the Hungarian uprising, almost every single newspaper and wire service carrying the story here, has corrobated that belief, that the revolt was carried out by the unity of the masses, not merely by a faction of white-collar workers. Do you agree with that?

DU BOIS: I do not. I do not believe those reports, and those are not the only reports that have come from Hungary. We have a situation here in the United States that when we get news of foreign countries we get the kind of news that certain persons in authority want us to have.

MORGAN: In all the papers, Dr. Du Bois?

DU BOIS: Oh, I would not say all the papers. I did not see all the papers and I don't suppose that many people did see all of the papers. Nevertheless, in spite of reports of that sort, I have seen reports of another sort. I do not believe that that first quotation which you read was a quotation which showed just what was happening in Hungary.

MORGAN: Do you think that the newspapers in America for the most part report foreign affairs truthfully? Do you think we are getting a full picture of what is happening in the world?

DU BOIS: No, I certainly do not.

MORGAN: There are something like ten thousand newspapers in America. There are 9,000 magazines. There are 3,000 radio stations. What do you think the percentage is of those that are telling the whole story?

DU BOIS: I don't know. I couldn't attempt to say. But let me tell you one experience that I had. When I first went to Russia in 1926, I landed at Kronstadt, which was a dead city with weeds growing among the cobblestones, with only a few people, ragged and walking dejectedly through the streets, with only a few ships rotting in the harbor. I stayed there only about a day and then I went to Leningrad and about a week later I got to Moscow. When I got to Moscow I found a copy of the *New York Times* which had been published on the very day that I landed in Kronstadt. And the *New York Times* said that revolution had broken out in Kronstadt and the streets were flowing with blood.

MORGAN: You are saying then in this specific instance the *New York Times* slanted its news. Which paper do you read?

DU BOIS: I read the *New York Times.*

MORGAN: Why don't you, for instance, read the *Daily Worker?* Do you think the *Daily Worker* gives us a better picture of what is happening inside Soviet Russia today?

DU BOIS: Sometimes it does, but the *Daily Worker* hasn't the facilities to get at the news.

MORGAN: Let's talk about—excuse me, Dr. Du Bois—let's talk about the Russian press. You have by inference criticized the American press. What about the Russian press? How free is that and how much of the news in the Russian press is to be believed by somebody in Russia?

DU BOIS: I think that a good deal of it is to be believed. It is slanted, it is controlled, but take, for instance, one thing. We usually say that the American press is poisoning the Russian people with regard to the Americans, so that they are getting altogether a false idea. I think that anybody who goes to Russia will find out that the Russians are very well disposed to Americans there. They are not hating them. They don't believe that they have horns. They have continually something nice to say about them. The young man who was my interpreter when I was there in 1949 not only told me about his education and so forth but one of his ambitions was to come to the United States. He had a great admiration for many things, not for all things, but for many things in the United States. I didn't have the heart to tell him that he couldn't come here.

MORGAN: One final question on the whole newspaper situation. Let's go back again to the Hungarian revolt. You say we have not heard the full story of it, and yet tonight you are on a television program in the largest city in the world, in which you are able to say this. Do you think the same courtesy would be extended to somebody in Russia who held a viewpoint that was different from what was in the press and what was the government viewpoint?

DU BOIS: That depends. In some cases not and in other cases yes. In this specific case I think that recently the press in Russia has been a great deal freer. Remember, however, the situation that you had there at the beginning of the twentieth century when you had people who were perhaps 90 percent illiterate, were poor, were diseased, were superstitious, you were trying to bring that people up to a state where they could form a socialist government, and you had to do that by discipline. Now that discipline included being careful of the kind of news that you let them have, that you wanted to have. It included a great deal of curtailment of their liberty. The result, however, has shown itself in what the Russians are today, shown itself first in an extraordinary system of education. The city of New York has no such system of education as Moscow. Now that education has gone on, it has spread, until the people have demanded more liberties, and they are getting more liberties, and in the future as they become more intelligent and effective, they will get still more. I do not think that the Russian press today is as curtailed and one-sided as the American press, but I do know that of course it is curtailed.

MORGAN: A short question, Dr. Du Bois. Are you a religious person?

DU BOIS: That depends on what you call a religious person.

MORGAN: By your definition.

DU BOIS: I belong to no church.

MORGAN: You belong to no church?

DU BOIS: No.

MORGAN: All right. Let's turn to some other items in your resume. In 1948 you were dismissed by the National Association for the Advanced of Colored People, an organization you helped found back in 1909. How come the firing?

DU BOIS: It came, I think, from a misunderstanding on both sides. At the age of 75, after I had served the NAACP and Atlanta University for long periods, I was retired for age. The NAACP suggested that I come back to them. At first I did not pay much attention to it and then at last I met at their invitation with a number of their officers. They wanted me to come back. They didn't want to limit what I was going to do. They said they wanted me to do what I pleased, but to come back at a reasonable salary and be on their staff. Now I think that what they meant there was that they wanted to afford me an easy approach to death and they probably thought that there wasn't much more that I could do or wanted to do. Now I, on the other hand, misunderstood that as meaning that they wanted me to do what work I could and I started in, perhaps rather impatiently, to do a whole lot of things. I wrote two or three books. I wrote columns in newspapers. I lectured at universities. I wrote the Appeal to the United Nations and pretty soon I was getting into con—well, controversy—with the secretary. Now since I had been away from there ten years that organization had grown and it had become tightly organized. I don't think I realized then how tight the organization is and perhaps has to be in associations like that.

MORGAN: Dr. Du Bois, I am sorry to cut you off, but I would like to read you this. Do you know Mr. Henry Lee Moon, the public relations director of the NAACP? I assume you do.

DU BOIS: Yes.

MORGAN: We talked with Mr. Moon today. I break in because I think maybe we can get the information you were giving us in your reaction to this. This is what he told us today. He said: "Dr. Du Bois was a tremendous influence on the Negroes of my generation. His generation was during the thirties and early forties. He truly inspired us and nurtured all that had intellectual aspirations. He held our banner aloft. Most of us still have great reverence for him. But we feel that he in recent years has departed from his original position, and is pursuing a path that we of the NAACP do not choose to follow. Very, very few of us go along with him today." What is your reaction to that?

DU BOIS: I have no dispute with that at all. Of course, nobody has the same outlook on life and the development of the world today that they had in the thirties. We have had tremendous changes. But I think it would be unfair to say that the controversy concerning me in the NAACP had anything to do directly with my different views. It was rather the matter of whether the NAACP was going to have any hand in the development of Africa. I had come back with the idea that we were going to carry on the work that I had been doing, with regard to the Pan-African Congresses, and I held one Congress after I came back there. But many people in the NAACP said that we had enough trouble in the United States without seeking troubles and problems in Africa and they didn't want that part to go on. So that I think was the basic difference. I don't think that the difference concerning my political outlook came up until after I was dismissed.

MORGAN: In our final minutes, sir, I'd like to turn from William Du Bois the historian to find out about William Du Bois the apparently sprightly octogenarian. As the question that is always asked of elderly people, sir, what is the secret of your long and obviously healthy life?

DU BOIS: Well, as I told a number of interviewers not long ago, first it is care with regard to your grandfathers, and then, secondly, it is getting enough sleep.

MORGAN: Do you smoke or drink, sir? Any vices?

DU BOIS: I think I average three cigarettes a day, and I have a jigger of whiskey usually every night before I go to bed.

MORGAN: And how is your appetite?

DU BOIS: Fairly good, although my wife complains about it.

MORGAN: One final question, sir. If you were writing your epitaph, and I sincerely hope you won't be, what would you set down?

DU BOIS: Well, the thing that I would want to be remembered for would be my writing and my teaching. I have liked teaching. I left the NAACP to go back to teaching and then found as I had found before, that it wasn't quite as ideal a job as I wanted. Then I have always wanted to express myself in writing. We began with the school paper which was gotten out by hand in the high school in 1883 and it has ended with the trilogy which you brought attention to. I have tried to write with some success. I have tried to teach.

MORGAN: Thank you very much, Dr. Du Bois, for spending this half hour with us. Whatever else may be said of William Du Bois' philosophies, it is only when his views cannot be aired, only when they are denied utterance because they are unpopular views, only when there is silence and solemn agreement, does this country then stand in danger.

The following is the text of Du Bois' remarks at his 90th birthday celebration held at the Roosevelt Hotel and attended by some 2,000 people.

NINETIETH BIRTHDAY SPEECH

March 2, 1958

The most distinguished guest on this festive occasion is none other than my great-grandson, Arthur Edward McFarlane II, who was born this last Christmas day. He has kindly consented to permit me to read to you a bit of advice, which, as he remarked with a sigh of resignation, great-grandparents are supposed usually to inflict on the helpless young.

This then is my word of advice. As men go, I have had a reasonably happy and successful life. I have had enough to eat and drink, have been suitably clothed, and, as you see, have many friends. But the thing which has been the secret of whatever I have done is the fact that I have been able to earn a living by doing the work which I wanted to do and work which the world needed. I want to stress this. You will soon learn, my dear young man, that most human beings spend their lives doing work which they hate and work which the world does not need. It is therefore of prime importance that you early learn what you want to do, what you can do, and whether or not the world needs this service.

Here in the next twenty years your parents can be of use to you. You will soon begin to wonder just what parents are for, beside interfering with your natural wishes. Let me therefore tell you: parents and their parents are inflicted upon you in order to show you what kind of a person you are, what sort of world you live in, and what the persons who dwell here need for their happiness and well-being.

It was my unusual good fortune in the first twenty-five years of my life, to learn by effort and hard competition who I was; what I wanted to do; what the world needed done; and what part of this I could do. In those years I had seen the United States, North and South; I had lived in England, Holland, France, Germany, and Italy; I had listened to the advice of some of the world's greatest minds and I had heard from the lips of human beings just what their problems were. Beside this I had seen the Atlantic Ocean, the high Alps at Berne, the Venus of Milo and the Sistine Madonna. I had heard the Ninth Symphony and the shriek of the Valkyrs. Then I came home prepared and willing to work.

It was then, in the summer of 1892, sixty-six years ago, that I made a quite unconscious choice. I chose to begin my life work for the satisfaction of doing it and the need of its being done, and not for the money I was going to be paid for doing it. This was no great and advertised occasion; I asked no advice and none was proffered. Yet I chose without hesitancy or question. It was in this wise: after borrowing money to pay for postage stamps, I wrote around the nation and offered my services. The response was slow and unenthusiastic. But at last three offers came. Wilberforce University in Ohio offered me $750 a year as a teacher. Tuskegee Institute asked me what I would charge to teach there; and a state school in Missouri offered me $1,050. I utterly ignored the extra $300 offered by Missouri. I went to Wilberforce not because of any martyr complex, but because I knew something about Wilberforce. I knew that in 1787, eleven years after the nation had declared "that all men are created equal," two black men were on their knees praying to God in the Church of St. George's in Philadelphia. While St. George's was glad to see Negroes practice the true religion, it did not like them to clutter up the aisles of this fashionable church and to assail God with such vehemence. Two deacons therefore approached these black men and whispered gently that it would be more seemly if they would finish their prayers in the balcony. The balcony was much nearer heaven than the main floor. But these Negroes were stubborn. They said: "No, we are going to finish our prayers right here and now. Then we are going to get up and leave this church and we are never coming back." So one of these men, Richard Allen, left the white Methodist church and founded the African Methodist Episcopal Church which today is one of the largest Negro organizations in the world. And one of Allen's successors, Bishop Daniel Payne, bought a site in Southern Ohio and founded a college called Wilberforce and Wilberforce in 1892 offered me a job of teaching which I hastened to accept because Wilberforce was near the center of the Negro population of this nation and because I immediately planned to develop there a university like the University of Berlin for the uplift of the Negro race in America, a job which the world needed. Quite incidentally, Wilberforce offered me enough to live on during this work. The fact that Missouri offered me $300 more seemed to me then of no importance whatsoever.

Right here, my esteemed great-grandson, may I ask you to stick a pin. You will find it the fashion in the America where eventually you will live and work, to judge that life work by the amount of money it brings you. This is a grave mistake. The return from your work must be the satisfaction which that work brings you and the world's need of that work. With this, life is heaven or as near heaven as you can get. Without this—with work which you despise, which bores you, and which the world does not need—life is hell. And believe me, many a $25,000 a year executive is living in just such a hell today. Income is not greenbacks. It is satisfaction; it is creation; it is beauty; it is the supreme sense of a world of men going forward, lurch and stagger though it may, but slowly, inevitably, going forward, and you, yourself, standing with your hand on the wheels, make this choice. Then, my son, never hesitate, never falter.

And now comes a word of warning. This satisfaction, even at best, will never be complete, since nothing on earth can be perfect. The forward pace of the world which you are pushing will be painfully slow. Indeed, let's face it, it may for a day even fall backward. But what of that? The difference between a hundred and a thousand years is less than you now think. But doing what must be done, that is eternal, even when it walks with poverty and pain.

> And I care not to garner while others
> Know only to harvest and reap,
> For mine is the reaping of sowing,
> Till the spirit of rest gives me sleep.

His ninety-first birthday was celebrated in Peking. On that day he delivered a speech to the world over Peking radio.

MY TENTH DECADE

When in Peking, my 91st birthday was given national celebration. I pled for unity of China and Africa and my speech was broadcast to the world:

By courtesy of the government of the 600 million people of the Chinese Republic, I am permitted on my 91st birthday to speak to the people of China and Africa and through them to the world. Hail, then, and farewell, dwelling places of the yellow and black races. Hail human kind!

I speak with no authority; no assumption of age nor rank; I hold no position, I have no wealth. One thing alone I own and that is my own soul. Ownership of that I have even while in my own country for near a century I have been nothing but a "nigger." On this basis and this alone I dare speak, I dare advise.

China after long centuries has arisen to her feet and leapt forward. Africa, arise, and stand straight, speak and think! Act! Turn from the West and your slavery and humiliation for the last 500 years and face the rising sun.

Behold a people, the most populous nation on this ancient earth, which has burst its shackles, not by boasting and strutting, not by lying about its history and its conquests, but by patience and long suffering, by blind struggle, moved up and on toward the crimson sky. She aims to "make men holy; to make men free."

But what men? Not simply the mandarins but including mandarins; not simply the rich, but not excluding the rich. Not simply the learned, but led by knowledge to the end that no man shall be poor, nor sick, nor ignorant; but that the humblest worker as well as the sons of emperors shall be fed and taught and healed and that there emerge on earth a single unified people, free, well and educated.

You have been told, my Africa: My Africa in Africa and all your children's children overseas; you have been told and the telling so beaten into you by rods and whips, that you believe it yourselves, that this is impossible; that mankind can rise only by walking on men; by cheating them and killing them; that only on a doormat of the despised and dying, the dead and rotten, can a British aristocracy, a French cultural elite or an American millionaire be nurtured and grown.

This is a lie. It is an ancient lie spread by church and state, spread by priest and historian, and believed in by fools and cowards, as well as by the downtrodden and the children of despair.

Speak, China, and tell your truth to Africa and the world.

What people have been despised as you have? Who more than you have been rejected of men? Recall when lordly Britishers threw the rickshaw money on the ground to avoid touching a filthy hand. Forget not the time when in Shanghai no Chinese man dare set foot in a park which he paid for. Tell this to Africa, for today Africa stands on new feet, with new eyesight, with new brains and asks: Where am I and why?

The Western sirens answer: Britain wheedles; France cajoles; while America, my America, where my ancestors and descendants for eight generations have lived and toiled; America loudest of all, yells and promises freedom. If only Africa allows American investment!

Beware Africa, America bargains for your soul. America would have you believe that they freed your grandchildren; that Afro-Americans are full American citizens, treated like equals, paid fair wages as workers, promoted for desert and free to learn and travel across the world.

This is not true. Some are near freedom; some approach equality with whites; some have achieved education; but the price for this has too often been slavery of mind, distortion of truth and oppression of our own people.

Of 18 million Afro-Americans, 12 million are still second-class citizens of the United States, serfs in farming, low-paid laborers in industry, and repressed members of union labor. Most American Negroes do not vote. Even the rising six million are liable to insult and discrimination at any time.

But this, Africa, relates to your descendants, not to you. Once I thought of you Africans as children, whom we educated Afro-Americans would lead to liberty. I was wrong. We could not even lead ourselves, much less you. Today I see you rising under your own leadership, guided by your own brains.

Africa does not ask alms from China nor from the Soviet Union nor from France, Britain, nor the United States. It asks friendship and sympathy and no nation better than China can offer this to the Dark Continent. Let it be freely given and generously. Let Chinese visit Africa, send their scientists there and their artists and writers. Let Africa send its students to China and its seekers after knowledge. It will not find on earth a richer goal, a more promising mine of information.

On the other hand, watch the West. The new British West

Indian Federation is not a form of democratic progress but a cunning attempt to reduce these islands to the control of British and American investors. Haiti is dying under rich Haitian investors who with American money are enslaving the peasantry. Cuba is showing what the West Indies, Central and South America are suffering under American big business.

The American worker himself does not always realize this. He has high wages and many comforts. Rather than lose these, he keeps in office by his vote the servants of industrial exploitation so long as they maintain his wage. His labor leaders represent exploitation and not the fight against the exploitation of labor by private capital. These two sets of exploiters fall out only when one demands too large a share of the loot.

This China knows. This Africa must learn. This the American Negro has failed so far to learn. I am frightened by the so-called friends who are flocking to Africa. Negro Americans trying to make money from your toil, white Americans who seek by investment and high interest to bind you in serfdom to business as the Near East is bound and as South America is struggling with. For this America is tempting your leaders, bribing your young scholars, and arming your soldiers. What shall you do?

First, understand! Realize that the great mass of mankind is freeing itself from wage slavery, while private capital in Britain, France, and now in America, is still trying to maintain civilization and comfort for a few on the toil, disease and ignorance of the mass of men. Understand this, and understanding comes from direct knowledge. You know America and France, and Britain to your sorrow. Now know the Soviet Union, but particularly know China.

China is flesh of your flesh, and blood of your blood. China is colored and knows to what a colored skin in this modern world subjects its owner. But China knows more, much more than this: she knows what to do about it. She can take the insults of the United States and still hold her head high. She can make her own machines, when America refuses to sell her American manufactures, even though it hurts American industry, and throws her workers out of jobs. China does not need American nor British missionaries to teach her religion and scare her with tales of hell. China has been in hell too long, not to believe in a heaven of her own making. This she is doing.

Come to China, Africa, and look around. Invite Africa to come, China, and see what you can teach by just pointing. Yonder old woman is working on the street. But she is happy. She has no fear. Her children are in school and a good school. If she is ill, there is a hospital where she is cared for free of charge. She has a vacation with pay each year. She can die and be buried without taxing her family to make some undertaker rich.

Africa can answer: but some of this we have done; our tribes undertake public service like this. Very well, let your tribes continue and expand this work. What Africa must realize is what China knows; that it is worse than stupid to allow a people's education to be under the control of those who seek not the progress of the people but their use as means of making themselves rich and powerful. It is wrong for the University of London to control the University of Ghana. It is wrong for the Catholic church to direct the education of the black Congolese. It was wrong for Protestant churches supported by British and American wealth to control higher education in China.

The Soviet Union is surpassing the world in popular and higher education, because from the beginning it started its own complete educational system. The essence of the revolution in the Soviet Union and China and in all the "iron curtain" nations, is not the violence that accompanied the change; no more than starvation at Valley Forge was the essence of the American revolution against Britain. The real revolution is the acceptance on the part of the nation of the fact that hereafter the main object of the nation is the welfare of the mass of the people and not of the lucky few.

Government is for the people's progress and not for the comfort of an aristocracy. The object of industry is the welfare of the workers and not the wealth of the owners. The object of civilization is the cultural progress of the mass of workers and not merely of an intellectual elite. And in return for all this, communist lands believe that the cultivation of the mass of people will discover more talent and genius to serve the state than any closed aristocracy ever furnished. This belief the current history of the Soviet Union and China is proving true each day. Therefore don't let the West invest when you can avoid it. Don't buy capital from Britain, France and the United States if you can get it on reasonable terms from the Soviet Union and China. This is not politics; it is common sense. It is learning from experience. It is trusting your friends and watching your enemies. Refuse to be cajoled or to change your way of life, so as to make a few of your fellows rich at the expense of a mass of workers growing poor and sick and remaining without schools so that a few black men can have automobiles.

Africa, here is a real danger which you must avoid or return to the slavery from which you are emerging. All I ask from you is the courage to know; to look about you and see what is happening in this old and tired world; to realize the extent and depth of its rebirth and the promise which glows on your hills.

Visit the Soviet Union and visit China. Let your youth learn the Russian and Chinese languages. Stand together in this new world and let the old world perish in its greed or be born again in new hope and promise. Listen to the Hebrew prophet of communism:

Ho! every one that thirsteth; come ye to the waters; come, buy and eat, without money and price!

Again, China and Africa, hail and farewell!

MURDER AND DESTRUCTION FOR HUMAN PROGRESS

An Address at Rally for Peace and Disarmament, Toronto

February 7, 1960

From the beginning of time the chief occupation of human beings has been murdering each other and destroying the wealth which man has accumulated for his survival. This fact, while hidden by history and art so that most persons forget or deny it, has in our day become so clear and such an inescapable truth that we are at last compelled to admit that unless we give up war as our chief industry, human civilization will be set back hundreds of years or will end.

We have no reliable record of the world's wars. Since those

which are associated with the name of Napoleon there have been at least 300 wars, without including hundreds of minor and almost unknown conflicts. Ten of these were great wars, 50 were large conflicts, and 200 others were efforts to murder human beings and destroy property. Yet some of the great historians of our day call the hundred years from 1815 to 1914, the "hundred years of peace". They mean by this to distinguish between wars of Great European nations against each other and wars of Europeans against peoples of minor importance. This point of view I remember hearing Andrew Carnegie himself voice at one of the meetings of his peace organization. He was deploring the danger of war in Europe, but said the war in Turkey and the little wars in Africa and Asia were not the concern of his organization. This attitude is still widely prevalent and is a result of the war spirit which so dominates the world.

It lies beneath the assumption that most wars are wars of superior against inferior or wicked people whom we should despise or hate. From this point of view it is easy to conclude that any enemy is for that reason sub-human and despicable— "huns", "bolsheviks", "chinks", or "niggers". If they are not inferior in fact but simply people who disagree with us or who have been deceived, nevertheless we try by every means to make our citizens believe slanders which may be lies or at best misunderstandings. On such false bases probably most wars have been fought.

Wars in early days may have been isolated affairs, although the thought of the necessity of war must from earliest times have given rise to the feeling that brute force was widely necessary for progress. But it is certain today that practically all wars are interconnected and that current wars in Africa, Laos, Syria or Central America can all too easily cause the whole earth to be swept by a third world war.

This leads us to consider the actual causes of war. They arise from real or anticipated want of food and shelter; from defense against enemies, real or assumed; from desire of power to attack, for prestige or directing the thought or emotions of other peoples. All these causes call for investigation and proof, but seldom get them. Wars start on impulse, from lies, from fear. What man refuses so often to learn is what the real cause is or how far it is justified. Plunging blindly on, we repeat from year to year and century to century the same mistakes; and suffer the same results. We refuse to learn the truth or when we do learn, we do not teach this truth to our children so that they may avoid our errors. These results repeat themselves with horrible monotony; death of uncounted millions follows and not merely the death of the guilty, but of the innocent, the misled, the utterly mistaken. In addition to those who were actually striving for peace and justice. Such facts we often, almost usually, conceal.

I remember the one time when I saw war almost face to face. In 1918 just after the armistice, I was in France walking through the forest of the Argonne, where a battle had recently been fought. The worst results of that fearful slaughter had been removed. The corpses, the severed limbs, the ecstasy of pain. The human shrieks were stilled and the scenes of indescribable horror. But the signs of all this remained: the dried blood, the torn shoes, the shreds of uniform; I saw fire-arms, and blackened possessions; lost trinkets and twisted lead and iron. I knew too that a few miles over there soldiers were lying wearily in the sand to have their wounds healed and the lice and vermin picked out of their hair and off their skin.

I drove back the upsurge of tears and said to myself in determined joy: it is true that at least after this insane horror never again will war blast mankind, too many have seen too much. I was wrong.

In twenty little years the whole of mankind was gripped in the greatest war man ever knew. Even after that came other wars and rumors of war: until today we spend 100 times as much for war as for healing and education, and we face the threat of world-wide extermination. We do this even when we know well that most of the reality of war is concealed from us, and often by our own connivance. We refuse to contemplate what happens to women in war zones.

Why is one of the first acts of an invading army to erect whore houses and inspect soldiers for venereal disease? Why are prostitutes imported deliberately? Remember how Jane Addams was excoriated during the First World War when she revealed the well-known fact that soldiers were dosed with whiskey on the eve of battle?

Have any of you read that international report of how Korean women were treated and do you think that this was unusual? No. Drunkenness and gambling always have been twin sisters of war. Walk the streets of any modern city today and see the crippled and maimed; meet the insane, and visit if you dare, the jails and asylums. Do not deceive yourselves into thinking that disease and crime are not or have not always been the aftermath of war. What else can one expect of an era of murder, hate and dissipation inflicted on youth year after year and century after century? It is not a matter of nationality, or race or color; it is human nature and it keeps recurring. In my own country, after our revolutionary war, came crime and debauchery. After our war of 1812, came crime and debauchery. After our civil war came crime and debauchery. After our world wars came crime and debauchery, with some new names like juvenile delinquency.

Let us stop deceiving ourselves and refusing to face the truth. War must result in crime. You cannot teach murder and destruction to youth and reap unselfishness and high ideals. You cannot teach men to hate and expect them to love. Face then the question: is war ever necessary? Does it ever accomplish its avowed end? Can it be longer retained as a method of human progress? Once we ask this question and there comes the answer of despair: men say so long as human beings are as they are, so long we must be prepared to murder them and destroy their property. This conclusion by-passes the fundamental question of just how evil men need be, even the men we despise and hate. We hasten on to ask what laws and treaties can be had to make our enemies and our fellow-men worth living with. The answer must always be disappointing. It is not law that makes men do right but obedience to law; and obedience comes from wish and will and not from force and device. If the people of this world want to kill, maim and destroy, war is our inevitable and continuous future. But who believes this?

I have known the people of the Soviet Union for thirty-three years. I have watched them strive and stagger from starvation and bitter despair up to confidence and firm determination. Do they want war? They do not. I do not believe there is a nation on earth which wants war less. No modern people have suffered from war as they have. Nineteen million human lives they lost in the last war. Homes, schools, hospitals, factories and dreams perished between 1939 and 1945. They want no more war. They desperately want peace. Do the peoples of the Americas or of Britain, France, Spain or Italy want war? If the answer is no, as most of you answer, than all that is necessary is faith—faith in yourselves, faith in humanity, that faith in which for centuries you have declared unending belief. Right here you hesitate. Right here your faith fails. Right here you know there is something wrong with our thinking.

Who is it today that still wants war, even if they call it another name? Many of the world's great nations are still striving for something they do not call war but which is war. What is the colonial system, under which Great Britain came to rule the world, and set the example which France, Germany, Italy, Belgium and Holland followed? It was war of strong western people to control the land and cheap labor of eastern Europe, the Balkans, Asia, Africa, the sea isles and Central and South America. And even now as colonial peoples are gaining their freedom, what is the "foreign investment" to which the former imperial nations turn and which the United States leads in demanding? It is war conceived as taxation, and police power in countries too weak to resist, in order to make labor cheap and raw materials free. Let me remind you of 400 black miners lying dead in South Africa today. They worked like slaves at 75 cents a day in order to furnish gold and diamonds to London, Paris and New York. The copper output of Northern Rhodesia is worth $36,000,000 a year. Of this 17,000 black miners whose fathers once owned this land, got $37 a year each or $600,000; 1700 white artisans got $2,500,000, or $15,000 a year each and the right to vote. The balance over other costs of at least $20,-000,000 went to white investors in Europe and America. It is vast profit like this which makes west Europe and America support war and preparation for war under pretense of fearing communism and because of the real fear of losing profits in colonies and semi-colonies.

If you realize the threat of war today and if you want peace, and if you are convinced that the Soviet Union also wants peace, remember that the demand for continued war and preparation for war may rest on the consciences of big business which demands 75% profit on foreign investment. From them and not from socialists, demand peace, war no more.

LETTER OF APPLICATION FOR MEMBERSHIP IN THE COMMUNIST PARTY OF THE UNITED STATES

To Gus Hall,

Communist Party of the U.S.A.
New York, New York.

On this first day of October, 1961, I am applying for admission to membership in the Communist Party of the United States. I have been long and slow in coming to this conclusion, but at last my mind is settled.

In college I heard the name of Karl Marx, but read none of his works, nor heard them explained. At the University of Berlin, I heard much of those thinkers who had definitively answered the theories of Marx, but again we did not study what Marx himself had said. Nevertheless, I attended meetings of the Socialist Party and considered myself a Socialist.

On my return to America, I taught and studied for sixteen years. I explored the theory of Socialism and studied the organized social life of American Negroes; but still I neither read or heard much of Marxism. Then I came to New York as an official of the new NAACP and editor of the *Crisis Magazine.* The NAACP was capitalist orientated and expected support from rich philanthropists.

But it had a strong Socialist element in its leadership in persons like Mary Ovington, William English Walling and Charles Edward Russell. Following their advice, I joined the Socialist Party in 1911. I knew then nothing of practical Socialist politics and in the campaign of 1912, I found myself unwilling to vote the Socialist ticket, but advised Negroes to vote for Wilson. This was contrary to Socialist Party rules and consequently I resigned from the Socialist Party.

For the next twenty years I tried to develop a political way of life for myself and my people. I attacked the Democrats and Republicans for monopoly and disfranchisement of Negroes; I attacked the Socialists for trying to segregate Southern Negro members; I praised the racial attitudes of the Communists, but opposed their tactics in the case of the Scottsboro boys and their advocacy of a Negro state. At the same time I began to study Karl Marx and the Communists; I read *Das Kapital* and other

Communist literature; I hailed the Russian Revolution of 1917, but was puzzled at the contradictory news from Russia.

Finally in 1926, I began a new effort: I visited Communist lands. I went to the Soviet Union in 1926, 1936, 1949 and 1959; I saw the nation develop. I visited East Germany, Czechoslovakia and Poland. I spent ten weeks in China, traveling all over the land. Then, this summer, I rested a month in Rumania.

I was early convinced that Socialism was an excellent way of life, but I thought it might be reached by various methods. For Russia I was convinced she had chosen the only way open to her at the time. I saw Scandinavia choosing a different method, half-way between Socialism and Capitalism. In the United States I saw Consumers Cooperation as a path from Capitalism to Socialism, while England, France and Germany developed in the same direction in their own way. After the depression and the Second World War, I was disillusioned. The Progressive movement in the United States failed. The Cold War started. Capitalism called Communism a crime.

Today I have reached a firm conclusion:

Capitalism cannot reform itself; it is doomed to self-destruction. No universal selfishness can bring social good to all.

Communism—the effort to give all men what they need and to ask of each the best they can contribute—this is the only way of human life. It is a difficult and hard end to reach—it has and will make mistakes, but today it marches triumphantly on in education and science, in home and food, with increased freedom of thought and deliverance from dogma. In the end Communism will triumph. I want to help to bring that day.

The path of the American Communist Party is clear: It will provide the United States with a real Third Party and thus restore democracy to this land. It will call for:

1. Public ownership of natural resources and of all capital.
2. Public control of transportation and communications.
3. Abolition of poverty and limitation of personal income.
4. No exploitation of labor.
5. Social medicine, with hospitalization and care of the old.
6. Free education for all.
7. Training for jobs and jobs for all.
8. Discipline for growth and reform.
9. Freedom under law.
10. No dogmatic religion.

These aims are not crimes. They are practiced increasingly over the world. No nation can call itself free which does not allow its citizens to work for these ends.

W. E. B. DuBois

Before Du Bois left for Ghana, he wrote an article explaining the origin and purpose of the "Encyclopedia Africana." It was published on the front page of the magazine section of the Baltimore Afro-American, *October 21, 1961.*

ON THE BEGINNINGS OF THE PROJECT

In 1909 when I was teaching history and economics in the University of Atlanta, Georgia I proposed the preparation of an "Encyclopedia Africana".

I secured as members of the Board of Advisors, in addition to 52 American scholars: Sir Harry Johnston, K. C. B., England; Prof. W. M. Flinders Petrie, D.C.L., England; Prof. Giuseppe Sergi, Italy; Dr. J. Deniker, France; Prof. William James, L.L.D., Harvard; Prof. Franz Boas, Ph.D., Columbia; and many others.

However, I was never able to raise the funds to carry this enterprise forward.

$260,000

In 1934, the Phelps Stokes Fund initiated a new project to prepare and publish an "Encyclopedia of Colored People".

I was chosen as editor-in-chief and for the next ten years gave intermittent effort to this project, but again the necessary funds, which we estimated then at $260,000, could not be secured.

Perhaps it was too soon to expect so large an amount for so ambitious a project to be carried out by ourselves and built mainly on our own scholarship.

Nevertheless, a preparatory volume summarizing the effort was published in 1944.

In 1959, while I was in Ghana, West Africa, witnessing the inauguration of the independent republic, the President Dr. Kwame Nkrumah, asked me if I again would plan an "Encyclopedia Africana". I consented to do this and to consult personally and by letter a number of persons who might be interested in this project.

People and Race

My idea is to prepare and publish an encyclopedia not on the vague subject of race, but on the peoples inhabiting the continent of Africa.

I propose an encyclopedia edited mainly by African scholars, but I am anxious to have this encyclopedia a scientific production and not a matter of propaganda; and to have included among its writers the best students of Africa in the world.

I want, however, to have the encyclopedia written mainly from the African point of view from people who know and understand the history and culture of Africans.

My thought also is that it would be a great advantage if at this juncture the interest and research of the African intelligentsia be concentrated on the history of the past and the cultural remains of Africa; that this might direct their action away from political and tribal divisions, give them a body of truth to guide them and unite them in wide agreement as to what has happened on this continent and what can happen in the future.

Difficulties

I realize that this is going to involve difficulties: first, the comparatively small number of Africans who are scientific students of Africa and secondly, the attitude of European scholars towards Africans.

There is, I am sure, a great deal of interest, sympathy and good will among British, French, Belgian and German scholars towards the African peoples.

But there is also much prejudice and condescension and certain assumptions toward Africans almost inevitable among persons educated in Europe.

I am trying, therefore, first to get the advice of leading persons in the scientific world as to what the procedure should be to prepare and publish such an encyclopedia.

I propose that there should be established a secretariat for editing such an encyclopedia and that the Republic of Ghana should bear the expense of preparation and publication;

But should share the expenses with such other African governments as are willing to contribute;

That with the advice and cooperation of the best scholars in the world the secretariat should select an editorial board.

That the board should consist mainly of African scholars and should plan an encyclopedia from the African point of view, but as I have said before, on a strictly scientific basis.

Du Bois has most frequently been written of as a person one would not have necessarily liked to have known. Described as arrogant, egotistical, proud, difficult, stern, his image is a forbidding one. Yet, his writings reflect a warm, sometimes sentimental person, with a good sense of humor. He admitted himself that he did not relax easily with people, especially whites, and that a certain formality characterized most of his relationships. It is impossible to imagine anyone calling him "Bill," for example. One of his closest friends was Joel Spingarn, yet he addressed Spingarn as "Colonel," and Spingarn always addressed him as "Doctor."

Du Bois was acutely aware that he was not only controversial as a writer and thinker, but as a personality. Thus, his own explanations of his character and personality are most moving, because Du Bois, without defending himself or pleading a case, reveals what he was like inside and how it caused him pain.

The selection is the 16th chapter of The Autobiography, *"My Character."*

(*The Autobiography of W.E.B. Du Bois: A Soliloquy on Viewing My Life from the Last Decade of its First Century,* International Publishers, New York, 1968, pp. 277-88.)

MY CHARACTER

When I was a young man, we talked much of character. At Fisk University character was discussed and emphasized more than scholarship. I knew what was meant and agreed that the sort of person a man was would in the long run prove more important for the world than what he knew or how logically he could think. It is typical of our time that insistence on character today in the country has almost ceased. Freud and others have stressed the unconscious factors of our personality so that today we do not advise youth about their development of character; we watch and count their actions with almost helpless disassociation from thought of advice.

Nevertheless, from that older generation which formed my youth I still retain an interest in what men are rather than what they do; and at the age of 50, I began to take stock of myself and ask what I really was as a person. Of course I knew that self-examination is not a true unbiased picture; but on the other hand without it no picture is quite complete.

From childhood I tried to be honest; I did not mean to take anything which did not belong to me. I told the truth even when there was no call for the telling and when silence would have been golden. I did not usually speak in malice but often blurted out the truth when the story was incomplete and was therefore as seemed to me wrong. I had strict ideas about money and its earning. I worked and worked hard for the first 25 cents a week which I earned. I could never induce myself to gamble or take silly chances because I figured the loss vividly in fatigue and pain. Once on a French train I played the pea in a shell game and lost two dollars. Forty years later in Mexico I won two dollars on a horse race. These were my first and last games of chance.

I was careful about debt. My folk were poor but seldom in debt. I have before me a statement of my indebtedness, September 1, 1894, when I started on my first life job. My salary was $800 a year and my living expense I calculated at: Board $100; Room $35; Clothes $65; Books $100; Debts $350; Sundries $25 —Total $675; Savings $125. This proved too optimistic but still I kept out of debt. When I taught at Atlanta at a salary of $1,200 a year for 12 years, I owed nobody. I had a wife and child and each year I took them somewhere north so as to give them fresh air and civilization. It took every cent of my salary, together with small fees from lectures and writing, to pay our way and yet only once was I compelled to overdraw my salary for a month ahead.

Saving I neglected. I had had no experience in saving. My

mother's family with whom I lived as a child never had a bank account nor insurance; and seldom a spare dollar. I took out a small life insurance of $1,000 when I was 27. I was cheated unmercifully by the white Pennsylvania company in the fee charged because I was colored. Later after marriage I took out $10,000 of insurance in a Negro company, the Standard Life. Eventually the company went bankrupt and I lost every cent. I was then too old to obtain more insurance on terms which I could afford.

My income has always been low. During my 23 years with the NAACP, I received for the first five years $2,500 a year. For the next 18 years, $5,000. With savings from this I bought a home and then sold it later for an apartment building in Harlem. There were five apartments, one of which my family was to occupy and the others I calculated would pay me a permanent income. But the house was overpriced; neglected orders for expensive sewer repairs were overdue. The down payment which I could afford was low and the property was overloaded with three mortgages on which I had to pay bonuses for renewal. Downtown banks began to squeeze black Harlem property holders and taxes increased. With the depression, tenants could not pay or moved.

There was one recourse: to turn the property into a rooming house for prostitution and gambling. I gave it to the owners of the mortgages and shouldered the loss of all my savings at 60 years of age. In all this I had followed the advice of a friend skilled in the handling of real estate but who assumed that I was trying to make money and not dreaming of model housing conditions. As many of my friends have since informed me, I was a fool; but I was not a thief which I count to my credit.

I returned to Atlanta University in 1934 at a salary of $4,500 a year but still out of debt. When ten years later I was retired without notice, I had no insurance and but small savings. A white classmate, grandson of a railway magnate, berated me for not wishing to give up work. He could not conceive of a man working for 50 years without saving enough to live on the rest of his days. In money matters I was surely negligent and ignorant; but that was not because I was gambling, drinking or carousing; it was because I spent my income in making myself and my family comfortable instead of "saving for a rainy day." I may have been wrong, but I am not sure of that.

On one aspect of my life, I look back upon with mixed feelings; and that is on matters of friendship and sex. I couple them designedly because I think they belong together. I have always had more friends among women than among men. This began with the close companionship I had with my mother. Friends used to praise me for my attention to my mother; we always went out together arm in arm and had our few indoor amusements together. This seemed quite normal to me; my mother was lame, why should I not guide her steps? And who knew better about my thoughts and ambitions? Later in my life among my own colored people the women began to have more education, while the men imitated an American culture which I did not share: I drank no alcoholic beverages until I went to Germany and there I drank light beer and Rhine wine. Most of the American men I knew drank whiskey and frequented saloons which from my boyhood were out of bounds.

Indeed the chief blame which I lay on my New England schooling was the inexcusable ignorance of sex which I had when I went south to Fisk at 17. I was precipitated into a region, with loose sex morals among black and white, while I actually did not know the physical difference between men and women. At first my fellows jeered in disbelief and then became sorry and made many offers to guide my abysmal ignorance. This built for me inexcusable and startling temptations. It began to turn one of the most beautiful of earth's experiences into a thing of temptation and horror. I fought and feared amid what should have been a climax of true living. I avoided women about whom anybody gossiped and as I tried to solve the contradiction of virginity and motherhood, I was inevitably faced with the other contradiction of prostitution and adultery. In my hometown sex was deliberately excluded from talk and if possible from thought. In public school there were no sexual indulgences of which I ever heard. We talked of girls, looked at their legs, and there was rare kissing of a most unsatisfactory sort. We teased about sweethearts, but quite innocently. When I went South, my fellow students being much older and reared in a region of loose sexual customs regarded me as liar or freak when I asserted my innocence. I liked girls and sought their company, but my wildest exploits were kissing them.

Then, as teacher in the rural districts of East Tennessee, I was literally raped by the unhappy wife who was my landlady. From that time through my college course at Harvard and my study in Europe, I went through a desperately recurring fight to keep the sex instinct in control. A brief trial with prostitution in Paris affronted my sense of decency. I lived more or less regularly with a shop girl in Berlin, but was ashamed. Then when I returned home to teach, I was faced with the connivance of certain fellow teachers at adultery with their wives. I was literally frightened into marriage before I was able to support a family. I married a girl whose rare beauty and excellent household training from her dead mother attracted and held me.

I married at 29 and we lived together for 53 years. It was not an absolutely ideal union, but it was happier than most, so far as I could perceive. It suffered from the fundamental drawback of modern American marriage: a difference in aim and function between its partners; my wife and children were incidents of my main life work. I was not neglectful of my family; I furnished a good home. I educated the child and planned vacations and recreation. But my main work was out in the world and not at home. That work out there my wife appreciated but was too busy to share because of cooking, marketing, sweeping and cleaning and the endless demands of children. This she did naturally without complaint until our firstborn died—died not out of neglect but because of a city's careless sewage. His death tore our lives in two. I threw myself more completely into my work, while most reason for living left the soul of my wife. Another child, a girl, came later, but my wife never forgave God for the unhealable wound.

As I wandered across the world to wider and higher goals, I sensed two complaints against the pairing of the sexes in modern life: one, that ties between human beings are usually assumed to be sexual if a man and woman are concerned; and two, that normal friendships between men and women could not exist without sex being assumed to be the main ingredient. Also, if a man and woman are friends, they must be married and their friendship may become a cloying intimacy, often lasting 24 hours a day, with no outside friends of the opposite sex on pain of gossip, scandal and even crime engulfing the family. My travel and work away from home saved us from this. One difficulty of married life we faced as many others must have. My wife's life-long training as a virgin, made it almost impossible for her ever to regard sexual intercourse as not fundamentally inde-

cent. It took careful restraint on my part not to make her unhappy at this most beautiful of human experiences. This was no
easy task for a normal and lusty young man.

Most of my friends and helpers have been women; from my
mother, aunts and cousins, to my fellow teachers, students,
secretaries, and dreamers toward a better world. Sex indulgence
was never the cause or aim of these friendships. I do not think
my women friends ever gave my wife harm or unease. I was
thoughtful of her comfort and support and of her treatment in
public and private. My absence from home so much helped in
the household drudgery. I still make my own bed of mornings;
for many years I prepared my own breakfast, especially my
coffee; I always leave a bathroom cleaner than when I enter; but
sewing and sweeping I neglect. I have often wondered if her
limitation to a few women friends and they chiefly housekeep-
ers; and if her lack of contact with men, because of her conventional upbringing and her surroundings—if this did not make
her life unnecessarily narrow and confined. My life on the other
hand threw me widely with women of brains and great effort to
work on the widest scale. I am endlessly grateful for these
contacts.

My first married life lasted over half a century, and its ending
was normal and sad, with the loneliness which is always the
price of death. To fill this great gap, and let my work go on, I
married again near the end of my days. She was a woman 40
years my junior but her work and aim in life had been close to
mine because her father had long believed in what I was trying
to do. The faith of Shirley Graham in me was therefore inherited and received as a joy and not merely as a duty. She has
made these days rich and rewarding.

In the midst of my career there burst on me a new and
undreamed of aspect of sex. A young man, long my disciple and
student, then my co-helper and successor to part of my work,
was suddenly arrested for molesting men in public places. I had
before that time no conception of homosexuality. I had never
understood the tragedy of an Oscar Wilde. I dismissed my
co-worker forthwith, and spent heavy days regretting my act.

I knew far too few of my contemporaries. I was on occasion
incomprehensibly shy, and almost invariably loath to interrupt
others in seeking to explain myself. This in the case of my fellow
Negroes was balanced by our common experiences and shared
knowledge of what each other had lived through; but in the case

of white companions, and especially those newly met, we could not talk together, we lived in different worlds. We belonged to no social clubs, and did not visit the same people or even stand at the same liquor bars. We did not lunch together. I did not play cards, and could never get wildly enthusiastic even over baseball. Naturally we could not share stories of sex.

Thus I did not seek white acquaintances. I let them make the advances, and they therefore thought me arrogant. In a sense I was, but after all I was in fact rather desperately hanging on to my self-respect. I was not fighting to dominate others; I was fighting against my own degradation. I wanted to meet my fellows as an equal; they offered or seemed to offer only a status of inferiority and submission.

I did not for the most part meet my great contemporaries. Doubtless this was largely my own fault. I did not seek them. I deliberately refused invitations to spend weekends with Henry James and H. G. Wells. I did not follow up an offer of the wife of Havelock Ellis to meet him and Bernard Shaw. Later, when I tried to call on Shaw he was coy. Several times I could have met Presidents of the United States and did not. Great statesmen, writers and artists of America, I might have met, and in some cases, might have known intimately. I did not try to accomplish this. This was partly because of my fear that color caste would interfere with our meeting and understanding; if not with the persons themselves, certainly with their friends. But even beyond this, I was not what Americans called a "good fellow."

This too illustrates a certain lack of sympathy and understanding which I had for my students. I was for instance a good teacher. I stimulated inquiry and accuracy. I met every question honestly and never dodged an earnest doubt. I read my examination papers carefully and marked them with sedulous care. But I did not know my students as human beings; they were to me apt to be intellects and not souls. To the world in general I was nearly always the isolated outsider looking in and seldom part of that inner life. Partly that role was thrust upon me because of the color of my skin. But I was not a prig. I was a lusty man with all normal appetites. I loved "Wine, Women and Song." I worked hard and slept soundly; and if, as many said, I was hard to know, it was that with all my belligerency I was in reality unreasonably shy.

One thing I avoided, and that was envy. I tried to give the

other fellow his due even when I disliked him personally and disagreed with him logically. It became to me a point of honor never to refuse appreciation to one who had earned it, no matter who he was. I loved living, physically as well as spiritually. I could not waste my time on baseball but I could appreciate a home run. My own exercise was walking, but there again I walked alone. I knew life and death. The passing of my first-born boy was an experience from which I never quite recovered. I wrote:

> The world loved him; the women kissed his curls, the men looked gravely into his wonderful eyes, and the children hovered and fluttered about him. I can see him now, changing like the sky from sparkling laughter to darkening frowns, and then to wondering thoughtfulness as he watched the world. He knew no color-line, poor dear—and the veil, though it shadowed him, had not yet darkened half his sun. He loved the white matron, he loved his black nurse; and in his little world walked souls alone, uncolored and unclothed. I—yea, all men—are larger and purer by the infinite breadth of that one little life. She who in simple clearness of vision sees beyond the stars said when he had flown—"He will be happy There; he ever loved beautiful things." And I, far more ignorant, and blind by the web of my own weaving, sit alone winding words and muttering, "If still he be, and he be There, and there be a There, let him be happy, O Fate!"
>
> Blithe was the morning of his burial, with bird and song and sweet-smelling flowers. The trees whispered to the grass, but the children sat with hushed faces. And yet it seemed a ghostly unreal day—the wraith of Life. We seemed to rumble down an unknown street behind a little white bundle of posies, with the shadow of a song in our ears. The busy city dinned about us; they did not say much, those palefaced hurrying men and women; they did not say much—they only glanced and said "Niggers."

My religious development has been slow and uncertain. I grew up in a liberal Congregational Sunday School and listened once a week to a sermon on doing good as a reasonable duty. Theology played a minor part and our teachers had to face some searching questions. At 17 I was in a missionary college where religious orthodoxy was stressed; but I was more developed to meet it with argument, which I did. My "morals" were sound, even a bit puritanic, but when a hidebound old deacon inveighed against dancing I rebelled. By the time of graduation I was still a "believer" in orthodox religion, but had strong questions which were encouraged at Harvard. In Germany I became a freethinker and when I came to teach at an orthodox Methodist Negro school I was soon regarded with suspicion, especially when I refused to lead the students in public prayer. When I became head of a department at Atlanta, the engagement was held up because again I balked at leading in prayer, but the liberal president let me substitute the Episcopal prayer book on most occasions. Later I improvised prayers on my own. Finally I faced a crisis: I was using Grapsey's *Religion and Politics* as a Sunday School text. When Grapsey was hauled up for heresy, I refused further to teach Sunday School. When Archdeacon Henry Phillips, my last rector, died, I flatly refused again to join any church or sign any church creed. From my 30th year on I have increasingly regarded the church as an institution which defended such evils as slavery, color caste, exploitation of labor and war. I think the greatest gift of the Soviet Union to modern civilization was the dethronement of the clergy and the refusal to let religion be taught in the public schools.

Religion helped and hindered my artistic sense. I know the old English and German hymns by heart. I loved their music but ignored their silly words with studied inattention. Great music came at last in the religious oratorios which we learned at Fisk University but it burst on me in Berlin with the Ninth Symphony and its Hymn of Joy. I worshipped Cathedral and ceremony which I saw in Europe but I knew what I was looking at when in New York a Cardinal became a strike-breaker and the Church of Christ fought the Communism of Christianity.

I revered life. I have never killed a bird nor shot a rabbit. I never liked fishing and always let others kill even the chickens which I ate. Nearly all my schoolmates in the South carried pistols. I never owned one. I could never conceive myself killing a human being. But in 1906 I rushed back from Alabama to Atlanta where my wife and six-year old child were living. A mob had raged for days killing Negroes. I bought a Winchester double-barreled shotgun and two dozen rounds of shells filled with buckshot. If a white mob had stepped on the campus where

I lived I would without hesitation have sprayed their guts over the grass. They did not come. They went to south Atlanta where the police let them steal and kill. My gun was fired but once and then by error into a row of *Congressional Records*, which lined the lower shelf of my library.

My attitude toward current problems arose from my long habit of keeping in touch with world affairs by repeated trips to Europe and other parts of the world. I became internationally-minded during my four years at Harvard, two in college and two in the graduate school. Since that first trip in 1892, I have made 15 trips to Europe, one of which circled the globe. I have been in most European countries and traveled in Asia, Africa and the West Indies. Travel became a habit and knowledge of current thought in modern countries was always a part of my study, since before the First World War when the best of American newspapers took but small account of what Europe was thinking.

I can remember meeting in London in 1911 a colored man who explained to me his plan of leading a black army out of Africa and across the Pyrenees. I was thrilled at his earnestness! But gradually all that disappeared, and I began building a new picture of human progress.

This picture was made more real in 1926 when it became possible for me to take a trip to Russia. I saw on this trip not only Russia, but prostrate Germany, which I had not seen for 30 years. It was a terrible contrast.

By 1945 all these contacts with foreign peoples and foreign problems and the combination of these problems with the race problem here was forced into one line of thought by the Second World War. This strengthened my growing conviction that the first step toward settling the world's problems was Peace on Earth.

Many men have judged me, favorably and harshly. But the verdict of two I cherish. One knew me in mid-life for 50 years and was without doubt my closest friend. John Hope wrote me in 1918:

> Until the last minute I have been hoping that I would have an opportunity to be with you next Monday when you celebrate the rounding out of 50 years in this turbulent but attractive world. But now I am absolutely cer-

tain that I cannot come, so I am writing Mr. Shillady expressing my regret and shall have to content myself with telling you in this letter how glad I am that your 50th birthday is going to be such a happy one because you can look back on so much good work done. But not the good work alone. What you may look upon with greatest comfort is good intention. The fact that every step of the way you have purposed to be a man and to serve other people rather than yourself must be a tremendous comfort to you. Sometime soon if I chance to be back in New York I am going to have you take your deferred birthday dinner with *me.* You do not realize how much that hour or two which we usually spend together when I am in New York means to me.

Joel Spingarn said:

I should like to have given public expression by my presence and by my words, not merely to the sense of personal friendship which has bound us together for 15 years, but to the gratitude which in common with all other Americans I feel we owe you for your public service. It so happens that by an accident of fate, you have been in the forefront of the great American battle, not merely for justice to a single race, but against the universal prejudice which is in danger of clouding the whole American tradition of toleration and human equality.

I congratulate you on your public service, and I congratulate you also on the power of language by which you have made it effective. I know that some people think that an artist is a man who has nothing to say and who writes in order to prove it. The great writers of the world have not so conceived their task, and neither have you. Though your service has been for the most part the noble one of teacher and prophet (not merely to one race or nation but to the world), I challenge the artists of America to show more beautiful passages than some of those in *Darkwater* and *The Souls of Black Folk.*

Let one incident illustrate the paradox of my life.

Robert Morse Lovett was perhaps the closest white student friend I made at Harvard; when not long before his last visit to New York about 1950 he wanted to see and talk with me, he proposed the Harvard Club of which he was a member. I was not. No Negro graduate of Harvard was ever elected to membership in a Harvard club. For a while Jews were excluded, but no longer. I swallowed my pride and met Lovett at the Club. A few months later he died.

The body of Dr. W.E.B. Du Bois was laid to final rest with full military honors on the afternoon of August 29th [1963] at a spot some fifty yards from the pounding surf, beside the wall of The Castle, residence of the President of Ghana. Immediately following the interment, a last message to the world written by Dr. Du Bois was read to the thousands of assembled mourners. It was dated June 26, 1957, and had been given to his wife, Shirley Graham Du Bois, for safekeeping until the hour of his death.

This is the Message:

LAST MESSAGE

Dr. Du Bois to the World

It is much more difficult in theory than actually to say the last good-bye to one's loved ones and friends and to all the familiar things of this life.

I am going to take a long, deep and endless sleep. This is not a punishment but a privilege to which I have looked forward for years.

I have loved my work, I have loved people and my play, but always I have been uplifted by the thought that what I have done well will live long and justify my life; that what I have done ill or never finished can now be handed on to others for endless days to be finished, perhaps better than I could have done.

And that peace will be my applause.

One thing alone I charge you. As you live, believe in life! Always human beings will live and progress to greater, broader and fuller life.

The only possible death is to lose belief in this truth simply because the great end comes slowly, because time is long.

Good-bye.

BIBLIOGRAPHY

There does not as yet exist a complete bibliography of the writings of W.E.B. Du Bois. This one is compiled from three previously published bibliographies. The basic source was the pioneer bibliography compiled by S.I.A. Kotei, Ghana Library Board, Padmore Research Library on African Affairs, Accra, Ghana. The other two bibliographies were mimeographed lists which I found in the Du Bois files of James Aronson. Together the three comprise as complete a bibliography of Du Bois' writings as has been published to date. I personally examined most, but not all of the items mentioned. Therefore, there may be inadvertent inaccuracies in some of the dates which have been included.

The following bibliography of works by W.E.B. Du Bois has been organized in the following way: Periodical Articles; Books and Pamphlets; Articles in Books.

PERIODICAL ARTICLES

"Great Barrington Notes," New York *Globe* (April 14, 1883), p. 4.

"Great Barrington Notes," New York *Globe* (May 5, 1883), p. 1.

"Great Barrington Notes," New York *Globe* (May 26, 1883), p. 4.

"Great Barrington Notes," New York *Globe* (June 3, 1883), p. 1.

"Great Barrington Notes," New York *Globe* (June 30, 1883), p. 4.

"Great Barrington Notes," New York *Globe* (September 29, 1883), p. 1.

"Great Barrington Notes," New York *Globe* (October 29, 1883), p. 4.

"Great Barrington Notes," New York *Globe* (December 8, 1883), p. 4.

"Great Barrington Notes," New York *Globe* (December 29, 1883), p. 4.

"Great Barrington Notes," New York *Globe* (January 26, 1884), p. 4.

"From the Berkshire Hills," New York *Globe* (February 23, 1884), p. 4.

"Great Barrington Items," New York *Globe* (April 12, 1884), p. 4.

"From the Berkshire Hills," New York *Globe* (May 17, 1884), p. 4.

"Great Barrington Items," New York *Globe* (August 2, 1884), p. 1.

"Great Barrington Items," New York *Globe* (August 23, 1884), p. 4.

"Great Barrington Items," New York *Globe* (September 27, 1884), p. 4.

"Great Barrington Items," New York *Globe* (October 18, 1884), p. 1.

"Great Barrington Notes," New York *Freeman* (November 22, 1884), p. 4.

"Wedding Bells of Berkshire," New York *Freeman* (December 6, 1884), p. 4.

"Great Barrington Notes," New York *Freeman* (December 27, 1884), p. 1.

"Great Barrington Notes," New York *Freeman* (January 10, 1885), p. 1.

"Great Barrington Notes," New York *Freeman* (January 31, 1885), p. 4.

"Great Barrington Notes," New York *Freeman* (March 14, 1885), p. 1.

"Great Barrington Notes," New York *Freeman* (May 16, 1885), p. 4.

"Exchanges," Fisk *Herald,* III, iii (November, 1885), p. 8.

"Exchanges," Fisk *Herald,* III, iv (December, 1885), p. 6.

"Exchanges," Fisk *Herald,* III, ix (May, 1886), p. 9.

"Exchanges," Fisk *Herald,* III, x (June, 1886), p. 11.

"How I Taught School," Fisk *Herald,* IV, iv (December, 1886), pp. 9-10.

"Strivings of the Negro People," *Atlantic Monthly,* Vol. 80 (1897) pp. 194-8.

"The Problem of Amusement," *Southern Workman,* September, 1897.

"The Negroes of Farmville Virginia; a Social Study," *Bulletin of the United States Department of Labor,* Vol. 3 (January, 1898) pp. 1-38.

"The Study of the Negro Problems," *Annals of the American Academy of Political and Social Science,* Vol. 11, January, 1898) pp. 1-23.

"The Negro Schoolmaster in the New South," *Atlantic Monthly,* Vol. 83 (January, 1899) pp. 99-104.

"The Negro and Crime," *Independent,* Vol. 51 (May 18, 1899), pp. 1355-7.

"The Negro in the Black Belt: Some Social Sketches," *Bulletin of the United States Department of Labor,* IV (May, 1899), pp. 401-17.

"Two Negro Conventions," *Independent,* Vol. 51 (September 7, 1899), pp. 2425-7.

"The Suffrage Fight in Georgia," *Independent,* Vol. 51, (November 30, 1899), pp. 3226-8.

"The Negro Farmer," *Special Reports of the Census Office* (1900).

"The Twelfth Census and the Negro Problem" *Southern Workman,* Vol. 29 (May, 1900), pp. 305-9.

"The American Negro at Paris," *American Monthly Review of Reviews,* Vol. 22 (November, 1900), pp. 575-7.

"The Religion of the American Negro," *New World,* Vol. 9 (December, 1900), pp. 614-25.

"The Black North, a Social Study," *New York Times* (November 17, 24, December 1, 8, 15, 1901).

"The Freedman's Bureau," *Atlantic Monthly,* Vol. 87 (March, 1901), pp. 354-65.

"The Storm and Stress in the Black World," *Dial,* Vol. 30 (April 16, 1901), pp. 262-4.

"The Negro as He Really Is" *World's Work,* Vol. 2 (June, 1901), pp. 848-66.

"Results of Ten Tuskegee Conferences," *Harpers' Weekly,* Vol. 65 (June 22, 1901), p. 641.

"The Relation of the Negroes to the Whites in the South," *Annals of the American Academy of Political and Social Science,* Vol. 18 (July, 1901), pp. 121-40.

"The Negro Landholder of Georgia," *Bulletin of the United States Department of Labor* (July, 1901).

"The Evolution of Negro Leadership," *Dial,* July 1, 1901.

"The Burden of Negro Schooling," *Independent,* Vol. 53 (July 18, 1901), pp. 1167-8.

"The Savings of Black Georgia," *Outlook,* Vol. 69 (September 14, 1901), pp. 128-30.

"The Spawn of Slavery," *Missionary Review of the World,* Vol. 24 (October, 1901), pp. 737-45.

"The Freedmen and Their Sons" *Independent,* Vol. 53 (November 14, 1901), p. 2709.

"The Problem of Housing the Negro" *Southern Workman,* XXX, pp. 390-95, 486-93, 535-42, 601-4, 688-93; XXXI, 65-72 (July, September, December, 1901; February, 1902).

"The Work of Negro Women in Society," *Spelman Messenger,* XVIII, v (February, 1902), pp. 1-3.

"The Opening of the Library," *Independent,* LIV (April 3, 1902), pp. 809-10.

"The Trust of Girard College," *Nation,* LXXIV (January–June, 1902), p. 226.

"Of the Training of Black Men," *Atlantic Monthly,* Vol. 90 (September, 1902), pp. 289-97.

"Hopeful Signs for the Negro," *Advance,* Vol. 44 (October 2, 1902), pp. 327-8.

"Crime and Our Colored Population," *Nation*, LXXV (December 25, 1902), p. 499.

"The Atlanta University Conferences," *Charities*, X (May 2, 1903), pp. 435-9.

"The Laboratory in Sociology at Atlanta," *Annals of the American Academy of Political and Social Science*, Vol. 21 (May, 1903), pp. 160-3.

"Possibilities of the Negro," *McGirt's Magazine*, September, 1903.

"Training of Negroes for Social Power," *Outlook*, Vol. 75 (October 17, 1903), pp. 409-14.

"Possibilities of the Negro: The Advance Guard of the Race," *Booklovers*, Vol. 2 (July, 1903), pp. 2-15.

"The Negro Farmer, Negroes in the United States," United States Department of Commerce and Labor, *Bureau of the Census Bulletin*, Vol. 8 (1904), pp. 69-98.

"The Future of the Negro Race in America," *The East and the West*, II (London: January, 1904), pp. 4-19.

"The Atlanta Conferences," *Voice of the Negro*, Vol. 1 (March, 1904).

"The Development of a People," *The International Journal of Ethics*, XIV (April, 1904), pp. 521-3.

"The Negro Problem from the Negro Point of View: The Parting of the Ways," *World Today*, Vol. 6 (April, 1904), pp. 521-3.

"Diminishing Negro Illiteracy," *Nation*, LXXVIII (January–June, 1904), pp. 147-8.

"What Intellectual Training is doing for the Negro," *Missionary Review of the World*, Vol. 27 (August, 1904), pp. 578-82.

"Credo," *Independent*, Vol. 57 (October 6, 1904), p. 787.

"The Souls of Black Folk," *Independent*, LVII (November 17, 1904), p. 1152.

"The Negro Church," *Political Science Quarterly* (December, 1904).

"Debit and Credit," *Voice of the Negro*, Vol. 2 (January, 1905), p. 677.

"Sayings of Dr. W.E.B. Du Bois," reprinted from the Boston *Guardian* in *The Fraternal Union* (Fort Smith, Arkansas), III (February 16, 1905), p. 12.

"The Beginnings of Slavery," *Voice of the Negro*, II, ii (February, 1905), pp. 104-6.

"Slavery in Greece and Rome," *Voice of the Negro,* II, v (May, 1905), pp. 320-3.

"The Southerner's Problem," *Dial,* Vol. 38, (May, 1905), pp. 315-18.

"The Beginning of Emancipation," *Voice of the Negro,* II, vi (June, 1905), pp. 397-400.

"Serfdom," *Voice of the Negro,* II, vii (July, 1905), pp. 479-81.

"The Negro South and North," *Bibliotheca Sacra,* LXII (July, 1905), pp. 500-13.

"The Niagara Movement," *Voice of the Negro,* Vol. 2 (September, 1905), pp. 619-22.

"The Black Vote of Philadelphia," *Charities,* Vol. 15 (October, 7, 1905), pp. 31-5.

"The Problem of Tillman, Vardaman and Thomas Nixon, Jr.," *Central Christian Advocate,* XLIX (October 18, 1905), pp. 1324-5.

"The Negro Ideals of Life," *Christian Register,* LXXXIV (October 26, 1905), pp. 1197-9.

"Garrison and the Negro," *Independent,* Vol. 59 (December 7, 1905), pp. 1316-17.

"The Growth of the Niagara Movement," *Voice of the Negro,* Vol. 13 (January, 1906), pp. 43-5.

"The Economic Future of the Negro," *Publications of the American Economic Association,* 3rd series, Vol. 7 (February, 1906), pp. 219-42.

"White Teachers," *The Moon Illustrated Weekly,* (ca. February, 1906), reprinted in the Washington *Bee,* XXV (February 17, 1906), p. 4.

"Vardaman," *Voice of the Negro,* Vol. 3 (March, 1906), pp. 189-94.

"Liberia," *The Moon Illustrated Weekly,* Vol. 14 (March 2, 1906).

"South Africa," *The Moon Illustrated Weekly,* I, xiv (March 2, 1906), p. 3.

"Barbadoes," *The Moon Illustrated Weekly,* I, xiv (March 2, 1906), p. 3.

"Washington," *The Moon Illustrated Weekly,* I, xiv (March 2, 1906), p. 3.

"Boston, Mass.," *The Moon Illustrated Weekly,* I, xiv (March 2, 1906), pp. 3-4.

"Fort Smith, Ark.," *The Moon Illustrated Weekly,* I, xiv (March 2, 1906), p. 4.

"Springfield, Ohio," *The Moon Illustrated Weekly,* I, xiv (March 2, 1906), p. 4.

"Their Voices," *The Moon Illustrated Weekly,* I, xiv (March 2, 1906), pp. 4-5, 10.

"Vicksburg, Miss. Notes," *The Moon Illustrated Weekly,* I, xiv (March 2, 1906), p. 11.

"Memphis Solvent Savings Bank and Trust Co.," *The Moon Illustrated Weekly,* I, xiv (March 2, 1906), p. 12.

"Negro Literature," *The Moon Illustrated Weekly,* I, xiv (March 2, 1906), p. 16.

"Bibliography," *The Moon Illustrated Weekly,* I, xiv (March 2, 1906), p. 16.

"The Negro," *The Moon Illustrated Weekly,* I, xxx (June 23, 1906), p. 3.

"Aliens," *The Moon Illustrated Weekly,* I, xxx (June 23, 1906), p. 3.

"Disenfranchisement in Alabama," *The Moon Illustrated Weekly,* I, xxx (June 23, 1906), pp. 3-4.

"Lynching," *The Moon Illustrated Weekly,* I, xxx (June 23, 1906), pp. 4-5.

"Our Voices," *The Moon Illustrated Weekly,* I, xxx (June 23, 1906), pp. 5-6.

"North East," *The Moon Illustrated Weekly,* I, xxx (June 23, 1906), pp. 6-7.

"South East," *The Moon Illustrated Weekly,* I, xxx (June 23, 1906), p. 7.

"North Central," *The Moon Illustrated Weekly,* I, xxx (June 23, 1906), p. 7.

"North West," *The Moon Illustrated Weekly,* I, xxx (June 23, 1906), p. 7.

"South West," *The Moon Illustrated Weekly,* I, xxx (June 23, 1906), pp. 7, 10.

"Memphis News and Comment," *The Moon Illustrated Weekly,* I, xxx (June 23, 1906), p. 8.

"Atlanta Local News," *The Moon Illustrated Weekly,* I, xxx (June 23, 1906), p. 9.

"Faith," *The Moon Illustrated Weekly,* I, xxx (June 23, 1906), p. 12.

"Council and Ransom," *The Moon Illustrated Weekly*, I, xxx (June 23, 1906), p. 12.

"Wandering," *The Moon Illustrated Weekly*," I, xxx (June 23, 1906), p. 12.

"The Niagara Movement," *The Moon Illustrated Weekly*, I, xxx (June 23, 1906), p. 12.

"The Hampton Idea," *Voice of the Negro*, III, ix (September, 1906), pp. 632-6.

"Litany at Atlanta," *Independent*, Vol. 61 (October, 1906), pp. 856-8.

"St. Francis of Assisi," *Voice of the Negro*, III, x (October, 1906), pp. 419-26.

"The Color Line Belts the World," *Collier's*, XXVIII, iv (October 20, 1906), p. 30.

"L'Ouvrier Negre en Amerique" Revue Economique Internationale (Brussels), IV (November, 1906), pp. 298-348.

"Tragedy of Atlanta," *World Today*, Vol. 11 (November, 1906), pp. 1173-5.

"The President and the Soldiers," *The Voice*, III, xii (December, 1906), pp. 552-3.

"Africa," *Horizon*, Vol. 1 (January, 1907).

"The Magazines," *Horizon*, I, i (January, 1907), pp. 2-4.

"Subscription," *Horizon*, I, i (January, 1907), pp. 4-6.

"Books," *Horizon*, I, i (January, 1907), p. 6.

"Congo," *Horizon*, I, i (January, 1907).

"India," *Horizon*, I, i (January, 1907), p. 8.

"Roosevelt," *Horizon*, I, i (January, 1907), pp. 8-9.

"Moonshine," *Horizon*, I, i (January, 1907), pp. 9-10.

"The Magazines," *Horizon*, I, ii (February, 1907), pp. 3-4.

"Lagos," *Horizon*, I, ii (February, 1907), p. 10.

"The Song of the Snake," *Horizon*, I, ii (February, 1907), pp. 4-6.

"France," *Horizon*, I, ii (February, 1907), pp. 6-7.

"Socialist of the Path," *Horizon*, I, ii (February, 1907), p. 7.

"Negro and Socialism," *Horizon*, I, ii (February, 1907), pp. 7-8.

"India," *Horizon*, I, ii (February, 1907), pp. 8-9.

"Austria," *Horizon*, I, ii (February, 1907), pp. 9-10.

"The Value of Agitation," *Horizon*, Vol. I, iii (March, 1907), pp. 109-10.

"Books," *Horizon*, I, iii (March, 1907), p. 3.

"Periodicals," *Horizon*, I, iii (March, 1907), pp. 3-7.

"Hearken Theodore Roosevelt," *Horizon*, I, iii (March, 1907), pp. 7-8.

"Journeying," *Horizon*, I, iii (March, 1907), pp. 8-9.

"Back-Talk," *Horizon*, I, iii (March, 1907), p. 9.

"Indians," *Horizon*, I, iii (March, 1907), p. 10.

"Notes," *Horizon*, I, iii (March, 1907), p. 10.

"Magazines," *Horizon*, I, iv (April, 1907), pp. 3-5.

"Books," *Horizon*, I, iv (April, 1907), pp. 5-6.

"Africa," *Horizon*, I, iv (April, 1907), pp. 6-8.

"Unknown," *Horizon*, I, iv (April, 1907), pp. 8-9.

" 'Wittekind', " *Horizon*, I, iv (April, 1907), pp. 9-10.

"Magazines," *Horizon*, I, v (May, 1907), pp. 3-4.

"A Book," *Horizon*, I, v (May, 1907), pp. 4-5.

"The Lash," *Horizon*, I, v (May, 1907), pp. 5-6.

"March 25th, 1907," *Horizon*, I, v (May, 1907), pp. 6-8.

"Dying," *Horizon*, I, v (May, 1907), pp. 8-9.

"Record," *Horizon*, I, v (May, 1907), pp. 9-10.

" 'Nulla Dies' ," *Horizon*, I, v (May, 1907), p. 10.

"Sociology and Industry in Southern Education," *Voice of the Negro*, Vol. 4 (May, 1907).

"Magazines," *Horizon*, I, vi (June, 1907), pp. 3-4.

"Satyrland," *Horizon*, I, vi (June, 1907), p. 4.

"Africa," *Horizon*, I, vi (June, 1907), p. 5-7.

"Carpenters," *Horizon*, I, vi (June, 1907), p. 8.

"Brownsville," *Horizon*, I, vi (June, 1907), pp. 8-9.

"Books," *Horizon*, I, vi (June, 1907), pp. 9-10.

"Fuller," *Horizon*, I, vi (June, 1907), p. 10.

"The Magazines," *Horizon*, II, i (July, 1907), p. 3.

"The Case," *Horizon*, II, i (July, 1907), pp. 4-10.

"The Magazines," *Horizon*, II, ii (August, 1907), p. 4.

"A Rebuke," *Horizon*, II, ii (August, 1907), p. 4.

"The Shaven Lady," *Horizon*, II, ii (August, 1907), pp. 5-10.

"The Magazines," *Horizon*, II, iii (September, 1907), pp. 3-4.

"Niagara," *Horizon*, II, iii (September, 1907), pp. 4-6.

"The Road to Dalnally," *Horizon*, II, iii (September, 1907), pp. 7-8.

"Chains," *Horizon*, II, iii (September, 1907), pp. 8-9.

"Neglected Duty," *Horizon*, II, iii (September, 1907), p. 10.

"The Negro in Large Cities," a speech reprinted in large part in the New York *Evening Post* (September 30, 1907).

"The Magazines," *Horizon*, II, iv (October, 1907), p. 3.

"The Foreign View," *Horizon*, II, iv (October, 1907), pp. 4-6.

"Two Letters," *Horizon*, II, iv (October, 1907), pp. 6-8.

"News From Alabama," *Horizon*, II, iv (October, 1907), p. 8.

"Egypt," *Horizon*, II, iv (October, 1907), pp. 9-10.

"The Magazines for November," *Horizon*, II, v (November, 1907), p. 1.

"Books," *Horizon*, II, v (November, 1907), p. 2.

"Burton," *Horizon*, II, v (November, 1907), pp. 2-3.

"The Burden of Black Women," *Horizon*, II, v (November, 1907), pp. 3-5.

"My Country 'Tis of Thee," *Horizon*, II, v (November, 1907), pp. 5-7.

"The Running of the Bishop," *Horizon*, II, v (November, 1907), pp. 7-8.

"The Christmas Magazines," *Horizon*, II, vi (December, 1907), pp. 1-2.

"A Book," *Horizon*, II, vi (December, 1907), pp. 2-3.

"An Essay by A Southern White Boy," *Horizon*, II, vi (December, 1907), pp. 3-5.

"A Hero," *Horizon*, II, vi (December, 1907), p. 5.

"Report," *Horizon*, II, vi (December, 1907), p. 6.

"Clay," *Horizon*, II, vi (December, 1907), p. 7.

"1907: Debit and Credit," *Horizon*, III, i (January, 1908), p. 1.

"Magazine Articles of 1907," *Horizon*, III, i (January, 1908), p. 2.

"Books of 1907," *Horizon*, III, i (January, 1908), p. 2.

"New Year," *Horizon*, III, i (January, 1908), pp. 2-3.

"Books and Papers," *Horizon*, III, i (January, 1908), pp. 3-4.

"Peonage," *Horizon*, III, i (January, 1908), pp. 4-5.

"A Day in Africa," *Horizon*, III, i (January, 1908), pp. 5-6.

"Hubert," *Horizon*, III, i (January, 1908), pp. 6-7.

"Widgeon," *Horizon*, III, i (January, 1908), pp. 7-8.

"Magazines," *Horizon*, III, ii (February, 1908), p. 17.

"To Black Voters," *Horizon*, III, ii (February, 1908), pp. 17-18.

"Little Brother of Mine," *Horizon*, III, ii (February, 1908), pp. 18-20.

"The Song of America," *Horizon*, III, ii (February, 1908), pp. 20-1.

" 'Know Thy People' ," *Horizon*, III, ii (February, 1908), pp. 21-2.

"A Book," *Horizon,* III, ii (February, 1908), pp. 22-4.

"Reading," *Horizon,* III, iii (March, 1908), p. 1.

"Ava Maria," *Horizon,* III, iii (March, 1908), p. 2.

"Ida Dean Bailey," *Horizon,* III, iii (March, 1908), p. 2.

"Darwinism," *Horizon,* III, iii (March, 1908), pp. 5-6.

"Bryan," *Horizon,* III, iii (March, 1908), p. 7.

"Mulattoes," *Horizon,* III, iii (March, 1908), pp. 7-8.

"Articles and Books," *Horizon,* III, iv (April, 1908), pp. 1-2.

"Prayer of the Bantu," *Horizon,* III, iv (April, 1908), p. 3.

"Taft," *Horizon,* III, iv (April, 1908), pp. 3-6.

"Charles Cuthbert Hall," *Horizon,* III, iv (April, 1908), pp. 6-7.

"The Southern Electorate," *Horizon,* III, iv (April, 1908), pp. 7-8.

"Race Friction Between Black and White," *American Journal of Sociology,* XIII (May, 1908), pp. 834-8.

"Periodicals for May," *Horizon,* III, v (May, 1908), p. 1.

"Well-Wisher," *Horizon,* III, v (May, 1908), p. 1-3.

"Negro Soldiers and Others," *Horizon,* III, v (May, 1908), pp. 3-8.

"Books and Periodicals," *Horizon,* III, vi (June, 1908), pp. 1-2.

"Taft," *Horizon,* III, vi (June, 1908), pp. 2-5.

"Union," *Horizon,* II, vi (June, 1908), pp. 5-6.

"Twelfth Night," *Horizon,* III, vi (June, 1908), pp. 6-7.

"El Dorado," *Horizon,* III, vi (June, 1908), pp. 7-8.

"Free," *Horizon,* IV, i (July, 1908), p. 1.

"The Horizon," *Horizon,* IV, i (July, 1908), pp. 1-4.

"The Negro Voter—Talk Number One," *Horizon,* IV, i (July, 1908), pp. 4-7.

"An African on His Race," *Horizon,* IV, i (July, 1908), pp. 7-8.

"The Guarantors," *Horizon,* IV, ii (August, 1908), p. 1.

"Negro Vote—Talk Number Two," *Horizon,* IV, ii (August, 1908), pp. 1-5.

"Talk Number Three," *Horizon,* IV, ii (August, 1908), pp. 5-8.

"Niagara Movement," *Horizon,* IV, iii (September, 1908), pp. 1-3.

"The Negro Vote—Talk Number Four," *Horizon,* IV, iii (September, 1908), pp. 4-6.

"Talk Number Five," *Horizon,* IV, iii (September, 1908), pp. 7-8.

"A Reply," *Horizon,* IV, iii (September, 1908), p. 9.

"Books and Periodicals," *Horizon,* IV, iv (October, 1908), pp. 1-3.

"100-21-79," *Horizon,* IV, iv (October, 1908), pp. 4-6.

"The Negro Vote—Talk Number Six," *Horizon,* IV, iv (October, 1908), pp. 6-8.

"From Abroad," *Horizon,* IV, iv (October, 1908), p. 8.

"The Christ of the Andes," *Horizon,* IV, v & vi (November and December, 1908), pp. 1-10.

"Politics," *Horizon,* IV, v & vi (November and December, 1908), pp. 11-12.

"Liberia," *Horizon,* IV, v & vi (November and December, 1908), p. 13.

"The New Horizon," *Horizon,* IV, v & vi (November and December, 1908), p. 14.

"Georgia Negroes and their Fifty Millions of Savings," *World's Work,* Vol. 18 (May, 1909), pp. 11550-4.

"National Committee on the Negro," *Survey,* Vol. 22 (June 12, 1909), pp. 407-9.

"Long in Darke," *Independent,* Vol. 67 (October 21, 1909), pp. 917-18.

"Fifty Years Among the Black Folk," *New York Times,* (December 12, 1909), p. 64.

"The Optimist," *Horizon* (February, 1910).

"The Negro and the YMCA," *Horizon* (March, 1910).

"Better South," *Horizon* (March, 1910).

"The Economic Aspects of Race Prejudice," *Editorial Review* (May, 1910).

"Godfrey of Bouillon," *Horizon* (June, 1910).

"Reconstruction and its Benefits," *American Historical Review,* Vol. 15 (July, 1910), pp. 781-99.

"Marrying of Black Folk," *Independent,* Vol. 69 (October 13, 1910), pp. 812-13.

"Negro Property," *World To-Day* (August, 1910).

"The Souls of White Folks," *Independent* (August 18, 1910).

"Forty Years of Freedom," *Missionary Review of the World* (June, 1911).

"The Economics of Negro Emancipation," *Sociological Review* (October, 1911).

"A Hymn to the Peoples," *Independent,* Vol. 71 (August 24, 1911), pp. 401-3.

"The First Universal Races Congress," *Independent,* Vol. 71 (August, 1911), pp. 401-3.

"Upbuilding of Black Durham," *World's Work,* Vol. 23 (January, 1912), pp. 334-35.

"The Rural South," *American Statistical Association Publications* (March, 1912).

"The Social Effects of Emancipation," *Survey* (February 1, 1913).

"Socialism and the Negro Problem," *New Review* (February 1, 1913).

"Negro in Literature and Art," *Annals of American Academy,* Vol. 49 (September, 1913), pp. 233-7.

"Of the Culture of White Folk," *Journal of Race* (April, 1917).

"The African Roots of War," *Atlantic Monthly,* Vol. 115 (May, 1915), pp. 707-14.

"The Passing of Jim Crow," *Independent* (July 14, 1917).

"The Negro's Fatherland," *Survey* (November 10, 1917).

"Eternal Africa," *Nation* (September 25, 1920).

"On Being Black," *New Republic,* Vol. 21 (February 18, 1920), pp. 338-41.

"Republicans and the Black Voter," *Nation,* Vol. 110 (June 5, 1920), pp. 757-8.

"Eternal Africa," *Nation,* Vol. 111 (September 25, 1920), pp. 350-2.

"E.D. Morel," *Nation,* Vol. 112 (May 25, 1921), p. 749.

"A Second Journey to Pan-Africa," *New Republic,* Vol. 29 (December 7, 1921), pp. 39-42.

"The Object of the Pan-African Congress," *African World* (1921-22), p. 99.

"Social Equality and Racial Intermarriage," *World Tomorrow* (March, 1922).

"The Negro as a National Asset," *Homiletic Review,* Vol. 86 (1923), pp. 52-8.

"The South and a Third Party," *New Republic,* Vol. 33 (1923), pp. 138-41.

"Back to Africa," *Century,* Vol. 105 (February, 1923), pp. 339-48.

"The Segregated Negro World," *World Tomorrow* (May, 1923).

"Making a Living: What the Negro Faces," *World Tomorrow* (May, 1923).

"The Hosts of Black Labor," *Nation*, Vol. 116 (May 9, 1923), pp. 539-48.

"Can the Negro Serve the Drama?" *Theatre* (July, 1923).

"Diuturni Silenti," *Fisk Herald*, Col. XXXIII (1924).

"The Negro Takes Stock," *New Republic*, Vol. 38 (January 2, 1924).

"The Dilemma of the Negro," *American Mercury*, Vol. 3 (October, 1924), pp. 179-85.

"The Primitive Black Man," *Nation*, Vol. 119 (December 17, 1924), pp. 673-6.

"Liberia and Rubber," *New Republic*, Vol. 44 (November 18, 1925), pp. 326-9.

"Georgia: Invisible Empire State," *Nation*, Vol. 120 (January 21, 1925), pp. 63-7.

"What is Civilization," *Forum*, Vol. 73 (February, 1925), pp. 178-88.

"Britain's Negro Problem in Sierra Leone," *Current History*, Vol. 21 (February, 1925).

"The Black Man Brings His Gifts," *Survey*, Vol. 53 (March, 1925), pp. 655-7.

"Worlds of Colour," *Foreign Affairs*, Vol. 3 (April, 1925), pp. 523-44.

"France's Black Citizen's in West Africa," *Current History*, Vol. 22 (July, 1925), pp. 559-64.

"The Social Origins of American Negro Art," *Modern Quarterly* (October-December, 1925).

"Negroes in College," *Nation*, Vol. 122 (March 3, 1926), pp. 228-30.

"The Shape of Fear," *North American Review*, Vol. 223 (June, 1926), pp. 291-304.

"Hampton Strike," *Nation*, Vol. 125 (November 2, 1927), pp. 471-2.

"Is Al Smith Afraid of the South?" *Nation*, Vol. 127 (October 17, 1928), pp. 392-4.

"Race Relations in the US," *Annals of the American Academy of Political and Social Science*, Vol. 140 (November, 1928), pp. 6-10.

"The Celebrated Case of the Eleko of Lagos. . . ." The *Philadelphia Tribune* (August 6, 1931).

"West African Natives . . . Exported Cocoa," The *Philadelphia Tribune* (September 19, 1931).

The Wide, Wide World, *Louisiana Weekly* (September 19, 1931).

"The Story of Cocoa," *Louisiana Weekly* (September 9, 1931).

"Will the Church Remove the Color Line," *Christian Century*, Vol. 48 (December 9, 1931), pp. 1554-6.

"Education and Work," *Journal of Negro Education*, Vol. 1 (April, 1932), pp. 60-74.

"Liberia, the League and the United States," *Foreign Affairs*, Vol. 11 (July, 1933), pp. 682-95.

"A Negro Nation within the Nation" *Current History*, Vol. 42 (June, 1935), pp. 265-70.

"Does the Negro Need Separate Schools?" *Journal of Negro Education*, Vol. 4 (July, 1935), pp. 382-5.

"Inter-racial Implications of the Ethiopian crisis," *Foreign Affairs*, Vol. 14 (October, 1935), pp. 89-92.

"Social Planning for the Negro, Past and Present," *Journal of Negro Education*, Vol. 5 (January, 1936), pp. 110-25.

"A Forum of Fact and Opinion," *Pittsburgh Courier* (February 8, 1936; February 29, April 11, April 18, April 25, May 21, June 13, August 29, December 5, November 20, 1937).

"Black Africa Tomorrow," *Foreign Affairs*, Vol. 17 (1938), pp. 100-10.

"How Negroes Have Taken Advantage of Educational Opportunities Offered By Friends," *Journal of Negro Education* (1938).

"The Revelation of St. Orgne the Damned," *Fisk News* (November-December, 1938).

"The Position of the Negro in the American Social Order, *Journal of Negro Education*, Vol. 8 (1939), pp. 551-70.

"The Negro Scientist," *American Scholar*, Vol. 8 (July, 1939), pp. 309-20.

"Pushkin," *Phylon*, Vol. 1 (1940).

"Moton of Hampton and Tuskegee," *Phylon*, Vol. 1 (1940).

"Review of Events in African History, a Supplement to Atlantic Charter and Africa from an American Standpoint, *Phylon*, Vol. 3, Fourth Quarter (1942).

"The Realities in Africa," *Foreign Affairs*, Vol. 21 (July, 1943), pp. 721-32.

"Africa at the Peace Table," *Negro Digest*, Vol. 1 (August, 1943).

"Segregation," *Phylon*, Vol. 4 (1943).

"A Great Singer," *Phylon*, Vol. 4 (1943).

"Reconstruction, Seventy-Five Years After," *Phylon*, Vol. 4 (1943).

"Scholarly Delusion," *Phylon*, Vol. 4 (1943).

"A Report to the General Education Board," *Atlanta University Publications*, No. 22 (1943).

"Prospect of a World without Race Conflict," *American Journal of Sociology*, Vol. 49 (March, 1944), pp. 450-6.

"Phylon: Science or Propaganda," *Phylon*, Vol. 5 (1944).

"Mercer Cook," *Phylon*, Vol. 5 (1944).

"Jacob and Esau," *Talladegan* (November, 1944).

"The Winds of Time," *Chicago Defender* (May 12, 1945; June 30, 1945; September 1, 1945; September 22, 1945; September 29, 1945; October 20, 1945; November 10, 1945, etc.).

"What He (FDR) Meant to the Negro," *New Masses* (April 24, 1945).

"Bound By the Color Line," *New Masses* (February 12, 1946).

"Past Africa," *People's Voice* (March 8, 1946).

"Colonies and Moral Responsibility," *Journal of Negro Education* (Summer, 1946).

"The Future and Function of the Private Negro College," *Crisis* (August, 1946).

"Common Objectives," *Soviet Russia Today* (August, 1946).

"Crisis at Fisk," *Nation*, Vol. 163 (September 7, 1946), pp. 269-70.

"Three Centuries of Discrimination," *Crisis*, Vol. 54 (1947), pp. 362-3, 379-80.

"Pioneers in the Struggle Against Segregation," *Survey Graphic*, Vol. 36 (January, 1947), p. 90.

"Behold the Land," *New Masses* (January 14, 1947).

"Jan Christiaan Smuts: Story of a Tyrant," *New Masses* (March 4, 1947).

"Can the Negro Expect Freedom by 1965?" *Negro Digest* (April, 1947).

"The Most Hopeful State in the World," *Soviet Russia Today* (November, 1947).

"Race Relations in the United States, 1917-1947," *Phylon*, Vol. 9 (1948).

"John Hope, Scholar and Gentleman," *Crisis*, Vol. 55 (1948), pp. 270-1.

"The Riot in South Africa, *New Africa*, Vol. 8 (January, 1948).

"A Programme of Emancipation for Colonial People," *Howard University Studies in the Social Sciences*, Vol. 6 (1948), pp. 96-103.

"Pan-Africa," *People's Voice* (March 8, 1947 and March 6, 1948).

"From McKinley to Wallace: My Fifty Years as a Political Independent," *Masses and Mainstream*, (August, 1948), pp. 3-13.

"The Negro Since 1900: a Progress Report," *The New Times Magazine* (November 21, 1948), pp. 54-7, 59.

"This is Africa Today," *National Guardian*, Vol. 1 (November 29, 1948).

"Africa for the Europeans," *National Guardian*, Vol. 1 (December 6, 1948).

"Black Africa Fights Back," *National Guardian*, I, ix (December 13, 1948), p. 9.

"The Freeing of India," *Crisis*, Vol. 54 (1949).

"Watch Africa, Watchword for Thinking People," *National Guardian*, Vol. 21 (January 3, 1949).

"Africa Today," *New Africa*, Vol. 8 (February, 1949).

"Ethiopia and Eritrea," *New Africa*, Vol. 8 (February, 1949).

"Africa, a 'Natural' for the Plunderers," *National Guardian*, Vol. 22 (March, 1949).

"The Freedom to Learn," *Lawyers Guild Review* (Spring, 1949).

"Colonial Peoples and the Fight for Peace," *New Africa*, Vol. 8 (April, 1949).

"To Save the World, Save Africa," *New Africa*, Vol. 8 (May, 1949).

"None Who Saw Paris Will Ever Forget," *National Guardian*, I, xxxi (May 16, 1949), p. 12.

"The Freedom to Learn," *Midwest Journal*, Vol. 2 (Winter, 1949).

"Let's First Learn to Rule Ourselves," *National Guardian*, I, xiv (August 22, 1949), p. 3.

"The Moscow Peace Congress," *National Guardian*, I, 1 (September 26, 1949), p. 12.

"Statement on the Conviction of Communist Leaders," *National Guardian*, II, ii (October 24, 1949), p. 7.

"The Role of West Africa," *The Crescent*, Vol. 24 (Spring, 1950).

"Background and Significance of the Seretse Khama Case," *New Africa*, Vol. 19 (April, 1950).

"Government and Freedom," *Harlem Quarterly* (Spring, 1950).

"Repression Madness Rules South Africa." *New Africa*, Vol. 4 (May-June, 1950).

"A Portrait of Carter G. Woodson," *Masses and Mainstream* (June, 1950).

"African Youth at Prague," *New Africa*, Vol. 9 (July-September, 1950).

"This is the Heart of the 1950 Election Campaign: 'There Can Be No Progress Without Peace.' " *National Guardian*, II, xlv (October 4, 1950), p. 8.

"[The] US Needs No More Cowards," *National Guardian*, III, i (October 25, 1950), p. 1.

"Money Buys American Elections," *National Guardian*, III, viii (December 13, 1950), p. 6.

"The Big Problem: To Get the Truth to the People," *National Guardian*, III, xiv (January 24, 1951), p. 8.

"Why John Brown's Soul Marches On," *National Guardian*, III, xvii (February 14, 1951), p. 5.

"Editing the Crisis," *Crisis*, Vol. 58 (March, 1951).

"There Must Come A Vast Social Change in the United States," *National Guardian*, III, xxxviii (July 11, 1951), p. 5.

"A Call to Courage," *National Guardian*, III, i (October 3, 1951), p. 1.

"The Choice that Confronts America's Negroes," *National Guardian*, IV, xvii (February 13, 1952), p. 7.

" 'He Knew the Comman Man . . . Followed His Fate,' " *National Guardian*, IV, xxi (March 16, 1952), p. 4.

"Come On Out—The Dream is Ours," *National Guardian*, IV, xxviii (May 1, 1952), p. 6.

"We Cry Aloud To Those Sleeping in the Wilderness, Awake, Awake, . . ." *National Guardian*, IV, xxxviii (July 10, 1952), p. 4.

"The Negro Voter and the 1952 Elections," *National Guardian*, IV, xlvii (September 11, 1952), pp. 6-7.

"On a Nation Going Mad," *National Guardian*, V, vii (December 4, 1952), p. 3.

"Pan-Colored," *Spotlight on Africa*, Vol. 12 (January, 1953).

"The Hard-Bit Man in the Loud Shirts," *National Guardian*, V, xiv (January 22, 1953), p. 8.

"Du Bois on the Collection of Honest News," *National Guardian*, V, xv (January 29, 1953), pp. 1, 3.

"Color Lines," *National Guardian*, V, xvii (February 12, 1953), p. 7.

"On Cats, Public Manners and the Education of Educators," *National Guardian*, V, xx (March 23, 1953), p. 8.

"The Commonsense Party," *National Guardian*, V, xxiv (April 6, 1953), p. 8.

"The Right to Speak Up Implies the Right to Keep Silent," *National Guardian*, V, xxviii (May 4, 1953), p. 7.

"Of a Man Born of the People" (review of *Born of the People*, by Luis Taruc), *National Guardian*, V, xxxiii (June 8, 1953), p. 6.

"On the Right to Express and Hear Unpopular Opinion," *National Guardian*, V, xxxi (May 25, 1953), p. 3.

"An Epitaph for Senator Taft," *National Guardian*, V, xlv (August 10, 1953), p. 1.

"Why Vote ALP," *National Guardian*, V, xlvii (September 14, 1953), p. 3.

"Du Bois Scans His Crystal Ball," *National Guardian*, V, xlviii (September 21, 1953), p. 4.

"1876 and After: Democracy and American Negroes," *National Guardian*, VI, xvi (February 15, 1954), pp. 4-5.

"The Great Tradition in English Literature," *National Guardian*, VI, xx (March 8, 1954), p. 7.

"Cannot This Paralyzed Nation Awake?" *National Guardian*, VI, xxv (April 12, 1954), p. 1.

"A Third Party—Or Even a Second," *National Guardian*, VI, xxx (May 17, 1954), p. 1.

"We Rejoice and Tell the World . . . But We Must Go Further," *National Guardian*, V, xxxii (May 31, 1954), p. 5.

"Seeds of Destruction" (review of the book by Cedric Belfrage), *National Guardian*, VII, i (October 25, 1954), p. 4.

"Africa and the American Negro Intelligentsia," *Presence Africaine* (December, 1954–January, 1955).

"American Negroes and Africa," *National Guardian*, VII, xvii (February 14, 1955), p. 5.

"Ethiopia: State Socialism Under an Emperor," *National Guardian*, VII, xviii (February 21, 1955), p. 4.

"The Sudan—Three Critical Years Ahead," *National Guardian*, VII, xix (February 28, 1955), p. 5.

"The Black Union of French Africa," *National Guardian*. VII, xx (March 7, 1955), p. 5.

"Uganda—And the Prisoner of Oxford," *National Guardian*, VII, xxi (March 14, 1955), p. 5.

"British West Africa: 35,000,000 Free?" *National Guardian*, VII, xxii (March 21, 1955), p. 5.

"The Belgian Congo: Copper Cauldron," *National Guardian*, VII, xxiii (March 28, 1955), p. 5.

"Pan-Africa, A Mission in my Life," *United Asia*, Vol. 7 (April, 1955).

"Kenya: The War That Can't Be Won," *National Guardian*, VII, xxiv (April 4, 1955), p. 5.

"Declaration of Independence Near?" *National Guardian*, VII, xxvi (April 18, 1955), p. 5.

"What is Wrong with the United States?" *National Guardian*, VII, ix (May 9, 1955), p. 6.

"Dr. Du Bois Insists State Department Give Him Passport," *National Guardian*, VII, ii (October 10, 1955), p. 10.

"The Wealth of the West vs. a Chance for Exploited Mankind," *National Guardian*, VIII, vi (November 28, 1955), p. 3.

"Sound Sense from a Sage," *National Guardian*, VIII, vii (December 5, 1955), p. 2.

"Let's Restore Democracy to America," *National Guardian*, VIII, xi (January 2, 1956), pp. 1, 3.

"The Negro in America Today," *National Guardian*, VIII, xiii (January 16, 1956), p. 3.

"How United Are Negroes?" *National Guardian*, VIII, xiv (January 23, 1956), pp. 6-7.

"A Bitter Battle is Shaping Up," *National Guardian*, VIII, xv (January 30, 1956), p. 4.

"The Rape of Africa, *The American Negro* (February, 1956).

"Democracy in America," *National Guardian*, VIII, xvii (February 13, 1956), pp. 1-2.

"The Political Power of the South," *National Guardian*, VIII, xx (March 5, 1956), p. 4.

"The Theory of a Third Party," *National Guardian,* VIII, xxiii (March 26, 1956), p. 4.

"[The] Cure for America's Disaster Lies Within Ourselves," *National Guardian,* VIII, xxxiv (June 11, 1956), p. 3.

"Clean Out the Congress," *National Guardian,* VIII, xxxvi (June 25, 1956), p. 5.

"I Won't Vote," *Nation,* Vol. 183 (October 20, 1956), pp. 324-5.

"Africa's Choice," *National Guardian,* IX, ii (October 29, 1956), p. 10.

"Colonialism and the Russian Revolution," *New World Review* (November, 1956).

"Reform the Senate or Lose Your Democracy," *National Guardian,* IX, iii (November 5, 1956), p. 3.

"National Guardianship," *National Guardian,* IX, vii (December 3, 1956), p. 6.

"Negro History Centenaries," *National Guardian,* IX, xiii (January 14, 1957), p. 8.

"Will the Great Gandhi Live Again?" *National Guardian,* IX, xvii (February 11, 1957), pp. 6-7.

"The Collier's Story: It had $4,000,000 But It Died," *National Guardian,* IX, xix (February 25, 1957), p. 9.

"A Future for Pan-Africa: Freedom, Peace, Socialism," *National Guardian,* IX, xxi (March 11, 1957), p. 7.

"Negroes and Socialism" *National Guardian,* IX, xxviii (April 29, 1957), p. 12.

"The Present Leadership of American Negroes," *National Guardian,* IX, xxxi (May 20, 1957), p. 7.

"Colombo: No Peace Delegate from the US," *National Guardian,* IX, xxxiv (June 10, 1957).

"The Man Who Wrote 'Lift Every Voice and Sing,' "*National Guardian,* IX, xxxvi (June 24, 1957), p. 7.

"Watchword for Negroes: Register and Vote," *National Guardian,* IX, xxxviii (July 8, 1957), p. 4.

"Does 'All Deliberate Speed' Mean 338 Years?" *National Guardian,* X, iii (November 4, 1957), p. 3.

"A Vista of Ninety Fruitful Years," *National Guardian,* X, xviii (February 17, 1958), p. 7.

"To An American Born Last Christmas Day," *National Guardian,* X, xxi (March 10, 1958), p. 4.

"The Real Reason Behind Robeson's Persecution," *National*

Guardian, X, xxxviii (July 7, 1958), p. 6.

"The Independocrat at the Dinner Table," *National Guardian*, XI, iii (July 7, 1958), p. 5.

"The Future of All Africa Lies in Socialism," *National Guardian*, XI, iii (December 22, 1958), p. 7.

"The Prime Minister of Ghana," *Mainstream*, Vol. 10 (December 22, 1958).

"The Africans and the Colonialist Tactic," *New Times*, No. 7 (February, 1959).

"China and Africa," *Peking Review*, Vol. 2 (March 3, 1959).

"The Vast Miracle of China Today," *National Guardian*, XI, xxxiv (June 8, 1959), p. 6.

"Forty Years of the USSR," *National Guardian*, XI, xlvii (September 7, 1959), p. 8.

"Crusader Without Violence" (review of the book by L.D. Reddick), *National Guardian*, XII, iv (November 9, 1959), p. 8.

"The Lost Cities of Africa" (review of the book by Basil Davidson), *National Guardian*, XII, iv (November 16, 1959), p. 8.

"A Negro Student At Harvard at the End of the Nineteenth Century," *Massachusetts Review*, Vol. I (1960).

"The Lie of History as it is Taught Today," *National Guardian*, XII, xviii (February 15, 1960), pp. 5, 8.

"The World Must Wake Soon To Bar War in Africa," *National Guardian*, XII (September 29, 1960).

"Nigeria Becomes Part of Modern World," *National Guardian*, XIII (January 1961).

"What the Future Holds for Nigeria," *National Guardian*, XIII (January 23, 1961).

"The Negro People and the United States," *Freedomways* (Spring, 1961).

"American Negroes and Africa's Rise to Freedom," *National Guardian*, XIII (May 15, 1961).

"A Logical Program for a Free Congo," *National Guardian*, XIII (May 15, 1961).

"The Negro and the American Civil War," *Science and Society* (December, 1961).

"Conference on Encyclopedia Africana," *Freedomways* (Winter, 1963).

BOOKS AND PAMPHLETS

Morality Among Negroes in Cities (ed.). Atlanta, Atlanta University Press, Atlanta Study No. 1, 1896 (reprinted in *The Atlanta University Publications*, New York, Arno Press and the *New York Times*, 1968).

Suppression of the African Slave-Trade to the United States of America, 1638-1870. New York, Longmans, Green & Co., 1896 (reprinted by Schocken Books, New York, 1969).

Social and Physical Condition of Negroes in Cities (ed.). Atlanta, Atlanta University Press, Atlanta Study No. 2, 1897 (reprinted in *The Atlanta University Publications*. New York, Arno Press and the *New York Times*, 1968).

The Conservation of Races. Washington, D.C., The American Negro Academy, Occasional Paper No. 2, 1897.

Some Efforts of American Negroes for their Own Social Betterment (ed.). Atlanta, Atlanta University Press, Atlanta Study No. 3, 1898 (reprinted in *The Atlanta University Publications*. New York, Arno Press and the *New York Times*, 1968).

The Negro in Business (ed.). Atlanta, Atlanta University Press, Atlanta Study No. 4, 1899.

Memorial to the Legislature of Georgia Upon the Hardwick Bill (pamphlet), 1899.

The Philadelphia Negro. Philadelphia, Publishers for the University, 1899 (reprinted by Schocken Books, New York, 1967).

The College-Bred Negro (ed.). Atlanta, Atlanta University Press, Atlanta Study No. 5, 1900.

The Negro Common School, Georgia (ed.). Atlanta, Atlanta University Press, Atlanta Study No. 6, 1901.

The Negro Artisan (ed.). Atlanta, Atlanta University Press, Atlanta Study No. 7, 1902.

Some Notes on Negroes in New York City (ed.). Atlanta, Atlanta University Press, Atlanta Study, Special Number, 1903.

The Negro Church (ed.). Atlanta, Atlanta University Press, Atlanta Study No. 8, 1903 (reprinted in *The Atlanta University Publications*. New York, Arno Press and the *New York Times*, 1968).

The Souls of Black Folk. Chicago, A.C. McClurg & Co., 1903 (reprinted in several paperbound editions).

Possibilities of the Negro: The Advance Guard of Race. Philadelphia, Library Publishers, 1903.

Some Notes on Negro Crime Particularly in Georgia (ed.). Atlanta, Atlanta University Press, Atlanta Study No. 9, 1904 (reprinted in *The Atlanta University Publications.* New York, Arno Press and the *New York Times,* 1968).

A Select Bibliography of the American Negro for General Readers. Atlanta, Atlanta University Press, Atlanta Study No. 10, 1901, 1904.

Heredity and the Public School. Washington, D.C., Principals Association of the Colored Schools of Washington, D.C., March 25, 1904.

Of the Wings of Atlanta. New York, Ivan Earle, 1904.

The Black Vote of Philadelphia. New York, The Charity Organization Society, 1905.

The Negro South and North. Oberlin, Ohio, 1905.

Health and Physique of the Negro American (ed.). Atlanta, Atlanta University Press, Atlanta Study No. 11, 1906 (reprinted in *The Atlanta University Publications.* New York, Arno Press and the *New York Times,* 1968).

Economic Cooperation Among Negro Americans. Atlanta, Atlanta University Press, Atlanta Study No. 12, 1907.

The Negro in the South (with Booker T. Washington). Philadelphia, George W. Jacobs & Co., 1907.

The Negro American Family. Atlanta, Atlanta University Press, Atlanta Study No. 13, 1908 (reprinted in *The Atlanta University Publications.* New York, Arno Press and the *New York Times,* 1968).

Efforts for Social Betterment Among Negro Americans. Atlanta, Atlanta University Press, Atlanta Study No. 14, 1909 (reprinted in *The Atlanta University Publications.* New York, Arno Press and the *New York Times,* 1968).

John Brown. Philadelphia, G.W. Jacobs, 1909 (reprinted by International Publishers, New York, 1962).

The College-Bred Negro American (ed., with A.G. Dill) Atlanta, Atlanta University Press, Atlanta Study No. 15, 1910 (reprinted in *The Atlanta University Publications.* New York, Arno Press and the *New York Times,* 1968).

Race Prejudice. New York, The Republican Club, 1910.

The Common School and the Negro American (ed., with A.G.

Dill). Atlanta, Atlanta University Press, Atlanta Study No. 16, 1911 (reprinted in *The Atlanta University Publications.* New York, Arno Press and the *New York Times,* 1968).

The Quest of the Silver Fleece: A Novel. Chicago, A.C. McClurg & Co., 1911 (reprinted by Mnemosyne Publishing Co., Miami, Florida, 1969).

The Social Evolution of the Black South. Washington, D.C., American Negro Monograph Co., 1911.

The Negro American Artisan (ed., with A.G. Dill). Atlanta, Atlanta University Press, Atlanta Study No. 17, 1912 (reprinted in *The Atlanta University Publications.* New York, Arno Press and the *New York Times,* 1968).

Disfranchisement. New York, National American Woman Suffrage Assocation, 1912.

Morals and Manners Among Negro Americans (ed., with A.G. Dill). Atlanta University Press, Atlanta Study No. 18, 1914 (reprinted in *The Atlanta University Publications.* New York, Arno Press and the *New York Times,* 1968).

The Negro. New York, Henry Holt & Co., 1915.

Darkwater: Voices from within the Veil. New York, Harcourt, Brace & Howe, 1920 (reprinted by Schocken Books, New York, 1969).

The Gift of Black Folk. Boston, Stratford Co., 1924.

The Amenia Conference. Amenia, New York, Troutbeck Press, (Troutbeck Leaflets No. 8), 1925.

Race Relations in the United States. Philadelphia, Donald Young, 1928.

Dark Princess: A Romance. New York, Harcourt, Brace & Co., 1928.

Shall the Negro Be Encouraged to Seek Cultural Equality? Chicago, Chicago Forum, 1929.

Africa, Its Geography, People and Products. Girard, Kansas, Haldeman-Julius, 1930.

Africa, Its Place in Modern History. Girard, Kansas, Haldeman-Julius, 1930.

Black Reconstruction. New York, Harcourt, Brace & Co., 1935 (reprinted by World Publishing Co.).

What the Negro has Done for the United States and Texas. Washington, D.C., Government Printing Office, 1936.

A Pageant in Seven Decades, 1868-1938. Atlanta, Atlanta University, 1938.

The Revelation of Saint Orgne, The Damned. Nashville, Hemphill Co., 1939.

Black Folk: Then and Now. New York, Henry Holt & Co., 1939.

Dusk of Dawn. New York, Harcourt, Brace & Co., 1945 (reprinted by Schocken Books, New York, 1968).

Color and Democracy. New York, Harcourt, Brace & Co., 1945.

Encyclopedia of the Negro: Preparatory Volume. New York, Phelps-Stokes Fund, 1945.

An Appeal to the World. New York, National Association for the Advancement of Colored People, 1947.

The World and Africa. New York, The Viking Press, 1947 (enlarged edition, with additional material, published by International Publishers, New York, 1965).

I Speak for Peace. New York, September 24, 1950.

I Take My Stand for Peace. New York, Masses and Mainstream, 1952.

In Battle for Peace: The Story of my 83rd Birthday (with comment by Shirley Graham) New York, Masses and Mainstream, 1952.

The Story of Benjamin Franklin. Vienna, Austria, Secretariat of the World Council for Peace, 1956.

The Ordeal of Mansart (the first volume of the trilogy *The Black Flame*). New York, Mainstream Publishers, 1957.

Mansart Builds a School (the Second volume of *The Black Flame* trilogy). New York, Mainstream Publishers, 1959.

The Riddle of the Sphinx. London, Abelard-Schuman, 1959.

Africa in Battle Against Colonialism, Racialism, Imperialism. Chicago, Afro-American Books, 1960.

Worlds of Color (the third volume of *The Black Flame* trilogy). New York, Mainstream Publishers, 1961.

Information Report (For Cooperation Toward an Encyclopedia Africana). Accra, Ghana, 1962.

Socialism Today—On China and Russia. Chicago, Afro-American Books, 1964.

The Immortal Child—Background on Crises in Education. Chicago, Afro-American Books, 1964.

The Damnation of Women—Prediction on Fatherless and Dependent Children. Chicago, Afro-American Books, 1964.

The Autobiography of W.E.B. Du Bois: A Soliloquy on Viewing

My Life from the Last Decade of its First Century. New York, International Publishers, 1968.

ARTICLES IN BOOKS

"The Enforcement of the Slave Trade Laws," in [The] American Historical Association *Annual Report . . . for the Year 1891.* Washington, D.C., Government Printing Office, 1892.

"Careers Open to College-Bred Negroes," in *Two Addresses.* Nashville, Fisk University, 1898.

"The Talented Tenth," in Booker T. Washington (ed.), *The Negro Problem.* New York, James Pott Co., 1903 (reprinted by Arno Press and the *New York Times,* 1968).

"The Negro Farmer," in Twelfth Census of the US: 1900 Special Reports, *Supplementary Analysis and Derivative Tables.* Washington, D.C., Government Printing Office, 1906.

"The Negro in America," in *The Encyclopedia Americana,* Frederick Converse Beach ed. New York, Vol. 11, 1904.

"Atlanta University," in Kelly Miller *et. al., From Servitude to Service.* Boston, American Unitarian Association, 1905, pp. 153-97.

"Religion in the South," in Booker T. Washington and W.E.B. Du Bois, *The Negro in the South.* Philadelphia, George W. Jacobs & Co., 1907.

"The Economic Revolution in the South," in Booker T. Washington and W.E.B. Du Bois, *The Negro in the South.* Philadelphia, George W. Jacobs & Co., 1907.

"Politics and History" and "The Evolution of the Race Problem," in *Proceedings of the National Negro Conference, New York, May 31–June 1, 1909.* New York, National Negro Conference, 1909.

"The Negro Race in the US of A," in G. Spiller (ed.), *Papers on Interracial Problems.* London, P.S. King & Son; Boston, World's Peace Foundation, 1911.

"Documentary Review of 1911 NAACP Conference," in *The NAACP,* by Warrent D. St. James. New York, Exposition Press, 1958.

"Resolution du Deuxième Congres Pán-Africain, 1921," in *La Question des Noirs aux Etats-Unis* by Frank Louis Schoell. Paris, Payot, 1923.

"Introduction" to *Bronze: A book of Verse,* by Georgia Douglas Johnson. Boston, B.J. Brummer Co., 1922.

"Georgia, Invisible Empire State," in E.H. Gruening (ed.), *The United States: A Symposium.* New York: boni and Liveright, 1923.

"The Negro Mind Reaches Out," in Alain Locke (ed.), *The New Negro: An Interpretation.*

"The Negro Citizen," in Charles S. Johnson (ed.), *The Negro in American Civilization.* New York: Holt, 1930.

"Black America," in F.J. Ringel (ed.), *America as Americans See It.* New York: Harcourt, Brace, 1932.

"The Significance of Henry Hunt," in *Founders and Annual Report Number, Fort Valley* (Georgia) *State College Bulletin,* October, 1940.

"A Program for Negro Land-Grant Colleges," *Proceedings, Nineteenth Annual Conference, Presidents of Negro Land Grant Colleges,* November, 1941. Chicago, 1941.

"A Report to the General Education Board, 1943," in W.E.B. Du Bois (ed.), *Report of the First Conference of Negro Land-Grant Colleges for Coordinating a Program of Social Studies.* Atlanta: Atlanta University, 1943.

"My Evolving Program for Negro Freedom," in Rayford W. Logan (ed.), *What the Negro Wants.* Chapel Hill, N.C.: University of North Carolina Press, 1944.

"A Voyage to Liberia," in Carlos H. Baker (ed.), *The American Looks at the World.* New York: Harcourt, Brace, 1944.

"The Black Man and Albert Schweitzer," in A.A. Roback (ed.), *The Albert Schweitzer Jubilee Book.* Cambridge, Mass.: Sci-Art, 1945.

"The Pan-African Movement," in George Padmore (ed.), *Colonial and . . . Colored Unity.* Manchester, England: Pan-African Federation, 1947.

"A Program of Emancipation for Colonial Peoples," in Merze Tate (ed.), *Trust and Non-Self-Governing Territories.* Washington, D.C.: Howard University Press, 1948.

"The Nature of Intellectual Freedom," in Daniel S. Gillmor (ed.), *Speaking of Peace.* New York: National Council of the Arts, Sciences, and Professions, 1949.

"That Outer, Whiter World of Harvard," in W. Bentinck-Smith (ed.), *The Harvard Book*. Cambridge, Mass.: Harvard University Press, 1953.

"Pan-Africanism: A Mission in My Life," in *Africa and the Modern World: A Symposium*. Bombay: Associated Advertisers and Printers, 1955.

"200 Years of Segregated Schools," in Louis Harap (ed.), *Jewish Life Anthology, 1946-1956*. New York: Jewish Life Magazine, 1956.

"Liberia, the League, and the United States," in *Africa Seen by American Negroes*. Paris: Présence Africaine, 1958.

"The Negro and Socialism," in Helen L. Alfred (ed.), *Toward a Socialist America: A Syposium of Essays*. New York: Peace Publications, 1958.

The following is a brief bibliography of books, by other authors, that were used by the editor in compiling this work. ✓

Baker, Ray Stannard, *Following the Color Line: American Negro Citizenship in the Progressive Era*. New York, Harper Torchbook, 1964.

Fishel, Leslie H., & Quarles, Benjamin, eds., *The Negro American: A Documentary History*. New York, William Morrow & Co. 1967.

Johnson, James Weldon, *Black Manhattan*. New York, Arno Press and the *New York Times*, 1968.

Logan, Rayford W., *The Betrayal of the Negro: From Rutherford B. Hayes to Woodrow Wilson*. New York, Collier Books, 1965.

Meier, August, *Negro Thought in America; 1880–1915: Racial Ideology in the Age of Booker T. Washington*. Ann Arbor, The University of Michigan Press, 1963.

INDEX

Figures in italics indicate references for Volume II

Abd-el Krim, 547
Abolition, nullified by capitalism, *695*
Abolition Society, 196, 204, 211
Abolitionism, 388, *441, 471, 474*
 Negro participation in, 359, 388-89, *691*
 See also Civil War
Abolitionists
 colleges founded by, 397
 and race riots, 200-1
Abron, *578*
Abyssinia, 457, *187-88, 204, 476, 599*
 language of, 480
 trade of, 458
Abyssinian Baptist Church, 289
Acheson, Dean, 121
Adams, Henry, *422*
Addams, Jane, 65, *611, 718*
Adenauer, Konrad, *673*
Adger, Rev. Dr. J. B., 286
Adler, Felix, *693*
Aemilius Paullus, 410-11
Aeschylus, *357*
AF of L, *see* American Federation of
 Labor
Africa, *164, 228, 229, 335*
 achievements of, 453
 agriculture in, 466, 483
 and America, *620, 688-89, 713, 714*
 animal worship in, 254
 art in, 308-9, 447, 470, 481-83
 artisanship in, 335-38
 and big business, *675*
 bourgeoisie in, *294-95*
 bush of, *349*
 cannibalism in, 483
 and capitalism, *659-60, 675, 712*
 cattle raising in, 467
 and China, *661, 682, 694, 695, 713, 714-15, 716*
 civilization of, compared to Europe, *188, 303, 473*
 climate of, *473*
 communications in, *497-98*
 conquest of, *557-58*
 culture of, 35-36, 307-12, 464-84, *473, 476*
  compared to Europe, *495, 497-98*
 Du Bois's arrival in, *342-44, 490-91*
 and the East, *661, 694*
 economic value of, 457-58
 enslavement of, 461

European control of in nineteenth
 century, *554*
European goals in, *189*
European wars over, 452-63, 455
Europe's seizure of, 453-54, 461, *697*
exploitation of, 458
failure to integrate, 253, 466
family structure in, 474-76
fetishism in, 254, 476-77
folklore of, 480
freeing of, *693-94*
governmental forms in, 253, 475-76, 483
history of, 35-36, 463-64, *473, 693*
 denial of, *549*
and imperialism, 452, *66*
industrial arts in, 467-72, 481, 483
industrial significance of, *620*
invasions of, 466, *476*
iron smelting in, 306-7, 470-71
languages of, 480
leadership of, *694*
lessons for Europe, *497, 498*
liberation struggles in, *621*
marriage in, 474, 476
monotheism in, 476, 477
motherhood in, 513-14
music in, *574*
need to unite, *682*
needs of, 461
Negro studies of, 449
parable of, *32-34*
partition of, *187*
polygamy in, 474
polytheism in, 476
Portugal's seizure of, *187*
poverty in, *498*
primitive communism in, 126, 252, *654, 689*
private property in, 252-53, 475
prostitution in, *498*
religions of, 253-54, 476-80
rise of, *693, 694*
and Russia, 135, *694, 695, 716*
effect of slave trade on, 308
slavery in, *475*
and socialism, 136, *658*
sorcery in, 254
spell of, *350-51*
trade in, 471-74, 483
vegetation of, *348*

Index

About the Editor

Julius Lester is the author of three adult books, two juveniles, one of which, *To Be a Slave,* was runner-up for the Newbery Prize. He has also recorded two albums of his own songs. He has contributed articles and reviews to many publications, including the *New York Times Sunday Book Review, Evergreen Review, Liberation, Nickle Review, Black Review,* and *Ebony,* He has a radio program on WBAI-FM in New York, where he makes his home.